XB-70 VALKYRIE PILOT'S FLIGHT OPERATING INSTRUCTIONS

©2006-2010 Periscope FIlm LLC
All Rights Reserved
ISBN #978-1-935700-35-7
www.PeriscopeFilm.com

Originally Published by the USAF and NASA

INTERIM FLIGHT MANUAL

USAF SERIES XB-70A AIRCRAFT

CONTRACT AF33(600)-42058
CONTRACT AF33(657)-12395

CHANGE NOTICE

LATEST CHANGED PAGES SUPERSEDE
THE SAME PAGES OF PREVIOUS DATE

Insert changed pages into basic
publication. Destroy superseded pages.

- Commanders are responsible for bringing this publication to the attention of all personnel cleared for operation of subject aircraft.

PUBLISHED UNDER AUTHORITY OF THE
SECRETARY OF THE AIR FORCE

See T.O. 01-1-2A for correct status of
Flight Manuals, Safety Supplements, and
Flight Crew Checklists

This publication is incomplete without
Confidential Supplement, T.O. 1B-70(X)A-1A

31 AUGUST 1964
CHANGED 25 JUNE 1965

T.O. 1B-70(X)A-1

TABLE OF CONTENTS

			PAGE
Section	I	DESCRIPTION	1-1
Section	II	NORMAL PROCEDURES	2-1
Section	III	EMERGENCY PROCEDURES	3-1
Section	IV	AUXILIARY EQUIPMENT	4-1
Section	V	OPERATING LIMITATIONS	5-1
Section	VI	FLIGHT CHARACTERISTICS	*
Section	VII	SYSTEMS OPERATION	7-1
Appendix	I	PERFORMANCE DATA	*

*Refer to Confidential Supplement, T.O. 1B-70(X)A-1A, for this information.

T.O. 1B-70(X)A-1

THESE PAGES TELL YOU HOW TO USE THE MANUAL.

SCOPE. This manual contains the necessary information for safe and efficient operation of the XB-70A. These instructions provide you with a general knowledge of the airplane, its characteristics, and specific normal and emergency operating procedures.

SOUND JUDGMENT. Instructions in this manual are for a crew (pilot and copilot) inexperienced in the operation of this airplane. This manual provides the best possible operating instructions under most circumstances, but it is a poor substitute for sound judgment. Multiple emergencies, adverse weather, terrain, etc, may require modification of the procedures.

PERMISSIBLE OPERATIONS. The Flight Manual takes a "positive approach" and normally states only what you can do.

HOW TO BE ASSURED OF HAVING LATEST DATA. Refer to T.O. 0-1-1-2A which lists all current Flight Manuals, Safety Supplements, and Checklists. Its frequency of issue and brevity assures an accurate, up-to-date listing of these publications.

STANDARDIZATION AND ARRANGEMENT. Standardization assures that the scope and arrangement of all Flight Manuals are identical. This manual is divided into seven fairly independent sections and an appendix to simplify reading it straight through or using it as a reference manual. Some text pages are left partially blank to facilitate future changes to this manual.

SAFETY SUPPLEMENTS. Information involving safety will be promptly forwarded to you by Safety Supplements. Supplements covering loss of life will get to you in 48 hours by TWX, and those concerning serious damage to equipment, within 10 days by mail. The title page of the Flight Manual and the title block of each Safety Supplement should also be checked to determine the effect they may have on existing supplements. You must remain constantly aware of the status of all supplements. Current supplements must be complied with, but there is no point in restricting your operation by complying with a replaced or rescinded supplement.

CHECKLISTS. The Flight Manual contains only amplified checklists. Abbreviated checklists have been issued as separate technical orders. (Refer to the back of the title page for the T.O. number of your latest checklist.) Line items in the Flight Manual and checklists are identical with respect to arrangement and item number. Whenever a Safety Supplement affects the abbreviated checklist, write in the applicable change on the affected checklist page. As soon as possible, a new checklist page incorporating the supplement will be issued. This will keep handwritten entries of Safety Supplement information in your checklist to a minimum.

HOW TO GET PERSONAL COPIES. Each flight crew member is entitled to personal copies of the Flight Manual, Safety Supplements, and Checklists. The required quantities should be ordered before you need them to assure their prompt receipt. Check with your supply personnel; it is their job to fulfill your Technical Order requests. Basically, you must order the required quantities on the Publication Requirements Table (T.O. 0-1-1-2). Technical Orders 00-5-1 and 00-5-2 give detailed information for properly ordering these publications. However, distribution of this manual is limited and is controlled by B-70 SPO. The listing for this manual in the Air Force Technical Manual Index will carry a code "H," designating that distribution is limited to a "need to know," "need to have" basis. Make sure a system is established at your base to deliver these publications to the flight crews immediately upon receipt.

T.O. 1B-70(X)A-1

FLIGHT MANUAL BINDERS. Loose-leaf binders and sectionalized tabs are available for use with your manual. These are obtained through local purchase procedures and are listed in the Federal Supply Schedule (FSC Group 75, Office Supplies, Part 1). Check with your supply personnel for assistance in securing these items.

WARNINGS, CAUTIONS, AND NOTES. The following definitions apply to "Warnings," "Cautions," and "Notes" found throughout the manual.

WARNING
Operating procedures, techniques, etc, which will result in personal injury or loss of life if not carefully followed.

CAUTION
Operating procedures, techniques, etc, which will result in damage to equipment if not carefully followed.

NOTE
An operating procedure, technique, etc, which is considered essential to emphasize.

YOUR RESPONSIBILITY - TO LET US KNOW. Every effort is made to keep the Flight Manual current. However, we cannot correct an error unless we know of its existence. In this regard, it is essential that you do your part. Comments, corrections, and questions regarding this manual are welcomed. These should be forwarded through your Command Headquarters to:

San Antonio Air Materiel Area
Kelly AFB, Texas
Attn: SANB

Send copies to the following addresses:

Headquarters ASD,
Wright-Patterson AFB, Ohio
Attn: ASZO

Air Force Systems Command
Wright-Patterson AFB, Ohio
Attn: B-70 SPO, SANBS

North American Aviation, Inc.
Dept. 278 Technical Services
Los Angeles International Airport
Los Angeles 9, California

T.O. 1B-70(X)A-1

SAFETY SUPPLEMENT SUMMARY

Safety Supplements are numbered as follows: 1SS-1, 1SS-2, etc. The supplements you receive should follow in sequence and if you find you are missing one, check T.O. 01-1-2A to see whether the supplement was issued and, if so, is still in effect. It may have been replaced or rescinded before you received your copy. If it is still active, see your Publication Distribution Officer and get your copy. It should be noted that a supplement number will never be used more than once.

SAFETY SUPPLEMENTS REPLACED BY THIS CHANGE OR RESCINDED

NUMBER	DATE	SHORT TITLE	DISPOSITION

(NONE)

ACTIVE SAFETY SUPPLEMENTS

This portion is to be filled in by you when you receive your Flight Manual and to be added to as you receive additional supplements. Refer to T.O. 0-1-1-2A for latest information if any questions arise. Supplements outstanding at the time of preparation of this page have been listed below for your convenience.

NUMBER	DATE	SHORT TITLE

(NONE)

This page intentionally left blank

T.O. 1B-70(X)A-1

XB-70A

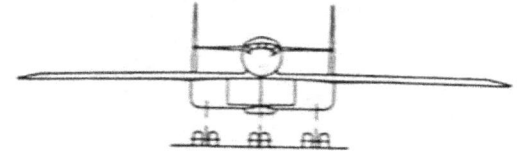

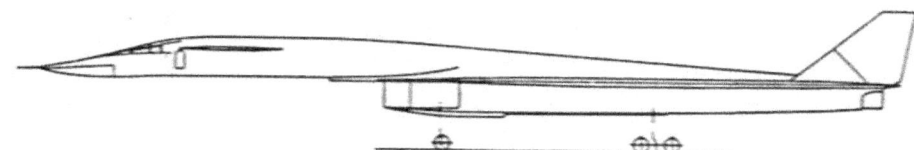

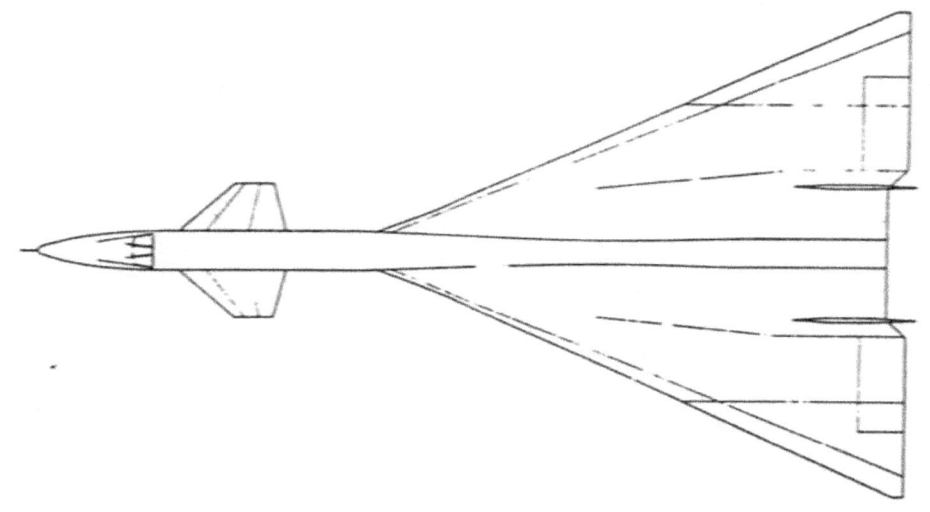

T.O. 1B-70(X)A-1

SECTION I

DESCRIPTION

TABLE OF CONTENTS	PAGE		PAGE
Airplane	1-1	Landing Gear System	1-97
Engines	1-20	Nose Wheel Steering System	1-103
Engine Afterburner System	1-33	Wheel Brake System	1-104A
Oil Supply System	1-33	Drag Chute System	1-108
Accessory Drive System (ADS) . . .	1-33	Central Air Data System (CADS)	1-110
Air Induction Control System (AICS)	1-35	Instruments	1-110
Fuel Supply System	1-40B	Annunciator (Indicator, Caution, and Warning) Lights	1-117
Electrical Power Supply System	1-54	Emergency Equipment	1-118
Hydraulic Power Supply Systems	1-72	Windshield	1-124
Nitrogen Systems	1-76	Entrance Door	1-126
Flight Control System	1-78	Seats and Escape Capsules	1-126
Canard Flap System	1-90	Auxiliary Equipment	1-135
Wing Tip Fold System	1-90		

AIRPLANE.

The XB-70A "Valkyrie," designed and built by the Los Angeles Division of North American Aviation, Inc, is a two-place prototype high-altitude supersonic bomber. As a prototype, its mission is to demonstrate the aerodynamic capabilities and technical feasibility of the design. The airplane is characterized by a long forward fuselage section, with a canard mounted aft of the crew compartment, a thin delta wing which incorporates folding wing tips used as ventral surfaces, twin rudders, and a divided engine air inlet below the fuselage. Power is supplied by six afterburner-equipped turbojet engines arranged side by side at the rear of the fuselage. Armament equipment is not provided.

SPECIAL FEATURES.

The nose section of the fuselage and the crew and electronic equipment compartment areas are of riveted titanium frames and skin, with H-11 steel (tool steel) longerons. The fuselage center section and the multispar wings have a skin of brazed stainless steel honeycomb sandwich. The wings are welded to the wing root section. The aft section of the fuselage, in the engine area, uses titanium and high alloy steel joined by welding and riveting. All high-pressure fluid line connections are brazed; the

T.O. 1B-70(X)A-1

GENERAL ARRANGEMENT

1. PITOT BOOM
2. MOVABLE WINDSHIELD RAMP
3. PILOT'S ESCAPE CAPSULE
4. COPILOT'S ESCAPE CAPSULE
5. ENTRANCE DOOR
6. OXYGEN CONVERTER-CONTAINER (2)
7. CANARD
8. GROUND EMERGENCY ESCAPE HATCH
9. IFF ANTENNA
10. FLAPS
11. UHF ANTENNA
12. RETRACTABLE ANTICOLLISION LIGHT
13. TACAN ANTENNA
14. FUSELAGE FUEL TANK (TYPICAL)
15. WING FUEL TANK (TYPICAL)
16. MAIN LANDING GEAR (RETRACTED)
17. DRAG CHUTE COMPARTMENT
18. RUDDER
19. YJ93-GE-3 ENGINE (6)
20. SEGMENTED ELEVONS (TYPICAL BOTH SIDES)
21. COMBINATION WING TIP AND TAIL LIGHT (TYPICAL BOTH TIPS)
22. FOLDING WING TIP (TYPICAL BOTH SIDES)
23. WING TIP FOLD POWER HINGE (TYPICAL BOTH SIDES)
24. ENGINE ACCESSORY DRIVE SYSTEM COMPARTMENT (TYPICAL)
25. INLET BYPASS DOORS (TYPICAL)
26. VARIABLE INLET
27. NOSE GEAR (RETRACTED)
27A. ENVIRONMENTAL SYSTEM EMERGENCY RAM AIR SCOOP (RETRACTED)
28. ENVIRONMENTAL CONTROL SYSTEM EQUIPMENT COMPARTMENT
29. ELECTRONIC EQUIPMENT COMPARTMENT
30. CREW COMPARTMENT
31. FORWARD EQUIPMENT COMPARTMENT
32. LOCALIZER ANTENNA
33. LANDING LIGHT
34. AUXILIARY LANDING LIGHT
35. TACAN ANTENNA
36. IFF ANTENNA
37. UHF ANTENNA
38. MARKER BEACON ANTENNA
39. GROUND COOLING CONNECTION
40. RETRACTABLE ANTICOLLISION LIGHTS
41. SINGLE - POINT REFUELING RECEPTACLE (RIGHT SIDE ONLY)
42. WEAPONS BAY
43. EXTERNAL ELECTRICAL POWER RECEPTACLE (AC)
44. HYDRAULIC AND GASEOUS NITROGEN GROUND-TEST-FILLER CONNECTIONS

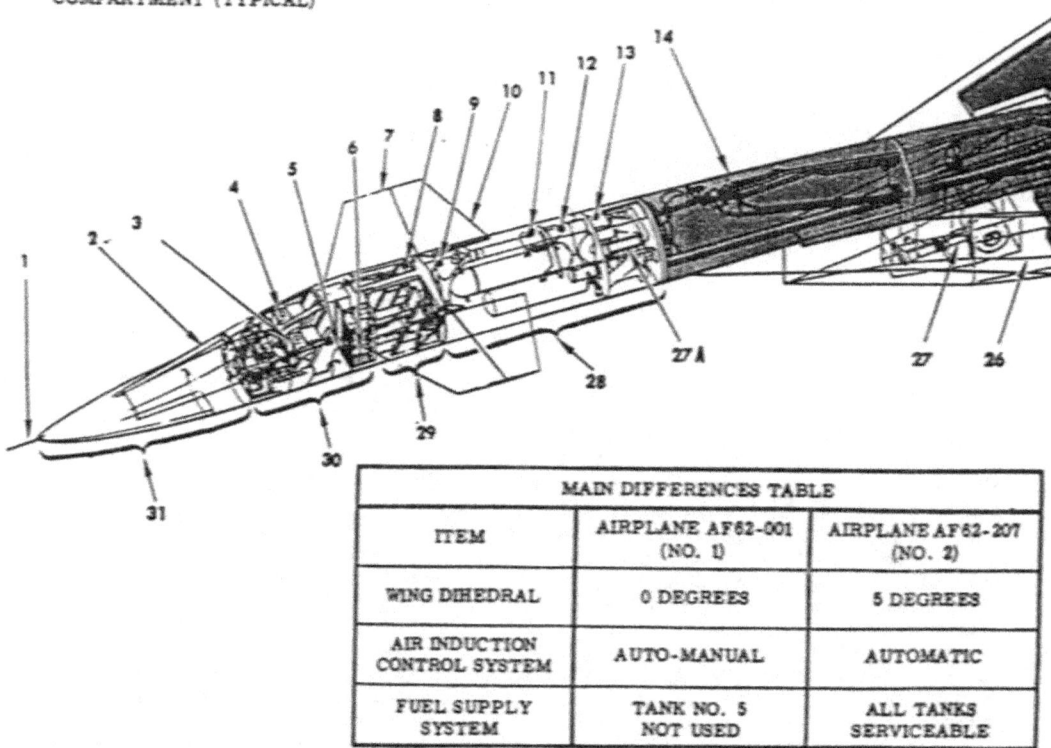

MAIN DIFFERENCES TABLE		
ITEM	AIRPLANE AF62-001 (NO. 1)	AIRPLANE AF62-207 (NO. 2)
WING DIHEDRAL	0 DEGREES	5 DEGREES
AIR INDUCTION CONTROL SYSTEM	AUTO-MANUAL	AUTOMATIC
FUEL SUPPLY SYSTEM	TANK NO. 5 NOT USED	ALL TANKS SERVICEABLE

Figure 1-1 (Sheet 1 of 2)

Changed 25 June 1965

T.O. 1B-70(X)A-1

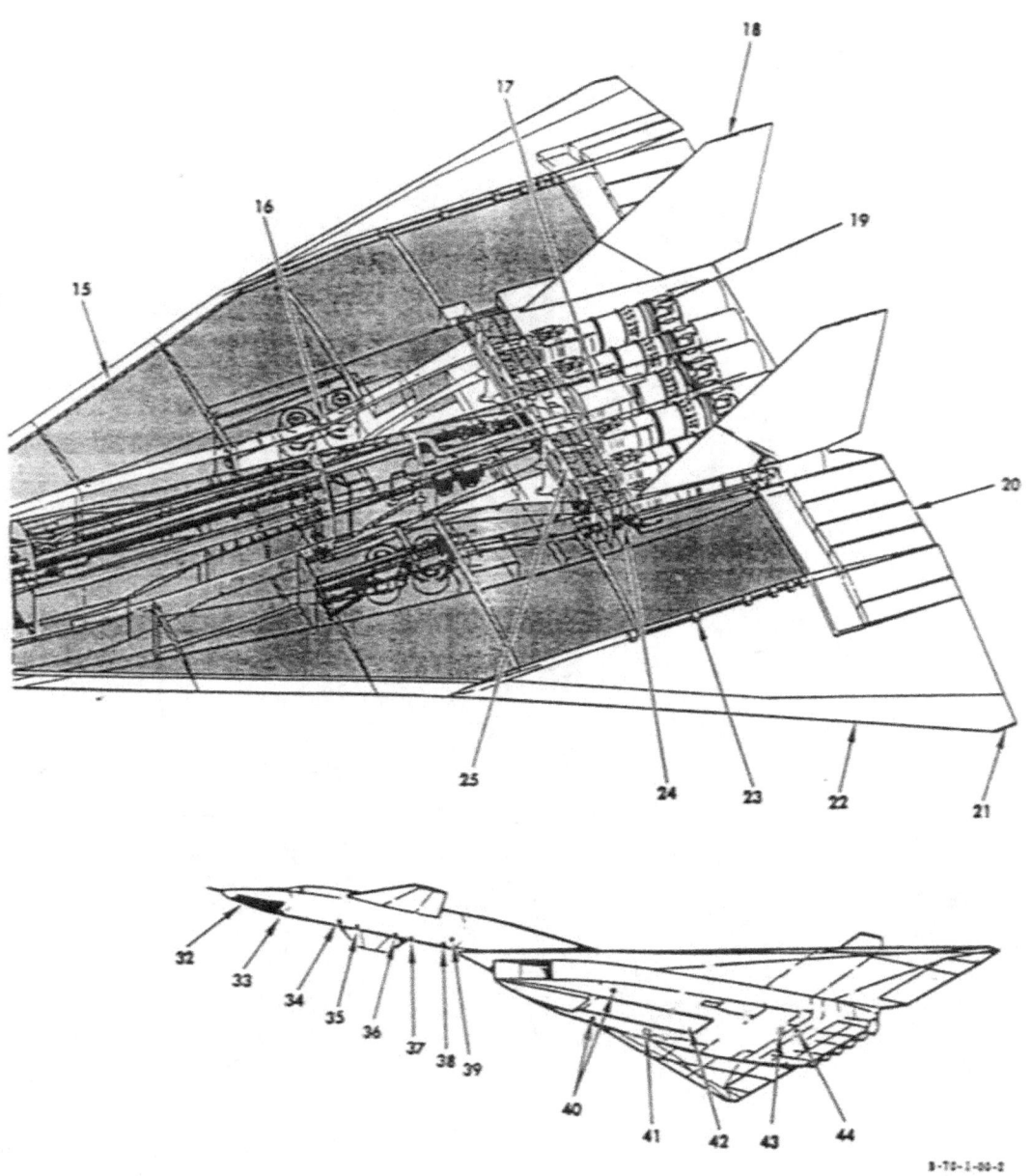

Figure 1-1 (Sheet 2 of 2)

T.O. 1B-70(X)A-1

CREW COMPARTMENT (typical)
CAPSULES NOT SHOWN

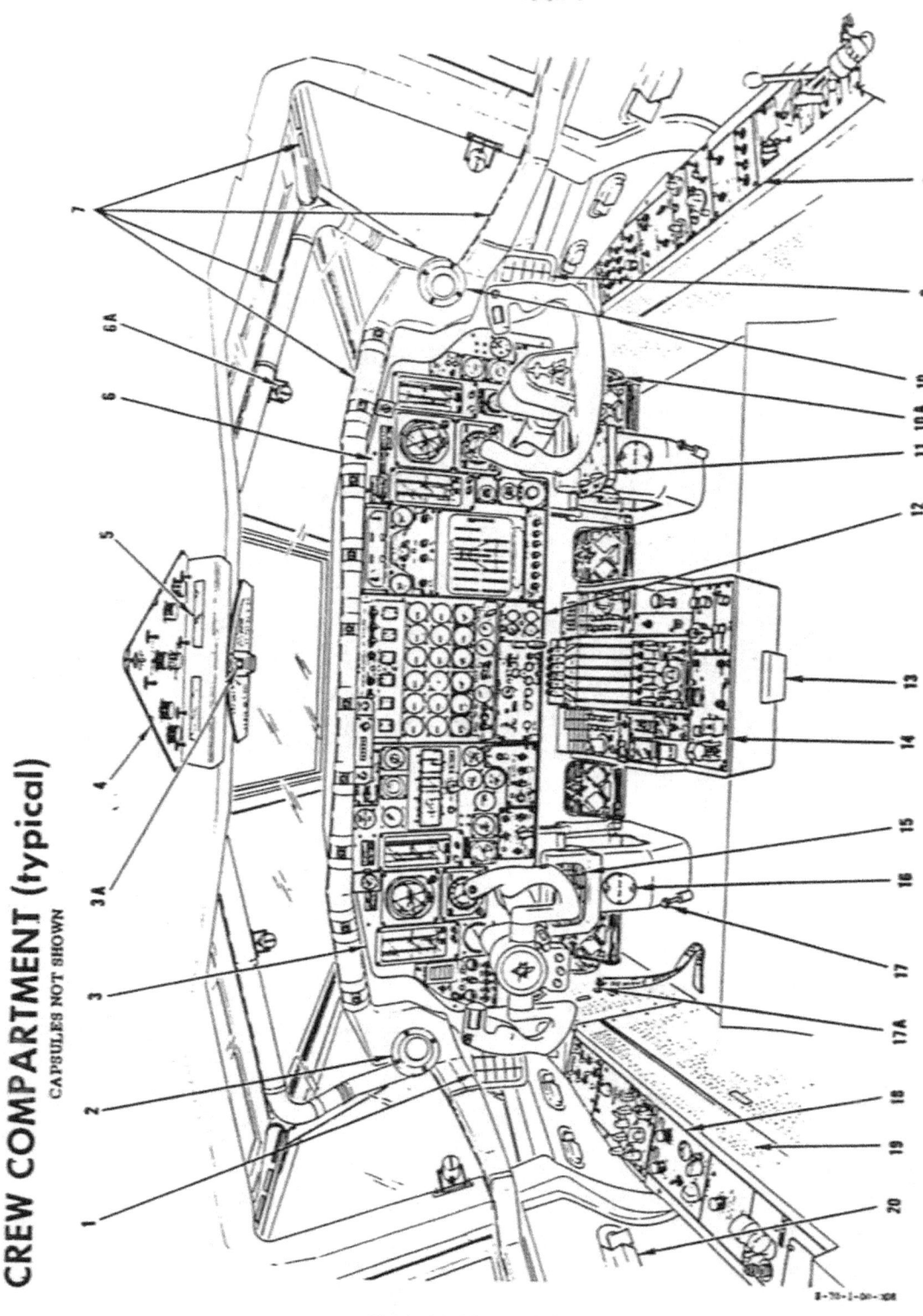

Figure 1-2 (Sheet 1 of 2)

Changed 25 June 1965

T.O. 1B-70(X)A-1

11. AICS CONTROL PANEL *
12. CENTER INSTRUMENT PANEL
13. CONSOLE RELEASE HANDLE
14. CENTER CONSOLE
15. ADJUSTABLE AIR OUTLET (TYPICAL, BOTH SIDES)
16. RUDDER PEDAL ADJUSTMENT KNOB (TYPICAL, BOTH SIDES)
17. CONTROL COLUMN RELEASE PEDAL (TYPICAL, BOTH SIDES)
17A. GROUND ESCAPE HATCH INITIATOR MAINTENANCE SAFETY PIN
18. PILOT'S CONSOLE
19. AIR RECIRCULATION TRANSPIRATION WALL (TYPICAL)
20. CONSOLE FLOODLIGHT (TYPICAL)

* AIRPLANE AF62-001

1. PILOT'S ADJUSTABLE AIR OUTLET
2. PILOT'S "EYEBALL" AIR OUTLET
3. PILOT'S INSTRUMENT PANEL
3A. MANUAL EMERGENCY LANDING GEAR LEVER *
4. OVERHEAD PANEL
5. OVERHEAD PANEL FLOODLIGHTS
6. COPILOT'S INSTRUMENT PANEL
6A. DEFOGGING SYSTEM THERMAL SWITCH (TYPICAL)
7. FIXED AIR OUTLETS (TYPICAL)
8. COPILOT'S CONSOLE
9. COPILOT'S ADJUSTABLE AIR OUTLET
10. COPILOT'S "EYEBALL" AIR OUTLET
10A. FIXED AIR OUTLET (TYPICAL, BOTH SIDES)

Figure 1-3 (Sheet 2 of 2)

Changed 25 June 1965

T.O. 1B-70(X)A-1

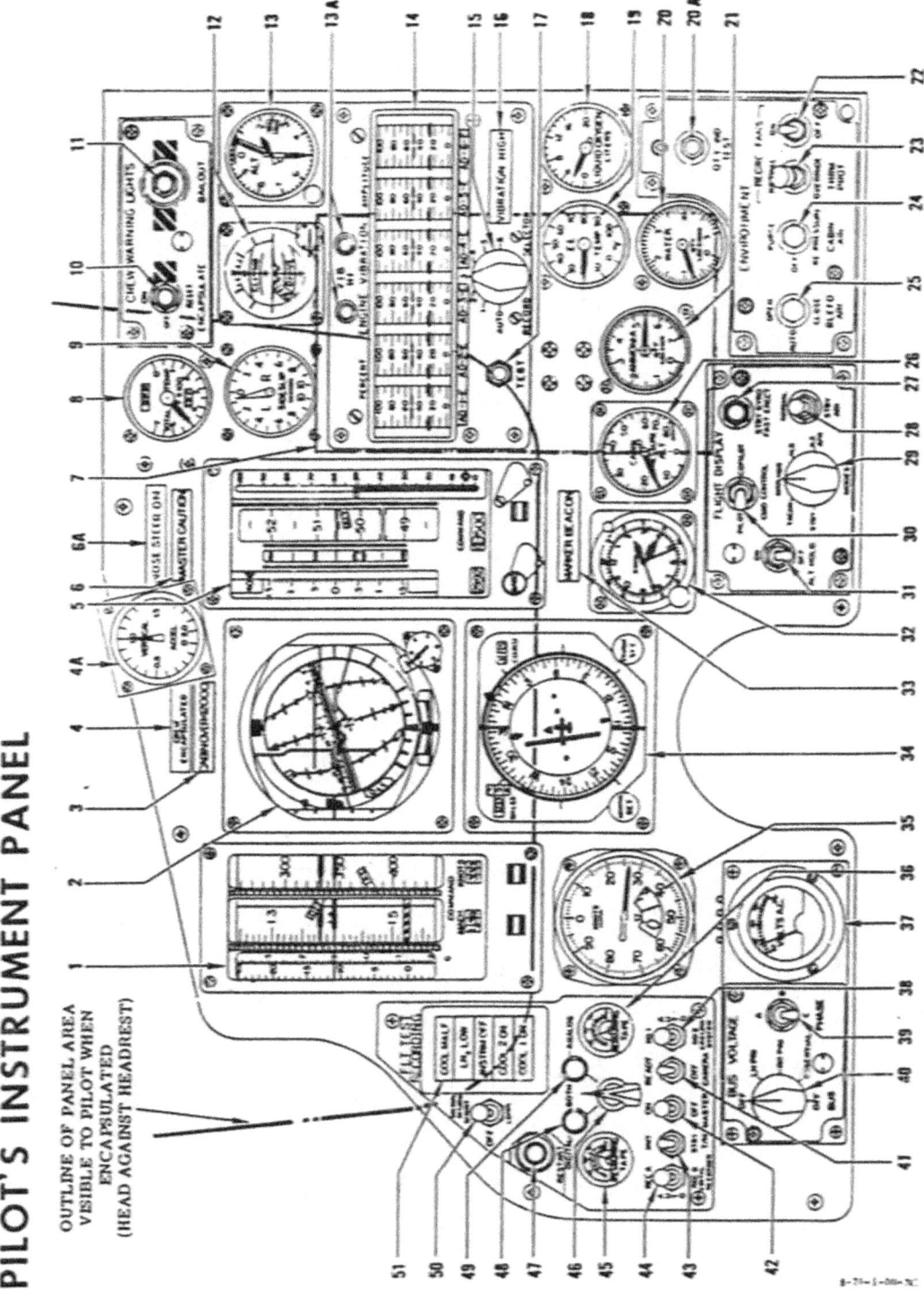

PILOT'S INSTRUMENT PANEL

OUTLINE OF PANEL AREA
VESIBLE TO PILOT WHEN
ENCAPSULATED
(HEAD AGAINST HEADREST)

Figure 1-3 (Sheet 1 of 2)

Changed 25 June 1965

T. O. 1B-70(X)A-1

1. AIRSPEED – MACH NUMBER INDICATOR
2. ATTITUDE DIRECTOR INDICATOR
3. CABIN OVER 42,000 FEET CAUTION LIGHT
4. CREW ENCAPSULATED INDICATOR LIGHT
4A. VERTICAL ACCELEROMETER (SHROUD-MOUNTED)
5. ALTITUDE – VERTICAL VELOCITY INDICATOR
6. MASTER CAUTION LIGHT
6A. NOSE WHEEL STEERING ON INDICATOR LIGHT
7. LETDOWN CHART HOLDER LOCATION (PLUG-IN)
8. TOTAL TEMPERATURE GAGE
9. SIDESLIP INDICATOR
10. ENCAPSULATE CAUTION LIGHT SWITCH
11. BAIL-OUT WARNING LIGHT BUTTON
12. STANDBY ATTITUDE INDICATOR
13. STANDBY ALTIMETER
13A. ENGINE-ADS VIBRATION CAUTION LIGHTS*
14. ENGINE-ADS GEARBOX VIBRATION INDICATORS (TYPICAL)
15. ENGINE-ADS VIBRATION RECORD SELECTOR SWITCH
16. ENGINE-ADS VIBRATION CAUTION LIGHT †
17. ENGINE-ADS VIBRATION INDICATOR TEST BUTTON
18. LIQUID OXYGEN QUANTITY GAGE
19. ELECTRONIC EQUIPMENT COMPARTMENT AIR TEMPERATURE GAGE
20. WATER QUANTITY GAGE
20A. QUANTITY GAGES TEST BUTTON
21. AMMONIA QUANTITY GAGE
22. AIR RECIRCULATING FAN SWITCH
23. AIR RECIRCULATING FAN THERMAL PROTECTION OVERRIDE SWITCH

24. CABIN AIR SWITCH
25. BLEED AIR SWITCH
26. CABIN PRESSURE ALTIMETER
27. STANDBY GYRO FAST ERECT BUTTON
28. ATTITUDE DIRECTOR INDICATOR SELECTOR SWITCH
29. FLIGHT DIRECTOR MODE SELECTOR SWITCH
30. COMMAND CONTROL SWITCH
31. FLIGHT DIRECTOR SYSTEM ALTITUDE HOLD SWITCH
32. CLOCK
33. MARKER BEACON INDICATOR LIGHT
34. HORIZONTAL SITUATION INDICATOR
35. STANDBY AIRSPEED INDICATOR
36. ANALOG TAPE REMAINING INDICATOR
37. AC VOLTMETER
38. INSTRUMENTATION PACKAGE COOLING SYSTEM SELECTOR SWITCH
39. AC VOLTMETER PHASE SELECTOR SWITCH
40. AC VOLTMETER BUS SELECTOR SWITCH
41. CAMERA SWITCH
42. INSTRUMENTATION MASTER SWITCH
43. TELEMETERING SWITCH
44. DIGITAL RECORDER SELECTOR SWITCH
45. DIGITAL TAPE REMAINING INDICATOR
46. RECORDING SYSTEM SELECTOR SWITCH
47. RECORDING RESTART BUTTON
48. DIGITAL RECORD INDICATOR LIGHT
49. ANALOG RECORD INDICATOR LIGHT
50. INTERVAL RECORD SWITCH
51. INSTRUMENTATION CAUTION AND INDICATOR LIGHTS

* AIRPLANE AF62-207
† AIRPLANE AF62-001

Figure 1-3 (Sheet 2 of 2)

Changed 25 June 1965

T. O. 1B-70(X)A-1

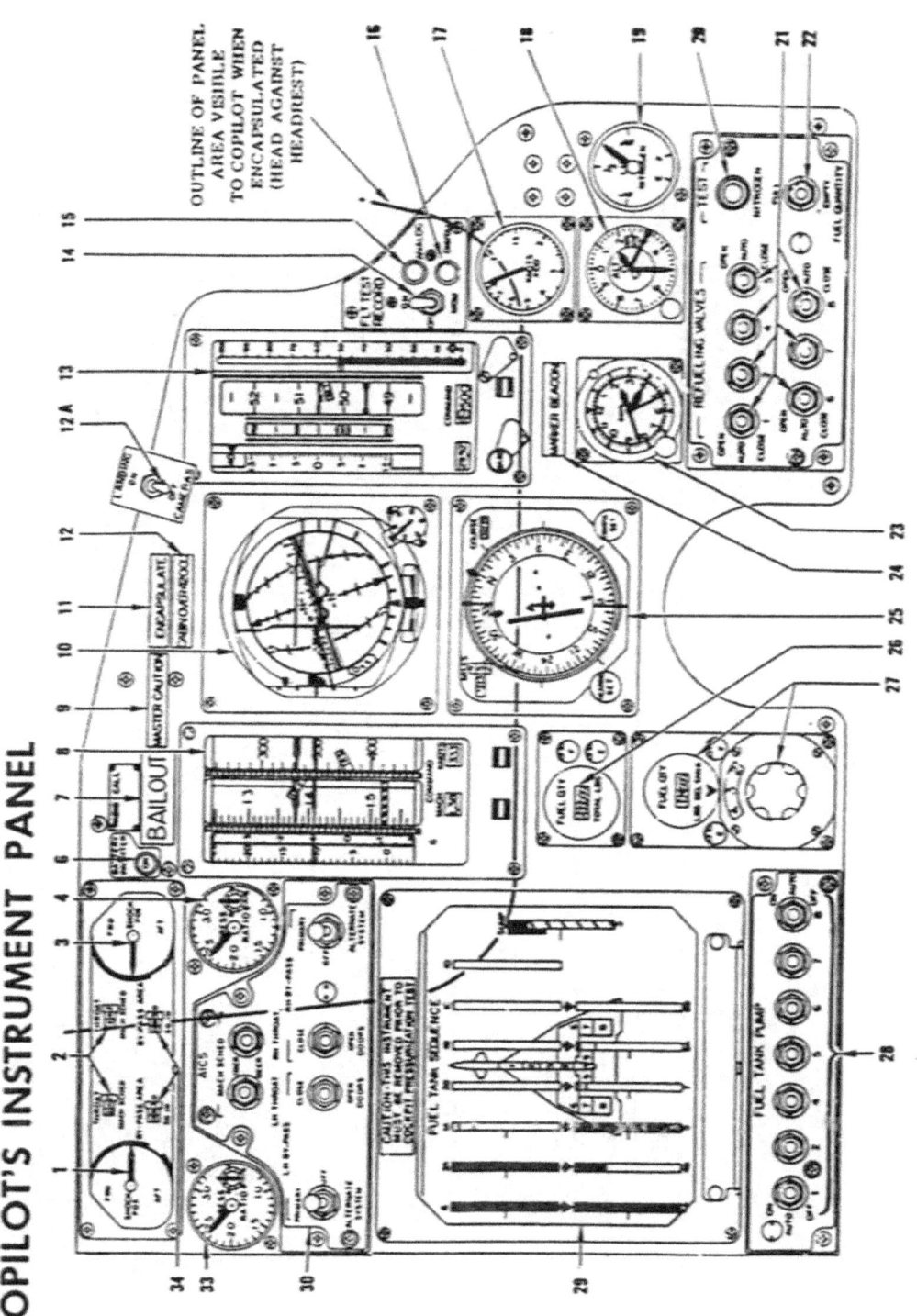

Figure 1-4 (Sheet 1 of 2)

T. O. 1B-70(X)A-1

1. LEFT INLET SHOCK WAVE POSITION INDICATOR
2. LEFT AND RIGHT INLET THROAT MACH SCHEDULE INDICATORS
3. RIGHT INLET SHOCK WAVE POSITION INDICATOR
4. RIGHT INLET PRESSURE RATIO GAGE *
5. DELETED
6. BATTERY INVERTER INDICATOR LIGHT*
7. BAIL-OUT WARNING LIGHT
8. AIRSPEED-MACH NUMBER INDICATOR
9. MASTER CAUTION LIGHT
10. ATTITUDE DIRECTOR INDICATOR
11. ENCAPSULATE CAUTION LIGHT
12. CABIN OVER 42,000 FEET WARNING LIGHT
12A. LANDING CAMERA SWITCH (SHROUD MOUNTED)*
13. ALTITUDE - VERTICAL VELOCITY INDICATOR
14. INSTRUMENTATION RECORD SWITCH
15. ANALOG RECORD INDICATOR LIGHT
16. DIGITAL RECORD INDICATOR LIGHT
17. STANDBY AIRSPEED INDICATOR
18. STANDBY ALTIMETER

19. LIQUID NITROGEN QUANTITY INDICATOR (FUEL PRESSURIZATION AND INERTING SYSTEM)
20. LIQUID NITROGEN QUANTITY INDICATOR TEST BUTTON
21. REFUELING VALVE SWITCHES
22. FUEL QUANTITY INDICATOR TEST SWITCH
23. CLOCK
24. MARKER BEACON INDICATOR LIGHT
25. HORIZONTAL SITUATION INDICATOR
26. TOTAL FUEL QUANTITY INDICATOR
27. SELECTED FUEL TANK QUANTITY INDICATOR AND SELECTOR KNOB
28. FUEL TRANSFER PUMP SWITCHES
29. FUEL TANK SEQUENCE INDICATOR
30. AICS PANEL (TYPICAL)
31. DELETED
32. DELETED
33. LEFT INLET PRESSURE RATIO GAGE
34. LEFT AND RIGHT INLET BYPASS AREA INDICATORS

* Airplane AF62-001

Figure 1-4 (Sheet 2 of 2)

Changed 25 June 1965

T.O. 1B-70(X)A-1

CENTER INSTRUMENT PANEL

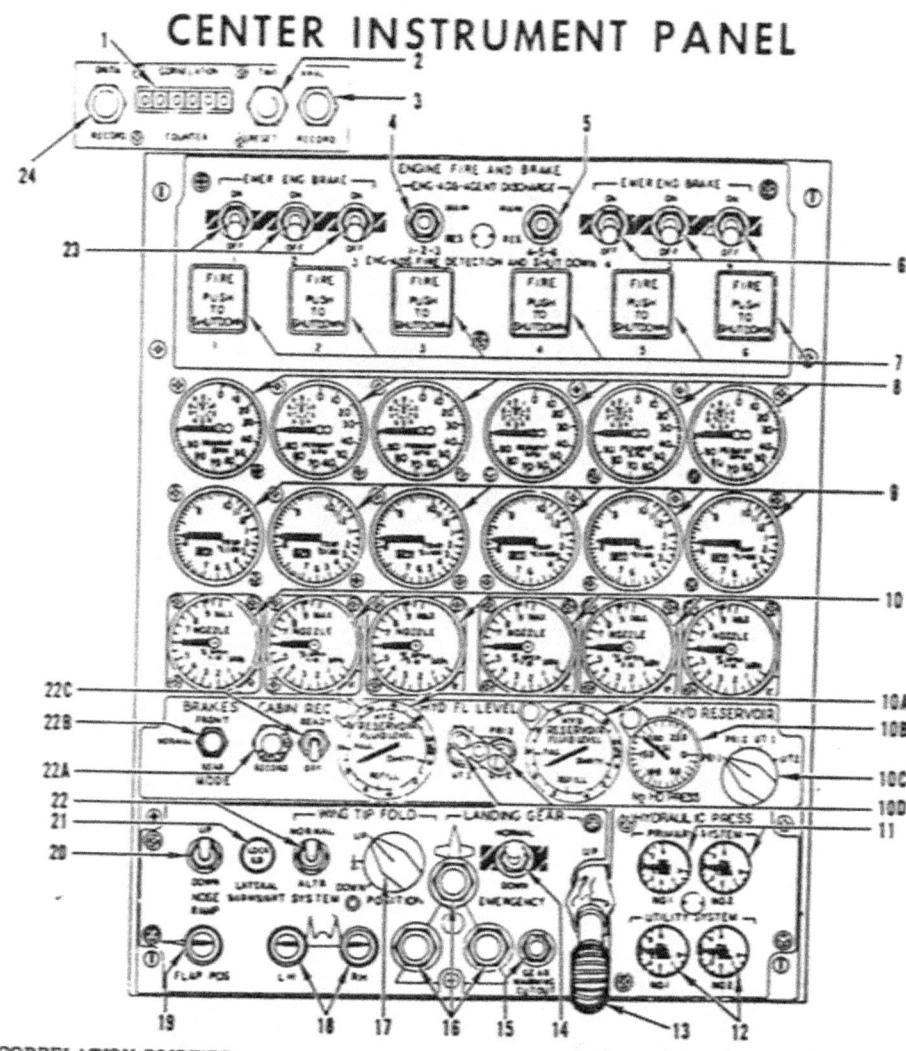

1. CORRELATION COUNTER
2. CORRELATION TIME AND COUNTER RESET BUTTON
3. ANALOG RECORDER INDICATOR LIGHT
4. FIRE EXTINGUISHER AGENT DISCHARGE SWITCH (NO. 1, 2, AND 3 ENGINES)
5. FIRE EXTINGUISHER AGENT DISCHARGE SWITCH (NO. 4, 5, AND 6 ENGINES)
6. ENGINE EMERGENCY BRAKE SWITCHES
7. FIRE WARNING LIGHTS/ENGINE SHUTDOWN BUTTONS
8. TACHOMETERS
9. EXHAUST TEMPERATURE GAGES
10. PRIMARY EXHAUST NOZZLE POSITION INDICATORS
10A. HYDRAULIC RESERVOIR FLUID LEVEL INDICATORS
10B. HYDRAULIC RESERVOIR GASEOUS NITROGEN HEAD PRESSURE GAGE
10C. HYDRAULIC RESERVOIR HEAD PRESSURE SELECTOR SWITCH
10D. HYDRAULIC RESERVOIR FLUID LEVEL SELECTOR SWITCHES
11. PRIMARY HYDRAULIC SYSTEM PRESSURE GAGES
12. UTILITY HYDRAULIC SYSTEM PRESSURE GAGES
13. LANDING GEAR HANDLE
14. LANDING GEAR EMERGENCY LOWERING SWITCH
15. LANDING GEAR AUDIBLE WARNING SYSTEM CUTOUT BUTTON
16. LANDING GEAR POSITION LIGHTS
17. WING TIP POSITION SELECTOR SWITCH
18. WING TIP POSITION INDICATORS
19. FLAP POSITION INDICATOR
20. NOSE RAMP SWITCH
21. LATERAL BOBWEIGHT INDICATOR*
22. WING TIP FOLD MODE SWITCH
22A. CABIN RECORDER INDICATOR LIGHT
22B. WHEEL BRAKE MODE SWITCH
22C. CABIN RECORDER SWITCH
23. ENGINE EMERGENCY BRAKE SWITCHES
24. DIGITAL RECORDER INDICATOR LIGHT

* Airplane AF62-001

Figure 1-5

Changed 25 June 1965

T.O. 1B-70(X)A-1

OVERHEAD PANEL AND LANDING GEAR EMERGENCY LEVER

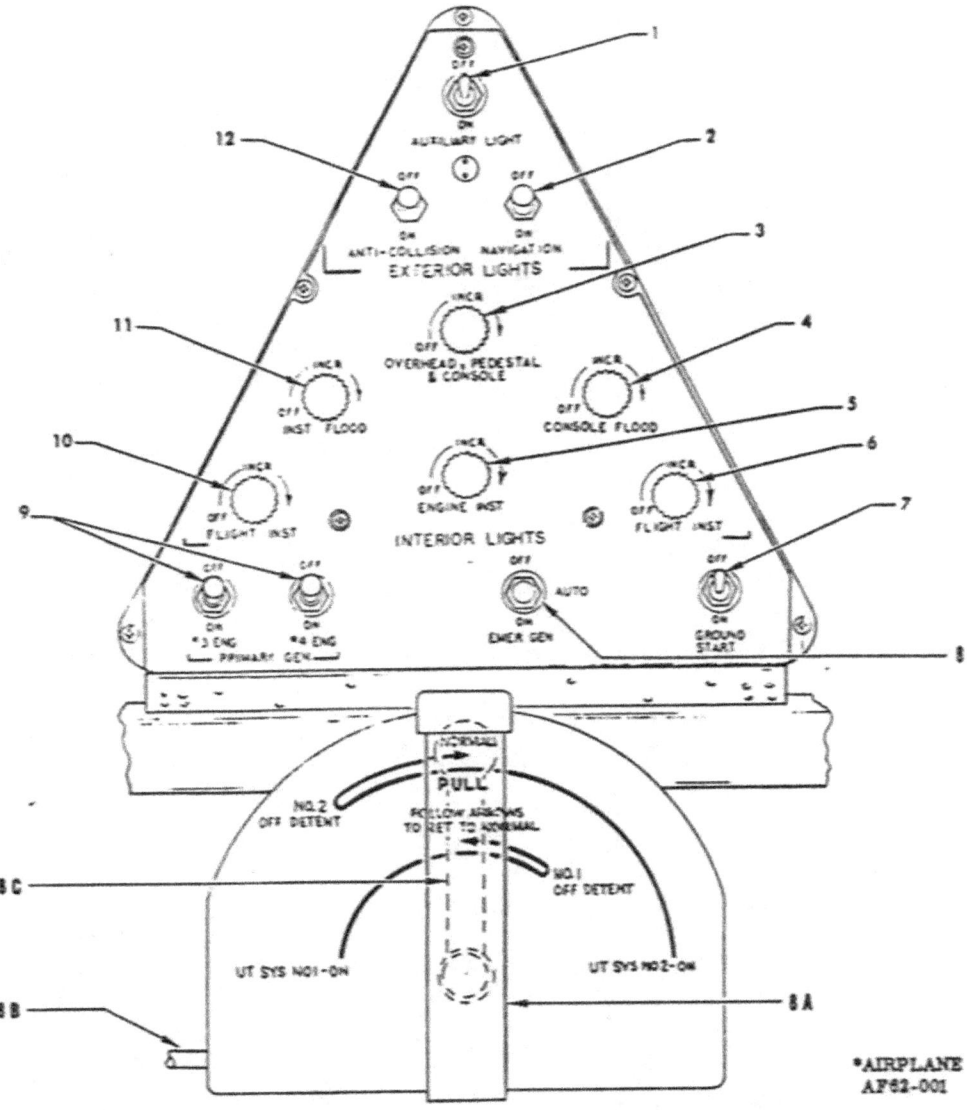

1. AUXILIARY LANDING AND TAXI LIGHT SWITCH
2. NAVIGATION LIGHT SWITCH
3. OVERHEAD, PEDESTAL, AND CONSOLE INDIRECT LIGHT SWITCH AND RHEOSTAT
4. CONSOLE FLOODLIGHT SWITCH AND RHEOSTAT
5. ENGINE INSTRUMENT INDIRECT LIGHT SWITCH AND RHEOSTAT
6. COPILOT'S FLIGHT INSTRUMENT INDIRECT LIGHT SWITCH AND RHEOSTAT
7. ENGINE GROUND START SWITCH
8. EMERGENCY GENERATOR SWITCH
8A. GEAR EMERGENCY LEVER COVER GUARD*
8B. TELEFLEX TO HANDLE IN ELECTRONIC EQUIPEMENT COMPARTMENT *
8C. MANUAL EMERGENCY LANDING GEAR LEVER*
9. PRIMARY GENERATOR SWITCHES
10. PILOT'S FLIGHT INSTRUMENT INDIRECT LIGHT SWITCH AND RHEOSTAT
11. INSTRUMENT PANEL FLOODLIGHT SWITCH AND RHEOSTAT
12. ANTICOLLISION LIGHT SWITCH

*AIRPLANE AF62-001

Figure 1-6

Changed 25 June 1965

T.O. 1B-70(X)A-1

CENTER CONSOLE

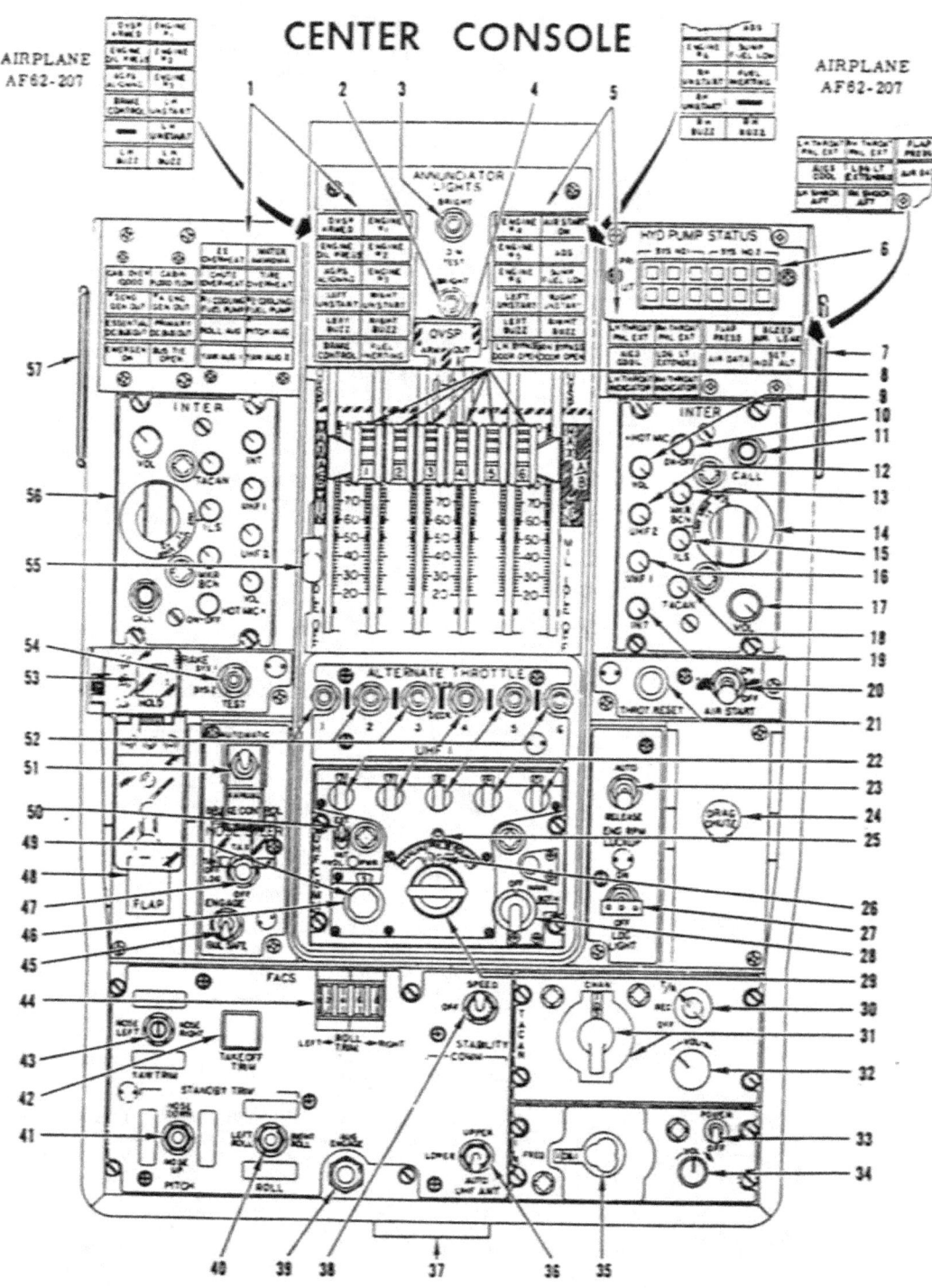

Figure 1-7 (Sheet 1 of 2)

T.O. 1B-70(X)A-1

1. ANNUNCIATOR LIGHTS
2. ANNUNCIATOR LIGHT INTENSITY SWITCH
3. ANNUNCIATOR LIGHT TEST SWITCH
4. ENGINE OVERSPEED ARMING LEVER
5. ANNUNCIATOR LIGHTS
6. HYDRAULIC PUMP STATUS INDICATORS
7. UHF FREQUENCY CARD HOLDER
8. THROTTLES
9. HOT MICROPHONE VOLUME KNOB
10. HOT MICROPHONE ON-OFF SWITCH
11. INTERCOM CALL BUTTON
12. UHF NO. 2 MIXER SWITCH
13. MARKER BEACON MIXER SWITCH
14. FUNCTION SELECTOR SWITCH
15. ILS MIXER SWITCH
16. UHF NO. 1 MIXER SWITCH
17. MASTER VOLUME KNOB
18. TACAN MIXER SWITCH
19. INTERCOM MIXER SWITCH
20. AIR START SWITCH
21. THROTTLE RESET BUTTON
22. VHF MANUAL FREQUENCY SELECTOR KNOBS
23. ENGINE RPM LOCKUP SWITCH
24. DRAG CHUTE HANDLE
25. UHF MANUAL - PRESET-GUARD SLIDING SELECTOR
26. UHF CHANNEL INDICATOR
27. LANDING LIGHT SWITCH
28. UHF FUNCTION SWITCH
29. UHF CHANNEL SELECTOR KNOB
30. TACAN FUNCTION SWITCH
31. TACAN CHANNEL SELECTOR SWITCH
32. TACAN VOLUME KNOB (INOPERATIVE)
33. ILS POWER SWITCH
34. ILS VOLUME KNOB (INOPERATIVE)
35. ILS FREQUENCY SELECTOR KNOB
36. UHF ANTENNA SELECTOR SWITCH
37. CONSOLE RELEASE HANDLE
38. FLIGHT AUGMENTATION CONTROL SYSTEM SPEED STABILITY SWITCH
39. FLIGHT AUGMENTATION CONTROL SYSTEM ENGAGE BUTTON
40. STANDBY TRIM ROLL SWITCH
41. STANDBY TRIM PITCH SWITCH
42. TAKE-OFF TRIM BUTTON/LIGHT
43. YAW TRIM SWITCH
44. PRIMARY ROLL TRIM KNOB
45. NOSE WHEEL STEERING ENGAGE SWITCH
46. UHF VOLUME KNOB (INOPERATIVE)
47. NOSE WHEEL STEERING SELECTOR SWITCH
48. FLAP HANDLE
49. UHF TRANSMITTER POWER OUTPUT KNOB
50. UHF MODULATION SELECTOR SWITCH (INOPERATIVE)
51. WHEEL BRAKE CONTROL SWITCH
52. ALTERNATE THROTTLE SWITCHES
53. WHEEL BRAKE HOLD SWITCH
54. WHEEL BRAKE TEST SWITCH
55. THROTTLE FRICTION LEVER
56. INTERCOM PANEL (SAME AS ITEMS 9 THRU 19)
57. UHF FREQUENCY CARD HOLDER

NOTE

Horizontal bar or cover of each blank annunciator light is illuminated during light test to identify it as an unused light.

Figure 1-7 (Sheet 2 of 2)

Changed 25 June 1965

T. O. 1B-70(X)A-1

PILOT'S CONSOLE

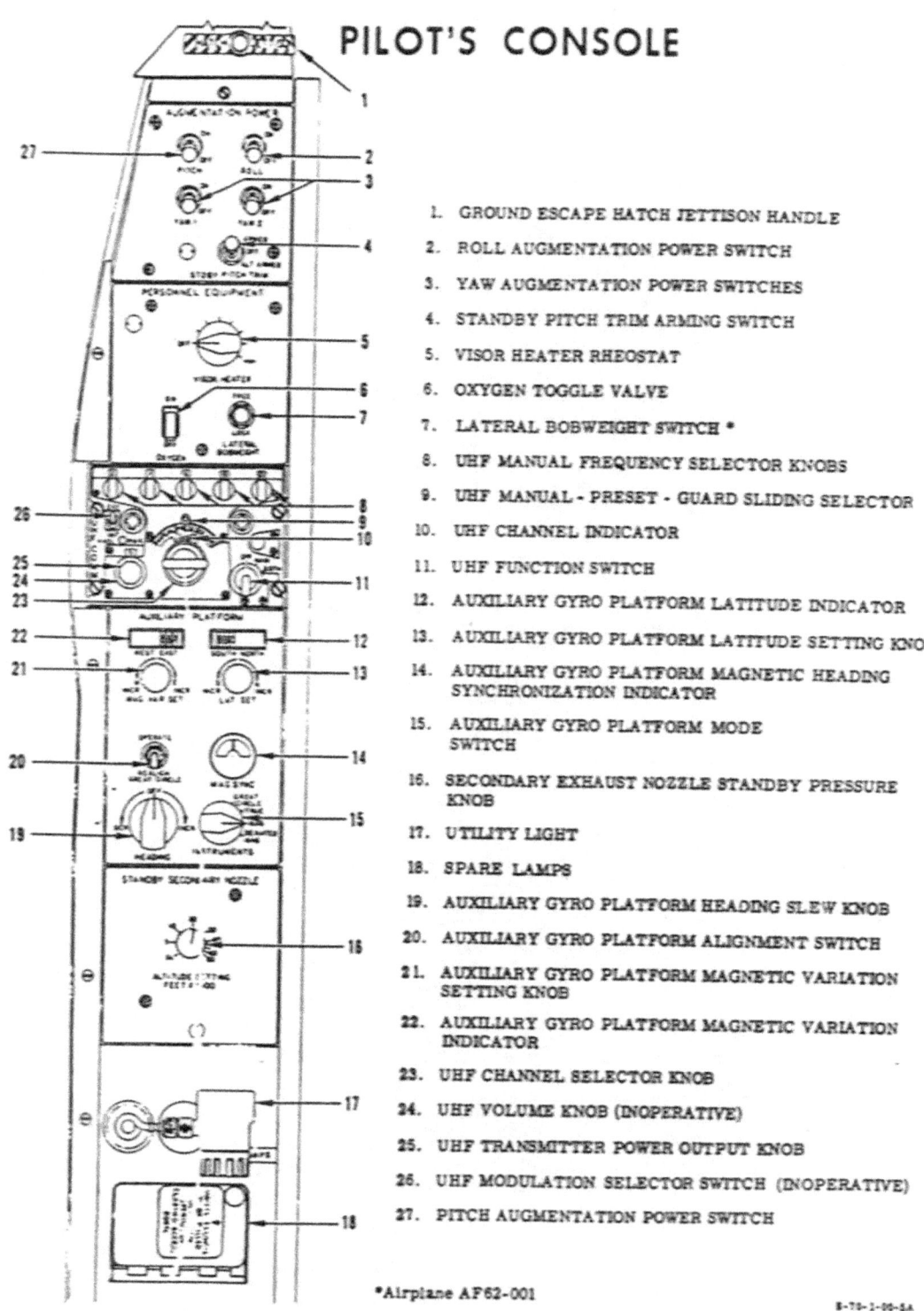

1. GROUND ESCAPE HATCH JETTISON HANDLE
2. ROLL AUGMENTATION POWER SWITCH
3. YAW AUGMENTATION POWER SWITCHES
4. STANDBY PITCH TRIM ARMING SWITCH
5. VISOR HEATER RHEOSTAT
6. OXYGEN TOGGLE VALVE
7. LATERAL BOBWEIGHT SWITCH *
8. UHF MANUAL FREQUENCY SELECTOR KNOBS
9. UHF MANUAL - PRESET - GUARD SLIDING SELECTOR
10. UHF CHANNEL INDICATOR
11. UHF FUNCTION SWITCH
12. AUXILIARY GYRO PLATFORM LATITUDE INDICATOR
13. AUXILIARY GYRO PLATFORM LATITUDE SETTING KNOB
14. AUXILIARY GYRO PLATFORM MAGNETIC HEADING SYNCHRONIZATION INDICATOR
15. AUXILIARY GYRO PLATFORM MODE SWITCH
16. SECONDARY EXHAUST NOZZLE STANDBY PRESSURE KNOB
17. UTILITY LIGHT
18. SPARE LAMPS
19. AUXILIARY GYRO PLATFORM HEADING SLEW KNOB
20. AUXILIARY GYRO PLATFORM ALIGNMENT SWITCH
21. AUXILIARY GYRO PLATFORM MAGNETIC VARIATION SETTING KNOB
22. AUXILIARY GYRO PLATFORM MAGNETIC VARIATION INDICATOR
23. UHF CHANNEL SELECTOR KNOB
24. UHF VOLUME KNOB (INOPERATIVE)
25. UHF TRANSMITTER POWER OUTPUT KNOB
26. UHF MODULATION SELECTOR SWITCH (INOPERATIVE)
27. PITCH AUGMENTATION POWER SWITCH

*Airplane AF62-001

Figure 1-8

T.O. 1B-70(X)A-1

COPILOT'S CONSOLE

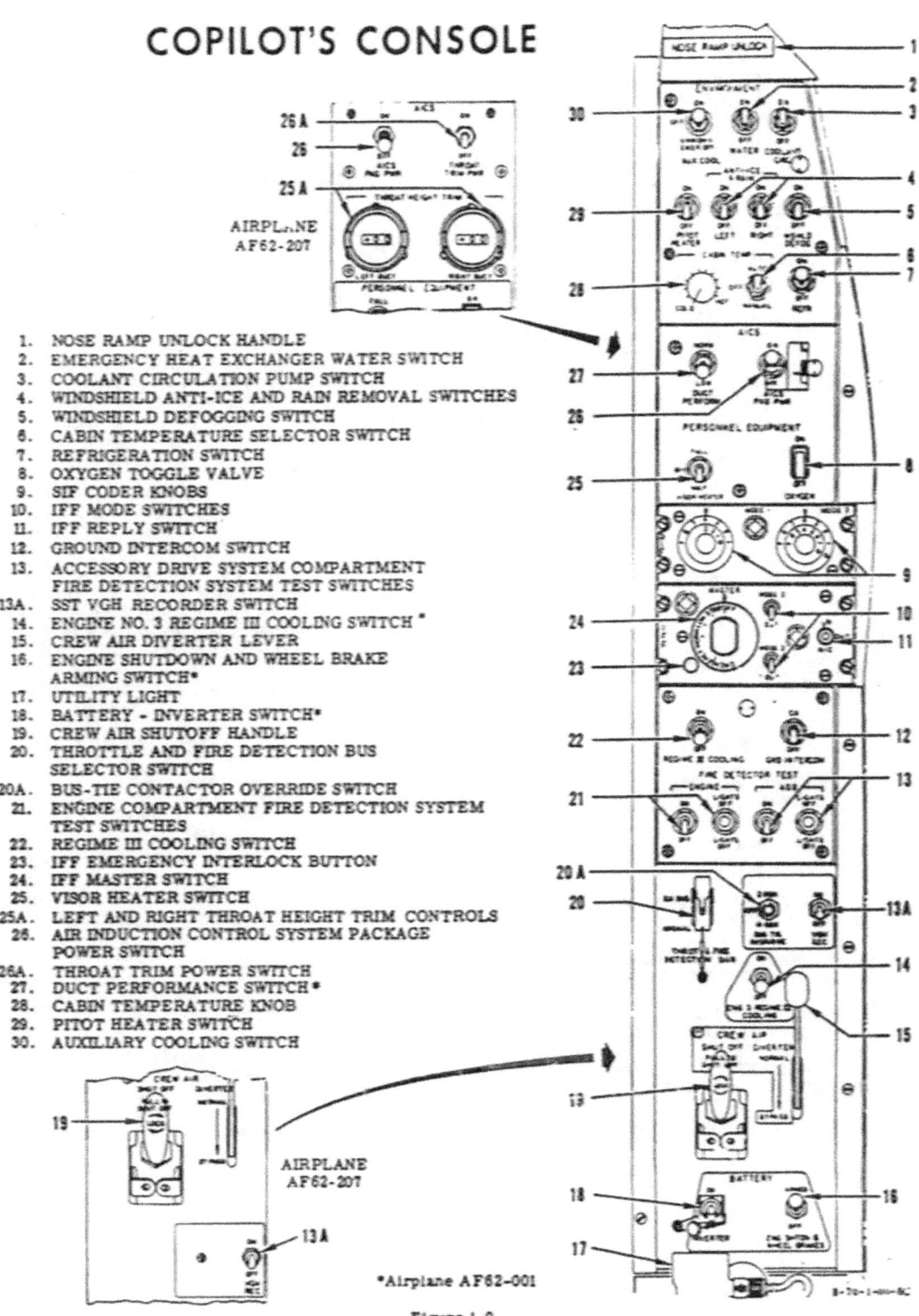

1. NOSE RAMP UNLOCK HANDLE
2. EMERGENCY HEAT EXCHANGER WATER SWITCH
3. COOLANT CIRCULATION PUMP SWITCH
4. WINDSHIELD ANTI-ICE AND RAIN REMOVAL SWITCHES
5. WINDSHIELD DEFOGGING SWITCH
6. CABIN TEMPERATURE SELECTOR SWITCH
7. REFRIGERATION SWITCH
8. OXYGEN TOGGLE VALVE
9. SIF CODER KNOBS
10. IFF MODE SWITCHES
11. IFF REPLY SWITCH
12. GROUND INTERCOM SWITCH
13. ACCESSORY DRIVE SYSTEM COMPARTMENT FIRE DETECTION SYSTEM TEST SWITCHES
13A. SST VGH RECORDER SWITCH
14. ENGINE NO. 3 REGIME III COOLING SWITCH*
15. CREW AIR DIVERTER LEVER
16. ENGINE SHUTDOWN AND WHEEL BRAKE ARMING SWITCH*
17. UTILITY LIGHT
18. BATTERY - INVERTER SWITCH*
19. CREW AIR SHUTOFF HANDLE
20. THROTTLE AND FIRE DETECTION BUS SELECTOR SWITCH
20A. BUS-TIE CONTACTOR OVERRIDE SWITCH
21. ENGINE COMPARTMENT FIRE DETECTION SYSTEM TEST SWITCHES
22. REGIME III COOLING SWITCH
23. IFF EMERGENCY INTERLOCK BUTTON
24. IFF MASTER SWITCH
25. VISOR HEATER SWITCH
25A. LEFT AND RIGHT THROAT HEIGHT TRIM CONTROLS
26. AIR INDUCTION CONTROL SYSTEM PACKAGE POWER SWITCH
26A. THROAT TRIM POWER SWITCH
27. DUCT PERFORMANCE SWITCH*
28. CABIN TEMPERATURE KNOB
29. PITOT HEATER SWITCH
30. AUXILIARY COOLING SWITCH

*Airplane AF62-001

Figure 1-9

Changed 25 June 1965

T. O. 1B-70(X)A-1

AICS CONTROLS
COPILOT'S CONTROL PEDESTAL
(AIRPLANE AF62-001)

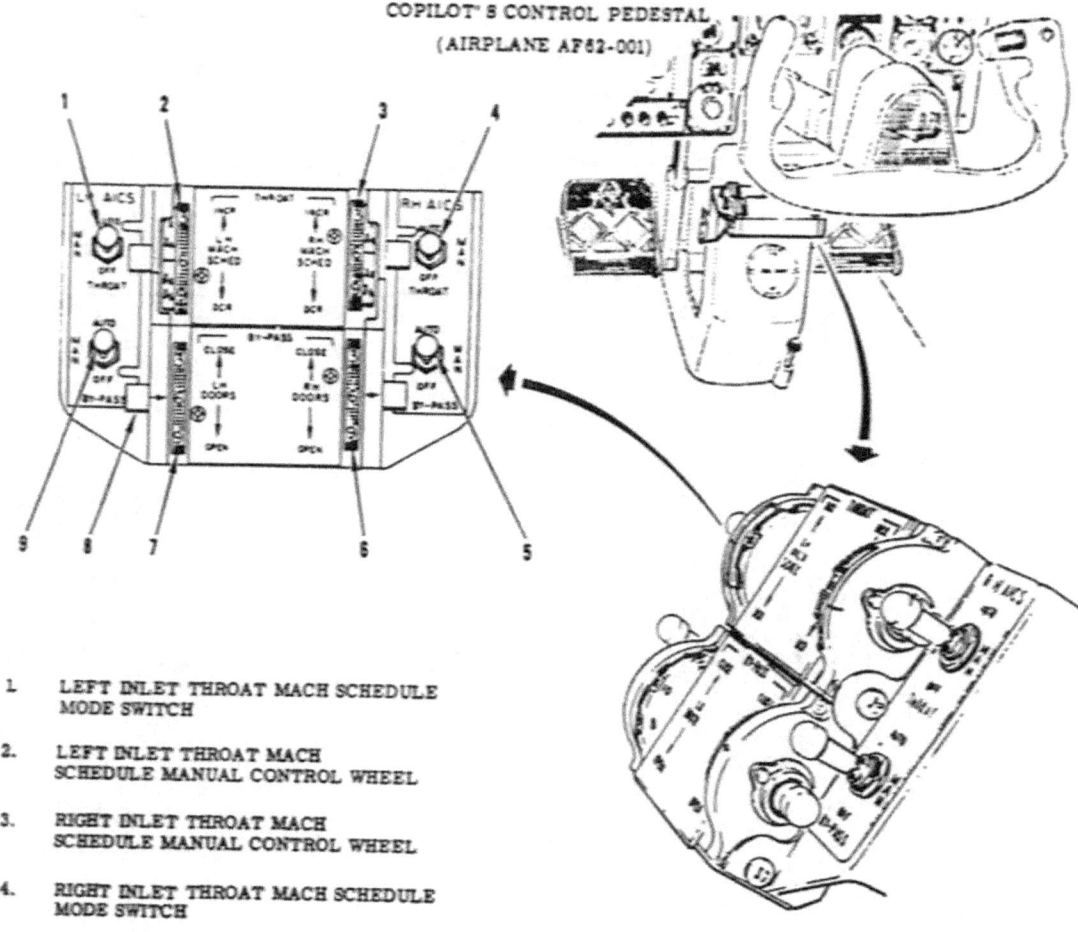

1. LEFT INLET THROAT MACH SCHEDULE MODE SWITCH
2. LEFT INLET THROAT MACH SCHEDULE MANUAL CONTROL WHEEL
3. RIGHT INLET THROAT MACH SCHEDULE MANUAL CONTROL WHEEL
4. RIGHT INLET THROAT MACH SCHEDULE MODE SWITCH
5. RIGHT INLET BYPASS DOOR MODE SWITCH
6. RIGHT INLET BYPASS DOOR MANUAL CONTROL WHEEL
7. LEFT INLET BYPASS DOOR MANUAL CONTROL WHEEL
8. WHEEL POTENTIOMETER (4) - FLIGHT TEST INSTRUMENTATION
9. LEFT INLET BYPASS DOOR MODE SWITCH

NOTE

The bypass area reference numbers on the inside face of the bypass door manual control wheel are typical for both bypass door control wheels.

Figure 1-10 (Sheet 1 of 2)

Changed 25 June 1965

T. O. 1B-70(X)A-1

COPILOT'S INSTRUMENT PANEL

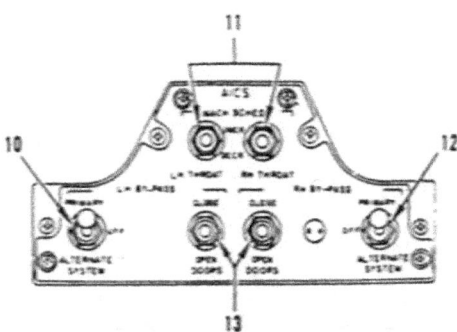

(AIRPLANE AF62-001)

(AIRPLANE AF62-207)

10. LEFT INLET BYPASS DOOR STANDBY SYSTEM SELECTOR SWITCH
11. LEFT AND RIGHT INLET THROAT MACH SCHEDULE STANDBY SWITCHES
12. RIGHT INLET BYPASS DOOR STANDBY SYSTEM SELECTOR SWITCH
13. LEFT AND RIGHT INLET BYPASS DOOR STANDBY SWITCHES

14. LEFT INLET AICS MODE SWITCH
15. DUCT PERFORMANCE SWITCH
16. LEFT AND RIGHT INLET THROAT MACH SCHEDULE STANDBY SWITCHES
17. RIGHT INLET AICS MODE SWITCH
18. AICS RESET SWITCH/LIGHT
19. LEFT AND RIGHT INLET BYPASS DOOR STANDBY SWITCHES

COPILOT'S CONSOLE

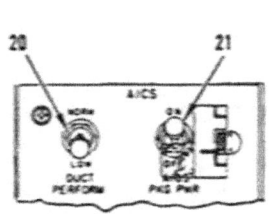

(AIRPLANE AF62-001)

20. DUCT PERFORMANCE SWITCH
21. AIR INDUCTION CONTROL SYSTEM PACKAGE POWER SWITCH
22. AIR INDUCTION CONTROL SYSTEM PACKAGE POWER SWITCH
23. THROAT TRIM POWER SWITCH
24. THROAT HEIGHT TRIM CONTROLS
25. THROAT HEIGHT TRIM INDICATORS
26. THROAT HEIGHT TRIM CONTROL KNOBS
27. THROAT HEIGHT TRIM CONTROL KNOB LOCK (TYPICAL)

(AIRPLANE AF62-207)

Figure 1-10 (Sheet 2 of 2)

T. O. 1B-70(X)A-1

CONTROL WHEELS

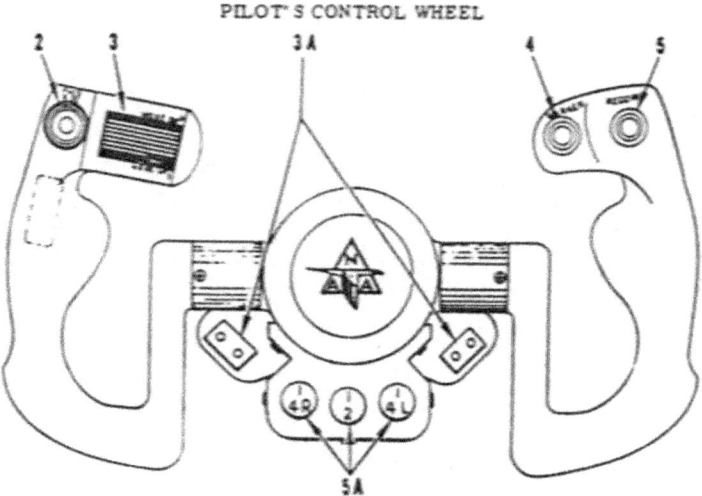

PILOT'S CONTROL WHEEL

NOTE
Use applicable stop selector pin to obtain desired wheel rotation. For a 3/4 turn stop, use opposite 1/4 selector pin. (To select stop, push pin in and turn left 90 degrees. To release, turn pin right 90 degrees. Pin is spring-loaded out.)

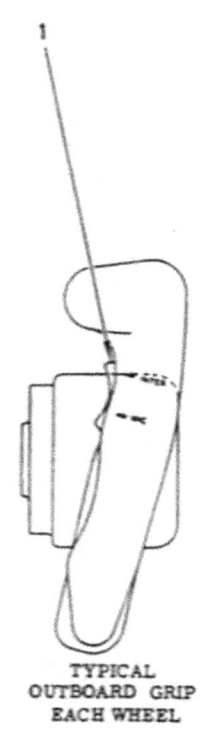

TYPICAL OUTBOARD GRIP EACH WHEEL

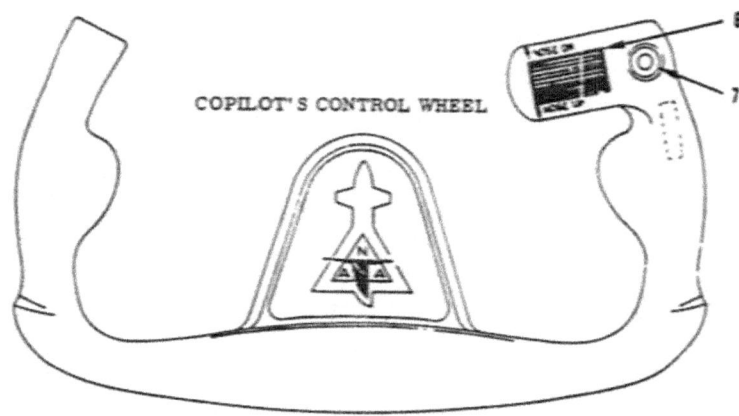

COPILOT'S CONTROL WHEEL

1. INTERCOM-MICROPHONE SWITCH
2. FLIGHT AUGMENTATION CONTROL SYSTEM DISENGAGE BUTTON
3. PRIMARY PITCH TRIM KNOB
3A. WHEEL ROTATION STOPS (INSTRUMENTATION INSTALLATION)
4. EVENT MARKER BUTTON
5. INSTRUMENTATION RECORD BUTTON
5A. WHEEL ROTATION STOP SELECTOR PINS
6. PRIMARY PITCH TRIM KNOB
7. FLIGHT AUGMENTATION CONTROL SYSTEM DISENGAGE BUTTON (ROLL AND PITCH ONLY)

Figure 1-11

Changed 25 June 1965

T.O. 1B-70(X)A-1

WING TIP AND LANDING GEAR EMERGENCY CONTROLS AND GROUND TEST PANEL
(IN ELECTRONIC EQUIPMENT COMPARTMENT)

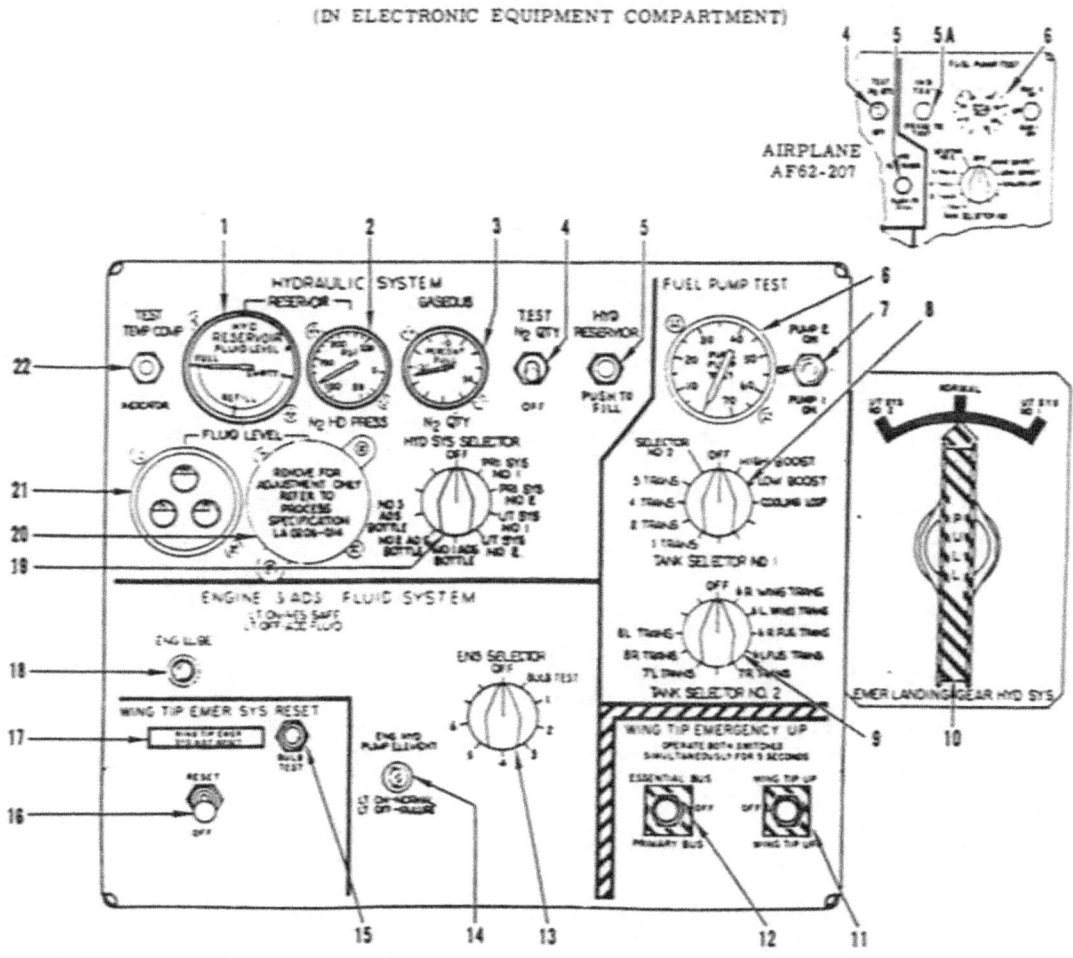

1. HYDRAULIC RESERVOIR FLUID LEVEL INDICATOR *
2. HYDRAULIC RESERVOIR NITROGEN HEAD PRESSURE GAGE *
3. GASEOUS NITROGEN QUANTITY INDICATOR
4. GASEOUS NITROGEN QUANTITY INDICATOR TEST SWITCH
5. HYDRAULIC RESERVOIR GROUND SERVICING BUTTON
5A. FUEL PUMP GAGE TEST BUTTON
6. FUEL PUMP TEST GAGE
7. FUEL PUMP TEST SWITCH
8. FUEL TANK PUMP SELECTOR SWITCH NO. 1
9. FUEL TANK PUMP SELECTOR SWITCH NO. 2
10. MANUAL EMERGENCY LANDING GEAR HANDLE (TYPICAL)
11. WING TIP EMERGENCY-UP SWITCH
12. WING TIP EMERGENCY-UP POWER SELECTOR SWITCH
13. ENGINE FLUID SELECTOR SWITCH
14. ENGINE HYDRAULIC PUMP ELEMENT INDICATOR LIGHT
15. WING TIP CAUTION LIGHT TEST BUTTON
16. WING TIP EMERGENCY-UP SYSTEM RESET SWITCH
17. WING TIP EMERGENCY-UP SYSTEM NOT RESET CAUTION LIGHT
18. ENGINE OIL TANK FLUID LEVEL INDICATOR LIGHT
19. HYDRAULIC SYSTEMS SELECTOR SWITCH
20. TEMPERATURE COMPENSATING UNIT AND REFERENCE INDICATOR (MAINTENANCE ONLY) *
21. POWER UNIT (MAINTENANCE ONLY)
22. FLUID LEVEL INDICATOR TEMPERATURE COMPENSATOR TEST SWITCH (MAINTENANCE ONLY) *

* AIRPLANE AF62-001

Figure 1-12

low-pressure system line connections are welded.

The hydraulically powered flight control systems have an electronic control augmentation system which automatically compensates control surface movements for the prevailing flight conditions. Elevons at the wing trailing edge, outboard of the engines, are segmented to reduce air-load bending effects. The wing tips can be folded down to increase directional stability at high Mach numbers. The movable canard is geared to the elevons for increased pitch control. Flaps, for use in take-offs and landings, are on the trailing edge of the canard.

The tricycle landing gear has dual steerable nose wheels and four wheels on each main gear bogie. An additional wheel on each main gear supplies speed sensing for the automatic braking system. Simultaneously deployed drag chutes reduce the landing roll. A cooling system reduces the temperature in the landing gear and drag chute compartments.

An air induction control system varies the internal geometry of the inlets to maintain the required airflow to the engines at all flight conditions. Six accessory drive system gearboxes, each shaft-driven by a corresponding engine, are mounted in separate compartments forward of the engines. These gearboxes drive the hydraulic pumps, and each of the two inboard gearboxes drives an ac generator. Fuel is carried in integral tanks in the fuselage center section and inboard wing panels. The fuel system is pressurized and inerted by nitrogen. Intertank fuel transfer sequencing is automatic.

The airplane has two windshields: a movable outer windshield and a fixed inner windshield. The outer windshield is raised to form a smooth unbroken fuselage contour for low drag during high-speed flight and is lowered for maximum over-the-nose vision during low speeds.

The pilot and copilot sit side by side in individual escape capsules. Each capsule has a self-contained oxygen and pressurization system, affording complete crew protection during and following ejection. The capsules also can be closed, if necessary, for crew protection in an in-flight emergency. Limited control of the airplane and engines for an emergency descent is available when the capsules are closed. During ejection, capsule stabilization devices and a parachute are deployed automatically. Survival equipment is stowed in each capsule.

AIRPLANE DIMENSIONS.

The over-all dimensions of the airplane with the airplane on the landing gear, at normal weight and tires and gear struts at specified inflation, are as follows:

Span . . . . 105 feet
Length (including
 pitot boom) . . . . 193 feet 5 inches
Height (to top of
 rudders) . . . . . 30 feet 9 inches

For the minimum turning radius and ground clearance, see figure 2-4.

AIRPLANE WEIGHT.

The airplane is in the 500,000-pound weight class. For detailed weight information, refer to "Weight Limitations" in Section V.

T.O. 1B-70(X)A-1

ENGINES.

Six General Electric YJ93-GE-3 turbojet engines incorporating afterburners are mounted side by side in individual compartments across the rear of the fuselage. Each engine and engine compartment is identified in the conventional manner from left to right, with left outboard as No. 1.

NOTE
For additional information, refer to the Confidential Supplement, T.O. 1B-70(X)A-1A.

ENGINE CONTROLS.

THROTTLES.

The six throttle levers (8, figure 1-7), one for each engine, control various engine and fuel system functions in addition to selecting engine thrust. The throttles are in a quadrant on the center console, arranged and numbered to correspond with the respective engines. Grouping of the throttle levers permits individual control of each engine or simultaneous control, with one hand, of all six engines. The quadrant is calibrated in degrees of travel of the engine power lever on the engine fuel control. (These calibrations are not degrees of throttle lever travel, nor direct indications of percent rpm, but can be used as throttle position references.) For throttle quadrant markings versus thrust, see figure 2-6. An orange area on each side of the quadrant identifies the afterburner range.

Movement of each throttle is transmitted to the main fuel control of its corresponding engine by an electrical-mechanical servo system. The throttle is connected mechanically to a synchro transformer which responds to and senses changes in throttle settings. A synchro transmitter senses the setting of the main fuel control. The synchros electrically compare the throttle setting with that of the fuel control and supply an electrical signal to the thrust control amplifier whenever the throttle and fuel control settings do not agree. The amplifier, in turn, directs power to an electric motor in the thrust control actuator which repositions the setting of the main fuel control. When the fuel control setting corresponds to the throttle setting, the synchro signal to the control amplifier is shut off. In response to throttle movement in the afterburner range, the thrust control actuator changes the setting of the afterburner fuel control by positioning a servo system within the nozzle area control which is connected mechanically to the afterburner control. The throttle servo system normally receives power from the essential ac bus; however if this power is not available, a switch in the crew compartment permits the throttle servo circuits to be powered by the right primary ac bus. Individual circuits, one for each engine, provide an emergency means of increasing or decreasing thrust if a throttle servo system fails. (Refer to "Alternate Throttle Switches" in this section.)

When electrical power is available and the throttles are moved from OFF to IDLE, the engine start and ignition systems are armed, the fire wall fuel shutoff valve for the corresponding engine is opened, and the fuel cutoff valve in the corresponding main fuel control is opened. If pressure is available in each hydraulic system, moving the throttles from OFF to IDLE also starts the fuel boost pumps, the fuel cooling loop pumps, and permits transfer pump operation.

NOTE
To reduce hydraulic loads during ground starts, the boost pump and the cooling loop pump powered by the No. 1 primary hydraulic system are shut down when engines 1, 2, or 3 are started; during starting of engines 4, 5, or 6, the boost pump and cooling loop pump powered by

Changed 25 June 1965

T.O. 1B-70(X)A-1

ENGINE FUEL CONTROL SYSTEM

REFER TO CONFIDENTIAL SUPPLEMENT, T.O. 1B-70(X)A-1A

Figure 1-13

the No. 2 primary hydraulic system are shut down. (The boost pump powered by the No. 1 utility hydraulic system is not shut down during any engine start.)

A positive stop prevents inadvertent forward movement of the throttles from OFF to IDLE. The throttle must be lifted and moved forward over the stop and then pushed down into the IDLE position.

The desired thrust settings are obtained by advancing the throttles from IDLE. If a downward pressure is applied to the top of the throttles and maintained as they are advanced, the MIL (Military Thrust) detent will feel like a positive stop, preventing inadvertent throttle movement into the afterburner range. The afterburners are engaged when the throttles are moved up a ramp from the MIL position to MIN A/B. (Refer to "Engine Afterburner System" in this section.)

NOTE
Having the throttles for three engines on either side, or all six throttles in the range from IDLE to below MIN/AB, completes the water control circuits for the fuel-cooling heat exchanger in the cooling loop. (Refer to "Fuel Supply System" in this section.)

Advancing the throttles in the afterburner range of the quadrant increases afterburner fuel flow and thrust until the positive stop at the MAX A/B position is reached. Whenever a throttle is advanced beyond the 88-degree marking of the quadrant, a throttle-actuated switch opens the circuit from the regime III cooling switch to the corresponding engine compartment cooling system. This automatically changes the engine compartment cooling to regime II if regime III had been selected. (Refer to "Engine Compartment Cooling System" in this section.) To retard the throttles within the afterburner range, an upward force should be applied to the throttles as they are moved back. This upward force makes the MIN A/B detent in the quadrant feel like a positive stop,

preventing inadvertent afterburner shutdown. A downward force on the throttles permits them to be retarded from the MIN A/B detent, down the ramp in the quadrant into the Military Thrust range.

The extra thrust required for take-offs when ambient temperature is over 50°F can be obtained by advancing the throttles through the MAX A/B stop into the OVSP (overspeed) position. Moving the throttles to this position increases engine speed to 104% rpm. Before the throttles can be placed in OVSP, overspeed protection in the thrust control system must be removed by use of the overspeed arming lever.

NOTE
The throttles cannot be advanced to OVSP unless the overspeed circuits have been armed prior to moving the throttles to the MAX A/B position.

Because throttles 3 and 4 contact and unlatch the overspeed arming lever before they reach the OVSP stop, additional force is required to move these throttles to OVSP. When the throttles are at OVSP, the thrust control actuators set the main fuel controls at the overspeed setting to provide increased rpm. As throttles 3 and 4 are retarded from OVSP into the afterburner range, the overspeed lever automatically resets the overspeed lockout circuit.

CAUTION
Overspeed operation is limited to certain take-off conditions. (Refer to "Engine Limitations" in Section V.) Reduced turbine life and premature turbine replacement can result from improper or excessive overspeed operation.

When the throttles are moved to OFF to shut down the engines, the fuel cutoff valve in the corresponding main fuel control is closed, the firewall fuel shutoff valve for the corresponding engine is closed, and the various control circuits actuated by throttle movement from OFF to IDLE are de-energized. Moving a throttle to OFF during any portion of the starting cycle will abort the start of the related engine by de-energizing the ignition and starting control circuits. The engine emergency braking system which is used to prevent a dead engine from windmilling at excessive rpm can be engaged only if the throttle for the respective engine is at OFF. The throttles must be lifted and moved back over the positive stop at IDLE to the OFF position.

CAUTION
To prevent possible engine vibration, the following throttle technique is recommended during ground and flight operations: When making throttle bursts from IDLE to MIL (or greater), accelerate to 80% to 90% rpm, and hold this speed long enough to observe stable rpm. If vibration is within limits, accelerate engine to throttle position as required. (During all flight conditions where flight idle is greater than 80% rpm, throttle movements are unrestricted.)

THROTTLE FRICTION LEVER.

Adjustment of throttle travel friction is controlled by a lever (55, figure 1-7) that moves within a slot on the left side of the throttle quadrant. Moving the lever forward increases the travel friction of all throttles simultaneously; moving the lever aft decreases the friction.

ENGINE OVERSPEED ARMING LEVER.

Actuation of the overspeed arming lever (4, figure 1-7), at the forward end of the throttle quadrant, releases protective stops within the thrust control system, allowing engine overspeed to 104% rpm for extra thrust during take-offs at ambient temperatures over 50°F. When overspeed operation is required, the arming lever must be pushed down and pulled back to latch in the arm position.

As a result, the solenoid-actuated overspeed stops on the thrust control actuator on each engine are retracted by right primary ac bus power, and the throttle quadrant stop at the MAX A/B position is unlocked so that the throttles can be advanced to OVSP. A caution light indicates that the overspeed lockout stops have been disengaged. The overspeed lever is pushed off the armed position latch by throttles 3 and 4 when they are advanced from MAX A/B to OVSP. This automatically resets the overspeed lockout provisions when throttles 3 and 4 are retarded from OVSP to MAX A/B.

NOTE
- When the overspeed arming lever is armed, or if throttles 3 and 4 are at OVSP, the other throttles can be moved in and out of the overspeed range without resetting the overspeed lockout.
- The overspeed arming lever should be armed before the throttles are advanced from IDLE; however, overspeed arming can be engaged at other throttle settings up to about 10 degrees from the MAX A/B stop.

CAUTION
Refer to "Engine Limitations" in Section V for restrictions on use of engine overspeed.

ENGINE RPM LOCKUP SWITCH.

Refer to the Confidential Supplement, T.O. 1B-70(X)A-1A.

ALTERNATE THROTTLE SWITCHES.

The alternate throttle switches (52, figure 1-7), on the center console, permit emergency thrust control if failure occurs in the throttle servo system. An alternate switch is provided for each throttle. The switches are number-identified and aligned behind the corresponding throttles. Separation guards between the switches prevent inadvertent actuation of adjacent switches. Each is a jog-type switch, spring-loaded from the INCR (increase) and DECR (decrease) positions to the center (off) position. The alternate throttle switches normally receive power from the right primary ac bus. If this power is not available, the emergency battery* can be energized to power the alternate throttle switch circuits. The thrust control circuits actuated by the alternate switches are independent of the throttle servo control systems; and when an alternate switch is engaged, the servo system of the corresponding throttle is disconnected. Use of an alternate switch routes electrical control power directly to an electric motor in the corresponding thrust control actuator. This motor is independent of the servo-throttle-controlled motor and repositions the main fuel control in response to switch movement. The thrust control actuator responds to alternate switch operation at about the same rate as a fast throttle movement. Holding a switch at INCR (forward) increases thrust; the thrust is decreased by holding the switch at DECR (aft). When the desired thrust setting is obtained, as indicated by rpm or primary nozzle position, the alternate throttle switch should be released to off. Small changes in the thrust settings can be made by "jogging" the switch.

The thrust range of alternate switch operation is from Idle to Maximum Afterburner, when the corresponding throttle is positioned between the IDLE and MAX A/B stops. If an alternate switch is used for a full-travel thrust increase or decrease, the switch should be held at the desired position for about 3 seconds. After the engine stabilizes, the switch should be "jogged" to INCR or DECR to obtain the correct rpm.

NOTE

The throttle does not move to correspond to the new thrust settings established by the alternate switch, and co-ordinated movement of throttle and alternate switch is not necessary in the Idle to Maximum Afterburner thrust range. However, because various systems are controlled by throttle-actuated switches within the quadrant, it is desirable to have the throttle setting match the thrust obtained by the alternate switch.

A limit switch in the thrust control actuator prevents alternate switch operation from decreasing thrust below Idle. This precludes inadvertent engine shutdown when the switch is held at DECR. If intentional engine shutdown is necessary when thrust is controlled by an alternate switch, the switch should be used to reduce thrust to Idle, and then the corresponding throttle retarded to OFF. (This shuts down the engine by closing the firewall fuel shutoff valve.)

CAUTION

If the throttle is moved to OFF before Idle thrust is obtained, possible fuel system damage may occur when the fuel shutoff valve closes at a high thrust setting.

However, on the airplane* with the emergency battery-inverter, the alternate throttle switches can be used to shut down the engines. After the battery is activated and the engine shutdown and wheel brake arming switch is at ARMED, holding the alternate throttle switch at DECR bypasses the limit switch and shuts down the engine by shutting off fuel at the main fuel control unit. (Refer to "Emergency Battery-inverter System" in this section.)

---

* Airplane AF62-001

T.O. 1B-70(X)A-1

Engine overspeed can be obtained by use of the alternate switch without using the battery*. However, to permit switch control in this area, the overspeed arming lever must be armed and the corresponding throttle moved to OVSP before the switch is held at INCR.

CAUTION

Overspeed operation with the alternate throttle switch is not recommended. Because overspeed is for take-off only, use of an alternate switch at this time would constitute starting a flight with a known failure.

An operational check of each alternate throttle switch is made before flight by holding each switch momentarily at INCR and then at DECR. The throttles must be at IDLE during this preflight check; and when the switches are moved, engine rpm should respond accordingly. To restore thrust control to the throttles following any use of the alternate throttle switches, the throttle reset button must be pressed.

ESCAPE CAPSULE THROTTLE RETARD BUTTONS.

Two throttle retard buttons (figure 1-36), one in each escape capsule, permit the thrust of all engines to be reduced to idle after the capsules are closed for an in-flight emergency. A retard button is mounted on the emergency descent flight control grip in each capsule. The grip, which also has a trim button for emergency flight control, is stowed in the upper left survival kit in the capsule. (Refer to "Escape Capsules" in this section.) The grip is removed from its mounting clip and hand-held for actuation of the throttle retard button. The retard button is effective only after the doors of the related capsule are closed. When the retard button in either capsule is held in, the throttle servo systems for all engines are disconnected and electrical power is supplied directly to all thrust control actuators through the alternate throttle control. The actuators simultaneously drive all main fuel controls toward a decrease condition to reduce thrust from that determined by the throttle settings. (The throttles do not move to correspond to the thrust settings obtained by using the retard button.) The thrust control actuator responds to retard button operation at about the same rate as a fast throttle movement, and the amount of thrust decrease depends upon the length of time a retard button is held depressed. (A thrust reduction from maximum to idle requires holding the button depressed for about 3 seconds.) When the desired thrust is obtained, the button should be released. A limit switch in each thrust control actuator prevents the retard buttons from decreasing thrust below idle. The first tap of the throttle retard button moves the engine inlet throat panels and bypass doors to a fail-safe position. If a retard button is used during a temporary in-flight encapsulation, normal throttle control can be regained after the capsule is opened by using the throttle reset button to disengage the retard button control circuit. Inlet reaction upon decapsulation is a function of the sequence of encapsulation and decapsulation. (Refer to "Inlet Reaction Upon Decapsulation" in Section VII.) The throttle retard buttons receive power from the right primary ac bus.

THROTTLE RESET BUTTON.

The throttle reset button (21, figure 1-7), on the center console, returns thrust control to the throttle following actuation of a corresponding alternate throttle switch. The reset button also must be used to regain throttle control if an escape capsule throttle retard button was operated during a temporary in-flight emergency encapsulation. Momentarily pressing the reset button

---

*Airplane AF62-001

Changed 25 June 1965

T.O. 1B-70(X)A-1

re-engages the throttle servo systems which had been disengaged as a result of actuating any alternate throttle switch or either escape capsule throttle retard button and restores normal throttle thrust control. The throttle reset button does not re-engage automatic operation of the inlet throat panels and bypass doors following use of a throttle retard button.

If an alternate throttle switch is engaged because of suspected throttle servo system failure and a subsequent check of throttle operation is desired, the reset button must be used. The button also must be used to provide normal throttle operation after the preflight operational check of the alternate throttle switches. Normally, the reset button receives power from the essential ac bus; but if this power is not available, a switch in the crew compartment permits the button to receive its power from the right primary ac bus.

NOTE
Before the reset button is pressed, the applicable throttles should be positioned to correspond to the thrust setting obtained through use of an alternate throttle switch or a throttle retard button. This will preclude undesirable thrust response when the throttle servo system is re-engaged.

ENGINE EMERGENCY BRAKE SWITCHES.

Refer to the Confidential Supplement, T.O. 1B-70(X)A-1A.

THROTTLE AND FIRE DETECTION BUS SELECTOR SWITCH.

Refer to "Electrical Power Supply System" in this section.

ENGINE SHUTDOWN AND WHEEL BRAKE ARMING SWITCH.*

Refer to "Electrical Power Supply System" in this section.

---

* Airplane AF62-001

VARIABLE STATOR SYSTEM.

Refer to the Confidential Supplement, T.O. 1B-70(X)A-1A.

VARIABLE EXHAUST NOZZLE SYSTEM.

Refer to the Confidential Supplement, T.O. 1B-70(X)A-1A.

ENGINE HYDRAULIC SYSTEM.

Refer to the Confidential Supplement, T.O. 1B-70(X)A-1A.

ENGINE FLUID SELECTOR SWITCH.

This 8-position switch (13, figure 1-12), on the ground test panel in the electronic equipment compartment, is used on the ground to test the engine fluid systems. Switch positions 1 through 6 represent engine numbers. When any of these positions is selected, a simultaneous check can be made of the lube oil level and the engine hydraulic pump element operation for the corresponding engine by observing the adjacent fluid level and pump element indicator lights. Both of these indicator lights are tested by turning the selector switch to its BULB TEST position. The engine fluid selector switch receives power from the right primary ac bus.

ENGINE HYDRAULIC PUMP ELEMENT INDICATOR LIGHT.

The engine hydraulic pump element indicator light (14, figure 1-12), on the ground test panel in the electronic equipment compartment, works in conjunction with the engine fluid selector switch to show proper operation of the engine hydraulic pumps. The light comes on during engine ground operation if both elements of the engine hydraulic pump on the engine selected by engine fluid selector switch are operating properly. A failure of one of the pump elements is indicated if the light does not come on. This indicator light is powered by the right primary ac bus, and can be tested by using the BULB TEST position of the engine fluid selector switch.

ENGINE COMPARTMENTS.

The six individual engine compartments are separated from each other by a stainless steel wall. A cooling shroud around each engine is attached to the engine. It serves as a heat shield to protect the structure, and ducts the cooling air around the engine and out the exhaust nozzle. Fire protection for the engine compartments is provided by the fire detection and extinguishing systems. (Refer to "Emergency Equipment" in this section.)

ENGINE COMPARTMENT COOLING SYSTEM.

There are three independent sources of cooling air for the engine compartment. (See figure 1-14.) Outside air is used during the speed range up to between Mach 0.45 to Mach 0.70 (regime I cooling); inlet bypass air normally is used during the speed range of about Mach 0.45 to Mach 2.9 (regime II cooling). During operation at speeds above Mach 2.9 (regime III cooling), inlet boundary layer bleed air is ducted to the engine compartment by pilot selection. Operation of the engine compartment cooling system for regimes I and II is automatic and operates on pressure differentials and temperature modulation. However, regime III cooling can be selected only by a switch in the crew compartment.

Ambient air, used during regime I cooling, is drawn in from the outside through doors (spring-loaded to the open position) in the bottom of the fuselage and is expelled between the exhaust nozzles. The ground cooling doors automatically close when the compartment pressure increases. During regime II cooling, inlet air drawn from the duct just ahead of each engine flows through two bypass valves which modulate to control cooling airflow and prevent excessive compartment pressures. The cooling air flows inside the engine shroud and is expelled between the primary and secondary engine exhaust nozzles. During regime II cooling, the boundary layer bleed air from the inlet perforated ramp panels is ducted between the shroud and the structure. This air is exhausted overboard between the engine shroud and the fuselage skin. During regime III cooling, the regime III switch, working in conjunction with individual throttle switches, closes the inlet bypass valves and boundary layer bleed diverter valves, and diverts the boundary layer bleed airflow into the engine compartment through spring-loaded check valves. Switching to regime III cooling can be accomplished for each engine only if its throttle is below the 88-degree mark on the throttle quadrant. If a fire warning light/engine shutdown button is pressed, the respective inlet boundary layer bleed diverter valve is opened and the inlet bypass valve is closed to limit engine compartment cooling airflow. (Refer to "Emergency Equipment" in this section.) The inlet bypass valves also are closed when the engine brake switch is used.

Regime III Cooling Switch.

The regime III cooling switch (22, figure 1-9), on the copilot's console, receives power from the right primary ac bus and controls the regime III circuit for all engines. The two-position switch is mechanically latched at OFF and must be pulled out before it can be moved to ON. The switch must be at OFF below Mach 2.9. Additional switches, mechanically opened

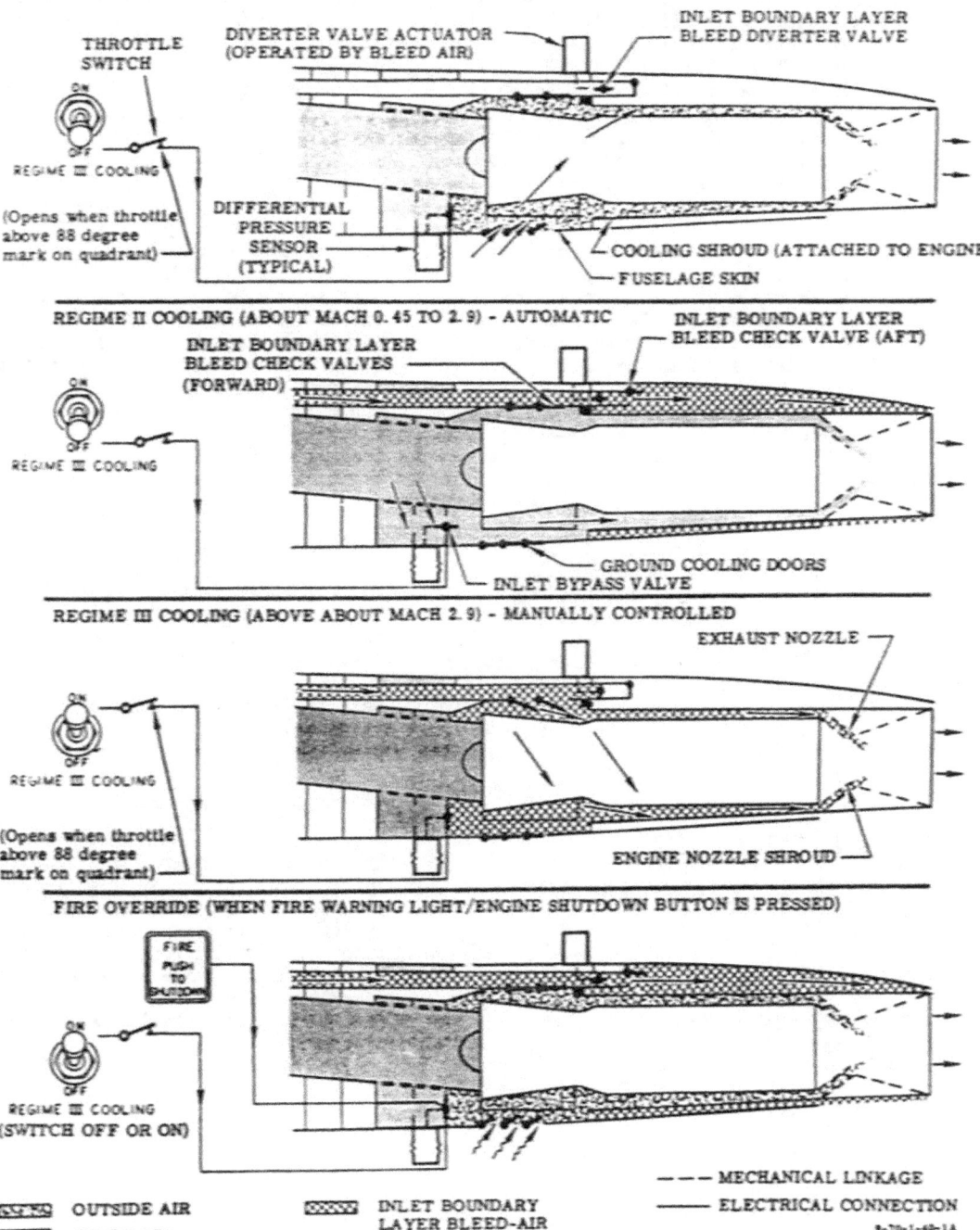

Figure 1-14

T.O. 1B-70(X)A-1

by each throttle, de-energize the regime III cooling circuit for an engine compartment when the respective throttle is positioned above the 88-degree mark. Moving the regime III cooling switch to ON, when the throttles are below 88 degrees, first closes the inlet bypass valves and then positions the inlet boundary layer bleed air diverter valves. This routes inlet boundary layer bleed air between the engine and the shroud and out the engine exhaust nozzle.

CAUTION
Do not move the regime III cooling switch to ON at speeds below Mach 2.9, as the engine compartment may become overheated. Below Mach 2.9, there is insufficient boundary layer bleed airflow for cooling.

Moving the switch to OFF or moving the throttles above 88 degrees de-energizes the regime III cooling system and permits regime II automatic cooling.

CAUTION
Switch-over from regime III to regime II cooling requires about 45 seconds before the throttles may be moved above the 88-degree mark.

An additional regime III cooling switch * (14, figure 1-9) on the copilot's console operates the same as the other regime III cooling switch but only controls the regime III circuit for engine number 3.

ENGINE IGNITION SYSTEM.

Refer to the Confidential Supplement, T.O. 1B-70(X)A-1.

THROTTLES.

Refer to "Engine Controls" in this section.

GROUND START SWITCH.

Refer to "Engine Starting System" in this section.

―――――――――――――――――――

*Airplane AF62-001

AIR START SWITCH.

The two-position air start switch (20, figure 1-7), on the center console, is used to energize the ignition system for air starts. The air start switch also can be used, in addition to the ground start switch, to provide high-energy ignition during low-temperature ground starts. The switch is mechanically latched in the OFF position and must be pulled out before it can be moved to ON. When the switch is ON, power is supplied to energize both circuits of the ignition system on any engine that has its throttle set at IDLE or above. (Essential ac bus power energizes the high-energy ignition circuit, and right primary ac bus power energizes the low-energy circuit.) The air start caution light is illuminated when the air start switch is ON. As soon as a start is obtained, the air start switch must be returned to OFF to de-energize the ignition system.

AIR START CAUTION LIGHT.

The air start caution light (5, figure 1-7) is on the center console. This placard-type light is illuminated by essential ac power when the air start switch is ON. It serves as a reminder that the air start ignition must be turned off manually.

ENGINE STARTING SYSTEM.

The engine ground starting system is hydraulically driven and electrically controlled. Hydraulic and electrical power for starting is supplied from external power sources or from an operating engine. The engines are not equipped with starters because the starting system permits the engine-driven primary hydraulic system pumps on the accessory drive gearboxes to function as hydraulic motors during starting to crank the engines. A single switch in the crew compartment initiates the starting system for all engines simultaneously; however, selection of the particular engine to be started and arming of the individual starting system requires the corresponding throttle to be moved from OFF to IDLE. Once the starting system for the selected engine is engaged, the low energy (4-joule) ignition system is energized and the start cycle is controlled automatically by a speed sensing switch that is mounted on and driven by the gearbox. When the start is initiated, the speed sensing switch depressurizes the hydraulic pumps normally driven by the engine to reduce engine cranking loads.

NOTE
To ensure adequate hydraulic pressure and flow for the hydraulic system starting the engine, the cooling loop pump and the boost pump on the same hydraulic system are shutdown automatically during starting.

The speed switch also opens a motor bypass valve for the primary hydraulic pressure applied to the primary system (from an operating engine) to bypass directly to the primary system pump. The hydraulic pressure actuates valving to change the pump function from that of a pump to a motor, and the pressure drives the pump. (Internal valving permits the pump to rotate in the same direction during pumping or motoring.) The pump provides starting torque to the engine by driving the accessory gearbox which, in turn, cranks the engine through the power transmission shaft and the engine transfer and inlet gearboxes. During the start an overspeed control automatically shuts off hydraulic pressure to the pump if it begins to overspeed. When the engine attains a speed of about 35% rpm, the speed sensing switch de-energizes the ignition. In addition, it closes the motor bypass valve so that the primary system pump reverts to its pumping function. Until the engine reaches idle rpm the pump is kept at a low output condition to minimize torque loads on the engine.

Because both primary hydraulic systems are independent of each other, with the primary system No. 1 pumps driven by engines 1, 2, 3, and the primary system No. 2 pumps driven by engines 4, 5, and 6, only the three engines on the same side can be started from a single hydraulic pressure source. An external hydraulic power source connection is provided for each primary hydraulic system. (See figure 1-37.) The hydraulic power applied to either connection is used to start the corresponding bank of three engines. If primary hydraulic pressure supplied by an operating engine is used for starting, the other two engines on the same side can be started with this pressure.

A separate switch is used to energize the ignition for air starts. This circuit is independent of the ground start circuit. (Refer to "Engine Ignition System" in this section.) There is no specific stop-start control; but the starting cycle for any engine can be shut down, if desired, by retarding the corresponding throttle to OFF.

GROUND START SWITCH.

The two-position ground start switch (7, figure 1-6), on the overhead panel, is used to initiate engine ground starts. The switch is spring-loaded from ON to OFF and is effective only when the weight of the airplane is on the gear. Holding the switch momentarily at ON energizes the start system and the low-energy (4-joule) ignition system of any engine which has its throttle at IDLE. Power from the right primary ac bus then is supplied through a holding circuit to the speed sensing switch on the accessory drive gearbox of each engine being started. The speed sensing switch then

T.O. 1B-70(X)A-1

controls the starting sequence and automatically shuts down the starting system, de-energizes the ignition, converts the primary pump from the cranking to the pumping mode and pressurizes the hydraulic system when engine speed reaches about 35% rpm. Fuel boost pumps and cooling loop pumps are restarted automatically when the start circuit is de-energized. Although the starting cycle is automatic after the momentary actuation of the ground start switch, the start can be aborted whenever necessary by retarding the throttle to OFF.

THROTTLES.

Refer to "Engine Controls" in this section.

AIR START SWITCH.

Refer to "Engine Ignition System" in this section.

ENGINE INDICATORS.

TACHOMETERS.

Six tachometers (8, figure 1-5), one for each engine, are on the center instrument panel. These instruments are mounted side by side, corresponding to the respective engines. Each tachometer shows engine speed in percent of Military Thrust rpm, which is considered 100 percent. The main scale on the tachometer is not calibrated above 100 percent rpm and therefore does not show the percent rpm for the take-off overspeed condition. (Dial limit markings include the overspeed range.) A subdial, calibrated from 0 to 9 in one percent increments, permits a more accurate reading of engine speed. Each tachometer is powered by an engine-driven tachometer generator in the accessory pod of its respective engine.

EXHAUST TEMPERATURE GAGES.

The six exhaust temperature gages (9, figure 1-5), one for each engine, are arranged side by side on the center instrument panel, corresponding to the position of their respective engines. Each gage indicates turbine discharge temperature in degrees centigrade. Temperature indications are obtained from the thermocouples located aft of the turbine and supplied directly to the gage. The exhaust temperature gage systems use essential ac bus power, and an "OFF" indication appears in a window on the dial face when electrical power is not applied to the gage.

PRIMARY EXHAUST NOZZLE POSITION INDICATORS.

Refer to "Variable Exhaust Nozzle System" in Section I of the Confidential Supplement, T.O. 1B-70(X)A-1A.

ENGINE IDENTIFICATION CAUTION LIGHTS.

A placard-type engine identification caution light (1 and 5, figure 1-7) is illuminated simultaneously with the engine oil pressure caution light or the accessory drive system oil pressure caution light to indicate the specific location of either oil pressure failure. The identification lights are on the center console and are powered by the essential ac bus. All six engine identification lights and the two oil pressure (engine and accessory drive system) caution lights should be illuminated before any engine is started if electrical power is on the airplane. After

T.O. 1B-70(Y)A-1

each engine is started, and the engine and accessory gearbox oil pressures are adequate, the corresponding engine identification light goes out.

NOTE

After the first engine is started, the accessory drive system oil pressure caution light comes on to show low oil pressure in any gearbox only if the corresponding throttle is above IDLE. However, lack of gearbox oil pressure when the throttle is at IDLE is shown by having only an engine identification light come on.

ENGINE OIL PRESSURE CAUTION LIGHT.

The placard-type engine oil pressure caution light (1, figure 1-7), on the center console, is illuminated with the applicable engine identification light to show low oil pressure at the number 2 bearing of the corresponding engine. (The number 2 bearing is the critical bearing.) This light and all engine identification lights should be on before any engine is started and external electrical power is on the airplane. After the first engine is started and engine oil pressure is adequate, the light goes out. During the starting cycle of each of the other engines, the light comes on when a throttle is moved from OFF to IDLE and goes out when the engine builds up adequate oil pressure. (The engine identification light for the engine being started goes out simultaneously with the engine oil pressure caution light, if the corresponding accessory drive gearbox oil pressure also is adequate.) If the engine oil pressure caution light comes on, the affected engine must be shut down to preclude engine damage and the light goes out when the respective throttle is retarded from IDLE to OFF. This caution light is powered by the essential ac bus.

ENGINE OVERSPEED ARMED CAUTION LIGHT.

The placard-type overspeed armed caution light (1, figure 1-7) is on the center console. It is illuminated by essential ac bus power when the overspeed arming lever is moved aft to the armed position. Illumination of this light indicates that the overspeed lockout stops in the thrust control system have been disengaged so that the throttles can be advanced to the OVSP position. The light goes out when the overspeed lever is returned to its unarmed position.

ENGINE AND ACCESSORY DRIVE SYSTEM GEARBOX VIBRATION INDICATORS.

The six vibration indicators (14, figure 1-3), one for each engine-gearbox installation, are mounted side by side in a panel on the pilot's instrument panel. These instruments, which are numbered to correspond to the respective engine and accessory drive gearbox, permit vibrations to be monitored for indications of mechanical unbalance or deterioration. (Refer to "Engine - Accessory Drive System Gearbox Vibration" in Section VII.) Each vibration indicator has two vertically moving pointers. The right pointer is for the engine; the left is for the corresponding accessory drive system gearbox. The pointers of each indicator are read against a vertical scale that is calibrated in 10-percent increments from 0 to 100 percent. (Each 10-percent increment corresponds to a 1-mil peak-to-peak vibration displacement.) The indicators receive signals from vibration pickups which generate a voltage proportional to the vibration. The engine pickup is at the compressor rear frame and the gearbox pickup is on the gearbox-mounted primary hydraulic pump.

1-32

T.O. 1B-70(X)A-1

A preflight check of the vibration indicators can be made by using the test button (17, figure 1-3), below the indicators. When the button is pushed before engine start, all 12 pointers should read 75 percent. (The vibration caution light should come on when the test button is pushed.) The test button also can be used for limited testing of the indicating system during engine operation. The record selector switch, below the indicators, controls the selection of vibration signals to the flight test data system, and does not affect indicator operation. (Refer to "Flight Test Instrumentation" in Section IV.) The vibration indicating system receives power from the right primary ac bus.

VIBRATION CAUTION LIGHT.

The placard-type vibration caution light (16, figure 1-3), on the pilot's instrument panel, comes on if the vibration of any engine or accessory drive system gearbox is over 50 percent (5 mils peak-to-peak). (The affected engine or gearbox is identified from the vibration indicator.) If the vibration caution light comes on during steady-state operation, the applicable emergency procedures must be used to preclude damage to the affected engine or gearbox.

NOTE
The master caution light does not come on when the vibration caution light is on.

The vibration caution light also comes on when the vibration indicating system test button is pushed. The light is powered by the right primary ac bus.

NOTE
Airplane AF62-207 has two neon bulb vibration caution lights (13A, figure 1-3) instead of the placard-type caution light.

ENGINE AFTERBURNER SYSTEM.

Refer to the Confidential Supplement, T.O. 1B-70(X)A-1A.

OIL SUPPLY SYSTEM.

Refer to the Confidential Supplement, T.O. 1B-70(X)A-1A.

ENGINE FLUID SELECTOR SWITCH.

Refer to "Engine Hydraulic System" in this section.

ENGINE OIL TANK FLUID LEVEL INDICATOR LIGHT.

The engine oil tank fluid level indicator light (18, figure 1-12), on the ground test panel in the electronic equipment compartment, is marked "ENG LUBE," and works in conjunction with the engine fluid selector switch. The light comes on if the oil level is safe in the tank selected by the engine fluid selector switch. If the light does not come on, the oil level is low. The light is powered by the right primary ac bus and can be tested by the engine fluid selector switch.

ACCESSORY DRIVE SYSTEM (ADS).

The accessory drive system, which includes six independent engine-driven gearbox assemblies, drives the hydraulic power system pumps and the ac generators. During engine ground starts the accessory drive system also serves as an input system to crank the engines. (The combination of accessory drive, hydraulic, and electrical systems is considered as the secondary power generating system or SPGS.) The six accessory drive system gearbox assemblies are mounted in individual compartments, each forward of its corresponding engine.

NOTE
The accessory drive system compartments and components are number-identified according to the standard engine identification practice, with the left outboard as No. 1.

Fire protection is provided for each accessory drive system compartment by

Changed 25 June 1965   1-33

T.O. 1R-70(X)A-1

the fire detection and fire extinguishing systems. (Refer to "Emergency Equipment" in this section.) Each gearbox is driven by its corresponding engine through a power transmission shaft. The shaft, which is driven from the power take-off pad on the engine transfer gearbox, permits fore and aft relative motion between the engine and the gearbox caused by temperature differences. Both ends of the shaft have diaphragm-type joints which allow for some misalignment of the gearbox with the engine. A shear section in the engine gearbox protects the engine if the gearbox fails or if other overload conditions occurs.

Each accessory drive gearbox drives two gearbox-mounted hydraulic pumps (a primary hydraulic system pump and a utility system pump) and a gearbox-mounted, centrifugally operated speed switch which controls electrical circuits to provide automatic sequencing of the engine ground starting cycle. (Refer to "Engine Starting System" in this section.) In addition, No. 3 and No. 4 gearboxes each drive an ac generator through a constant-speed drive unit. The constant-speed drives convert the variable engine-gearbox speed to a constant 8000 rpm for proper ac generator operation. (Refer to "Electrical Power Supply System" in this section.) Gear trains in the gearboxes provide the different drive speeds required by the gearbox-driven accessories. For the engine ground starting mode of gearbox operation, two overrunning clutches in the gearbox provide automatic gear train selection.

An oil reservoir mounted on each gearbox supplies lube oil for the corresponding gearbox assembly including the speed switch, and where applicable, the constant speed drive and the ac generator. This oil also is used as an operating fluid for the constant-speed drive. Gaseous nitrogen pressurizes and inerts each accessory gearbox and gearbox oil system. (Refer to "Nitrogen Systems" in this section.) The nitrogen increases the useful life of gearbox oil during high-temperature operation by minimizing oxidation, and the pressure augments the lube pumps to improve the altitude performance of the gearbox oil system. Oil from each gearbox flows through an oil cooler that is cooled by fuel in the airplane fuel supply system cooling loop. (Refer to "Fuel Supply System" in this section.) Oil system failure in any gearbox is indicated by a caution light in the crew compartment. (See figure 1-37 for accessory drive gearbox oil specifications.)

ACCESSORY DRIVE SYSTEM (ADS) OIL PRESSURE CAUTION LIGHT.

The placard-type ADS oil pressure caution light (5, figure 1-7), on the center console, comes on to show low oil pressure in any ADS gearbox. (The affected gearbox is identified by simultaneous illumination of an engine identification light.) With external power on the airplane, the ADS caution light and all engine identification lights should be on before any engine is started. After the first engine is started and gearbox oil pressure is adequate, the ADS caution light goes out. During the starting cycle of each of the other engines, the ADS light comes on when a throttle is moved from OFF to IDLE and goes out when the oil pressure of the corresponding gearbox is satisfactory. (The engine identification light for the engine being started goes out when engine oil pressure and oil pressure in the corresponding ADS gearbox are adequate.) Illumination of the ADS caution light also may represent a gearbox or power transmission shaft failure, or loss of a nitrogen pressurization system. The light is powered by the essential ac bus.

T.O. 1B-70(X)A-1

ENGINE IDENTIFICATION CAUTION LIGHTS.

Refer to "Engine Indicators" in this section.

ENGINE AND ACCESSORY DRIVE SYSTEM GEARBOX VIBRATION INDICATORS.

Refer to "Engine Indicators" in this section.

VIBRATION CAUTION LIGHT.

Refer to "Engine Indicators" in this section.

AIR INDUCTION CONTROL SYSTEM (AICS).

Air is supplied to the engines through two separate variable-geometry inlets below the fuselage. One inlet supplies air for the three left engines, and the other supplies the three right engines. To maintain inlet efficiency during supersonic flight, each has an adjustable throat and a variable bypass system. The adjustable throat consists of three movable panels on the inboard side of the inlet to change the throat size from 48 inches wide to 19 inches (depending on the schedule). The bypass system removes excess inlet air and consists of six pairs of bypass doors in the duct upper surface just ahead of the engines. Each pair of doors is interconnected. (One door of each pair of bypass doors opens downward and the other opens upward.) The bypass doors provide from "0" to 2400 square inches of bypass area. The throat panels are hydraulically operated and electrically controlled.

Airplane AF62-001, has two control systems for the inlets. The normal system permits either automatic or manual operation of the throat panels and bypass doors. The normal system uses hydraulic power from both utility systems No. 1 and 2 but will operate with only utility system No. 1 available. The standby system permits only manual control of the throat panels and bypass doors. It is powered by two electrical and two hydraulic systems and can function if one electrical and one hydraulic system is lost.

Airplane AF62-207, also has two control systems for the inlets. The automatic system permits only automatic operation of the throat panels and bypass doors. It uses hydraulic power from both utility systems No. 1 and 2 but will operate with only utility system No. 1 available. The standby system permits manual control of the throat panels and bypass doors. It is powered by two electrical and two hydraulic systems and can function if one electrical and one hydraulic system is lost. The standby system has an emergency function wherein the automatic system is de-energized and the throat panels and bypass doors are driven to predetermined positions (throats to 39 inches and bypass doors full open).

For both airplanes, there is a capsule mode of operation. When either the pilot or copilot encapsulates and actuates this mode of operation, the throat panels and bypass doors are driven to predetermined positions (throats to 39 inches and bypass doors full open). Inlet reaction upon decapsulation depends on the sequence of encapsulation and decapsulation. (Refer to "Inlet Reaction Upon Decapsulation" in Section VII.)

During flight above Mach 2, it is desirable for the shock wave to be positioned in the inlet to ensure high pressure recovery and maximum engine thrust. Also, if the shock wave moves forward out of the inlet (a condition known as "unstart"), engine thrust decreases and engine flame-out can occur. To recover from an "unstart" condition, opening the variable throat and bypass doors as required draws the shock wave back into the inlet. Above airplane Mach 1.5, pressure fluctuations called buzz can occur in the inlets. This buzz can vary from light to moderate. If the buzz is prolonged, the inlet and/or engines can be damaged. Normal operation will be restored by proper operation of both the throat panels and bypass doors. During subsonic flight, the inlet functions as a fixed intake duct, with the bypass doors closed and the throat wide open.

The air induction control system sensors and computers are air-cooled and pressurized automatically by a packaged dual cooling system, using a gaseous and liquid nitrogen heat sink. This self-contained cooling package is in the aft

Changed 25 June 1965

weapons bay. The air induction control system actuators are cooled by the landing gear and drag chute compartment ethylene glycol/water cooling system. (See figure 4-4.) Caution lights and indicators in the crew compartment indicate any system malfunction or abnormal operations.

AIR INDUCTION CONTROL SYSTEM CONTROLS AND INDICATORS - AIRPLANE AF62-001.

AIR INDUCTION CONTROL SYSTEM PACKAGE POWER SWITCH.

The two-position air induction control system power switch (21, figure 1-9) on the copilot's console receives power from the right primary ac and essential ac busses. The switch is mechanically latched at ON and must be pulled out before it can be moved. Also a spring-loaded guard must be raised to permit moving the switch out of ON. When the switch is ON, power is supplied to the cooled components of the air induction control system. Moving the switch to OFF turns off the cooled components and protects the components from damage in the event of cooling system failure. The switch should be left at ON at all times except when the AICS coolant caution light comes on.

NOTE

The air induction control system package power switch must be at ON 25 minutes prior to manual or automatic operation of the air induction control system.

DUCT PERFORMANCE SWITCH.

The two-position duct performance switch (27, figure 1-9), on the copilot's console, is used to provide inlet stability during maneuvering flight. The switch should be at NORM while manually controlling the inlets, or during stable flight when the inlets are controlled automatically. If maneuvering flight is anticipated and the inlets are being controlled automatically, the switch should be moved to LOW. This lowers inlet efficiency by increasing the throat width slightly. The switch should be returned to NORM after stable flight has been resumed. The duct performance switch, which receives power from the right primary ac bus, is latched mechanically at its LOW position and must be pulled out before it can be moved to NORM.

THROAT MACH SCHEDULE MODE SWITCHES.

The two throat Mach schedule mode switches (1 and 4, figure 1-10), one for each inlet, are on the copilot's control pedestal and receive power from the right primary ac bus. The three-position switches are mechanically latched at MAN and OFF and must be pulled out before they can be moved. Moving the switches to AUTO provides automatic control and hydraulic operation of the respective inlet throat panels. Moving the switches to MAN permits manual control of the panels with a manual control wheel for each inlet. Moving the switches to OFF locks the master cylinder to prevent erratic operation and also provide an anchor point for the standby system linkage. The OFF position is used whenever the standby system is required.

THROAT MACH SCHEDULE MANUAL CONTROL WHEELS.

The two throat Mach schedule manual control wheels (2 and 3, figure 1-10), one for each inlet, are on the copilot's control pedestal and receive power from the right primary ac bus. The rim of each wheel is marked with two sets of numbers. The outer set of numbers on each wheel are reference numbers that represent Mach. (For example, reference number 2.6 represents Mach 2.6.) The reference numbers increase as the wheels are rolled forward towards INCR. Rolling the wheels aft towards DCR decreases the reference numbers. The inner set of numbers on each wheel are restart numbers 0, 3, 6, and 9. The four restart numbers are used to restart the inlets at various speeds. During automatic operation of the air induction control system, both manual control wheels must be maintained at the proper restart number depending on the airplane Mach. This is referred to as "updating." The "updating" schedule is as follows: Between Mach 1.7 and 2.3, use restart number 0; between Mach 2.3 and 2.6, use restart number 3; between Mach 2.6 and 2.9, use restart number 6;

above Mach 2.9, use restart number 9. The wheels control the throat panels only when the throat Mach schedule mode switches are at MAN. Rolling the wheels forward towards INCR, moves the panels outboard to decrease the throat width; and rolling the wheels aft towards DCR, moves the panels inboard to increase the throat width.

BYPASS DOOR MODE SWITCHES.

Two bypass door mode switches (5 and 9, figure 1-10), one for each inlet, are on the copilot's control pedestal and receive power from the right primary ac bus. The three-position switches are mechanically latched at MAN and OFF and must be pulled out before they can be moved. Moving the sivtches to AUTO provides automatic control and hydraulic operation of the respective bypass doors. Moving the switches to MAN permits manual control of the doors with a manual control wheel for each inlet. Moving the switches to OFF locks the master cylinder to prevent erratic operation and also provide an anchor point for the standby system linkage. The OFF position is used whenever the standby system is required.

BYPASS DOOR MANUAL CONTROL WHEELS.

Two bypass door manual control wheels (6 and 7, figure 1-10), one for each inlet, are on the copilot's control pedestal and receive power from the right primary ac bus. The wheels are marked on the side with reference numbers that represent hundreds of square inches. (For example, reference number 8 represents 800 square inches bypass area.) The reference numbers increase as the wheels are rolled aft towards OPEN. Rolling the wheels forward towards CLOSE decreases the reference numbers. Restart numbers (3, 6 and 9) on the rim of the wheels are restart positions used to restart the inlets at various speeds. During automatic operation of the air induction control system, both manual control wheels must be maintained at the proper restart number depending on the airplane Mach. This is referred to as "updating." The "updating" schedule is as follows: below Mach 2.6, use restart number 3; between Mach 2.6 and 2.9, use restart number 6; above Mach 2.9, use restart number 9. The wheels control the bypass doors only when the bypass door mode switches are at MAN. Rolling the wheels forward towards CLOSE, closes the bypass doors which moves the shock wave forward in the inlet. Rolling the wheels aft towards OPEN, opens the bypass doors which moves the shock wave aft in the inlet.

THROAT MACH SCHEDULE STANDY SWITCHES.

The two throat Mach schedule standby switches (32, figure 1-4), one for each inlet, are on the copilot's instrument panel and receive power from the right primary ac or essential ac bus. Each three-position switch is spring-loaded to the center (OFF) position. Holding either switch at INCR or DECR electrically positions the control linkage to hydraulically move the throat panels of the respective inlet. This panel movement establishes the throat width necessary for proper operation at a selected Mach. The throat Mach schedule mode switches should be at OFF when these switches are to be used in flight.

BYPASS DOOR STANDBY SWITCHES.

Two bypass door standby switches (30, figure 1-4), one for each inlet, are on the copilot's instrument panel and receive power from the right primary ac or essential ac bus. Each three-position switch is spring-loaded to the center (OFF) position. Holding either switch at CLOSE or OPEN electrically positions the control linkage to hydraulically move the bypass door servos of the respective inlet which either opens or closes the doors. Moving the switch to CLOSE closes the bypass doors which moves the shock wave forward in the inlet and moving the switch to OPEN opens the bypass doors which moves the shock wave aft in the inlet. The OPEN position also will stop inlet buzz. Releasing the switch to the center (OFF) position stops the bypass doors at the position where the switch is released. The bypass door mode switches should be at OFF and the bypass door standby system selector switches must be at PRIMARY or ALTERNATE when the bypass door standby switches are to be used in flight.

T.O. 1B-70(X)A-1

BYPASS DOOR STANDBY SYSTEM SELECTOR SWITCHES.

The two three-position bypass door standby system selector switches (5, and 31, figure 1-4), one for each inlet, are on the copilot's instrument panel and receive power from both the right primary ac bus and the essential ac bus. The switches are mechanically latched at OFF and must be pulled out before they can be moved from OFF. Moving the switch to PRIMARY selects the right primary and essential ac busses and the bypass door electrical controls powered by these busses. Moving the switch to ALTERNATE selects a duplicate set of bypass door electrical controls powered by these busses. The switch, normally set at OFF, is moved first to PRIMARY in case of a malfunction requiring the standby system. However, in case of a malfunction of the primary standby system, moving the switch to ALTERNATE restores control of the bypass doors. Moving the switch to OFF, when using the standby switches, centers the electrical actuator. The switch must be at OFF when in the automatic mode to provide low-rate operation of the bypass doors.

ESCAPE CAPSULE THROTTLE RETARD BUTTONS.

Refer to "Engine Controls" in this section.

SHOCK WAVE POSITION INDICATORS.

Two shock wave position indicators (1 and 3, figure 1-4), one for each inlet, are on the copilot's instrument panel and indicate the location of the shock wave in the inlet. Each indicator system requires power from the right primary ac and essential ac busses and reacts to signals received from taps in the respective inlet walls which sense the shock wave location. The pointer moves on a scale which has the two extremes marked "FWD" and "AFT". The position of the pointer between the two extremes indicates the location of the shock wave in the inlet.

BYPASS AREA INDICATORS.

Two bypass area indicators (34, figure 1-4), one for each inlet, are on the copilot's instrument panel. Each shows the total area in square inches of the respective inlet bypass openings. The area indicated is accurate to within 30 square inches. The indicators are electrically powered by a synchro transformer on the respective bypass door linkage.

THROAT MACH SCHEDULE INDICATORS.

Two throat Mach schedule indicators (2, figure 1-4), one for each inlet is on the copilot's instrument panel. Each indicator gives a relative indication of throat size, by showing the airplane Mach number required for the particular throat width. The indicators are electrically powered by a synchro transformer on the respective throat panel linkage.

INLET PRESSURE RATIO GAGES.

Two inlet pressure ratio gages (4 and 33, figure 1-4), one for each inlet, are on the copilot's instrument panel and indicate the ratio of inlet static pressure to pitot pressure. The gages are powered by the right primary ac bus. In case of a power failure or main control system failure, the pointers will remain at the position they were in when the failure occurred. The gages indicate inlet efficiency. An increase in pressure ratio reading indicates forward movement of the shock wave. A decrease in reading indicates aft movement of the shock wave.

AIR INDUCTION CONTROL SYSTEM COOLANT CAUTION LIGHT.

The air induction control system coolant caution light (5, figure 1-7), on the center console, is powered by the essential ac bus. This placard-type light comes on to show "AICS COOL" in case of a failure or malfunction of either the primary or secondary cooling systems for the air induction control system. The operation of this light when the master caution light is pressed determines which system of the cooling system has failed. If pressing the master caution light puts out the AICS coolant caution light, only the primary system has failed, and the secondary system is still operating. However, if pressing the master caution light does not put out the coolant caution light, both systems have failed. (Refer to "Air Induction Control System Emergency Operation" in Section III.)

T.O. 1B-70(X)A-1

THROAT POSITION INDICATOR-OUT CAUTION LIGHTS.

Two placard-type throat position indicator-out caution lights (5, figure 1-7), one for each inlet, are on the center console. The lights are powered by the essential ac bus and come on to show "LH or RH THROAT INDICATOR" in case of a failure of the respective throat Mach schedule indicator.

INLET UNSTART CAUTION LIGHTS.

Four placard-type duct unstart caution lights (1 and 5, figure 1-7), two for each inlet, are on the center console. The lights are powered by the right primary ac and essential ac busses. Both lights come on if the shock wave moves forward out of the respective inlet. Each light associated with a given inlet is controlled by a separate unstart sensor system. If one sensor system or its light fails, the other light still will come on when an unstart condition develops. Opening the bypass and decreasing the throat Mach schedule after the unstart caution light is on will restart the inlet by drawing the shock wave back into the inlet, and the light will go out.

NOTE

The lights are inoperative when both throat Mach schedule indicators are at Mach 2.17 or less. Anytime one or both throat Mach schedule indicators are at Mach 2.17 or above, the lights will be operative.

THROAT PANEL EXTENDED CAUTION LIGHTS.

Two placard-type throat panel extended caution lights (5, figure 1-7), one for each inlet, are on the center console. The lights are powered by the essential ac bus. The lights come on to show "LH or RH THROAT PNL EXTENDED" when the respective throat Mach schedule indicator is more than Mach 2.17, and the airplane speed is below Mach 1.1 and the anticollision light switch is ON.

INLET BUZZ CAUTION LIGHTS.

Four placard-type buzz caution lights (1 and 5, figure 1-7), two for each duct,

are on the center console. The lights are powered by the right primary ac and essential ac busses. Both lights come on if a buzz condition is detected in the respective inlet. Each light associated with a given inlet is controlled by a separate buzz sensor system. If one sensor system or its light fails, the other light still will come on when a buzz condition develops. Opening the bypass doors, or reducing airspeed will help to eliminate the buzz, and the light will go out after about 15 seconds delay.

CAUTION

Immediate action to eliminate buzz must be taken when the buzz caution light comes on; otherwise structural damage may occur.

BYPASS DOOR-OPEN CAUTION LIGHTS.

Two placard-type bypass door-open caution lights (1 and 5, figure 1-7), one for each inlet, are on the center console. The lights are powered by the right primary ac and essential ac busses. The lights come on to show "LH or RH BYPASS DOOR OPEN" when the respective bypass doors are open below Mach 0.4 and below 8,000 feet.

AIR INDUCTION CONTROL SYSTEM CONTROLS AND INDICATORS - AIRPLANE AF62-207.

AIR INDUCTION CONTROL SYSTEM PACKAGE POWER SWITCH.

Except for the fact that it does not have a spring-loaded guard, this switch (25A, figure 1-9) is the same as on Airplane AF62-001. (Refer to "Air Induction Control System Controls and Indicators - Airplane AF62-001" in this section.)

DUCT PERFORMANCE SWITCH.

The three-position duct performance switch (15, figure 1-10) on the copilot's instrument panel is used to provide inlet stability for various flight conditions. The switch is effective only when the automatic mode of the AICS is being used. The NORM position should be used during normal flight and maneuvering. The HIGH position should be used only above Mach 2.8 with limited maneuvering capability.

Changed 25 June 1965

1-39

T.O. 1B-70(X)A-1

The LOW position should be selected in anticipation of engine shutdowns, unusual flight maneuvers, and when disturbance of inlet airflow could be expected by such conditions as storm fronts, turbulent air conditions, or passage of another aircraft. The switch receives power from the right primary ac bus. It is latched mechanically at its LOW position and must be pulled out before it can be moved to NORM or HIGH.

AICS MODE SWITCHES.

The two AICS mode switches (14 and 17, figure 1-10), one for each inlet, are on the copilot's instrument panel. They receive power from the essential ac bus or right primary ac bus. Moving the switches to AUTO provides automatic operation of the throat panels and bypass doors. With the switches at STBY, the panels and doors must be manually controlled. Moving the switches to EMER, causes the throat panels and bypass doors to move to predetermined, fixed positions (throat panels to 39 inches and bypass doors full open.) The switches are mechanically latched at EMER and must be pulled out before they can be moved to MAN or AUTO.

THROAT MACH SCHEDULE STANDBY SWITCHES.

These two switches (16, figure 1-10), one for each inlet, are on the copilot's instrument panel. They receive power from the essential ac bus or right primary ac bus. The AICS mode switches should be at STBY when these switches are used in flight. Holding the switches at either INCR or DCR causes the throat panels to move in the direction of throat width necessary for proper operation at a selected Mach. Moving the switches also changes the throat Mach schedule indicators to show the airplane Mach number for the particular throat width. Each three-position switch is spring-loaded to the center (OFF) position.

BYPASS DOOR STANDBY SWITCHES.

These three-position switches (19, figure 1-10) are on the copilot's instrument panel. They receive power from the essential ac bus or right primary ac bus. The AICS mode switches should be at STBY when these switches are used in flight. Holding the switches at either CLOSE or OPEN causes corresponding movement of the bypass doors. Movement of the doors toward open causes the shock wave aft in the inlet. Movement of the doors toward close causes the shock wave to move forward. Releasing the switches to the center (OFF) position stops the bypass doors at the position where the switches are released. Moving the switches also changes the bypass area indicators to show the total area of the bypass door openings. The switches are spring-loaded to the center position.

ESCAPE CAPSULE THROTTLE RETARD BUTTONS.

Refer to "Engine Controls" in this section.

THROAT TRIM POWER SWITCH.

The throat trim power switch (26A, figure 1-9) is on the copilot's console. With the switch at ON, power is available to the throat height trim adjustment controls. The switch receives power from the right primary ac bus.

THROAT HEIGHT TRIM CONTROLS.

The throat height trim controls (25A, figure 1-9 and 24, figure 1-10), one for each inlet, are on the copilot's console. Each control has a trim indicator, trim control knob, and trim control knob lock. Each indicator will read from +00 to +45 in one direction and -00 to -45 in increments of 05 in the other direction. The righthand counter of each indicator has "V" marks between 0 and 5. The numbers and "V" marks in the minus direction are red. The trim control knobs can move the throat panels a maximum of 4 inches either side of the scheduled position. The knobs when rotated clockwise cause the indicator readings to increase in or toward the plus value. The trim control lock knob when moved clockwise locks the trim control knob and prevents it being moved inadvertently. The controls can be used to vary throat height trim only when the throat trim power switch is ON and when the AICS is in automatic mode of operation.

AICS RESET SWITCH/LIGHT.

The AICS reset switch/light (18, figure 1-10) is a push-button type switch with

1-40

Changed 25 June 1965

integral light located on the copilot's instrument panel. During automatic operation of the AICS, the light will come on and read "AICS RESET" when an unstart or buzz condition develops in either inlet. If a buzz condition develops below Mach 2.0, the affected inlet will shift from fixed bypass control to low performance shock control and the doors will move to the position commanded by the shock control to eliminate the buzz. If a buzz or unstart condition develops above Mach 2.0 the throat panels for the affected inlet will be driven 8 inches in the open direction and shock control for the affected inlet will shift to low performance, causing the bypass doors to be driven open until restart occurs. After the unstart or buzz condition is eliminated, the light will remain on, as a reminder that the bypass doors or bypass doors and throat panels are not on their normal schedule. Pressing the switch/light momentarily will then return the affected inlet to normal operation. The switch/light receives power from the essential ac bus and right primary ac bus. The switch/light is also used prior to take-off for checking the positions of the throat and bypass door master cylinders. If the light comes on when pressed, the cylinders are at their take-off positions.

SHOCK WAVE POSITION INDICATORS.

These indicators (1 and 3, figure 1-4) are the same as on Airplane AF62-001. (Refer to "Air Induction Control System Controls and Indicators - Airplane AF62-001" in this section.)

BYPASS AREA INDICATORS.

These indicators (34, figure 1-4) are the same as on Airplane AF62-001. (Refer to "Air Indication Control System Controls and Indicators - Airplane AF62-001" in this section.)

THROAT MACH SCHEDULE INDICATORS.

These indicators (2, figure 1-4) are the same as on Airplane AF62-001. (Refer to "Air Induction Control System Controls and Indicators - Airplane AF62-001" in this section.)

INLET PRESSURE RATIO GAGE.

For flight test purposes, this airplane has only a left inlet pressure ratio gage, which is the same as on Airplane AF62-001. (Refer to "Air Induction Control System Controls and Indicators - Airplane AF62-001" in this section.)

AIR INDUCTION CONTROL SYSTEM COOLANT CAUTION LIGHT.

This light (5, figure 1-7) is the same as on Airplane AF62-001. (Refer to "Air Induction Control System Controls and Indicators - Airplane AF62-001" in this section.)

INLET UNSTART CAUTION LIGHTS.

These lights (1 and 5, figure 1-7) are, with one exception, the same as on Airplane AF62-001. The exception is that the lights are inoperative when the throat Mach schedule indicators are at Mach 2.06 or less. (Refer to "Air Induction Control System Controls and Indicators - Airplane AF62-001" in this section.)

THROAT PANEL EXTENDED CAUTION LIGHTS.

These lights (5, figure 1-7) are the same as on Airplane AF62-001. (Refer to "Air Induction Control System Controls and Indicators - Airplane AF62-001" in this section.

INLET BUZZ CAUTION LIGHTS.

These lights (1 and 5, figure 1-7) are the same as on Airplane AF62-001. (Refer to "Air Induction Control System Controls and Indicators - Airplane AF62-001" in this section.)

SHOCK AFT CAUTION LIGHTS.

The shock aft caution lights (5, figure 1-7), one for each inlet, are on the center console. The placard-type lights will come on to read "LH (or RH) SHOCK AFT" when the shock wave is aft of a predetermined limit. The lights also will come on at low airspeed (below Mach 0.7) when the bypass doors are not fully closed. The lights are powered by the essential ac bus.

THROAT PANEL EXTENDED CAUTION LIGHTS.

Two placard-type throat panel extended caution lights (5, figure 1-7), one for each inlet, are on the center console. The lights are powered by the essential ac bus. The lights come on to show "LH or RH THROAT PNL EXT" when the respective throat panel position is 40 inches (±1 inch) or less (throat Mach schedule indicator is more than Mach 2.11) and the airplane speed is below Mach 0.7.

FUEL SUPPLY SYSTEM.

The fuel supply system (figure 1-16) includes 11 integral tanks: five in the fuselage and three in each wing. The tanks are numbered 1 through 5 in the fuselage, and 6 right, 6 left, 7 right, 7 left, 8 right and 8 left in the wing. (The No. 5 tank is not used on Airplane AF62-001.)

The right tanks and left tanks with the same number function as one tank. Fuel transfer is manually and automatically sequenced. All fuel is transferred to tank No. 3, which is the sump tank, for delivery to the engines. Indicators are provided for monitoring the fuel transfer sequence. The boost pumps supply the fuel to the engines from the tank No. 3. A cooling loop in the fuel supply system uses fuel as a coolant for the fluids in various systems. Liquid nitrogen, converted to a gas, is supplied to the fuel tank vent space by the fuel pressurization and inerting system to provide positive fuel tank pressures within structural limits. The nitrogen gas also maintains the oxygen concentration below the minimum that could cause autoignition of the fuel vapors. The vent system prevents excessive build-up of tank pressures.

The fuel tanks are serviced by single-point refueling. (Refer to "Single-point Pressure Refueling System" in Section IV.) Fuel specifications are shown in figure 1-37, and fuel quantities are shown in figure 1-15.

FUEL MANAGEMENT SYSTEM.

The fuel management system automatically controls the operation of the fuel transfer system to maintain the airplane center-of-gravity within limits, and supplies fuel quantity indications. Fuel control modules and capacitance-type tank units start and stop the fuel transfer pumps in a predetermined sequence and operate the fuel sequence and quantity indicators. The fuel management system also provides low sump tank (tank No. 3) level warning. Switches on the instrument panel permit manual selection of the transfer pumps in case of failure of the automatic operation. Operation of the quantity indicating portion of the system can be tested by a switch on the instrument panel.

FUEL TRANSFER SYSTEM.

All fuel is transferred to tank No. 3 (sump tank) by the fuel transfer system. (See figure 1-16.) Each tank has two or more hydraulically driven fuel transfer pumps to supply fuel to tank No. 3. With a full fuel load, moving any throttle out of OFF starts the transfer pumps in tanks No. 2 and 6 when the fuel transfer pump switches are at AUTO. Operation of the fuel transfer pumps in the proper sequence is controlled automatically by the fuel management system or manually controlled by fuel transfer pump switches on the instrument panel. Manual control of the fuel transfer pump switches overrides the automatic operation. (See figure 3-7 for proper fuel transfer sequence.) Two fuel level control valves in tank No. 3 control the flow of fuel into this tank. The upper fuel level control valve (preset at the fuel level of tank No.3) regulates the transfer of fuel from the aft tanks (tanks No. 4 through 8). The lower fuel level control valve in tank No. 3, (preset 5,000 pounds below the upper fuel level control valve) regulates the transfer of fuel from the forward tanks (tanks No. 1 and No. 2). The transfer pumps in tanks No. 1 and/or No. 2 supply fuel to tank No. 3 if the transfer rate from the aft tanks does not meet engine requirements and if the fuel level in tank No. 3 drops below the

T.O. 1B-70(X)A-1

FUEL QUANTITY DATA

REFER TO CONFIDENTIAL SUPPLEMENT, T.O. 1B-70(X)A-1A

Figure 1-15

T.O. 1B-70(X)A-1

FUEL SUPPLY SYSTEM
AIRPLANE AF62-001

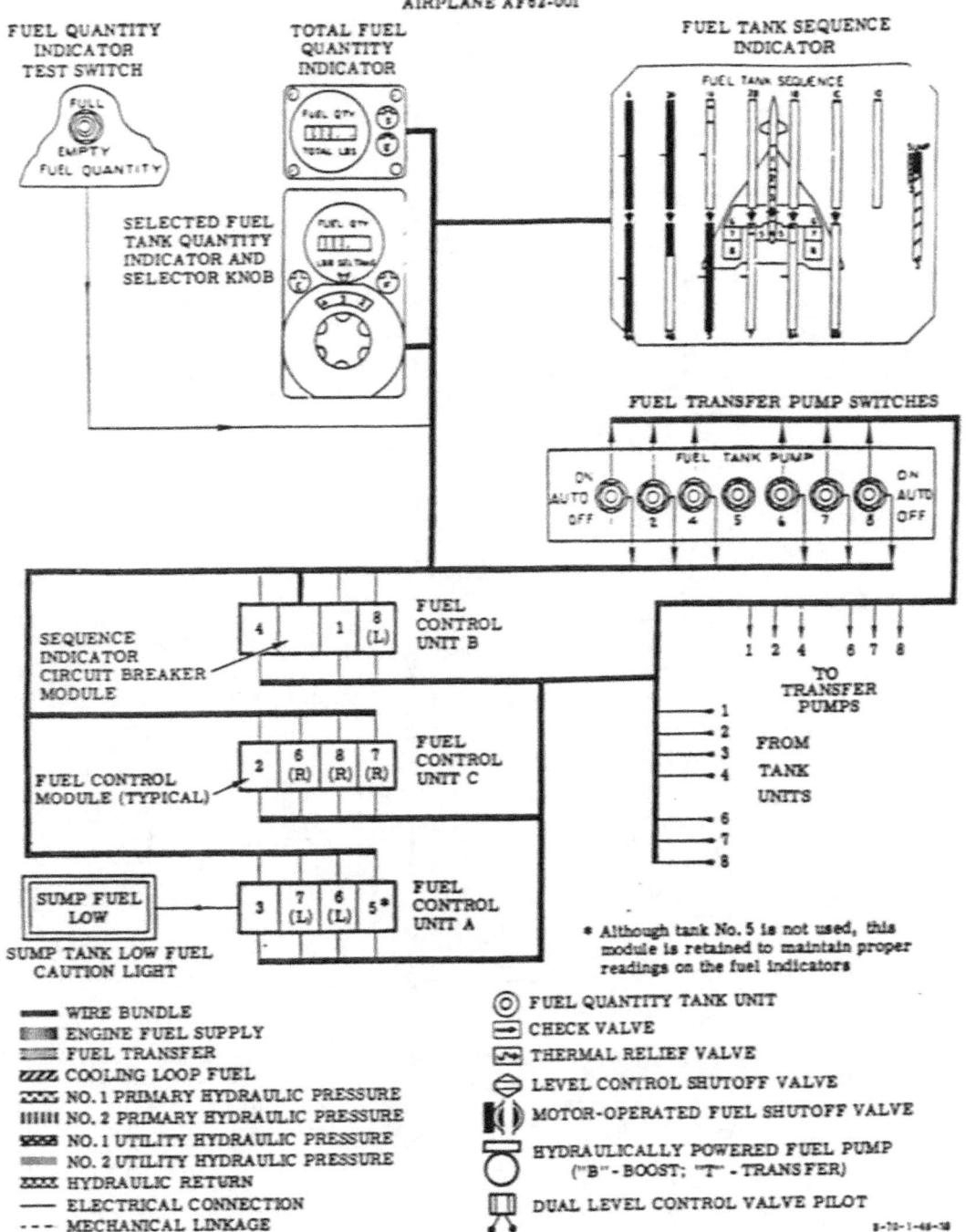

Figure 1-16 (Sheet 1 of 4)

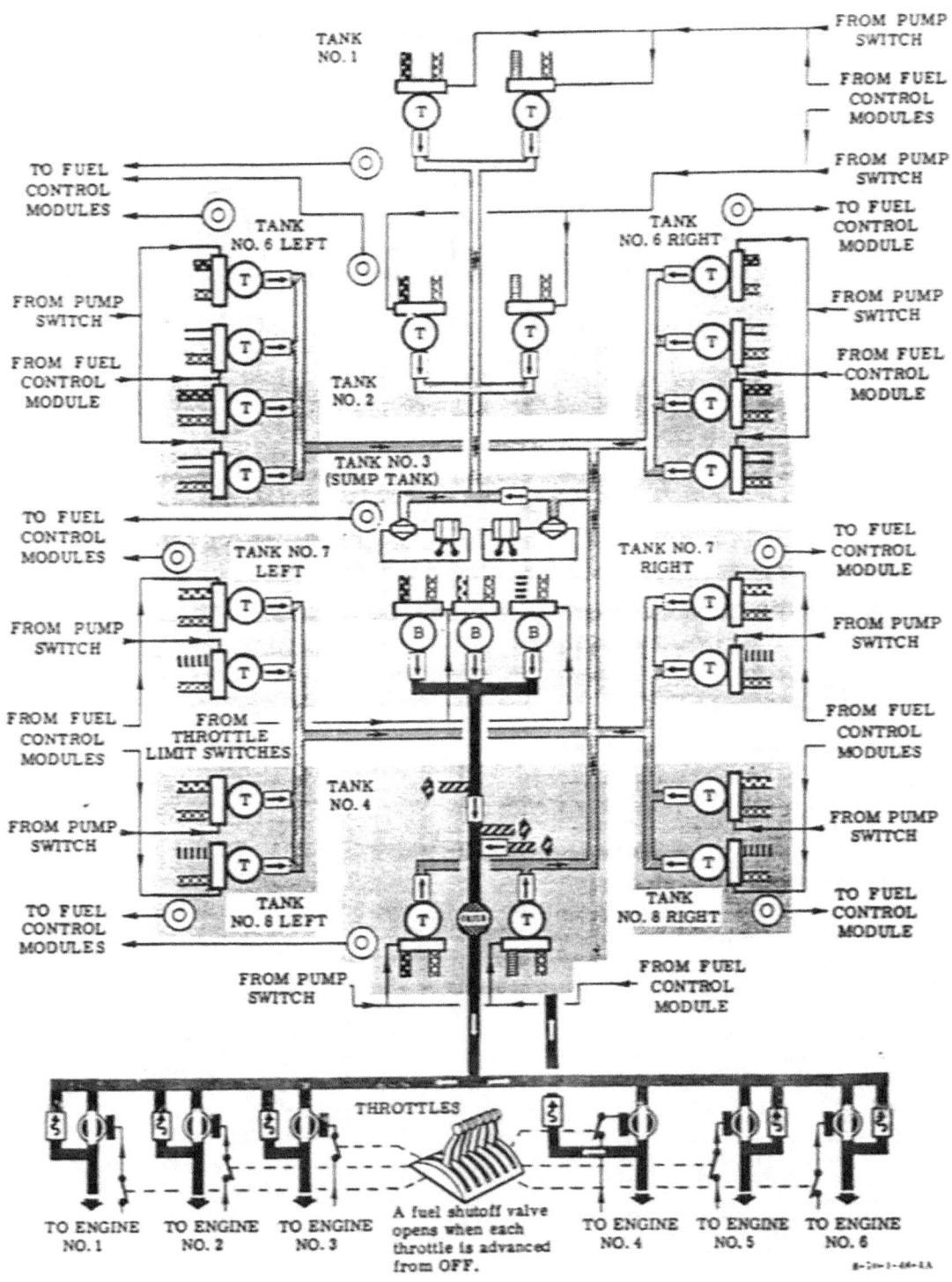

Figure 1-16 (Sheet 2 of 4)

T.O. 1B-70(X)A-1

FUEL SUPPLY SYSTEM
AIRPLANE AF62-207

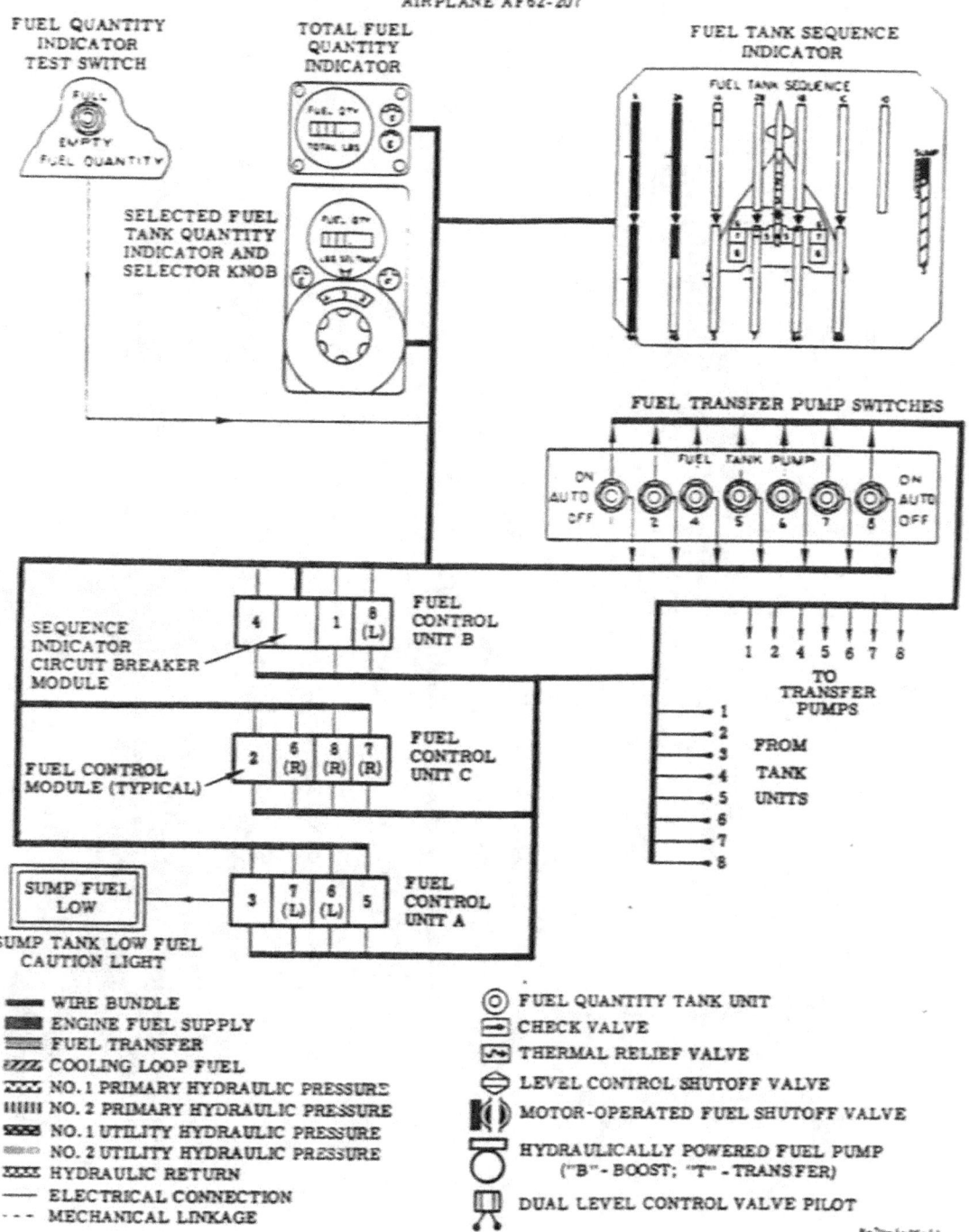

Figure 1-16 (Sheet 3 of 4)

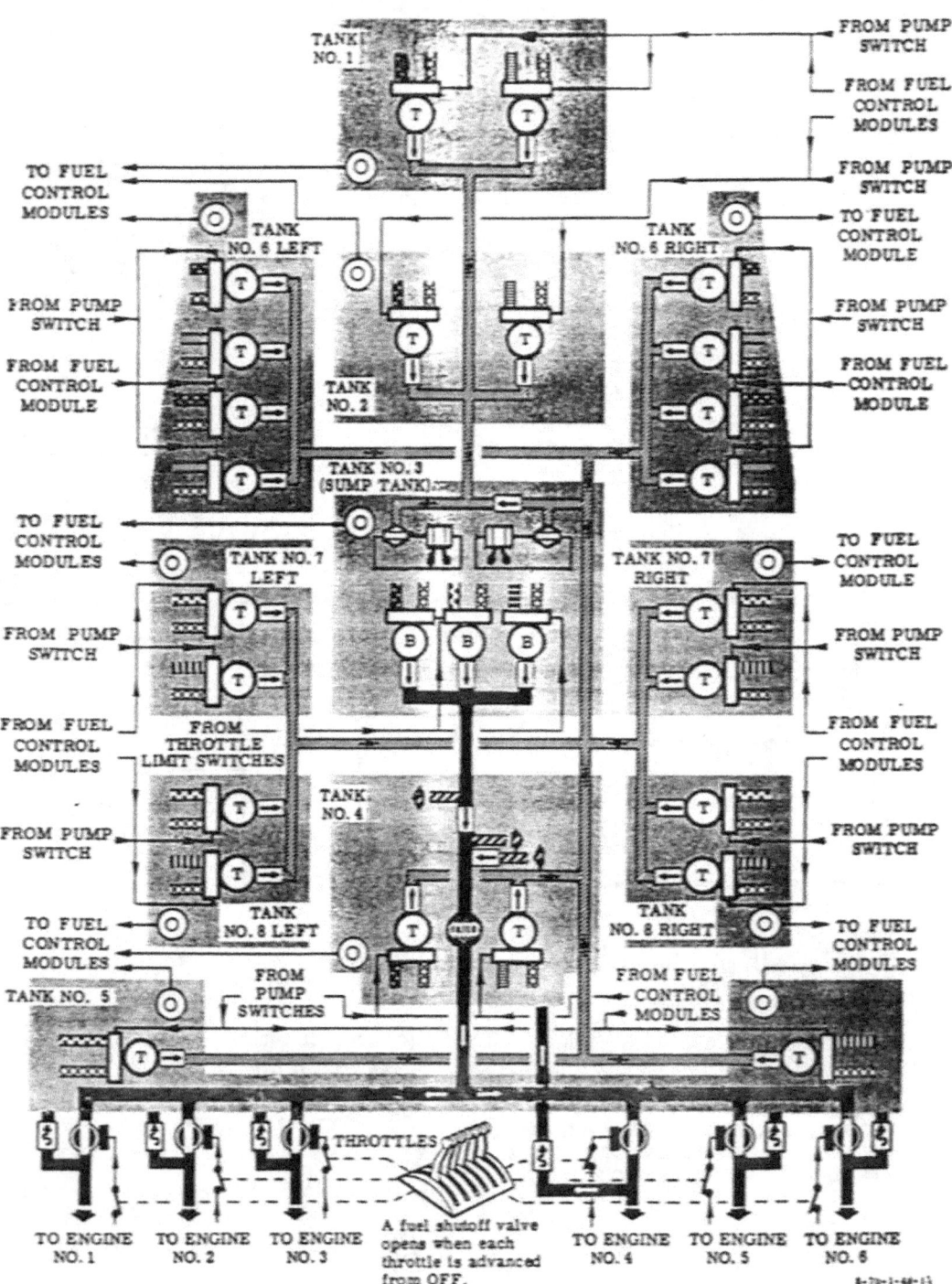

Figure 1-16 (Sheet 4 of 4)

T.O. 1B-70(X)A-1

lower fuel level control valve. A caution light in the crew compartment comes on whenever the fuel level in tank No. 3 falls below a preset level. Fuel from the forward tanks cannot flow through the upper fuel level control valve. However, fuel from the aft tanks can flow through either of the fuel level control valves, with flow normally being through the upper fuel level control valve.

FUEL CONTROL MODULES.

Each tank has a fuel control module which is the master fuel quantity measuring device for that tank. This module, receiving signals from the tank units, provides fuel quantity indications and automatic control of the fuel management system. The modules are mounted in the fuel control units in the electronic equipment compartment. (See figure 1-17.)

Each module has half of the tank unit-module bridge circuit and half of the indicator-module bridge circuit. Both of these bridge circuits must be balanced to show the correct reading on the fuel quantity and sequence indicators.

A change of the fuel level in any tank unbalances the tank unit-module bridge circuit. This causes the fuel control module to rebalance this circuit. However, this action unbalances the indicator-module bridge circuit which then is rebalanced so the indicators show the correct reading. All bridge circuit rebalancing is automatic.

NOTE
Although tank No. 5 is not used on Airplane AF62-001, the fuel control module for this tank is retained in the fuel management system to complete the indicator circuits and does not effect the indicated fuel quantity.

The fuel transfer pumps in tanks No. 1, 2, 4, and 8 are automatically started and stopped at intermediate fuel levels by switches in the fuel control modules. These switches operate solenoid control valves that control the hydraulic power to the transfer pumps. In addition, the module for tank No. 3 incorporates a switch to automatically turn on the sump fuel low caution light at a predetermined setting. Three adjustments (marked "E", "T", and "F") on the top front of each module are used to calibrate each module during initial installation by the ground crew. An indicator on the front of each fuel control module shows the approximate percent of fuel remaining in the corresponding tank. Also, marks on the indicator bezel show where the transfer pumps are turned on. Each fuel tank unit has two independent sensing elements (identified as circuits I and II) either of which can be selected by a tank unit selector switch on the front of each fuel control module. This switch determines which circuit will be used in the tank unit-module bridge circuit. The fuel control module circuit breaker power switch on the front of the module supplies fuel and defuel ac bus power to its module and respective tank units.

Spare fuel control modules for tanks No. 1, 2, 3, 4, and 5 are carried in the fuel control units to permit replacing a faulty module during flight. (See figure 3-8 for module replacement.) These spare modules are calibrated by the ground crew to match the module they replace and require no further adjustment.

NOTE
The fuel control modules must not be adjusted during flight, as incorrect sequencing or fuel quantity indication will occur.

A fuel sequence indicator circuit breaker power switch module, mounted in one of the fuel control units, supplies essential fuel and defuel ac bus power

T.O. 1B-70(X)A-1

FUEL CONTROL UNITS AND FUEL CONTROL MODULES

(IN ELECTRONIC EQUIPMENT COMPARTMENT)

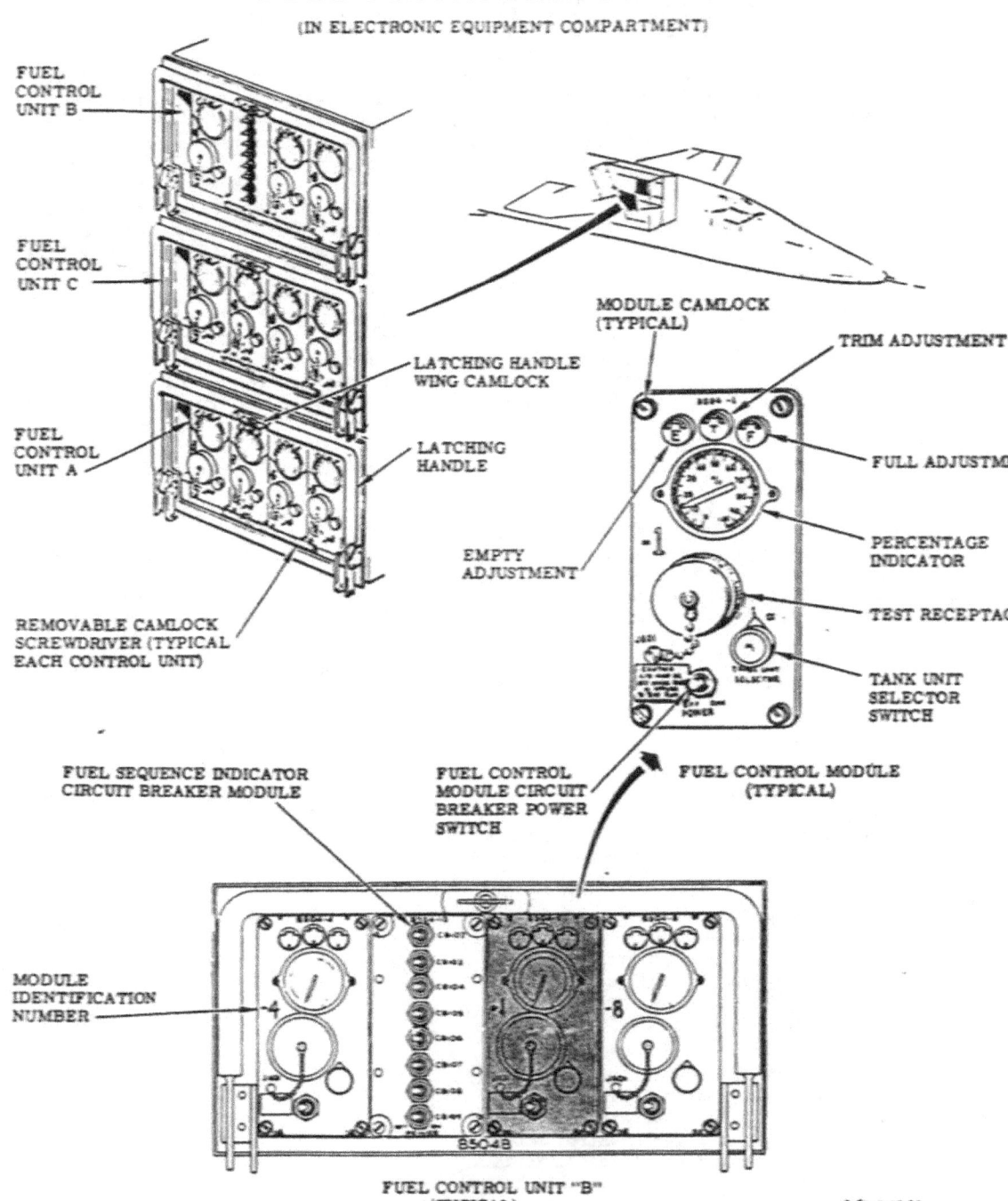

Figure 1-17

T.O. 1B-70(X)A-1

to the fuel sequence indicator circuit in both the fuel control modules and the fuel sequence indicator.

FUEL TRANSFER PUMPS.

The fuel transfer pumps in each fuel tank transfer fuel into tank No. 3 (sump tank) which in turn supplies fuel to the engines and to the fuel cooling loop. Tanks No. 1, 2, 4, and 5 have two transfer pumps each; tanks No. 7 and 8 have four transfer pumps each; and tank No. 6 has eight transfer pumps.

NOTE

Tank No. 5 is not used on Airplane AF62-001 and does not have transfer pumps.

The transfer pumps are hydraulically driven by pressure from either the No. 1 or No. 2 hydraulic system, primary or from the No. 1 or No. 2 utility hydraulic system. A single hydraulic system failure can cause the loss of only half the number of transfer pumps in any tank.

Electrical power from the primary or essential fuel and defuel ac busses is used to actuate the solenoid control valves of the hydraulic motors. These control valves open or close in response to signals from the fuel control module to start or stop the transfer pumps at intermediate fuel levels.

Automatic control of the transfer pumps is provided by the fuel management system or manual control is provided by the fuel transfer pump switches on the instrument panel. All transfer pumps within a specific tank are controlled by the respective fuel transfer pump switch. The transfer pumps are started automatically in sequence by the fuel management system when the fuel transfer pump switches are at AUTO (provided by hydraulic power is available) and any throttle is advanced from OFF. The transfer pumps in tanks No. 1, 2, 4, and 8 are stopped and restarted automatically at intermediate fuel levels in the proper sequence by the fuel management system. However, after a fuel tank is empty, the fuel transfer pumps continue to run until turned off by the corresponding fuel transfer pump switch.

CAUTION

If the fuel transfer pumps are not turned off when the tank is empty, pump damage may occur.

During ground test operations, the transfer pumps can be tested by the fuel pump selector and test switch on the ground test panel in the electronic equipment compartment. (Refer to "Fuel Pump Test System" in this section.)

FUEL BOOST PUMPS.

Fuel is supplied to all six engines by three boost pumps in a compartment in tank No. 3. These centrifugal-type pumps are driven by hydraulic motors. For reliability, each boost pump is independently driven by separate hydraulic systems. Primary No. 1 and No. 2 and utility No. 1 hydraulic systems supply the hydraulic power. Each pump is controlled by a solenoid valve powered from the primary fuel and defuel ac bus. The boost pumps operate when throttles are advanced to IDLE, provided hydraulic power is available. Two of the pumps are installed at the bottom of the tank and the third pump is mounted at a higher level. During starting, the boost pump using the same hydraulic system as the engine being started, is shut down automatically. The tank is constructed to contain fuel within the pump compartment to enable the higher pump to continue to supply fuel to the engines during negative-G conditions. Each boost pump can be tested for proper operation on the ground by means of test switches on the ground test panel in the electronic equipment compartment. (Refer to "Fuel Pump Test System" in this section.)

T.O. 1B-70(X)A-1

COOLING FUEL LOOP.

The cooling loop in the fuel tanks uses fuel as a heat sink to remove heat from various fluid systems and for control of the fuel tank pressurization and inerting system control package. (See figure 1-18.) Fuel for the cooling loop is delivered by the fuel boost pumps from the engine fuel supply line to the two cooling loop pumps in tank No. 3. A check valve permits the cooling loop pumps to draw fuel directly from tank No. 3 in case the fuel boost pumps fail. The pressure rise through the cooling loop pumps provides the required rate of fuel circulation through the cooling loop system. A check valve in the main fuel supply line prevents the cooling loop fuel from being recirculated through the loop. A portion of the fuel discharged from the cooling loop pumps is delivered to the fuel tank pressurization and inerting system control package. This fuel is used to control operation of the vent and nitrogen regulator valves, and heat from the fuel is used to change the liquid nitrogen into a gas. (Refer to "Fuel Tank Pressurization and Inerting System" in this section.) Cooling loop fuel from the pressurization and inerting system control package is returned directly to tank No. 3. The remaining fuel, after flowing through the various heat exchangers in the cooling loop, is returned to the engine supply line to supply fuel to the engines. (If the fuel demands of the engines exceed cooling loop output, the additional requirements are supplied by fuel from the fuel boost pumps. If engine fuel demands are less than the cooling loop flow, the excess fuel is relieved into tank No. 3 through relief valves.) The fuel that has passed through the fluid systems heat exchangers in the cooling loop flows through a fuel-cooling heat exchanger before returning to the engine fuel supply line. This heat exchanger (water boiler) uses water from the air conditioning and pressurization system to cool the heated fuel in the cooling loop. (See figure 4-1.) The exchanger keeps the temperature of the cooling loop fuel below 260°F. Water flow through the heat exchanger is controlled by throttle position and is modulated according to cooling loop fuel temperature. The water control circuits are engaged only when the throttles for three engines on either side, or all six throttles are in the IDLE to below MIN A/B range. This permits water control valves to open so that when the temperature of the incoming cooling loop fuel is about 240°F water flows through the heat exchanger in proportion to fuel temperature, with maximum water flow becoming available when the fuel temperature is about 255°F. During afterburner operation, however, the fuel flow is sufficient to keep the fuel cool, and the water to the heat exchanger is shut off.

COOLING LOOP PUMPS.

The two centrifugal-type cooling loop pumps, mounted in tank No. 3, are hydraulically driven and electrically controlled. The No. 1 cooling loop pump is powered by the No. 1 primary hydraulic system; the No. 2 pump by the No. 2 primary hydraulic system. With hydraulic pressure and electrical power available, the cooling loop pumps are started when any throttle is advanced from OFF to IDLE. However, to reduce hydraulic system demands during engine start, the No. 1 cooling loop pump is shut down as engines 1, 2, or 3 are started, and the No. 2 pump is shut down during starting of engines 4, 5, or 6. The shutdown pump is restarted automatically by the speed sensing switch on the accessory drive gearbox when the start circuit is de-energized. Caution lights in the crew compartment indicate cooling loop pump failure, or when the pumps are shut down. The cooling loop pumps are controlled by primary fuel and defuel ac bus power.

COOLING FUEL LOOP

* Refer to "Environmental Systems" in Section IV.

8-70-1-48-11

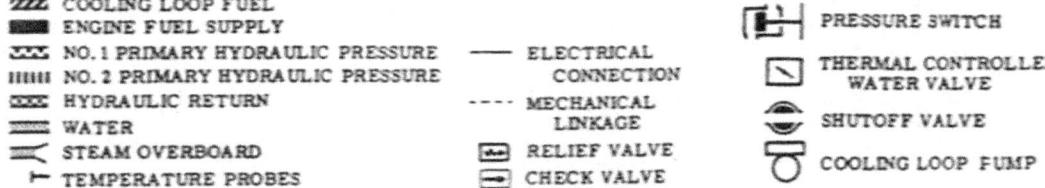

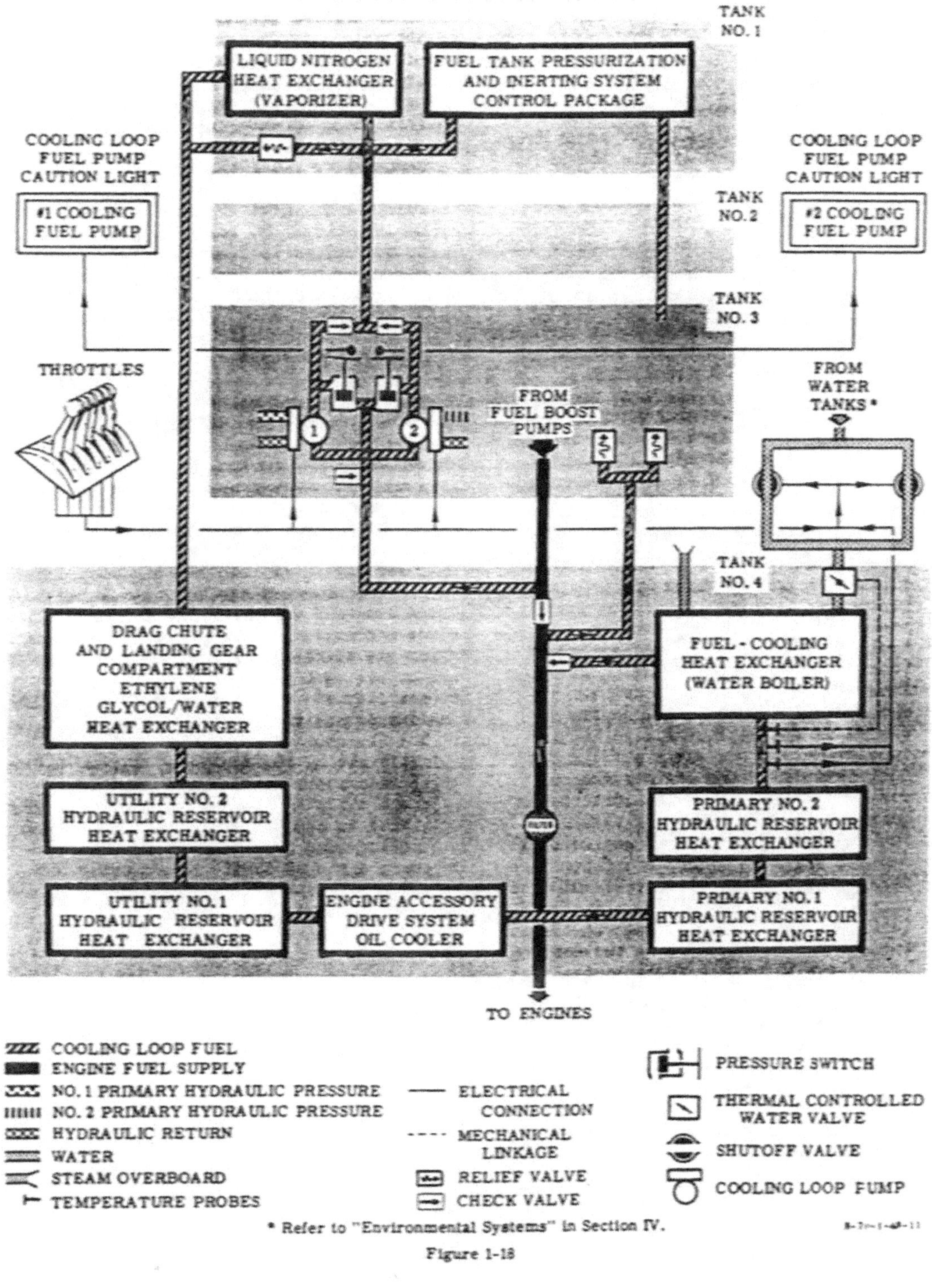

Figure 1-18

T.O. 1B-70(X)A-1

FUEL FILTER.

All fuel supplied to the engines passes through a single filter element. Filter element bypass valves maintain fuel flow to the engines if the filter element becomes clogged. In addition, each engine has fuel filters.

FIRE WALL FUEL SHUTOFF VALVES.

An electric-motor-driven (essential ac bus) fire wall shutoff valve is in the fuel line to each engine. Each valve is controlled by the position of its corresponding throttle. Advancing the throttle from OFF opens the shutoff valve, and retarding the throttle to OFF closes the shutoff valve. The shutoff valve also closes when the corresponding fire warning light/engine shutdown button is pressed. (Refer to "Emergency Equipment" in this section.)

NOTE
After a fire warning light/engine shutdown button is pressed (which closes the corresponding fuel shutoff valve), the throttle of the affected engine must be moved to OFF to preclude the reopening of the valve if a second fire warning light/engine shutdown button is pressed.

The firewall fuel shutoff valves receive electrical power from the essential ac bus.

THERMAL RELIEF VALVES.

A thermal relief valve in each engine fuel inlet line is located between the fire wall fuel shutoff valve and the engine. The relief valves prevent excessive line pressures due to heating of the fuel after an in-flight emergency or normal ground engine shutdown. The valve in No. 4 engine inlet line relieves excessive pressures into tank No. 4. On Airplane AF62-001, all other valves relieve back into the lines, and on Airplane AF62-207, the other valves relieve the excessive pressures into tank No. 5.

FUEL TANK PRESSURIZATION AND INERTING SYSTEM.

The fuel tank pressurization and inerting system automatically regulates the supply of nitrogen used to pressurize the fuel tanks and maintain the inert condition of the deaerated fuel. The system also maintains fuel transfer pump inlet pressures, provides tank pressure relief, and minimizes fuel boil-off during flight. Cooling loop fuel is used for operation of the pressurization and inerting system which is controlled by the pressurization and inerting control package. Two negative-pressure relief valves and one positive-pressure relief valve prevent excessive pressure differential between the fuel tanks and ambient pressures should the pressurization and inerting system fail.

All components of the pressurization and inerting system are located in the No. 1 fuel tank except the main vent lines connecting all fuel tanks. Common lines are used for both venting and pressurizing. The main vent lines may be filled completely by thermal expansion of the fuel or by fuel entering these lines during maneuvering flight or ground servicing. However, the vent lines are sloped to a low point in the venting system (in the sump area of tank No. 4).

The liquid nitrogen for the system is stored in two pressure tanks which are connected in parallel and are filled at a single-point filler connection. (See figure 1-37 for nitrogen specifications.) An indicator in the crew compartment indicates the amount of liquid nitrogen in the storage tanks and a caution light in the crew compartment comes on when the liquid nitrogen pressure or quantity is low, or if the fuel vent space pressure is low.

When the cooling loop pumps start operating, the control package directs cooling loop fuel to actuate the overboard vent and nitrogen regulator valves. These valves open or close as fuel tank and atmospheric pressures vary. When the regulator valve opens, liquid nitrogen flows to the heat exchanger (vaporizer) which utilizes heat from the cooling loop fuel to change the liquid nitrogen into a gas. (A bypass valve in the cooling loop, connected in parallel with the nitrogen heat exchanger, bypasses the cooling loop fuel if the heat exchanger becomes obstructed.) The gaseous nitrogen is distributed through the main vent lines to the fuel tanks to maintain the inert condition of the fuel that was achieved during refueling, and to provide a slight positive pressure in the fuel tanks. With altitude changes, the pressure differential between the fuel tank vent space pressure and atmospheric pressure is sensed by the control package. As a result, the control package either supplies nitrogen gas to increase the fuel tank pressures, or opens the overboard vent valve to decrease tank pressures. When the nitrogen pressure in the fuel tanks rises above atmospheric pressure, the nitrogen regulator valve closes, stopping the flow of nitrogen to the heat exchanger. If the fuel tank pressure increases above atmospheric pressure by a preset amount, the overboard vent valve opens to relieve the excess pressure.

The overboard vent valve opens in flight only to relieve excessive fuel tank pressure caused by rapid climbs or fuel heating. During ground servicing, when the pressurization and inerting system is inoperative, the overboard vent valve is open. Incoming fuel which has been deaerated before it enters the tanks forces the air in the tanks overboard through the overboard vent valve. A check valve in the overboard vent line prevents outside air from entering the fuel tanks through the open vent valve.

Two negative tank pressure relief valves in the overboard vent line admit air directly into tank No. 1 to prevent excessive negative tank pressures if the pressurization and inerting system fails to supply sufficient gaseous nitrogen to the fuel tanks. A positive tank pressure relief valve, also in the overboard vent line, prevents excessive tank pressures if the overboard vent valve fails to open.

FUEL SUPPLY SYSTEM CONTROLS AND INDICATORS.

FUEL TRANSFER PUMP SWITCHES.

The seven fuel tank pump switches (28, figure 1-4), one for each tank (except tank No. 3), are arranged horizontally on the copilot's instrument panel. Each switch is numbered to correspond with a tank, and controls the operation of the transfer pumps in the respective tank.

NOTE

The fuel transfer pump switch for tank No. 5 is inoperative on Airplane AF62-001.

When the switches are at AUTO, the fuel management system automatically controls the fuel transfer pumps in a predetermined sequence. Moving a switch to ON, provides manual control of the fuel transfer pumps in the corresponding tank, overriding the automatic sequence and manually sequencing fuel flow. After a tank has emptied, the corresponding pump switch must be moved to OFF to conserve transfer pump life.

CAUTION

If the pump switch is not turned OFF when the tank is empty, pump damage may occur.

If the fuel tank pump switches are used for manual control of the transfer

Changed 25 June 1965

T.O. 1B-70(X)A-1

pumps, they must be subsequently returned to the AUTO position at the end of the sequence step which was in progress at the time they were switched to ON. The primary fuel and defuel ac bus and the essential fuel and defuel ac bus supply power through the transfer pump switches to the fuel pump control circuits.

REFUELING VALVE SWITCHES.

Refer to "Single-point Pressure Refueling System" in Section IV.

FUEL QUANTITY INDICATOR TEST SWITCH.

The fuel quantity indicator test switch (22, figure 1-4), on the copilot's instrument panel is used to test operation of the total fuel quantity indicator, the selected tank fuel quantity indicator, the fuel control modules, and the fuel sequence indicator. When the switch is actuated, it checks all three indicating systems and fuel control modules simultaneously. The test switch is spring-loaded from FULL and EMPTY to the center (OFF) position. The switch substitutes a given capacitance into the circuitry. When the switch is held in the FULL or EMPTY position, the indicators should drive towards full or empty indications, depending on the test position selected. Because tank No. 5 is not used on Airplane AF62-001, strip 5 on the fuel sequence indicator remains black (indicating an empty tank), and the selected tank quantity indicator will show zero fuel quantity when the tank No. 5 position is selected on this airplane. When the switch is released to OFF, the indicators should return to their original readings. If the indicators do not move or return to their previous setting, the indicating system is faulty. The test switch circuit receives power from the right primary dc bus.

TOTAL FUEL QUANTITY INDICATOR.

The total fuel quantity indicator (26, figure 1-4), on the copilot's instrument panel, is a digital indicator, displaying in pounds the total remaining fuel. The fuel quantity, indicated in 500-pound increments, is gaged by capacitance-type tank units in all of the tanks. The signals from the tank units are integrated by the fuel control modules to provide an indication of total fuel. The indicator is powered by the primary fuel and defuel ac bus. To the right of the counter are two adjustments, labeled "E" and "F", for adjusting the indicator for installation errors during maintenance and initial installation. Operation of the total fuel quantity indicator can be checked by the fuel quantity indicator test switch. (Refer to "Fuel Quantity Indicator Test Switch" in this section.)

SELECTED FUEL TANK QUANTITY INDICATOR AND SELECTOR KNOB.

The selected fuel tank quantity indicator (27, figure 1-4), on the copilot's instrument panel, is a digital-type counter calibrated in hundreds of pounds. When the rotary selector knob below the indicator has been set for one of the individual tanks, the fuel quantity in that tank is displayed on the indicator to the nearest 100 pounds. Because tank No. 5 is not used on Airplane AF62-001, the selected tank quantity indicator will read zero at the No. 5 position on this airplane. The left or right wing tanks (6L, 6R, 7L, 7R, 8L, and 8R) may be selected individually. The number of the tank selected is indicated in the center of a moving dial above the selected knob. Directly above the selected knob are two adjustments, labeled "E" and "F", for adjusting the indicator for installation errors during maintenance and initial installation.

The tank selector normally is positioned to correspond to the tank being used, as shown by the fuel sequence indicator strip. By monitoring the selected tank indicator, it is possible to determine if fuel has started to transfer from the tank selected.

Changed 25 June 1965

The indicating system is powered by the essential fuel and defuel ac bus. The fuel quantity indicator signals originate in capacitor-type sensing units in each tank. The capacitance is continuously measured, calibrated, and converted to a fuel quantity reading on the indicator by the fuel control modules. Operation of the selected tank quantity indicator can be checked by the fuel quantity indicator test switch. (Refer to "Fuel Quantity Indicator Test Switch" in this section.)

FUEL TANK SEQUENCE INDICATOR.

The fuel tank sequence indicator (29, figure 1-4), on the copilot's instrument panel, is used to monitor the sequence of fuel transfer and usage. The sequence indicator has 14 tape strips arranged in two rows, one above the other, to represent the fuel usage sequence.

The strips on the upper half of the indicator represent the fuel forward of the center of gravity, with the exception of tank No. 6 which is near the center of gravity, and the lower strips represent fuel aft of the center of gravity. The white portion of the strip represents the amount of fuel remaining in the tank. As the tank empties, the white part of the strip recedes and the black part of the strip is exposed. When the tank is empty or the portion of fuel in a tank represented by that strip is used, the entire strip will be black. (Because tank No. 5 is not used on Airplane AF62-001, strip 5 remains black on this airplane to indicate the empty tank.) The fuel represented by a lower strip is used following the fuel represented by the strip above it. If part of the total fuel in a tank is used at different times during the fuel sequence, the strip number representing that tank is followed by an A, B, C, or D in the order of usage. During automatic fuel sequencing, strip 6 on the upper left of the indicator is the first to recede. When strip 6 is completely black, tank No. 6 is empty and the white of strip 4A begins to recede, indicating tank No. 4 is transferring. The next strip in sequence is 2A. The sequence continues from top to bottom and from left to right throughout the fuel sequence. (Fuel transfer sequence is shown in figure 3-6.) Four black dash marks at the top of the white strips make it possible to observe initial movement of strips 1A, 2A, 4A, 5, 6, 7, and 8A. The tape strip for tank No. 3 is white with black diagonal strips. This strip also shows black as the tank empties. The tape strip for tank No. 3 moves up and down as fuel level in the tank varies. At the top left of this strip is a green marker which represents the normal range of strip movement between the high level control valve and the low level control valve. The vertical strip for tank No. 3 will not drop below the green marker unless the automatic sequence fails or until all other tanks have emptied. Operation of the fuel tank sequence indicator can be checked by the fuel quantity indicator test switch. (Refer to "Fuel Quantity Indicator Test Switch" in this section.)

Signals for the fuel tank sequence indicator originate in the capacitance-type tanks units in each tank. These signals are continuously summed and converted to fuel tank sequence indications by the fuel control modules. The sequence indicator circuit breaker power switch module (in the electronic equipment compartment) supplies power from the essential fuel and defuel ac bus to the fuel tank sequence indicator.

FUEL PUMP SHUTOFF SWITCH.

The two-position fuel pump shutoff switch is used during maintenance operations to de-activate all fuel pumps simultaneously. The switch is recessed in a panel at the corner of the aisle leading to the ground escape hatch. A hinged plate covers the switch, and a clip on the inner face of the plate prevents it from closing when the switch is at its OFF position. The switch must be at NORM for normal operation of the fuel pumps.

LIQUID NITROGEN QUANTITY INDICATOR AND TEST BUTTON.

The nitrogen quantity indicator (19, figure 1-4), on the copilot's instrument panel, indicates the quantity of fuel inerting liquid nitrogen in the storage containers. A push-button test switch (20, figure 1-4), below the indicator, is used to test operation of the indicator. When the button is pressed, the indicator pointer should rotate counterclockwise towards E (empty). When the button is released, the pointer should return to its previous setting. If the pointer fails to move or does not return to its previous setting, the indicating system is faulty. The nitrogen quantity indicator and test button receive power from the essential ac bus.

FUEL INERTING CAUTION LIGHT.

The placard-type fuel inerting caution light (5, figure 1-7), on the center console, indicates fuel tank inerting and pressurization system failures. The fuel inerting light comes on if fuel inerting nitrogen pressure is low, if the fuel vent space pressure is low, or if the liquid nitrogen quantity is low. If the light comes on, it will be necessary to reduce speed, if Mach 2.4 has been exceeded, and maintain altitude for a sufficient time to decrease the vent space temperature to a safe limit before descending. When the caution light comes on, a latching circuit keeps the light on until it is reset on the ground.

NOTE
When testing the liquid nitrogen quantity indicator, the fuel inerting caution light will come on if the indicator pointer is allowed to go below 1/4. Therefore, to avoid the need of resetting the fuel inerting caution light circuitry, the liquid nitrogen quantity indicator test button should only be held long enough to cause the indicator pointer to start to move counterclockwise.

The fuel inerting light is powered by the essential ac bus.

SUMP TANK LOW FUEL LEVEL CAUTION LIGHT.

This placard-type caution light (5, figure 1-7), on the center console, comes on when the fuel level of the No. 3 (sump) tank has dropped to 21,000 pounds. The light also indicates a fuel sequence malfunction if fuel is not transferring to the No. 3 tank and total fuel remaining is more than 21,000 pounds. The light is powered by the essential ac bus.

COOLING LOOP FUEL PUMP CAUTION LIGHTS.

Two placard-type cooling loop fuel pump caution lights (1, figure 1-7), one for each cooling loop pump, are on the center console. When either of the cooling loop fuel pumps fails, the corresponding caution light illuminates. The lights are powered by the essential fuel and defuel ac bus.

CAUTION
When either cooling loop fuel pump caution light comes on, the flight should be aborted because failure of the remaining pump would stop the flow of cooling fuel through the cooling loop. As a result, subsequent failure of accessory drive systems and electrical generating system can occur, as well as overheating of the fluid systems that are cooled by the cooling loop.

NOTE
A cooling loop fuel pump caution light comes on after the ground start switch is moved to ON when starting each engine. When the speed sensing switch in the accessory drive gearbox automatically de-energizes the start circuits, the cooling loop fuel pump caution light goes out.

FUEL PUMP TEST SYSTEM.

The fuel boost and transfer pumps in the fuel tanks, and the cooling loop pumps can be individually tested when all throttles are at OFF by use of switches and a fuel pump test gage on the ground test panel in the electronic equipment compartment. The test system uses power from the primary fuel and defuel ac bus.

T.O. 1B-70(X)A-1

FUEL TANK PUMP SELECTOR SWITCH NO. 1.

The 12-position fuel tank pump selector switch number 1 (8, figure 1-12) is on the ground test panel in the electronic equipment compartment and selects the fuel transfer pumps in tanks No. 1 through No. 5, and the fuel boost or cooling loop pumps to be checked. The SELECTOR NO. 2 position transfers the selection of fuel pumps to be tested to fuel tank selector switch number 2. Turning the switch to any of the other marked positions and holding the fuel pump test switch at either of its test positions operates the respective pump. The pressure of the pump being tested is shown on the fuel pump test gage.

NOTE

Because tank No. 5 is not used on Airplane AF62-001, the 5 TRANS position of the selector switch is inoperative on this airplane.

FUEL TANK PUMP SELECTOR SWITCH NO. 2.

The 12-position fuel tank pump selector switch number 2 (9, figure 1-12) is on the ground test panel in the electronic equipment compartment and selects the fuel transfer pumps to be checked in tanks No. 6 through No. 8. Before the selector switch number 2 will operate, selector switch number 1 must be at its SELECTOR NO. 2 position. Turning the selector switch to any of the marked positions, and holding the fuel pump test switch at either of its test positions operates the respective pump. The pressure of the pump being tested is shown on the fuel pump test gage.

FUEL PUMP TEST SWITCH.

The 3-position fuel pump test switch (7, figure 1-12) is on the ground test panel in the electronic equipment compartment. The switch is spring-loaded to OFF. After setting the tank selector, moving and holding the switch at PUMP 1 ON or PUMP 2 ON starts the selected pump.

FUEL PUMP TEST GAGE.

The fuel pump test gage (6, figure 1-12) is on the ground test panel in the electronic equipment compartment. The gage shows the output pressure (in psi) of the fuel pump selected when the fuel pump test switch is at either of the on positions. The fuel pump test gage on Airplane AF62-207 can be tested during maintenance operations by a push button (5A, figure 1-12), on the ground test panel, next to the gage. Proper operation of the gage is indicated by counterclockwise movement of the gage pointer when the test button is held in, and the return of the pointer to its previous setting when the button is released.

ELECTRICAL POWER SUPPLY SYSTEM.

The electrical power supply is essentially an ac system which also supplies dc power, through transformer-rectifiers, for the dc equipment. Power is supplied by two primary ac generators, one driven by the accessory drive gearbox of engine No. 3 and the other by the No. 4 gearbox. A hydraulically driven emergency ac generator provides power to the critical circuits in case both primary gearbox-driven generators fail. The electrical power supply system does not have a storage battery. The primary ac generators supply 240/416 volt, 400 cycle electrical power, which permits use of low-weight power transmission feeders, which is reduced to 115/200 volts by step-down transformers and then supplied to the airplane system busses. An external power receptacle permits the application of power to the complete electrical system for ground operations, and another receptacle is used when electrical power is needed only for towing, fueling, or defueling.

WARNING

The high voltages generated and distributed throughout the airplane are dangerous and can cause serious or fatal injuries. When power is on the airplane, proper precautions must be taken to avoid contacting a "hot" wire or exposed terminals or connections.

1-54   Changed 25 June 1965

T.O. 1B-70(X)A-1

ELECTRICAL CONDUIT FAULT SENSING SYSTEM.

The electrical wiring routed through the fuel tanks or other critical areas is installed in metal conduits with insulated liners having a copper conductor laminated between two sections. If a wire becomes exposed because of abrasion or chafing, the conduit fault sensing system gives an indication of the fault before the wire shorts to the metal conduit or allows sufficient time for protective devices to function. Two neon bulbs in the electronic equipment compartment, one for the master power and one for the external power feeder junction, indicate a fault. A switch for testing the conduit fault sensing system indicator lights is located below the bulbs. (The fault sensing system is basically an indicating system for maintenance personnel and is powered by the right primary ac bus.)

PRIMARY AC GENERATING SYSTEM.

The primary ac generating system consists of two 60 kva ac generators; one is driven by the No. 3 engine-driven accessory drive gearbox and the other by the No. 4 engine gearbox. Each generator is mounted on and driven by a gearbox-mounted constant-speed drive. The generators are 3-phase oil-cooled, self-excited, brushless, 240/416-volt ac, 400-cycle units. (The 240/416 volts ac is stepped down to 115/200 volts ac and then delivered to the airplane system busses.) The minimum generator cut-in speed is about 58% engine rpm.

Normal operation is with both generators operating in parallel; however, each generator and its controls can operate as a single generating system. The generators are protected from abnormal operating conditions by generator control and protective circuits and by feeder fault sensing systems. A faulty generator is removed automatically from the bus power feeder and the remaining good primary generator can supply power to both bus power feeders. (Refer to "AC Power Distribution" in this section.) Temporary overvoltage or undervoltage faults that take the generator "off the line" will be automatically reset by an automatic cycling reset circuit. The automatic reset circuit will cycle the faulty generator three times in an attempt to clear the fault. If the fault is not cleared after the third try, the reset circuit locks the affected generator off the bus power feeder and de-energizes the generator.

CONSTANT-SPEED DRIVES.

Because most electronic equipment requires a constant ac frequency, each primary ac generator is driven by a constant-speed drive (CSD) which maintains the generator at a constant 8000 rpm throughout the range of various engine speeds. (Refer to "Accessory Drive System (ADS)" in this section.) One constant-speed drive is mounted on and driven by each of the inboard (No. 3 and No. 4) engine accessory drive system gearboxes. The CSD consists of a hydraulic transmission controlled by an electromechanical governor. With this speed control and the voltage regulator, the average load of one generator will not be more than 3 kva greater than the other generator when they are operating in parallel. The constant-speed drive contains two governors, the basic governor and the limit governor. Normal output speed control is maintained by the basic governor. Any possible malfunction resulting in output overspeed or underspeed is controlled or limited by the limit governor.

EMERGENCY AC GENERATOR.

The hydraulically driven 10 kva emergency ac generator supplies 3-phase, 115/200-volt, 400-cycle ac power to the essential ac bus if the left primary ac bus power is not available as the result of a malfunction in the primary generating system.

T.O. 1B-70(X)A-1

The emergency generator is driven by a hydraulic motor using No. 2 utility hydraulic system pressure. A switch in the crew compartment permits automatic or selective operation of the emergency generator. When the emergency generator is on, the essential ac bus is automatically disconnected from the left primary ac bus. If the left primary ac bus is inoperative, the emergency generator control circuit is completed and the emergency generator automatically supplies electrical power to the essential ac bus only. A relay, providing a one-second delay, permits the emergency generator to attain the required operating speed before assuming control of the essential ac bus. As a back-up, another relay provides a five-second delay to ensure that the emergency generator has reached normal operating speed if the one-second delay relay should fail. If the primary generating system has again assumed the electrical load, the emergency generator will remain on the essential ac bus for five seconds, then is automatically cut off by a third relay. The emergency generator is prevented from cutting in and out by these relays, in case the primary generating system momentarily fails. A caution light indicates operation of the emergency ac generator.

AC POWER DISTRIBUTION.

The ac power supplied by the primary generators is delivered to the busses by generator transmission feeders through step-down transformers. (The left bus power feeder is powered by the No. 3 generator; the right bus power feeder is powered by the No. 4 generator.) During normal operation, both generators operate in parallel through two bus-tie contactors. The bus-tie contactors are in series and connect the two bus power feeders to permit paralleling the generators or to permit one generator to supply power to both bus power feeders if one generator fails. Also the bus-tie contactors provide a means of splitting the busses should a bus fault occur on one bus. A fault on either primary bus power feeder during parallel operation of the two primary generators causes the bus-tie contactors to open and split the busses. When the bus-tie contactors are open and both primary generators are operating, each generator will supply power only to its corresponding bus power feeder. When the bus-tie contactors open, a caution light in the crew compartment is illuminated.

The 240/416 volts ac power is generated to reduce the conductor weight of the bus power feeders to the two step-down transformers (left and right) in the electronic equipment compartment. The step-down transformer output is 115/200 volts ac and is divided into several load busses to permit the separation of generator loads in case of nonparallel operation of generators, to reduce the total load for emergency generator operation, or for operation of essential systems during ground towing and refueling. The left step-down transformer supplies power directly to the left primary ac bus; the right step-down transformer supplies power directly to the right primary ac bus. The ac power distribution is shown schematically in figure 1-19.

LEFT PRIMARY AC BUS.

The left primary ac bus receives its power from both the No. 3 and 4 generators when the bus-tie contactors are closed. If the bus-tie contactors open because of a fault, the bus will be powered by the No. 3 generator. The left primary ac bus is energized when external power is connected. It cannot be powered by the emergency generator.

RIGHT PRIMARY AC BUS.

The right primary ac bus can be powered from both the No. 3 and 4 generators or external power when the bus-tie contactors are closed. If the bus-tie contactors open because of a fault, the bus will be powered by the No. 4 generator. The right primary ac bus cannot be powered by the emergency generator.

T.O. 1B-70(X)A-1

ESSENTIAL AC BUS.

In normal operation the essential ac bus receives power (primary generator or external source) from the left primary ac bus. However, when the emergency generator is operating, the essential ac bus is automatically transferred from the left primary ac bus to the emergency generator.

GROUND TOW AC BUS.

The ground tow ac bus furnishes power to those ac electrical circuits necessary for ground towing. This bus is energized by power (primary generator or external source) from the right primary ac bus or by external ground tow or fueling and defueling power through the ac and dc power receptacle. When ground tow ac power is applied, the ac tow bus is automatically disconnected from the right primary ac bus.

PRIMARY AND ESSENTIAL FUEL AND DEFUEL AC BUSSES.

The primary and essential fuel and defuel ac busses are energized by power (primary generator or external source) from the right primary ac and essential ac busses, respectively. Both fuel and defuel busses also can be energized by an external fuel and defuel ground power unit through the ground tow power receptacle. When power is supplied by the fuel and defuel ground power unit, only the fuel busses and the tow busses are powered.

INSTRUMENT AC BUS.

The instrument ac bus, which furnishes power to the air data computer synchronizer and the horizontal situation indicators, receives 26-volt ac power from the essential ac bus through the instrument step-down transformer. Loss of the instrument ac bus is indicated only by the erratic displays of the horizontal situation indicators. (Refer to "Erratic Operation of the Attitude Director and Horizontal Situation Indicators" in Section IV.)

DC POWER DISTRIBUTION.

RIGHT PRIMARY DC BUS.

The right primary dc bus receives 28-volt dc power from the right primary transformer-rectifier which is connected to and converts the ac power from the right primary ac bus. (The right primary dc bus cannot be powered by the emergency generator.) A caution light indicates loss of voltage on the right primary dc bus.

ESSENTIAL DC BUS.

The essential dc bus receives 28-volt dc power from the essential transformer-rectifier which is connected to and converts the ac power from the essential ac bus. Loss of dc voltage is indicated by illumination of a caution light.

GROUND TOW DC BUS.

The ground tow dc bus furnishes power to those dc electrical circuits necessary for ground towing. This bus is energized by power (primary generator or external source) from the essential dc bus or by external power through the ac and dc power receptacle. When external ground tow power, or fuel and defuel power is applied, the tow dc bus is disconnected automatically from the essential dc bus.

ELECTRICALLY OPERATED EQUIPMENT.

See figure 1-19.

EXTERNAL AC ELECTRICAL POWER RECEPTACLE.

Access to the external ac power receptacle is through an access door on the bottom of the airplane next to the No. 3 accessory drive system compartment. (See 4, figure 1-37.) When external ac

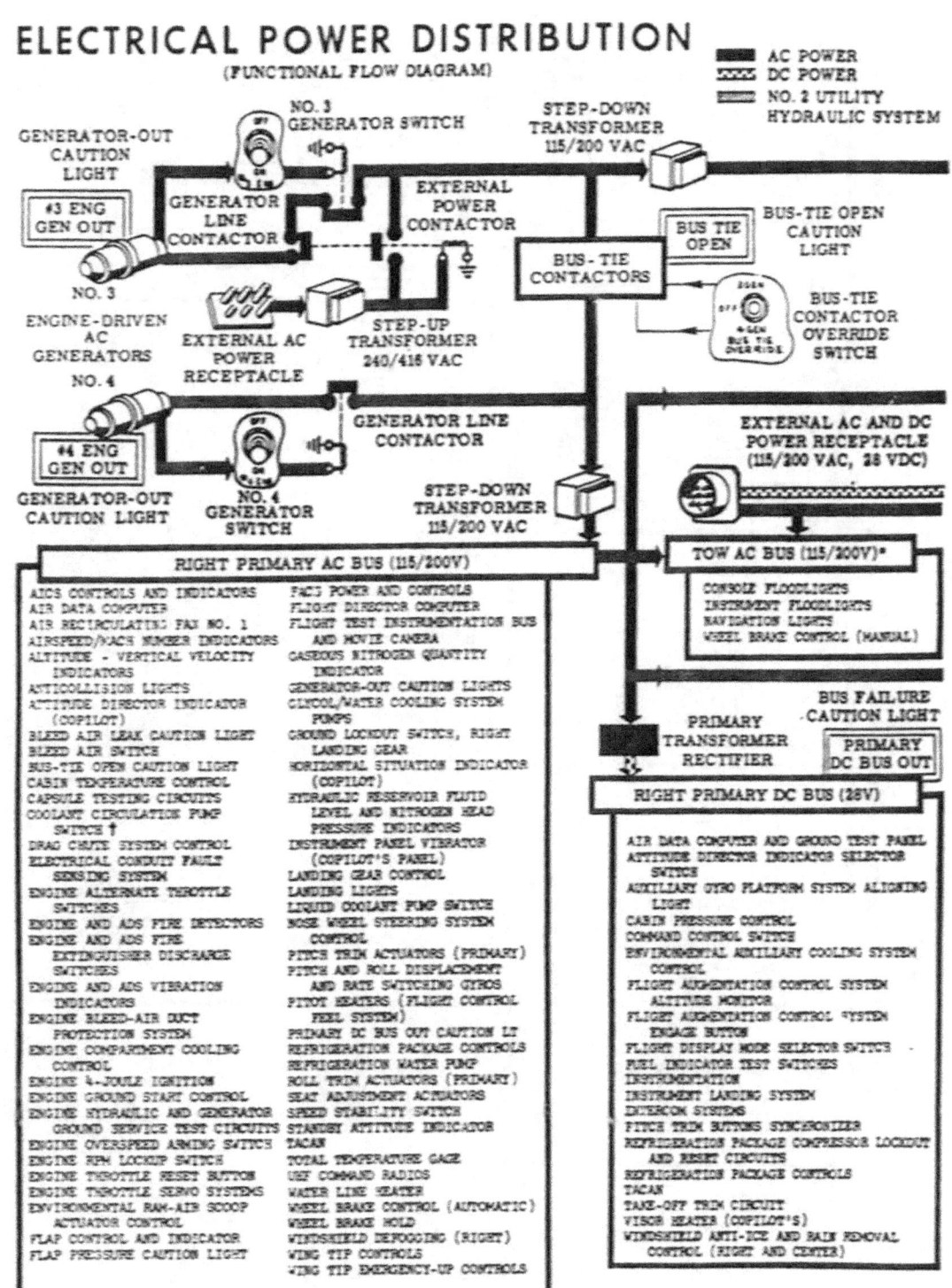

Figure 1-19 (Sheet 1 of 2)

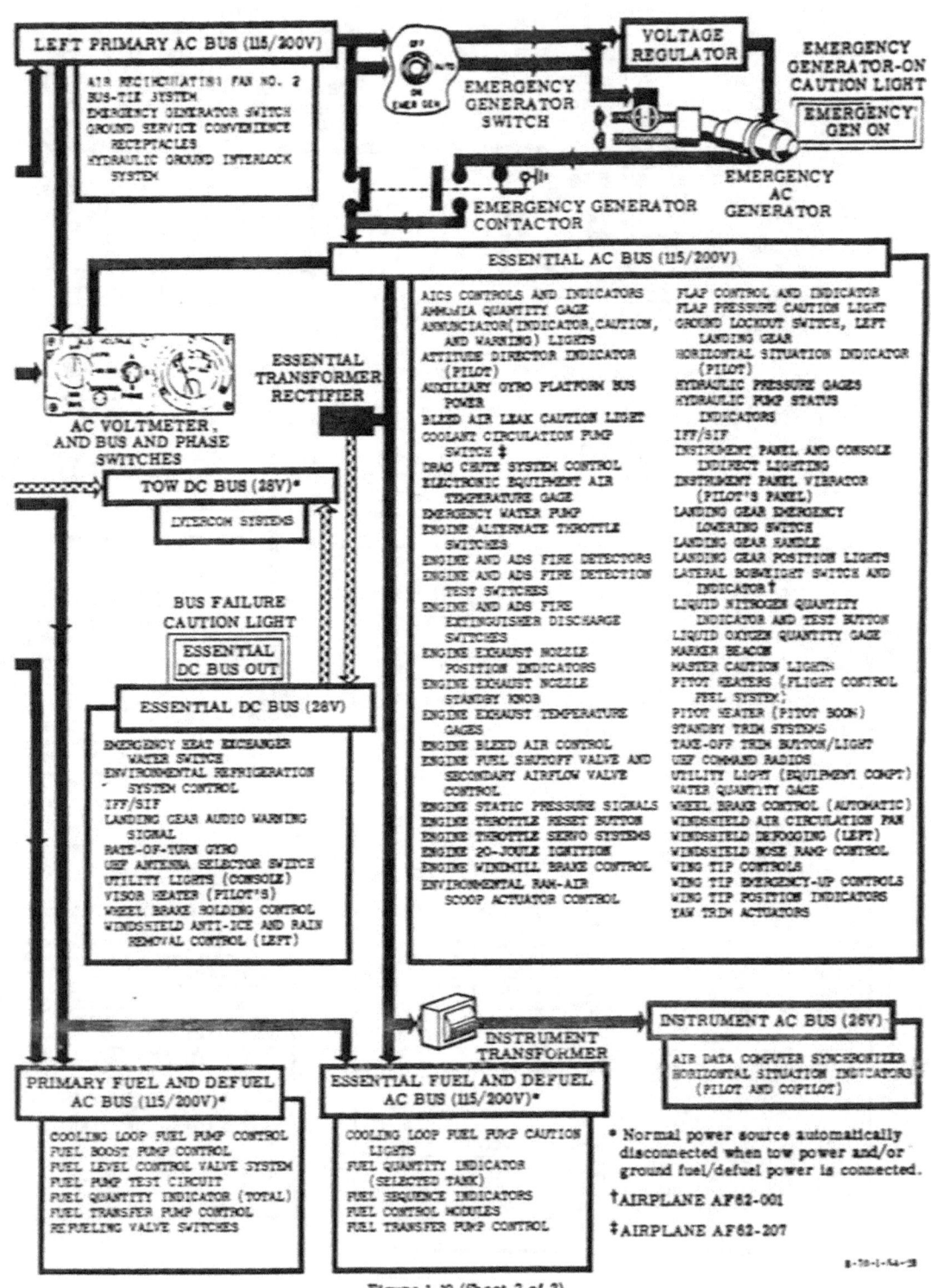

Figure 1-19 (Sheet 2 of 2)

T.O. 1B-70(X)A-1

power is connected to the airplane, all electrical busses (ac and dc) are energized, provided the ground air conditioner is supplying cooling air flow or the recirculating fan switch is ON. The external ground power unit supplies 115/200-volt ac power to a step-up transformer which increases the voltage to 240/416 for transmission by the generator feeders to the step-down transformers in the electronic equipment compartment. After No. 4 engine is started, No. 4 generator parallels the external electrical power source. When the No. 4 generator is up to cut-in speed (engine rpm about 58%), external electrical power is automatically removed from the power transmission feeders. External electric power cannot power the airplane busses if the busses are being supplied by the airplane generating system.

CAUTION

Electrical equipment cooling must be maintained during external power operation.

External electric power must be supplying the airplane busses to permit the external hydraulic power to supply the airplane hydraulic systems. When external power is applied, either of the two feeder fault neon indicators is illuminated if a fault disconnects either primary generator from the electrical busses by its related differential protection system. (The two feeder fault indicators, one for each primary generator system, are on the right side of the electronic equipment compartment.) If an unbalanced electrical condition occurs in the external power feeder system, the feeder fault circuit for the No. 3 generator automatically removes the external power from the airplane busses.

EXTERNAL AC AND DC ELECTRICAL POWER RECEPTACLE.

The ac and dc external power receptacle supplies 115/200-volt ac power and 28-volt dc power for ground towing, fueling, and defueling operations. The receptacle is on the left landing gear strut door. (See 18, figure 1-37.) The ground tow power unit supplies ac and dc power through the receptacle to the tow ac and dc busses only. When the fuel and defuel ground power unit is supplying power through the receptacle, the tow ac and dc busses, and the primary and essential fuel and defuel busses are energized.

CIRCUIT BREAKERS AND FUSES.

The ac and dc electrical distribution circuits are protected by push-to-reset trip-free circuit breakers. This type of circuit breaker, after being tripped requires a cooling period before it can be reset. The circuit breakers are in the electronic equipment compartment. (See figure 1-20.) Fuses are used for protection of individual phases of some lightly loaded 3-phase ac circuits. The fuses also are in the electronic equipment compartment.

ELECTRICAL POWER SUPPLY SYSTEM CONTROLS AND INDICATORS.

PRIMARY GENERATOR SWITCHES.

Two primary generator switches (9, figure 1-6) are on the overhead panel. Each controls its respective gearbox-driven ac generator and is mechanically latched in the ON position. The switch must be pulled out before it can be moved to OFF. Generator output is not available unless the generator switch is in the ON position. If a malfunction is known or suspected, the corresponding primary generator switch should be turned OFF. A primary generator will go off the line when the windmilling speed of the corresponding engine is below about 52% to 58% rpm, and the respective generator switch must be cycled from ON to OFF to ON after an air start to obtain generator output if windmilling speeds were low.

1-60   Changed 25 June 1965

T.O. 1B-70(X)A-1

BUS-TIE CONTACTOR OVERRIDE SWITCH.

The three-position bus-tie contactor override switch (20A, figure 1-9), is on the copilot's console. If a fault has opened the bus-tie contactors (bus-tie open caution light on), and one primary generator is still on the line, the override switch can be used to close the contactors so that the remaining generator will power both bus feeders. The switch should be held momentarily at the 3 GEN position if the No. 3 generator is operating; the 4 GEN position is used when the No. 4 generator is the remaining good generator. The override switch, which is mechanically latched in the OFF position and must be raised before it can be actuated, is spring-loaded to OFF from each of the other positions. Normally, the switch should be used only if the contactors were opened because of a known fault, such as shutdown of an engine (No. 3 or 4) or a generator. The override switch must not be used to close the bus-tie contactors if both generators are operating.

EMERGENCY GENERATOR SWITCH.

The three-position emergency generator switch (8, figure 1-6), on the overhead panel, controls operation of the hydraulically driven emergency ac generator. The switch is mechanically latched in the AUTO position, and it must be pulled out to be moved to either the ON or OFF positions. When the switch is at AUTO

This page intentionally left blank

(normal position), the emergency generator remains off the line as long as the left primary ac bus is energized. If this bus power fails, the emergency generator then is engaged automatically to power the essential ac bus.

NOTE
A one-second delay relay, with a five-second delay backup relay, allows the emergency generator to come up to the required speed before being applied to the essential ac bus.

If left primary ac bus power is restored while the switch is at AUTO, the emergency generator is shutdown automatically.

NOTE
A five-second delay relay keeps the emergency generator in control of the essential ac bus for five seconds after left primary ac bus power is restored. This prevents the emergency generator from cycling on and off in response to voltage fluctuations of the left primary ac bus.

Moving the switch to ON disconnects the left primary ac bus from the essential ac bus, and engages the emergency generator to power the essential ac bus. The OFF position keeps the emergency generator off the line by interrupting the voltage regulator field control. When the switch is at either OFF or at AUTO (emergency generator not on), the valve controlling hydraulic flow (No. 2 utility system) to the generator drive motor is energized closed. However, a bleed-flow of hydraulic pressure is maintained through the closed valve for slow rotation of the generator. If the emergency generator switch is moved to ON, or if the left primary ac bus fails when the switch is at AUTO, the control valve is de-energized and opens to supply full hydraulic pressure to the generator drive motor.

AC VOLTMETER AND VOLTMETER PHASE AND BUS SELECTOR SWITCHES.

The ac voltmeter (37, figure 1-3) on the pilot's instrument panel indicates the voltage of each phase of the essential ac, the right primary ac, or the left primary ac bus. The voltmeter indication is determined by the setting of the bus selector switch (40, figure 1-3) and the phase selector switch (39, figure 1-3), which are adjacent to the voltmeter. The voltages indicated are line voltage of the selected phase.

PRIMARY GENERATOR-OUT CAUTION LIGHTS.

Two placard-type generator-out caution lights (1, figure 1-7), one for each gearbox-driven primary generator, are on the center console. If primary generator output is not available, the corresponding generator-out light is illuminated by essential ac or right primary ac bus power. If an overvoltage or undervoltage has taken the generator "off the line," the generator reset circuit automatically makes three attempts to reset; and the caution light goes out when a reset is obtained. The generator-out caution light also is illuminated if the corresponding primary generator switch is OFF.

EMERGENCY GENERATOR-ON CAUTION LIGHT.

The placard-type emergency generator-on caution light (1, figure 1-7), on the center console, comes on whenever the emergency generator is operating and supplying power to the essential ac bus. This caution light is powered by the right primary ac bus. If this bus fails, the light is powered by the essential ac bus.

ESSENTIAL DC BUS-OUT CAUTION LIGHT.

The placard-type essential dc bus-out caution light (1, figure 1-7), on the center console, comes on when there is no power on the essential dc bus. The systems lost when the essential dc bus-out caution light comes on are shown on figure 1-19. This light is powered by the essential ac bus.

T.O. 1B-70(X)A-1

CIRCUIT BREAKER AND FUSE PANELS (Typical)
IN ELECTRONIC EQUIPMENT COMPARTMENT
(LOCATOR DRAWINGS SHOW CIRCUIT BREAKER PANEL IDENTIFICATION NUMBERS)

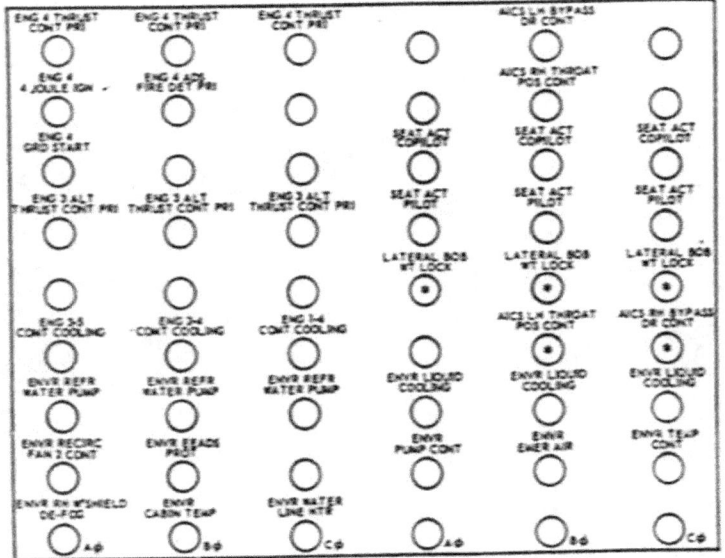

* AIRPLANE AF62-001

Figure 1-20 (Sheet 1 of 8)

Changed 25 June 1965

T. O. 1B-70(X)A-1

LEFT SIDE

RIGHT SIDE

* AIRPLANE AF62-207

Figure 1-20 (Sheet 2 of 8)

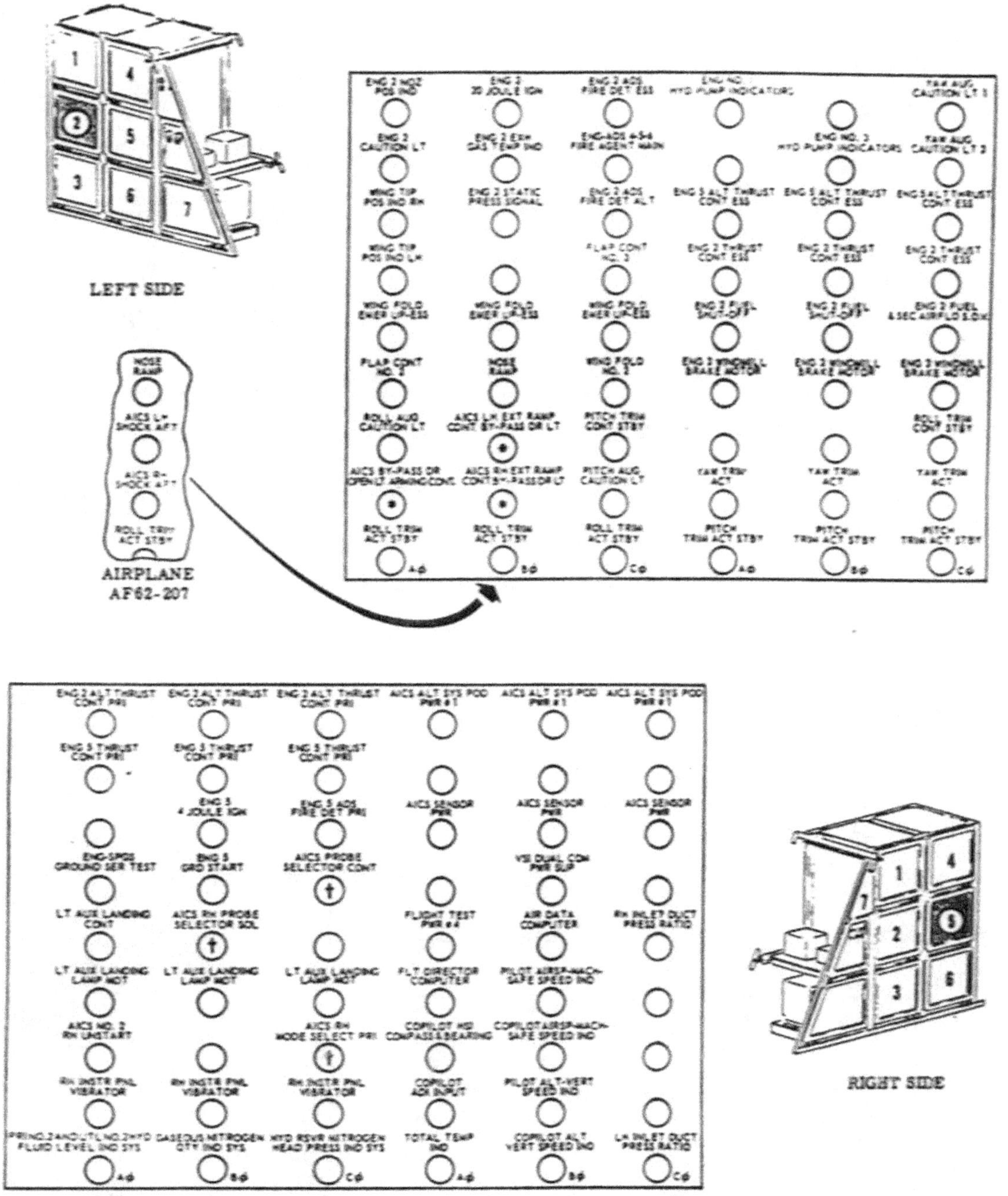

T.O. 1B-70(X)A-1

Figure 1-20 (Sheet 3 of 8)

* AIRPLANE AF62-001
† AIRPLANE AF62-207

T.O. 1B-70(X)A-1

LEFT SIDE

* AIRPLANE AF62-001
† AIRPLANE AF62-207

RIGHT SIDE

Figure 1-20 (Sheet 4 of 8)

Changed 25 June 1965

T.O. 1B-70(X)A-1

LEFT SIDE

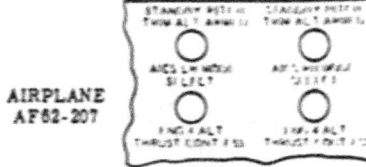

AIRPLANE
AF62-207

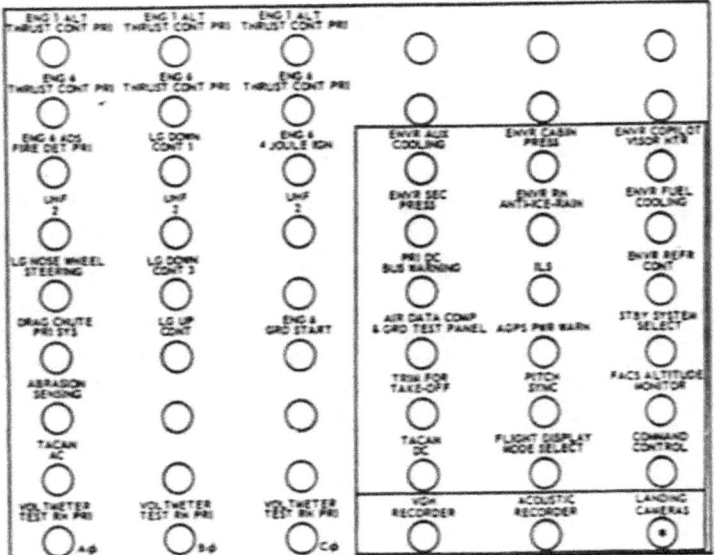

RIGHT SIDE

* AIRPLANE AF62-001

Figure 1-20 (Sheet 5 of 8)

T. O. 1B-70(X)A-1

LEFT SIDE

RIGHT SIDE

* AIRPLANE AF62-001
† AIRPLANE AF62-207

Figure 1-20 (Sheet 6 of 8)

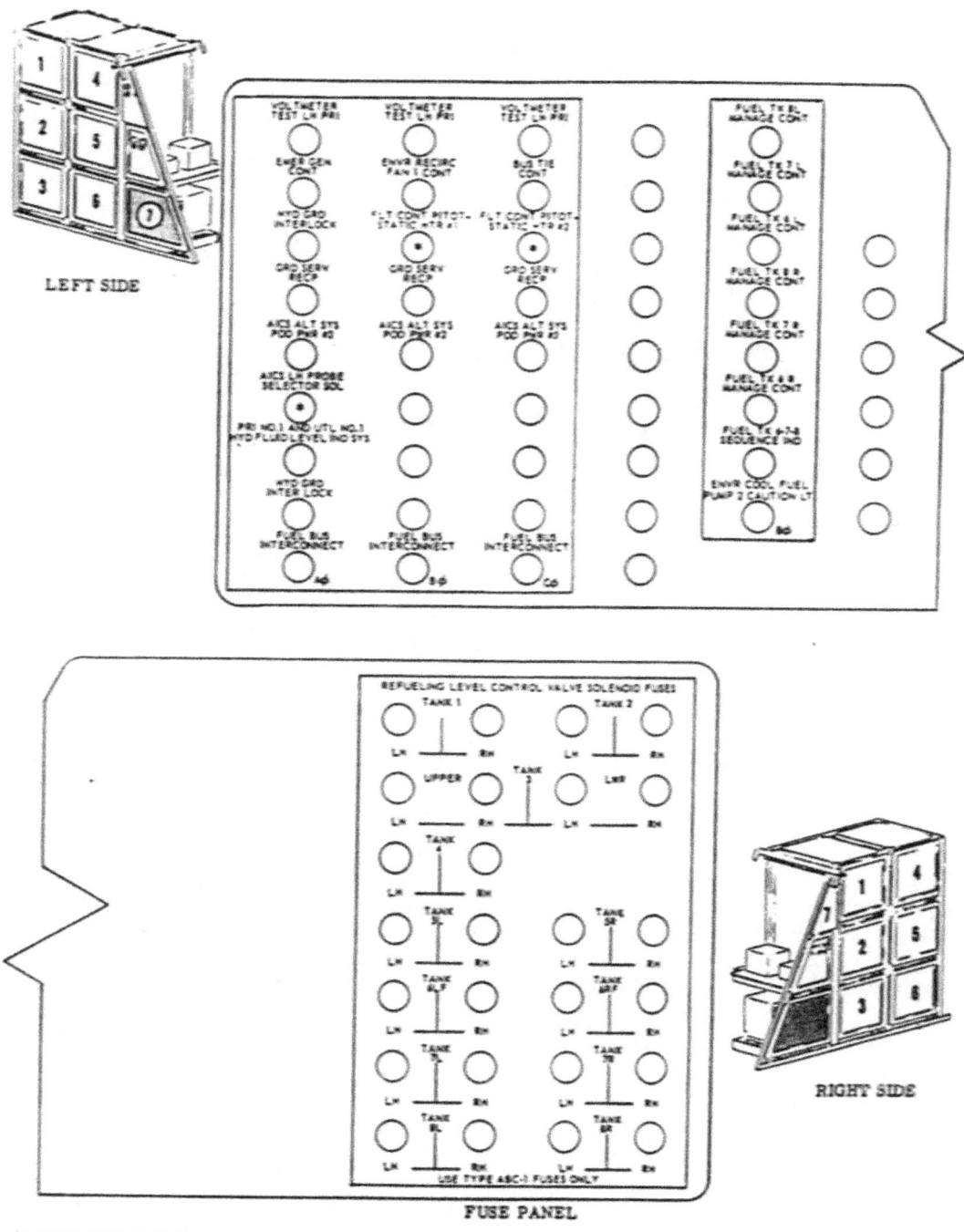

*AIRPLANE AF62-207

Figure 1-20 (Sheet 7 of 8)

T.O. 1B-70(X)A-1

RIGHT SIDE

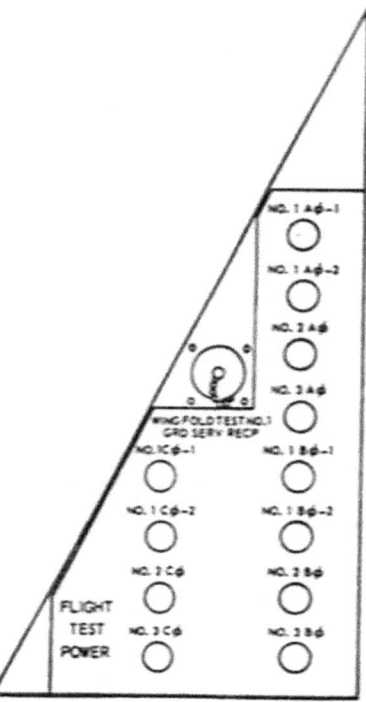

Figure 1-20. (Sheet 8 of 8)

T.O. 1B-70(X)A-1

PRIMARY DC BUS-OUT CAUTION LIGHT.

The placard-type primary dc bus-out caution light (1, figure 1-7), on the center console, comes on when there is no power on the primary dc bus. The systems lost when the primary dc bus-out caution light comes on are shown on figure 1-19. The light is powered by the right primary ac bus. If the right primary ac bus fails, the light is powered by the essential ac bus.

BUS-TIE OPEN CAUTION LIGHT.

The placard-type bus-tie open caution light (1, figure 1-7), on the center console, is powered by the right primary or the essential ac bus. The light comes on when the left and right generating systems have been separated by the open bus-tie contactors. Once the bus-tie contactors have opened because of system fault, they will remain open until reset on the ground, or if closed by using the bus-tie override switch. If the No. 4 engine primary generator fails while the bus-tie contactors are open, the right primary electrical system will not be powered. If the No. 3 engine primary generator fails while the bus-tie contactors are open, only the left primary ac bus will be lost as the emergency generator will come on and provide power for the essential bus. The right primary bus will be supplied by No. 4 generator.

THROTTLE AND FIRE DETECTION BUS SELECTOR SWITCH.

This two position switch (20, figure 1-9), on the copilot's console, is used to transfer the electrical power source of the throttle servo system and fire detection circuits to the right primary ac bus upon failure of essential ac bus power. When the switch is at NORMAL, the throttle, throttle reset, and fire detection circuits are connected to the essential ac bus; when the switch is at its RH BUS position, these circuits are transferred to the right primary ac bus. The switch is safety-wired at NORMAL, and should not be moved to RH BUS unless essential ac bus power is not available.

EMERGENCY BATTERY-INVERTER SYSTEM.*

Emergency electrical power for thrust control, shutting down the engines, raising the wing tips, and wheel brake control is supplied by a 28-volt dry-charged nickel cadmium emergency battery and inverter system. (See figure 1-21.) The battery is in a deactivated state until needed. The battery is activated by firing a squib in the battery to release the electrolite for the battery. After the battery is activated (which requires 3 to 5 seconds), on, dc power is supplied to the battery inverter and is available for engine shutdown and wheel brake control. The emergency battery dc power is converted to 115-volt, 400-cycle, three-phase ac power by the battery inverter for alternate throttle control and for the wing tip emergency-up circuits. An indicator light in the crew compartment shows when the battery inverter is powered. When the emergency battery-inverter is turned on, relays are energized by the battery to transfer the circuits of the equipment to be operated, from their normal source of power to the emergency source of power.

BATTERY-INVERTER SWITCH.

The two-position battery-inverter switch (18, figure 1-9), on the copilot's console, controls power from the dry cell battery to activate the emergency battery and also controls power from the emergency battery after it has been activated. Moving the switch to ON causes power from a 6-volt dry cell battery to fire a squib in the emergency battery which releases the electrolite and activates the battery. This provides dc electrical power to the engine shutdown and wheel brake arming switch, and to the battery inverter. The output of the battery inverter provides ac electrical power to the alternate throttle control circuits (allowing thrust

---

* Airplane AF62-001

1-70

EMERGENCY BATTERY-INVERTER SYSTEM

(AIRPLANE AF62-001)

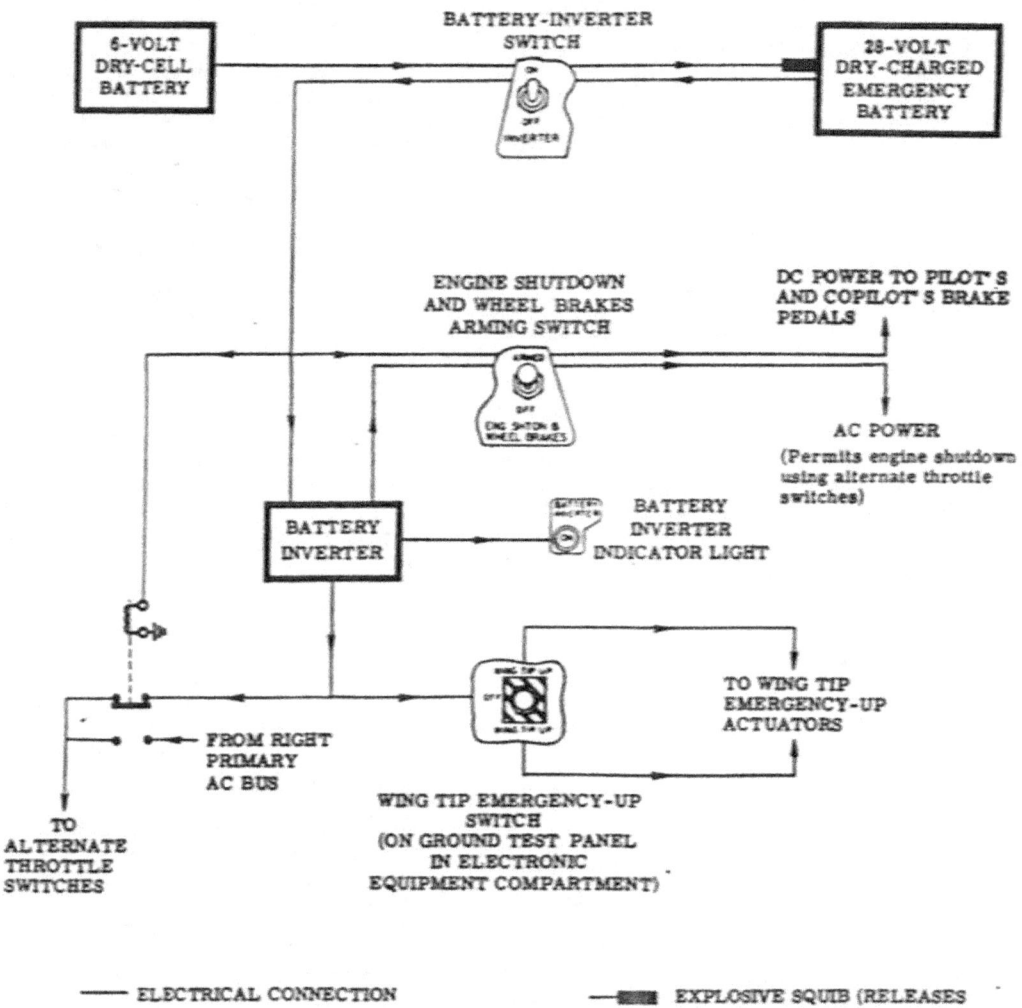

Figure 1-21

decrease to IDLE), and to the wing tip emergency-up circuits. The switch also can be used to turn off the battery inverter to conserve battery power when it is not required after the battery has been activated. The switch is safety-wired in the OFF position.

ENGINE SHUTDOWN AND WHEEL BRAKE ARMING SWITCH.

The two-position arming switch (16, figure 1-9), on the copilot's console, is mechanically latched at OFF and must be pulled out before it can be moved to ARMED. Moving the switch to ARMED after the emergency battery is activated and battery-inverter switch is ON, provides 28-volt dc power for brake control, and enables the alternate throttle switches to be used to shut down the engines. The positioning of this switch does not effect emergency battery power to the battery inverter.

CAUTION

To preclude inadvertent engine shutdown when using the alternate throttle switches, the engine shutdown and wheel brake arming switch must not be at its ARMED position in flight.

BATTERY INVERTER INDICATOR LIGHT.

The battery inverter indicator light (6, figure 1-4), on the copilot's instrument panel, is a neon bulb powered by the battery inverter. The light comes on after the emergency battery is activated to show that the battery inverter is powered and on the line.

HYDRAULIC POWER SUPPLY SYSTEMS.

The hydraulic systems (figure 1-22) consist of two independent primary systems (identified as primary systems No. 1 and No. 2) and two independent utility systems (identified as utility systems No. 1 and No. 2). The hydraulic system pumps are driven by and mounted on the engine-driven accessory drive system gearboxes. The primary hydraulic pumps also operate as hydraulic motors for starting the engines. (Refer to "Engine Starting System" in this section.) Each of the four separate hydraulic systems is powered by three pumps arranged so that primary system No. 1 and utility system No. 1 are driven by engines 1, 2, and 3, and primary system No. 2 and utility system No. 2 are driven by engines 4, 5, and 6. Failure of one primary system, one utility system, or of any three pumps or engines will not cause a loss of hydraulic power essential for safe flight and landing. The normal operating pressure range of the system is 3800 psi to 4200 psi. A hydraulic pressure gage is provided for each independent power system, and a status indicator is provided for each pump. Each of the four hydraulic systems has its own separate reservoir and associated nitrogen pressurization system. A heat exchanger in each reservoir uses cooling loop fuel to cool the hydraulic fluid returned from the various systems. (Refer to "Fuel Supply System" in this section.) Some hydraulically powered systems are supplied simultaneously by primary systems No. 1 and No. 2 or utility systems No. 1 and No. 2 while others have a selector valve to permit manual selection of the paralleling system. (See figure 1-22.) Although the No. 1 and No. 2 systems may serve the same units, there is no direct interconnection of the two systems.

The hydraulic ground power unit connections are forward of the No. 2 accessory drive system compartment. Four self-sealing couplings permit ground filling, flushing, and functional testing of the hydraulic systems and permit the application of hydraulic pressure for starting the engines on the ground.

NOTE

The external hydraulic power unit cannot supply the airplane hydraulic system unless external electric power is on the airplane electrical busses.

The reservoir fluid level of each hydraulic system is shown selectively by an indicator on the ground test panel in the electronic equipment compartment or on the center instrument panel. Hydraulic fluid specification is listed in figure 1-37.

HYDRAULIC PUMPS.

Hydraulic power is supplied by four individual hydraulic systems, with three pumps in each system. Twelve pump status indicators, one for each hydraulic pump are in the crew compartment. One primary system pump and one utility system pump are mounted on and driven by each of the engine-driven accessory drive gearboxes. Pumps for primary system No. 1 and utility system No. 1 are driven by gearboxes No. 1, 2, and 3; and pumps for primary system No. 2 and utility system No. 2 are driven by gearboxes 4, 5, and 6. Each pumping system supplies the pressure requirements at all engine speeds. The pumps are the positive displacement type with a variable output. The normal operating pressure range is 3800 psi to 4200 psi. The pumps are cooled and lubricated by the circulating hydraulic fluid. Each pumping system has a master pump and two slave pumps. The master pumps for both systems are on engines No. 2 and 5. The master pump supplies the continuous demand of the system, and the slave pumps operate at no flow until the capability of the master pump has been exceeded. When the capacity of the master pump is exceeded, the output of the two slave pumps automatically becomes available to meet the additional demands. However, the two slave pumps may not share the additional load equally, as the output of these pumps can vary. The engines are started with hydraulic power supplied from a ground

This page intentionally left blank

T.O. 1B-70(X)A-1

power unit connected to the primary system on the same side as the engine being started (No. 1 system left side, No. 2 system right side) or from an operating engine on the same side. (Refer to "Engine Starting System" in this section.)

HYDRAULIC PRESSURE GAGES.

The pressure in each of the four hydraulic systems is indicated on four individual gages (11 and 12, figure 1-5) on the center instrument panel. The pressure gages are powered by the essential ac bus. The gages are calibrated in 500 psi increments from 0 to 6000 psi.

HYDRAULIC RESERVOIR FLUID LEVEL INDICATORS AND INDICATOR SELECTOR SWITCHES.

Two hydraulic reservoir fluid level indicators and indicator selector switches (10A, and 10D, figure 1-5) are on the center instrument panel. Each indicator shows the fluid level in either of two hydraulic reservoirs according to the setting of the adjacent indicator selector switch. The left indicator shows the primary system No. 1 reservoir fluid level when the left selector switch is at PRI 1, and shows the utility system No. 1 reservoir level when the switch is at UT 1. The right indicator shows reservoir fluid level in the primary system No. 2 or utility system No. 2 when the right selector switch is at PRI 2 or UT 2, respectively. A bezel on each indicator is graduated in 10-percent increments, from 0 to 200. The 100-percent (FULL) reading indicates a fully-serviced system during static, on-the-ground conditions. Indicator readings above or below the 100 percent mark can occur as the result of normal operational demands on the respective system. A center-pivoted bar joins the two selector switches and causes a diagonal movement of both switches when either is moved. This prevents simultaneous selection of fluid level indications for both primary or both utility systems. However, if such a selection is necessary, the switch bar can be pulled off its pivot pin to permit unrestricted movement of the selector switches. The hydraulic reservoir fluid level indicator system is powered by the right primary ac bus.

HYDRAULIC SYSTEM SELECTOR SWITCH.

The hydraulic system selector switch (19, figure 1-12) is on the ground test panel in the electronic equipment compartment. The 8-position selector switch is used to check hydraulic reservoir fluid level*, hydraulic reservoir nitrogen head pressure*, and engine hydraulic-accessory drive system gaseous nitrogen quantity. The PRI SYS NO. 1, PRI SYS NO. 2, UT SYS NO. 1, and UT SYS NO. 2 positions are used for checking the hydraulic systems*; the NO. 1 ADS BOTTLE, NO. 2 ADS BOTTLE, and NO. 3 ADS BOTTLE positions are used for checking ADS gaseous nitrogen quantity. The selector switch receives power from the essential and right primary ac busses. When the selector switch is moved to OFF, the hydraulic reservoir fluid level indicator* and the gaseous nitrogen quantity indicator stay at the last setting, and the reservoir nitrogen head pressure gage* goes to 0.

GASEOUS NITROGEN QUANTITY INDICATOR TEST SWITCH.

Refer to "Nitrogen Systems" in this section.

HYDRAULIC RESERVOIR FLUID LEVEL INDICATOR.*

The hydraulic reservoir fluid level indicator (1, figure 1-12), on the ground test panel in the electronic equipment compartment, is powered by the right primary ac bus. The indicator shows the fluid level in each of the four hydraulic reservoirs, depending on the setting of the hydraulic systems selector switch.

*Airplane AF62-001

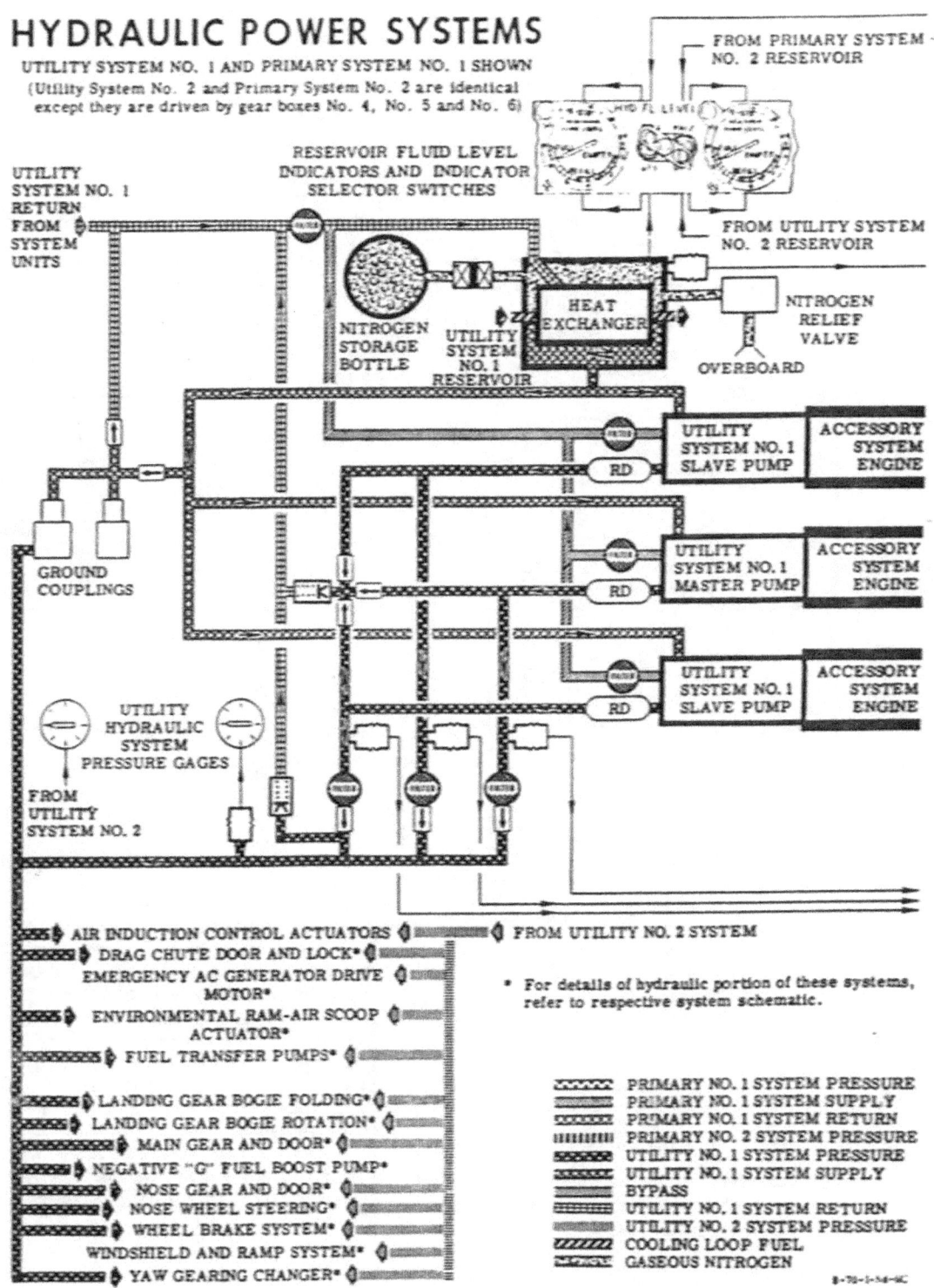

Figure 1-22 (Sheet 1 of 2)

T.O. 1B-70(X)A-1

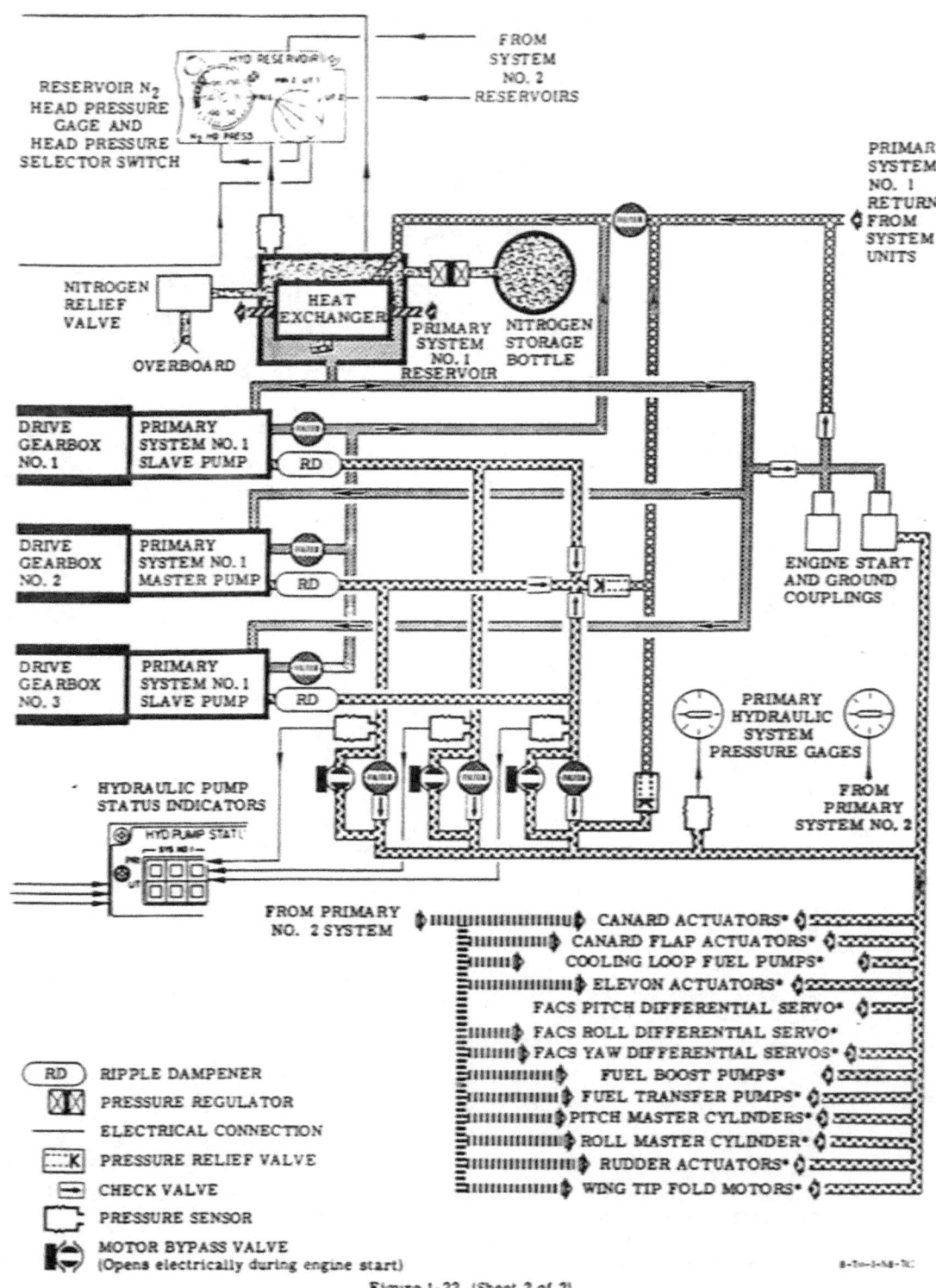

Figure 1-22 (Sheet 2 of 2)

Changed 25 June 1965

T.O. 1R-70(X)A-1

GASEOUS NITROGEN QUANTITY INDICATOR.

Refer to "Nitrogen Systems" in this section.

HYDRAULIC RESERVOIR GASEOUS NITROGEN HEAD PRESSURE GAGE.

Refer to "Nitrogen Systems" in this section.

HYDRAULIC PUMP STATUS INDICATORS.

The electromechanical hydraulic pump status indicators (6, figure 1-7), are grouped together on the center console, and actuated by the essential ac bus. There is a separate indicator for each hydraulic pump in both the No. 1 and No. 2 primary and utility hydraulic systems. The indicators show green when the respective hydraulic pump pressure is normal. If the pump pressure is either too high (above 4650 + 0 - 100 psi) or too low (below 2600 ±150 psi), the respective indicator shows yellow and causes the master caution light to come on. (A high-pressure condition also can be noted on the pressure gage.) However, if the pump pressure returns to normal, the indicator will show green again and the master caution light will go out. The indicators are arranged to represent the pumps on each engine, i.e. the two indicators at the left side of the panel represent pumps on engine No. 1 and the two indicators at the right of the panel represent pumps on engine No. 6; the other indicators between represent the pumps on the other respective engines.

NOTE

When the indicators are not energized, they show green.

The primary pump status indicator, for the respective engine, will change to green when a ground start is initiated. Between 35% and 38% engine rpm, the indicator changes to yellow. The indicator is yellow while the pump is kept at a low output condition during engine acceleration, then turns green at about 57% to 59% engine rpm. If the indicator does not respond as described, the start must be aborted as there is a malfunction of the start control system.

NITROGEN SYSTEMS.

LIQUID NITROGEN SYSTEM.

Refer to "Fuel Tank Pressurization and Inerting System" in this section.

GASEOUS NITROGEN SYSTEMS.

NITROGEN SYSTEMS FOR DRAG CHUTE AND LANDING GEAR COMPARTMENT COOLING SYSTEM AND ENGINE HYDRAULIC AND ACCESSORY DRIVE SYSTEMS.

Three separate gaseous nitrogen systems automatically supply nitrogen gas to pressurize and inert the accessory drive gearbox lubricating systems, the engine hydraulic systems, AICS electric motors, and the coolant tank for the drag chute and landing gear compartment cooling system. The nitrogen supply bottle No. 1 is in No. 1 accessory drive system compartment, bottle No. 2 in No. 5 accessory drive system compartment, and bottle No. 3 in No. 6 accessory drive system compartment. Bottle No. 1 supplies nitrogen to the engine hydraulic reservoirs on engines No. 1 and 4 and to the accessory drive gearboxes in compartments No. 1 and 4. Bottle No. 2 supplies the engine hydraulic reservoirs on engines No. 2 and 5, the accessory drive gearbox in compartments No. 2 and 5, and the coolant tank. Bottle No. 3 supplies the engine hydraulic reservoirs on engines No. 3 and 6 and to the accessory drive gearbox in compartments No. 3 and 6. Pressurizing the accessory drive gearboxes and engine hydraulic systems prevents cavitation of the system pumps. Inerting the systems extends

T.O. 1B-70(X)A-1

the life of the system fluids at high operating temperatures. Pressurizing the liquid coolant tank prevents premature boiling of the liquid coolant in the reservoir and lines during a mission. The loss of nitrogen system No. 2 could result in overheating of the landing gear and drag chute compartments. The loss of any of the three nitrogen systems could cause loss of two gearboxes and their associated accessories and sluggish engine reaction to changes in thrust settings resulting from poor exhaust nozzle action. Because the engine hydraulic systems and the electrical power generating systems are not supplied by one common nitrogen supply, failure of one nitrogen system cannot result in complete electrical or hydraulic power loss, or cause a reduction in performance of all engines. The three nitrogen systems are filled at a single-point filler valve forward of the No. 2 accessory compartment. The nitrogen quantity of each bottle is indicated selectively by a gage on the ground test panel in the electronic equipment compartment. (See figure 1-37 for gaseous nitrogen specifications.) Satisfactory performance of the electrical, hydraulic, accessory drive and engine systems indicates sufficient nitrogen supply.

HYDRAULIC RESERVOIR NITROGEN SYSTEMS.

Four separate gaseous nitrogen systems, one for each hydraulic reservoir, provide a head pressure of 150 to 185 psi in the reservoirs to maintain a positive supply of hydraulic fluid to the pumps, and to prevent oxygen contamination of the fluid. Nitrogen is supplied to each reservoir from an individual supply bottle. Individual filler valves, forward of the No. 2 accessory drive system compartment, are provided for each of the four supply bottles. Nitrogen relief valves prevent over-pressurization of the the reservoirs, and check valves prevent interflow between systems after servicing. The quantity in each system is shown by an indicator on the ground test panel in the electronic equipment compartment. The pressure in each system is shown by an indicator on the ground test panel in the electronic equipment compartment*, and one in the crew compartment. Gaseous nitrogen specifications are shown in figure 1-37.

*Airplane AF62-001

GASEOUS NITROGEN SYSTEMS CONTROLS AND INDICATORS.

Hydraulic Systems Selector Switch.

Refer to "Hydraulic Power Supply Systems" in this section.

Gaseous Nitrogen Quantity Indicator Test Switch.

The two-position gaseous nitrogen quantity indicator test switch (4, figure 1-12) is on the ground test panel in the electronic equipment compartment. This switch, which is spring-loaded to OFF, is used to test the gaseous nitrogen quantity indicator when the hydraulic systems selector switch is not at OFF. Holding the indicator test switch at TEST causes the pointer to move towards 0, and when the switch is released to OFF, the pointer should return to its previous reading. The test switch receives power from the right primary ac bus.

Hydraulic Reservoir Head Pressure Selector Switch.

The 4-position reservoir head pressure selector switch (10C, figure 1-5), on the center instrument panel, selects which hydraulic system reservoir nitrogen head pressure will be shown on the nitrogen head pressure gage. When the switch is at PRI 1, PRI 2, UT 1, or UT 2 the gage shows the head pressure in the corresponding reservoir.

Hydraulic Reservoir Gaseous Nitrogen Head Pressure Gages.

Two hydraulic reservoir head pressure gages (2, figure 1-12 and 10B, figure 1-5), one on the ground test panel in the electronic equipment compartment* and one on the center instrument panel, show the nitrogen pressure in each of the four hydraulic reservoirs, depending on the setting of the hydraulic systems selector switch in the electronic equipment compartment or the reservoir head pressure selector switch in the crew compartment, respectively. The selsyn-type gages are calibrated from 0 to 250 psi in 10 psi increments, and are powered by the right primary ac bus.

Changed 25 June 1965   1-77

T.O. 1B-70(X)A-1

Gaseous Nitrogen Quantity Indicator.

The gaseous nitrogen quantity indicator (3, figure 1-12) is on the ground test panel in the electronic equipment compartment. The indicator shows the percentage of gaseous nitrogen in each of the four hydraulic reservoir nitrogen head pressure storage bottles or in each of the three ADS nitrogen system storage bottles, as selected by the hydraulic systems selector switch. The quantity indicator is calibrated in 10-percent graduations and is powered by the right primary ac bus.

FLIGHT CONTROL SYSTEM.

The flight control system mechanically controls full-powered hydraulic actuators to position the twin rudders, a movable canard, and two elevons. (See figure 1-23.) The elevons are on the trailing edge of the wing outboard of the engines and are segmented to reduce spanwise bending effects. Pitch control is provided by symmetrical movement of the elevons with simultaneous movement of the canard. Use of both the elevons and canard maintains control effectiveness relatively constant throughout the speed range. (The canard is more effective than the elevons at high speeds; the elevons are more effective at low speeds.) Roll control is provided by differential movement of the elevons. The rudders move about a diagonal hinge line. Directional stability at high speeds is improved by the folding wing tips. Flaps for use during take-off and landing are on the trailing edge of the canard. (Refer to "Wing Tip Fold System" and "Canard Flap System" in this section.)

NOTE
- When the wing tips are folded, the elevon segments mounted on the folding portion of the wing move to a fixed neutral position.
- When the flaps are lowered, the canard moves to its leading edge full down position and all pitch control is obtained through the elevons.

Conventional rudder pedals and column-mounted control wheels are provided for the pilot and copilot. Control movements mechanically reposition hydraulic control valves at the control surface actuators. These valves then direct hydraulic pressure to the actuators which move the surface. As the surface reaches the selected position, a follow-up mechanism automatically returns the control valves to neutral, shutting off the hydraulic flow to the actuators. Hydraulic pressure to the flight control system is supplied simultaneously by the independent No. 1 and No. 2 primary hydraulic systems. (Refer to "Hydraulic Power Supply Systems" in this section.) Each elevon segment has two individual actuators, one powered by the No. 1 primary hydraulic system, the other by the No. 2 primary hydraulic system. The actuator control valves of each elevon are mechanically interconnected for simultaneous operation of the actuators. The canard has two separate tandem actuators and each rudder has a tandem actuator. Each canard actuator and each rudder actuator is supplied with hydraulic power from both the primary hydraulic systems simultaneously. The control valves of the rudder actuator are mechanically interconnected, as are the canard actuator control valves, to ensure coordinated movement of both corresponding actuators if one fails.

A flight augmentation control system is connected to the flight control system which provides full-time, three-axes stability augmentation throughout all flight conditions. The flight augmentation control system transforms pilot inputs and airplane motion into electrical signals which drive the control surfaces through servos to produce the desired damping and maneuver control.

Because of its extreme length, the mechanical portion of the flight control system is designed to reduce system friction and to minimize control surface movements induced by vibrations and fuselage flexing. A tension regulator maintains proper control cable tension by compensating for airframe deflection and the effects of temperature changes. (The regulator does not induce control surface movement.) Friction forces in the elevon control system are reduced by hydraulically-powered master cylinders serving as boosters in the mechanical portion of the pitch and roll system. The master cylinders receive power simultaneously from both primary hydraulic systems. From the master cylinders, the elevon system is joined to the surface actuator control valves through a mechanical mixer. The mixer is a linkage which converts control wheel rotation and flight augmentation control system roll servo deflection to differential elevon operation for roll control and movement of the control column and flight augmentation control system pitch servo deflection to symmetrical operation of the elevons for pitch control. Pitch and roll movements can be applied simultaneously or individually. Roll control inputs will not cause pitch changes. An ancillary control operates in parallel with the mechanical portion of the elevon control system between the master cylinder augmentation servos and the elevon actuators. The ancillary control is an electrical backup system which provides elevon control if this portion of the mechanical system fails. At high Mach numbers, a bobweight in the roll control system is engaged to apply elevon movements as a result of lateral accelerations.* Use of the bobweight counteracts the negative dihedral effect that occurs when the wing tips are folded full down. (Refer to "Folding Wing Tips" in Section VI for further details on bobweight operation.) The rudder control linkage incorporates a yaw gearing changer that is hydraulically positioned by the landing gear system. The changer automatically increases rudder travel from the normal ±3 degrees to ±12 degrees when the gear is down. This variation in rudder travel ensures adequate directional control at low speeds without excessive control sensitivity at high speeds. Full rudder pedal travel is used to obtain either rudder travel range, and the actuator rate limits prevent abrupt changes of pedal-to-rudder gearing.

Artificial feel is built into the flight control system to simulate feel at the controls, since the irreversible characteristics of hydraulic actuation prevent the transmission of airloads to the controls. The spring-type artificial feel bungees in the roll and yaw systems provide system centering as well as proper control feel. The pitch system artificial feel has a dynamic pressure bellows (Q bellows) which varies the feel forces with changes in airspeed. The trim systems operate directly on the flight control system linkage, changing the neutral (no load) position of the controls and repositioning the surfaces.

ANCILLARY CONTROL.

The ancillary control is an automatic electrical backup system for a portion of the elevon control system. (See figure 1-23.) The ancillary system operates in parallel with the mechanical linkage of the elevon control system between the master cylinders and the elevon actuators. (This linkage includes the mechanical mixer.) In the event of failure of this mechanical linkage, the ancillary control electrically positions the ancillary actuator in response to master cylinder and differential servo control movements. The ancillary actuators are on the inboard elevon actuator of the inboard elevon segment only. Electrical signals representing movements of the controls through the pitch and roll master cylinders and movements of the flight augmentation control system pitch and roll differential servos are sent to the ancillary control unit. The control unit compares these signals with signals from the ancillary actuators which indicate elevon position. A corrected control signal from the control unit is then transmitted to the ancillary actuators. These actuators mechanically

---

*Airplane AF62-001

T.O. 1B-70(X)A-1

FLIGHT CONTROL SYSTEM

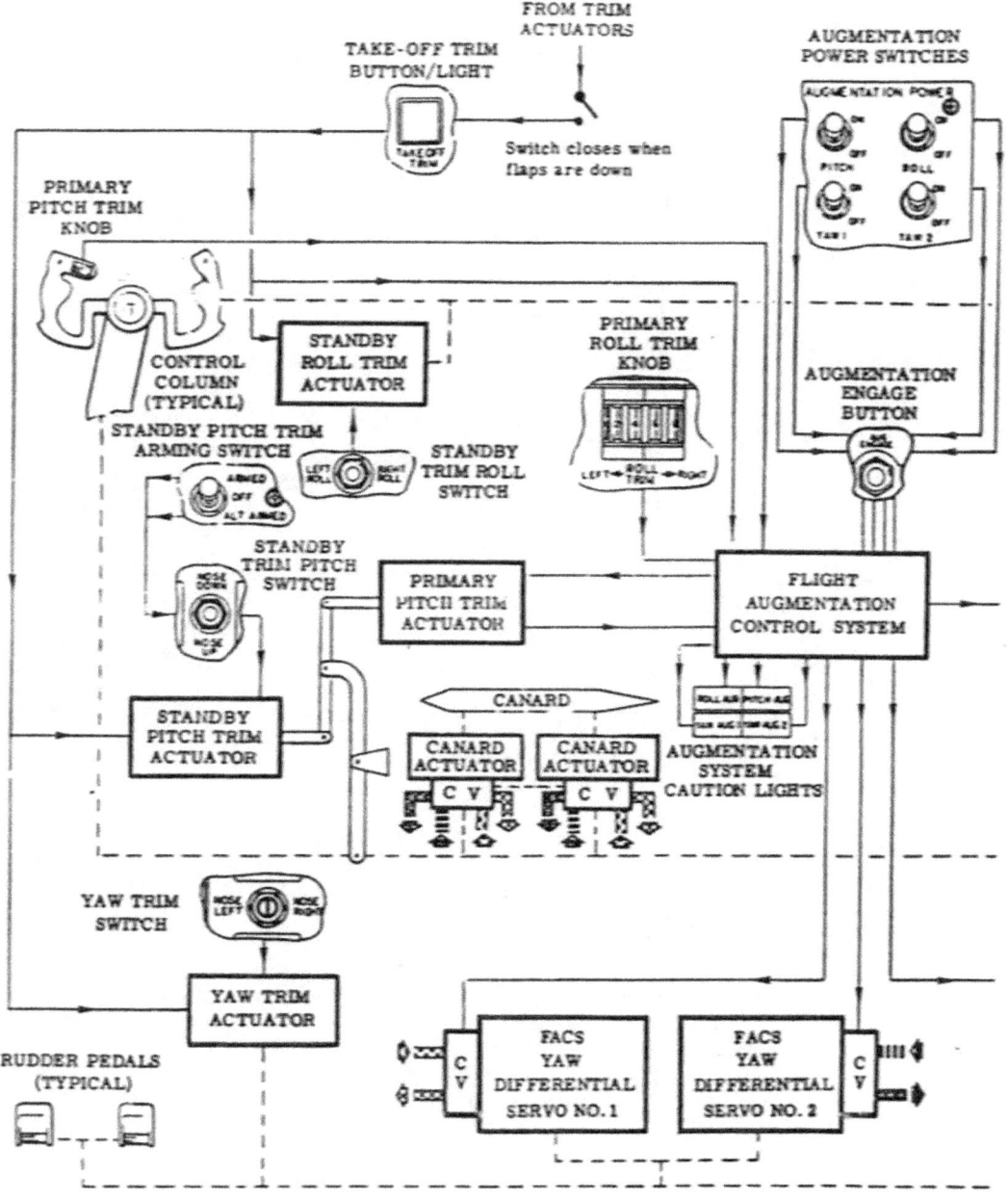

Figure 1-23 (Sheet 1 of 2)

T.O. 1B-70(X)A-1

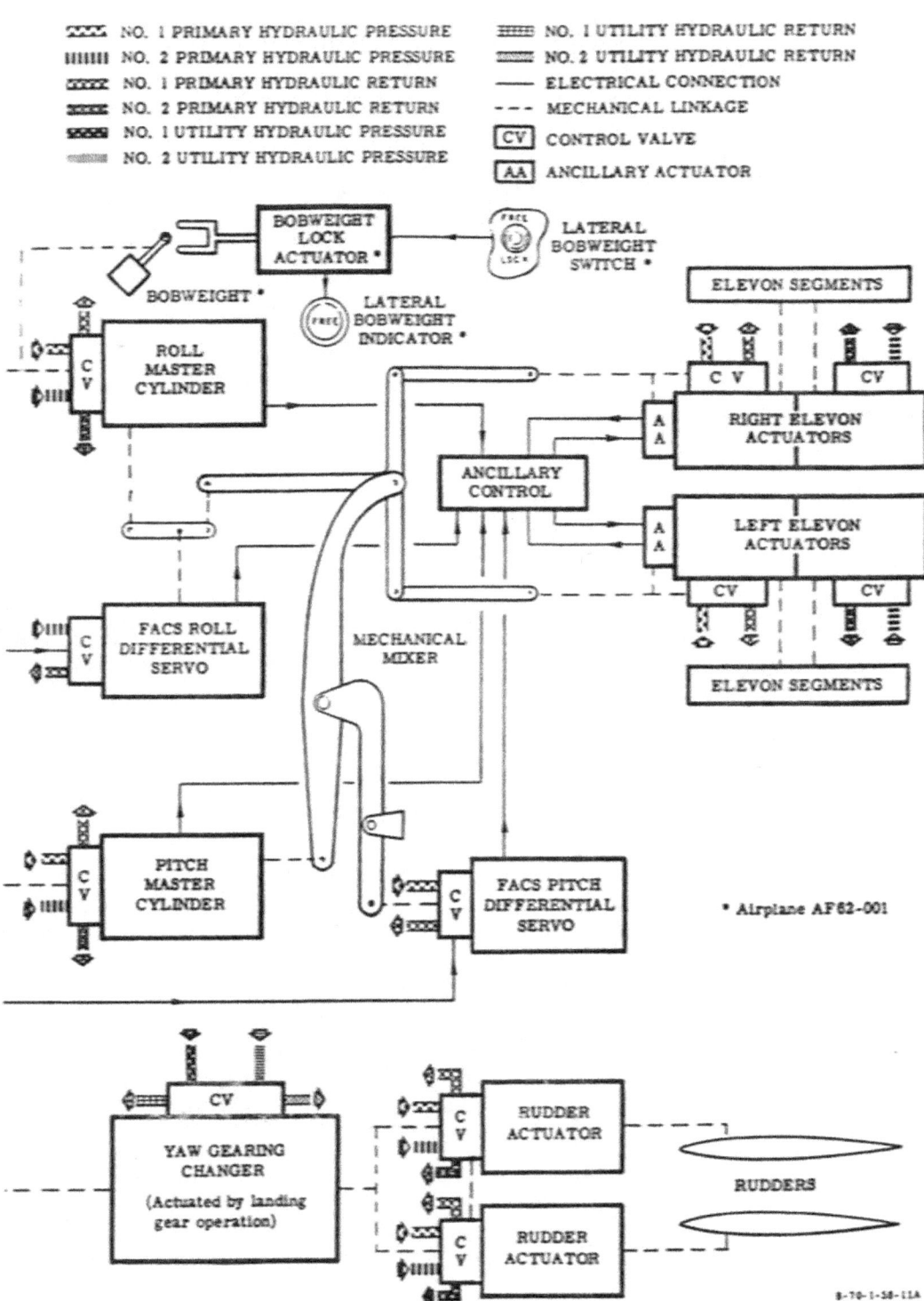

Figure 1-23 (Sheet 2 of 2)

position the hydraulic control valves of the elevon actuators so that elevon movement corresponds to control movements applied to the master cylinders and differential servos. The pitch control signals from the ancillary control unit are electrically in phase with each other, thereby driving the ancillary actuators in unison. Roll signals from the control unit are electrically 180 degrees out of phase with each other to drive the ancillary actuators differentially. The ancillary control is powered by the right primary ac bus through the roll flight augmentation control system and is operative only if the roll augmentation system is powered.

FLIGHT AUGMENTATION CONTROL SYSTEM (FACS).

The flight augmentation control system automatically varies control surface movements to compensate for changes in flight conditions and airplane motion. The augmentation system, which should be engaged during all phases of flight (including take-off and landing), provides airplane damping about all three axes, improved pitch and roll maneuverability, and is used in the primary roll trim and take-off trim systems. Electrical signals from the central air data computer representing airplane speed and altitude are transmitted to a computer in the augmentation system through independent electronic channels. Through identical, independent channels, the augmentation computer receives signals that represent movements of the control wheels and control columns. Dual rate gyros for the pitch, roll, and yaw axes provide signals for controlling damping about these axes; and dual accelerometers sense acceleration in the pitch axis. The rate gyros and the accelerometers produce output signals with a voltage that is proportional to the rate of motion or acceleration sensed by these units.

NOTE

The rate gyros and accelerometers are included in a signal generator assembly which is mounted as a package in a tank containing a preformed block of ice for in-flight cooling of the assembly. (See figure 1-37 for ice servicing requirements.)

The pitch axis damping also compensates for the effects of fuselage bending. Both the pitch and yaw signals are altitude-corrected. The pitch system provides increased speed stability by moving the elevons in response to signals from the air data system that are proportional to the Mach number and to the rate of Mach number change. A speed stability package can be engaged to provide pitch system speed corrections during supersonic flight. As a result, both elevons are moved up with an increase in Mach number and down when Mach number is decreased. (The control column can be pushed forward for speed increase and pulled back for speed decrease.) The augmentation computer compares all input signals with airplane response and sends corrective signals to actuate the augmentation differential servos for increasing or decreasing control surface movement. The differential servos (one for pitch, one for roll, and two for yaw) have servo valves which, when energized by the signals from the augmentation computer, direct pressure from No. 1 and No. 2 primary hydraulic systems to move the pitch and roll servo output shafts. These shafts are connected to the mechanical portion of the flight control system aft of the master cylinders. (See figure 1-23.) Movement of the servos, therefore, repositions the flight control system linkage to change the position of the control surfaces through the surface actuators. Dual tandem differential servos are used in the pitch and roll systems and are controlled by dual independent electrical signals from the augmentation computer. The roll differential servo also is actuated by the primary roll trim inputs. The yaw augmentation system has two single independent differential servos, each controlled by a separate yaw channel of the computer. The output shafts of the yaw servos are mechanically connected through a walking beam to the flight control system.

Switches permit individual disengagement of the pitch, roll, or both yaw augmentation channels, or all may be disengaged simultaneously. In addition, automatic disengagement of pitch or roll augmentation occurs if hydraulic or electric power fails, or if there is a malfunction within the augmentation control system. This disengagement locks the respective pitch or roll servo in the center neutral position and the yaw servo at its position at time of disengagement. Electronic balancers in the augmentation pitch and roll channels prevent gradual or intermittent signal differences between the corresponding channels from causing nuisance disengagement of the servos.

If a system malfunction occurs, the balancer action results in control surface movement at a safe rate until the system is automatically disengaged or selectively shut off. The automatic disengagement is made if the balancer control limit is exceeded for three seconds. Yaw augmentation is not disengaged automatically if a yaw channel fails, because the limited output of the yaw servo prevents even a "hard over" failure to cause excessive control surface movements. Following a failure of one yaw channel, the remaining channel is capable of providing adequate damping. If hydraulic or electric power to a yaw differential servo fails, the output shaft of the servo locks automatically in the position existing at the time of the failure. The use of dual channels, each by independent electrical circuits, and dual servos provides additional fail-safe capabilities in the augmentation system. The monitor circuits which disengage the system if electrical or hydraulic power fails also prevent system engagement if adequate power is not available. Individual caution lights in the crew compartment (one for pitch, roll, and each of the two yaw augmentation channels) indicate system failure or system disengagement.

TRIM SYSTEMS.

The pitch, roll, and yaw control systems have electrically controlled and actuated trim systems. Standby trim systems are provided in case of failure in the primary pitch and roll trim systems. The trim systems mechanically reposition the linkage of the feel system to a new neutral (no load) position and repositions the control surfaces and controls. Primary pitch and roll trim is applied through the primary pitch trim actuator and the flight augmentation control system roll differential servo respectively. The primary roll trim system is inoperative if the flight augmentation control system is disengaged and the primary pitch trim is inoperative if unpowered. The trim response to these primary systems is proportional to trim control movement. The yaw, primary pitch, standby pitch, and standby roll trims are applied directly by individual constant rate trim actuators. The trim actuators, each driven by an integral electric motor, are connected to and mechanically reposition the zero force position of the respective control system. The primary and standby pitch trim actuators mechanically reposition the artificial feel bungee to move the control column zero force position, which moves the canard and elevons at the same time through the control system.

NOTE
- When the flaps are lowered, the canard moves to its zero degree position and pitch trim then moves only the elevons.
- The primary pitch trim system is inoperative when the standby pitch trim system is engaged.

When the flight augmentation control system roll differential servo is actuated by the primary roll trim system, the roll portion of the flight control system positions the hydraulic control valves, and hydraulic pressure to the elevon actuators moves the elevons differentially to the trim position. The yaw trim actuator and the standby roll trim actuator mechanically reposition the respective artificial-feel bungees to move the pedals or the control wheels to a new, neutral (no load) position.

NOTE

Use of the standby roll trim system does not deactivate the primary roll trim system. The trim settings obtained by the standby system increase or decrease those of the primary system.

Trim travel of the control surfaces is the same as the travel obtainable with normal control movements in pitch and equal to half travel in roll. A single control permits all trim systems to be energized simultaneously with the airplane on the ground, to establish the required take-off trim settings. A trim switch in each escape capsule actuates the standby pitch and roll trim systems for control of the airplane while the crew is encapsulated during an inflight emergency.

FLIGHT CONTROLS AND INDICATORS.

CONTROL WHEELS AND COLUMNS.

Each of the dual conventional, column-mounted control wheels (figure 1-11) has a primary pitch trim knob, a flight augmentation control disengage button, and an intercom/microphone switch. (The pilot's wheel is a special flight test wheel with additional switches.) The control wheels and columns are mechanically connected to the hydraulic actuator control valves through the master cylinders and a mixer assembly to move the elevons symmetrically as elevators or differentially as ailerons. Movement of the column also mechanically positions the canard actuator control valves. Each column can be manually or ballistically stowed in the forward position. Manual stowage of the column aids access to each seat for crew movement on the ground or during flight and prevents the column from interfering with capsule door closure during manual encapsulation. Ballistic column stowage occurs as part of the ballistic encapsulation sequence. (Refer to "Seats and Escape Capsules" in this section.) When the column is stowed, it is disengaged from the pitch system linkage; roll control is not disengaged.

CAUTION

The column can be ballistically stowed only once during flight. Re-engagement of the column is accomplished by pulling the column aft. Proper realignment and subsequent operation of the control column is assured by a linkage alignment slot.

CONTROL COLUMN RELEASE PEDALS.

Each control column is released for manual stowing by pressing a release pedal (17, figure 1-2) at the base of each control column pedestal, on the outboard side. Pressing the pedal operates a mechanical linkage that disengages the control column from the pitch control system, pulls the column forward, and latches the column in stowed position.

NOTE

Roll control is not disengaged when the column is stowed.

The column is re-engaged by pulling it aft until an alignment slot is engaged.

RUDDER PEDALS.

Dual conventional hanging-type rudder pedals (figure 1-2) are mechanically linked to both rudder actuator hydraulic control valves. Toe action on the rudder pedals applies the wheel brakes. Rudder pedal movement also controls nose wheel steering. (Refer to "Nose Wheel Steering System" in this section.)

RUDDER PEDAL ADJUSTMENT KNOBS.

Each pair of rudder pedals is adjusted fore and aft by rotating a knob (16, figure 1-2) on the respective control pedestal below the control column. Both paired pedals are adjusted, simultaneously, forward when the knob is rotated clockwise, and aft when the knob is rotated counterclockwise.

PRIMARY PITCH TRIM KNOBS.

Two rotary knobs (3 and 6, figure 1-11), one on the outboard grip of each control wheel, control the primary pitch trim system using right primary ac bus power. Rotating either knob towards NOSE UP or NOSE DN energizes the primary pitch trim actuator. When the flaps are up, the trim actuator causes both the canard and elevons to move to the desired trim setting. When the flaps are lowered, the canard is moved to its zero degree position and all pitch trim action is obtained through the elevons. The trim actuator moves the control surfaces in proportion to the amount of trim knob rotation.

Trimming stops when the surfaces are trimmed an amount proportional to knob rotation or when the surfaces have reached their limit of travel. Although the primary pitch trim knobs do not have fixed stops, mechanically actuated limit switches are opened, cutting off power to the actuator when the trim linkage travel limits have been reached. Because the primary pitch trim knobs have no neutral setting and can be rotated continuously, use of either knob after trim has been applied results in an increase or decrease from the previously obtained trim position.

CAUTION

Simultaneous operation of both primary pitch trim knobs in opposite directions should be avoided. If this is done inadvertently, a compensator in the circuit prevents trim actuator damage.

NOTE

The primary pitch trim knobs are inoperative and the primary system is locked out when the standby pitch trim is used. To re-engage the primary system, the standby pitch trim arming switch must be moved to OFF.

PRIMARY ROLL TRIM KNOB.

A serrated knob (44, figure 1-7), on the center console, controls the primary roll trim circuit by right primary ac bus power. The knob is effective when the roll augmentation power switch is ON and the augmentation engage button has been pressed. A channel-type guard prevents inadvertent actuation of the knob. Index numbers on the knob show the degrees and direction of trim applied. When the roll trim knob is rotated towards LEFT or RIGHT, simultaneous signals are sent to each of the two roll channels in the flight augmentation control system. Signals from these channels cause the roll differential servo to position the elevons differentially at the desired trim setting. Trim movement of the elevons is in proportion to the amount of knob rotation. Rotating the knob 150 degrees in either direction from its neutral setting (0 index mark) provides full trim movement of the elevons in the corresponding direction. Trim action stops when the surfaces are trimmed an amount proportional to knob rotation or when the travel limits of the roll differential servos are reached.

NOTE
- The primary roll trim system remains operative if the standby roll trim is engaged and subsequent use of the primary roll trim knob does not deactivate the standby system. Therefore, additive roll trim action from both systems can exist simultaneously.
- The primary roll trim knob is returned to its neutral setting when the trim for take-off button is actuated on the ground or when the flight augmentation control system engage button is pressed with roll augmentation not engaged. This prevents transient roll action during engagement of the augmentation.

YAW TRIM SWITCH.

Yaw trim is controlled by a three-position switch (43, figure 1-7) on the center console. The switch has a channel-type guard to prevent inadvertent operation and receives power from the essential ac bus. It is spring-loaded from the NOSE LEFT and NOSE RIGHT positions to the center (OFF) position. When the switch is held at NOSE LEFT or NOSE RIGHT, the yaw trim actuator is energized and repositions the yaw control system artificial feel bungee at a constant rate. The bungee mechanically changes the neutral (no load) position of the rudder pedals. Yaw trim action stops when the switch is released to OFF, or when the travel limits of the yaw trim actuator are reached.

NOTE
There is no standby yaw trim system.

TAKE-OFF TRIM BUTTON/LIGHT.

Pressing the square take-off trim button (42, figure 1-7), on the center console, trims all the control surfaces to the proper setting for takeoff. A green light in the button comes on when the correct trim positions are obtained; however, because the flaps must be down for take-off, the light is illuminated to show take-off trim only if the flaps are down. The light and the switches in the trim for take-off button receive power from the essential ac bus. The take-off trim circuit is effective only when the weight of the airplane is on the gear, if the standby pitch trim arming switch is at ARMED, and if the pitch and roll augmentation power switches are ON. When the take-off trim button is held down, the primary roll and pitch trim systems are energized by primary ac bus power, and the yaw trim and the standby roll and pitch trim systems are energized by essential ac bus power. This moves all controls and control surfaces to the take-off trim positions. When the button is released, the light goes out; but the trim remains at the take-off settings.

NOTE
- Use of the primary or standby trim switches after take-off trim is set, changes the trim positions of the surfaces.
- The take-off trim position of the rudders is neutral; the elevons are neutral differentially with the trailing-edge of both symmetrically down.

STANDBY PITCH TRIM ARMING SWITCH.

The three-position standby pitch trim arming switch (4, figure 1-8), which provides two modes of control of standby pitch trim, is on the pilot's console. Moving the switch to either ARMED or ALT ARMED places the standby pitch trim system in a ready condition. With the switch at OFF, standby pitch trim is not available. The ARMED position is the normal position of the switch directing essential ac bus power to the standby trim pitch switch through the up or down standby trim control relays. If a failure occurs in this circuit, moving the arming switch to ALT ARMED bypasses the trim control relays and supplies essential ac bus power directly to the standby pitch trim actuator. The arming switch is mechanically latched at OFF and must be pulled out before the ALT ARMED position can be selected.

CAUTION
The trim actuator power through the trim control relays is shut off if the actuator reaches its travel limits. Because this travel limit protection is bypassed when the arming switch is at ALT ARMED, full trimming should be avoided to prevent possible structural damage.

The standby pitch trim arming switch must be used to transfer trim control from the standby system back to the primary system. The primary pitch trim system is re-engaged by moving the arming switch to OFF. The switch must be at ARMED for the take-off trim button to be effective. The emergency descent control grip trim buttons in the escape capsules are connected in parallel with the standby trim systems and are inactive unless the standby pitch trim arming switch is at ARMED.

1-86

T.O. 1B-70(X)A-1

STANDBY TRIM PITCH SWITCH.

This three-position switch (41, figure 1-7), on the center console, is used to obtain pitch trim if the primary trim system fails. The switch is spring-loaded to the center (OFF) position from the NOSE DOWN and NOSE UP positions. A channel-type guard prevents inadvertent switch actuation. The standby trim pitch switch is effective only if the standby pitch trim arming switch is at either its ARMED or ALT ARMED position. When the standby trim switch is held at NOSE DOWN or NOSE UP, essential ac bus power energizes the standby pitch actuator accordingly for the desired trim response. (The standby actuator moves at a constant rate that is twice the rate provided by the primary system.) Trim action stops when the switch is released or when the actuator limit is reached.

NOTE

The primary pitch trim system is automatically locked out when the standby switch is used. The standby trim pitch circuit also may be controlled from either escape capsule through the trim switch on the emergency descent control grip which is connected in parallel with the standby pitch trim (ARMED only) circuit.

STANDBY TRIM ROLL SWITCH.

The three-position standby trim roll switch (40, figure 1-7), on the center console, is used for roll trim if the primary roll trim system fails. The switch is spring-loaded from its LEFT ROLL and RIGHT ROLL positions to the center (OFF) position and is protected by a channel guard. Holding the switch at either LEFT ROLL or RIGHT ROLL energizes the standby roll actuator which repositions the artificial-feel bungee in the roll system to mechanically change the neutral (no load) position of the control wheels. The standby trim roll switch receives power from the essential ac bus.

NOTE
- Actuation of the standby trim roll switch does not lock out the primary roll trim circuit. As a result, additive trim action from both roll trim systems can exist at the same time.
- The standby roll trim circuit also may be controlled from either escape capsule through the trim switch on the emergency descent control grip which is connected in parallel with the standby roll trim circuit.

ESCAPE CAPSULE TRIM BUTTONS.

Control of the airplane, after the crew has encapsulated, is accomplished by a trim button (figure 1-36) on the emergency descent control grip that is stowed in the upper left survival kit of each escape capsule. The grip must be removed from its mounting clip and hand-held. Each trim button is a five position (center neutral) momentary switch for pitch and roll trim. These trim buttons receive power from the essential ac bus and control movement of the canard and elevons. The escape capsule trim buttons are connected in parallel with the standby pitch and roll trim switches.

CAUTION
- Pitch trim cannot be obtained by forward or aft movement of the trim button on the emergency descent control grip, unless the standby pitch trim arming switch is at ARMED.
- The trim button circuits are "hot" if the capsule doors are open or closed.

1-87

T.O. 1B-70(X)A-1

FLIGHT AUGMENTATION CONTROL SYSTEM POWER SWITCHES.

Four augmentation power switches (2, 3, and 27, figure 1-8), one for pitch augmentation, one for roll augmentation and one for each of the two identical yaw augmentation channels, are on the pilot's console. When a power switch is ON, power from the right primary ac bus is available for corresponding circuits of the flight augmentation control system. These circuits can then be engaged by pressing the engage button. (Until the circuits are engaged, the flight augmentation control system caution lights are illuminated.) All four power switches must be ON for normal operation of the flight augmentation control system. Each power switch is mechanically latched in the ON position and must be pulled out before being moved to OFF. Moving a power switch to OFF disconnects the corresponding augmentation circuit. The power switches should be left at the ON position, although they can be used to selectively disconnect an individual augmentation circuit.

NOTE

If the pitch and roll power switches are OFF, the take-off trim system is inoperative.

FLIGHT AUGMENTATION CONTROL SYSTEM ENGAGE BUTTON.

The augmentation engage button (39, figure 1-7), on the center console, supplies power from the right primary ac bus to engage the flight augmentation control system. Electric and hydraulic power must be available to the augmentation system for engagement. The button can engage only those channels of the augmentation system which have been placed in the standby condition as a result of the corresponding augmentation power switches being at ON. When all the power switches are ON, momentarily pressing the button engages all augmentation channels simultaneously. The button energizes the yaw monitor circuit to engage the yaw channel and energizes engage relays in the pitch and roll systems. These relays open solenoid-operated valves which direct hydraulic pressure to the augmentation system pitch and roll differential servos. (Holding circuits keep the relays energized if adequate hydraulic pressure is maintained at the servos.) When the augmentation channels are engaged, the corresponding flight augmentation control system caution lights go out.

NOTE

When the engage button is pressed, a solenoid recenters the primary roll trim knob at its 0 (no trim) position if roll is not previously engaged. This recentering of the primary trim system prevents transient roll effects during engagement of the augmentation.

If a hydraulic or system malfunction disengages pitch or roll augmentation, the engage button can be used in an attempt to re-engage the faulty system. The malfunction must be corrected before the engage button can complete the re-engagement. If the system malfunction has not cleared when the engage button is used, the effected system is disengaged in about 3 seconds after the button is momentarily pressed.

FLIGHT AUGMENTATION CONTROL SYSTEM DISENGAGE BUTTONS.

The pitch, roll, and yaw circuits of the flight augmentation control system are disengaged simultaneously by pressing the disengage button (2, figure 1-11) on the outboard grip of the pilot's control wheel. A similar button (7, figure 1-11) on the outboard grip of the copilot's control wheel simultaneously disengages the pitch and roll augmentation circuits only. Both disengage buttons receive power from the right primary ac bus.

1-88

T.O. 1B-70(X)A-1

SPEED STABILITY SWITCH.

This two-position switch (38, figure 1-7), on the center console, is powered by the right primary ac bus. When the switch is moved to the SPEED position, the speed stability signals are introduced into the pitch augmentation system and provide corrections to the control surfaces through the pitch differential servos. When the switch is in the OFF position, speed stability signals from the central air data system are zeroed out providing no corrections to the pitch differential servos.

LATERAL BOBWEIGHT SWITCH.*

The three-position bobweight switch (7, figure 1-8), on the pilot's console, is used to engage or disengage the bobweight in the roll control system. The switch is spring-loaded to OFF from the FREE and LOCK positions. It is mechanically latched at OFF and must be pulled out before another position can be selected. When the switch is held for 3 seconds at LOCK, the lateral bobweight actuator locks the bobweight and prevents it from responding to lateral accelerations. Therefore, the bobweight does not affect operation of the roll system when it is locked.

NOTE

It is possible that when the bobweight switch is moved to LOCK, the bobweight lock actuator could overrun the locked position and release the bobweight. This would be indicated by the bobweight indicator showing FREE after LOCK had been selected. Locking the bobweight then requires pulsing the bobweight switch towards FREE until the indicator shows LOCKED.

Holding the switch at FREE for 3 seconds allows the actuator to release the bobweight so that it can cause the roll system to move the elevons in response to lateral acceleration forces. The FREE position should be used only at certain speeds to compensate for the negative dihedral effects produced when the wing tips are folded full down. The bobweight switch receives power from the essential ac bus.

FLIGHT AUGMENTATION CONTROL SYSTEM CAUTION LIGHTS.

The four placard-type augmentation system caution lights (1, figure 1-7), on the center console, are powered by the essential ac bus. One light is for pitch augmentation, one for roll augmentation, and one for each of the two yaw channels. The lights come on to indicate improper operation of the respective yaw system or that the pitch or roll system is disengaged. With all augmentation power switches ON, the four caution lights remain illuminated until the systems have been engaged by the augmentation engage button. Subsequent illumination of the pitch or roll augmentation caution light indicates that the corresponding augmentation system is disengaged. If either yaw augmentation caution light comes on, the indicated yaw channel may be inoperative. The primary roll trim system is inoperative if the roll augmentation caution light is on.

LATERAL BOBWEIGHT INDICATOR.*

An electromechanical indicator (21, figure 1-5), on the center instrument panel, shows "FREE" when the lateral bobweight is unlocked, and "LOCKED" when the bobweight is locked. The indicator is actuated by essential ac bus power through limit switches when the bobweight actuator is moved to either position. Diagonal stripes appear while the actuator is at an intermediate position or if the indicator is not energized.

*Airplane AF62-001

1-89

CANARD FLAP SYSTEM.

Auxiliary lift is obtained by the two-position flaps on the trailing edge of the canard. The flaps are electrically controlled and hydraulically operated. Flap extension time from full-up (0 degrees) to full-down (20 degrees) is about 10 to 20 seconds, depending on air loads. The flaps retract in about 10 seconds. There are no intermediate flap positions. The flaps are held in the up position by hydraulic pressure. During high-speed flight, a decrease in the flap system normal hydraulic pressure, or an increase in the return hydraulic pressure indicates air loads are causing the flaps to "creep" down. A caution light shows this change in flap system hydraulic pressure. When the flaps are lowered, a mechanical linkage causes the canard to return to a zero-degree position from any surface position and all pitch control is obtained through the elevons. An indicator in the crew compartment shows flap full-up or full-down position. Because the flap system has dual electrical control and dual hydraulic system actuation, no emergency flap system is provided. The flap system is shown in figure 1-24.

CANARD FLAP SYSTEM CONTROL AND INDICATORS.

FLAP HANDLE.

The airfoil-shaped flap handle (48, figure 1-7), on the center console, is recessed in a guard to prevent inadvertent actuation. A spring-loaded cover plate must be raised to permit moving the flap handle to the FLAP DOWN position. Moving the handle to FLAP UP or FLAP DOWN supplies right primary ac or essential ac bus power to the two hydraulic control valves that direct pressure from No. 1 and No. 2 primary hydraulic systems to the flap actuators.

FLAP POSITION INDICATOR.

The flap position indicator (19, figure 1-5), on the center instrument panel, is powered by the essential ac bus. It is an electromechanical indicator with a pictorial-type flap symbol to display the full-up or full-down positions of the flap. Diagonal "barber pole" lines appear when the flaps are in transit or if a power failure occurs.

FLAP PRESSURE CAUTION LIGHT.

The flap pressure caution light (5, figure 1-7), on the center console, is powered by the right primary ac and essential ac busses. This light indicates that during high-speed flight, air loads are forcing the flaps downward and causing hydraulic pressure within the flap actuators to increase or decrease. When the hydraulic pressure falls below a preset amount, or when the return pressure increases above a preset amount, pressure switches on the flap actuators close, causing the flap pressure light to come on. When the light comes on, the airplane must be slowed to the flap-lowering speed. (Refer to "Flap Lowering Speed" in Section V.)

NOTE

The flap pressure caution light can illuminate to show hydraulic pressure fluctuations above or below the preset amounts only when the flap handle is in the FLAP UP position.

WING TIP FOLD SYSTEM.

The wing tips, which are folded down to increase directional stability primarily during transonic and supersonic flight conditions, offer the design advantage of providing this additional stability without the need of a large fixed vertical surface. The electrically controlled, hydraulically actuated wing tip fold system moves the tips to

Changed 25 June 1965

CANARD FLAP SYSTEM

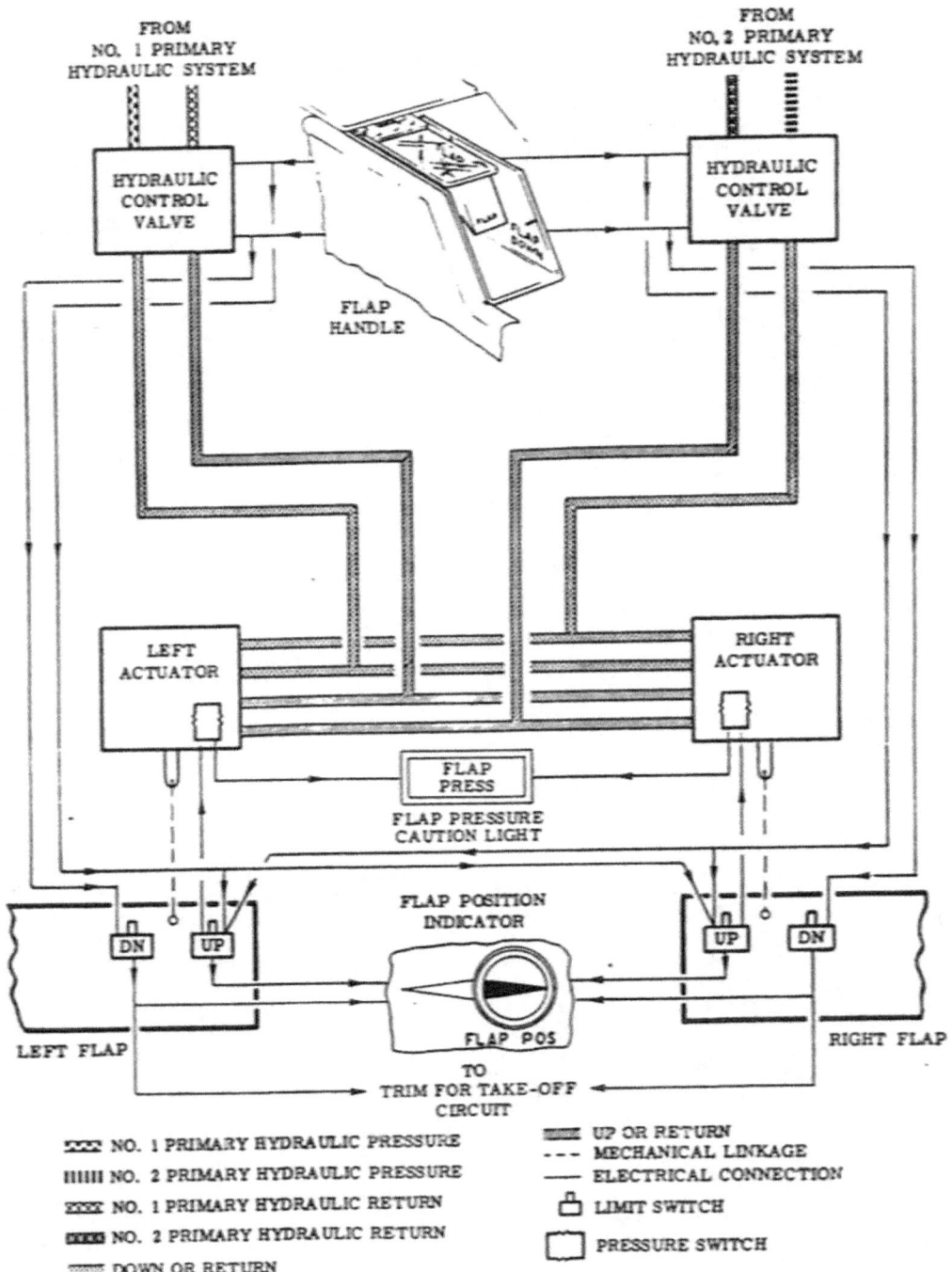

Figure 1-24

either of two fold settings from the normal up position. Both tips operate simultaneously, with each tip positioned by six power hinge drives. These multiple hinges are driven by reversible hydraulic motors through a gearbox and a drive shaft assembly. The motors in each wing are independently powered by the No. 1 and No. 2 primary hydraulic systems. Automatic friction braking of the drive shaft maintains tip position during power-off ground operations and overcomes air-load fluctuations during flight. Tip movement between the full-up and full-down positions (for either lowering or retracting) requires about 65 seconds; between the full-up and the one-half positions requires about 25 seconds; and between the one-half and full-down position takes about 40 seconds. (These operating times are increased following prolonged periods of cold soaking.)

NOTE

Lockout switches on each main landing gear strut prevent wing tip fold operation on the ground.

In normal operation, when the wing tip system is engaged, power from both the right primary ac and essential ac busses energize selected position solenoid-operated pilot valves to open. These valves direct hydraulic control pressure from both primary hydraulic systems to the directional and flow control valves for the drive motors. The directional control valve ports system pressure to the hydraulic motors. The motors turn the drive shafts, which move the multiple hinges in the selected direction to position the wing tips. The flow control valves regulate both incoming and outgoing hydraulic flow to the motors, controlling motor speed and maintaining a uniform rate of movement of the wing tips. Mechanical linkage interconnects the directional control valves of the two hydraulic motors in each wing, assuring simultaneous operation of both hydraulic motors. Approximately one degree before the tips reach the selected position, a feedback linkage actuates a limit switch assembly which de-energizes the pilot valve solenoids, permitting the valves to close. This cuts off hydraulic control pressure which would keep the control valves open. As the wing tips continue to the selected position, the feedback linkage repositions the control valves which in turn shut off hydraulic flow to the hydraulic motors. An alternate method of wing tip operation is provided when a failure is known or suspected in normal operation. Unlike the normal mode, the alternate mode when engaged energizes all pilot valve solenoids to open at the half-down position. A change of wing tip position is accomplished, when using the alternate mode, by de-energizing the opposite directional solenoids with the other pilot valves remaining energized to port hydraulic control pressure to the motor directional control valves. The hydraulic motors are then driven by hydraulic system pressure in the direction selected. As the tips approach the selected position, limit switches, engaged by the feedback linkage, re-energize the de-energized solenoids, permitting the related pilot valves to port hydraulic control pressure to the opposite side of the hydraulic directional control valves. Hydraulic control pressure to fold and/or raise the tips is sent to the hydraulic control valves in equal proportions which neutralizes the actuating control pressure. The positioning of the control valves by the feedback mechanism shuts off hydraulic flow to the hydraulic motors.

When the wing tips fold, the outer two segments of each elevon are positioned automatically to a neutral position and remain in this position while the tips are down. Because the wing tip fold system is operated by dual electrical and hydraulic systems, no single system failure will prevent wing tip operation. An emergency-up system is provided to raise the tips if a multiple failure occurs when they are in either down position. (The tip emergency-up system must be reset before normal operation of the wing tip fold system can be restored.) Indication of the three wing tip positions appears in the crew compartment. The wing tip fold system is shown schematically in figure 1-25.

T.O. 1B-70(X)A-1

WING TIP FOLD SYSTEM CONTROLS AND INDICATORS.

WING TIP POSITION SELECTOR SWITCH.

Wing tip position is selected by a three-position rotary switch (17, figure 1-5), on the center instrument panel. This switch, which must be used in conjunction with the wing tip fold mode switch, supplies right primary ac and essential ac bus power to control the wing tip hydraulic pilot valve solenoids. When the selector switch is moved to its UP, 1/2, or DOWN position, appropriate pilot valve solenoids position pilot valves which port hydraulic pressure to the hydraulic control valves, to activate the fold mechanisms. When the tips reach the selected position, feedback linkage mechanically centers the control valves, cutting off hydraulic flow to the motors which stops the folding process. The feedback linkage is held in either of the two extreme travel positions by a mechanical stop on a cam in the gearbox. This assures the holding of the wing tip in the selected position.

WING TIP FOLD MODE SWITCH.

This two-position switch (22, figure 1-5), on the center instrument panel, provides two methods for controlling the wing tip fold system. When the mode switch is in NORMAL and the wing tip position selector switch is moved, electrical power from the right primary ac and essential ac busses energizes the appropriate hydraulic pilot valve solenoids to actuate the wing tips. The ALTR position of the mode switch is used if proper tip operation is not obtained or if a failure of the normal mode is suspected. With the mode switch in the ALTR position, movement of the wing tip position selector switch to UP energizes the up pilot valve solenoids and de-energizes the full-down pilot valve solenoids. The energized pilot valves then port hydraulic control pressure to the up sides of the hydraulic motors. When the tips reach the full up (zero degree) position, the solenoids remain energized and hydraulic pressure aids in holding the tip in the position selected. When the selector switch is moved to DOWN, with the mode switch at ALTR, the full-down solenoids are energized porting hydraulic control pressure to the down side of the hydraulic motors. System hydraulic pressure is supplied to the hydraulic motor which drives and holds the tip in the full down position. Moving the selector switch to 1/2 for selection of the half-down tip position from either the up or down setting energizes the appropriate pilot valve solenoids sending hydraulic control pressure to the selected side of the hydraulic motors. When the tips reach the half-down position, the opposite solenoids are energized, hydraulic pressure to the motors is equalized, and wing tip movement is stopped.

WING TIP EMERGENCY-UP POWER SELECTOR SWITCH.

The wing tip emergency-up power selector switch (12, figure 1-12), on the ground test panel in the electronic equipment compartment, permits selection of ac power for the wing tip emergency-up system. The switch, which must be operated in conjunction with the wing tip emergency-up switch, selects primary ac bus power in the PRIMARY BUS position and essential ac bus power in the ESSENTIAL BUS position. The switch is spring-loaded to the OFF (center) position.

CAUTION
- This switch must be operated simultaneously with the wing tip emergency-up switch. It must not be held in the selected position longer than 5 seconds to prevent overheating of the electric motors in the tip emergency-up system.

- Once the emergency-up system has been used, operation of any other mode cannot be obtained until the system has been reset.

The power selector switch also must be actuated to provide power for the tip emergency-up system reset switch and to test the bulbs in the emergency system caution light.

Changed 25 June 1965

1-93

T.O. 1B-70(X)A-1

WING TIP FOLD SYSTEM
LEFT SIDE SHOWN - RIGHT SIDE TYPICAL

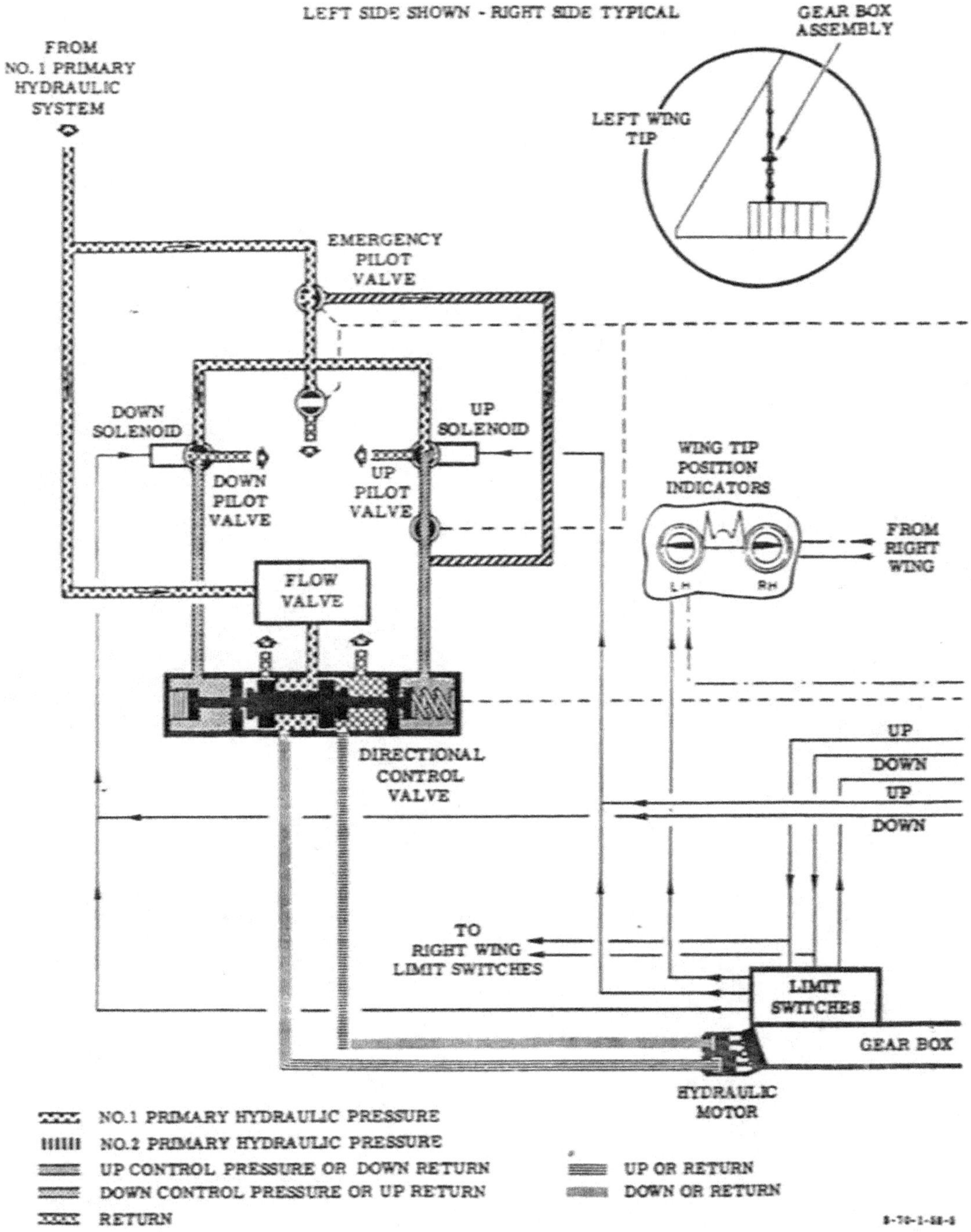

Figure 1-25 (Sheet 1 of 2)

This page intentionally left blank

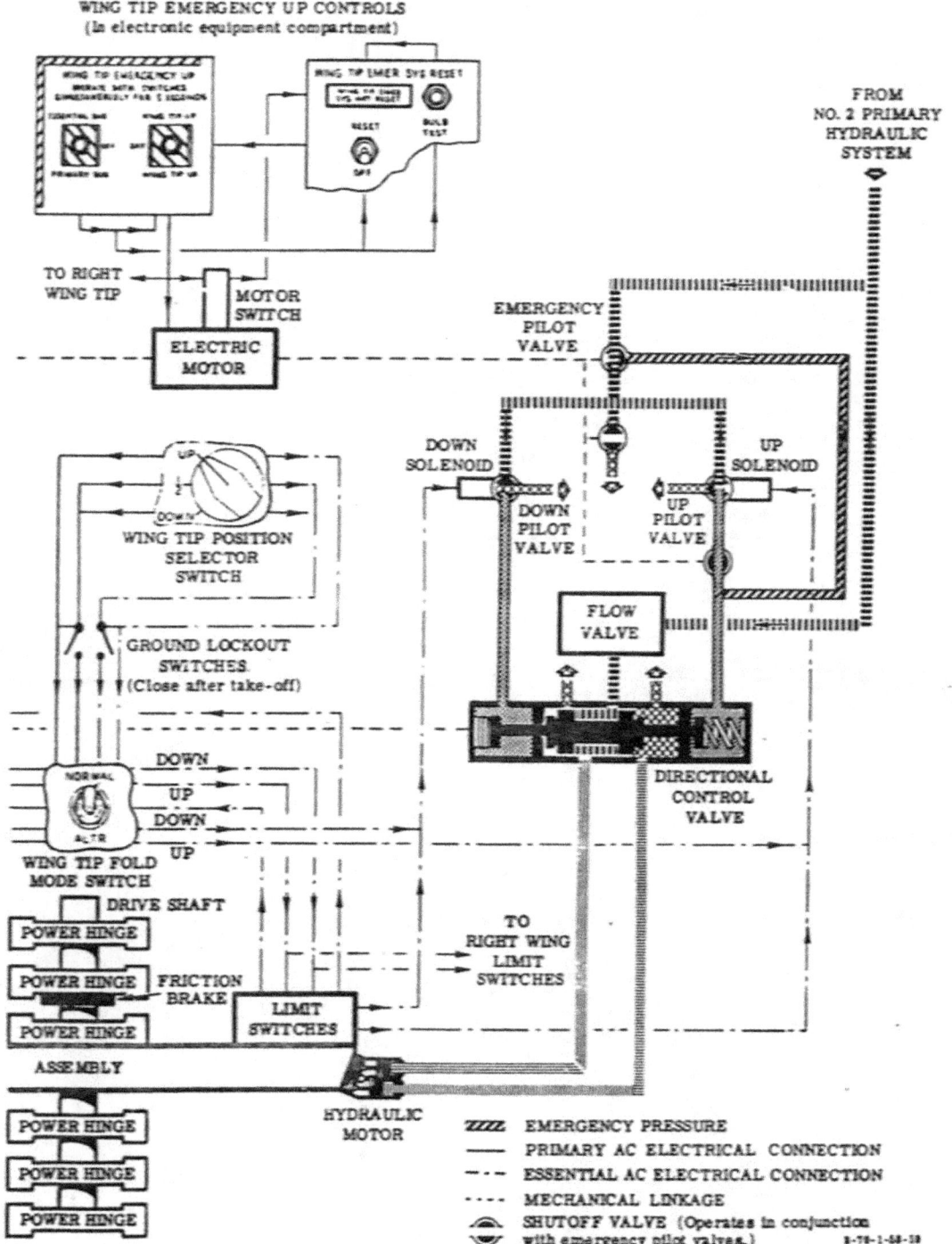

Figure 1-25 (Sheet 2 of 2)

This page intentionally left blank

T.O. 1P-70(X)A-1

WING TIP POSITION INDICATORS.

The two wing tip position indicators (18, figure 1-5), on the center instrument panel, are powered by the essential ac bus and display the wing tip positions. A symbolic wing tip in each indicator shows the full-up, 1/2, or full-down positions of the wing tips. As the tips reach the selected position, limit reach the selected position, limit switches are closed to energize the position indicator. Diagonal "barber pole" lines appear when the tips are in transit, if an essential ac bus failure occurs, or if the tips are not in any of the three selective positions.

WING TIP EMERGENCY-UP SYSTEM NOT RESET CAUTION LIGHT AND LIGHT TEST BUTTON.

This placard-type caution light (17, figure 1-12), on the ground test panel in the electronic equipment compartment, comes on when the wing tip emergency-up system is engaged. The light remains on until the emergency-up system has been reset. A test button (15, figure 1-12) adjacent to the caution light permits a preflight operational test of the bulbs in the light. The emergency-up system power selector switch must be held at either ESSENTIAL BUS or PRIMARY BUS positions to supply the corresponding ac power for test button operation.

LANDING GEAR SYSTEM.

The retractable tricycle landing gear is electrically controlled and hydraulically actuated. (See figures 1-26 and 1-28.) Each four wheel bogie-type main gear retracts aft into the fuselage, outboard of the engine inlets. (The bogie folds and rotates before retraction.) A small fifth wheel on each bogie is used for the automatic wheel brake system speed sensing. The dual wheel nose gear retracts aft into the fuselage, behind the engine inlets. A yaw gearing changer reduces rudder travel from ±12 degrees to ±3 degrees when the landing gear retracts. The wheel well doors normally are closed after the gear is down and locked. A load limit switch on each main gear prevents retracting the gear when the weight of the airplane is on the gear. Electrical and hydraulic emergency gear lowering systems are provided. Normal gear lowering time is about 23 seconds, and normal retraction time is about 20 seconds. Gear emergency lowering time is about 36 seconds. When the landing gear is lowered, a strut overpressure bleed on all three landing gear shock struts bleeds off any build-up of excess strut pressure. After the landing gear is down and locked, the bogies are held in an 8-degree nose-high attitude until touchdown. Shimmy damping for the nose gear is accomplished by the interconnected nose wheels. The paired wheels on each bogie are corotated by a connecting torque tube.

Each corotating pair of wheels on each bogie have hydraulically operated, multiple-disc brakes with an automatic brake control system to prevent skidding the tires. A manual braking system is provided for brake emergencies. The gear compartments are cooled by a recirculating-type cooling system using ethylene glycol and water to reduce compartment in-flight temperatures. The steel wheels and extra high pressure tubeless tires used on both the main and nose gears are interchangeable. Each wheel has a combined thermal plug and pressure relief valve to bleed off tire pressures before the tire-burst limit is reached. The tires are filled with nitrogen. (See figure 1-37 for nitrogen specification.)

LANDING GEAR GROUND SAFETY PINS AND LOCKS.

Removable ground safety pins may be installed in the main and nose gear assemblies to prevent possible collapsing of the gear while the airplane is on the ground. (See figure 1-27.) Ground safety locks also are provided for the open position of the main and nose gear well doors. The pins and locks have regulation red warning streamers. All gear ground safety pins and locks must be removed before flight.

Changed 25 June 1965

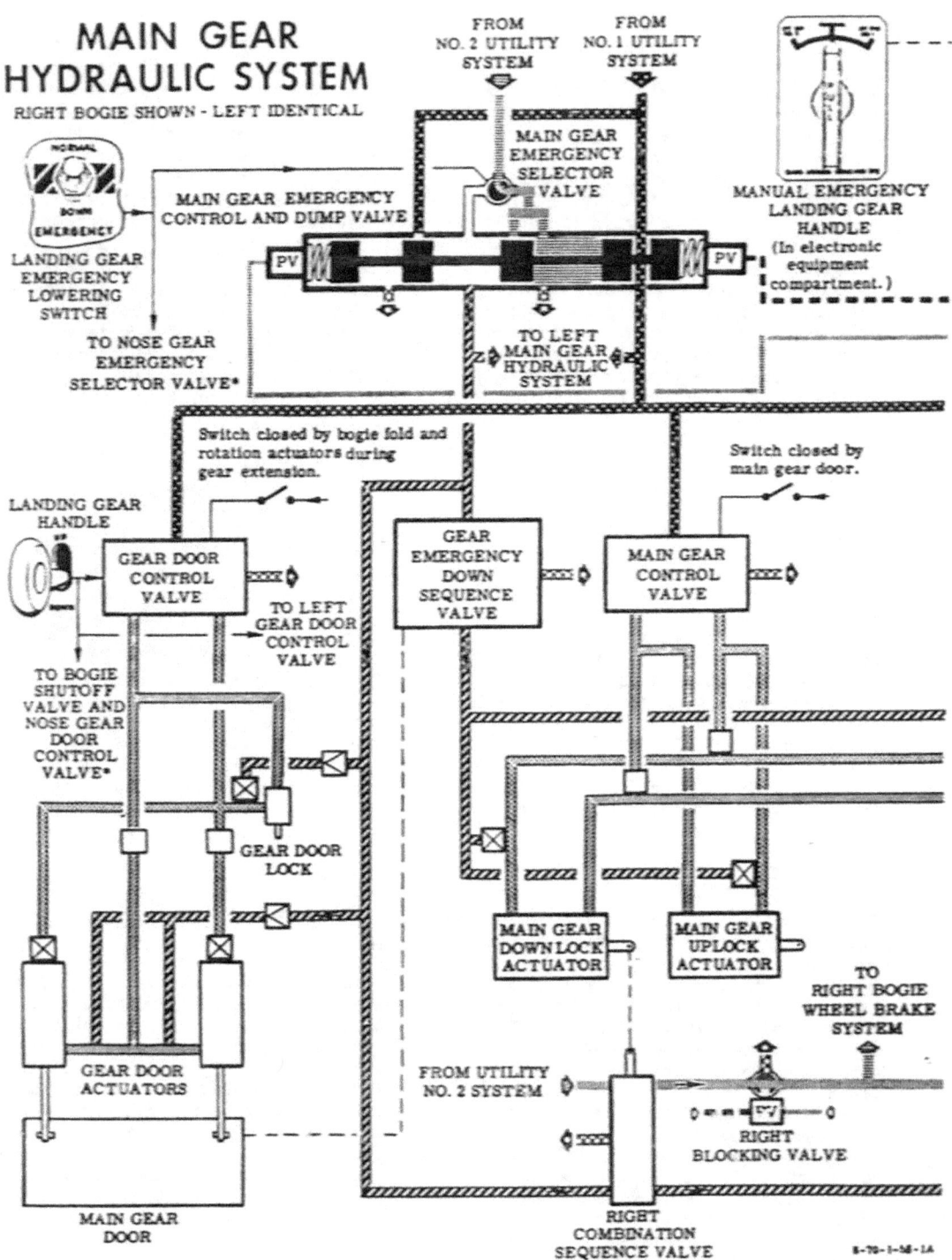

Figure 1-26 (Sheet 1 of 2)

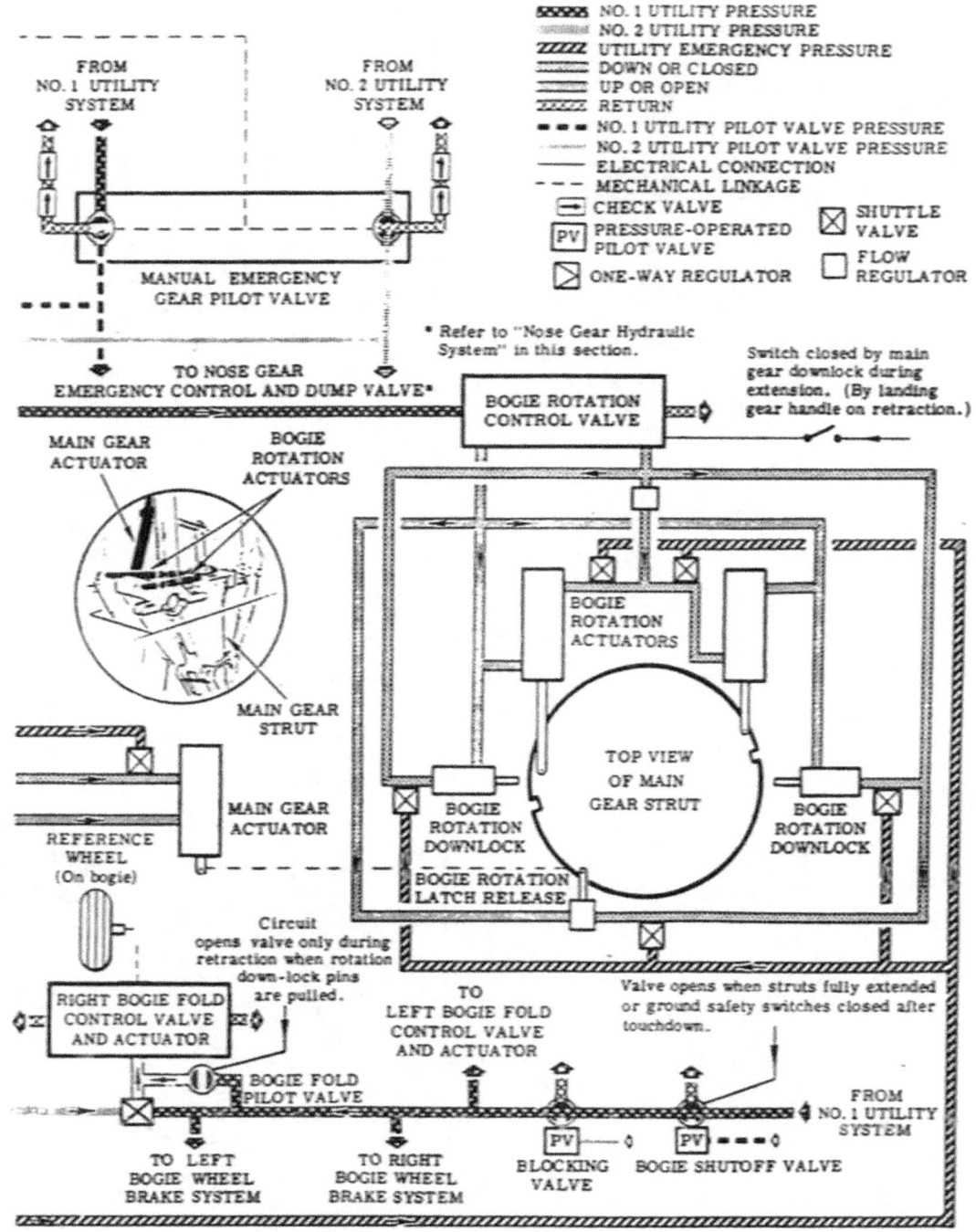

Figure 1-26 (Sheet 2 of 2)

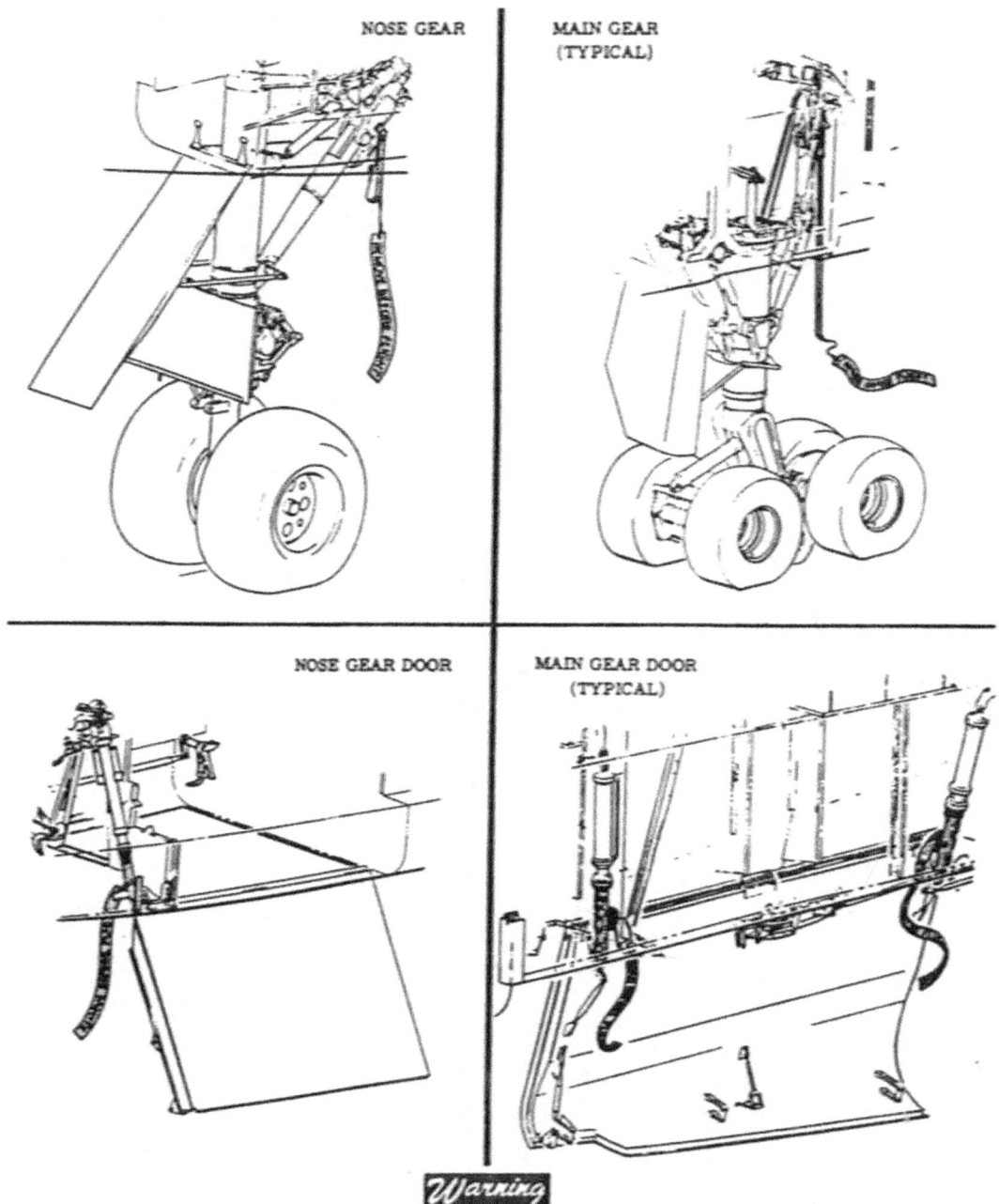

Figure 1-27

LANDING GEAR COMPARTMENT COOLING SYSTEM.

Refer to "Drag Chute and Landing Gear Compartments Cooling System" in Section IV.

LANDING GEAR SYSTEM CONTROLS AND INDICATORS.

LANDING GEAR HANDLE.

The landing gear handle (13, figure 1-5), on the center instrument panel, electrically controls the landing gear by right primary ac and essential ac bus power. The gear handle is mechanically latched and must be pulled out before it can be moved. When the airplane is airborne, moving the handle to UP energizes the landing gear door control valves so that the No. 1 utility hydraulic system pressure opens the gear doors. After gear doors are open, No. 1 and No. 2 utility hydraulic system pressure is applied to release the downlocks, fold and rotate the bogies, and retract the landing gear. (No. 1 utility hydraulic system releases the downlocks, rotates the bogies, retracts the landing gear, and sequences the bogie folding. The hydraulic pressure that sequences bogie folding is controlled by a bogie shutoff valve, a pressure-controlled blocking valve, and a bogie fold pilot valve. The shutoff and blocking valves are open when the main gear is down and locked; the pilot valve is open only during retraction, when the rotation downlock pins are pulled. The No. 2 utility hydraulic system, controlled by a combination sequence valve and a pressure-controlled blocking valve, folds the bogies while they are being rotated.) Both main gear bogies fold and rotate simultaneously before the main gear starts to retract. When all gears are retracted and the uplocks closed, the gear doors close and the gear hydraulic system is depressurized. Moving the landing gear handle to DOWN energizes the landing gear door control valves so that the No. 1 utility pressure opens the gear doors. After the gear doors open, pressure is applied to release the gear uplocks and lower the nose and main gears. When the gear is down and locked, the main gear bogies rotate and unfold simultaneously. (Normally, the bogies are unfolded by the No. 2 utility hydraulic system. If this is not available, No. 1 utility system is applied automatically to unfold the bogies.) After the bogies are unfolded and in landing position, the gear doors close. System pressure is maintained when the gear is down.

NOTE
- If the landing gear handle is accidentally moved to UP on the ground, the gear will not retract and the handle must be moved to DOWN then UP to retract the gear when airborne.
- The landing gear handle must be at DOWN after the landing gear has been lowered by the emergency lowering switch or by the manual emergency handle to permit automatic braking.

LANDING GEAR EMERGENCY LOWERING SWITCH.

The two-position landing gear emergency lowering switch (14, figure 1-5), on the center instrument panel, is mechanically latched at NORMAL and must be pulled out before it can be moved to DOWN. The switch receives power from the essential ac bus and is used to lower the gear in case the normal system fails or the electrical contacts of the gear handle fail. Moving the emergency switch to DOWN activates the main and nose gear hydraulic system emergency control valves through additional electrical circuits. This supplies No. 2 utility hydraulic system pressure for gear extension sequence and nose wheel steering. The switch should be at its NORMAL position for normal operation of the gear. No means are provided for emergency retraction of the gear. Moving the switch to DOWN while on the ground prior to shutdown, or with auxiliary power attached, opens the gear doors. Also, moving the switch to NORMAL closes the doors.

WARNING
Warn ground crew to stand clear of the landing gear doors before moving the landing gear emergency lowering switch to NORMAL. The doors will close rapidly if there is power on the airplane or when power is applied to the airplane and the switch is already at NORMAL.

MANUAL EMERGENCY LANDING GEAR HANDLE.

The three-position emergency handle (10, figure 1-12) is next to the ground test panel in the electronic equipment compartment. The handle is used for mechanically selecting the No. 1 or the No. 2 utility hydraulic system to lower the landing gear if the gear cannot be lowered by the normal system. On Airplane AF62-207, handle must be pulled before it can be turned. On Airplane AF62-001, the handle is connected to a Teleflex cable and bellcrank system that permits operation of the handle from a lever in the crew compartment. On this airplane, the handle still can be moved directly at the electronic equipment compartment if necessary (ground test purposes, for example) without disturbing the position of the remote lever. The handle need not be pulled out before turning. Turning the handle to UT SYS NO. 1 directs No. 1 utility hydraulic system pressure to lower the gear; turning the handle to UT SYS NO. 2 directs No. 2 utility hydraulic system pressure to lower the gear. The nose wheel steering system also operates from the No. 2 utility system when the handle is at UT SYS NO. 2. The handle should be at the NORMAL position for all normal operations.

NOTE

Returning the handle to NORMAL after selecting UT SYS NO. 1 to lower the gear, depressurizes the landing gear system and the bogie may drift towards the folded position and give an unsafe indication. However, when the handle is returned to UT SYS NO. 1 for landing, the bogie returns to the proper position.

CAUTION

If two hydraulic pumps in the No. 2 utility hydraulic system have failed and the emergency ac generator has been engaged, only the UT SYS NO. 1 position of handle should be selected. This is necessary to avoid overloading the No. 2 utility hydraulic system, which powers the emergency generator.

---

*Airplane AF62-001

MANUAL EMERGENCY LANDING GEAR LEVER.*

This lever (3A, figure 1-2 and figure 1-6) just forward of the overhead panel, allows the pilot or copilot to mechanically select the No. 1 or the No. 2 utility hydraulic system for lowering the landing gear in an emergency without leaving the seat. The lever is connected to the manual emergency landing gear handle in the electronic equipment compartment by a Teleflex cable, a bellcrank, and an actuating rod. A plate just above the lever is labeled to indicate lever positioning and directional movements. The lever is guarded in the center NORMAL position by a cover labeled "MANUAL EMER LG CONTROL" on each side, and "PULL" on the bottom. The cover guard is hinged at its forward end and snaps around the ball tip of the lever. The guard is also secured to the lever by a safety wire. The aft end of the guard is open so that the finger can be inserted and pulled downward to break the safety wire and expose the lever for use. Whenever the lever is at NORMAL, the guard can be returned to its original position by raising the aft end to snap around the lever tip.

When the lever is moved left (counter-clockwise) 90 degrees to engage the No. 1 system, or right (clockwise) 90 degrees to engage the No. 2 system, a detent will be felt about halfway through the turn. More pressure is then required to continue the lever through the turn. This is because during the first half of the turn (approximately 45 degrees) the slotted actuating rod, moved by the bellcrank, merely rides across the arm attached to the manual emergency landing gear handle. At this halfway point, the end of the slot in the actuating rod picks up the arm and pushes or pulls (depending upon which way the lever is turned) for position selection. This linkage arrangement makes it possible to turn the manual emergency landing gear handle in the electronic equipment compartment without moving the remote lever in the crew compartment. When turning the lever from UT SYS NO. 1-ON to NORMAL, the lever must be turned first to NO. 1 OFF DETENT and then back to NORMAL. The same procedure is used in turning lever from UT SYS NO. 2-ON to NORMAL (NO. 2 OFF DETENT then NORMAL). To facilitate the correct movements, the plate is

Changed 25 June 1965

marked "FOLLOW ARROWS TO RET TO NORMAL". For additional information on operation of the manual emergency landing gear system, refer to "Manual Emergency Landing Gear Handle" in this section.

LANDING GEAR DOOR SWITCH.

The two-position gear door switch, which is recessed at the corner of the ground escape hatch aisle, is used primarily during maintenance operations to actuate the gear doors. If electrical and hydraulic power are available and the landing gear handle is at DOWN, the main and nose gear doors can be opened by moving the door switch to the DOORS OPEN position. The switch also is used for specific in-flight emergency procedures to reduce hydraulic requirements after the gear is down by preventing the gear doors from closing. If the gear handle is DOWN, the landing gear warning system (light in gear handle and audio signal) is actuated when the gear door switch is at DOORS OPEN, regardless of the gear position. For normal operation of the gear doors during gear operation cycles, the door switch must be at NORM. A hinged plate which covers the gear door switch cannot be closed when the switch is at the DOORS OPEN position.

LANDING GEAR POSITION LIGHTS.

The down-and-locked position of the gear is indicated by three green indicator lights (16, figure 1-5) on the center instrument panel. These lights are powered by the essential ac bus and each is on only when its corresponding gear is in the down-and-locked position. The lights may be dimmed by the annunciator light dimmer switch.

LANDING GEAR WARNING LIGHT.

The red light in the plastic knob of the landing gear handle (13, figure 1-5) is illuminated by essential ac bus power when the landing gear handle is moved to UP and warns of an unlocked condition of the landing gear or wheel well doors when the gear is retracted. The light goes out when all gears and doors are up and locked. When the landing gear handle is moved to DOWN, the red light comes on and then goes out when all gears are down and locked, regardless of the gear door positions. Whenever the landing gear door switch is moved to the DOORS OPEN position and the gear handle is DOWN, the gear warning light comes on, regardless of gear position. The light also comes on if the throttle for No. 4 engine is out of the afterburner range and the airplane is below about 8,000 feet altitude and below 250 knots IAS and the gear is not down and locked. The light in the handle comes on in conjunction with the audio warning signal heard in the headset.

LANDING GEAR AUDIO WARNING SIGNAL.

An audio warning in both headsets provides an indication of unsafe landing gear condition when the airplane is below about 8,000 feet altitude, and below 250 knots IAS, and No. 4 throttle is out of the afterburner range. The warning signal sounds until the landing gear handle is moved to DOWN and all gears reach their down-and-locked position or the warning system control button is pressed. When the gear handle is DOWN and the landing gear door switch is moved to the DOORS OPEN position, the audio warning signal is actuated. The warning signal is powered by the essential dc bus.

LANDING GEAR AUDIBLE WARNING SYSTEM CUTOUT BUTTON.

A warning system cutout button (15, figure 1-5), on the center instrument panel, is used to turn off the audible warning signal when desired. An increase in airspeed above 260 knots IAS, or an increase in altitude above 9,000 feet, automatically resets the warning circuit for the landing gear.

This page intentionally left blank

TIRE OVERHEAT CAUTION LIGHT.

Refer to "Drag Chute and Landing Gear Compartments Cooling System" in Section IV.

NOSE WHEEL STEERING SYSTEM.

Nose wheel steering is hydraulically operated and electronically controlled. It is selectively engaged and is normally operated by No. 1 utility hydraulic system. A shuttle valve in the hydraulic system permits steering operation from the No. 2 utility hydraulic system (after manual emergency landing gear handle is moved to UT SYS NO. 2, or the landing gear emergency lowering switch is moved to DOWN) in case of a failure of the No. 1 utility hydraulic system. (Refer to "Landing Gear Emergency Lowering Switch" in this section.) Steering is controlled by the rudder pedals, which furnish command signals to an electronic control unit. These signals are proportional to pedal movement from a neutral pedal position. The control unit in turn provides differential current to a steering control valve which directs hydraulic pressure to a steering actuator to obtain the desired nose wheel steering. The steering actuator travel is selected by a switch in the crew compartment and permits the nose wheels to be turned about 58 degrees each side of center for taxiing, or about 35 degrees for take-off and landing. A load switch disengages the nose wheel steering system when the weight of the airplane is off both main gear. The system also is automatically disengaged in case of a failure in the steering system which would cause a hard-over signal. However, the nose wheel steering remains engaged when only the nose wheels lift off and the main gear is still on the ground, but hydraulic power is removed from the steering actuator. The nose wheel steering system is shown in figure 1-28.

NOSE GEAR TORQUE LINK.

The nose gear shock strut and nose wheel assembly are connected by a torque link ("scissors") which keeps the strut and wheel assembly aligned. The nose gear has a spring-loaded lever-type lock just above the tow bar connection. The lock is pushed aft by the tow bar to disengage the wheel assembly and permits the wheel assembly to rotate 360 degrees. Removing the tow bar releases the lock to engage the wheel assembly when it is aligned. If the lock is not engaged, the spring-loaded lock drops in place as the wheel assembly starts to caster during taxiing or when the rudder pedals are moved through neutral with the steering engaged.

NOSE WHEEL STEERING SELECTOR SWITCH.

The three-position nose wheel steering selector switch (47, figure 1-7), on the center console, has OFF, TAXI, and TAKE-OFF LDG positions. The switch receives power from the right primary ac bus and permits selection of two different travel limits for nose wheel steering. Moving the switch to TAXI selects a maximum nose wheel steering travel of about 58 degrees each side of center. Moving the switch to TAKE-OFF LDG selects a maximum nose wheel steering travel of about 35 degrees each side of center. Moving the switch to OFF disengages the nose wheel steering system, permitting the nose wheels to caster. After moving the switch from OFF to either position, the nose wheel steering must be engaged with the nose wheel steering engage button. However, moving the nose wheel steering selector switch between the TAXI and TAKE-OFF LDG positions does not disengage the nose wheel steering.

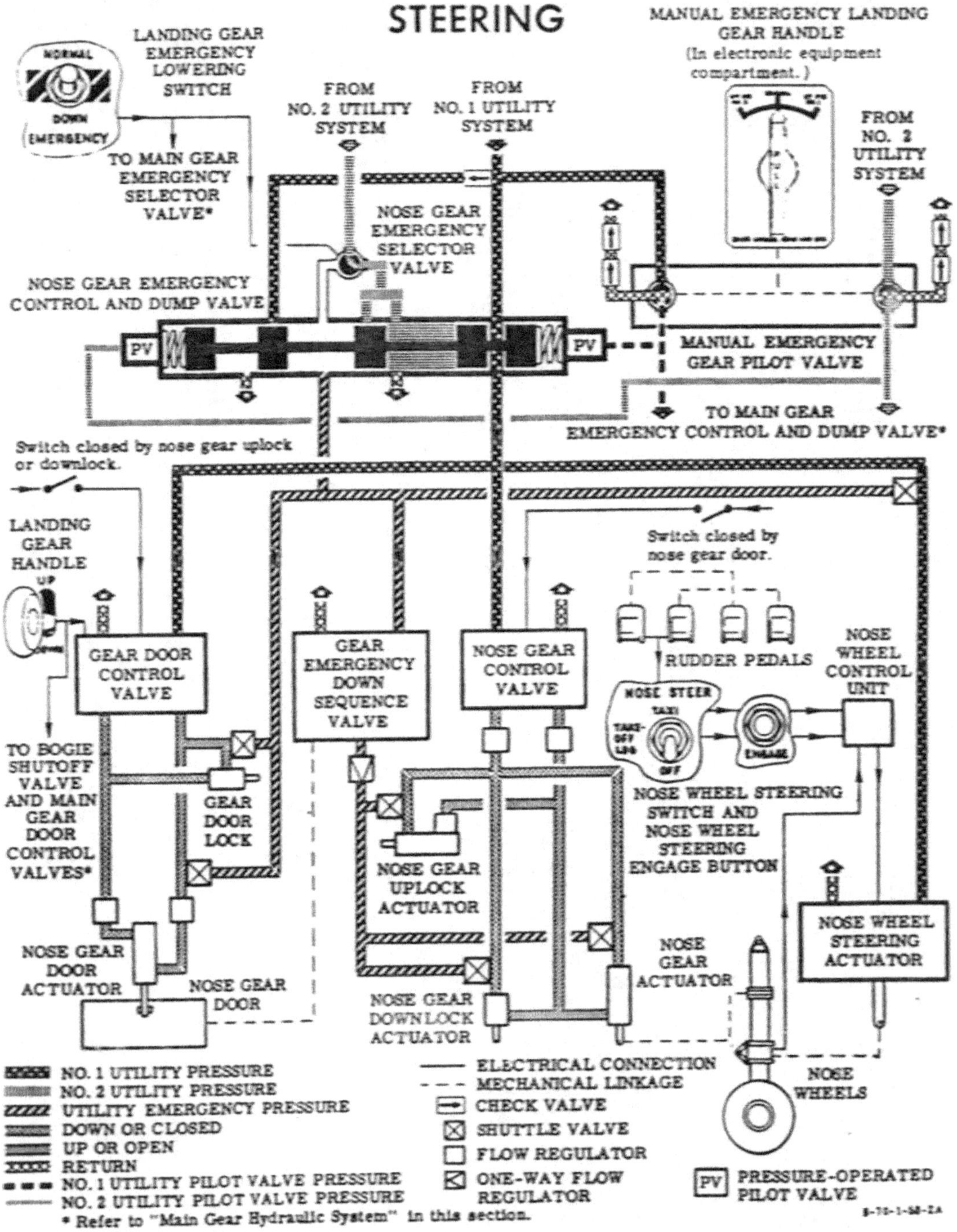

Figure 1-28. Nose Gear Hydraulic System and Nose Wheel Steering

This page intentionally left blank

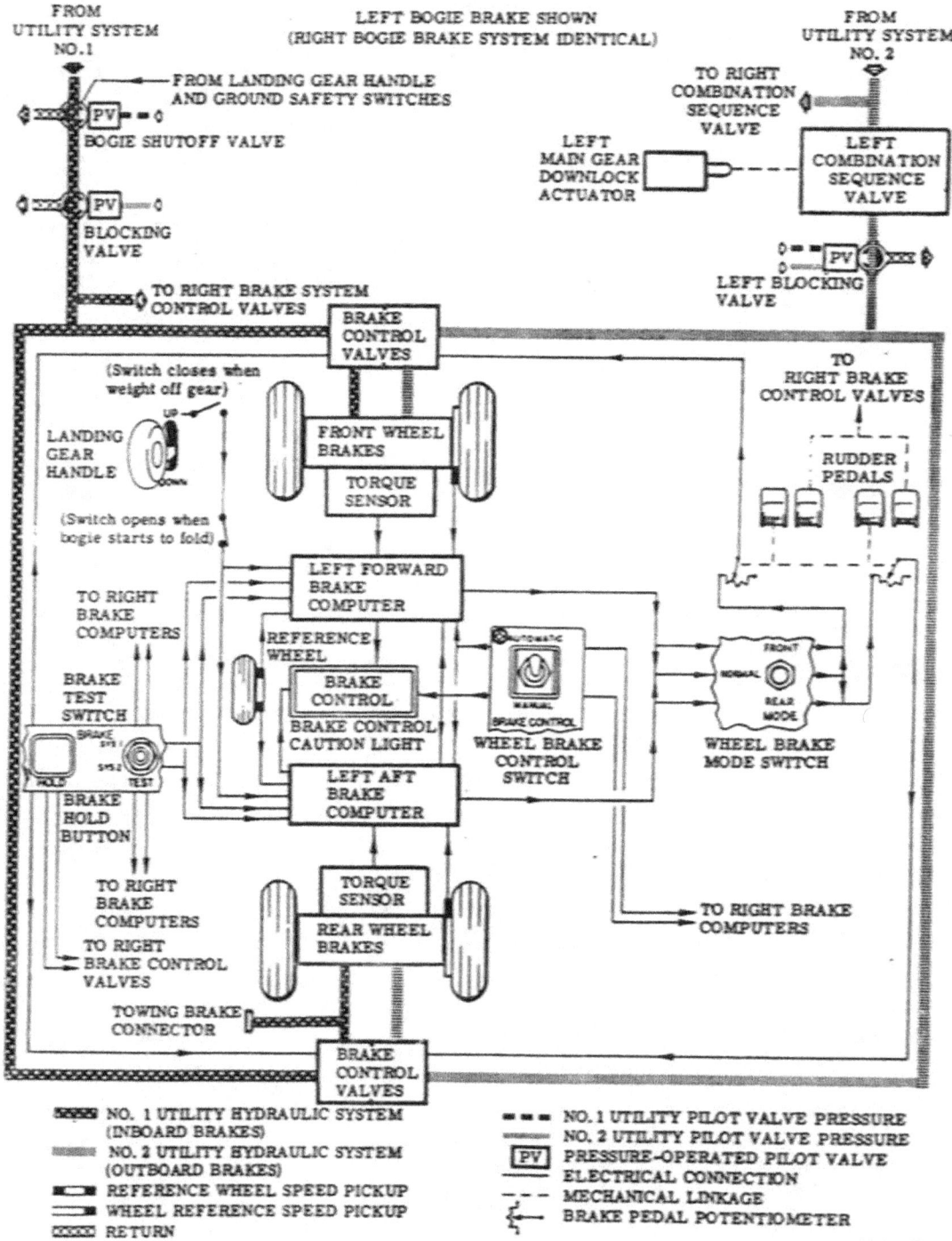

Figure 1-29

T.O. 1B-70(X)A-1

During manual braking, the hydraulic pressure applied to the brakes is proportional to the position of the pedal. On the airplane* with the emergency battery-inverter system, the battery can be activated to provide emergency electrical power for manual brake operation. (Refer to "Emergency Battery-inverter System" in this section.) A brake holding system applied by a combination button and indicator light, by-passes the brake control circuitry to hold the brakes on when the airplane is stopped. A caution light in the crew compartment indicates a malfunction of the automatic brake control system. During landing gear retraction, when landing gear handle is moved to UP, brakes are automatically applied to stop main gear wheel rotation before the wheels enter the wheel well. The brakes then are released when the bogie starts to fold. The brake system is shown in figure 1-29.

AUTOMATIC BRAKE SYSTEM.

The automatic wheel brake system, using brake computers and sensors, provides a fully automatic brake control by limiting the brake pressure so that maximum braking is obtained with no tire skidding. A small reference wheel on each bogie, preloaded to maintain runway contact, provides a reference speed for the computers. Each of the four brake installations has a separate automatic control. The automatic brake system is engaged or disengaged by a switch in the crew compartment. When selected, the automatic braking is put into operation by applying toe pressure on the rudder pedals. This pressure on the pedals monitors the brake computer signal to the brake control valves. The computers, using inputs from the brake torque sensors, reference wheel, and braked wheel speed sensors transmit computed signals to the brake limiters. The limiters compare the computer signals with the predetermined allowable braking limits and provide control signals that will not exceed these limits to the brake control valves. Brake pressure is then applied as necessary by the brake control valves.

TOWING BRAKE SYSTEM.

An externally controlled auxiliary towing brake system can be connected to provide an emergency stop during towing operations using the rear brake of each bogie. Two trailers, one attached to the rear of each bogie, are towed by the airplane. Quick-disconnects make the necessary connections from the trailers to the airplane. The towing brake controls and operator's seat are on the trailer that attaches to the right bogie. The trailer on the left bogie carries an auxiliary power unit to supply electrical power for the airplane lighting and intercom systems. Both trailers are interconnected electrically to provide simultaneous operation of the brakes. The system can only be used for a single emergency stop while towing. After use, the towing brake system must be reset before it can be used again.

WHEEL BRAKE SYSTEM CONTROLS AND INDICATORS.

WHEEL BRAKE CONTROL SWITCH.

The two-position wheel brake control switch (51, figure 1-7), on the center console, receives power from the essential and right primary ac busses and selects the mode of braking. The switch normally should be set at AUTOMATIC to provide fully automatic brake control

---

* Airplane AF62-001

in the automatic brake system. It may
not be necessary to change to manual to
obtain braking when the light is on.
However, after landing, be prepared to
change to manual braking if a change in
brake effectiveness is noticed. The
light also comes on when the brake
control switch is at MANUAL, or when
the wheel brake test switch is moved
to either test position if there is a
failure of the electrical power supply
in the brake control system.

DRAG CHUTE SYSTEM.

Two 28-foot, ring-slot type parachutes, packed in separate deployment bags, are stowed in a compartment on the upper surface of the wing on the centerline, inboard of the vertical stabilizers. (See 17, figure 1-1.) An integral-type riser and trunnion fitting attach the drag chutes to the airplane. Two pilot chutes (one a spring-loaded type which pulls out the main pilot chute) also are stowed in the compartment. The main pilot chute pulls out both drag chutes simultaneously. Two doors which close the compartment are hydraulically opened. These doors must be manually closed by the ground crew. The pilot chute ground safety pin protrudes through the door and must be removed after the chutes are installed. The drag chute system is controlled by power from both the primary ac and essential ac busses and by hydraulic pressure from both No. 1 and No. 2 utility systems operating a tandem actuator. (See figure 1-30.) The drag chute attachment hook is kept unlocked during flight to permit drag chute jettisoning in case of accidental opening of the doors.

During the deployment sequence, the hook closes before the doors open. Deployment and jettison of the drag chutes are controlled by a handle in the crew compartment. The drag chute compartment is cooled to prevent overheating by engine and aerodynamic heating. In case of a cooling system failure, a caution light warns of a compartment overheat condition.

DRAG CHUTE COMPARTMENT COOLING SYSTEM.

Refer to "Drag Chute and Landing Gear Compartments Cooling System" in Section IV.

DRAG CHUTE HANDLE.

The two-position drag chute handle (24, figure 1-7), shaped like an inflated chute, is on the center console. The handle has STOWED JETTISON and DEPLOY positions and is mechanically latched at each position. The handle must be pulled up before it can be moved. With the handle normally at STOWED JETTISON, the drag chute attachment hook is kept open so the drag chutes will jettison if the drag chute compartment doors accidently open in flight. Lifting and moving the handle to DEPLOY mechanically operates a right primary ac and essential ac bus powered control switch which directs No. 1 and No. 2 utility hydraulic pressure to close the attachment hook and open the compartment doors. When the doors open, the small spring-loaded pilot chute is thrust vertically into the slip stream and pulls out the main pilot chute. The main pilot chute pulls out both drag chutes simultaneously. (The inflated drag chute canopies trail about 68 feet behind the airplane.) After the chutes have been deployed, they may be jettisoned by lifting the handle and moving it to STOWED JETTISON. This opens the attachment hook and jettisons the drag chutes. The drag chute compartment doors remain open until manually closed by the ground crew. Refer to Section V for maximum drag chute deployment speeds and minimum jettisoning speeds.

DRAG CHUTE COMPARTMENT OVERHEAT CAUTION LIGHT.

Refer to "Drag Chute and Landing Gear Compartments Cooling System" in Section IV.

DRAG CHUTE HYDRAULIC SYSTEM

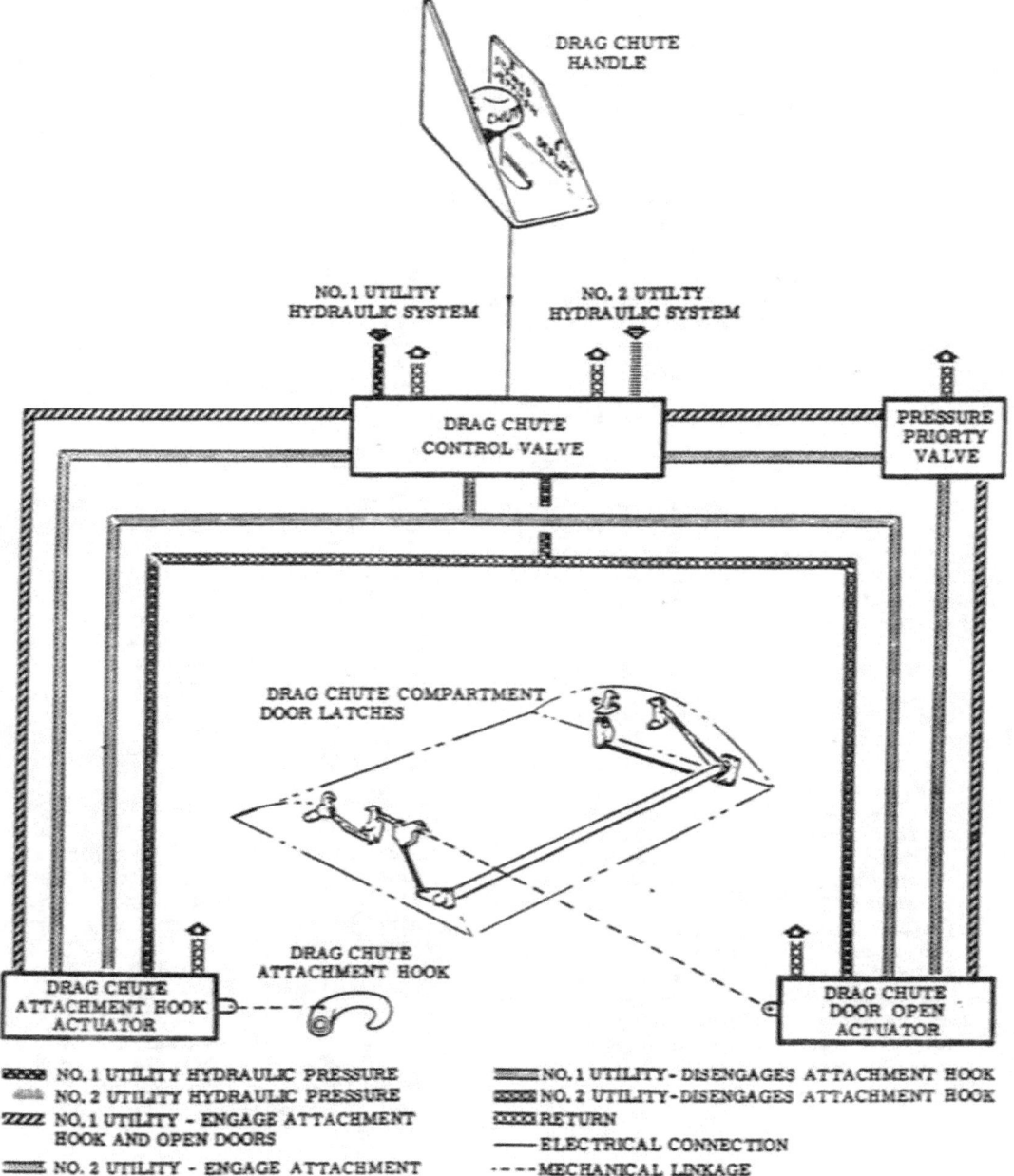

Figure 1-30

T.O. 1B-70(X)A-1

CENTRAL AIR DATA SYSTEM (CADS).

The central air data system furnishes aerodynamic data, in the form of usable electrical signals, for operation of various airplane and engine systems and for certain flight instruments. The system receives pitot and static pressures from the pitot-static probe in the nose boom and receives total air temperature data from a temperature probe on the underside of the fuselage. The pressure and temperature inputs are transmitted to an electromechanical air data computer which is powered by the right primary ac and dc busses. It converts this pneumatic and electrical input data into electrical signals which can be used by the applicable systems and instruments. Computer output signals represent prevailing Mach number, vertical velocity, pressure altitude, computed static pressure, and true airspeed, Mach rate of change, and altitude rate of change. The systems which depend on applicable output signals from the center air data system are: the anticollision light circuit, landing and taxi light circuit engine nozzle area controls, engine fuel controls, flight augmentation control system, air induction control system*, flight director computer, landing gear warning system, altitude - vertical velocity indicator, airspeed-Mach number indicator, and auxiliary gyro platform system. Critical functions of the system (flight augmentation control system and engine static pressure outputs) are provided with an altitude monitor circuit which indicates a malfunction. When a failure occurs, a caution light comes on and the system automatically switches to fixed outputs for the flight augmentation control system and to the engine exhaust nozzle standby control. Failure flags in the vertical scale indicators also provide an indication of air data system power failure, signal interruption, or some types of instrument malfunction.

AIR DATA SYSTEM CAUTION LIGHT.

The placard-type air data caution light (5, figure 1-7), on the center console, comes on to indicate air data computer altitude circuit failure or power failure to the air data computer. (This does not necessarily indicate a failure in the airspeed, Mach, or altitude rate portions of the central air data system.) The light receives power from the essential ac bus.

INSTRUMENTS.

The instruments covered here are those which are not an integral part of a complete system. For information on those instruments which are in particular systems, refer to applicable paragraphs in this section and Section IV.

PITOT-STATIC SYSTEMS.

The pitot-static system supplies pitot and static air pressures to the central air data system, the standby altimeters, and the standby airspeed indicators. The pitot-static probe is in the fixed boom at the nose of the airplane. An electrical heater provides probe anti-icing. (Refer to "Environmental Systems" in Section IV.)

AIRSPEED-MACH NUMBER INDICATORS.

Two airspeed-Mach number indicators (1, figure 1-3; 8, figure 1-4; and figure 1-31), one on the pilot's instrument panel and one on the copilot's instrument panel, are powered by the right primary ac bus. In addition to showing airspeed and Mach number, each indicator shows angle of attack and vertical acceleration(G). Airspeed and Mach number signals are supplied to the indicators by the central air data system. Angle of attack data is supplied from a vane-type sensor on the pitot boom, and acceleration signals are transmitted from a remote accelerator near the airplane center of gravity.

---

*Airplane AF62-001

Changed 25 June 1965

This page intentionally left blank

AIRSPEED/MACH NUMBER INDICATOR
(Typical)

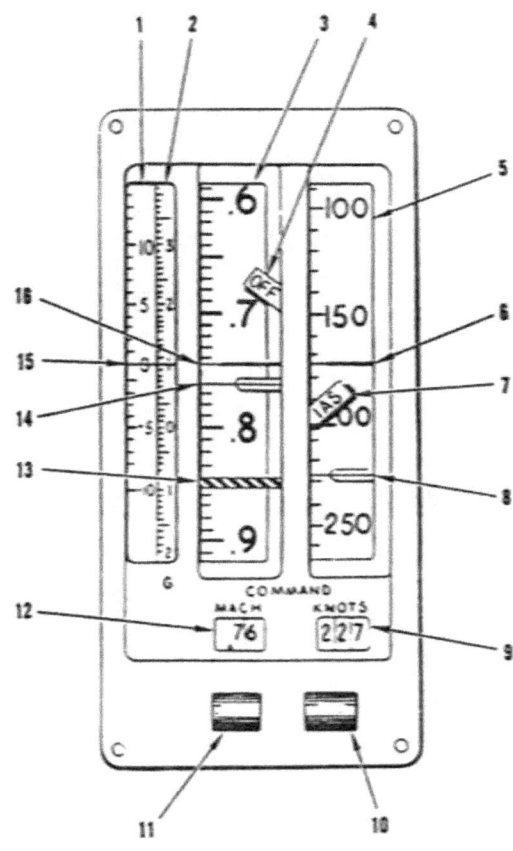

1. ANGLE OF ATTACK SCALE
2. ACCELERATION (G) SCALE
3. MACH SCALE
4. POWER OFF WARNING FLAG (MACH)
5. AIRSPEED SCALE
6. FIXED INDEX LINE (AIRSPEED)
7. AIRSPEED WARNING FLAG (POWER OFF)
8. COMMAND AIRSPEED MARKER
9. COMMAND AIRSPEED READOUT WINDOW
10. COMMAND AIRSPEED SLEWING SWITCH
11. COMMAND MACH SLEWING SWITCH
12. COMMAND MACH READOUT WINDOW
13. MAXIMUM ALLOWABLE MACH MARKER
14. COMMAND MACH MARKER
15. FIXED INDEX LINE (ANGLE OF ATTACK AND ACCELERATION)
16. FIXED INDEX LINE (MACH)

Figure 1-31

Airspeed is displayed on a vertically moving scale and is read against a fixed index line. The airspeed scale is calibrated in 10-knot increments. Mach number is read from the vertically moving Mach scale against a fixed index line. The Mach scale is calibrated in increments of 0.01 Mach number.

NOTE
For airspeed and Mach number correction data, refer to "Position Error Correction" in Part 1 of Appendix I.

Maximum allowable Mach number for prevailing flight altitude is indicated by a diagonally striped marker that moves vertically over the Mach scale. Whenever the maximum allowable Mach number is greater than the range visible on the Mach scale, the marker is out of view at the bottom of the scale. The marker remains hidden until the maximum allowable Mach number is within about 0.2 Mach number of the airplane Mach. Then, as the airplane Mach number increases, the marker moves up toward the Mach scale fixed index line. The airplane is at the maximum allowable Mach number when the marker is aligned with the Mach scale index line.

Angle of attack is read from a vertically moving scale against a fixed index line. The angle of attack scale is calibrated in 1-degree increments.

NOTE
The indicator shows indicated angle of attack, not true angle of attack.

The vertically moving acceleration scale is read against the same fixed index line as the angle of attack scale. The acceleration scale is calibrated in 0.1G increments.

Each airspeed-Mach number indicator also displays command Mach and command airspeed. Command settings are shown by two markers and two direct-reading digital counters. One command marker is on the Mach scale and one is on the airspeed scale. The command digital counters, one for Mach and one for airspeed, are visible through readout windows below the respective scales.

Each command marker is slaved to its respective scale, moving with it to show the command display continuously. However, if a command setting is not within the range visible on the moving scale, the marker remains at the top or bottom of the scale until the command setting is within range. Command Mach is selected by a slewing switch below the command Mach readout window; command airspeed is selected by a slewing switch below the command airspeed readout window. Moving either slewing switch up or down from its center (OFF) position increases or decreases respectively, the corresponding command setting. The rate of command setting change varies with the amount of switch movement. When a slewing switch is released to the spring-loaded center position, the command setting changing action stops immediately. The command airspeed slewing switch also can be locked in a position right of center. When this side position is selected, the command airspeed marker becomes centered at the airspeed scale fixed index line. As a result, the command airspeed then represents airplane airspeed, and the command airspeed readout window provides a continuous direct digital indication of airplane airspeed.

NOTE
Actuation of a slewing switch on one indicator changes the corresponding command setting on both indicators, with the "master" indicator (pilot's or copilot's) determined by the setting of the command control switch on the pilot's instrument panel. The slewing switches on the "slaved" indicator become inoperative.

If electrical power to the indicator system fails, or is not available, a warning flag appears across the Mach scale and another across the airspeed scale.

T.O. 1B-70(X)A-1

ALTITUDE-VERTICAL VELOCITY INDICATORS.

Two altitude-vertical velocity indicators (5, figure 1-3; 13, figure 1-4; and figure 1-32), one on the pilot's instrument panel and one on the copilot's instrument panel, are powered by the right primary ac bus. Each indicator shows vertical velocity and three altitude displays: gross altitude, sensitive altitude, and vernier altitude. Data signals for the altitude-vertical velocity indicators are supplied by the central air data system.

Vertical velocity is indicated by a triangular index. When the rate of climb or dive is less than 2000 feet per minute, the index moves against a fixed scale that is calibrated in 100-feet per minute increments. When the climb or dive rate exceeds 2000 feet per minute, the index is stopped above or below the fixed scale. Vertical velocity then is read from the index against a moving scale that appears above or below the fixed vertical velocity scale. (The upper moving scale is for climb; the lower scale is for dive.) The calibrations on the moving scales are not visible when the index is moving against the fixed scale.

Gross altitude is presented on the right side of the indicator and is shown by the gross altitude index which moves vertically against a fixed scale. The gross altitude scale is calibrated in 1000-foot increments. Sensitive altitude is read from the vertically moving altitude scale against a fixed index line. This altitude scale is calibrated in 500-foot increments. The vernier altitude scale, which is an endless tape calibrated in 50-foot increments, is read against the fixed vernier altitude index line. The vernier scale rotates through its entire range for each 1000-foot change of sensitive altitude on the altitude scale. When the altitude scale is at a whole 1000-foot increment, the vernier scale reads 0; when the altitude scale is between 1000-foot increments, the vernier scale shows the altitude. (The vernier scale reading must be added to the sensitive altitude reading to obtain total altitude.) Because sensitive altitude is presented in 500-foot increments, the vernier scale shows 500 feet whenever the sensitive altitude scale is at a 500-foot mark. The 0-foot and 500-foot markings on the vernier altitude scale are distinguished by white circles.

The altitude-vertical velocity indicator also has provisions for displaying command altitude. The command altitude is indicated by two markers and a direct reading digital counter. (One marker is on the sensitive altitude scale and one is on the gross altitude scale. The digital counter is visible through the command altitude readout window below the sensitive altitude scale.) The command altitude marker on the sensitive altitude scale is slaved to the scale, moving with it to show command altitude continuously. However, if the command altitude is not within the range visible on the scale, the marker remains at the top or bottom of the scale until the command altitude is within range. Command altitude is selected by a slewing switch below the command altitude readout window. Moving the switch up or down from the center (OFF) position increases or decreases respectively, the command altitude. The rate of command altitude change varies with the amount of switch movement. When the slewing switch is released to the spring-loaded center position, the command altitude changing action stops immediately. The slewing switch also can be locked in a position right of center. When this side position is selected, the command altitude marker on the sensitive altitude scale becomes centered at the fixed index line. As a result, the command altitude then represents airplane altitude and the command altitude

ALTITUDE - VERTICAL VELOCITY INDICATOR
(Typical)

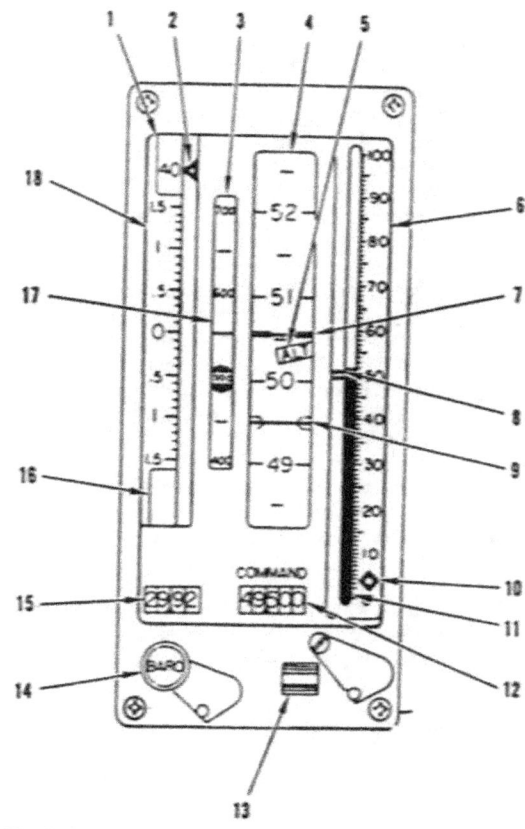

1. VERTICAL VELOCITY MOVING SCALE (CLIMB)
2. VERTICAL VELOCITY INDEX
3. VERNIER ALTITUDE SCALE
4. ALTITUDE SCALE (SENSITIVE ALTITUDE)
5. ALTITUDE WARNING FLAG (POWER OFF)
6. GROSS ALTITUDE SCALE
7. FIXED INDEX LINE (SENSITIVE ALTITUDE)
8. COMMAND ALTITUDE MARKER (GROSS ALTITUDE)
9. COMMAND ALTITUDE MARKER (SENSITIVE ALTITUDE)
10. TARGET ALTITUDE MARKER (NOT IN USE)
11. GROSS ALTITUDE INDEX (MOVABLE)
12. COMMAND ALTITUDE READOUT WINDOW
13. COMMAND ALTITUDE SLEWING SWITCH
14. BAROMETRIC PRESSURE SET KNOB
15. BAROMETRIC PRESSURE READOUT WINDOW
16. VERTICAL VELOCITY MOVING SCALE (DIVE)
17. VERNIER ALTITUDE FIXED INDEX LINE
18. VERTICAL VELOCITY FIXED SCALE

Figure 1-32

T.O. 1B-70(X)A-1

readout window provides a continuous direct digital indication of airplane altitude.

NOTE

Actuation of the slewing switch on one indicator changes the command altitude on both indicators, with the "master" indicator (pilot's or copilot's) determined by the setting of the command control switch on the pilot's instrument panel. The slewing switch on the "slaved" indicator becomes inoperative.

The altitude indications can be corrected for prevailing barometric pressure by using the barometric pressure set knob on the face of the indicator. A digital counter, visible through the readout window above the set knob, shows the pressure reading inserted by the knob. If electrical power to the indicator fails, or is not available, a warning flag (labeled "ALT") appears over the sensitive altitude scale.

NOTE

The diamond-shaped target altitude marker is inoperative and remains fixed on the gross altitude scale.

COMMAND CONTROL SWITCH.

Refer to "Flight Director System" in Section IV.

HORIZONTAL SITUATION INDICATORS (HSI).

Refer to "Flight Director System" in Section IV.

ATTITUDE DIRECTOR INDICATORS (ADI).

Refer to "Flight Director System" in Section IV.

ATTITUDE DIRECTOR INDICATOR SELECTOR SWITCH.

Refer to "Flight Director System" in Section IV.

STANDBY ATTITUDE INDICATOR.

The standby attitude indicator (12, figure 1-3), on the pilot's instrument panel, displays pitch and roll information relative to a fixed miniature airplane. The airplane attitude is shown accurately through 360 degrees of roll and ±82 degrees of pitch. Acceleration and deceleration cause slight errors in pitch indications which are most noticeable on take-off. Pitch and roll attitudes are shown by the circular motion of a universally mounted sphere. The miniature reference airplane is always in proper relationship to the simulated earth, horizon, and sky areas of the background sphere. On the sphere, the horizon is represented by a solid white line, the sky by a light gray area, and the earth by a dull black area. Horizontal markings with 5 degrees of separation on the face of the sphere show accurate airplane attitudes up to 82 degrees of climb or dive. The 30-and 60-degree lines are identified with figures. Bank angles are read on a semicircular bank scale on the upper half of the instrument. The pitch trim knob on the indicator electrically rotates the sphere to the proper position in relation to the miniature airplane to correct for pitch attitude changes. This adjustment is necessary because the level-flight attitude varies with weight and speed. The standby attitude gyro supplies pitch and roll angle information to the pilot's standby attitude indicator at all times, and to the copilot's attitude director indicator and to the flight director computer only when the attitude director indicator selector switch is at STBY. An attitude warning flag (labeled "OFF") appears when power is removed or interrupted and also remains in view for about one minute after right primary ac bus power is applied initially. The normal erection cycle takes about one minute.

WARNING

A slight reduction in power, or failure of certain electrical components within the system will not cause "OFF" to appear even though the system is not functioning properly. Therefore, periodically in flight, the attitude indications given should be checked against other flight instruments.

If a fast erection of the gyro is required, use of the fast erection button erects the gyro in about 10 to 15 seconds. There are no manual gyro caging provisions because the system cages automatically. If the pitch limits of the instrument are extended, the sphere will tumble, reversing the normal sky and earth reference, but still providing an accurate indication of airplane attitude. As soon as the airplane returns within limits, the sphere automatically rolls back to its normal position. However, after prolonged accelerations or adverse flight conditions, accumulation of standby gyro precession can cause false indications on the standby attitude indicator. When necessary, use the standby gyro fast erect button to realign the gyro after checking with other flight instruments or the horizon for normal level-flight attitude.

STANDBY GYRO FAST ERECT BUTTON.

The standby gyro fast erect button (27, figure 1-3), on the pilot's instrument panel, is powered by the right primary ac bus. The button provides fast erection for the pilot's standby attitude gyro, and must be pushed in and held for 10 to 15 seconds to complete the gyro erection cycle.

STANDBY AIRSPEED INDICATORS.

The two standby airspeed indicators (35, figure 1-3; 17, figure 1-4), one on the pilot's instrument panel and one on the copilot's instrument panel, are conventional airspeed indicators. The airspeed is indicated in knots by a pointer read against a fixed dial scale ranging from 100 to 850. In case of a complete central air data system failure, the standby airspeed indicators will still operate.

STANDBY ALTIMETERS.

Two standby altimeters (13, figure 1-3; 18, figure 1-4), one on the pilot's instrument panel and one on the copilot's instrument panel are conventional altimeters with the standard 100-, 1000-, and 10,000-foot pointers, barometric pressure window, and barometric setting knob. In case of a complete central air data system failure, the standby altimeters will still operate.

TOTAL TEMPERATURE GAGE.

The total temperature gage (8, figure 1-3), on the pilot's instrument panel, shows outside airstream total temperature. The temperature is indicated in degrees Fahrenheit, by a pointer on a scale ranging from 0 to 700 degrees, in 50-degree increments, and also by digits in the upper window in the dial. The window indication provides a more accurate reading. A temperature sensing probe on the underside of the fuselage supplies signals directly to the gage. The total temperature gage system is powered by the right primary ac bus. If electrical power is not available to the gage, "OFF" appears in the lower window in the dial.

T.O. 1B-70(X)A-1

CLOCKS.

The type A-13A, 8-day clocks (32, figure 1-3 and 23, figure 1-4) on the pilot's and copilot's instrument panels are hand-wound, and each has a winding knob on the lower left section of the bezel. Clockwise rotation of the winding knob winds the clock. To set the hour and minute hands the winding knob must be pulled out. A start-stop-reset button on the upper right section of the bezel controls the sweep second hand and a minute totalizer hand. Pressing this button starts the second and minute totalizer hands. Pressing the button a second time stops both hands. Pressing the button the third time resets both hands to the 12 o'clock position and places the clock in readiness for again measuring elapsed time.

ANNUNCIATOR (INDICATOR, CAUTION, AND WARNING) LIGHTS.

Malfunctions, marginal operating conditions, or the status of certain systems are indicated by placard-type annunciator lights (1 and 5, figure 1-7) on the center console and instrument panels. Some lights give specific information, while others direct attention to other indicators in the crew compartment. Each placard-type light has two bulbs to ensure illumination if one bulb fails. A transformer in each light circuit steps down the bus voltage to 6.3 volts for light operation.

NOTE
For detailed information on specific annunciator lights, refer to applicable system descriptions in this section and in Section IV.

MASTER CAUTION LIGHTS.

The two placard-type master caution lights (6, figure 1-3 and 9, figure 1-4), one on the pilot's instrument panel and one on the copilot's instrument panel, are powered by the essential ac bus. Both master caution lights come on simultaneously when any individual system annunciator light comes on, with the exception of the following lights: trim for take-off, bail-out, brake control, fire-warning/engine shutdown, landing gear warning, landing gear position, vibration, and air start on. The master caution lights also come on if any hydraulic pump status indicator turns yellow. When the master caution lights come on, the specific malfunctioning system should be determined by referring to the lights or indicators on the annunciator light panel and one of the master caution lights must be pressed momentarily. This extinguishes both master caution lights and the master caution light system is ready for another fault signal.

NOTE
If neither master caution light is pressed, both stay on as long as the malfunction exists. (The specific annunciator light also remains on as long as the indicated condition exists.) If the indicated condition clears, or is transient, the master caution lights and the specific annunciator light go out.

ANNUNCIATOR LIGHTS INTENSITY SWITCH.

Annunciator light intensity is controlled by a three-position switch (2, figure 1-7) on the center console. The switch is spring-loaded from BRIGHT and DIM to a center neutral position. Momentarily holding the switch at the BRIGHT or DIM position closes holding relays to maintain the annunciator lights at the selected intensity. The lights cannot be dimmed unless the engine instrument indirect lighting is on and instrument flood lighting is at or below 80 percent of full brightness. Increasing the brightness of the instrument floodlights above 80 percent of full brightness or turning the engine instrument lights off automatically cancels the dimming action, and the annunciator lights will come on bright. Electrical power for the intensity switch is provided by the essential ac bus.

T.O. 1B-70(X)A-1

ANNUNCIATOR LIGHT TEST SWITCH.

A three-position switch (3, figure 1-7) on the center console tests the bulbs in the annunciator lights as well as the individual components in the lighting circuits. Holding the switch at BRIGHT or DIM tests the lights at the selected intensity. The switch is spring-loaded to the center (OFF) position. When the annunciator light dim circuit has been engaged, the lights can only be tested dim in either position of the test switch. When dimming is cancelled, the lights can be tested either bright or dim by selecting the appropriate test switch position. The essential ac bus supplies power for the test switch.

EMERGENCY EQUIPMENT.

ENGINE AND ACCESSORY DRIVE SYSTEM COMPARTMENT FIRE DETECTION SYSTEM.

The fire detection system is a continuous type with a dual sensing circuit in each engine compartment and a dual sensing circuit in each accessory drive system compartment. The individual dual circuits operate independently to provide system reliability. Both of the circuits would have to fail to give a false warning. Red warning lights in the crew compartment indicate a fire and/or overtemperature condition in an engine compartment or its respective accessory drive system compartment.

FIRE WARNING LIGHTS/ENGINE SHUTDOWN BUTTONS.

The six fire warning lights are integral with the engine shutdown buttons (7, figure 1-5) on the center instrument panel. The buttons are flush with the panel and each is numbered to correspond to its respective engine and accessory drive system compartment. Illumination of any individual fire warning light indicates a fire or overheat condition in the corresponding engine or accessory drive compartment. The illuminated button should be pushed in to a locked position (about 3/8 inch) to shut down the engine. Pushing the button closes the corresponding fire wall shutoff valve, which stops fuel flow to the engine. Also, when the button is pressed, the bypass air valve is locked closed, the boundary layer bleed diverter valve is locked opened, and the fire extinguisher discharge circuit is armed for the corresponding engine and accessory drive compartment. The fire warning light remains on until the fire goes out or the overheat condition is eliminated. However, once a shutdown button is pushed it remains in until the system is reset on the ground, or it will be released if another shutdown button for a compartment on the same side is pressed.

CAUTION

- Before another shutdown button is pressed, the throttle of the first engine must be retarded to OFF. This prevents the fire wall shutoff valve from opening when the first button is reset by actuation of the second button.
- The engine cannot be restarted while the shutdown button is in. If subsequent emergency actuation of another shutdown button on the same side is necessary, the first button will be released; and a restart of its corresponding engine then is possible if windmill brake has not been actuated. Such a restart is not recommended because the bypass valve remains closed, the boundary layer bleed diverter valve remains open (preventing adequate engine compartment cooling above Mach 0.7), and the fire or overheat condition may reoccur.

The fire warning light/engine shutdown button circuits normally are powered by the essential ac bus. If this power is not available, a switch in the crew compartment permits these circuits to be powered by the right primary ac bus.

1-118

Changed 25 June 1965

T.O. 1B-70(X)A-1

ENGINE AND ACCESSORY DRIVE SYSTEM COMPARTMENT FIRE DETECTION SYSTEM TEST SWITCHES.

The engine and accessory drive system fire detection test switches (21 and 13, figure 1-9) are on the copilot's console and are powered by the essential ac bus. There are two switches (a power switch and a test switch) for checking the engine fire detection circuits and two for checking the accessory drive system circuits. Each LIGHTS OFF position of the test switches checks one of the dual circuits in the corresponding fire detection system. Each system is tested by moving the power switch to ON. With the corresponding circuit test switch in the center (OFF) position, all fire warning lights should come on. The circuit test switch then is moved to one of the LIGHTS OFF positions and the lights should go out. When the lights go out, the test switch should be moved through the center position, (the lights come on if the switch is centered) to the other LIGHTS OFF position. If all lights go out with the switch in this position the circuits are satisfactory. When the test switch is returned to the center position, the lights come back on. The power switch is then moved to OFF (lights go out).

NOTE

The engine circuits and accessory drive system circuits cannot be tested at the same time as they both illuminate the same fire warning light.

THROTTLE AND FIRE DETECTION BUS SELECTOR SWITCH.

Refer to "Electrical Power Supply System" in this section.

ENGINE AND ACCESSORY DRIVE SYSTEM COMPARTMENT FIRE EXTINGUISHER SYSTEMS.

There are two separate fire extinguishing systems, one for the engines and accessory drive system compartments of engines 1, 2, and 3 and another for engines and accessory drive system compartments of engines 4, 5, and 6. (See figure 1-33.) Each system has two storage containers (each containing 64 pounds of agent), in insulated compartments behind the main landing gear wheel well. A pressure gage is mounted on each container. (These gages cannot be checked by the pilot during preflight.) To provide cooling for the storage containers, dry ice can be added to the container compartments if high-speed flight is anticipated. The extinguishing agent is dibromodifluoromethane (CBr_2F_2) pressurized to 600 psi with nitrogen. The system discharges the extinguishing agent into the selected engine compartment and the corresponding accessory drive system compartment simultaneously. The extinguishing agent of the selected container is discharged in about two seconds.

FIRE EXTINGUISHER AGENT DISCHARGE SWITCHES.

Two fire extinguisher discharge switches (4 and 5, figure 1-5), one for engines 1, 2, and 3 and one for engines 4, 5, and 6, are on the center instrument panel. The switches are spring-loaded from either MAIN or RES to a center off position. When a fire warning light/engine shutdown button is pushed in, the fire extinguisher circuit for the specific engine is armed. Subsequent movement of the appropriate discharge switch to MAIN, ignites a cartridge within the frangible-disc type discharge valve of one extinguisher agent storage container. When the cartridge is ignited, the frangible disc is ruptured and the extinguishing agent is discharged by nitrogen pressure into the selected accessory drive system and engine compartments. If use of one container does not extinguish the fire, moving the discharge switch to RES discharges the second container to the selected compartment. The extinguisher discharge circuits normally are powered by the right primary ac bus. If this power is not available, the essential ac bus automatically powers these circuits.

Changed 25 June 1965

ENGINE AND ACCESSORY DRIVE SYSTEM COMPARTMENT FIRE EXTINGUISHING SYSTEM

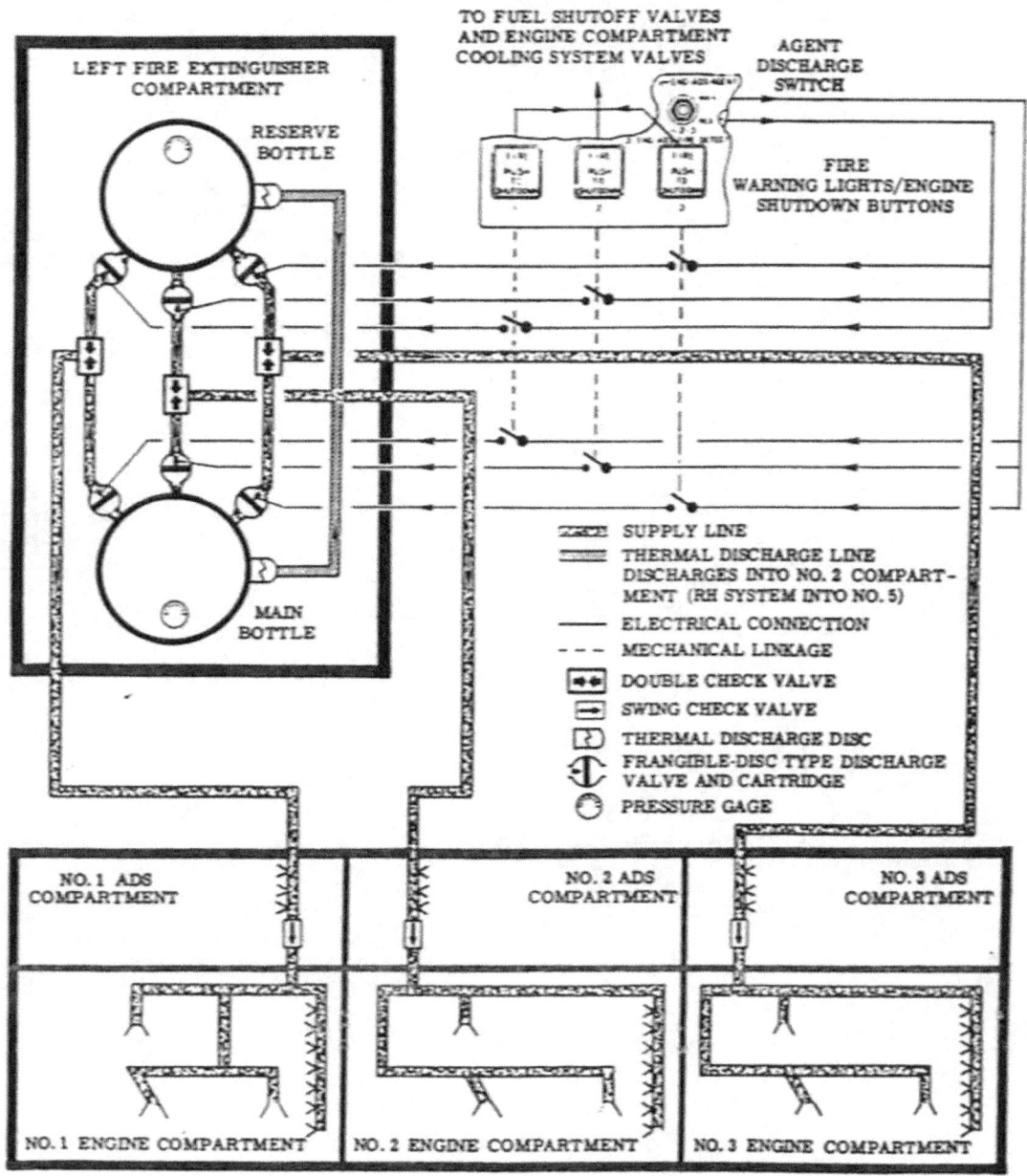

Figure 1-33

T.O. 1B-70(X)A-1

GROUND EMERGENCY ESCAPE HATCH.

The ground emergency escape hatch is on the top of the fuselage on the right side of the electronic equipment compartment. (See figure 1-34.) The hatch can be force-jettisoned by a ballistic remover actuated by any of three "T" handles, two internal and one external. One internal jettison handle (1, figure 1-8) is forward of the pilot's console. The other (figure 1-34) is in a compartment on the left side of the ground escape aisle, below the escape hatch. The external jettison handle (figure 1-34), stowed behind an access door on the lower right side of the fuselage, is attached to a 20-foot cable to permit ground personnel to stand clear when the handle is actuated. Each handle is connected to a mechanically actuated initiator which is fired when its corresponding handle is pulled and causes the hatch remover to fire. (The initiators actuated by the pilot's jettison handle and the external jettison handle fire pressure-actuated initiators which, in turn, fire the remover. The initiator in the ground escape aisle fires the remover directly.) A ground maintenance safety pin may be installed in each handle-actuated initiator. All these safety pins must be removed before flight.

The hatch also can be removed manually from the inside by unlocking the hatch locks with a handle stowed next to the internal jettison handle compartment. (See figure 1-34.) The hatch lock release handle must be attached to a small lever on the hatch-locking mechanism and pulled down to unlock the hatch. When the hatch has been released manually, it can be pushed up and aft for removal. (The ground escape hatch weighs about 155 pounds.)

GROUND ESCAPE ROPES.

Two ground escape ropes provide a means of escape from the airplane while it is on the ground. These 3/8-inch-diameter nylon ropes are long enough to reach the ground from either the entrance door or the ground escape hatch. Each escape rope has a hand strap attached to the housing of a descent device called a Sky Genie. The rope is wound around the center shaft in the Sky Genie. The rate of descent depends on the number of rope turns around the center shaft, which can be checked through the transparent housing of the Sky Genie. (Maintenance personnel must rerig the unit if there are not four or five turns around the shaft.) Both escape ropes are stowed in a fabric container on the bulkhead forward of the entrance door. (See figure 3-2.) One end of each rope is anchored to a common bracket on the fuselage structure. A pip pin is tied to the rope about 11 feet from the anchored end. If escape is to be made through the entrance door, the pip pin must be inserted into a fitting just above the door opening and the free end of the rope dropped out the door opening. If escape is to be made through the ground escape hatch, the pip pins are not used, as the ropes extend from the anchor point through the hatch opening, over the leading edge of the right canard. (See figure 3-6.)

CAUTION

There should be a minimum of slack rope between the genie and attachment point of the rope to reduce the G-load when the user jumps free of the airplane.

NOTE

Descent may be stopped by grasping the free end of the rope below the Sky Genie.

HAND FIRE EXTINGUISHER.

A Type A-20 portable bromochloromethane (CB) fire extinguisher is mounted on the inside of the entrance door for use in case of internal fires. (See figure 3-2.) The extinguishing agent (CB) is pressurized to between 150 and 175 psi. The pressure is indicated by a gage on the extinguisher. Discharge of the

Changed 25 June 1965

GROUND EMERGENCY ESCAPE HATCH

WARNING
ALL INITIATOR MAINTENANCE SAFETY
PINS MUST BE REMOVED BEFORE FLIGHT

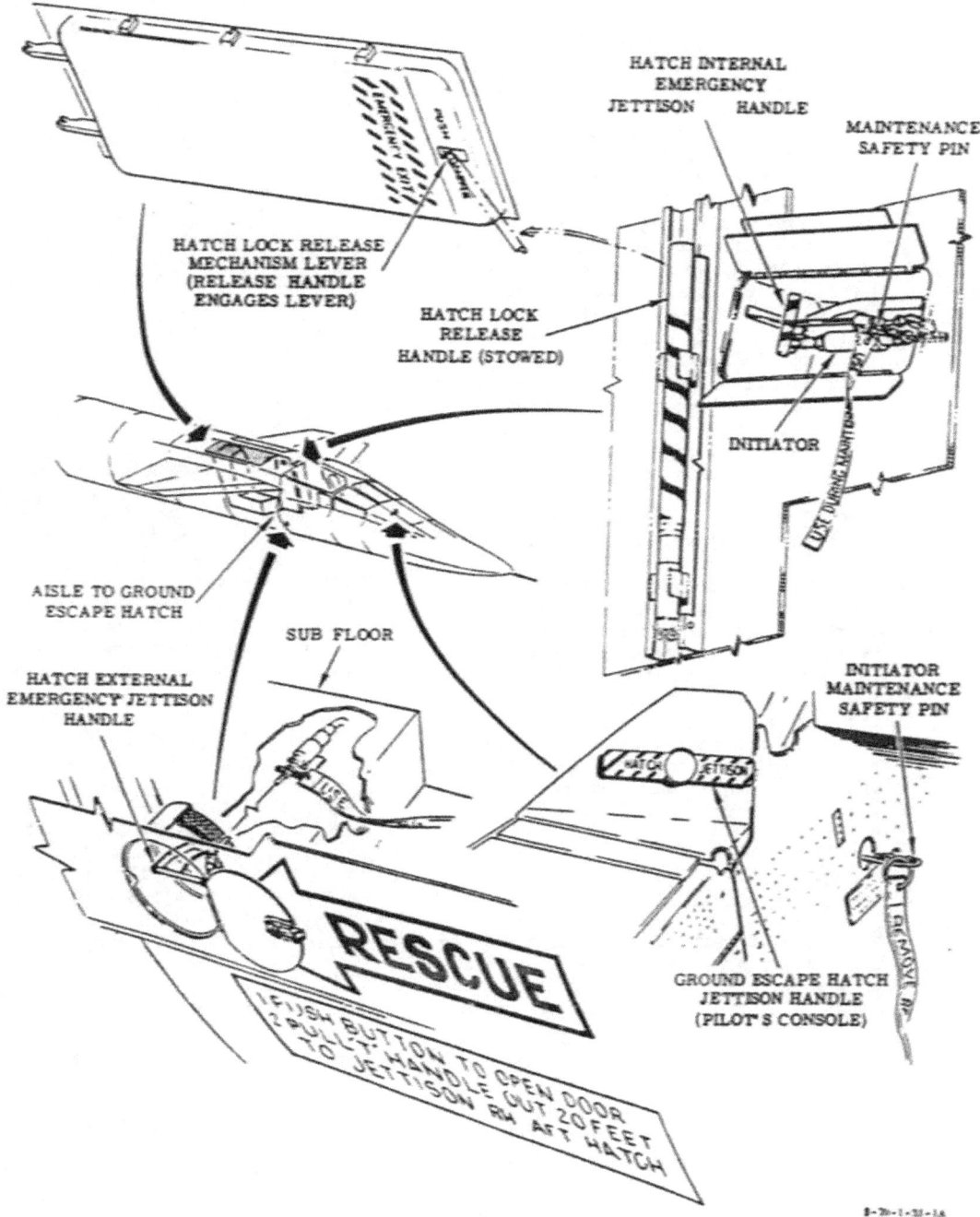

Figure 1-34

T.O. 1B-70(X)A-1

agent is controlled by a trigger-type handle on the top of the extinguisher which permits one-hand operation. The extinguisher can be used for any type of fire.

WARNING

Prolonged (5 minutes or more) exposure to high concentrations of bromochloromethane (CB) or products of its decomposition should be avoided. Bromochloromethane is an anesthetic agent of moderate intensity. It is safer to use than previously used fire extinguishing agents (carbon tetrachloride, methylbromide). However, especially in confined spaces, adequate respiratory and eye protection from excessive exposure, including the use of oxygen when available, should be sought as soon as the primary fire emergency permits.

Bromochloromethane is highly corrosive to some metals, paints, and plastic materials. Therefore, if the extinguisher starts to leak, it can be made harmless by being discharged from an inverted position. This releases the pressurizing gas charge with a minimum discharge of fluid. (Cover the nozzle with a cloth or aim into a receptacle to catch any discharged liquid.) Return the depressurized extinguisher to its bracket, and make suitable entry in the Form 781 (or equivalent) so that the unit will be replaced.

BAIL-OUT WARNING SYSTEM.

The bail-out warning system permits the pilot to instruct the copilot to encapsulate and eject from the airplane. The system also provides the pilot with a visual indication that the copilot has encapsulated.

ENCAPSULATE CAUTION LIGHT SWITCH.

The three-position encapsulate caution light switch (10, figure 1-3) on the pilot's instrument panel is mechanically latched in the OFF position and must be pulled out before it can be moved to either ON or RESET. The switch is used by the pilot to reset the IFF circuit and instruct the copilot to encapsulate. Moving the switch to ON illuminates the encapsulate light on the copilot's instrument panel and gives the pilot and copilot a hot intercom microphone. The RESET position is used after decapsulation to turn off the IFF and reset the IFF circuit for the next encapsulation. The switch is spring-loaded from RESET to OFF and receives power from the essential ac bus.

BAIL-OUT WARNING LIGHT BUTTON.

The bail-out warning light button (11, figure 1-3), on the pilot's instrument panel, receives power from the essential ac bus. If a decision is made to eject, the pilot pushes the bail-out button before he encapsulates. This illuminates the copilot's bail-out warning light. The button also provides a hot intercom microphone in each escape capsule.

ENCAPSULATE CAUTION LIGHT.

The placard-type encapsulate caution light (11, figure 1-4), on the copilot's instrument panel, is powered by the essential ac bus. The light comes on to instruct the copilot to encapsulate when the pilot activates the encapsulate caution light switch or when the pilot's escape capsule doors close.

CREW ENCAPSULATED INDICATOR LIGHT.

The placard-type crew encapsulated indicator light (4, figure 1-3), on the pilot's instrument panel, receives power from the essential ac bus. It comes on when the copilot's escape capsule doors close and shows the pilot that the copilot has encapsulated.

T.O. 1B-70(X)A-1

BAIL-OUT WARNING LIGHT.

The placard-type bail-out warning light (7, figure 1-4) is on the copilot's instrument panel. The light is powered by the essential ac bus and illuminates when the pilot pushes the bail-out warning light button to instruct the copilot to bail out.

WINDSHIELD.

The windshield assembly includes a fixed inner windshield, a movable outer windshield, and two fixed side windows. The use of a movable windshield permits an unbroken fuselage contour for low drag at high-speed flight with improved visibility during low speed. The fixed inner windshield, which provides the pressure barrier for cabin pressurization, consists of a front panel, two windshield side panels, and three overhead panels. The fixed windshield panels are laminated and the front and side panels contain a transparent, electrically heated film to defog the glass. (Refer to "Fixed Windshield Defogging" in Section IV.) The movable windshield which consists of three upper and two side panels is controlled by a switch in the crew compartment. The panels of this windshield are single-pane, full-tempered glass. The nose ramp is attached to and moves with a two position, hydraulically actuated movable windshield. A hydraulically operated linkage, attached to the forward edge of the windshield, raises and lowers the windshield and ramp. (See figure 1-35.) The movable windshield has a fixed pivot at the lower aft edge and a rotating pivot at the forward upper edge. The windshield and nose ramp assembly is sealed to the adjacent structure by a metal bellows at the aft end and a silicone-rubber fabric seal along the sides and front. This sealing prevents dust and moisture from entering the air gap between the inner fixed windshield and the outer movable windshield. The movable windshield and nose ramp are raised to a 14-degree windshield slope to form the unbroken fuselage contour and are lowered to 24-degree windshield slope for visibility. The airplane may be flown at supersonic speeds with the windshield and nose ramp down if maximum range is not a requirement.

CAUTION

Sustained operation with the windshield down at speeds above Mach 2.5 may result in deterioration of the inner windshield glass edge attachment bonds and inner layer.

The two fixed side windows are on each side of the fuselage aft of the movable windshield. The side windows have inner and outer glass panels separated by an air gap. A defogging system is provided for the air gap between the movable and fixed windshield and air gap between the fixed side window panels. (Refer to "Movable Windshield Defogging" in Section IV.)

NOSE RAMP SWITCH.

The two-position nose ramp switch (20, figure 1-5), on the center instrument panel, is powered by the essential ac bus. The UP and DOWN positions of the switch control the nose ramp solenoid control valve to direct No. 2 utility hydraulic system pressure to the nose ramp actuator and uplock cylinder. When the nose ramp switch is moved to UP, hydraulic pressure first raises the ramp then locks the uplock. A limit switch de-energizes the solenoid valve when the windshield and ramp are up and locked. The windshield and ramp are held in the up position by the uplock. When the windshield nose ramp switch is moved to DOWN, the hydraulic pressure first unlocks the uplock; then the actuator lowers the ramp. The actuator acts as a mechanical stop for the down position of the windshield and ramp, and hydraulic pressure is maintained to hold the windshield and ramp down.

1-124

MOVABLE WINDSHIELD AND RAMP SYSTEM

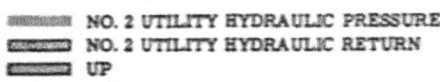

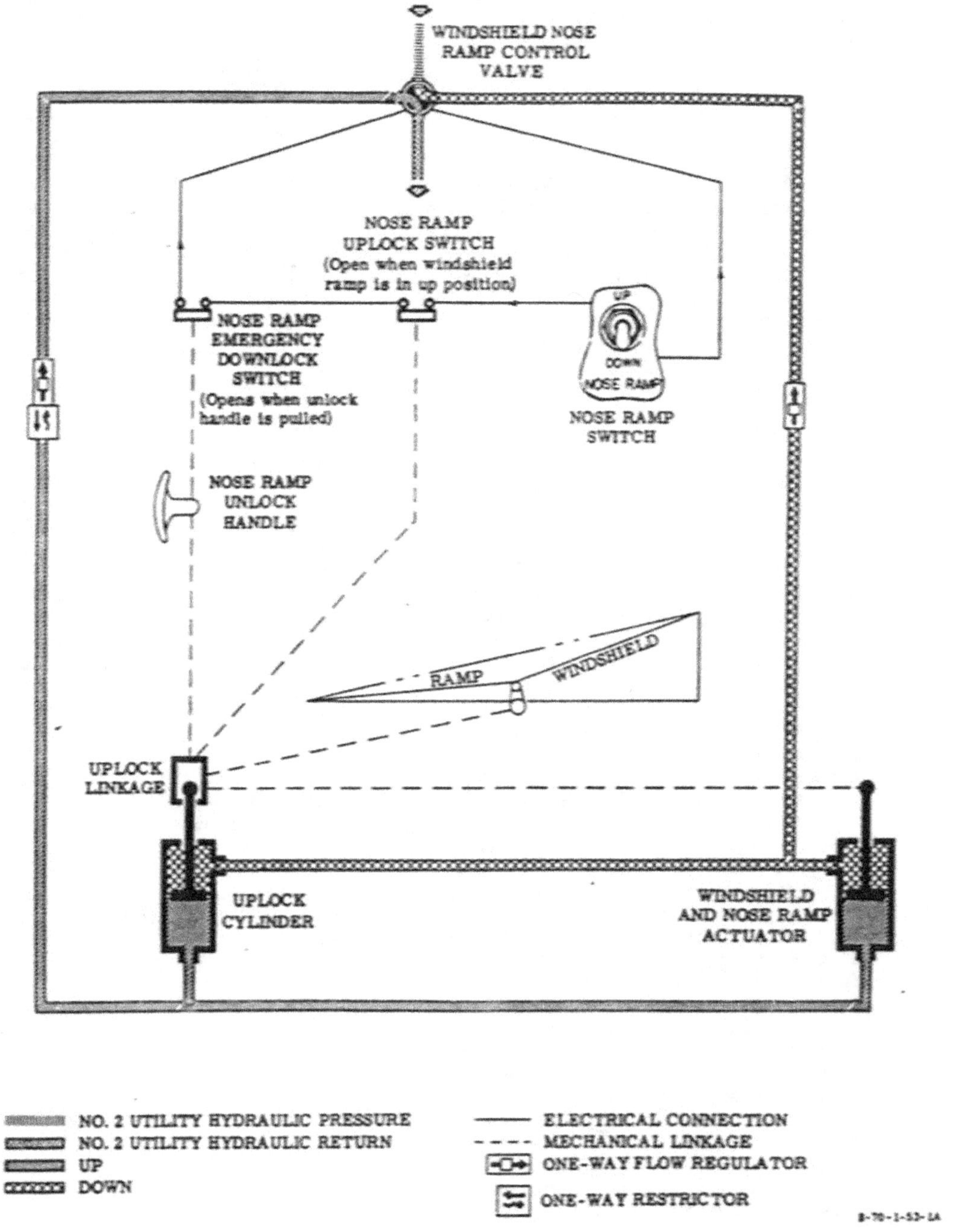

Figure 1-35

T.O. 1B-70(X)A-1

NOSE RAMP UNLOCK HANDLE.

The nose ramp unlock handle (1, figure 1-9) ahead of the copilot's console is used to lower the windshield if the normal control system fails. When the handle is pulled out about 4 inches, the unlock is released mechanically. Air loads then force the windshield and nose ramp to the down position. To ensure full downlock engagement of the nose ramp, the handle must be pulled at airspeeds above 300 knots IAS at 1G at any altitude. The mechanism engages an emergency downlock linkage which locks the windshield and nose ramp in the down positions. A downlock switch, in the nose ramp up-circuit, is opened when the handle is pulled to prevent operation and damage to the downlock linkage if subsequent operation of the nose ramp is attempted before resetting the downlock.

CAUTION

After use, the unlock handle and downlock linkage must be reset on the ground before the next mission.

ENTRANCE DOOR.

The inward opening plug-type crew entrance door (5, figure 1-1) is on the left side of the fuselage, forward of the canard. An inflatable and dynamic pressure seal actuated by the secondary pressurization system seals the door. The door is opened from the outside by a flush handle near the top center of the door. The handle is released from its recess by a push plate on the handle. When the handle is out of its recess, rotating it clockwise about 45 degrees releases the latches and seal pressure so the door can be opened. After the door is opened, the exterior handle must be stowed in its recess by pressing the handle in and rotating it about 45 degrees counterclockwise. When the handle is over the recess it must be pressed in to engage a latch.

CAUTION

- Before the door is closed from inside, the exterior handle must be stowed flush to prevent damage.

- The air recirculating fans must be off before attempting to open or close the door. Fan operation will prevent door opening or will cause the door to slam closed.

Latching the door from the inside is accomplished by turning an exposed handle clockwise about 45 degrees to CLOSE after the door is shut. The door is opened from the inside by turning the handle to OPEN.

WARNING

Before leaving by the door, which is about 17 feet above ground level, make sure an adequate ladder is in place. (Refer to "Emergency Ground Escape" in Section III for emergency exit without a ladder.)

SEATS AND ESCAPE CAPSULES.

A combination seat and escape capsule at each crew station permits ejection from the airplane and provides crew protection during and after ejection. (See figure 3-5 for ejection speeds and altitudes.) The capsule also provides in-flight pressurization protection during emergencies.

SEATS.

The pilot's and copilot's seats are an integral part of their respective capsules. (See figure 1-36.) Both seats are identical and each is equipped with a combination shoulder harness and restraint harness with buckles on the lap belt and on the chest strap. An inertia reel is part of the restraint harness and is controlled by a lever on

1-126

the seat. A contoured seat cushion and back pad are attached to the seat. The headrest and armrests are faced with energy absorbent material. Vertical adjustment of the seat is done electrically. Folding armrests can be raised by lifting the armrest or lowered by pushing a lever attached to the front of each. Personal leads are fitted into a disconnect block at the lower center forward edge of the seat. The emergency oxygen "green apple" also is located in this area. Upon initiation of encapsulation, the seat retracts into the capsule and the forward portion of the seat bottom rotates upward to aid in proper leg positioning. The seat is locked when in either the extended or retracted position and can be manually released by a lever on the seat right console.

SHOULDER HARNESS INERTIA REEL.

The gas-operated multidirectional-type shoulder harness inertia reel below the headrest of the seat has a manual control to permit selection of reel locking. The reel automatically locks the shoulder harness when the straps are pulled from the reel with an acceleration of 2G to 3G in any direction. This locking depends only on the speed at which the straps are pulled from the reel and not on the load imposed upon the reel itself. During encapsulation, when the seat is ballistically retracted into the capsule, gas pressure to the inertia reel retracts and locks the shoulder harness.

ESCAPE CAPSULES.

Each escape capsule (figure 1-36), with the seat inside, permits safe crew ejection and provides crew in-flight pressurization protection for emergencies. A ballistic rocket catapult supplies the necessary propulsion to eject the capsule and occupant from the airplane. Each capsule has self-contained oxygen and pressurization systems. The capsule can be closed manually at any time or is closed ballistically when the handgrips are raised and both heel pedals pressed. Upon ballistic encapsulation, the respective control column is stowed automatically, the seat is retracted into the capsule, and the pair of clamshell doors close from the top and bottom. Closing of the doors automatically inflates the capsule seals and actuates the capsule pressurization system. If the intercom and IFF are set up before encapsulating, closing the capsule doors turns on the emergency IFF and provides hot mike intercom to permit crew communication after encapsulation. (The hot mike intercom system and emergency IFF also are turned on when either the encapsulate caution light switch or bail-out warning light switch is actuated.) An emergency descent control grip, incorporating a trim switch and engine retard button, is in each capsule for control of the airplane while the crew is encapsulated. (Refer to "Inlet Reaction Upon Decapsulation" in Section VII.) Windows in the capsule and capsule doors provide a view of the flight instruments after the capsules are closed and a view of the recovery chute, impact bladder, and approaching terrain after ejection. (The instrument panel area visible through the capsule windows with the head against the headrest is shown in figures 1-3 and 1-4. By unlocking the inertia reel and putting head close to the window, the entire instrument panel can be seen.) Upon ejection, chaff is released and stabilization booms with small parachutes automatically extend to stabilize the capsule. If ejection occurs above 15,500 feet, an aneroid device prevents deployment of the capsule recovery parachute until this altitude is reached. At the preset altitude, the aneroids initiate deployment of the pilot chute which pulls out the capsule recovery chute. A warning light in each capsule comes on at parachute deployment altitude to alert the occupant that the parachute should have deployed at this time. Manual controls are provided to substitute for the

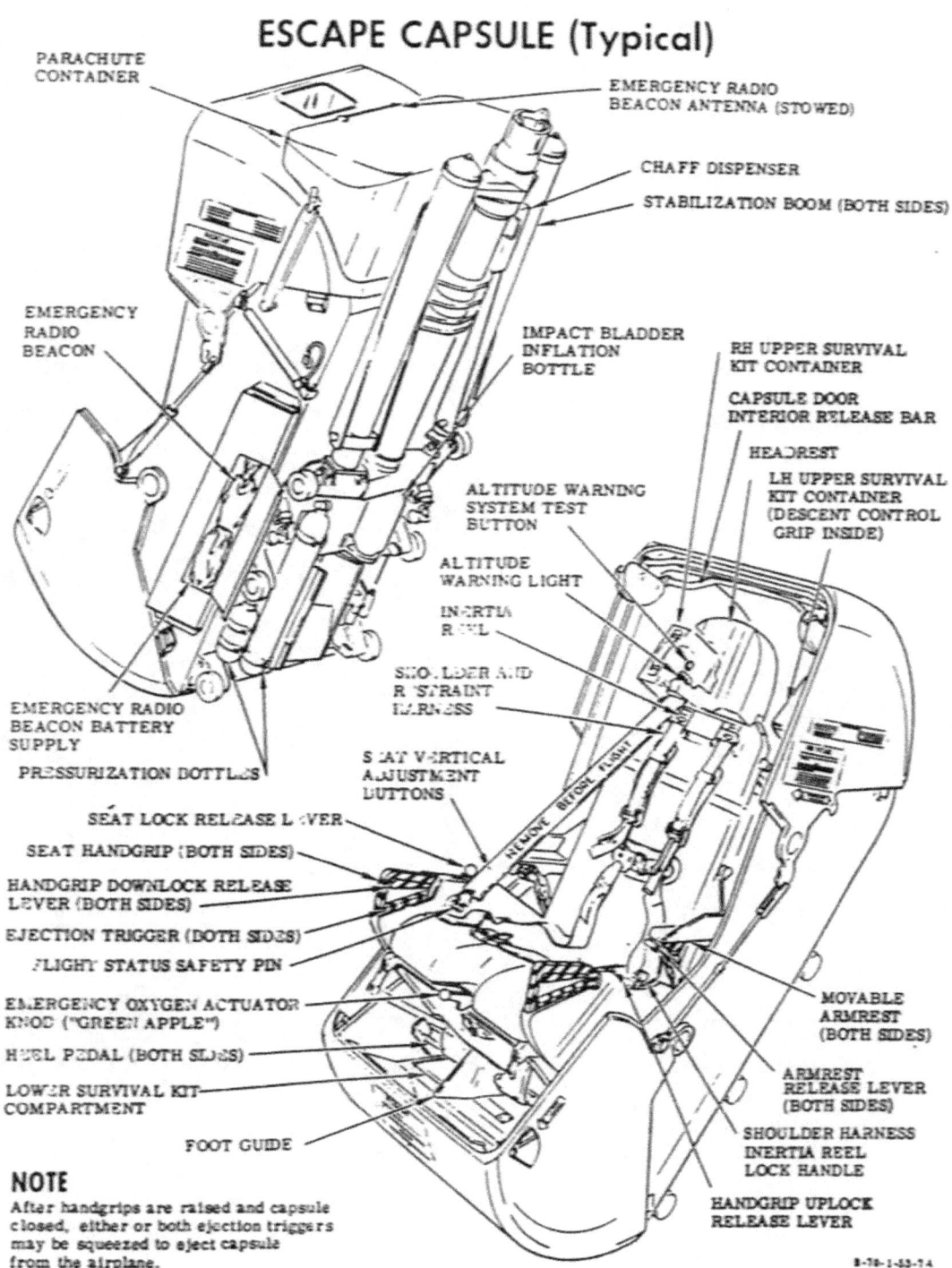

Figure 1-36 (Sheet 1 of 2)

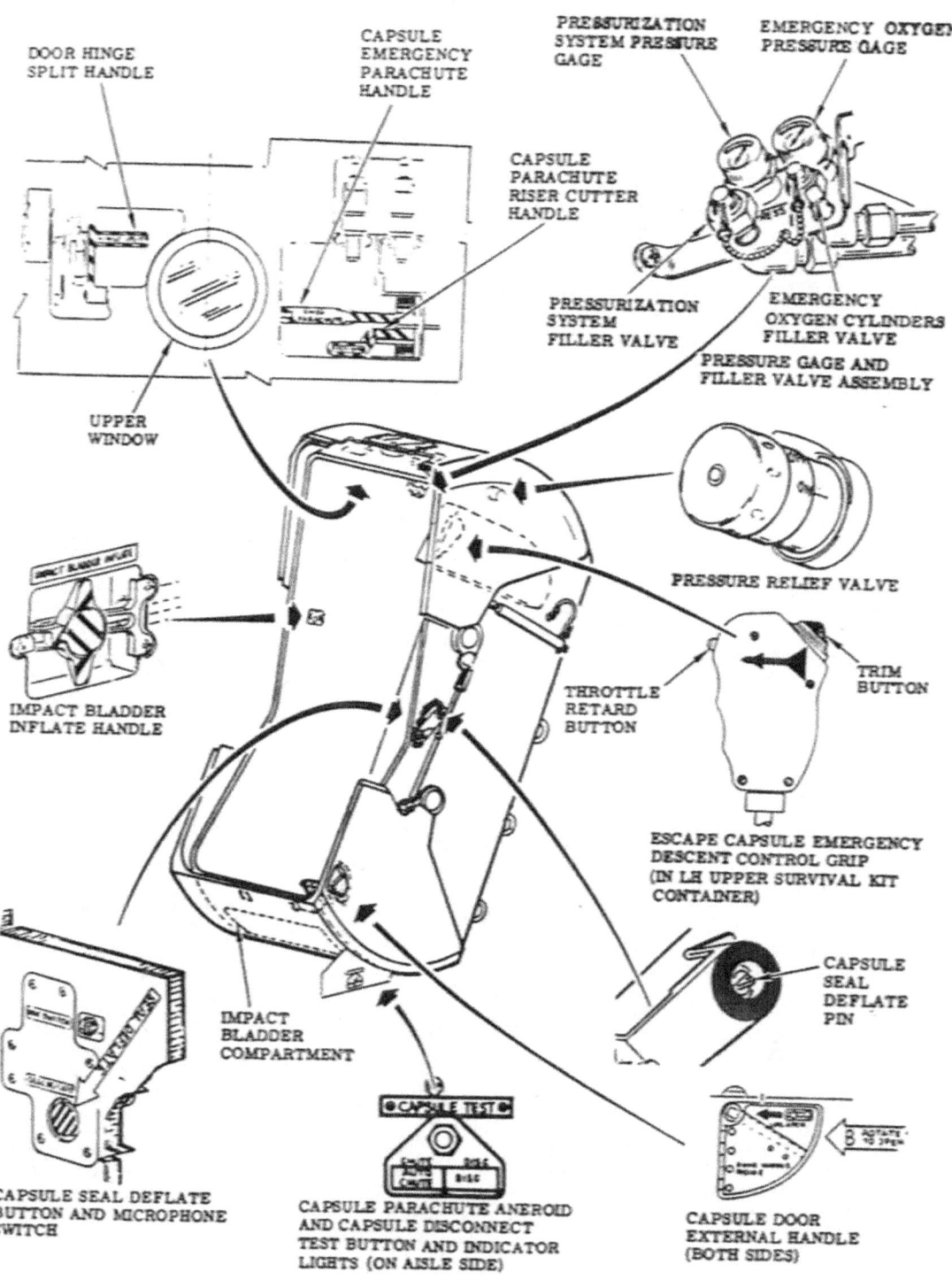

Figure 1-36 (Sheet 2 of 2)

automatic functions if required. Also during chute deployment, the impact bladder on the bottom of the capsule is automatically inflated. Plugs in the bladder blow out on impact with ground or water to cushion the landing and prevent rebound. Controls are provided for releasing one riser of the chute and opening the doors after the capsule lands. Survival equipment is carried in the capsule, and the capsule is designed to float with the doors upward, in case of a water landing.

ESCAPE CAPSULE VENTILATION AND PRESSURIZATION SYSTEM.

Refer to "Escape Capsule Pressurization System" in Section IV.

CAPSULE VENTILATION PLUG.

The round ventilation plug is in the center of the capsule upper door and is accessible only when the door is closed. The plug is sealed with an "O" ring, and is released internally by rotating it counterclockwise to the stop (about 1/8 turn). The plug can then be pulled into the capsule and reinstalled when desired.

ESCAPE CAPSULE COMMUNICATION EQUIPMENT.

Refer to "Communication and Associated Electronic Equipment" in Section IV.

EMERGENCY RADIO BEACON SYSTEM.

The self-contained emergency radio beacon system is in a container on the left exterior of the capsule. The system is automatically activated after ejection when the cover of the parachute container is released. The radio then transmits a continuous distress signal during the parachute descent of the capsule. After the capsule lands, the radio and its battery can be disconnected and removed from the container by the crew member to be used as a homing beacon after extending the stowed antenna and reconnecting the battery lead. If, after landing, transmission is not desired, the attached lanyard switch must be inserted in its chamber to shut off the transmitter and conserve the battery.

ESCAPE CAPSULE STABILIZATION SYSTEM.

Two telescopic booms on the back of the capsule, and parachutes that extend from the booms, furnish aerodynamic stabilization of the capsule after ejection until deployment of the capsule recovery parachute. The capsule stabilization system is actuated by trippers as the capsule travels up the guide rails during ejection. The trippers mechanically fire two initiators, and the gas from these initiators actuates integral boom cartridges to furnish gas pressure to unfold and extend the two telescopic stabilization booms. After a time delay of 1-1/2 seconds, the stabilization parachutes are released from the ends of the booms to augment low-speed free-fall stability.

ESCAPE CAPSULE IMPACT BLADDER SYSTEM.

An inflatable bladder is installed within a covered compartment on the lower portion of the capsule. A half-second delay after deployment of the capsule recovery parachute, the compartment cover is ballistically released automatically by gas pressure from an initiator. The initiator gas pressure also opens a valve on a 3000 psi nitrogen bottle. One-half second later, the nitrogen from the bottle begins to inflate the bladder. Complete inflation of the bladder requires four seconds. The bladder has blowout plugs to permit controlled release of pressure and prevent capsule rebound on landing. A manual means of inflating the bladder from inside the capsule is provided and should be actuated only when the capsule doors are closed and should be used only during parachute descent if a malfunction of the automatic system occurs.

CAPSULE ALTITUDE WARNING SYSTEM.

The capsule self-contained altitude warning system, in the upper right survival kit, is battery powered and provides a warning light after ejection when the capsule reaches the parachute operating altitude (15,500 ±500 feet pressure altitude). The system is mechanically armed during ejection by a tripper, and aneroid controlled after ejection. The aneroid, set to operate at the proper altitude, fires a gas cartridge which operates a pressure switch to turn on the warning light. The light can be tested by a push button in the capsule. Position of the trippers can be visually checked before flight.

Capsule Altitude Warning System Test Button.

The capsule altitude warning system push-to-test button (figure 1-36) is on the upper right survival kit in the capsule. The button receives power from the battery in the survival kit. Pushing the button tests the bulbs in the warning light and checks the battery.

Capsule Altitude Warning System Warning Light.

The placard-type capsule altitude warning system warning light (figure 1-36) is on the upper-right survival kit in the capsule. The light is powered by the battery in the survival kit after the system is armed and the altitude of the capsule is below parachute operating altitude (15,500 ±500 feet pressure altitude).

SURVIVAL KITS.

Each capsule has three survival equipment storage compartments. There are two small suitcase types, one on each side of the capsule at headrest level and one large compartment beneath the capsule floor. Each smaller survival kit can be removed from the capsule by actuating a release on the inside of the Compartment. These kits have carrying handles and are opened by releasing the latches on the handle end. The two small compartments have energy absorbent material on the sides facing inboard. The large survival kit compartment is accessible by removing the two heel pedals, foot guide, and unlatching the cover.

SEAT AND CAPSULE SAFETY PINS.

A single ball-lock type ground safety pin, inserted in a hole in the right side of the seat, prevents the handgrips from being raised. This flight status safety pin is attached to a red streamer marked "REMOVE BEFORE FLIGHT." The streamer is attached to a spring-loaded roller in the headrest which retracts the streamer and pin when not in use.

WARNING

The pin must not be pulled and then released, because the streamer reels in with considerable force and could damage equipment or cause personnel injury.

Maintenance safety pins, used during maintenance and check-out of the seat and capsule, also have a red streamer attached. These streamers are marked "USE DURING MAINTENANCE ONLY" and are interconnected where possible. All of these pins must be checked for removal before flight.

SEAT AND CAPSULE CONTROLS.

Seat Handgrips.

Ballistic encapsulation is initiated by raising the seat handgrips. (See figure 1-36.) The mechanically interconnected handgrips are latched in the down position to prevent them from being raised accidentally. Rotation upward and aft

T.O. 1B-70(X)A-1

of the right or left handgrip on the seat exposes the ejection trigger in each handgrip. When a handgrip is raised, mechanical linkage fires initiators. These initiators actuate a thruster to retract the seat into the capsule and lock it, retract and lock the shoulder harness, unlock and ballistically stow the control column, and provide pressure for closing the capsule doors. The capsule doors will not close automatically during the ballistic encapsulation cycle until the occupant presses both heels back against the two heel pedals.

Ejection Triggers.

An ejection trigger (figure 1-36) is within a guard in the lower part of each handgrip. As the handgrips are raised, the triggers are exposed. The seat must be retracted into the capsule before the triggers are operative. After the handgrips are raised and the seat is retracted, squeezing either the right or the left trigger fires initiators which cause the hatch over the capsule to be jettisoned and the capsule catapult cartridge to fire which ejects the capsule. When the capsule is within 6 inches of leaving the top of the guide rails, the rocket motor is ignited. While the capsule is moving up the guide rails, trippers activate the stabilization boom system, the recovery parachute system, and changes over to the capsule-mounted oxygen supply.

Heel Pedals.

The heel pedals (figure 1-36) below the front edge of the seat permit the capsule to close as part of the ballistic encapsulation cycle only after the occupant's feet are properly positioned. When the seat has been retracted into the capsule as the result of raising the seat handgrips, pressing both heels back against the pedals allows gas pressure to actuate a thruster which closes and locks the capsule doors. The door closure activates the capsule seals and pressurization system, and puts the hot mike intercom system into operation. The pedals are removed to gain access to the survival equipment compartment under the seat by pressing a release on each pedal.

Handgrip Downlock Release Lever.

A spring-loaded handgrip latch release lever is in the upper portion of each handgrip to permit raising the handgrips. (See figure 1-36.) The release lever is actuated automatically by the fingers when the handgrip is raised.

Handgrip Uplock Release Lever.

A spring-loaded handgrip uplock release lever (figure 1-36), on the left console of each seat unlocks and permits the lowering of the handgrips to the unarmed position after ballistic encapsulation if immediate ejection is not anticipated. Pressing the lever forward into the console unlocks both handgrips and permits them to be rotated forward and down to their stowed position.

WARNING

Do not contact the ejection triggers while stowing the handgrips as the ejection triggers will fire the capsule if accidentally squeezed.

NOTE

When the handgrips have been stowed following ballistic encapsulation, they must be rotated upward and aft again to expose the triggers before ejection can be accomplished.

Control Column Release Pedals.

Refer to "Flight Control Systems" in this section.

1-132

T.O. 1B-70(X)A-1

Capsule Door Interior Release Bar.

The door interior release bar (figure 1-36) on the upper door permits manual control of the capsule doors. When the doors are open, pulling the horizontal bar down unlatches the capsule doors. Changing the direction of pull from downward to forward closes the doors.

NOTE
The control column must be stowed before manual encapsulation, to provide control column clearance.

The doors are opened by pulling the release bar back and up to unlock and raise the upper door. As the doors are interconnected, both doors will open. However, after the impact bladder inflates following an ejection, the lower door is latched in the closed position and only the upper door will open. The latch may also be manually released externally.

Seat Lock Release Levers.

A spring-loaded seat lock release lever (figure 1-36) on the right console of each seat permits manual retraction or extension of the seat. Moving the lever aft releases the seat locks permitting repositioning of the seat. When the seat retracts, or handgrips are raised, the armrests are raised automatically.

Armrest Release Levers.

The armrest release levers (figure 1-36), on the forward edge of each folding armrest, are marked "PUSH." Pushing in on the lever permits the armrest to be lowered. The lever does not have to be pushed to raise the armrest.

Emergency Descent Control Grip.

The emergency descent control grip (figure 1-36) is mounted in a clip inside the door of the upper left survival kit in each capsule. The grip is hand-held and contains a trim button and throttle retard button. Refer to "Flight Control Systems" and "Engine Controls" in this section.

Seat Vertical Adjustment Buttons.

The two right primary ac bus-powered seat vertical adjustment push buttons (figure 1-36) on the right console of each seat are color-coded red and black. Pushing the red (forward) button energizes an electrical actuator to lower the seat, and pushing the black (aft) button raises the seat. When the seat is retracted, the buttons are inoperative.

Capsule Emergency Oxygen Actuator Knob ("Green Apple").

Refer to "Oxygen System" in Section IV.

Shoulder Harness Inertia Reel Lock Handle.

The inertia reel lock can be manually controlled by a two-position handle on the seat left console. (See figure 1-36.) Moving the handle forward to LOCK prevents further extension of the shoulder harness. It is recommended that the shoulder harness be locked manually during maneuvers and flight in rough air or as a safety precaution in case of a forced landing. The shoulder harness is set for automatic locking when the handle is at UNLOCKED. Once the reel has locked automatically, the handle must be moved to LOCK and back to UNLOCKED to release the reel. The shoulder harness can be loosened after ballistic locking (such as during encapsulation) without unlocking the reel by unsnapping the strap ends and pulling up on the two loops near the chest plate buckle.

T.O. 1B-70(X)A-1

Capsule Emergency Parachute Handle.

A handle (figure 1-36) to manually deploy the capsule parachute is in a recess on the inside roof of the capsule. The handle is marked "EMERG PARACHUTE" and is painted yellow and black. Pulling down on the handle releases a latch and fires an initiator which deploys the parachute and, as a backup system, extracts the parachute compartment door latch pins. When the handle is released, it springs back in the recess and exposes the riser cutter handle.

Capsule Parachute Riser Cutter Handle.

The handle (figure 1-36) is used to collapse the chute to prevent the dragging of the capsule on the ground or water during windy conditions. This handle is protected by the capsule emergency parachute handle to prevent inadvertent actuation. The handle is yellow with black strips and marked "RISER CUTTER." Pulling the handle down, after the emergency parachute handle has been pulled down and released, fires an initiator that retracts a pin to release one of the parachute risers.

WARNING

The riser cutter handle must not be used until ground or water contact is made.

Impact Bladder Inflate Handle.

If the impact bladder automatic inflation system fails, manual inflation can be accomplished with the impact bladder inflate handle. (See figure 1-36.) The yellow, black-striped "T" handle is in a recess in the right inside wall of the capsule. Next to the handle is a decal which reads "IMPACT BLADDER INFLATE." By pushing the button in the center of the handle and pulling the handle inboard, an initiator is fired which releases the bladder compartment lid. The gas pressure which releases the lid also opens the valve on the 3000 psi nitrogen bottle to inflate the bladder. Inflation of the bladder can be checked through the lower door window.

WARNING

The impact bladder inflate handle must be used only when the capsule doors are closed during parachute descent to prevent damaging the bladder.

Capsule Seal Deflate Button.

Refer to "Escape Capsule Pressurization System" in Section IV.

Capsule Pressure Relief Valve.

Refer to "Escape Capsule Pressurization System" in Section IV.

Capsule Door Hinge Split Handles.

Two hinge split handles are at the top of the capsule. The internal capsule door hinge split handle (figure 1-36) is on the inside roof of the capsule and the external hinge split handle is outside on the top of the capsule. The L-shaped handles are yellow with black stripes and marked "HINGE SPLIT." Pulling either handle fires an initiator which splits the hinge pins of both capsule doors and permits the doors to be pushed off of the capsule. The handles should be used only as a last resort to decapsulate. Once the hinge pins are split, the doors cannot be replaced without special tools. The primary use of the handles is for ground exit after ejection.

WARNING

If either door hinge split handle is used in the airplane, and ejection is necessary, the loose capsule doors would cause an extremely hazardous condition.

1-134

T.O. 1B-70(X)A-1

Capsule Door External Handles.

The external door handles (figure 1-36), one on each side of the lower door, permit opening the upper capsule door from the outside by rescue personnel after dumping seal pressure. (Refer to "Emergency Entrance" in Section III.) The handles are held in place by formed covers which must be opened before the handles can be moved. It is necessary to operate only one handle to open the upper capsule door.

NOTE

Capsule seal pressure should be released before attempting to open the capsule door, by pulling the seal deflate pin on the capsule.

Capsule Parachute Aneroid and Capsule Disconnect Test Button.

The capsule parachute aneroid and disconnect test button (figure 1-36), on a vertical panel below the capsule, receives power from the right primary ac bus. Pressing the button during preflight, lights both the capsule parachute aneroid and capsule disconnect indicator lights if the aneroids are operative and the capsule-to-airplane disconnects are properly engaged.

Microphone Switch.

Refer to "Escape Capsule Communications" in Section IV.

CAPSULE INDICATORS.

Capsule Pressurization and Emergency Oxygen Pressure Gages.

Refer to "Escape Capsule Pressurization System" and "Escape Capsule Oxygen System (Emergency Oxygen System)" in Section IV.

Capsule Parachute Aneroid Indicator Light.

The placard-type parachute aneroid indicator light (figure 1-36), powered by the right primary ac bus, is on a panel under the capsule. When the adjacent test button is pressed during preflight, this light comes on to indicate that the capsule parachute deploy system aneroids are in a safe, operative condition.

Capsule Disconnect Indicator Light.

The placard-type capsule disconnect indicator light, (figure 1-36), powered by the right primary ac bus, is on a panel under the capsule. When the adjacent test button is pressed during preflight, this light comes on to indicate that the capsule-to-airplane disconnects are properly engaged.

Encapsulate Caution Light.

Refer to "Bail-out Warning System" in this section.

Crew Encapsulated Indicator Light.

Refer to "Bail-out Warning System" in this section.

AUXILIARY EQUIPMENT.

The following auxiliary equipment and systems are described in Section IV: environmental systems; electronic equipment cooling system; drag chute and landing gear compartments cooling system; communication and associated electronic equipment; lighting equipment; oxygen systems; navigation equipment; single-point pressure refueling system; and miscellaneous equipment.

1-135

T. O. 1B-70(X)A-1

SERVICING DIAGRAM

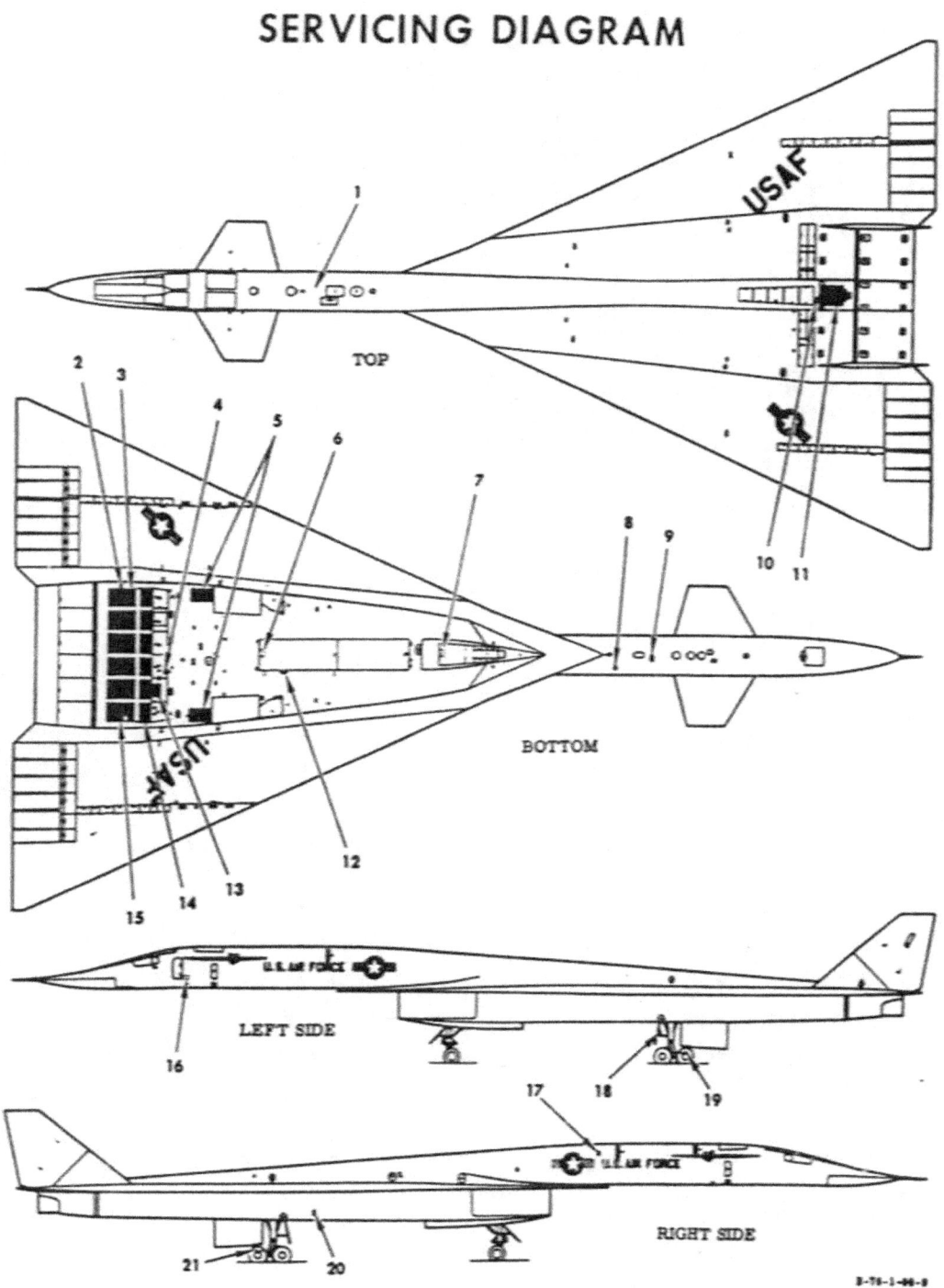

Figure 1-37 (Sheet 1 of 2)

T. O. 1B-70(X)A-1

1. REFRIGERATION PACKAGE SERVICING (ZONYL LUBRICANT AND FREON- IN ENVIRONMENTAL EQUIPMENT COMPARTMENT)
2. ENGINE LUBRICATION OIL FILLER (ENGINE NO. 6)
3. ENGINE HYDRAULIC OIL FILLER (ENGINE NO. 6)
4. EXTERNAL ELECTRICAL POWER RECEPTACLE (AC ONLY)
5. FIRE EXTINGUISHER CYLINDERS AND DRY ICE CONTAINERS
6. AIR INDUCTION CONTROL SYSTEM ENVIRONMENTAL PACKAGE FILLERS (GASEOUS AND LIQUID NITROGEN — IN WEAPONS BAY)
7. FLIGHT AUGMENTATION CONTROL SYSTEM SENSOR COOLER (ICE CONTAINER AND WATER FILLER — IN WHEEL WELL)
8. GROUND COOLING CONNECTION
9. WATER TANK AND ANHYDROUS AMMONIA FILLERS
10. DRAG CHUTE COMPARTMENT LATCH HANDLE
11. DRAG CHUTE COMPARTMENT
12. ETHYLENE GLYCOL FILLER
13. HYDRAULIC SYSTEM GROUND-TEST-FILLER CONNECTIONS (HYDRAULIC FLUID AND HYDRAULIC RESERVOIR GASEOUS NITROGEN)
14. ACCESSORY DRIVE SYSTEM LUBRICATION OIL RESERVOIR FILLERS (6 PLACES)
15. ENGINE LUBRICATION OIL AND ENGINE HYDRAULIC OIL FILLERS (ENGINES NO. 1 THROUGH NO. 5)
16. LIQUID OXYGEN, GASEOUS OXYGEN, OXYGEN-NITROGEN FILLERS (IN CREW COMPARTMENT)
17. FUEL INERTING SYSTEM LIQUID NITROGEN FILLER
18. EXTERNAL ELECTRICAL POWER RECEPTACLE (GROUND TOW, FUEL AND DEFUEL AC AND DC ONLY)
19. TOWING BRAKE HYDRAULIC POWER CONNECTION
20. SINGLE-POINT REFUELING RECEPTACLE
21. TOWING BRAKE HYDRAULIC POWER CONNECTION

SPECIFICATIONS

FUEL (JP-6)	MIL-J-25656 (No alternate fuel recommended)
ENGINE LUBRICATION OIL	MIL-L-9236 (Plus an additive)
ENGINE HYDRAULIC OIL	GE81406 (Versilube F-50)
ACCESSORY DRIVE SYSTEM LUBRICATION OIL	MIL-L-7808
HYDRAULIC FLUID	HTHF-70
LIQUID NITROGEN	MIL-N-6011, GRADE A TYPE II
GASEOUS NITROGEN	MIL-N-6011, GRADE A TYPE I
GASEOUS NITROGEN AND OXYGEN	MIL-N-6011, GRADE A TYPE I (40%) AND MIL-O-27210, TYPE I (60%)
LIQUID OXYGEN	MIL-O-27210, TYPE II
GASEOUS OXYGEN	MIL-O-27210, TYPE I
ETHYLENE GLYCOL	UNION CARBIDE PART NO. PM 2251
ANHYDROUS AMMONIA	MIL-O-A-445a
DEMINERALIZED WATER	Water not exceeding the equivalent of 10 parts per million by weight of sodium chloride at a "ph" value of 6.5 to 7.5. Maximum solid content in water will not exceed 5 parts per million by weight.
ICE (Shaped to fit container)	Ice made from the above water
FIRE EXTINGUISHING AGENT (Dibromodifluoromethane)	MIL-D-4540
DRY ICE	COMMERCIAL GRADE
FREON F-11	DUPONT COMMERCIAL GRADE
ZONYL E-91 LUBRICANT	DUPONT COMMERCIAL GRADE

Figure 1-37 (Sheet 2 of 2)

This page intentionally left blank

T.O. 1B-70(X)A-1

SECTION II

NORMAL PROCEDURES

TABLE OF CONTENTS	PAGE		PAGE
Preparation for Flight	2-1	Cruise	2-32B
Preflight Check	2-3	Deceleration	2-33
Before Starting Engines	2-12	Descent	2-34D
Starting Engines	2-13	Before Landing	2-35
Before Taxiing	2-17	Landing	2-35
Taxiing	2-21	Go-around	2-38
Before Lineup	2-23	After Landing	2-40
Take-off	2-24	Engine Shutdown	2-40
After Take-off - Climb	2-27	Before Leaving Airplane	2-41
Acceleration	2-28	Strange Field Procedure	2-41
AICS Change-over	2-32A	Abbreviated Checklist	2-41

NOTE

To show which of the crew is to accomplish each step, code letters appear in this section after each step as follows: (P) pilot and (CP) copilot. If no code letter appears, the step is accomplished by the pilot. In the cases where the pilot or copilot reads, the steps are not coded unless the step must be performed by both crew members.

PREPARATION FOR FLIGHT.

FLIGHT RESTRICTIONS.

Refer to Section V for detailed airplane and engine limitations.

FLIGHT PLANNING.

Refer to Appendix I to determine the fuel quantity, engine settings, and airspeeds that are required to complete the proposed mission.

TAKE-OFF AND LANDING DATA.

Refer to Parts 2 and 10 of Appendix I for the information necessary to fill out the Take-off and Landing Data card in T.O. 1B-70(X)A-1CL-1, before each flight.

NOTE
Take-off ground roll may be considered unclassified provided that it is not correlated with gross weight and configuration. This will avoid the necessity for classifying the clearance because of the inclusion of take-off ground roll.

WEIGHT AND BALANCE.

Refer to Section V for weight and balance limitations. For loading information, refer to the weight and balance form. Before each flight, check take-off and anticipated landing gross weight and balance. Complete Form 365F for weight and balance clearance.

Changed 25 June 1965

T.O. 1B-70(X)A-1

EXTERIOR INSPECTION

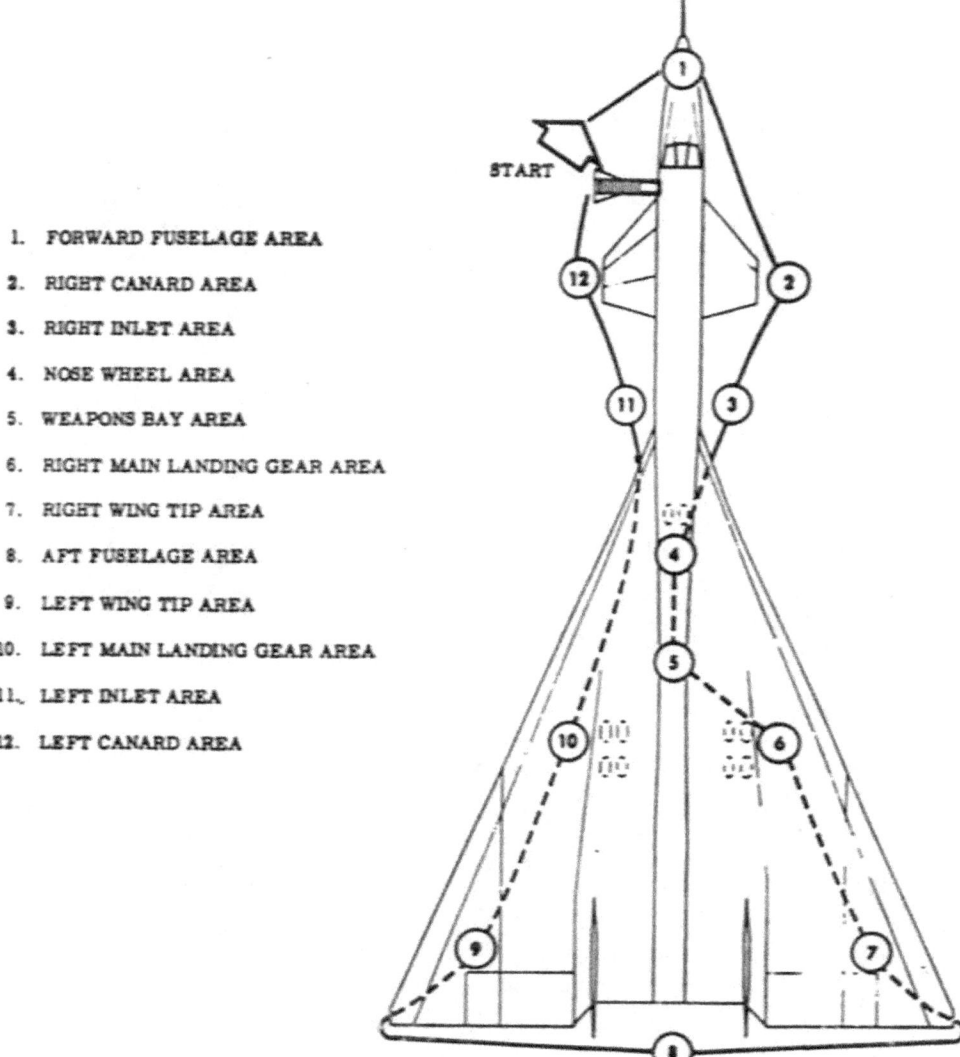

1. FORWARD FUSELAGE AREA
2. RIGHT CANARD AREA
3. RIGHT INLET AREA
4. NOSE WHEEL AREA
5. WEAPONS BAY AREA
6. RIGHT MAIN LANDING GEAR AREA
7. RIGHT WING TIP AREA
8. AFT FUSELAGE AREA
9. LEFT WING TIP AREA
10. LEFT MAIN LANDING GEAR AREA
11. LEFT INLET AREA
12. LEFT CANARD AREA

For detailed checks to be performed, refer to "Preflight Check" in this section.

Figure 2-1

T.O. 1B-70(X)A-1

CHECKLIST.

Refer to page ii for additional information on this subject. AFR 60-9 requires each flight crew member to refer directly to the checklist during specified ground and flight operations.

ENTRANCE.

Normal entrance is through a door on the left side of the fuselage, just forward of the canard. The door opens inward and is hinged on the forward edge. Before the door can be reached, an adequate ladder must be in place. See figure 2-2 for entrance door opening and closing procedures.

PREFLIGHT CHECK.

BEFORE EXTERIOR INSPECTION.

1. Form 781 (or equivalent) - Check. Check aircraft form for engineering and maintenance status, and make sure the airplane has been serviced properly for the intended mission. Check that a foreign object inspection has been made. For servicing points, see figure 1-37.

EXTERIOR INSPECTION.

Because of the size and complexity of this airplane, it is assumed that maintenance personnel have completed the required preflight inspections. The exterior inspection performed by the flight crew is only an inspection of readily accessible and flight safety items and is based on the flight crew accepting the airplane for flight with emphasis on the items affecting safety of flight. Check the airplane as outlined in figure 2-1. Information on non-accessible items is listed in the "Preflight Inspection Record." Ground crew will be at the airplane to discuss the status of the airplane and its systems.

NOTE
While performing the exterior inspection, check for overall condition, cleanliness, and signs of fluid leaks; make sure all vents, ducts, and ports are clear; and all access doors and panels are secure.

1. Forward fuselage area.
    a. Lower fuselage area - Check.
    b. Antennas - Check.
    c. Landing and auxiliary landing and taxi lights - Check retracted.
    d. Pitot boom - Check cover removed.
2. Flight canard area.
    a. Right flap - Check.
    b. Fuselage area - Check.
    c. Antennas - Check.
3. Right inlet area - Inspect from opening.
    a. Check that inlet alignment markings (throat wide open) are visible.
    b. Inlet pitot-static probes - Check covers removed.
4. Nose wheel area.
    a. Gear and gear door ground safety pins and locks - Check installed.

NOTE
The ground safety pins and locks will be removed and displayed by the ground crew when called for by the pilot.

    b. Nose wheels and tires - Check. Visually inspect tires for proper inflation for present gross weight, for signs of slippage, and for damage.
    c. Wheel chocks - Check removed.
    d. Nose gear strut - Check.
    e. Total temperature probes - Check covers removed.
5. Weapons bay area.
    a. Inspect weapons bay area as required.
    b. Anticollision lights - Check retracted.

ENTRANCE

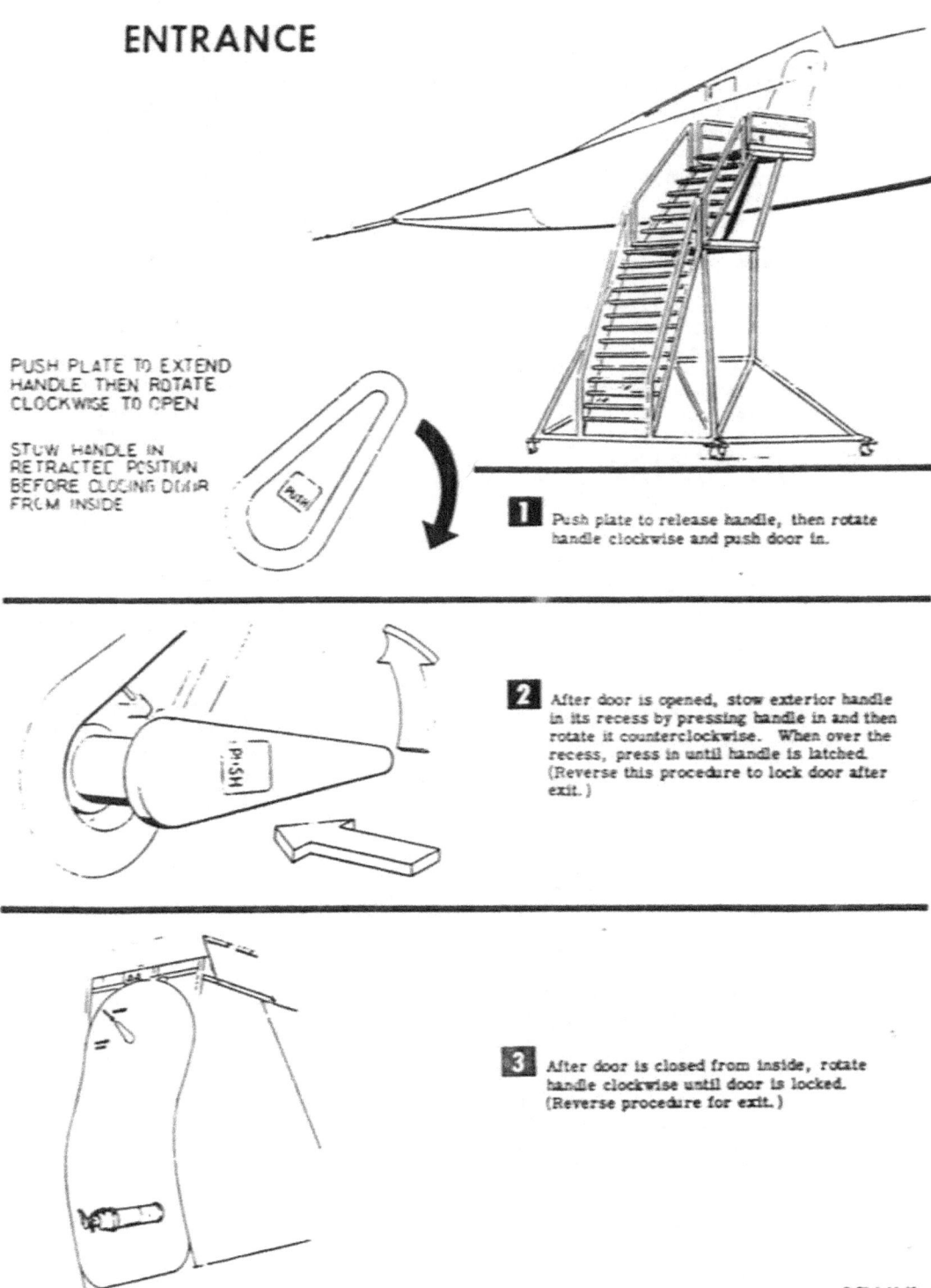

PUSH PLATE TO EXTEND HANDLE THEN ROTATE CLOCKWISE TO OPEN

STOW HANDLE IN RETRACTED POSITION BEFORE CLOSING DOOR FROM INSIDE

1 Push plate to release handle, then rotate handle clockwise and push door in.

2 After door is opened, stow exterior handle in its recess by pressing handle in and then rotate it counterclockwise. When over the recess, press in until handle is latched. (Reverse this procedure to lock door after exit.)

3 After door is closed from inside, rotate handle clockwise until door is locked. (Reverse procedure for exit.)

Figure 2-2

T.O. 1B-70(X)A-1

6. Right main landing gear area.
    a. Gear and gear door ground safety pins and locks - Check installed.

    NOTE
    The ground safety pins and locks will be removed and displayed by the ground crew when called for by the pilot.

    b. Wheels and tires - Check.
        Visually inspect tires for proper inflation for present gross weight, for signs of slippage, and for damage.
    c. Wheel chocks - Check in place.
    d. Main gear strut - Check.
7. Right wing tip area.
    Inspect the right wing tip, elevon, and navigation light.
8. Aft fuselage area.
    a. Elevons - Check.
        Check elevon segments for proper alignment.
    b. Engine exhaust nozzles - Check for condition and uniformity of area.
    c. Engine ground cooling doors - Check open.
    d. Rudder surfaces - Check.
    e. Drag chute safety pin - Check removed.
        The drag chute safety pin should have been removed by the ground crew and shown to the pilot.
    f. External electrical and hydraulic power - Connected and operating.
9. Left wing tip area.
    Inspect the left wing tip, elevon, and navigation light.
10. Left main landing gear area.
    a. Gear and gear door ground safety pins and locks - Check installed.

    NOTE
    The ground safety pins and locks will be removed and displayed by the ground crew when called for by the pilot.

    b. Wheels and tires - Check.
        Visually inspect tires for proper inflation for present gross weight, for slippage, and for damage.
    c. Wheel chocks - Check in place.
    d. Main gear strut - Check.

11. Left inlet area - Inspect from opening.
    a. Check that inlet alignment markings (throat wide open) are visible.
    b. Inlet pitot-static probes - Check probe covers removed.
12. Left canard area.
    a. Left flap - Check.
    b. Fuselage area - Check.
    c. Antennas - Check.

BEFORE INTERIOR INSPECTION.

1. External electrical and hydraulic power, ground intercom, and ground cooling units connected and operating.
    Check that ac and dc electrical power and power to all hydraulic systems is available.

    CAUTION
    The ground cooling units must be on to provide proper cooling to internal equipment.

    NOTE
    Local magnetic variation for the auxiliary gyro platform system must have been set manually before connecting external electrical power. This ensures correct great circle alignment.

T.O. 1B-70(X)A-1

INTERIOR INSPECTION.

CREW ENTRY AREA.

With ground crew personnel aboard the airplane until after engine start, the flight crew should make the following inspection:

NOTE
The entrance door must remain latched open with the dust cover installed until after engine start.

1. Descent devices (Sky Genies) and escape ropes - Check.
   Make sure rope is wound 4 or 5 turns around center shaft of the Sky Genie. If more or less than 4 or 5 turns have been wound around the shaft, have ground crew properly wind the rope and reinstall the Sky Genie in its receptacle.

2. Ground emergency escape hatch - Check hatch secure and hatch unlock handle stowed.
   Make sure maintenance safety pin is removed from hatch jettison handle initiator in ground escape aisle.

3. Ventilated suit converter tanks - Check at 110 to 150 psi.

4. Capsule altitude warning aneroid trippers - Check.
   The arm of the altitude warning aneroid tripper of each capsule must extend through the hole in the canted bulkhead.

T.O. 1B-70(X)A-1

5. Central air data system ground test panel - Check.
   Make sure the air data ground test selector switch on the air data ground test panel (on the bulkhead immediately behind the pilot's capsule) is at NORMAL and the test caution light is out.
6. Fire extinguisher - Check.
   Check hand fire extinguisher mounting and gage pressure (150 to 175 psi).

FORWARD COCKPIT AREA.

NOTE

Windshield glass panels must be checked for any flaws or damage, as these could cause total crazing of the glass during flight.

1. Landing gear handle - Check DOWN and area below handle clear.

NOTE

The area between the landing gear handle and the center console must be free of foreign objects before raising the console. This precludes the possibility of the landing gear handle being moved to UP when the console is raised to permit the crew to enter the seats.

2. Walk-around oxygen bottle - Check.
3. Capsule, seat, and harness - Check. (P and CP)
   a. Capsule parachute aneroid and capsule disconnect test button - Press.
      Press the test button and check that both the aneroid and disconnect indicator lights come on.
   b. Flight status safety pin - Check inserted.
      Make sure flight status safety pin is inserted in the seat right console and all other seat and capsule safety pins (9) have been removed.
   c. Seat handgrips - Check down.
      The handgrips must be full down and stowed.
   d. Capsule doors - Check latched open.
   e. Heel pedals - Check attached and unrestricted. (Move one at a time.)
   f. Capsule emergency parachute and riser cutter handles - Secured.
      The capsule emergency parachute and riser cutter handles must be up and secure.
   g. Capsule pressurization system and oxygen pressure gages - Check in green area.
   h. Capsule altitude warning light - Test.
   i. Survival kits - Check.
      Check that upper survival kits are secure and the compartment doors are latched, and that the lower survival kit door is fastened.
   j. Seat position - Check forward and locked.
   k. Shoulder harness inertia reel lock handle - UNLOCKED.
   l. Personal leads, restraint harness and safety belt - Connect.
      Refer to "Oxygen System Preflight Check" in Section IV.
   m. Center console - Lower and latch.
      After entering the seats, lower and latch the console.

PILOT'S INTERIOR INSPECTION. (COPILOT READS.)

1. UHF 1 - On and selected.
1A. TACAN function switch - REC and channel selected.

NOTE

The TACAN requires 2-minute warm up.

1B. ILS power switch - OFF.
1C. AGPS circuit breakers - In.
   Have ground crew in electronic equipment compartment engage AGPS circuit breakers.

2. IFF - Check OFF. (CP)
3. Ground intercom switch - ON. (CP)
4. Standby pitch trim arming switch - ARMED.
5. No. 1 and No. 2 primary hydraulic systems - Check. (3800 psi minimum)

T.O. 1B-70(X)A-1

6. Intercom panel - Set and Check.
   - Master volume knob - As desired.
   - UHF mixer switch - Pull.
   - Intercom function selector switch - UHF.
   - Hot mike mixer switch - Push (OFF).
   - Call button - Push, check, then release.
   - TACAN mixer switch - As required.
   - ILS mixer switch - As required.
   - Marker beacon mixer switch - As required.
7. Capsule and seat - Encapsulated checks. (P and CP)

   NOTE
   Have ground crew standby to report control surface movement.

   a. Seat - Unlock and retract.

   WARNING
   Flight status safety pin must remain in the seat right console and handgrips must remain stowed to prevent inadvertent handgrip and trigger actuation.

   b. Emergency descent control grip - Check.
      Remove emergency descent control grip from clip in upper left survival kit. Move and hold control grip trim switch at its NOSE UP and NOSE DOWN positions to check pitch trim and at the LWD and RWD positions to check roll trim.

   NOTE
   The check of each capsule trim switch must be made separately. Standby pitch trim arming switch must be at ARMED to permit the escape capsule emergency descent control grip trim switch to operate in the pitch trim system.

   c. Emergency descent control grip - Stow properly.
      Carefully stow grip in mounting clip. (Be sure the airplane symbol on the grip is pointing forward.) Close and latch survival kit door.

   d. Capsule doors - Close manually.
   e. Capsule windows - Condition and clean.
   f. Crew encapsulated (P) and encapsulated (CP) caution lights - Check on.
   g. Communications - Check.
      - Check hot mike status while encapsulated.
      - Capsule microphone switch - Press to test transmit function.
   h. Seal deflate button - Press until latched.
   i. Capsule doors - Open and check upper door latched.
   j. Seal - Pull forward and locked.
8. Encapsulate caution light switch - Momentarily at RESET and release to OFF.
9. Crew encapsulated (P) and encapsulate (CP) caution lights - Check out.
10. Control columns - Engage. (P and CP) Pull control columns aft until engaged.
11. Rudder pedals - Adjust. (P and CP)
12. Secondary exhaust nozzle stand-by pressure knob - Set to field elevation.
13. Auxiliary gyro platform system mode switch - MAG.
14. Auxiliary gyro platform alignment switch - Check at OPERATE.
15. Auxiliary gyro platform magnetic variation indicator - Check.
    Check that correct local magnetic variation is shown on the variation indicator. If the variation shown is incorrect, realign.
16. Auxiliary gyro platform latitude setting knob - Set.
    Set local latitude into latitude indicator.
17. UHF 2 - On and set.
    a. UHF function switch - MAIN. (P UHF 2; CP UHF 1)
    b. UHF channel selector knob - As required. (P UHF 2; CP UHF 1)

Changed 25 June 1965

T.O. 1B-70(X)A-1

c. UHF manual-preset-guard sliding selector - As required. (P UHF 2; CP UHF 1)
d. UHF transmitter power switch - As required. (P UHF 2; CP UHF 1)
e. Manual frequency selector knobs - As required. (P UHF 2; CP UHF 1)

18. Lateral bobweight switch* - Momentarily at LOCK.
19. Oxygen toggle valve - ON and check.

NOTE

* Oxygen mask must be on and connected before moving oxygen toggle to ON.
* Refer to "Oxygen System Preflight Check" in Section IV.

20. Visor heater switch - As required. (P and CP)
21. Augmentation power switches - ON. The yaw 1, yaw 2, pitch, and roll augmentation power switches should be ON.
22. (Deleted)
23. (Deleted)
24. Ground escape hatch jettison handle - Check in and maintenance safety pin removed.
25. AC voltages - Check; then return voltmeter bus selector switch to ESSENTIAL.
    To check the external electrical power supply, move bus selector switch to each bus position, and check ac voltage through each phase. When check has been completed leave the bus selector switch at ESSENTIAL.
26. Instrumentation panels - Set. (P and CP)

NOTE

All recording switches must be at OFF before turning on the instrumentation master switch.

27. Flight instruments - Checked and set as required. (P and CP)
28. Flight display switches - Set.
29. Cabin over 42,000 feet warning lights Out. (P and CP)
30. Master caution lights - Check on. (P and CP)

31. Total temperature gage - Check off flag cleared and gage reading near ambient.
32. Encapsulate switch - ON; check hot mike and encapsulate light on; RESET; then OFF and note encapsulate light out.
33. Bailout button - Press; check bailout light on and hot mike; then release and note bailout light out.
34. Vibration panel - Test and record selector set at 4.
    When the vibration test button is pushed, all 12 vibration indicator pointers should read 75 percent and the vibration caution light should come on.
35. Electronic equipment air temperature gage - Check below 60°F.
36. Ammonia, water and liquid oxygen quantity gages - Check and test.
    When the quantity gages test button is pressed, the pointers of the ammonia, water and liquid oxygen quantity gages should move towards "0". When test button is released, pointers should return to previous indication if gages are functioning properly.
36A. Bleed air switch - AUTO.
37. Cabin air switch - OFF.
38. Air recirculating fan thermal protection override switch - NORMAL.
39. Air recirculating fan switch - OFF.
40. Interior and exterior light switches - As required.
41. No. 3 and 4 generator switches - OFF.
42. Emergency generator switch - AUTO.
42A. Manual emergency landing gear lever* - NORMAL and cover guard secured and safetied.
43. Engine emergency brake switches - Check OFF.

CAUTION

If engine emergency brake switches were at ON, the engines must be checked and brakes reset before a start can be attempted.

44. Fire extinguisher agent discharge switches - Center (OFF).
45. Fire warning lights - Out and button flush.
    Check that all fire warning lights/engine shutdown buttons are flush with the panel and have not been pressed.

*Airplane AF62-001

46. Exhaust temperature gages - Check. Off warning flags must be out of view.
47. (Deleted)
47A. Hydraulic reservoir nitrogen head pressure and fluid level - Check. Use selector switches to check nitrogen head pressure and fluid level in each hydraulic reservoir.
47B. Cabin recorder switch - As required.
47C. Wheel brake mode switch - NORMAL.
48. Nose ramp switch - DOWN.
49. Wing tip fold controls - Mode switch NORMAL, and position selector switch UP. Check indicators.
50. (Deleted)
51. Landing gear emergency lowering switch - Check NORMAL.
52. Landing gear position lights - Check green.
53. Annunciator lights - Test and check. Hold annunciator light test switch momentarily at BRIGHT, then DIM, check lights, and release switch to center.

NOTE
Check that all annunciator lights are out except the following: engine identification lights (6), engine oil pressure, accessory drive system, cooling fuel pump, No. 3 engine generator out, No. 4 engine generator out, water-ammonia, roll and pitch augmentation, 1 and 2 yaw augmentation, and both master caution lights.

54. Hydraulic pump status indicators - Check yellow.
55. Engine overspeed arming lever - OUT. (forward).
56. Throttles - OFF.
57. Alternate throttle switches - Check centered (OFF).
58. Throttle reset button - Press and release.
    Press throttle reset button to ensure that alternate throttle circuits are not energized.
59. Air start switch - Check OFF.
60. Wheel brake hold button - Push. Lift guard and momentarily press the wheel brake hold button, then release. Check that indicator light in button comes on.
61. Wheel brake control switch - MANUAL and check brake control caution light on.
62. Nose wheel steering selector switch - OFF.
62A. Nose wheel steering engage switch - FAIL SAFE.
63. Flap handle - Check FLAP UP and indicator showing flaps up.
64. Engine rpm lockup switch - RELEASE.
65. Drag chute handle - STOWED JETTISON.
66. UHF antenna selector switch - AUTO.
67. Both UHF radios - Check. (P and CP)
68. Intercom function selector switch - UHF 1.
69. Flight augmentation control system speed stability switch - OFF.
70. TACAN - Check operation.
71. AGPS - Check.

COPILOT'S INTERIOR INSPECTION. (PILOT READS).

1. Fuel tank pump switches - OFF.

T.O. 1B-70(X)A-1

2. Fuel quantity indicators - Check and test.

Hold fuel quantity indicator test switch at EMPTY. The fuel sequence indicator strips 6, 4A, 2A, 1A, 7, 8A and 3 should immediately display black, followed by the tank secondary strips 4B, 2B, 1C, 1D, and 8B. The total and selected tank fuel quantity indicators should go to zero. All strips should be black in about 35 seconds or the system is faulty.

NOTE

If any strip remains white or does not move with actuation of the test switch, select the corresponding tank on the fuel tank selector knob. Should the selected fuel tank quantity indicator drive towards zero, the fuel sequence indicator system is faulty. No movement of the selected fuel tank quantity indicator counter indicates a faulty indicating system.

If the selected tank zero value does not appear in 30 seconds, or if the total fuel quantity zero value does not appear in 3 minutes, the system is faulty. All indicators must return to their original readings when the test switch is released to OFF.

3. Refueling valve switches - AUTO.
4. Liquid nitrogen quantity indicator - Check and test.

Press test button and then release. Indicator pointer should go towards "E" and return to previous reading.

NOTE

Do not hold test button long enough to permit gage to indicate below 1/4 to prevent the fuel inerting caution light from coming on and necessitating a reseting of the caution light circuitry.

5. Nose ramp unlock handle - Check in.

6. Environmental switches - OFF.
   - Auxiliary cooling switch - OFF.
   - Emergency heat exchanger water switch - OFF.
   - Coolant circulation pump switch - OFF.
   - Pitot heater switch - OFF.
   - Windshield anti-ice and rain removal switches - OFF.
   - Windshield defogging switch - OFF.
   - Cabin temperature selector switch - OFF.
   - Refrigeration switch - OFF.

CAUTION

Refrigeration switch must be OFF to prevent damage to the Freon compressor during low engine thrust settings.

7. (Deleted)
8. Duct performance switch* - NORM.
9. Air induction control system package power switch - ON.

NOTE

- If air induction control system coolant caution light remains on for about 3 minutes, move air induction control system package power switch to OFF momentarily (about 1 second), then back to ON. The light should go out. This assures operation on the No. 1 system.
- The switch must be on at least 25 minutes before operating the air induction control system.

9A. Throat trim power switch† - OFF.
9B. Throat height trim controls† - Check at +00.

---

*Airplane AF62-001
†Airplane AF62-207

T.O. 1B-70(X)A-1

10. Oxygen toggle valve - ON and check.

> **NOTE**
> - Oxygen mask must be on and connected before moving oxygen toggle to ON.
> - Refer to "Oxygen System Preflight Check" in Section IV.

11. IFF master switch - STDBY.
12. Regime III cooling switch - Check OFF.

> **CAUTION**
> To prevent overheating of all engines, the regime III cooling switch must remain at OFF until flight speed and altitude require regime III cooling.

13. Fire detection systems - Test. Test engine compartment fire detection system by moving engine compartment test switch to ON and hold light test switch momentarily at each LIGHTS OFF position and releasing to center. Return test switch to OFF. Test accessory drive system compartment fire detection system by moving ADS test switch to ON and hold light test switch momentarily at each LIGHTS OFF position and releasing to center. Return test switch to OFF.

> **NOTE**
> The fire warning lights should come on when either system test switch is moved to ON and should go out when the corresponding light test switch is held at LIGHTS OFF. The engine compartment and accessory drive system compartment fire detection systems cannot be tested simultaneously because both systems use the same warning lights.

14. Throttle and fire detection bus selector switch - Check safetied at NORMAL.

> **CAUTION**
> If the throttle and fire detection bus selector switch is at RH BUS, or is not safetied, a ground crew check of circuit may be necessary.

14A. Bus-tie contactor override switch - Check OFF.
14B. VGH recorder switch - OFF.
15. Engine No. 3 regime III cooling switch* - Check OFF.

> **CAUTION**
> To prevent overheating engine No. 3, the engine No. 3 regime III cooling switch must remain at OFF until flight speed and altitude require regime III cooling.

16. Crew air shutoff handle - As desired.
17. Crew air diverter lever - NORMAL.
18. Battery-inverter switch* - Check safetied at OFF.

> **WARNING**
> If the battery-inverter switch was at ON or not safetied, the battery has been activated and must be replaced before flight.

19. Engine shutdown and wheel brakes arming switch* - Check OFF.

BEFORE STARTING ENGINES. (PILOT READS.)

AICS CHECKOUT - AIRPLANE AF62-001.

1. No. 1 and No. 2 utility hydraulic systems - Check.
   The ground hydraulic power unit must be supplying sufficient hydraulic pressure. (3800 psi minimum)

---

* Airplane AF62-001

2. Throat - Check and set for take-off, as follows:
   a. Throat wheels - Both full aft; then both throat mode switches - MAN.
   b. Throat wheels - Both forward to Mach 1.80.
      Move both throat wheels forward to obtain Mach 1.80 on throat Mach schedule indicators.
   c. Throat standby switches - Hold both down at DECR to obtain Mach 1.70, then up at INCR to obtain Mach 1.90.
      Hold both throat standby switches down at DECR to obtain Mach 1.70 then up at INCR to obtain Mach 1.90 on throat Mach schedule indicators.
   d. Throat wheels - Both full aft. Throat Mach schedule indicators should stop above 1.70. However, if they stop below 1.70, hold both throat standby switches up at INCR to increase throat Mach schedule indicators to above 1.70.
   e. Throat standby switches - Hold both down to DECR until throat Mach schedule indicators stop.
   f. Throat mode switches - Both OFF.
3. Bypass - Check and set for take-off as follows:
   a. Bypass wheels - Both full forward; then both bypass mode switches - MAN.
   b. Bypass wheels - Both aft to OPEN (bypass door open caution lights on).
      Move both bypass wheels aft until bypass area is 400 square inches.
   c. Bypass standby system selector switches - Both PRIMARY.
   d. Bypass standby switches - Hold both up at CLOSE to obtain 300, then hold both down at OPEN to obtain 500.
      Hold both bypass standby switches as required until bypass area is 300 square inches, then 500 square inches.
   e. Bypass standby system selector switches - Both ALTERNATE.
   f. Bypass standby switches - Hold both up at CLOSE to obtain 300 then hold both down at OPEN to obtain 500.
      Hold both bypass standby switches as required until bypass area is 300 square inches, then 500 square inches.
   g. Bypass standby system selector switches - Both OFF.
   h. Bypass wheels - Both full forward until bypass area indicators stop.
   i. Bypass mode switches - Both OFF.

AICS CHECKOUT - AIRPLANE AF62-207.

1. No. 1 and No. 2 utility hydraulic systems - Check.
   The ground hydraulic power unit must be supplying sufficient hydraulic pressure (3800 psi minimum).
2. Duct performance switch - NORM.
3. AICS mode switches - Both AUTO.
4. AICS reset switch/light - Press and hold.
   Press and hold switch/light until completion of step 8.
5. Throat Mach schedule standby switches (reset switch/light held pressed) - Both up to INCR until throat Mach schedule indicators read 1.80, then both down to DCR until both throat Mach schedule indicators read 1.67.
6. Bypass door standby switches (reset switch/light held pressed) - Both down to OPEN until positive doors-open indication is obtained, then up to CLOSE until doors close; check both shock-aft caution lights out.
7. AICS mode switches (reset switch/light held pressed) - Both STBY.
8. AICS reset switch/light - Check on.
   If the light is on, the throat panels and bypass doors are properly rigged. If the light is out, the bypass doors are not properly rigged and must be corrected before flight.
9. AICS reset switch/light - Release.

STARTING ENGINES.

   CAUTION
   • See figure 2-3 for engine exhaust wake temperature, velocity, and sound-pressure level danger areas.
   • On Airplane AF62-001, the throat and bypass door mode switches must be at OFF, the throat manual control wheels full aft, the bypass door manual control wheels full for-

T.O. 1B-70(X)A-1

ward, the throat Mach schedule at 1.67, and the bypass area closed for engine start.
- On Airplane AF62-207, the AICS mode switches must be at STBY, the throat Mach schedule at 1.67, and the bypass area closed for engine start.

NOTE
- The normal starting sequence is: engines No. 4, 6, 5, 3, 1, 2.
- When the first throttle is moved from OFF to IDLE, the cooling loop fuel pump caution light (for the pump powered by the primary hydraulic system being used for starting) goes out. However, as each engine is started, one cooling loop fuel pump caution light comes on and stays on until engine rpm is between 35 and 40 percent. (The No. 1 cooling loop fuel pump caution light comes on during starting of engine No. 1, 2, or 3; the No. 2 cooling loop fuel pump caution light comes on during starting of engine No. 4, 5, or 6.)
- After the first engine is started, and during the start of each successive engine; observe that engine and ADS oil pressure lights come on when each throttle is advanced to IDLE and go out after start. This provides a check on the pressure switches and the electrical circuits.

1. Nose boom cover and locks, canard strips, and drag chute safety pin - Check removed.
   Make sure ground crew has removed pitot boom cover, ground locks from pitot boom instrumentation units, canard leading edge protection strips, and drag chute compartment safety pin.

2. Wheel chocks - Have ground crew check in place.
3. Windshield defogging switch - ON.
4. No. 2 primary hydraulic system pressure - 4000 psi minimum.
   Check that ground hydraulic power unit is supplying sufficient hydraulic pressure for a start. (Minimum 4000 psi.)
5. Have ground crew check No. 4 engine run area clear.
6. Engine No. 4 throttle - Check OFF.
   Throttle must be OFF to ensure that engine fuel control, fire wall fuel shutoff valve, and throttle controlled starting circuits are off.
7. Engine No. 4 alternate throttle switch - Hold at DECR momentarily.
   This disconnects the throttle servo system so that the engine fuel control will not respond to throttle movement.
8. Engine No. 4 throttle - IDLE.
   Advancing throttle to IDLE opens the fire wall fuel shutoff valve and arms the engine start and ignition circuits.

NOTE
The No. 2 cooling loop fuel pump caution light goes out when No. 4 throttle is moved from OFF to IDLE.

9. Ground start switch - ON momentarily.
   Holding switch momentarily at ON and releasing to OFF provides ignition and causes starting system to motor the engine. (Engine cannot light-off because the fuel cutoff valve in the engine fuel control is closed.)

CAUTION
Observe ignition system duty cycle limits to prevent possible damage to ignition unit.

   a. Primary hydraulic pump No. 4 status indicator - Check green.
   b. No. 2 cooling loop fuel pump caution light - Check on.
10. Throttle reset button - Press (after rpm stabilizes).
    Press reset button to restore normal throttle control of the engine fuel control and to open the fuel cutoff valve in the engine fuel control.

T.O. 1B-70(X)A-1

NOTE

Engine light-off occurs about 8 to 10 seconds after reset button is pressed.

11. Engine No. 4 exhaust temperature gage - Monitor.

    If engine light-off does not occur within about 20 seconds after throttle reset button is pressed, retard throttle to OFF.

    CAUTION

    - Primary hydraulic pump No. 4 status indicator must change from green to yellow below 40% rpm, or move throttle OFF.
    - If exhaust temperature reaches the start limit and continues to rise, engine must be shut down to prevent over-temperature. (See figure 5-1.) <u>Do not</u> attempt re-start of engine.

12. At IDLE rpm, check utility and primary hydraulic pump status indicators for engine No. 4 green, and check the following caution lights out:
    - Engine oil pressure
    - ADS
    - No. 2 cooling fuel pump
    - Engine No. 4 identification

13. Engine No. 4 engine instruments - Within limits.

    Engine rpm should increase steadily, with the throttle at IDLE, to about 60% rpm. Engine should accelerate to idle rpm in about 45 seconds. Make sure all No. 4 engine indicators are within limits. Check No. 4 exhaust nozzle position indicator at 65 to 75 percent.

14. Start engine No. 6, then No. 5. Use steps 6 through 13 for starting engines No. 6 and 5. (Substitute "engine No. 6" and "engine No. 5" when applicable.)

    NOTE

    - Engines No. 4 and 6 must be at idle rpm while starting engine No. 5.

    - After engines No. 4, 5, and 6 are started, have ground crew change hydraulic ground power unit to the No. 1 primary hydraulic system.

15. No. 1 primary hydraulic system pressure - 4000 psi minimum.

    Check that ground hydraulic power unit is supplying sufficient hydraulic pressure for a start. (Minimum 4000 psi.)

16. Start engines No. 3, No. 1, then No. 2.

    Use steps 5 through 13 for starting engines No. 3, 1, and 2. (Substitute "engine No. 3," "engine No. 1," and "engine No. 2" where applicable.)

    NOTE

    Engines No. 1 and 3 must be at idle rpm while starting engine No. 2.

17. No. 4 engine primary generator switch - ON and check voltages.

    Check that No. 4 generator-out caution light goes out. Check each phase (A, B, and C) for each ac bus (LH PRI, RH PRI, and ESSENTIAL). Voltage should be 115 volts ±3 volts.

18. External electrical power - OFF.

    Have ground crew turn off external electrical power.

19. No. 3 engine primary generator switch - ON.

    Check that No. 3 generator-out caution light goes out.

20. No. 4 engine primary generator switch - OFF and check voltages.

21. No. 4 engine primary generator switch - ON and check voltages.

    Check that No. 4 generator-out and bus tie open caution lights out. Check each phase (A, B, and C) for each ac bus (LH PRI, RH PRI, and ESSENTIAL). Voltage should be 115 volts ±3 volts.

22. Both cooling fuel pump caution lights - Out.

23. Electrical and hydraulic ground power units - Have ground crew disconnect.

173

T.O. 1B-70(X)A-1

DANGER AREAS

REFER TO CONFIDENTIAL SUPPLEMENT, T.O. 1B-70(X)A-1A

Figure 2-3

T.O. 1B-70(X)A-1

30. Vibration record selector knob - AUTO.
31. No. 4 engine primary generator switch - ON.
    Check that No. 4 generator-out caution light goes out.
32. AC voltages - Check 115 volts ±3 volts.
    Check each phase (A, B, and C) of ac voltage for each ac bus (LH PRI, RH PRI, and ESSENTIAL). Voltage should be 115 volts ±3 volts.
33. External electrical power - OFF.
    Have ground crew turn off external electrical power.
34. No. 3 engine primary generator switch - ON.
    Check that No. 3 generator-out caution light goes out.
35. No. 4 engine primary generator switch - OFF and check voltages.
36. No. 4 engine primary generator switch - ON.
    Check that No. 4 generator-out and bus tie open caution lights out.
37. AC voltages - Check 115 volts ±3 volts.
    Check each phase (A, B, and C) of ac voltage for each ac bus (LH PRI, RH PRI, and ESSENTIAL). Voltage should be 115 volts ±3 volts.
38. Electrical and hydraulic ground power units - Have ground crew remove.

MANUAL START.

A manual start should be used instead of the normal start procedure for any engine having a history of hot-start tendencies. The manual start procedure reduces the probability of a hot start by allowing the engine to be motored before fuel is supplied to the engine. The steps of the normal start procedure that apply before the start is initiated and after engine light-off also apply when making a manual start. If a manual start is necessary, proceed as follows:

1. Normal pre-start procedures - Complete.
2. Throttle (applicable engine) - Check OFF.
    Throttle must be OFF to ensure

Changed 30 November 1964   175   2-16A/2-16

This page intentionally left blank

T.O. 1B-70(I)A-1

24. Cabin temperature controls - MANUAL and full HOT. (CP)
    Set cabin temperature selector switch to MANUAL and temperature knob to its full HOT position.
25. Have ground crew check hot air flow from crew compartment heater overboard vent.
26. Bleed air switch - CLOSE, and have ground crew check that no air is flowing from heater overboard vent.
27. Bleed air switch - OPEN, and have ground crew check hot air flow from heater overboard vent.
28. Bleed air switch - AUTO.
29. Cabin temperature controls - AUTO, temperature as desired. (CP)
    Set cabin temperature selector switch to AUTO and temperature knob at its 10 o'clock position.
30. Engine-ADS vibration record selector switch - AUTO.

BEFORE TAXIING. (COPILOT READS).

1. Emergency generator switch - ON.
   Check that emergency generator-on caution light comes on and monitor No. 2 utility hydraulic system pressure.
2. Essential ac bus voltages - Check 115 volts ±3 volts.
   Check voltage for each phase (A, B, and C) of the essential ac bus.
3. Emergency generator switch - AUTO.
   Check that emergency generator-on caution light goes out in about 5 seconds.
4. Essential ac bus voltages - Check.
   Check voltage for each phase (A, B, and C) of the essential ac bus. Voltage should be 115 volts ±3 volts.
5. (Deleted)

Changed 25 June 1965

2-17

T.O. 1B-70(X)A-1

6. Trim and flight augmentation control system - Check and have the ground crew report surface movements.

CAUTION
The nose wheel steering switch must be at OFF to prevent wearing the nose wheel tires when the rudder pedals are moved.

NOTE
- Three ground crewmen are required to assist checking the movement and position of the control surfaces. One man should be stationed out from and to the rear of each wing tip, and one out from the left side of the fuselage, opposite the canard. Ground crew will report control surface movement and position to the flight crew. Any discrepancies should be investigated and corrected before flight.
- During flight control system check, a momentary pressure fluctuation will be noticed in both primary hydraulic systems as controls or trim systems are actuated. Also check flight controls for proper movement when trim is actuated.

a. Control columns and wheels - Check for freedom of movement. Move control columns to the forward and rear limits and rotate control wheels to the full left and right limits.
b. Rudder pedals - Check for freedom of movement. Move rudder pedals the full limit of travel right and left.
c. Primary pitch trim knob - Check inoperative. (P and CP)

NOTE
The primary pitch trim system became disengaged when the emergency descent control grip trim switch was used.

d. Standby trim pitch switch - NOSE UP, then NOSE DOWN. Hold the standby trim pitch switch alternately at the NOSE UP and NOSE DOWN positions. Leave trim near neutral.
e. Standby pitch trim arming switch - OFF. (Standby pitch trim is inoperative.)
f. Standby pitch trim arming switch - ALT ARMED.
g. Standby trim pitch switch - NOSE UP, then NOSE DOWN. Hold the standby trim pitch switch alternately at the NOSE UP and NOSE DOWN positions to check trim operation on the ALT ARMED circuit. Check primary pitch trim knobs inoperative.

CAUTION
When the standby pitch trim arming switch is at ALT ARMED, power to the trim actuator is not shut off automatically when the actuator exceeds control travel limits. Therefore, to prevent possible structural damage, do not trim for full elevon travel when the arming switch is at ALT ARMED, or continue trimming after control column has stopped.

2-18

T.O. 1B-70(X)A-1

h. Standby pitch trim arming switch - OFF then ARMED.
   Return arming switch to ARMED, hesitating momentarily at OFF, to re-engage the primary pitch trim systems.

   NOTE
   Some control column motion may occur.

i. Primary pitch trim knob - NOSE DN, then NOSE UP then neutral. (P and CP)
   Rotate primary pitch trim knob towards NOSE DN until ground crew verifies the canard leading edge and elevons are trimmed full down. Then rotate trim knob towards NOSE UP until ground crew verifies canard leading edge and elevons are trimmed full up.

j. Yaw trim switch - NOSE LEFT then NOSE RIGHT.
   Hold the yaw trim switch at NOSE LEFT and NOSE RIGHT then neutralize.

k. Standby trim roll switch - LEFT ROLL, RIGHT ROLL, then neutral.
   Hold the standby trim roll switch at the LEFT ROLL and RIGHT ROLL positions until full corresponding elevon trim travel has been reached then neutralize.

l. Flight augmentation control system engage button - Press.
   Press button to re-engage augmentation system. Check all augmentation caution lights out.

m. Primary roll trim knob - LEFT, RIGHT, then leave knob about 4 degrees off center.

n. Copilot's flight augmentation control system disengage button - Press. (CP)
   Press the disengage button on the copilot's wheel to check operation of the disengage circuit. Pitch and roll augmentation caution lights should come on.

   NOTE
   Only the pitch and roll augmentation are disengaged when the copilot's disengage button is pressed.

o. Flight augmentation control system engage button - Press and note that primary roll trim knob recenters.
   Press button to re-engage augmentation system. Check all augmentation caution lights out and that primary roll trim knob centers.

p. Pilot's flight augmentation control system disengage button - Press.
   The disengage button on the pilot's wheel should be pressed to check operation of disengage circuit. All augmentation caution lights should come on.

7. Flight controls - Check lateral bobweight.*
   a. Lateral bobweight switch - Hold at FREE until bobweight indicator shows FREE.
   b. Turn control wheel full left and release. Observe the residual oscillation (about 2 or 3 cycles) around center.
   c. Lateral bobweight switch - Hold at LOCK until bobweight indicator shows LOCKED.
   d. Turn control wheel full right and release. There should be no residual oscillation.

8. Flight controls - Check elevons and canard. Have ground crew report.
   a. Pull control wheel full aft and hold. (Canard leading edge goes up 6 degrees.) Then turn control wheel full left and check left elevons up and right elevons down. Then turn control wheel full right and check left elevons down and right elevons up. Then neutralize elevons.

---

* Airplane AF62-001

2-19

T.O. 1B-70(X)A-1

b. Push control wheel full forward. (Canard leading edge goes to 0 degrees.) Then pull control wheel back to neutral.
9. Flight controls - Check rudders. Have ground crew report.
   a. Full right, full left, then neutral.
10. Flap handle - FLAP DOWN.
    a. Have ground crew check canard leading edge goes to 0 degrees.
    b. Move control wheel forward and aft, and have ground crew verify that canard leading edge remains at 0 degrees.
10A. Interior check - Ground crew. Have ground crew make the following checks in the electronic equipment and crew compartments.
    a. S-band radar beacon switch - ON. Moving switch from ST-BY to ON engages the directional radar transmitter used as a positioning device for the telemetering range. (Switch is on left side of electronic equipment compartment, below CADS computer shelf.)
    b. Manual emergency landing gear handle - NORMAL, and check connecting linkage* from emergency gear lever in crew compartment.
    c. Fuel pump test switch and tank selectors - OFF.
    d. ADS nitrogen quantity - Check.
    e. Wing tip emergency-up reset system - Switches OFF, light tested and out.
    f. Wing tip emergency-up switches - OFF.
    g. Aft bulkhead door - Closed and latched.
    h. Circuit breakers - Check.
    i. Capsule thrust control test lights† and descent thrust safe light - Out.
    j. Electrical feeder fault indicator bulbs - Test and out.
    k. Engine windmill brake reset switches - OFF (centered).
    l. Electrical conduit fault sensing indicator bulbs - Test and out.
    m. Fuel tank unit selector switches - I.

n. Fuel control module circuit breaker power switches - Check ON.
   The circuit breaker power switch on each module must be ON except the switch for No. 5 module on Airplane AF62-001, which should be safetied OFF.

NOTE

The sequence indicator circuit breaker power switches on the sequence indicator circuit breaker power switch module also must be ON, except No. 5 on Airplane AF62-001, which should be safetied OFF.

CAUTION

After the preceding checks in the electronic equipment compartment, are completed, the compartment door must be closed and latched.

o. Liquid coolant pump switch - ON.
p. Landing gear door switch - NORM.
q. Fuel pump switch - NORM.
r. Tape recorder - ON.
s. Capsule hatch remover hoses - Check connected.

11. Take-off trim button - Press. Press and hold trim button until light comes on, then release.

NOTE

It may be necessary to manually move the controls slightly if the trim for take-off indicator light fails to come on.

12. Alternate throttle switches - Check. With throttles at IDLE, individually check each alternate throttle switch by holding it momentarily at INCR and noting rpm increase of corresponding engine. Then hold switch at DECP until rpm decreases to idle setting (60% rpm). Monitor engine instruments during check.
13. Throttle reset button - Press and check throttles. When check of alternate throttle switches is complete, momentarily

---
*Airplane AF62-001
†Airplane AF62-207

2-20

Changed 25 June 1965

T.O. 1B-70(X)A-1

press reset button to restore normal throttle control. Then advance and retard throttles momentarily to verify reset.

NOTE

Before pressing throttle reset button, make sure all engines are at idle rpm.

14. Have ground crew stand by to close entrance door.
15. Crew air shutoff handle - As desired. (CP)
16. Auxiliary cooling switch - ON. (CP)

CAUTION

Ammonia quantity is sufficient for 40 minutes of ground operation in addition to that required for normal and in-flight emergency operation.

16A. Coolant circulation pump switch - ON. (CP)
   The water-ammonia caution light will come on.
17. Both UHF radios - OFF.
   The UHF radios must be OFF whenever cooling is interrupted because of heat generated.
18. Ground cooling unit - Have ground crew set to full bypass.

NOTE

The electronic equipment overheat caution light will come on.

CAUTION

If steps 19 and 20 are delayed over 2 minutes, the ground cooling unit must be turned back on to prevent overheating of the electronic equipment.

19. Entrance door - Have ground crew close and lock.

NOTE

The door must be closed and locked to arm the door and hatch seal pressurization.

20. Air recirculating fan switch - ON and check electronic equipment overheat caution light out.
21. Electronic equipment temperature gage - If below 80°F, have ground cooling unit disconnected.
22. Both UHF radios - ON.
23. (Deleted)
24. (Deleted)
25. Landing gear safety pins, wheel chocks and clear airplane for taxi - Ground crew.
   Ground crew will remove the three landing gear safety pins and wheel chocks. The three landing gear safety pins will be displayed where the pilot can see and count them.
26. Nose wheel steering selector switch - TAXI.
27. Nose wheel steering engage switch - ENGAGE, check nose wheel steering-on indicator light on, then move switch to FAILSAFE.
28. Hydraulic pressures, fluid levels, and pump status indicators - Check.
29. Ground intercom - Have ground crew disconnect.
29A. AGPS magnetic and great circle headings - Check.
29B. AGPS mode switch - MAG.
30. Release brakes.
   Apply brakes and release pedals. Check that brake hold light goes out.

TAXIING.

CAUTION

- Before taxiing be sure there is proper clearance for the airplane. (See figure 2-4 for minimum turning radius and ground clearance.)
- To prevent structural damage while turning during taxiing, refer to recommended maximum turning speeds in Section V.

NOTE

- Over-the-nose vision (with windshield nose ramp retracted) to

Changed 25 June 1965

2-21

T.O. 1B-70(X)A-1

MINIMUM TURNING RADIUS AND GROUND CLEARANCE

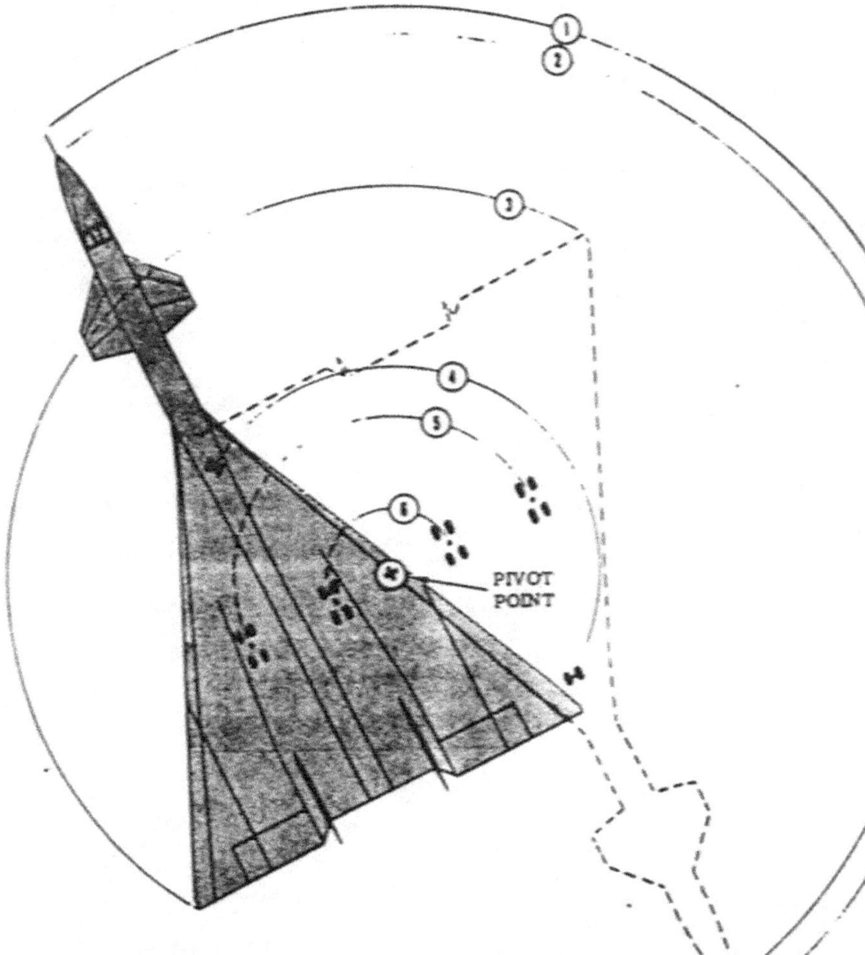

TURNING RADIUS BASED ON NOSE WHEELS TURNED 58 DEGREES FROM CENTER. (NOSE WHEEL STEERING SWITCH AT TAXI POSITION)

1. PITOT BOOM   142 FEET
2. NOSE   134 FEET
3. WING TIP   97 FEET
4. NOSE GEAR   54 FEET
5. LEFT MAIN GEAR 40 FEET
6. RIGHT MAIN GEAR 17 FEET

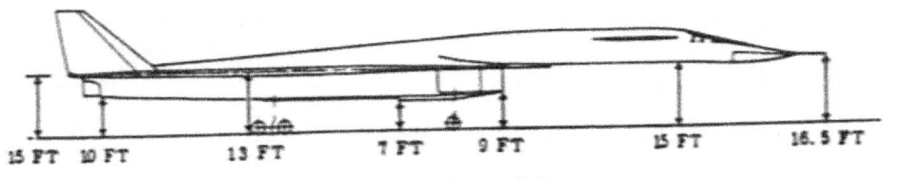

Figure 2-4

T.O. 1B-70(X)A-1

runway level is about 90 feet in front of airplane.
- The idle thrust of six engines is adequate for taxiing. Directional control should be maintained with nose wheel steering rather than with differential thrust or braking.

During taxiing, perform the following:

1. Brakes - Check during initial taxi roll and monitor hydraulic pressure.
2. Nose wheel steering - Check.
3. Turn needle, ADI, and HSI - Check. (P and CP)
   Check proper indications of attitude director and horizontal situation indicators.
4. Wheel brake control switch - AUTOMATIC.
5. Wheel brake test switch - Check.
   Check operation of each automatic brake system by holding the wheel brake test switch at SYS 1 then SYS 2 and applying brakes when switch is at each position. Check that brake control caution light is out at each position. Release switch to center (OFF).

BEFORE LINEUP.

After taxiing to the take-off area, come to a complete stop and do the following:

1. AC voltages - Check.
   Check each phase (A, B, and C) of ac voltage for each ac bus (LH PRI, RH PRI, and essential). Voltage should be 115 volts ±3 volts. When the check is over, leave the bus selector switch at ESSENTIAL.
2. Air induction control system - Check. (CP)
   Bypass area should be 0000 square inches and throat Mach schedule indicator should be at 1.67.
3. Secondary exhaust nozzle standby pressure knob - Check set at field elevation.

   CAUTION
   If the nozzle standby knob is improperly set, the automatic transfer of the ambient pressure signal to the nozzle standby circuit in the event of central air data computer failure may cause loss of thrust.

4. Liquid nitrogen quantity indicator - Check quantity. (CP)
5. IFF master switch - NORMAL. (CP)
6. Tires and brakes - Have ground crew check.
   Ground crew will check brake temperatures and visually check tires for cuts and abrasions and proper inflation.
7. Flight controls - Check for freedom of movement.
8. Canard flaps - Have ground crew check position.
9. Take-off trim button - Press.
   Press and hold trim button until light comes on, then release.

   NOTE
   It may be necessary to move the controls slightly to make the trim for take-off light come on.

10. Hydraulic pressures, fluid levels, and pump status indicators - Check.
11. Take-off data - Review.
12. Engine overspeed arming lever - OUT.

    NOTE
    When take-off conditions (ambient air temperature above 50°F) require engine overspeed (104% rpm) operation to provide extra thrust, the overspeed arming lever should be pulled back to its armed (ARM) position before the throttles are advanced from IDLE. The overspeed armed caution light comes on when the overspeed arming lever is armed. After the overspeed light comes on push either master caution light to extinguish both master caution lights and to reset master caution light circuit.

Changed 25 June 1965

2-23

T.O. 1B-70(X)A-1

13. Anticollision light switch - ON.

    CAUTION
    Operation of the anticollision lights on the ground should be limited as much as possible, as the bulbs can be damaged by overheating.

    NOTE
    Operation of the anticollision lights on the ground shall be held to a minimum because ground emergency vehicles have similar lights. The operation of the anticollision lights could confuse and hamper ground rescue operations.

14. Ammonia and water quantity gages - Check.
    Check that sufficient amounts of ammonia and water are available for completion of the mission.

    CAUTION
    If ammonia is below 275 pounds, or water is below 4000 pounds, abort the flight until ammonia or water tank is refilled.

15. Bypass area and throat Mach - Check both bypass areas closed and both throat Mach indicators at 1.67. (CP)
16. AICS:
    a. Bypass and throat mode switches* - Check all OFF. (CP)
    b. AICS mode switches† - Check both STBY. (CP)
17. Fuel quantity:
    a. Tanks 8L and 8R - Check quantity at 13,500 pounds or less.* (CP)
    b. Tank 5 - Check quantity at 26,000 pounds or less.† (CP)
       If fuel quantity in specified tank is above the recommended level, move corresponding fuel pump switch to ON until fuel level is reduced.
18. Fuel tank pump switches - AUTO. (CP)
    Move No. 6 fuel pump switch to AUTO and check increase in tank No. 3 quantity, then move all remaining fuel pump switches to AUTO.
19. Tank No. 3 - Check at high level. (CP)
    Make sure fuel is transferring properly to No. 3 (sump) tank. The sump tank tape will indicate full if proper transfer is taking place.
20. Ground intercom - Have ground crew disconnect.
21. Capsule flight status safety pins - Remove. (P and CP)
22. Pitot heater switch - ON. (CP)

TAKE-OFF.

    NOTE
    All take-off performance data should be determined prior to take-off. Normal take-off technique is that which will produce the results stated in the take-off data charts in Part 2 of Appendix I. See figure 2-5 for a typical take-off and initial climb pattern.

After lining up on the runway, proceed as follows:

1. Nose wheel steering selector switch - TAKE-OFF LDG.

    NOTE
    Nose wheel steering remains engaged when switch is moved from TAXI to TAKE-OFF LDG.

1A. Nose wheel steering engage switch - FAIL SAFE.
2. Throttles - Advance above 81% rpm.

    CAUTION
    To prevent possible engine vibration, the following "detented" throttle technique is recommended: When making throttle bursts from IDLE to MIL (or greater), accelerate to 80% to 90% rpm, and hold this speed long enough to observe stable rpm. If vibra-

*Airplane AF62-001
†Airplane AF62-207

2-24   Changed 25 June 1965

T.O. 1B-70(X)A-1

TAKE-OFF AND INITIAL CLIMB
(Typical)

NOTE
- Refer to Part 2 of Appendix I for take-off distances and speeds for all gross weights.
- Nose wheel lift off speed 20 knots less than take-off speed.

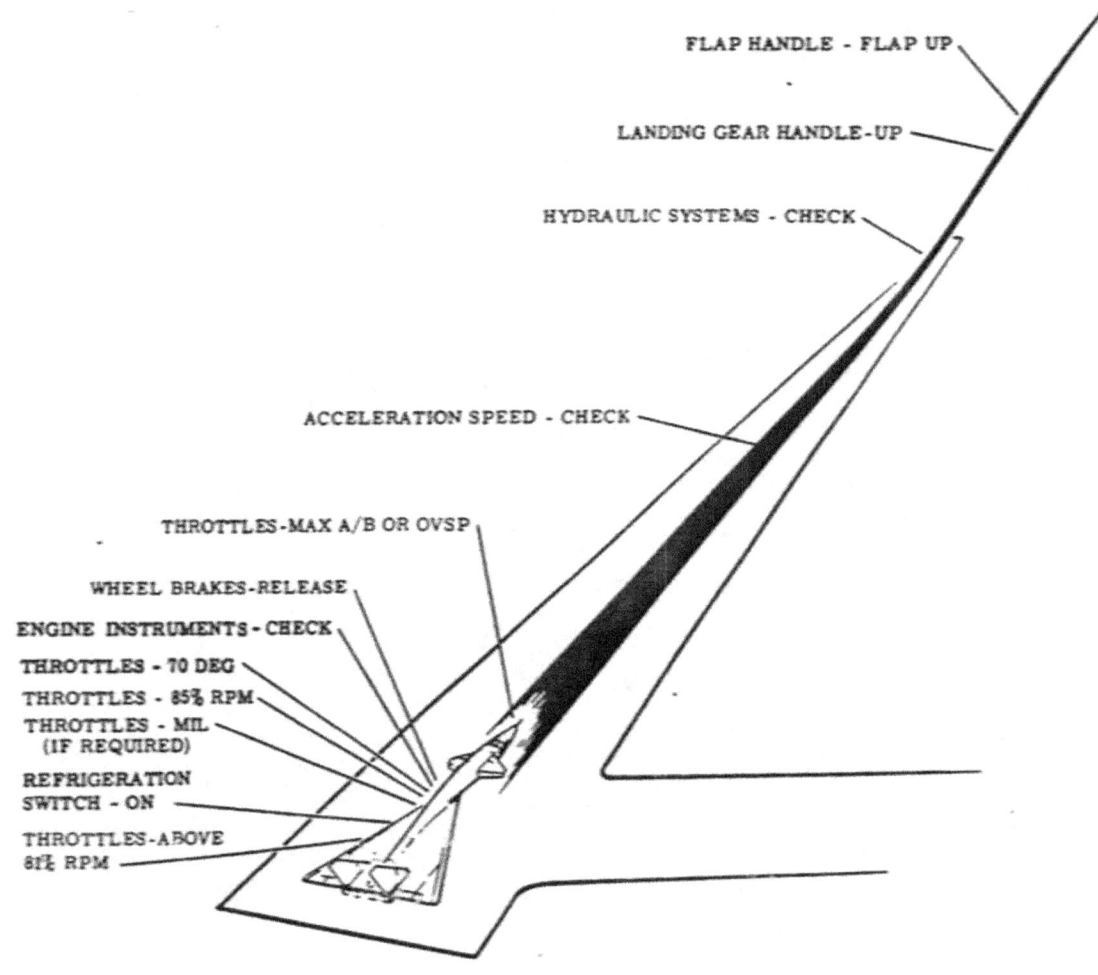

Figure 2-5

T.O. 1B-70(X)A-1

tion is within limits, accelerate engine to throttle position as required. (During all flight conditions where flight idle is greater than 80% rpm, throttle movements are unrestricted.)

3. Refrigeration switch - ON. (CP)
   a. Electronic equipment air temperature gage - Check decreasing.
   b. Water-ammonia caution light - Out.

4. Throttles (if required) - MIL.
   If Military Thrust check has not been made before lineup, advance all throttles to MIL and allow engines to stabilize for 30 seconds. Make sure all conditions are correct and within limits, and check exhaust nozzle position indicators are at about 40 percent.

5. Throttles - 85% rpm.

6. Throttles - 70 degrees.
   Advance throttles 3 and 4 rapidly to MIN A/B and, after afterburner light-off, continue to advance throttles to 70 degrees. Repeat procedure for engines 2 and 5, then for engines 1 and 6.

   CAUTION
   - To preclude stalling the other engines if one engine stalls, engage only one afterburner at a time per inlet.
   - Because operation in the minimum afterburner range may cause unstable combustion, which could result in compressor stalls and/or engine flame-out, avoid afterburner operation with the throttle between the 61- and 70-degree settings. (Refer to "Minimum Afterburner Instability" in Section VII.)

7. Engine instruments - Check.

8. Wheel brakes - Release.
   Use nose wheel steering for directional control at speeds up to nose wheel lift-off (approximately 10 knots IAS below take-off speed). It is not recommended that directional control be maintained by use of wheel brakes because braking action greatly increases the take-off roll.

9. Throttles - MAX A/B or OVSP.
   Advance all throttles simultaneously to MAX A/B or, if above 50°F and overspeed is required, through the MAX A/B setting to OVSP. Monitor engine instruments.

   CAUTION
   Selected overspeed operation should not be used for take-off below 50°F. Overspeed limitations given in Section V should not be exceeded, as damage to the engine turbine section can result.

   NOTE
   - To go into overspeed after the throttles have been moved to MAX A/B, the throttles must be retarded slightly (to release the overspeed solenoids), the overspeed arming lever placed in ARMED, and then the throttles moved to the overspeed position.
   - The pointers of the exhaust nozzle position indicators should be within the green arc for maximum afterburner or in the yellow arc for overspeed operation.

10. Acceleration speed - Check.

    NOTE
    - The acceleration should be checked and a decision made to either continue take-off or to abort. (Refer to Part 2 of Appendix I for acceleration and refusal speeds.)
    - At about 20 knots IAS below recommended take-off speed for the gross weight, begin to rotate the airplane at such a rate that it will assume the pitch angle required for lift-off at the recommended take-off speed.
    - Maintain take-off attitude after breaking ground until sufficient air-speed and altitude are attained to prevent settling back onto the runway.

Changed 25 June 1965

T.O. 1B-70(X)A-1

WARNING

The airplane should not be rotated to take-off attitude before nose wheel lift-off speed has been attained. A high angle of attack prior to take-off speed will reduce acceleration and increase take-off distance.

AFTER TAKE-OFF - CLIMB.

NOTE
- For the recommended climb speeds and the time, fuel and distance requirements, refer to Parts 3 and 4 of Appendix I. During climbs through both altitude regions, a transonic acceleration phase is necessary.
- During flight, continually monitor the fuel tank corresponding to the fuel sequence indicator strip being used.

1. Hydraulic systems - Check.
   Check hydraulic pressures, fluid levels, and pump status indicators.
2. Landing gear handle - UP, below 300 knots IAS.
   Check gear position lights.

NOTE
When the landing gear is retracted, the rudder travel is reduced automatically. (The ±12 degrees of rudder travel available when the gear is down is reduced to ±3 degrees when the gear is up.)

CAUTION
Landing gear and doors should be completely up and locked before gear-down limit speed is reached; otherwise, excessive air loads may damage the doors and gear operating mechanism and prevent subsequent operation. If the landing gear handle has been moved to UP while the weight of the airplane was still on the gear, the handle must be placed in the DOWN position and then returned to UP (with weight off the gear) before gear can retract.

3. Flap handle - FLAP UP, below 270 knots IAS.
   Move flap handle to FLAP UP before reaching flap-down limit airspeed. There will be a nose down trim change as the flaps are raised. Check flap position indicator and flap pressure caution lights out.
4. Electrical and hydraulics - Check.
   Check voltages, and hydraulic pressures, fluid levels, and pump status indicators.
5. Cabin altitude and oxygen - Check.
   a. Cabin pressure altimeter - Check at 8,000 feet when airplane is above 8,000 feet.
6. Auxiliary cooling switch - OFF, if electronic equipment air temperature in green arc. (CP)
7. Ammonia, water, oxygen, and nitrogen quantities - Check.
8. Fuel system - Check. (CP)
   a. Fuel sequencing - Check.
   b. Fuel tank pump switches - Check empty tanks OFF.
9. AICS mode switches* - Both AUTO. (CP)
10. Wing tips - ½ at Mach 0.95 or 400 knots, IAS, whichever is lower.
    a. Wing tip fold mode switch - Check NORMAL.

NOTE
Do not use ALTR position to lower the wing tips.

   b. Wing tip position selector switch - ½, check tip position indicators.

NOTE
A slight nose-up trim change occurs when the tips are lowered.

---

*Airplane AF62-207

Changed 25 June 1965

2-27

T.O. 1B-70(X)A-1

11. Electrical and hydraulics - Check.
    Check voltages, and hydraulic pressures, fluid levels, and pump status indicators.

ACCELERATION.

> NOTE
> * Refer to Part 5 of Appendix I for acceleration performance data.
> * Below Mach 2, disregard shock position indicator even though the pointers may ride in the red.

ACCELERATION - AUTO/MANUAL AICS (AIRPLANE AF62-001).

0.9 Mach

1. Bypass door standby system selector switches - Both PRIMARY. (CP)
2. Bypass door manual control wheels - Both forward; then both bypass door mode switches - MAN. (CP)

> NOTE
> Check bypass area closed and throat Mach schedule at 1.67.

3. AICS package power switch - Check ON. (CP)

> NOTE
> If package power switch was at OFF at this time, the system will require about 25 minutes to become fully operative after being turned on.

4. Duct performance switch - Check NORM. (CP)
5. Nose ramp switch - UP.
   Windshield nose ramp should be up before acceleration to minimize drag.

1.0 Mach

1. Bypass wheels - Both aft towards OPEN to increase bypass area to 200 square inches (CP).
2. Secondary exhaust nozzle area standby pressure knob - Set at 80.
   The secondary exhaust nozzle area standby pressure knob should be at 80 (80,000 feet) when passing through Mach 1.0 in acceleration. This will prevent nozzle damage resulting from excessive exhaust pressure build-up in the event of central air data system failure.
3. Engine rpm lockup switch - AUTO.
4. Flight augmentation control system - On.
   Press flight augmentation control system engage button momentarily. Check all flight augmentation control system caution lights out.
5. Anticollision light switch - OFF.

> NOTE
> Although the anticollision lights are turned off and retracted automatically above Mach 1.1, the anticollision light switch should be used to ensure that the lights are retracted for supersonic flight.

1.4 Mach

1. Wing tip position selector switch - DOWN and check tip position indicators.

> NOTE
> When the wing tips are lowered, a slight nose-up trim change occurs.

2. Bypass wheels - Both aft towards OPEN to increase bypass area to 400 square inches. (CP)
3. Fuel tank pump switches of empty tanks - Check OFF. (CP)

1.7 Mach

1. Emergency heat exchanger water switch - ON. (CP)
2. Pitot heater and windshield defogging switches - OFF. (CP)
3. Throat Mach schedule manual control wheels - Check both full aft to DCR. (CP)
4. Throat Mach schedule mode switches - Both AUTO. (CP)

> CAUTION
> Do not select automatic operation of the throats below Mach 1.7.

Changed 25 June 1965

T.O. 1B-70(X)A-1

SECONDARY EXHAUST NOZZLE STANDBY OPERATION

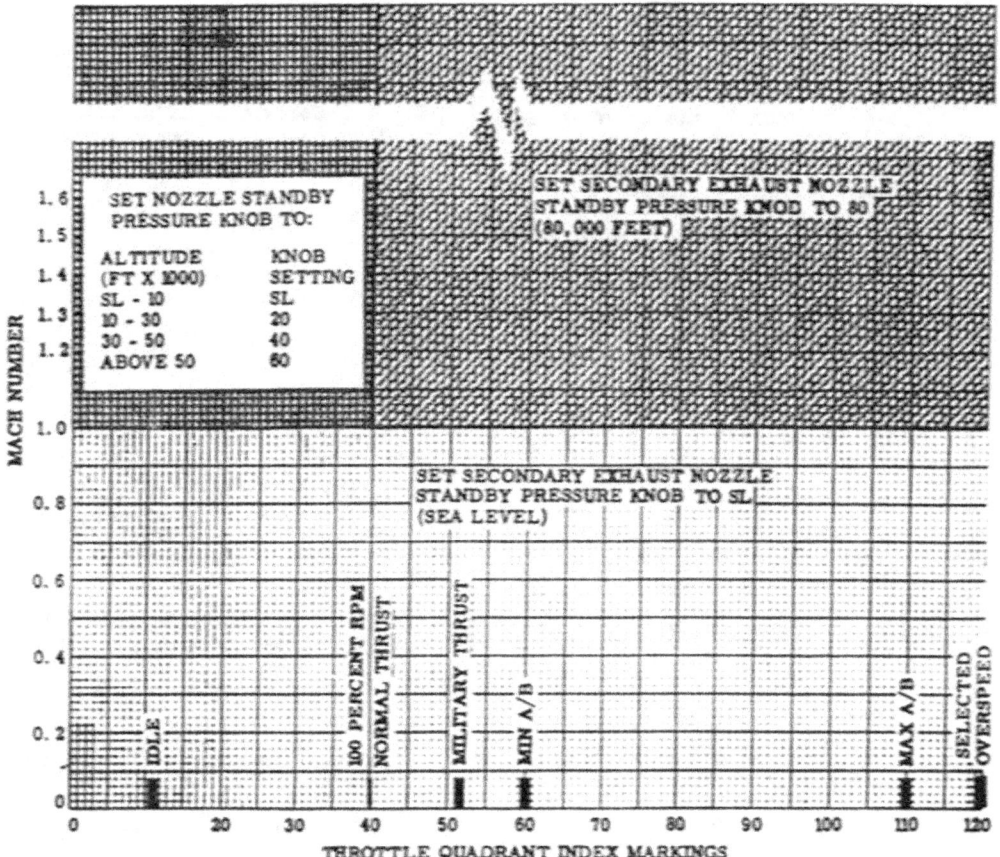

Caution

At take-off, set secondary nozzle standby pressure knob to field elevation.

NOTE

When maintaining a constant altitude, if any changes of thrust and Mach number are made, the secondary exhaust nozzle standby pressure knob may be set to correspond to airplane altitude.

Figure 2-6

T.O. 1B-70(X)A-1

5. Throat Mach schedule manual control wheels - Update both to restart number 0. (CP)
6. Exhaust temperature gages - Monitor as function of total temperature.
7. Fuel system - Check sequencing. (CP)

2.0 Mach

1. Bypass wheels - Both aft to position shocks in crosshatch, then forward to position shocks at bottom of green. (CP)

   NOTE
   Operation with the shock wave position indicator below the green arc should be avoided at all times. Operation with the indicator below the green arc will result in loss of engine thrust, and an engine stall may occur. Operation in the white arc or crosshatch also should be avoided except for buzz elimination, inlet restart, maneuvering flight, certain throttle changes, or asymmetrical engine operation.

2.3 Mach

1. Bypass wheels - Both forward to position shocks at bottom of green. (CP)
2. Throat wheels - Update both to restart number 3. (CP)
3. Exhaust temperature gages - Monitor as function of total temperature.

2.6 Mach

1. Throat wheels - Update both to restart number 6. (CP)
2. Lateral bobweight switch - Hold at FREE for 3 seconds then release to OFF and check bobweight indicator showing FREE.

2.9 Mach

1. Throat wheels - Update both to restart number 9. (CP)
2. Fuel tank pump switches of empty tanks - Check OFF. (CP)

ACCELERATION - MANUAL AICS (AIRPLANE AF62-001).

0.9 Mach

1. Bypass door standby system selector switches - Both PRIMARY. (CP)
2. Bypass door manual control wheels - Both forward; then both door mode switches - MAN. (CP)

   NOTE
   Check bypass areas closed and throat Mach schedule at 1.67.

3. AICS package power switch - Check ON. (CP)

   NOTE
   If package power switch was OFF at this time, the system will require about 25 minutes to become fully operative after being turned on.

4. Duct performance switch - Check NORM. (CP)
5. Nose ramp switch - UP.
   Windshield nose ramp should be up before acceleration to minimize drag.

1.0 Mach

1. Bypass wheels - Both aft towards OPEN to increase bypass area to 200 square inches. (CP)
2. Secondary exhaust nozzle area standby pressure knob - Set at 80.
   The secondary exhaust nozzle area standby pressure knob should be at 80 (80,000 feet) when passing through Mach 1.0 in acceleration. This will prevent nozzle damage resulting from excessive exhaust pressure build-up in the event of central air data system failure.
3. Engine rpm lockup switch - AUTO.
4. Flight augmentation control system - ON.
   Press flight augmentation control system engage button momentarily. Check all flight augmentation system caution lights out.

2-30   Changed 25 June 1965

T.O. 1B-70(X)A-1

WING TIP FOLD OPERATING SPEED

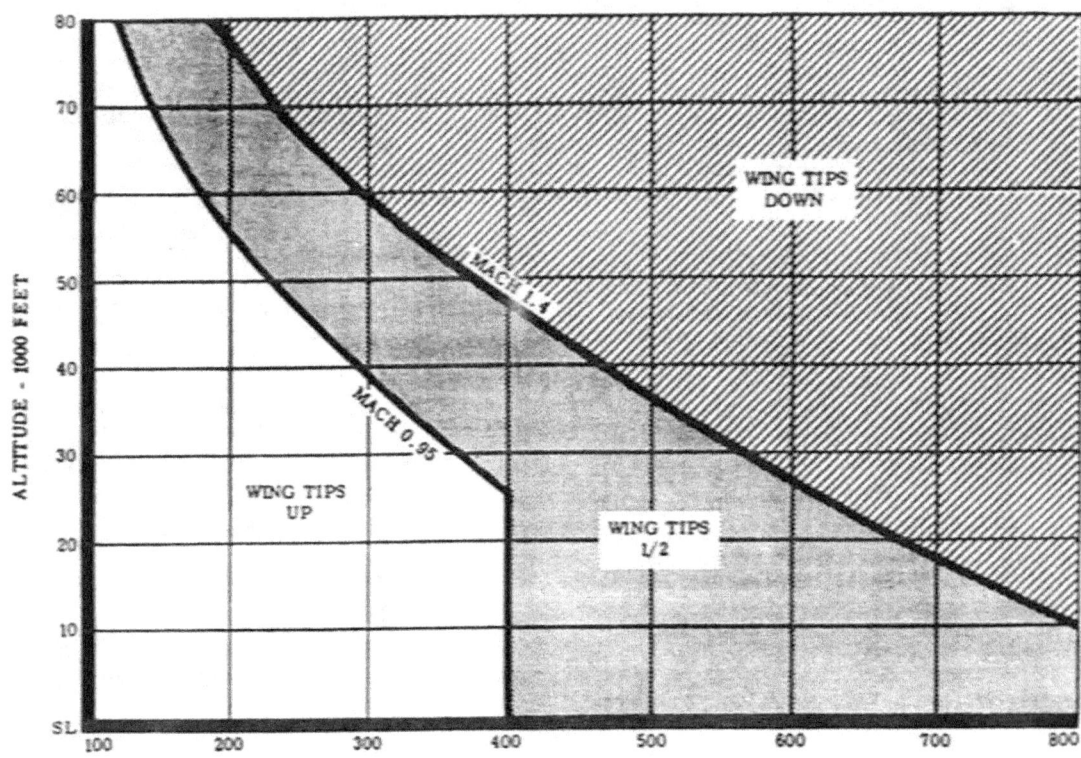

NOTE

CHANGE WING TIP POSITION AT 400 KNOTS IAS, MACH 0.95, OR MACH 1.4.

Figure 2-7

T.O. 1B-70(X)A-1

5. Anticollision light switch - OFF.

   NOTE
   Although the anticollision lights are turned off and retracted automatically above Mach 1.1, the anticollision light switch should be used to ensure that the lights are retracted for supersonic flight.

1.4 Mach

1. Wing tip position selector switch - DOWN and check tip position indicators.

   NOTE
   When the wing tips are lowered, a slight nose-up trim change occurs.

2. Bypass wheels - Both aft towards OPEN to increase bypass area to 400 square inches. (CP)
3. Fuel tank pump switches of empty tanks - Check OFF. (CP)

1.7 Mach

1. Emergency heat exchanger water switch - ON. (CP)
2. Pitot heater and windshield defogging switches - OFF. (CP)
3. Throat wheels - Check both full aft. (CP)
4. Throat mode switches - Both MAN. (CP)
5. Throat wheels - Both forward to schedule. (CP)
6. Exhaust temperature gages - Monitor as function of total temperature.
7. Fuel system - Check sequencing. (CP)

2.0 Mach

1. Bypass wheels - Both aft to position shocks in crosshatch, then forward to position shocks at bottom of green. (CP)

   NOTE
   Operation with the shock wave position indicator below the green arc should be avoided at all times. Operation with the indicator below the green arc will result in loss of engine thrust, and an engine stall may occur. Operation in the white arc or crosshatch also should be avoided except for buzz elimination, inlet restart, maneuvering flight, certain throttle changes, or asymmetrical engine operation.

2. Throat wheels - Both forward to schedule. (CP)

2.3 Mach

1. Bypass wheels - Both forward to position shocks at bottom of green arc. (CP)
2. Throat wheels - Both forward to schedule. (CP)
3. Exhaust temperature gages - Monitor as function of total temperature.

2.6 Mach

1. Bypass wheels - Both forward. (CP)
2. Throat wheels - Both forward to schedule. (CP)
3. Lateral bobweight switch - Hold at FREE for 3 seconds then release to OFF and check bobweight indicator showing FREE.

2.9 Mach

1. Bypass wheels - Both forward. (CP)
2. Throat wheels - Both forward to schedule. (CP)
3. Fuel tank pump switches of empty tanks - Check OFF. (CP)

ACCELERATION - AUTOMATIC AICS (AIRPLANE AF62-207).

0.9 Mach

1. AICS package power switch - Check ON. (CP)

   NOTE
   If package power switch was at OFF at this time, the system will require about 25 minutes to become fully operative after being turned on.

Changed 25 June 1965

T.O. 1B-70(X)A-1

2. Duct performance switch - Check NORM. (CP)
3. Bypass area - Check both closed. (CP)
4. Nose ramp switch - UP.
   Windshield nose ramp should be up before acceleration to minimize drag.
5. Throat Mach schedule indicators - Check that both are increasing from 1.67. (CP)

1.0 Mach

1. Secondary exhaust nozzle area standby pressure knob - Set at 80.
   The secondary exhaust area standby pressure knob should be at 80 (80,000 feet) when passing through Mach 1.0 in acceleration. This will prevent nozzle damage resulting from excessive exhaust pressure build-up in the event of central air data system failure.
2. Engine rpm lockup switch - AUTO.
3. Flight augmentation control system - ON.
   Press flight augmentation control system engage button momentarily. Check all flight augmentation control system caution lights out.
4. Anticollision light switch - OFF.

   NOTE
   Although the anticollision lights are turned off and retracted automatically above Mach 1.1, the anticollision light switch should be used to ensure that the lights are retracted for supersonic flight.

5. Bypass area - Check both closed. (CP)
   If bypass doors are opening, bypass area should not exceed 400 square inches.

1.4 Mach

1. Bypass area indicators - Check both at approximately 500 square inches. (CP)
2. Wing tip position selector switch - DOWN and check tip position indicators.

   NOTE
   When the wing tips are lowered, a slight nose-up trim change occurs.

3. Fuel tank pump switches of empty tanks - Check OFF. (CP)

1.7 Mach

1. Emergency heat exchanger water switch - ON. (CP)
2. Pitot heater and windshield defogging switches - OFF. (CP)
3. Exhaust temperature gages - Monitor as function of total temperature.
4. Fuel system - Check sequencing. (CP)

2.1 Mach

1. Bypass areas - Check that bypass doors are controlling shock position. (CP)

   CAUTION
   If bypass area exceeds 1200 square inches, put affected inlet in standby mode.

2. Throat Mach schedule indicators - Check both on schedule. (CP)

2.8 Mach

1. Fuel tank pump switches of empty tanks - Check OFF. (CP)
2. Duct performance switch - As required. (CP)
   Duct performance switch may be moved to HIGH, if desired, for high speed cruise flight.

AICS CHANGE-OVER (AIRPLANE AF62-001).

AUTO/MANUAL TO MANUAL AICS - ABOVE Mach 2.1.

To transfer from automatic throat-manual bypass operation of the air induction control system to manual throat and bypass operation during flight above Mach 2.1, proceed as follows:
1. Bypass wheels - Both aft towards OPEN to position shocks in crosshatch. (CP)
2. Throat wheels - Both forward towards INCR to maintain both throat Mach 0.1 Mach less than airplane Mach. (CP)

Changed 25 June 1965

3. Throat mode switches - Both MAN. (CP)
4. Throat wheels - Both as required. (CP)
5. Bypass wheels - Both as required. (CP)

MANUAL TO AUTO/MANUAL AICS - ABOVE MACH 2.1.

To transfer from manual throat and bypass operation to automatic throat-manual bypass operation during flight above Mach 2.1, proceed as follows:

1. Bypass wheels - Both aft towards OPEN to maintain shocks in crosshatch. (CP)
2. Throat wheels - Both aft towards DCR to maintain both throat Mach 0.1 Mach less than airplane Mach. (CP)
3. Duct performance switch - NORM. (CP)
4. Throat mode switches and bypass wheels - Both switches AUTO; both wheels forward towards CLOSE to maintain shocks in green arc. (CP)
5. Throat wheels - Both aft to update. (CP)

CRUISE.

CAUTION
- To prevent possible engine vibration, use recommended "detented" throttle technique as applicable.
- Because operation in the minimum afterburner range may cause unstable combustion, which could result in compressor stalls and/or engine flame-out, avoid afterburner operation with the throttle between the 61- and 70-degree settings. (Refer to "Minimum Afterburner Instability" in Section VII.)

For cruise data, refer to Parts 6 and 7 of Appendix I. At the desired cruise altitude, follow the mission cruise schedule. The best cruise thrust should be set for desired long range cruise and the Mach number maintained with proper attitude control. As fuel is used and the airplane becomes lighter, altitude will increase and a cruise climb condition will result.

CAUTION
The applicable fuel transfer pumps must be turned off (CP) after the corresponding tank is empty to prevent pump damage.

Above Mach 2.9, use the regime III cooling as required.

CAUTION
Before advancing the throttles above the 88-degree mark while in regime III cooling, move the regime III cooling switch to OFF and wait at least 45 seconds for system switchover.

Optimum cruise conditions will be maintained by applying trim corrections, cruise control and proper engine operation. Use proper wing tip positioning during cruise. Because of the high temperatures encountered in supersonic flight, proper environmental control must be maintained.

CRUISE - AUTO/MANUAL OR MANUAL AICS (AIRPLANE AF62-001).

1. Bypass wheels - Both as required. (CP)
2. Throat wheels; (CP)
   If AUTO/MAN - Update both to proper restart numbers.
   If MAN - Both as required to maintain schedule.
3. Electrical and hydraulics - Check. Check voltages and hydraulic pressures, fluid levels and pump status indicators.
4. Fuel system - Check. (CP) Check fuel sequencing and move fuel tank pump switches of empty tanks to OFF.
5. Ammonia, water, and liquid nitrogen - Check.
6. Cabin altitude and oxygen - Check.

MANEUVERING - AUTO/MANUAL AICS (AIRPLANE AF62-001).

BEFORE TURNS.

1. Bypass wheels - Both as required to position shocks in bottom of green arc. (CP)

T.O. 1B-70(X)A-1

AFTER ROLL-OUT.

1. Bypass wheels - Both as required. (CP)

MANEUVERING - MANUAL AICS (AIRPLANE AF62-001).

BEFORE TURNS.

1. Bypass wheels - Both aft towards OPEN to maintain shocks in crosshatch. (CP)
2. Throat wheels - Both aft towards DCR to maintain both throat Mach 0.1 less than airplane Mach. (CP)

AFTER ROLL-OUT.

1. Throat wheels - Both forward towards INCR to maintain both throat Mach at airplane Mach. (CP)
2. Bypass wheels - Both forward towards CLOSE as required. (CP)

THROTTLE CHANGES (IN OR OUT OF A/B) - AUTO/MANUAL AICS (AIRPLANE AF62-001).

When moving any or all throttles in or out of afterburner, accomplish the following to maintain stable inlet airflow:

BEFORE THROTTLE CHANGE.

1. Bypass wheels - Both aft towards OPEN to position shocks in crosshatch. (CP)

AFTER THROTTLE CHANGE.

1. Bypass wheels - Both forward towards CLOSE as required. (CP)

THROTTLE CHANGES (IN OR OUT OF A/B) - MANUAL AICS - (AIRPLANE AF62-001).

When moving any or all throttles in or out of afterburner, accomplish the following to maintain stable inlet airflow:

BEFORE THROTTLE CHANGE.

1. Bypass wheels - Both aft towards OPEN to position shocks in crosshatch. (CP)
2. Throat wheels - Both aft towards DCR to maintain both throat Mach 0.1 less than airplane Mach. (CP)

AFTER THROTTLE CHANGE.

1. Throat wheels - Both forward towards INCR to maintain both throat Mach at airplane Mach. (CP)
2. Bypass wheels - Both forward towards CLOSE as required. (CP)

CRUISE - AUTOMATIC AICS (AIRPLANE AF62-207).

1. Electrical and hydraulics - Check. Check voltages, and hydraulic pressures, fluid levels, and pump status indicators.
2. Fuel system - Check. (CP) Check fuel sequencing and move fuel tank pump switches of empty tanks to OFF.
3. Ammonia, water, and liquid nitrogen - Check.
4. Cabin altitude and oxygen - Check.

MANEUVERING - AUTOMATIC AICS (AIRPLANE AF62-207).

No action required.

THROTTLE CHANGES - AUTOMATIC AICS (AIRPLANE AF62-207).

No action required.

DECELERATION.

NOTE
For deceleration data, refer to Part 8 of Appendix I.

DECELERATION - AUTO/MANUAL AICS (AIRPLANE AF62-001).

Before Decelerating

Before beginning a deceleration from any airspeed, perform the following:

1. Bypass wheels - Both aft to position shocks in crosshatch. (CP)
2. Throat wheels - Update both to proper restart number. (CP)
3. Throttles - MIL.

Changed 25 June 1965

T.O. 1B-70(X)A-1

2.9 Mach

1. Bypass wheels - Both as required to maintain shocks in crosshatch. (CP)
2. Throat wheels - Update both to restart number 6. (CP)

2.6 Mach

1. Bypass wheels - Both as required to maintain shocks in crosshatch. (CP)
2. Throat wheels - Update both to restart number 3. (CP)
3. Lateral bobweight switch - LOCK; check bobweight indicator showing LOCKED.

2.3 Mach

1. Bypass wheels - Both as required to maintain shocks in crosshatch. (CP)
2. Throat wheels - Update both to restart number 0.

2.1 Mach

1. Throttles - 40 degrees or above.
2. Engine instruments - Check.
3. Duct performance switch - NORM. (CP)
4. Bypass wheels - Both forward as required to maintain shocks in green arc. (CP)
5. Throat wheels - Check both. (CP)
6. Fuel tank pump switches of empty tanks - Check OFF. (CP)

1.7 Mach

1. Bypass wheels - Check both. (CP)
2. Throat wheels - Both full aft. (CP)
3. Throat Mach schedule mode switches - Both MAN, then both OFF. (CP)
4. Emergency heat exchanger water switch - OFF. (CP)
5. Pitot heater and windshield defogging switches - ON. (CP)

1.4 Mach

1. Wing tip position selector switch - ½ and check tip position indicators.

    NOTE
    When the wing tips are raised, a slight nose-down trim change occurs.

2. Throttles - 40 degrees or above.

NOTE
If throttles cannot be maintained at 40 degrees or higher, accomplish the following:
- Cabin temperature selector switch - AUTO. (CP)
- Refrigeration switch - ON. (CP)
- Auxiliary cooling switch - OFF. (CP)
- Crew air shutoff handle - As required. (CP).

3. Engine rpm lockup switch - RELEASE.
4. Bypass wheels - Both forward towards CLOSE to obtain 400 square inches. (CP)

    If one engine in an inlet is shutdown, bypass area should be 700 square inches; with two engines out, 1100 square inches; and with three engines out, 1800 square inches.

5. Fuel tank pump switches of empty tanks - Check OFF. (CP)
6. Liquid nitrogen quantity - Check. (CP)
7. Secondary exhaust nozzle area standby pressure knob - Set to airplane altitude if below 100% engine rpm.
8. Engine rpm - Maintain engines 3 and 4 at or above 87%.

1.0 Mach

NOTE
If throttles cannot be maintained at 40 degrees or higher, accomplish the following:
- Cabin temperature selector switch - AUTO. (CP)
- Refrigeration switch - ON. (CP)
- Auxiliary cooling switch - OFF. (CP)
- Crew air shutoff handle - As required. (CP)

1. Bypass wheels - Both full forward. (CP)
2. Bypass door mode switches - Both OFF. (CP)

T.O. 1B-70(X)A-1

3. Bypass door standby system selector switches - Both OFF. (CP)
4. Secondary exhaust nozzle area standby pressure knob - Set to field elevation.
5. Nose ramp switch - DOWN.
6. Anticollision light switch - ON.

0.95 Mach

> NOTE
> If throttles cannot be maintained at 40 degrees or higher, accomplish the following:
> * Cabin temperature selector switch - AUTO. (CP)
> * Refrigeration switch - ON. (CP)
> * Auxiliary cooling switch - OFF. (CP)
> * Crew air shutoff handle - As required. (CP)

1. Wing tip position selector switch - UP and check tip position indicators.

> NOTE
> When the wing tips are raised, a slight nose-down trim change occurs.

2. Ammonia, water, oxygen, and liquid nitrogen quantity - Check.
3. Electrical and hydraulics - Check. Check voltages, and hydraulic pressures, fluid levels, and pump status indicators.
4. Fuel tank pump switches of empty tanks - Check OFF. (CP)
5. Engine rpm - Maintain engines 3 and 4 at or above 87%.

DECELERATION - MANUAL AICS (AIRPLANE AF62-001).

Before Decelerating

Before beginning a deceleration from any airspeed, perform the following:

1. Bypass wheels - Both aft towards OPEN to position shocks in crosshatch. (CP)
2. Throat wheels - Both aft towards DCR to maintain throat Mach 0.2 less than airplane Mach. (CP)
3. Throttles - MIL.

2.9 Mach

1. Bypass wheels - Both as required to maintain shocks in crosshatch. (CP)
2. Throat wheels - Both aft towards DCR to maintain throat Mach 0.2 less than airplane Mach. (CP)

2.6 Mach

1. Bypass wheels - Both aft towards OPEN to maintain shocks in crosshatch. (CP)
2. Throat wheels - Both aft toward DCR to maintain throat Mach 0.2 less than airplane Mach. (CP)
3. Lateral bobweight switch - LOCK; check bobweight indicator showing LOCKED.

2.1 Mach

1. Throttles - 40 degrees or above.
2. Engine instruments - Check.
3. Bypass wheels - Both forward towards CLOSE as required to position shocks in green arc. (CP)
4. Throat wheels - Both aft to maintain throat Mach 0.2 less than airplane Mach. (CP)
5. Fuel tank pump switches of empty tanks - Check OFF. (CP)

1.7 Mach

1. Bypass wheels - Check both. (CP)
2. Throat wheels - Both full aft. (CP)
3. Throat mode switches - Both OFF. (CP)
4. Emergency heat exchanger water switch - OFF. (CP)
5. Pitot heater and windshield defogging switches - ON. (CP)

1.4 Mach

1. Wing tip position selector switch - ½ and check tip position indicators.

> NOTE
> When the wing tips are raised, a slight nose-down trim change occurs.

2. Throttles - 40 degrees or above.

> NOTE
> If throttles cannot be maintained at 40 degrees

Changed 25 June 1965

2-34A

T.O. 1B-70(X)A-1

or higher, accomplish the following:
- Cabin temperature selector switch - AUTO. (CP)
- Refrigeration switch - ON. (CP)
- Auxiliary cooling switch - OFF. (CP)
- Crew air shutoff handle - As required. (CP)

3. Engine rpm lockup switch - RELEASE.
4. Bypass wheels - Both forward towards CLOSE to obtain 400 square inches. (CP)

If one engine in an inlet is shutdown, bypass area should be 700 square inches; with two engines out, 1100 square inches; and with three engines out, 1800 square inches.

5. Fuel tank pump switches of empty tanks - Check OFF. (CP)
6. Liquid nitrogen quantity - Check. (CP)
7. Secondary exhaust nozzle area standby pressure knob - Set to airplane altitude if below 100% engine rpm.
8. Engine rpm - Maintain engines 3 and 4 at or above 87%.

1.0 Mach

If throttle cannot be maintained at 40 degrees or higher, accomplish the following:
- Cabin temperature selector switch - AUTO. (CP)
- Refrigeration switch - ON. (CP)
- Auxiliary cooling switch - OFF. (CP)
- Crew air shutoff handle - As required. (CP)

1. Bypass wheels - Both full forward. (CP)
2. Bypass door mode switches - Both OFF. (CP)
3. Bypass door standby system selector switches - Both OFF. (CP)

4. Secondary exhaust nozzle area standby pressure knob - Set to field elevation.
5. Nose ramp switch - DOWN.
6. Anticollision light switch - ON.

0.95 Mach

NOTE
If throttle cannot be maintained at 40 degrees or higher, accomplish the following:
- Cabin temperature selector switch - AUTO. (CP)
- Refrigeration switch - ON. (CP)
- Auxiliary cooling switch - OFF. (CP)
- Crew air shutoff handle - As required. (CP)

1. Wing tip position selector switch - UP and check tip position indicators.

NOTE
When the wing tips are raised, a slight nose-down trim change occurs.

2. Ammonia, water, oxygen, and liquid nitrogen quantity - Check.
3. Electrical and hydraulics - Check. Check voltages and hydraulic pressures, fluid levels and pump status indicators.
4. Fuel tank pump switches of empty tanks - Check OFF. (CP)
5. Engine rpm - Maintain engines 3 and 4 at or above 87%.

DECELERATION - AUTOMATIC AICS (AIRPLANE AF62-207).

Before Decelerating

Before beginning a deceleration from any airspeed, perform the following:

1. Duct performance switch - NORM. (CP)
2. Throttles - MIL.

2.3 Mach

1. Throttles - 40 degrees or above.
2. Engine instruments - Check.

2-34B

Changed 25 June 1965

3. Bypass area - Check both. (CP)

BYPASS AREA VS TEMP AT MACH 2.3
(PERFORMANCE MODE-NORMAL)

Total temp (°F)	300	320	340	360	380
Amb temp (°F)	-90	-80	-70	-60	-50
Bypass area (sq in.)	620	660	710	750	790

WARNING

A bypass area greater than 860 square inches at Mach 2.3 indicates engine and/or inlet problems, and inlet should be biased before reaching Mach 2.2. Bias affected inlet one second for each 200 square inches of bypass area above 860.

2.0 Mach

1. Bypass area - Check both closing to 500 square inches plus bias. (CP). If a bypass door master cylinder had been biased from its normal rig position 1, 3, or 6 seconds because of engine problems, check the affected bypass area closing to 700, 1100, or 1800 square inches, respectively.
2. Throat Mach schedule indicator - Check both stopped at 2.13 Mach.
3. Throat trim power switch - OFF. (CP)

1.7 Mach

1. Emergency heat exchanger water switch - OFF. (CP)
2. Pitot heater and windshield defogging switches - ON. (CP)

1.4 Mach

1. Wing tip position selector switch - ½ and check tip position indicators.

NOTE

When the wing tips are raised, a slight nose-down trim change occurs.

2. Throttles - 40 degrees or above.

NOTE

If throttles cannot be maintained at 40 degrees or higher, accomplish the following:
* Cabin temperature selector switch - AUTO. (CP)
* Refrigeration switch - ON. (CP)
* Auxiliary cooling switch - OFF. (CP)
* Crew air shutoff handle - As required. (CP)

3. Engine rpm lockup switch - RELEASE.
4. Fuel tank pump switches of empty tanks - Check OFF. (CP)
5. Liquid nitrogen quantity - Check. (CP)
6. Secondary exhaust nozzle standby pressure knob - Set to airplane altitude if below 100% engine rpm.
7. Engine rpm - Maintain engines 3 and 4 at or above 87%.
8. Bypass area - Check both closing to 0 plus bias. (CP)
   If a bypass door master cylinder had been biased from its normal rig position 1, 3, or 6 seconds because of engine problems, check the affected bypass area closing to 700, 1100, or 1800 square inches, respectively.

1.0 Mach

1. AICS mode switches - Both STBY. (CP)
2. Bypass area - Check both closed. (CP)
3. Throat Mach schedule standby switches - Both down to DCR until throat Mach schedule is full open (1.67). (CP)
4. Secondary exhaust nozzle standby pressure knob - Set to field elevation.
5. Nose ramp switch - DOWN.
6. Anticollision light switch - ON.

T.O. 1B-70(X)A-1

.95 Mach

> **NOTE**
> If throttles cannot be maintained at 40 degrees or higher, accomplish the following:
> - Cabin temperature selector switch - AUTO. (CP)
> - Refrigeration switch - ON. (CP)
> - Auxiliary cooling switch - OFF. (CP)
> - Crew air shutoff handle as required. (CP)

1. Wing tip position selector switch - UP and check tip position indicators.

> **NOTE**
> When the wing tips are raised, a slight nose-down trim change occurs.

2. Ammonia, water, oxygen, and liquid nitrogen quantity - Check. (CP)
3. Electrical and hydraulics - Check. Check voltages, and hydraulic pressures, fluid levels, and pump status indicators.
4. Fuel tank pump switches of empty tanks - Check OFF. (CP)
5. Engine rpm - Maintain engines 3 and 4 at or above 87%.

DESCENT.

> **NOTE**
> For descent data, refer to Part 9 of Appendix I.

> **WARNING**
> Erroneous bearing information may exist during TACAN operations, therefore, TACAN bearing information must be verified constantly during penetrations or letdowns by using ground or airborne radar to cross-check readings.

Changed 25 June 1965

T.O. 1B-70(X)A-1

1. Engine rpm - Maintain engines 3 and 4 at or above 87%, or accomplish the following:
    a. Crew air shutoff handle - Pull. (CP)
    b. Auxiliary cooling switch - ON. (CP)
    c. Refrigeration switch - OFF. (CP)
    d. Cabin temperature selector switch - OFF. (CP)
2. Liquid nitrogen quantity gage - Check. (CP)
3. Landing gear - If lowered at this time, observe the following limits:
    0.82 Mach at 40,000 feet
    0.76 Mach at 35,000 feet
    0.70 Mach at 30,000 feet
    270 knots IAS at 20,000 feet or below.
4. Electrical and hydraulics - Check. Check voltages, and hydraulic pressures, fluid levels, and pump status indicators.

BEFORE LANDING.

During the final phase of the descent and approach to the field:

1. Brake control switch - AUTOMATIC.
2. Nose wheel steering selector switch - Check TAKE-OFF LDG.
3. Engine rpm lockup switch - Check RELEASE.
4. Fuel tank sequence and quantity indicators - Check and check empty tank pump switches OFF. (CP)
5. Landing data - Compute. Compute approach and touchdown speeds and landing distances before entering traffic pattern. (Refer to Part 10 of Appendix I for landing data.)

FLARE SPEED VS WEIGHT

GROSS WT LBS	CAS KNOTS	GROSS WT LBS	CAS KNOTS
460,000	219	340,000	192
440,000	215	320,000	186
420,000	210	310,000	184
400,000	206	300,000	181
380,000	201	290,000	178
360,000	197	280,000	175

6. Flight augmentation control system switches - OFF.
7. Landing gear handle - DOWN and check gear position lights.
    Extend gear below gear-down limit speed.
8. Flap handle - FLAP DOWN and check flap position indicator.
    Lower flaps below flap-down limit speed.
9. Electrical and hydraulics - Check. Check voltages, and hydraulic pressures, fluid levels, and pump status indicators.
10. Ammonia quantity gage - Check.
11. Auxiliary cooling switch - Check ON. (CP)
12. Refrigeration switch (if windshield anti-ice and rain removal switches are at ON) - OFF. (CP)

LANDING.

NORMAL LANDING.

NOTE
- See figure 2-8 for typical landing pattern.
- Refer to Part 10 of Appendix I for landing speeds and distances.

1. (Deleted)
2. Throttles - IDLE at touchdown. Retard all throttles simultaneously to IDLE at touchdown.

NOTE
Air induction control system coolant caution light will come on when weight is on the main gear. However, this does not indicate a malfunction.

3. Lower nose wheels.
4. Nose wheel steering engage switch - ENGAGE, then FAIL SAFE.

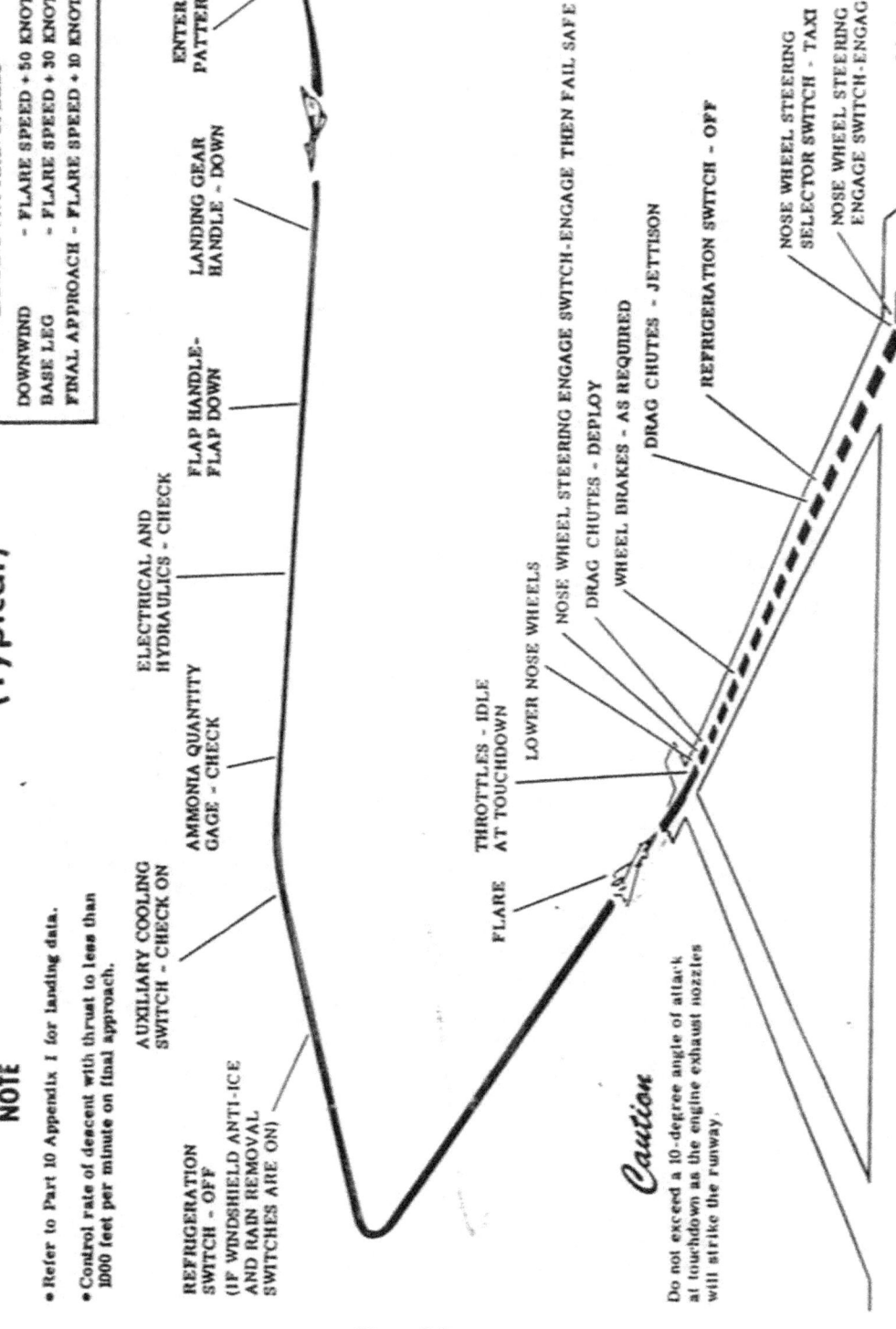

Figure 2-8

T.O. 1B-70(X)A-1

5. Drag chute handle - DEPLOY, below 220 knots IAS. (CP)
6. Wheel brakes - As required.

> **CAUTION**
> Avoid hard or excessive braking, unless necessary, as high operating temperatures and excessive tire wear can result.

7. Drag chute handle - STOWED JETTISON, between 60 and 70 knots IAS. (CP)
   It is recommended that the drag chutes be jettisoned at speeds between 60 and 70 knots IAS when required.

> **CAUTION**
> To avoid possible structural damage to the upper surface of the wing, do not jettison drag chutes below 60 knots IAS.

8. (Deleted)
9. Refrigeration switch - OFF after landing roll. (CP)
10. (Deleted)
11. Nose wheel steering selector switch - TAXI.
12. Nose wheel steering engage switch - ENGAGE.

NORMAL LANDING TECHNIQUE.

Following entry into the traffic pattern, lower the landing gear and the flaps below gear and flap down-limit speeds. Fly the traffic pattern at the previously computed airspeeds, adjusting throttles to control rate of descent. After rolling out of turn onto final approach, adjust thrust to maintain final approach speed for the specific landing gross weight to control rate of descent to touchdown at the desired speed. Retard the throttles to IDLE after touchdown. Normal landing touchdowns will be at about 10 degrees nose high.

> **CAUTION**
> Higher touchdown angles should be avoided, as the engine exhaust nozzles will strike the runway when the airplane is at an 11-degree attitude. Besides the angle-of-attack indicator, the windshield nose ramp can be used as a reference to indicate over-rotation. The windshield nose ramp angle is 11 degrees; therefore, when the ramp becomes horizontal during touchdown, the airplane is at 11 degrees angle of attack. Over-rotation will be indicated when the nose starts to blank out the horizon.

Approach thrust should not be reduced until the landing flare has been completed and the touchdown accomplished.

> **NOTE**
> A reduction in thrust during final approach or flare will result in a rapid increase in rate of descent.

Immediately after touchdown, move throttles to IDLE, lower the nose wheels to the runway, engage nose wheel steering, deploy the drag chutes, apply braking as required.

BRAKING TECHNIQUE.

Be prepared to start braking immediately after touchdown. This eliminates any time lag in decelerating if the drag chutes fail. Applying the necessary brake pedal force provides the desired braking. However, if maximum braking is required, apply and hold full brake pedal force.

Changed 25 June 1965

T.O. 1B-70(X)A-1

DRAG CHUTE OPERATION.

The drag chutes may be deployed at any speed after nose wheel touchdown up to 220 knots IAS. The effects of usage (i.e. runway abrasion and heat effects) can lower the strength of the chute to a point where failures may be encountered at speeds above 220 knots IAS. However, with properly inspected chutes, no failures of this type should occur at normal landing speeds or take-off speeds.

CAUTION
- To avoid possible structural damage to the upper surface of the wing, do not jettison drag chutes below 60 knots IAS.
- Avoid cross-wind taxiing with the drag chutes deployed to prevent damage to the wing and vertical tail surfaces caused by the drag chute attach cable.

LANDING WITHOUT DRAG CHUTES.

Landing without drag chutes will require greater landing distances. (Refer to Landing Distances Charts in Part 10 of Appendix I.) In case of drag chute failure, as indicated by the lack of deceleration within 4 to 6 seconds after deployment, immediately apply light moderate braking and gradually increase to heavy braking as required.

HEAVYWEIGHT LANDING.

For heavy gross weight landings, increase approach and touchdown speeds as given in Part 10, Appendix I.

CROSS-WIND LANDING.

In addition to normal landing procedures, the following should be accomplished, when landing in a crosswind. On final approach, crab airplane or drop a wing into the wind to keep lined up with the runway. Adequate rudder control is available for cross-wind landings; however, approach and touchdown speeds should be increased approximately one half the 90-degree crosswind component. Immediately before touchdown, level the wings and line up with the runway. After touchdown, lower nose wheels to the runway as soon as possible, engage nose wheel steering, and deploy the drag chutes. If yawing is encountered to the extent that directional control is marginal, the drag chutes should be jettisoned and directional control maintained by nose wheel steering and the use of the wheel brakes. Because of the inboard location of the engines, practically no advantage is gained by using asymmetrical thrust settings during a crosswind landing.

CAUTION
Avoid cross-wind taxiing with the drag chutes deployed to prevent damage to the wing and vertical tail surfaces caused by the drag chute attach cable.

SLIPPERY-RUNWAY LANDING.

On a slippery runway (wet or icy), braking effectiveness varies greatly. The runway conditions (rough or smooth surface) must be determined by ground personnel and the pilot advised accordingly. To keep the landing roll to a minimum, maintain proper approach, flare and touchdown speeds. A combination of rudder, nose wheel steering, and differential braking should be used for directional control. The drag chutes should be deployed as soon as possible after the nose wheels are lowered to the runway because braking effectiveness is reduced. Move the control column full aft for aerodynamic braking, then fly the nose down as the speed decreases.

GO-AROUND.

For a go-around procedure, see figure 2-9.

GO-AROUND (Typical)

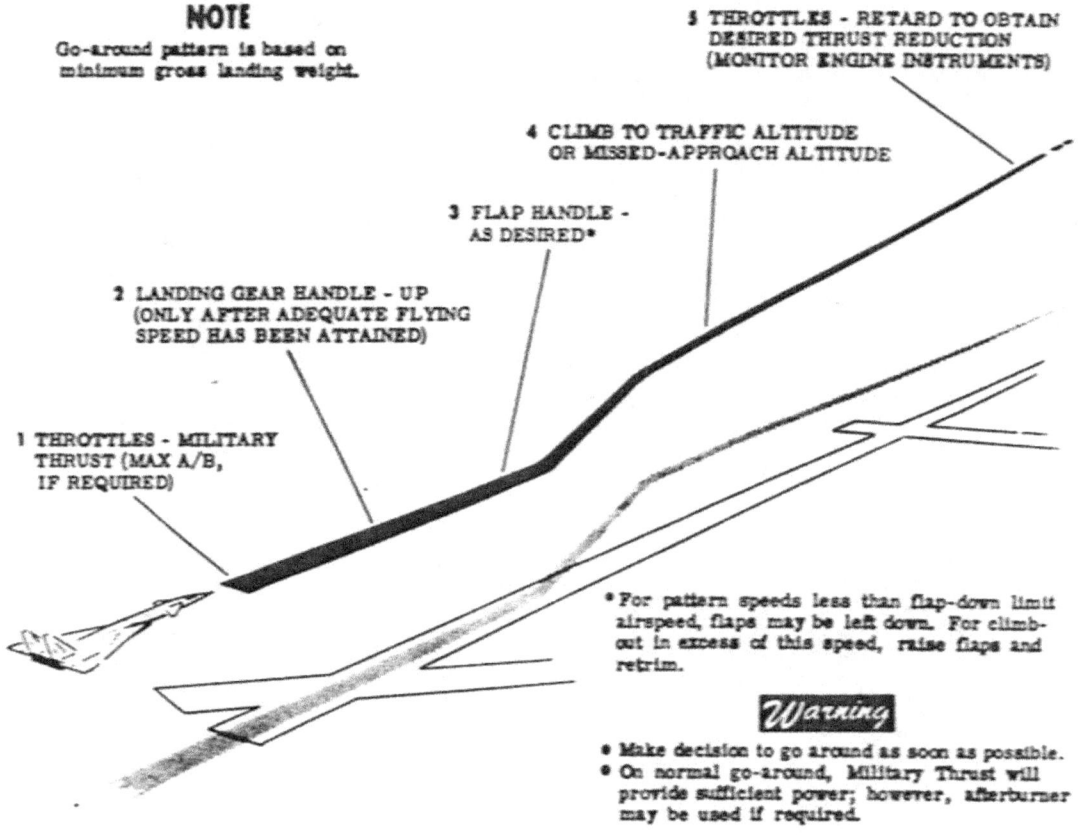

NOTE
Go-around pattern is based on minimum gross landing weight.

1. THROTTLES - MILITARY THRUST (MAX A/B, IF REQUIRED)
2. LANDING GEAR HANDLE - UP (ONLY AFTER ADEQUATE FLYING SPEED HAS BEEN ATTAINED)
3. FLAP HANDLE - AS DESIRED*
4. CLIMB TO TRAFFIC ALTITUDE OR MISSED-APPROACH ALTITUDE
5. THROTTLES - RETARD TO OBTAIN DESIRED THRUST REDUCTION (MONITOR ENGINE INSTRUMENTS)

*For pattern speeds less than flap-down limit airspeed, flaps may be left down. For climb-out in excess of this speed, raise flaps and retrim.

Warning

- Make decision to go around as soon as possible.
- On normal go-around, Military Thrust will provide sufficient power; however, afterburner may be used if required.

Figure 2-9

T.O. 1B-70(X)A-1

AFTER LANDING.

After clearing runway:

1. (Deleted)
2. (Deleted)
3. Anticollision light switch - OFF.
4. Flap handle - FLAP UP.
5. Seat safety pins - Install. (P and CP)

    Install flight status safety pins through the right console of each seat after checking seat handgrips down and stowed.

6. Electrical and hydraulics - Check and monitor.
7. TACAN and ILS - OFF. (CP)
8. Pitot heater switch - OFF. (CP)
9. Windshield anti-ice and rain removal switches - OFF. (CP)
10. Windshield defog switch - OFF. (CP)
11. IFF - OFF. (CP)

    Turn IFF off as soon after landing as possible. This will eliminate signals from taxiing or parked airplanes which would otherwise block the controller's scope and interfere with the control of airborne airplanes.

12. Brakes - Check.
    a. Check operation of each automatic brake system by holding the brake test switch at SYS 1 then SYS 2 and applying brakes when switch is at each position. Release switch to center (OFF).
    b. Brake control switch - MANUAL.

ENGINE SHUTDOWN.

NOTE

The engines must be operated for 3 minutes at or below 80% rpm before shutdown to stabilize engine temperatures. (Taxi time below 80% rpm may be included.) However, operation in the 75% to 78% rpm range should be avoided to prevent excessive engine vibration.

1. Wheel brake hold button - Engage. Press and hold the wheel brake hold button, release pedals, check brake hold light on, then release the wheel brake hold button.
2. Throttles - OFF. (Engines No. 6, 1, 2, in sequence.)

NOTE

- The engine oil pressure caution light coming on during engine shutdown (first five engines only) could indicate a possible failure of the firewall fuel shutoff valve to close.
- Check that applicable engine identification light comes on as each throttle is moved to OFF.

3. Air induction control system package power switch - OFF. (CP)
4. Fuel tank pump switches - All OFF. (CP)

Changed 25 June 1965

5. Emergency generator switch - OFF.
6. UHF radios - OFF. (P and CP)
7. Wheel chocks - Verify ground crew has installed.
8. Brakes - Press and release brake pedals.
   Keep feet off pedals after releasing brakes.
9. No. 5 throttle - OFF.
10. No. 3 primary generator switch - OFF.
11. No. 3 throttle - OFF.
12. Air recirculating fan switch - OFF.

NOTE

The air recirculating fans must be off to relieve the pressure so the entrance door can be opened and to prevent damage to the fans when the ground cooling unit is full on.

13. Auxiliary cooling switch - OFF. (CP)
14. Coolant circulation pump switch - OFF. (CP)
15. No. 4 throttle - OFF.
16. No. 4 primary generator switch - OFF.
17. Control columns - Stowed. (P and CP)
18. Oxygen toggle valve - OFF. (P and CP)
19. Flight status safety pins - Check installed. (P and CP)
   Make sure flight status safety pins are installed in the right console of each seat.

BEFORE LEAVING AIRPLANE.

Make the following checks before leaving the airplane:

1. Light switches - OFF.
2. Flight status safety pins - Check installed. (P and CP)
3. Form 781 (or equivalent) - Complete.

CAUTION

- Make appropriate entries covering any limits in the Flight Manual that have been exceeded. Entries also must be made when, in the pilot's judgement, the airplane has been exposed to unusual or excessive operations such as hard landings, excessive braking action during aborted take-offs, long and fast landings, etc.
- All high-speed flights must be recorded so that proper inspections and lubrication will be accomplished before the next flight. The high temperatures can dissipate lubricants from bearings, pins, etc.
- The remaining liquid nitrogen quantity should be recorded.
- Total engine flight time below Mach 2.00; between Mach 2.01 and 2.79; and above Mach 2.80 must be recorded.
- Total afterburner and overspeed operating time (flight or ground) must be recorded.
- Total engine ground time and ground time at Military and above must be recorded.

NOTE

- Breakdown of engine flight times, except overspeed, should be recorded to the nearest 5 minutes. Overspeed time should be recorded to the nearest 30 seconds.
- Breakdown of engine ground times, except overspeed should be recorded to the nearest 2 minutes. Ground overspeed time can be combined with flight overspeed time.

4. Communications tape recorder - Off.
5. Crew entrance dust cover - Check installed.

STRANGE FIELD PROCEDURE.

Because of the size and weight of the airplane, and the specialized servicing required, no strange-field procedures are recommended at this time.

ABBREVIATED CHECKLIST.

The abbreviated checklist is in T.O. 1B-70(X)A-1CL-1.

This page intentionally left blank

T.O. 1B-70(X)A-1

SECTION III

EMERGENCY PROCEDURES

TABLE OF CONTENTS	PAGE		PAGE
Introduction	3-2	Canard Flap Pressure Caution Light On	3-65
Engine Failure	3-2	Canard Flap System Emergency Operation	3-65
Ground Emergency Engine Shutdown	3-16	Wing Tip Fold System Emergency Operation	3-65
Fire	3-16A	Landing Gear Emergency Operation	3-67
Cabin Fire, Smoke, or Fumes	3-20	Automatic Braking System Failure	3-68
Crew Encapsulation	3-22	Nose Wheel Steering System Failure	3-68
Crew Decapsulation	3-23	Tire and/or Drag Chute Compartment Overheat Caution Light On	3-68
Ejection	3-24A	Windshield Nose Ramp Emergency Operation	3-69
Emergency Descent of Airplane	3-30	Central Air Data System Failure	3-69
Take-off and Landing Emergencies	3-31	Environmental Systems Emergency Operation	3-70
Emergency Ground Escape	3-33	Oxygen System Emergency Operation	3-73
Emergency Entrance	3-34	Loss of Hatch During Flight	3-73
Ditching	3-34	Caution and Warning Lights	3-73
Throttle System Malfunction	3-34	Abbreviated Checklist	3-73
Engine Exhaust Nozzle Failure	3-38		
Afterburner Failure	3-43		
Engine Oil Pressure Low	3-43		
Accessory Drive System Failure	3-43		
Excessive Engine or Accessory Drive System Gearbox Vibration	3-46A		
Air Induction Control System Emergency Operation	3-46B		
Fuel Supply System Failure	3-47		
Electrical Power System Failure	3-53		
Bus-tie Contactors Open	3-56		
Hydraulic Power System Failure	3-56A		
Nitrogen System Failure	3-58		
Flight Control System Failure	3-63		

Changed 25 June 1965

T.O. 1B-70(X)A-1

INTRODUCTION.

The procedures in this section are considered the best for coping with the various emergencies that may be encountered during operation of this airplane. A pilot with thorough knowledge of these procedures will be better able to cope with problems encountered. Even though the procedures are considered the best possible, sound judgement must be used when multiple emergencies, adverse weather, terrain clearance, etc are encountered.

NOTE
Because of various conditions that could arise, it is recommended that pilot and copilot agree on duty division beforehand to minimize time to accomplish the proper procedures.

ENGINE FAILURE.

NOTE
- All engine and engine-related procedures in this section are based on operation with throttle settings at 40 degrees or higher at the time the corrective action is started. Therefore, the procedures do not include the requirement to have all throttles at these settings before the engine RPM lockup is released. If throttle settings are below 40 degrees, however, the throttles must be advanced if rpm lockup release is required.

- Engine failure or shutdown affecting engines No. 3 and/or No. 4 may cause the respective primary generators to go off the line and the bus-tie contactors to open. Refer to "Bus-tie Contactors Open" in this section for additional information and procedures.

- Under certain conditions, low rpm and exhaust temperature indications may make it difficult to determine if engine flameout has occurred. If, as a result of such indications, engine operation is questionable, advance throttle to 40-degree setting. A corresponding increase in rpm will verify engine operation.

Although engine failures can result from numerous causes, they are normally associated with improper fuel scheduling or incorrect operating techniques. In this airplane the latter assumes special importance because the engines depend on correct operation of the variable-geometry inlet and because incorrect operation of one engine in either 3-engine bank can influence the operation of the other two engines served by the same inlet. Should an engine failure occur, the yaw resulting from unbalanced thrust is minimized because the engines are near the centerline which improves the flight safety aspects associated with this form of emergency.

If more than one engine fails, the hydraulic power available would be proportional to the number of operating engines remaining in either bank. Flight control system capability may be affected by any single engine failure or multiple engine failures in either left or right banks.

FLIGHT CHARACTERISTICS WITH PARTIAL THRUST.

DURING TAKE-OFF.

Engine failure during the take-off run can be critical and must be planned for before starting ground roll. Once the refusal speed has been reached or exceeded, normally the airplane is committed to completing the take-off. (Refer to Part 2 of Appendix I for refusal speeds and reduced thrust take-off performance.)

T.O. 1B-70(X)A-1

RECOMMENDED LEVEL FLIGHT LOITER - 3 ENGINES OUT

REFER TO CONFIDENTIAL SUPPLEMENT, T.O. 1B-70(X)A-1A

Figure 3-1

T.O. 1B-70(X)A-1

EMERGENCY EQUIPMENT

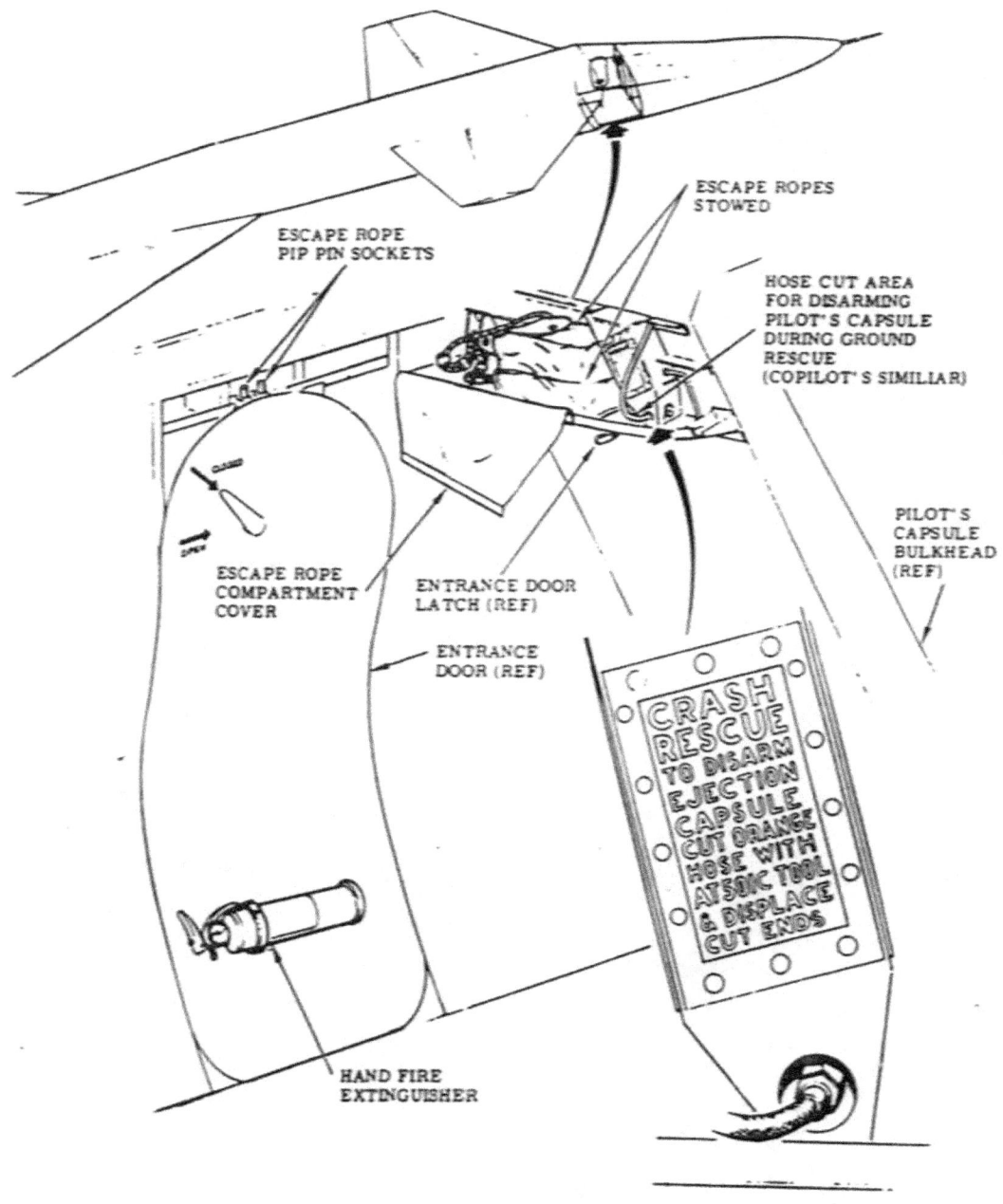

Figure 3-2 (Sheet 1 of 2)

T.O. 1B-70(X)A-1

SURVIVAL EQUIPMENT
(TYPICAL EACH ESCAPE CAPSULE)

REMOVABLE UPPER SURVIVAL EQUIPMENT CONTAINERS

REMOVABLE UPPER SURVIVAL EQUIPMENT CONTAINERS
RH   LH

EMERGENCY DESCENT CONTROL GRIP (REF)

SEALED BAG CONTAINING OVERCOAT

CONTAINER RELEASE BUTTON ACCESS HOLES

RAZOR BLADE

FILLER
RAZOR BLADE

SEALED BAG CONTAINING:
OVERBOOTS
MITTENS
SURVIVAL TROUSERS
SURVIVAL PARKA

LOWER SURVIVAL KIT COMPARTMENT

LOWER SURVIVAL KIT CONTAINER
PLASTIC WATER CONTAINER (5 QT)
WATER (1 PT)
SNARE WIRE (20 FT)
WHISTLE
SIGNAL MIRROR
HUNTING KNIFE
FLARE (MARK 13, MOD 0)
SEA MARKER DYE

LENSATIC COMPASS
FIRST AID KIT
WATER DESALTING KIT
ST RATIONS
FLARE (MARK 13, MOD 0)
FISHING KIT
MATCHES
LONG-BURNING CANDLES

LIFE RAFT (TYPE MB-4)
WATER (1PT)

Figure 3-2 (Sheet 2 of 2)

This page intentionally left blank

T.O. 1B-70(X)A-1

DURING SUBSONIC FLIGHT.

Adequate control is available to maintain straight and level flight with any single engine failure and to maintain controlled flight even with the maximum of three engines failed in either bank and with full afterburner thrust on the other three. However, the airplane performance is seriously affected at heavy gross weights with multiple engine failure. (See figure 3-1.)

DURING SUPERSONIC FLIGHT BELOW MACH 2.1.

Below Mach 2.1, the inlet has not been started and, as a result, the effects of engine failure are similar to those resulting from engine failure at subsonic speeds. However, inlet buzz may occur at speeds above Mach 1.5.

DURING FLIGHT ABOVE MACH 2.1.

In this speed range, the inlet normally will have been started, and there is a definite possibility a failed engine can cause inlet unstart and/or buzz. As a result of an inlet unstart, the airplane will pitch, roll, and yaw. However, sufficient control is available to maintain stabilized flight until normal operation is resumed. If engine failure is not accompanied by inlet unstart, the relatively mild effects of thrust loss occur.

CAUTION
The yaw, roll, and pitch caused by an unstarted inlet can unstart the opposite inlet. Recommended technique is to control the yawing, rolling, and pitching motions as quickly as possible. Restart the inlet as described in "Air Induction Control System Emergency Operation" in this section. Bypass door opening causes a nose-up trim change, and bypass door closing causes a nose-down trim change.

If engine failure occurs during afterburner operation, thrust can be reduced (if desired) to minimize asymmetrical thrust until directional control is regained.

ENGINE FAILURE DURING TAKE-OFF, ABORT.

It is recommended that the take-off run be aborted if an engine fails before reaching decision speed. (Decision speed must be determined before take-off. Refer to Part 2 of Appendix I for decision speeds.) The following procedures must be accomplished during an aborted take-off run:

1. All throttles - IDLE.
2. Drag chute handle - DEPLOY.
3. Wheel brakes - Apply.
4. Throttle (affected engine) - OFF.
5. Electronic equipment cooling - As required.
   a. Crew air shutoff handle - Unlock and pull up.
   b. Refrigeration switch - OFF.
   c. Auxiliary cooling switch - ON.
   d. Cabin temperature selector switch - OFF.

ENGINE FAILURE DURING TAKE-OFF, TAKE-OFF CONTINUED.

WARNING
If it is impossible to continue flight, do not attempt a forced landing on an unprepared surface. (Refer to "Ejection" in this section.)

If an engine thrust loss occurs and take-off is to be continued, continue the take-off as follows:

1. Alternate throttle switch (affected engine) - INCR.
2. Landing gear handle - UP.
   As soon as airplane is safely airborne, retract gear to improve rate of climb.

CAUTION
Do not retract gear until minimum control speed is reached. (See figure A2-4.)

3. Safe climb speed - Maintain.
   Until gear is fully retracted, maintain minimum safe climb.

Changed 25 June 1965

T.O. 1B-70(X)A-1

4. Throttle reset button - Push.
5. Throttle (affected engine) - OFF (if step 1 did not recover engine rpm). Moving the throttle to OFF closes the fire wall shutoff valve to stop fuel flow.
6. Flaps - As required.

NOTE
- Refer to "Engine Air Start" in this section if restart is contemplated.
- Refer to "Landing With One or More Engines Inoperative" in this section if restart is not possible.

ENGINE FAILURE OR SHUTDOWN - ABOVE MACH 2.1, AUTO/MANUAL OR MANUAL AICS (AIRPLANE AF62-001).

If an engine fails or must be shut down above Mach 2.1, proceed as follows:

1. Bypass wheels - Both aft to maintain shocks in crosshatch.
2. Engine rpm lockup switch - RELEASE.
3. Throttle (affected engine) - IDLE, and maintain shocks in crosshatch.
4. Throat:
   If AUTO - Check schedule.
   If MANUAL - Both throat wheels aft to maintain throat at 0.2 Mach less than airplane Mach.
5. Start normal deceleration and descent as required, with throttles (good engines) - MIL.
6. Throttle (affected engine) - OFF, and maintain shocks in crosshatch.
7. Engine emergency brake switch (affected engine) - ON, if required; maintain shocks in crosshatch.

CAUTION

Only one engine per inlet should be braked above Mach 1.5. This prevents the possibility of inducing continuous inlet buzz which could seriously affect airplane stability and control and could damage the engines and the inlet. Speed should be reduced to below Mach 1.5 before actuation of the brake for a second engine.

NOTE

The engine braking system is irreversible; therefore, the engine cannot be restarted after the emergency brake has been engaged.

8. Engine emergency brake switch - OFF. Move switch to OFF after rpm has stabilized at 22% or below.
9. Engine rpm lockup switch - AUTO.
10. Throttle (affected engine) - 40 degrees, if brake not used.

NOTE

If engine braking was not required, advance throttle of affected engine to 40 degrees, to provide fuel flow for proper cooling of engine lube oil system. (See figure 5-2.)

ENGINE FAILURE OR SHUTDOWN - BELOW MACH 2.1, AUTO/MANUAL OR MANUAL AICS (AIRPLANE AF62-001).

If an engine fails or must be shut down during flight below Mach 2.1, proceed as follows:

1. Bypass area (affected inlet):
   If SUPERSONIC - Wheel aft to obtain 700, 1100, or 1800 square inches. For first engine to be shut down, obtain 700 square inches; for second engine, 1100 square inches; and for third engine, 1800 square inches.
   If SUBSONIC - Check bypass area closed.
2. Engine rpm lockup switch - RELEASE.
3. Throttle (affected engine) - IDLE.
4. Throat - Check schedule.
5. Start normal deceleration and descent as required, with throttles (good engines) - MIL.
6. Throttle (affected engine) - OFF
7. Engine emergency brake switch (affected engine) - ON, if required.

CAUTION
Only one engine per inlet should be braked above Mach 1.5. This prevents the possibility of inducing

T.O. 1B-70(X)A-1

continuous inlet buzz which could seriously affect airplane stability and control and could damage the engines and the inlet. Speed should be reduced to below Mach 1.5 before actuation of the brake for a second engine.

NOTE

The engine braking system is irreversible; therefore, the engine cannot be restarted after the emergency brake has been engaged.

8. Engine emergency brake switch - OFF. Move switch to OFF after rpm has stabilized at 22% or below.
9. Engine rpm lockup switch (above Mach 1.4) - AUTO.
10. Throttle (affected engine) - 40 degrees, if brake not used.

NOTE

If engine braking was not required, advance throttle of affected engine to 40 degrees, to provide fuel flow for proper cooling of engine lube oil system. (See figure 5-2.)

ENGINE FAILURE OR SHUTDOWN - ABOVE MACH 2.1, AUTOMATIC OR STANDBY AICS (AIRPLANE AF62-207).

If an engine fails or must be shut down above Mach 2.1, proceed as follows:

1. Bypass area (affected inlet):
   If AUTO, duct performance switch - LOW.
   If STANDBY, bypass door standby switch - Down to maintain shock in crosshatch.
2. Engine rpm lockup switch - RELEASE.
3. Throttle (affected engine) - IDLE, and if affected inlet is in standby mode maintain shock in crosshatch.
4. Throat (affected inlet):
   If AUTO - Check schedule.
   If STANDBY, throat Mach schedule standby switch - Down to maintain throat at 0.2 Mach less than airplane Mach.
5. Start normal deceleration and descent as required, with throttles (good engines) - MIL.
6. Throttle (affected engine) - OFF, and if affected inlet is in standby mode maintain shock in crosshatch.
7. Bypass door standby switch (if affected inlet is in automatic mode) - Hold down 1, 3, or 6 seconds. If the inlet for the engine to be shut down is in automatic mode, hold the bypass door standby switch down for one second if only one engine is shut down; three seconds if two engines are shut down; and six seconds if three engines are shut down. This will bias the bypass door master cylinder from its normal rig position so that when the airplane is decelerating through approximately Mach 2.08 (AICS transfers from shock control to open loop control) the bypass doors will slowly open from their normal locked position of 500 square inches to approximately 700, 1100, or 1800 square inches (one, two, or three engines out).
8. Engine emergency brake switch (affected engine) - ON, if required, and if affected inlet is in standby mode maintain shock in crosshatch.

CAUTION

Only one engine per inlet should be braked above Mach 1.5. This prevents the possibility of inducing continuous inlet buzz which could seriously affect airplane stability and control and could damage the engines and the inlet. Speed should be reduced to below Mach 1.5 before actuation of the brake for a second engine.

NOTE

The engine braking system is irreversible; therefore, the engine cannot be restarted after the emergency brake has been engaged.

9. Engine emergency brake switch - OFF. Move switch to OFF after rpm has stabilized at 22% or below.
10. Engine rpm lockup switch - AUTO.

Changed 25 June 1965

T.O. 1B-70(X)A-1

11. Throttle (affected engine) - 40 degrees, if brake not used.

   NOTE
   If engine braking was not required, advance throttle of affected engine to 40 degrees, to provide fuel flow for proper cooling of engine lube oil system. (See figure 5-2.)

12. Duct performance switch (if affected inlet is in automatic mode) - NORM.

ENGINE FAILURE OR SHUTDOWN - BELOW MACH 2.1, AUTOMATIC OR STANDBY AICS (AIRPLANE AF62-207).

If an engine fails or must be shut down below Mach 2.1, proceed as follows:

1. Bypass area (affected inlet):
   If SUPERSONIC, bypass door standby switch - Hold down 1, 3, or 6 seconds. Hold the bypass door standby switch down for one second if only one engine is to be shut down; three seconds if two engines are to be shut down; and six seconds if three engines are to be shut down. If the affected inlet is in automatic mode, this will bias the bypass door master cylinder from its normal rig position so that when the airplane is decelerating through approximately Mach 2.08 (AICS transfers from shock control to open loop control) the bypass doors will slowly open from their normal locked position of 500 square inches to approximately 700, 1100, or 1800 square inches (one, two, or three engines out). If the affected inlet is in standby mode, this will cause the bypass doors to open to approximately 700, 1100, or 1800 square inches, respectively.

   If SUBSONIC - Check both bypass areas closed.

2. Engine rpm lockup switch - RELEASE.
3. Throttle (affected engine) - IDLE.
4. Throats - If one inlet is in standby mode and the other in automatic mode, adjust standby throat to obtain same throat Mach schedule indicator reading as for the automatic throat. If both throats are automatic, check indicators stopped at approximately Mach 2.1.

5. Start normal deceleration and descent as required, with throttles (good engines) - MIL.

6. Bypass (affected inlet):
   If SUPERSONIC, bypass door standby switch - As required to refine bypass area to 700, 1100, or 1800 square inches.

   Move switch as required to obtain 700 square inches for one engine out; 1100 square inches for two engines out; and 1800 square inches for three inches out.

7. Throttle (affected engine) - OFF.
8. Engine emergency brake switch (affected engine) - ON, if required.

   CAUTION
   Only one engine per inlet should be braked above Mach 1.5. This prevents the possibility of inducing continuous inlet buzz which could seriously affect airplane stability and control and could damage the engines and the inlet. Speed should be reduced to below Mach 1.5 before actuation of the brake for a second engine.

   NOTE
   The engine braking system is irreversible; therefore, the engine cannot be restarted after the emergency brake has been engaged.

9. Engine emergency brake switch - OFF. Move switch to OFF after rpm has stabilized at 22% or below.
10. Engine rpm lockup switch (above Mach 1.4) - AUTO.
11. Throttle (affected engine) - 40 degrees, if brake not used.

    NOTE
    If engine braking was not required, advance throttle of affected engine to 40 degrees, to provide fuel flow for proper cooling of engine lube oil system. (See figure 5-2.)

T.O. 1B-70(X)A-1

USE OF ENGINE WINDMILL BRAKING.

Engine windmill brake may be required as part of the engine shutdown procedure to prevent excessive windmill rpm of a dead engine which could cause destruction of the engine because of lack of proper lubrication, or excessive vibration.

CAUTION
- Above Mach 1.5, only one engine per inlet shall be braked. This prevents the possibility of inducing continuous inlet buzz which could seriously affect airplane stability and control, and could damage the engines and the inlet. If it becomes necessary to shut down a second engine in one inlet, reduce speed to below Mach 1.5 before actuation of the brake for the second engine.
- The engine braking system is <u>irreversible</u> in flight; therefore the engine cannot be restarted after the emergency brake has been engaged.

The windmill brake <u>must</u> be used if an engine is shutdown for any of the following reasons:

- Fire warning (above Mach 1.5).
- Engine or ADS gearbox vibration remains above limits after shutdown.
- Windmilling limits (22% rpm within 5 minutes) cannot be maintained following engine or ADS gearbox low oil pressure.

ENGINE AIR START.

For detailed air start requirements, see figure 3-3. Below 30,000 feet at low indicated airspeeds, the air start capabilities are limited by engine windmilling speed. During this condition, the drag of the accessory drive system reduces engine speed below that required to permit fuel flow through the pressurizing and drain valve to the fuel nozzles. Above 30,000 feet, the airspeed should exceed 400 knots IAS for consistent airstarts. Airstarts may be attempted whenever engine rpm is about 12% or above. If the rpm is too low for an air start attempt, the airspeed should be increased until the necessary rpm is obtained. Before attempting an air start, determine the cause of the engine failure. If a normal throttle servo system failure is suspected, attempt air start with applicable alternate throttle switch. A restart should not be attempted following a fire, or if the engine failure was caused by an obvious mechanical failure, such as indicated by the instrument indications or excessive vibration before the failure.

NOTE
Under certain conditions, low rpm and exhaust temperature indications may make it difficult to determine if an airstart light-off was obtained. If, as a result of such indications, light-off is questionable, advance throttle to 40-degree setting. A corresponding increase in rpm will verify engine operation.

AIR START - ABOVE MACH 2.1, AUTO/MANUAL OR MANUAL AICS (AIRPLANE AF62-001).

To accomplish an air start above Mach 2.1, proceed as follows:

NOTE
If desired, more than one engine per inlet may be started at the same time.

1. Bypass - Both wheels aft to maintain shocks in crosshatch.
2. Engine rpm lockup switch - RELEASE.
3. Throttles (all dead engines) - OFF

CAUTION
See figure 5-2 for engine windmilling time limits.

4. Throat:
   If AUTO - Check schedule.
   If MANUAL - Both throat wheels aft to maintain throat at 0.2 Mach less than airplane Mach.

Changed 25 June 1965

T.O. 1B-70(X)A-1

5. Air start switch - ON.

   NOTE

   Air start caution light comes on when the air start switch is ON.

6. Throttle (engine to be started) - IDLE, and maintain shocks in crosshatch.
7. Exhaust temperature gage (affected engine) - Monitor.

   NOTE

   - If light-off is not obtained within 15 seconds, move throttle (affected engine) and air start switch to OFF, then attempt another air start.

   - If start attempts are not successful, advance throttle (affected engine) and check corresponding primary nozzle indicator. If nozzle closure is noted, repeat start attempt at another airspeed and/or altitude. If nozzle did not respond, try start using applicable alternate throttle switch.

   - The use of an alternate throttle switch disengages the normal servo system of the corresponding throttle. Therefore, if a start is obtained with the alternate throttle switch, the normal system probably has failed and should not be re-engaged.

8. Air start switch - OFF, after light-off.
   Return air start switch to OFF as soon as engine lights off. Check air start caution light out.
9. Throttle (engine being started - 40 degrees or above.
10. Repeat steps 1 through 9 to start another engine in the same inlet.
11. Engine rpm lockup switch - AUTO (after last engine to be started stabilizes at 100% rpm).

AIR START - BELOW MACH 2.1, AUTO/MANUAL OR MANUAL AICS (AIRPLANE AF62-001).

To accomplish an air start below Mach 2.1, proceed as follows:

NOTE

If desired, more than one engine per inlet may be started at the same time.

1. Bypass area (affected inlet):
   If SUPERSONIC - Wheel aft to obtain 700, 1100, or 1800 square inches. With one engine out, bypass area should be 700 square inches; with two engines out, 1100 square inches; and with three engines out, 1800 square inches.
   If SUBSONIC - Check bypass area closed.
2. Engine rpm lockup switch - RELEASE.
3. Throttles (all dead engines) - OFF.

   CAUTION

   See figure 5-2 for engine windmilling time limits.

4. Throat - Check schedule.
5. Air start switch - ON.

   NOTE

   The air start caution light comes on when the air start switch is ON.

6. Throttle (engine to be started) - IDLE.
7. Exhaust temperature gage (affected engine) - Monitor.

   NOTE

   - If light-off is not obtained within 30 seconds, move throttle (affected engine) and air start switch to OFF, then attempt another start.

   - If start attempts are not successful, advance throttle (affected engine) and check corresponding primary nozzle indicator. If nozzle closure is noted, repeat start attempt at another airspeed and/or altitude. If nozzle does not respond, try start using applicable alternate throttle switch.

T.O. 1B-70(X)A-1

- The use of an alternate throttle switch disengages the normal servo system of the corresponding throttle. Therefore, if a start is obtained with the alternate throttle switch, the normal system probably has failed and should not be re-engaged.

8. Air start switch - OFF, after light-off.

    Return air start switch to OFF as soon as engine lights off. Check air start caution light out.

    NOTE
    If engine 3 or 4 is started, it may be necessary to cycle corresponding primary generator to restore generator operation.

9. Throttle (engine being started) - 40 degrees or above.
10. Bypass area (affected inlet) - Wheel forward as required.

NO. ENGINES OPERATING	AIRPLANE MACH NO.	BYPASS AREA (SQ. IN.)
2	1.0 to 2.1	700
1	1.0 to 2.1	1100

11. Repeat steps 1 through 10 to start another engine in the same inlet.

This page intentionally left blank

ENGINE AIR START ENVELOPE

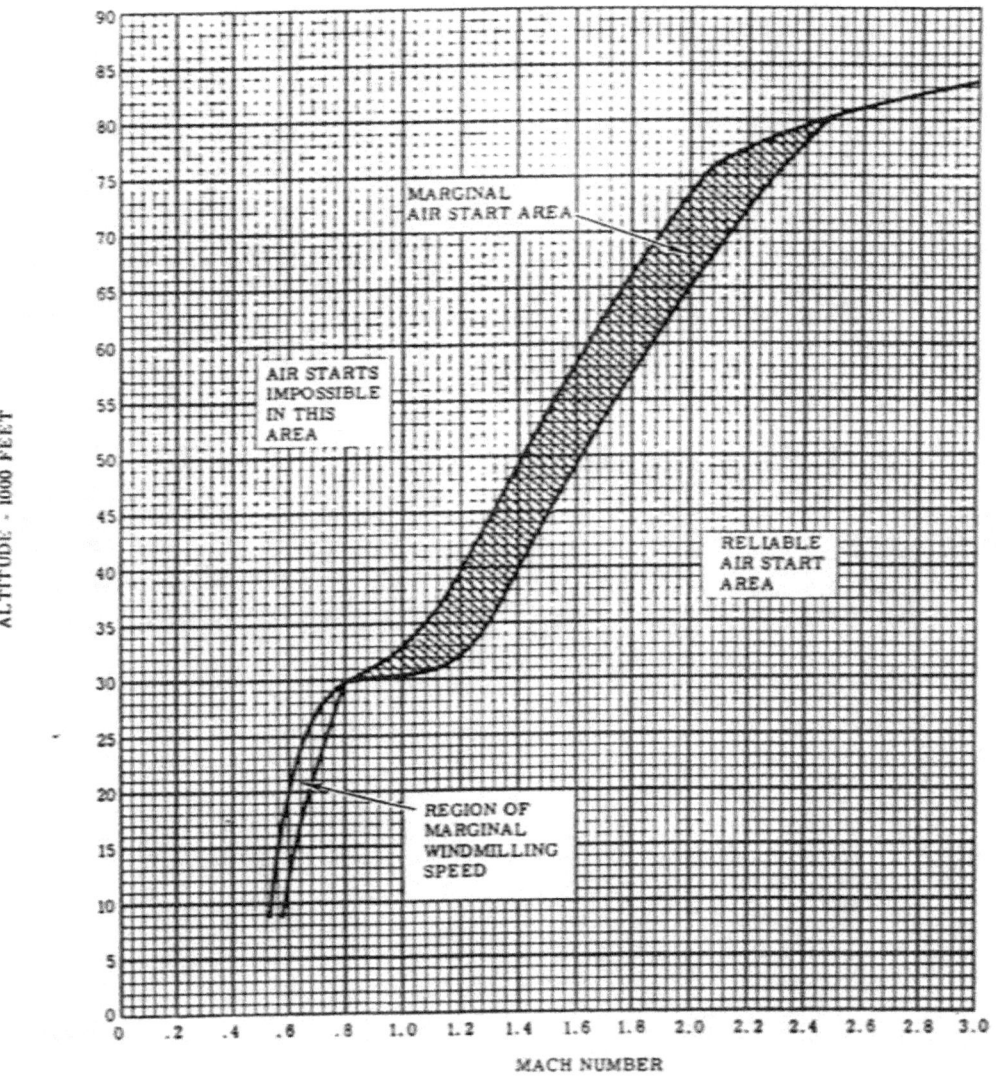

Figure 3-3

T.O. 1B-70(X)A-1

12. Engine rpm lockup switch (above Mach 1.4) - AUTO (after last engine to be started stabilizes at 100% rpm).

AIR START - ABOVE MACH 2.1, AUTOMATIC OR STANDBY AICS (AIRPLANE AF62-207).

To accomplish an air start above Mach 2.1, proceed as follows:

> **NOTE**
> If desired, more than one engine per inlet can be started at the same time.

1. Bypass (affected inlet):
   If AUTO, duct performance switch - LOW.
   If STANDBY, bypass door standby switch - Down to maintain shock in crosshatch.
2. Engine rpm lockup switch - RELEASE.
3. Throttles (all dead engines) - OFF.

> **CAUTION**
> See figure 5-2 for engine windmilling time limits.

4. Throat (affected inlet):
   If AUTO - Check schedule.
   If STANDBY, throat Mach schedule standby switch - Down to maintain throat at 0.2 Mach less than airplane Mach.
5. Air start switch - ON.

> **NOTE**
> Air start caution light comes on when the air start switch is ON.

6. Throttle (engine to be started) - IDLE, and if affected inlet is in standby mode maintain shock in crosshatch.
7. Exhaust temperature gage (affected engine) - Monitor.

> **NOTE**
> - If light-off is not obtained within 15 seconds, move throttle (affected engine) and air start switch to OFF, then attempt another air start.
> - If start attempts are not successful, advance throttle (affected engine) and check corresponding primary nozzle indicator. If nozzle closure is noted, repeat start attempt at another airspeed and/or altitude. If nozzle did not respond, try start using applicable alternate throttle switch.
> - The use of an alternate throttle switch disengages the normal servo system of the corresponding throttle. Therefore, if a start is obtained with the alternate throttle switch, the normal system probably has failed and should not be re-engaged.

8. Air start switch - OFF, after light-off.
   Return air start switch to OFF as soon as engine lights off. Check air start caution light out.
9. Throttle (engine being started) - 40 degrees or above, and if affected inlet is in standby mode maintain shock in crosshatch.
10. Repeat steps 1 through 9 to start another engine in the same inlet.
11. Engine rpm lockup switch - AUTO (after last engine to be started stabilizes at 100% rpm).
12. Duct performance switch (if affected inlet is in automatic mode) - NORM.

AIR START - BELOW MACH 2.1, AUTOMATIC OR STANDBY AICS (AIRPLANE AF62-207).

To accomplish an air start below Mach 2.1, proceed as follows:

> **NOTE**
> If desired, more than one engine per inlet may be started at the same time.

1. Bypass area (affected inlet):
   If SUPERSONIC, bypass door standby switch - Down as necessary to obtain 700, 1100, or 1800 square inches.
   With one engine out, bypass area should be 700 square inches; with two engines out, 1100 square inches; and with three engines out, 1800 square inches.
   If SUBSONIC - Check both bypass areas closed.

3-10

224

Changed 25 June 1965

T.O. 1B-70(X)A-1

2. Engine rpm lockup switch - RELEASE.
3. Throttles (all dead engines) - OFF.

CAUTION

See figure 5-2 for engine windmilling time limits.

4. Throats - If one inlet is in standby mode and the other in automatic mode, adjust standby throat to obtain same throat Mach schedule indicator reading as for the automatic throat. If both throats are automatic, check indicators stopped at approximately Mach 2.1.
5. Air start switch - ON.

NOTE

The air start caution light comes on when the air start switch is ON.

6. Throttle (engine to be started) - IDLE.
7. Exhaust temperature gage (affected engine) - Monitor.

NOTE

- If light-off is not obtained within 30 seconds, move throttle (affected engine) and air start switch to OFF, then attempt another start.

- If start attempts are not successful, advance throttle (affected engine) and check corresponding primary nozzle indicator. If nozzle closure is noted, repeat start attempt at another airspeed and/or altitude. If nozzle does not respond, try start using applicable alternate throttle switch.

- The use of an alternate throttle switch disengages the normal servo system of the corresponding throttle. Therefore, if a start is obtained with the alternate throttle switch, the normal system probably has failed and should not be re-engaged.

8. Air start switch - OFF, after light-off.

Return air start switch to OFF as soon as engine lights off. Check air start caution light out.

NOTE

If engine 3 or 4 is started, it may be necessary to cycle corresponding primary generator to restore generator operation.

9. Throttle (engine being started) - 40 degrees or above.
10. Bypass area (affected inlet) - UP, as required.

NO. ENGINES OPERATING	AIRPLANE MACH NO.	BYPASS AREA (SQ IN.)
2	1.0 to 2.1	700
1	1.0 to 2.1	1100

11. Repeat steps 1 through 10 to start another engine in the same inlet.
12. Engine rpm lockup switch (above Mach 1.4) - AUTO (after last engine to be started stabilizes at 100% rpm).

COMPRESSOR STALLS.

A compressor stall may be indicated by a rapid rise in exhaust temperature or a sudden abnormal opening of the primary exhaust nozzle.

NOTE

If compressor stall occurs, action necessary to get engine to idle (first three steps of compressor stall corrective procedures) should be completed as rapidly as possible. Check engine instruments for evidence of any out-of-limits conditions.

COMPRESSOR STALL - ABOVE MACH 2.1, AUTO/MANUAL OR MANUAL AICS (AIRPLANE AF62-001).

1. Bypass wheels - Both aft to maintain shocks in crosshatch.
2. Engine rpm lockup switch - RELEASE.
3. Throttle (affected engine) - IDLE, and maintain shocks in crosshatch.

T.O. 1B-70(X)A-1

4. Throat:
   If AUTO - Check schedule.
   If MANUAL - Both throat wheels aft to maintain throat at 0.2 Mach less than airplane Mach.
   If stall persists, perform steps 5 through 8.
5. Start normal deceleration and descent as required, with throttles (good engines) - MIL.
6. Throttle (affected engine) - OFF, and maintain shocks in crosshatch.

CAUTION

See figure 5-2 for engine windmilling time limits.

7. Engine rpm lockup switch - AUTO.
8. Throttle (affected engine) - 40 degrees.

NOTE

Advance throttle of affected engine to 40 degrees, to provide fuel flow for proper cooling of engine lube oil system until an air start is attempted.

COMPRESSOR STALL - BELOW MACH 2.1 AUTO/MANUAL OR MANUAL AICS (AIRPLANE AF62-001).

1. Bypass area (affected inlet):
   If SUPERSONIC - Wheel aft to obtain 700, 1100, or 1800 square inches.
   For one engine at IDLE, obtain 700 square inches; for second engine, 1100 square inches; and for third engine, 1800 square inches.
   If SUBSONIC - Check bypass area closed.
2. Engine rpm lockup switch - RELEASE.
3. Throttle (affected engine) - IDLE.
4. Throat - Check schedule; if stall persists, perform steps 5 through 8.
5. Start normal deceleration and descent as required, with throttles (good engines) - MIL.
6. Throttle (affected engine) - OFF, if stall persists.

CAUTION

See figure 5-2 for engine windmilling time limits.

7. Engine rpm lockup switch (above Mach 1.4) - AUTO.

8. Throttle (affected engine) - 40 degrees.

NOTE

Advance throttle of affected engine to 40 degrees, to provide fuel flow for proper cooling of engine lube oil system until an air start is attempted.

COMPRESSOR STALL - ABOVE MACH 2.1, AUTOMATIC OR STANDBY AICS (AIRPLANE AF62-207).

1. Bypass area (affected inlet):
   If AUTO, duct performance switch - LOW.
   If STANDBY, bypass door standby switch - Down to maintain shock in crosshatch.
2. Engine rpm lockup switch - RELEASE.
3. Throttle (affected engine) - IDLE, and if affected inlet is in standby mode maintain shock in crosshatch.
4. Throat (affected inlet):
   If AUTO - Check schedule.
   If STANDBY, throat Mach schedule standby switch - Down to maintain throat at 0.2 less than airplane Mach.
   If stall persists, perform steps 5 through 9.
5. Start normal deceleration and descent as required, with throttles (good engines) - MIL.
6. Throttle (affected engine) - OFF, and if affected inlet is in standby mode maintain shock in crosshatch.

CAUTION

See figure 5-2 for engine windmilling time limits.

7. Bypass door standby switch (if affected inlet is in automatic mode) - Hold down 1, 3, or 6 seconds.
   If the inlet for the engine being shut down is in automatic mode, hold the bypass door standby switch down for one second if only one engine is shut down; three seconds if two engines are shut down; and six seconds if three engines are shut down. This will bias the bypass door master cylinder from its normal rig position so that when the airplane is decelerating

3-12

T.O. 1B-70(X)A-1

through approximately Mach 2.08 (AICS transfers from shock control to open loop control) the bypass doors will slowly open from their normal locked position of 500 square inches to approximately 700, 1100, or 1800 square inches (one, two, or three engines out).

8. Engine rpm lockup switch - AUTO.
9. Throttle (affected engine) 40 degrees.

NOTE

Advance throttle of affected engine to 40 degrees, to provide fuel flow for proper cooling of engine lube oil system. (See figure 5-2.)

10. Duct performance switch (if affected inlet is in automatic mode) - NORM.

COMPRESSOR STALL - BELOW MACH 2.1, AUTOMATIC OR STANDBY AICS (AIRPLANE AF62-207).

1. Bypass area (affected inlet):
   If SUPERSONIC, bypass door standby switch - Hold down 1, 3, or 6 seconds.
   Hold the bypass door standby switch down for one second if only one throttle is to be moved to IDLE; three seconds for two throttles at IDLE; and six seconds for three engines at IDLE. If the affected inlet is in automatic mode, this will bias the bypass door master cylinder from its normal rig position so that when the airplane is decelerating through approximately Mach 2.08 (AICS transfers from shock control to open loop control) the bypass doors will slowly open from their normal locked position of 500 square inches to approximately 700, 1100, or 1800 square inches (one, two, or three engines at IDLE or out). If the affected inlet is in standby mode, this will cause the bypass doors to open to approximately 700, 1100, or 1800 square inches, respectively.
   If SUBSONIC - Check both bypass areas closed.

2. Engine rpm lockup switch - RELEASE.
3. Throttle (affected engine) - IDLE.

4. Throats - If one inlet is in standby mode and the other in automatic mode, adjust standby throat to obtain same throat Mach schedule indicator reading as for the automatic throat. If both throats are automatic, check indicators stopped at approximately Mach 2.1.

5. Start normal deceleration and descent as required. with throttles (good engines) - MIL.

6. Bypass area (affected inlet):
   If SUPERSONIC, bypass door standby switch - As required to refine bypass area to 700, 1100, or 1800 square inches.
   Move switch as required to obtain 700 square inches for one engine out; 1100 square inches for two engines out; and 1800 square inches for three engines out.

7. Throttle (affected engine) - OFF, if stall persists.

CAUTION

See figure 5-2 for engine windmilling time limits.

8. Engine rpm lockup switch (above Mach 1.4) - AUTO.
9. Throttle (affected engine) - 40 degrees.

NOTE

Advance throttle of affected engine to 40 degrees, to provide fuel flow for proper cooling of engine lube oil system.

MAXIMUM GLIDE.

For maximum glide distances and best glide speeds, refer to "Maximum Glide" in Section III of the Confidential Supplement, T.O. 1B-70(X)A-1A.

EJECTION VS FORCED LANDING.

It is not practical to predetermine the emergencies in which ejection is considered mandatory. This decision must be made by the pilot because his analysis of the situation, coupled with his knowledge of the airplane, provides the only information appropriate to such a decision. There are, however, several general conditions when a landing must

T.O. 1B-70(X)A-1

MAXIMUM GLIDE DISTANCES

REFER TO CONFIDENTIAL SUPPLEMENT, T.O. 1B-70(X)A-1A

Figure 3-4

T.O. 1B-70(X)A-1

not be attempted and ejection is necessary. The following conditions, for example, require ejection:

> **WARNING**
> If possible, before ejection, attempt to turn the airplane toward an area where injury to persons or damage to property on the ground or water is least likely to occur.

a. Airplane under control but flight cannot be maintained and a suitable landing surface is not available. Not being able to maintain flight normally is caused by excessive multiple engine failures. Depending upon various flight conditions, such as altitude, attitude, airspeed, and gross weight, excessive multiple engine failures can vary from a two-engine loss during takeoff to the in-flight loss of more than three engines. Unsuitable landing surfaces include rough terrain, insufficient runway length, or water.

> **WARNING**
> Under no circumstances should ditching be attempted, because the airplane design prevents successful ditching.

b. Nose gear cannot be lowered.
c. Landing gear cannot be lowered.
d. One main gear cannot be lowered.
e. Marginal stability combined with requirement for landing on a field with approaches over heavily populated areas.
f. Wing tips failed in the full-down position.
g. Loss of all electrical power (including emergency battery*).

LANDING WITH ONE OR MORE ENGINES INOPERATIVE.

In general, if one or two engines are inoperative, the pattern techniques to allow a safe touchdown and stop do not require any special landing procedures other than those noted in the hydraulic and electrical emergency procedures in this section. Also, any excess fuel should be burned up to reduce the landing weight. Care should be used in positioning the airplane on the downwind, base, and final approach, because altitude or airspeed corrections may require greater than normal throttle movement. Use normal pattern airspeeds. All turns in the pattern should be gentle. The decision to go around should be made as early as possible because of reduced acceleration. Do not retard throttles to IDLE until touchdown.

> **NOTE**
> - If either airplane gross weight and/or multiple engine failure combinations require that the throttles of the remaining engines be set near Military Thrust to stabilize flight, a balanced afterburner thrust condition should be set up in each bank, if possible, before establishing the downwind leg. This improves throttle setting flexibility during landing, and will ease go-around transition, if necessary.
> - The engine overspeed arming lever must be armed before final approach because overspeed arming cannot be engaged if any throttle is advanced to MAX A/B.
> - If only three engines are operating, afterburner is required on these engines, even at reduced gross weight. The heavyweight landing pattern and touchdown speeds should be used.

---

*Airplane AF62-001

T.O. 1B-70(X)A-1

GO-AROUND WITH ONE OR MORE ENGINES INOPERATIVE.

In case a go-around is necessary with one or more engines inoperative, use the following procedure:

1. Throttles (good engines) - As required.
2. Landing gear handle - UP.

> **CAUTION**
> Do not retract gear until minimum control speed is reached. (See figure A2-4.)

3. Flap handle - FLAP UP.
   Raise flaps when adequate airspeed is attained.

GROUND EMERGENCY ENGINE SHUTDOWN.

The engines can be shut down simultaneously or individually during ground emergencies without application of the ground equipment (electric and hydraulic power and ground cooling unit) that is required for a normal shutdown. Ground unit cooling for the electronic equipment is not needed for an emergency engine shutdown before flight, or after a flight at speeds less than Mach 2.

> **CAUTION**
> - If emergency engine shutdown is made after a flight at speeds above Mach 2, or during which emergency ram air was used, the electronic equipment can be damaged if ground cooling is not applied immediately after emergency shutdown.
> - To prevent possible fuel system damage, when making emergency shutdown, engine should be at low thrust setting, if possible, before throttle is moved to OFF.

GROUND EMERGENCY SHUTDOWN - ALL ENGINES.

If an emergency requires shutdown of all six engines, and the ground units are not connected, or it is not practical to have these units connected for the shutdown, proceed as follows:

1. Throttles (engines 1, 2, 5, and 6) - OFF.
   a. If emergency requires complete shutdown as soon as possible, proceed to step 3.
   b. If immediate shutdown is not required, proceed to step 2.
2. If time and conditions permit, proceed as follows while electrical power is available:
   a. Air induction control system package power switch - OFF.
   b. Flight augmentation control system - Engaged for 5 seconds.
   c. Yaw, pitch, and roll augmentation power switches - OFF.
   d. Fuel tank pump switches - All OFF.
   e. Refrigeration switch - OFF.
3. Throttles (engines 3 and 4) - OFF.
   Engines 3 and 4 are shut down last so electrical power will be available for shut down, and to close the fire wall fuel shutoff valves.

4. Emergency generator switch - OFF immediately.
   The emergency generator must be shut off as soon as possible after last throttle is moved to OFF to prevent possible electrical equipment damage.

GROUND EMERGENCY SHUTDOWN - ONE OR MORE ENGINES.

If an emergency requiring engine shutdown is confined to one engine or a group of engines (but not all engines), and the ground units are not connected, or it is not practical to have these units connected for the shutdown, proceed as follows

1. (Deleted)
2. Throttles (affected engines) - OFF.

T.O. 1B-70(X)A-1

3. Throttles (engines 1, 2, 5, and 6) - OFF, if desired.
   The remaining operating engines can be shutdown without use of external ground units, if desired.

   NOTE
   If engines 3 and 4 have been shut down because of the emergency, engine 5 or 6 should remain operating to supply hydraulic power for emergency generator.

4. If time and conditions permit, proceed as follows while electrical power is available:
   a. Air induction control system package power switch - OFF.
   b. Flight augmentation control system - Engaged for 5 seconds.
   c. Yaw, pitch, and roll augmentation power switches - OFF.
   d. Fuel tank pump switches - All OFF.
   e. Refrigeration switch - OFF.

5. Throttles (engines 3 and/or 4, or 5 or 6) - OFF.
   The engines driving the generators are shut down last so electrical power will be available for shut down, and to close the fire wall fuel shutoff valves.

6. Emergency generator switch - OFF immediately.
   The emergency generator must be shut off as soon as soon as possible after last throttle is moved to OFF to prevent possible electrical equipment damage.

FIRE.

The fire detector and extinguisher systems provide protection for each engine compartment and corresponding accessory drive system compartment. A fire or overheat condition in either an engine compartment, or corresponding accessory drive system compartment, illuminates the same fire warning light. Therefore, it cannot be determined by the light, in which compartment the fire or overheat condition exists. However, following the fire emergency procedure will eliminate the hazardous condition in either compartment.

NOTE
The fire warning light remains on for a minimum of 20 seconds after the fire goes out.

The portable fire extinguisher on the entrance door may be used for fires in the cabin area.

ENGINE OR ACCESSORY DRIVE SYSTEM COMPARTMENT FIRES - ON THE GROUND.

If an engine or accessory drive system compartment fire or overheat condition is indicated by illumination of a fire warning light and/or direct observation by the ground crew, proceed as follows:

T.O. 1B-70(X)A-1

1. Electrical power (airplane or external) - On.
2. Throttle (affected engine) - OFF.
3. Fire warning light/engine shutdown button (affected engine) - Push.
    Pushing the illuminated fire warning light/engine shutdown button:
    - Closes the corresponding firewall fuel shutoff valve.
    - Locks the engine compartment cooling air bypass air valves closed.
    - Locks the boundary layer bleed diverter valves open.
    - Arms the appropriate fire extinguisher agent discharge switch.
4. Fire extinguisher agent discharge switch - MAIN, if fire continues.
    Move appropriate agent discharge switch to MAIN if fire does not go out. The fire warning light should go out within 25 seconds after using the discharge switch if the fire or overheat condition no longer exists. If light remains on, proceed to step 5.
5. Fire extinguisher agent discharge switch - RES, if required.
    Discharge appropriate reserve extinguisher if fire warning light remains on.
6. Shut down other engines (3 or 4 last).
7. Emergency battery - inverter switch* - ON, if engines cannot be shut down.
8. Engine shutdown and wheel brake arming switch* - ARMED.
9. Alternate throttle switches - Hold at DECR to shut down engines.

---

*Airplane AF62-001

T.O. 1B-70(X)A-1

FIRE WARNING - TAKE-OFF GROUND ROLL.

If a fire warning light comes on during ground roll, and sufficient runway or overrun is available, abort the take-off. (Refer to "Engine Failure During Take-off, Abort" in this section.) Perform ground fire emergency procedures.

FIRE WARNING - ABOVE MACH 2.1, AUTO MANUAL OR MANUAL AICS (AIRPLANE AF62-001).

1. Bypass wheels - Both aft to maintain shocks in crosshatch.
2. Engine rpm lockup switch - RELEASE.
3. Throttle (affected engine) - IDLE, and maintain shocks in crosshatch.
4. Throat:
    If AUTO - Check schedule.
    If MANUAL - Both throat wheels aft to maintain throat at 0.2 Mach less than airplane Mach.
5. Start normal deceleration and descent as required with throttles (good engines) - MIL.
6. Throttle (affected engine) - OFF, and maintain shocks in crosshatch. If fire warning light remains on, proceed to step 7; if fire warning light goes out, proceed to step 9.
7. Fire warning light/engine shutdown button (affected engine) - Push.
    Pushing the illuminated fire warning light/engine shutdown button:
    - Closes the corresponding fire wall shutoff valve.
    - Closes and locks the engine compartment cooling air bypass air valves.
    - Locks the boundary layer bleed diverter valves open.
    - Arms the appropriate extinguisher agent discharge switch.
8. Fire extinguisher agent discharge switch - MAIN, 15 seconds after pushing fire warning light/engine shutdown button; then RES, if required.
    Wait 15 seconds after pushing button before moving appropriate discharge switch to MAIN, to allow cooling air bypass valves to close. The fire warning light should go out within 25 seconds after moving the discharge switch to MAIN if the fire or overheat condition no longer exists. If the fire warning light remains on, move the discharge switch to RES.

9. Engine emergency brake switch (affected engine) - ON, and maintain shocks in crosshatch.

CAUTION

Only one engine per inlet should be braked above Mach 1.5. This prevents the possibility of inducing continuous inlet buzz which could seriously affect airplane stability and control and could damage the engines and the inlet. Speed should be reduced to below Mach 1.5 before actuation of the brake for a second engine.

NOTE

The engine braking system is irreversible; therefore, the engine cannot be restarted after the emergency brake has been engaged.

10. Engine emergency brake switch (affected engine) - OFF.
    Move switch to OFF after rpm has stabilized at 22% or below.
11. Engine rpm lockup switch - AUTO.

FIRE WARNING - BELOW MACH 2.1, AUTO/MANUAL OR MANUAL AICS (AIRPLANE AF62-001).

1. Bypass area (affected inlet):
    If SUPERSONIC - Wheel aft to obtain 700, 1100, or 1800 square inches.
    For one engine at IDLE, obtain 700 square inches; for second engine, 1100 square inches; and for third engine, 1800 square inches.
    If SUBSONIC - Check bypass area closed.
2. Engine rpm lockup switch - RELEASE.
3. Throttle (affected engine) - IDLE.
4. Throat - Check schedule.
5. Start normal deceleration and descent as required, with throttles (good engines) - MIL.
6. Throttle (affected engine) - OFF. If fire warning light remains on, proceed to step 7; if fire warning light goes out, proceed to step 9.

T.O. 1B-70(X)A-1

7. Fire warning light/engine shutdown button (affected engine) - Push.
   Pushing the illuminated fire warning light/engine shutdown button:
   - Closes the corresponding fire wall fuel shutoff valve.
   - Closes and locks the engine compartment cooling air bypass air valves.
   - Locks the boundary layer bleed diverter valves open.
   - Arms the appropriate fire extinguisher agent discharge switch.
8. Fire extinguisher agent discharge switch - MAIN, 15 seconds after pushing fire warning light/engine shutdown button; then RES, if required.
   Wait 15 seconds after pushing button before moving appropriate discharge switch to MAIN to allow cooling air bypass valves to close. The fire warning light should go out within 25 seconds after moving the discharge switch to MAIN if the fire or overheat condition no longer exists. If the fire warning light remains on, move the discharge switch to RES.

   NOTE
   The 15-second wait is not required below Mach 0.45.

9. Engine emergency brake switch (affected engine) - ON, if above Mach 1.5.

   CAUTION
   Only one engine per inlet should be braked above Mach 1.5. This prevents the possibility of inducing continuous inlet buzz which could seriously affect airplane stability and control and could damage the engines and the inlet. Speed should be reduced to below Mach 1.5 before actuation of the brake for a second engine.

   NOTE
   The engine braking system is irreversible; therefore, the engine cannot be restarted after the emergency brake has been engaged.

10. Engine emergency brake switch (affected engine) - OFF.
    Move switch to OFF after rpm has stabilized at 22% or below.
11. Engine rpm lockup switch (above Mach 1.4) - AUTO.

FIRE WARNING - ABOVE MACH 2.1, AUTOMATIC OR STANDBY AICS (AIRPLANE AF62-207).

1. Bypass area (affected inlet):
   If AUTO, duct performance switch - LOW
   If STANDBY, bypass door standby switch - Down to maintain shock in crosshatch.
2. Engine rpm lockup switch - RELEASE.
3. Throttle (affected engine) - IDLE, and if affected inlet is in standby mode maintain shock in crosshatch.
4. Throat (affected inlet):
   If AUTO - Check schedule.
   If STANDBY, throat Mach schedule standby switch - Down to maintain throat at 0.2 Mach less than airplane Mach.
5. Start normal deceleration and descent as required, with throttles (good engines) - MIL.
6. Throttle (affected engine) - OFF, and if affected inlet is in standby mode maintain shock in crosshatch.
   If fire warning light remains on, proceed to step 7; if fire warning light goes out, proceed to step 9.
7. Fire warning light/engine shutdown button (affected engine) - Push.
   Pushing the illuminated fire warning light/engine shutdown button:
   - Closes the corresponding fire wall shutoff valve.
   - Closes and locks the engine compartment cooling air bypass air valves.
   - Locks the boundary layer bleed diverters valves open.
   - Arms the appropriate extinguisher agent discharge switch.
8. Fire extinguisher agent discharge switch - MAIN, 15 seconds after pushing fire warning light/engine shutdown button; then RES, if required.

Wait 15 seconds after pushing button before moving appropriate discharge switch to MAIN, to allow cooling air bypass valves to close. The fire warning light should go out within 25 seconds after moving the discharge switch to MAIN if the fire or overheat condition no longer exists. If the fire warning light remains on, move the discharge switch to RES.

9. Bypass door standby switch (if affected inlet is in automatic mode) - Hold down 1, 3, or 6 seconds. If the inlet for the engines being shut down is in automatic mode, hold the bypass door standby switch down for one second if only one engine is shut down; three seconds if two engines are shut down; and six seconds if three engines are shut down. This will bias the bypass door master cylinder from its normal rig position so that when the airplane is decelerating through approximately Mach 2.08 (AICS transfers from shock control to open loop control) the bypass doors will slowly open from their normal locked position of 500 square inches to approximately 700, 1100, or 1800 square inches (one, two, or three engines out).

10. Engine emergency brake switch (affected engine) - ON, and if affected inlet is in standby mode maintain shock in crosshatch.

CAUTION

Only one engine per inlet should be braked above Mach 1.5. This prevents the possibility of inducing continuous inlet buzz which could seriously affect airplane stability and control and could damage the engines and the inlet. Speed should be reduced to below Mach 1.5 before actuation of the brake for a second engine.

NOTE

The engine braking system is irreversible; therefore, the engine cannot be restarted after the emergency brake has been engaged.

11. Engine emergency brake switch - OFF. Move switch to OFF after rpm has stabilized at 22% or below.
12. Engine rpm lockup switch - AUTO.
13. Duct performance switch (if affected inlet is in automatic mode) - NORM.

FIRE WARNING - BELOW MACH 2.1, AUTOMATIC OR STANDBY AICS (AIRPLANE AF62-207).

1. Bypass area (affected inlet):
   If SUPERSONIC, bypass door standby switch - Hold down 1, 3, or 6 seconds.
   Hold the bypass door standby switch down for one second if only one throttle is to be moved to IDLE; three seconds for two throttles at IDLE; and six seconds for three throttles at IDLE. If the affected inlet is in automatic mode, this will bias the bypass door master cylinder from its normal rig position so that when the airplane is decelerating through approximately Mach 2.08 (AICS transfers from shock control to open loop control) the bypass doors will slowly open from their normal locked position of 500 square inches to approximately 700, 1100, or 1800 square inches (one, two, or three engines at IDLE or out). If the affected inlet is in standby mode, this will cause the bypass doors to open to approximately 700, 1100, or 1800 square inches, respectively.
   If SUBSONIC - Check both bypass areas closed.
2. Engine rpm lockup switch - RELEASE.
3. Throttle (affected engine) - IDLE.
4. Throats - If one inlet is in standby mode and the other in automatic mode, adjust standby throat to obtain same throat Mach schedule indicator reading as for the automatic throat. If both throats are automatic, check indicators stopped at approximately Mach 2.1.
5. Start normal deceleration and descent as required, with throttles (good engines) - MIL.
6. Throttle (affected engine) - OFF. If fire warning light remains on, proceed to step 7; if fire warning light goes out, proceed to step 9.

T.O. 1B-70(X)A-1

7. Fire warning light/engine shutdown button (affected engine) - Push.
   Pushing the illuminated fire warning light/engine shutdown button:
   - Closes the corresponding fire wall fuel shutoff valve.
   - Closes and locks the engine compartment cooling air bypass air valves.
   - Locks the boundary layer bleed diverter valves open.
   - Arms the appropriate fire extinguisher agent discharge switch.
8. Fire extinguisher agent discharge switch - MAIN, 15 seconds after pushing fire warning light/engine shutdown button; then RES, if required.
   Wait 15 seconds after pushing button before moving appropriate discharge switch to MAIN, to allow cooling air bypass valves to close. The fire warning light should go out within 25 seconds after moving the discharge switch to MAIN if the fire or overheat condition no longer exists. If the fire warning light remains on, move the discharge switch to RES.
9. Bypass (affected inlet):
   If SUPERSONIC, bypass door standby switch - As required to refine bypass area to 700, 1100, or 1800 square inches.
   Move switch as required to obtain 700 square inches for one engine out; 1100 square inches for two engines out; and 1800 square inches for three engines out.
10. Engine emergency brake switch (affected engine) - ON, if above Mach 1.5.

   CAUTION

   Only one engine per inlet should be braked above Mach 1.5. This prevents the possibility of inducing continuous inlet buzz which could seriously affect airplane stability and control and could damage the engines and the inlet. Speed should be reduced to below Mach 1.5 before actuation of the brake for a second engine.

   NOTE

   The engine braking system is irreversible; therefore, the engine cannot be restarted after the emergency brake has been engaged.

11. Engine emergency brake switch - OFF.
    Move switch to OFF after rpm stabilizes at 22% or below.
12. Engine rpm lockup switch (above Mach 1.4) - AUTO.

ENGINE FIRE DURING GROUND SHUTDOWN.

If an engine fire is observed by the ground crew, motor the affected engine as follows:

1. External electrical and hydraulic power - Check on.
   Motoring the engine requires right primary ac bus power and primary hydraulic power (for engines 1, 2 or 3, primary hydraulic system No. 1; for engines 4, 5 or 6, primary hydraulic system No. 2).
2. Throttle (affected engine) - OFF.
3. Alternate throttle switch (affected engine) - Hold at DECR momentarily.
4. Throttle (affected engine) - IDLE.
5. Ground start switch - ON.
   Moving the ground start switch to ON motors the engine to get rid of fuel fumes and clear the engine.
6. If fire persists, throttle (affected engine) - OFF.

WING OR FUSELAGE FIRE.

If a fire is confirmed in either wing section, or in a fuselage section other than the accessible crew and electronic equipment compartments and engine or accessory drive system compartments, abandon the airplane.

CABIN FIRE, SMOKE, OR FUMES.

Smoke and fumes are removed in time by the normal air recirculation system, however they can be removed faster by using these procedures.

T.O. 1B-70(X)A-1

NOTE

Do not encapsulate to escape the smoke and fumes, as the smoke and fumes trapped in the capsule could cause prolonged discomfort.

1. Oxygen masks on or face piece closed. If vision affected, proceed to step 7.
2. Cabin air switch - Hold at REPRESSURE.

CAUTION

If cabin altitude descends to below 6000 feet, release the cabin air switch to OFF.

   a. If smoke increases, release cabin air switch to OFF.
   b. If smoke clears, assume environmental control system operation is normal, and return to base.
3. Crew air shutoff handle - Unlock and pull up.
   Rotate crew air shutoff handle and pull up to close crew air shutoff valve.
     a. If smoke persists, proceed to step 4.
4. Decelerate and descend at 400 knots IAS minimum.
5. All non-essential electrical equipment - Off.
6. If fire is discovered, use portable fire extinguisher.

WARNING

Prolonged exposure (5 minutes or more) to high concentrations (pronounced irritation of eyes and nose) of bromochloromethane or its decomposition products should be avoided. Bromochloromethane, used in the portable fire extinguisher, is an anesthetic agent of moderate intensity. It is safer to use than previous fire extinguishing agents (carbon tetrachloride, methylbromide). However, especially in confined spaces, adequate respiratory and eye protection from excessive exposure, including use of oxygen, should be sought as soon as the primary fire emergency will permit.

CAUTION

Bromochloromethane is highly corrosive to some metals, paints, and plastic materials. Therefore, if the portable extinguisher starts to leak, it can be made harmless by being discharged from an inverted position. This releases the pressurizing gas charge with a minimum discharge of fluid. (Cover nozzle with a cloth or aim into a receptacle to catch any discharged liquid.) Return depressurized extinguisher to its bracket, and make suitable entry in Form 781 (or equivalent) so that unit will be replaced.

7. Cabin air switch - PURGE.
   Move cabin air switch to PURGE to bring in outside air to clear smoke and fumes.

NOTE

Cabin will dump pressure at the rate of one psi per second until cabin altitude equals actual flight altitude up to a maximum of 40,000 feet cabin altitude. This cabin altitude will be maintained providing airspeed is maintained above 400 knots IAS. Below 40,000 feet altitude, maintain at least 310 knots IAS unless descending, then 250 knots IAS is permissible.

8. Crew air shutoff handle - Unlock and push down.
   Rotate crew air shutoff handle and push down to open crew air shutoff valve.
     a. If smoke clears, hold cabin air switch at REPRESSURE until cabin altitude is less than 26,500 feet, then release.
     b. If smoke persists, or returns after clearing, move cabin air switch to PURGE, and proceed to step 10.

Changed 24 June 1965

3-21

T.O. 1B-70(I)A-1

9. Cabin pressure altimeter - Monitor.
   Monitor rise of cabin altitude and clearing of the air. The cabin altimeter should stabilize at 40,000 feet, or less.
10. Start emergency deceleration and descent as required.

EXCESSIVE AMMONIA FUMES.

If excessive ammonia fumes are noticed in the crew compartment, use the following procedure:

1. Oxygen masks check on or face piece closed.
2. Auxiliary cooling switch - AMMONIA EMER OFF.
3. Cabin air switch - PURGE.
4. Crew air shutoff handle - Unlock and push down.
   Rotate crew air shutoff handle and push down to open crew air shutoff valve.
5. (Deleted)
6. Start emergency deceleration and descent as required.

CREW ENCAPSULATION.

To encapsulate, proceed as follows:

NOTE
Ballistic encapsulation can be accomplished only once. However, manual encapsulation can be accomplished as often as necessary before or after ballistic encapsulation.

MANUAL ENCAPSULATION.

1. Encapsulate order. (Pilot)
   Move encapsulate caution light switch ON or use intercom to notify copilot to manually encapsulate. Watch for crew encapsulated indicator light to come on when copilot's capsule is closed. Receive copilot acknowledgement of the order.

   If time and conditions permit:
   a. Stow loose equipment.

   b. Standby pitch trim arming switch - Check ARMED.
      The standby pitch trim arming switch must be at ARMED to ensure operation of the trim switch on the emergency descent control grip in each capsule.
   c. Inlets* - Engage manual control.
      Inlets (Automatic AICS)† - No action required.
      Bypass door switches (Standby AICS)†- Both down to OPEN as required to position shocks in top of crosshatch.
   d. Throttles - MIL, or above.
   e. Engine rpm lockup switch - RELEASE.

   NOTE
   Releasing engine rpm lockup provides the capability of getting rid of an engine stall when using the throttle retard button on the capsule emergency descent control grip.

   f. Intercom push-pull switch - Pull out.
   g. IFF - Check at NORM or LOW; MODE 3 selector at code 77.
   h. UHF - Check settings so desired communications can be maintained.
   i. Pilot encapsulates first, and controls airplane unless immediate ejection is necessary.
2. Control column - Stow manually.
   Press control column release pedal and push control column forward to engage the stowage detent.
3. Seat - Unlock and retract.
   Move seat lock release lever aft and push seat back into capsule.
4. Capsule doors - Pull close.
   Pull feet into capsule and pull door handle down sharply and forward to close and latch capsule doors. The capsule will seal automatically and, if necessary, pressurize.

---

*Airplane AF62-001
†Airplane AF62-207

3-22

T.O. 1B-70(X)A-1

BALLISTIC ENCAPSULATION.

1. Encapsulate order. (Pilot)
   Move encapsulate caution light switch ON or use intercom to notify copilot to ballistically encapsulate. Watch for crew encapsulated indicator light to come on when copilot's capsule is closed. Receive copilot acknowledgement of order.

2. Seat handgrips - Pull up.
   This raises the seat handgrips, stows the control column, retracts the seat, and exposes the ejection triggers.

   WARNING
   - Do not touch either trigger when seat is retracted and handgrips are up, as seat is fully armed and catapult can fire.
   - Both heel pedals must be pressed back before capsule doors will close.

ENCAPSULATED DESCENT IN THE AIRPLANE.

1. Emergency descent control grip - Remove from upper left survival kit and use trim button as required.

2. Throttle retard button - As required. (P and CP)
   a. Pilot and copilot must press button momentarily and release to start movement of bypass doors and throat panels.

   NOTE
   When throttle retard button is used, the engine inlet bypass doors and throat panels move to a fail-safe position (throat opens to 39 inches and bypass area increases to 2400 square inches). The resultant bypass door opening causes an airplane nose-up trim change. Therefore, be prepared to apply nose down trim immediately after pressing throttle retard button.

   b. Press either button in short beeps to retard rpm slowly so that large changes in airplane trim do not occur.

   CAUTION
   To prevent inlet unstart, rpm must not be reduced to idle in less than 5 seconds.

   NOTE
   - All six engines are retarded simultaneously using the throttle retard button.
   - Throttle settings cannot be advanced until capsule is opened.

3. Seat handgrips - Unlock and stow.
   Unlock and lower handgrips to the stowed position if an immediate ejection is not expected.

   WARNING
   Do not touch ejection triggers because seat is fully armed and catapult could fire.

4. Decelerate and descend.
   Descend at 450 knots IAS minimum to a cabin altitude of 42,000 feet. Because of the limited control available, maintain a wings-level, descent.

CREW DECAPSULATION.

Decapsulate, one pilot at a time, as follows:

1. Copilot - Decapsulate.
   a. Seat handgrips - Unlock and stow.
      Unlock and lower handgrips to the stowed position, if not previously done.

      WARNING
      Do not touch ejection triggers because seat is fully armed and catapult could fire.

   b. Seal deflate button - Press.
      Press button until it latches, to deflate capsule seal.

Changed 25 June 1965

3-23

T.O. 1B-70(X)A-1

c. Capsule doors - Open.
   Pull door handle in and up, and raise upper door until latch is engaged.

d. Seat lock release lever - Unlock.
   Move seat lock release lever aft with the left hand, extend feet, and simultaneously rotate seat forward by pulling on the lip of the upper door with the right hand until the seat locks forward. (The seat lock lever can be released after initial movement of the seat.)

   NOTE
   Seat will not lock in forward position with handgrips raised or with lock release lever aft.

e. Control column - Re-engage.
   Pull control column aft until it engages the control system.

f. AICS mode switches* - All OFF.
   AICS mode switches† - Both STBY.

   NOTE
   AICS operation must be maintained in the standby mode, to ensure adequate throat and bypass door movement as required.

2. Pilot - Decapsulate.
   a. Emergency descent control grip - Stow.
      Stow grip carefully in its retaining clip on the upper left survival kit door, and close and latch the door. (Be sure airplane symbol on grip is pointing forward.)
   b. Seat handgrips - Unlock and stow.
      Unlock and lower handgrips to the stowed position, if not previously done.

      WARNING
      Do not touch ejection triggers because seat is fully armed and catapult could fire.

---
*Airplane AF62-001
†Airplane AF62-207

c. Seal deflate button - Press.
   Press button until it latches, to deflate capsule seal.

d. Capsule doors - Open.
   Pull door handle in and up, and raise upper door until latch is engaged.

e. Seat lock release lever - Unlock.
   Move seat lock release lever aft with the left hand, extend feet, and simultaneously rotate seat forward by pulling on the lip of the upper door with the right hand until the the seat locks forward. (The seat lock lever can be released after initial movement of the seat.)

   NOTE
   Seat will not lock in forward position with handgrips raised or with lock release lever aft.

f. Control column - Re-engage.
   Pull control column aft until it engages the control system.

3. All throttles - IDLE.

   NOTE
   This throttle adjustment will minimize undesirable thrust response when the throttles are re-engaged.

4. Throttle reset button - Press.
   Momentarily press reset button to re-engage normal throttle control of all engines, and check throttle response.

5. Air start switch - ON, if required.

6. (Deleted)

7. Bypass standby switches - As required.
   a. Above Mach 2.1, maintain shock in crosshatch.
   b. Below Mach 2.1, 700 square inches.

8. Throat standby switches - As required.
   a. Above Mach 2.1, throat Mach 0.2 less than airplane Mach.
   b. Below Mach 2.1, throat Mach to airplane Mach.

9. All throttles - MIL.
10. Air start switch - OFF, if used.

Changed 25 June 1965

T.O. 1B-70(X)A-1

11. Engine rpm lockup switch - As required.
12. Wing tips - As required.
13. Emergency descent control grip - Stow. (Copilot)
    a. Unlock and retract seat.
    b. Stow emergency descent control grip.
       Stow grip carefully in its retaining clip on the upper left survival kit door, and close and latch door. (Be sure airplane symbol on grip is pointing forward.)
    c. Unlock and extend seat.
14. Encapsulate switch - Momentarily at PESET.
15. IFF - Mode and code as briefed.

EJECTION.

NOTE.
See figure 3-5 for ejection procedure, capsule descent and landing procedures, and exit from the capsule.

If a decision has been made to eject use the following procedure:

WARNING
To prevent possible injury, stow emergency descent control grip if it is not already secured.

1. Bail-out order. (Pilot)
   Inform the copilot, by using intercom (or by pushing bail-out warning light button).
2. Encapsulate. (Pilot and copilot)
   Use ballistic encapsulation method (unless previously used) by pulling up either handgrip. As seat retracts, bring both feet back against their respective heel pedals.
3. Eject. (Copilot)
   a. Hear or see bail-out command.

T.O. 1B-70(X)A-1

b. Be sure pilot is encapsulated before ejecting.
c. Squeeze either or both triggers.
4. Eject. (Pilot)
   After copilot ejects, wait one second then eject by squeezing either or both triggers.

AFTER EJECTION.

During capsule descent after ejection and before landing, accomplish the following:

1. Capsule parachute - Check deployment.
   When altitude warning light comes on to indicate descent below 15,500 feet, visually check through window in top of capsule for parachute deployment. If parachute has not deployed (verified by capsule reaction or visually), pull emergency parachute handle.

   WARNING
   - Do not pull emergency parachute handle above 15,500 feet or before altitude warning light comes on, as parachute may be damaged.
   - If the emergency parachute handle is used, pull handle firmly only once as the riser cutter handle is exposed and armed.
   - Do not touch the riser cutter handle.

2. Impact bladder - Check inflation.
   After capsule parachute is deployed, visually check through the window in the lower door of the capsule for proper inflation of the impact bladder. If the impact bladder is not inflated, pull impact bladder inflate handle.

   WARNING
   Be seated with lap belt and shoulder harness fastened before ground impact.

ESCAPE CAPSULE GROUND LANDING AND EXIT.

After the capsule contacts the ground, proceed as follows:

1. Riser cutter handle - Pull.
   To prevent the possibility of the capsule being dragged by the parachute, pull riser cutter handle to spill air from the parachute.

   NOTE
   If capsule emergency parachute handle has not been used, it must be pulled to permit operation of the riser cutter handle.

2. Seal deflate button - Press.
   Press seal deflate button until it latches, to deflate capsule seal.
3. Door - Open.
   a. Pull door handle in and up and raise upper door. If position of capsule prevents opening door by this means, proceed to step 3b.

   NOTE
   Only the upper door will open when door handle is used if impact bladder has actuated.

   b. Hinge split handle - Pull, if necessary.
      Pull hinge split handle down to split hinge pins of each door so doors can be pushed off.
4. Survival equipment - Remove, if required.

This page intentionally left blank

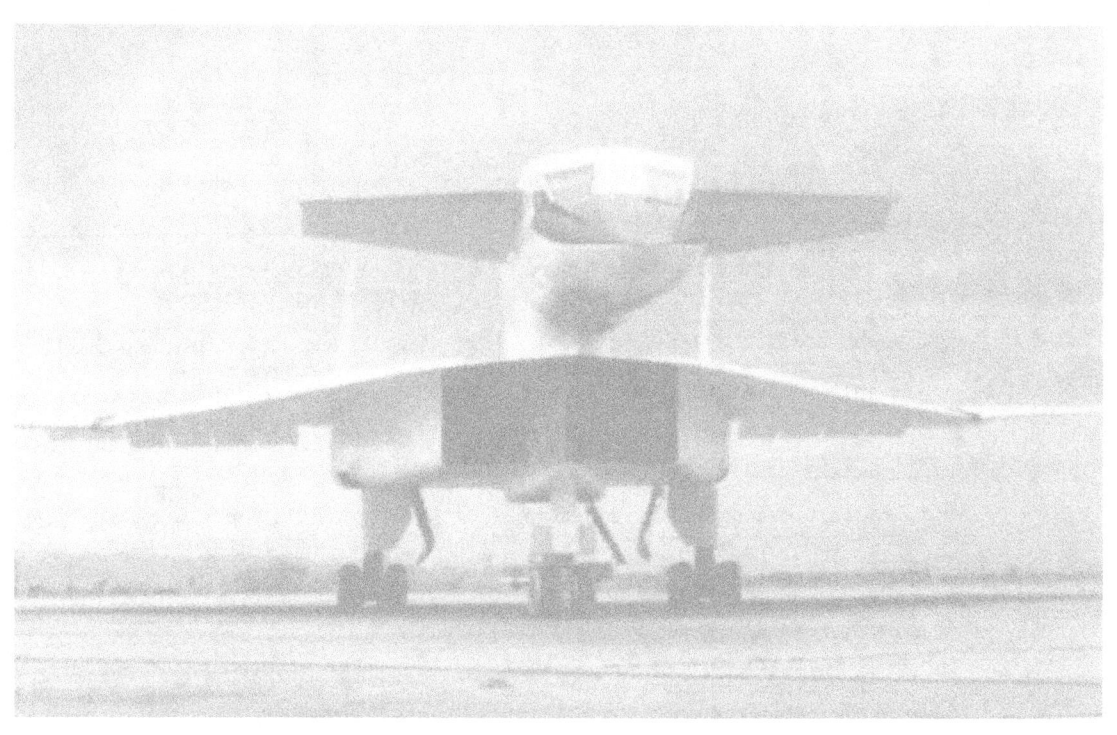

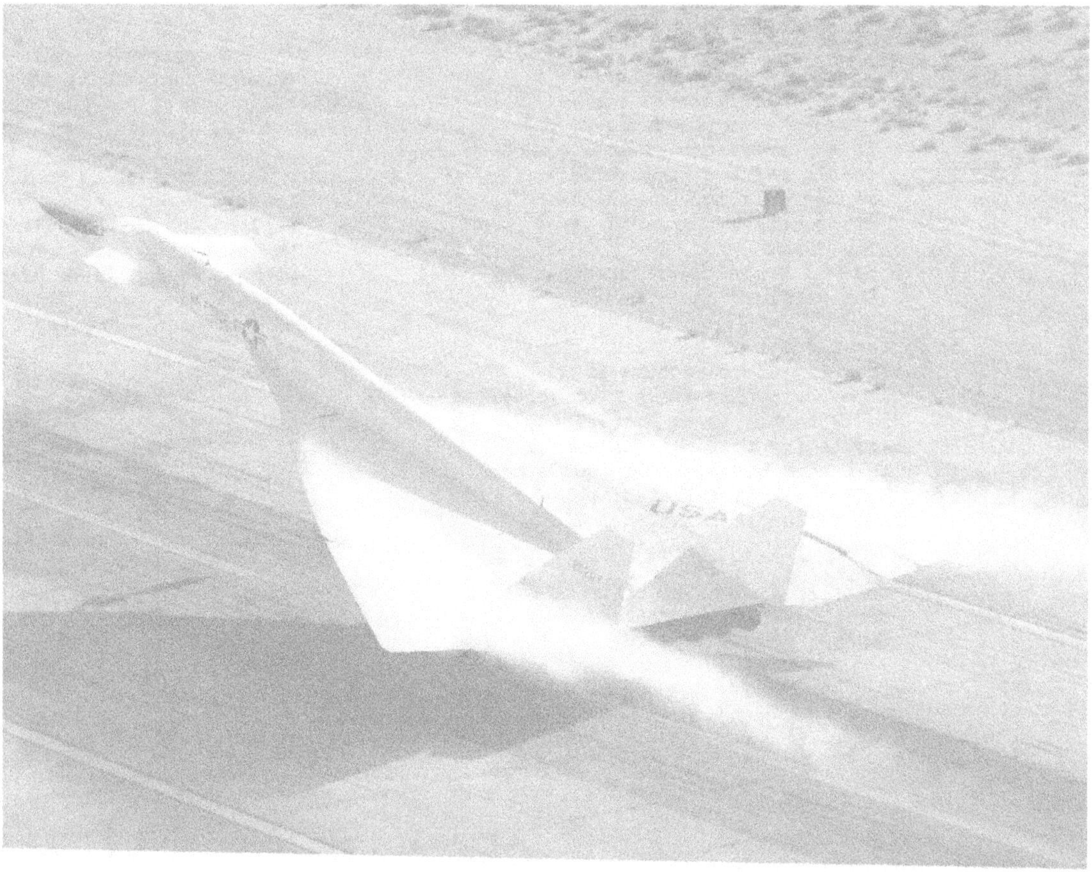

T.O. 1B-70(X)A-1

EJECTION

SAFE EJECTION ALTITUDES

Warning

Capsule must be ejected above the applicable altitude line.

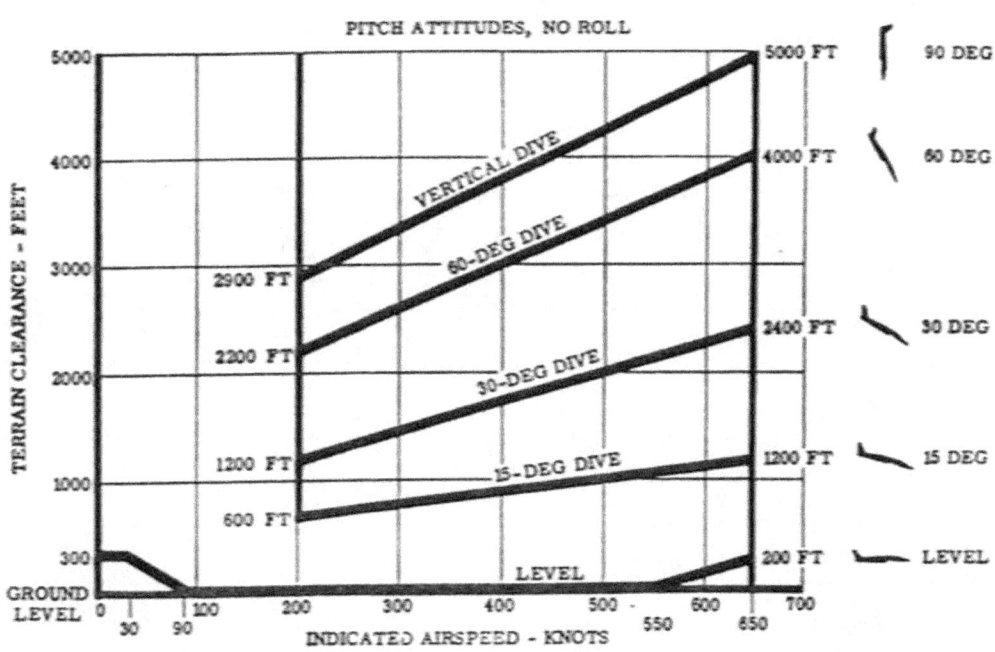

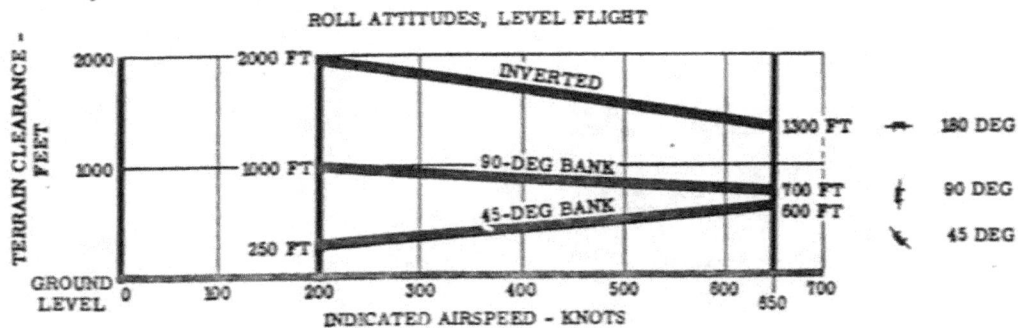

Figure 3-5 (Sheet 1 of 3)

T.O. 1B-70(X)A-1

PROCEDURES

(TYPICAL EACH ESCAPE CAPSULE)

1 Pull up either handgrip and, as seat retracts, bring both feet back against their respective heel pedals to encapsulate.

HANDGRIP DOWNLOCK RELEASE LEVER

EJECTION TRIGGER

2 Squeeze either or both triggers to eject escape capsule.

Steps 1 and 2 are all that are necessary for ejection. If time and conditions permit, pilot should do as much of the following as possible prior to encapsulating and ejecting.

- Stow all loose equipment.
- Move encapsulate caution light switch to ON and note that crew encapsulated light comes on.
- Establish intercom contact with copilot.
- Press bail-out button and receive confirmation from copilot.
- Brace for ejection after encapsulating (pilot and copilot):
    Arms braced in armrests
    Body erect
    Head hard against headrest

AFTER EJECTION

- Capsule parachute will open at 15,500 feet.
- Impact bladder inflates when parachute is deployed.
- If capsule parachute has not deployed when altitude warning light comes on, pull emergency parachute handle.

Warning

Do not pull emergency parachute handle above 15,500 feet, as parachute may be damaged.

- If impact bladder is not visible when viewed through the lower capsule door window, pull impact bladder inflate handle when landing is imminent.

Figure 3-5 (Sheet 2 of 3)

T.O. 1B-70(X)A-1

ESCAPE CAPSULE LANDING AND EXIT - (Ground landing)

1 After capsule contacts the ground, pull riser cutter handle to prevent dragging of capsule. (Emergency parachute handle must be pulled first.)

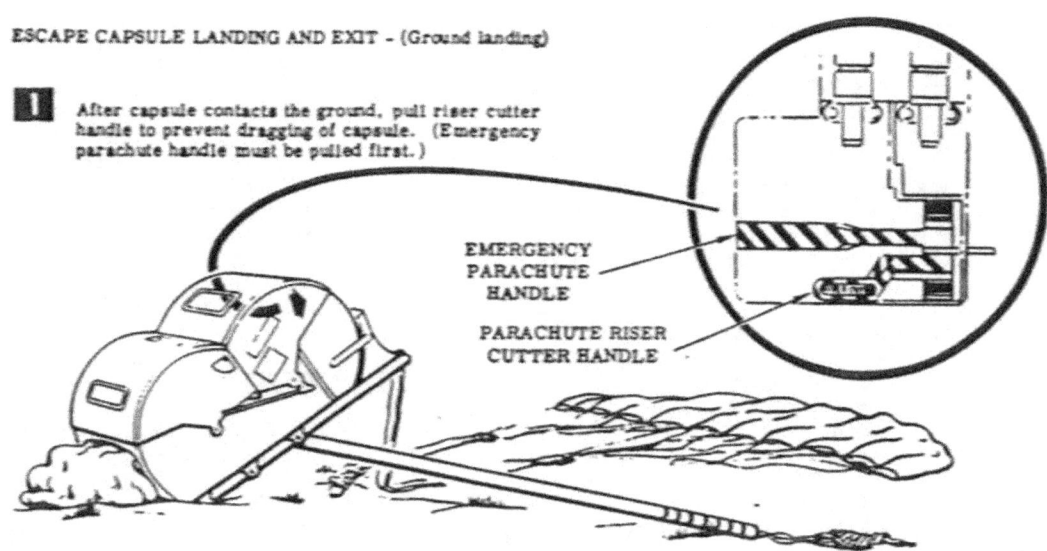

EMERGENCY PARACHUTE HANDLE

PARACHUTE RISER CUTTER HANDLE

2 Press seal internal deflate button. (On left side of capsule)

3 Pull and raise door interior release bar to open upper door. If door cannot be opened, proceed to step 4.

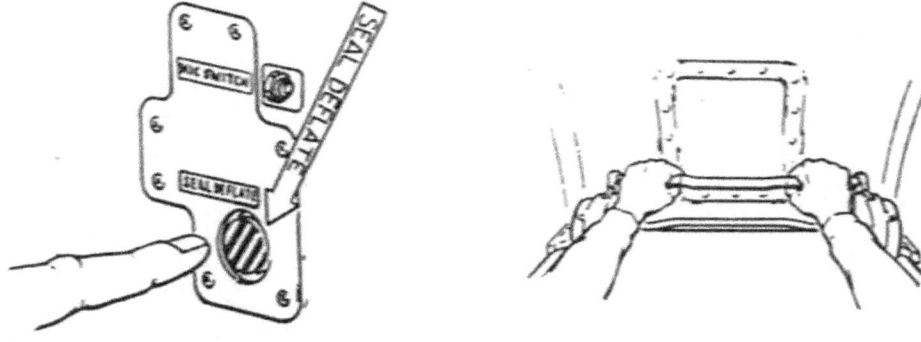

4 Pull door hinge split handle and push capsule doors off.

DOOR HINGE SPLIT HANDLE

Figure 3-5 (Sheet 3 of 3)

T.O. 1B-70(X)A-1

AFTER ESCAPE CAPSULE WATER LANDING.

The capsule floats upright with the doors facing upward. Top and bottom panels are painted with a high visibility paint to aid rescue. All survival equipment is contained in the capsule. Therefore, it is recommended that the occupant remain with the capsule until rescued. <u>After the capsule is in the water,</u> proceed as follows:

1. Riser cutter handle - Pull.
   To prevent the possibility of the capsule being dragged by the parachute, pull riser cutter handle to spill air from the parachute.

   NOTE
   - If emergency parachute handle has not been used, it must be pulled to permit operation of the riser cutter handle.
   - After the capsule rights itself, proceed to step 2.

2. Ventilation plug - Remove and retain.
   Remove ventilation plug from the capsule upper door and retain for possible reinstallation.
3. Capsule doors - Keep closed.
   Do not open the capsule doors and do not press the seal deflate button. However, if it is necessary to abandon the capsule immediately, refer to "Escape Capsule Water Exit" in this section.
4. Prepare to abandon capsule.
   a. Remove heel pedals from their sockets by grasping and squeezing and pulling the pedals.
   b. Remove foot guide.
      Press and pull pip pin from leading edge of guide.
   c. Open lower survival equipment compartment by turning and pulling the ring on compartment door.
   d. Remove the two packages from the compartment. (Open package marked "LIFE RAFT." The other package contains survival equipment.)

   e. If warm clothing is desired, remove equipment packages from right and left upper survival equipment compartments. Remove containers from the wall by pressing the release button through the hole in the outboard wall of each container, and sliding the container forward and inboard. Release electrical connection on aft end of left container. Remove and discard emergency descent control grip.

ESCAPE CAPSULE WATER EXIT.

1. Seal deflate button - Press.
   Press seal deflate button until it latches to deflate capsule seal.
2. Door - Open.
   a. Pull door handle in and up and raise upper door. If door cannot be opened, and capsule is to be abandoned, proceed to step 2b.

   NOTE
   Only the upper door will open when door handle is used if impact bladder has actuated.

   b. Hinge split handle - Pull, if necessary.
      Pull hinge split handle down to split hinge pins of each door so doors can be pushed off.
3. Abandon capsule.
   If it is necessary to use the life raft, proceed as follows:
   a. Hook or tie mooring lanyard to person.
   b. Hold life raft out of capsule and inflate.

c. Transfer survival equipment to life raft and secure to prevent loss.
d. Step gently into life raft.

EJECTION WITH CAPSULE DOORS OPEN (AFTER PULLING UP HANDGRIPS).

If capsule doors fail to close or cannot be closed, a last resort ejection is possible. Proceed as follows:

> **WARNING**
> - Seat must be retracted and locked before any ejection, to properly position the occupant for ejection and to unlock the ejection triggers.
> - Occupant of capsule with open doors should eject first.

1. Ejection trigger - Squeeze.
   Second capsule should not be ejected sooner than one second after the first.
2. Capsule parachute - Check deployment.
   When altitude warning light comes on to indicate descent below 15,500 feet, check for parachute deployment. If parachute has not deployed (verified by capsule reaction or visually), pull emergency parachute handle.

> **WARNING**
> - Do not pull emergency parachute handle above 15,500 feet or before altitude warning light comes on, as parachute may be damaged.
> - If the emergency parachute handle is used, pull handle firmly only once as the riser cutter handle is exposed and armed.
> - Do not touch the riser cutter handle.

3. Capsule doors - Close.
   Attempt to close capsule doors to permit inflation of impact bladder.
   a. If doors close, proceed to step 6.
   b. If doors cannot be closed, proceed to step 4.
4. Hinge split handle - Pull, and kick lower door off.

> **NOTE**
> Both doors come off when lower door is kicked off, however, doors must be at least 1/2 closed before they can be kicked off.

5. Door closure sensing valve lever - Push in and hold with right hand until step 6 is completed.
   Push in lever on left exterior of the capsule and hold until impact bladder is inflated.
6. Impact bladder inflate handle - Pull with left hand.
   After capsule doors are closed, (or doors removed and door closure sensing lever pushed) pull handle to inflate impact bladder.

> **CAUTION**
> Do not pull impact bladder handle above 15,500 feet, or before parachute opens, or before capsule doors are closed or removed, as the impact bladder pressure may bleed off, or structural damage may occur.

EMERGENCY DESCENT OF AIRPLANE.

If an emergency descent is necessary, proceed as follows:

> **NOTE**
> Refer to "Emergency Descent of Airplane" in Section III of T.O. 1B-70(X)A-1A for additional information.

1. Inlets - Adjust as required.

T.O. 1B-70(X)A-1

2. Throttles - IDLE.
3. Maintain maximum safe-G spiral, above 450 knots IAS.
4. Throttles (any two of four inboard engines) - Advance to obtain 87% rpm, or move refrigeration switch to OFF.

TAKE-OFF AND LANDING EMERGENCIES.

ABORTED TAKE-OFF.

Depending upon the severity of the situation, do as many of the following steps as necessary:

1. All throttles - IDLE.
   If sufficient runway remains to stop, move all throttles to IDLE.
2. Drag chute handle - DEPLOY.
3. Wheel brakes - Apply.

RUNWAY OVERRUN BARRIER.

Because of the size and weight of the airplane and landing gear placement, a successful barrier engagement is very unlikely.

TIRE FAILURE.

Tire failure during take-off normally creates more difficulty than during landing. Take-off speeds in general are higher, causing directional control problems in maintaining a straight ground track down the runway. Take-off abort procedures are recommended if tire failure occurs or is suspected before reaching decision speed. Effective braking not only is reduced, but additional stress is applied to the remaining tires on the same gear as the failed tire.

WARNING

If take-off is continued after a suspected tire failure, the landing gear should not be retracted until a visual report is received from a chase plane or from the tower. Make landing in accordance with "Nose Gear Tire Failure Landing" or "Main Gear Tire Failure" in this section.

NOSE GEAR TIRE FAILURE ON TAKE-OFF.

If nose gear tire failure occurs or is suspected during take-off, the take-off should be either aborted or continued, depending upon whether or not refusal speed has been reached. If abort procedures are followed, the control column should be held back to reduce nose gear tire load as much as possible during braking. It is recommended that minimum braking consistent with remaining runway be used to reduce nose gear tire loading. If nose gear tire failure occurs or is suspected above refusal speed, relieve nose wheel load with longitudinal control and continue take-off.

NOSE GEAR TIRE FAILURE LANDING.

If a landing is to be made with suspected or confirmed nose gear tire failure, proceed as follows:

1. Landing weight - Reduce.
   Burn off excess fuel to reduce weight and to move the CG as far aft as safely possible for landing.
2. Normal approach and touchdown.
3. Nose wheels - Hold off.
   Hold nose wheels off as long as possible.
4. Nose wheels - Touch down.
   When nose wheels touch down, maintain control column back pressure to lighten nose gear load.

T.O. 1B-70(X)A-1

5. Drag chute handle - DEPLOY.
6. Nose wheel steering switch - ENGAGE then FAIL SAFE.
7. Wheel brakes - Apply.
   Use minimum braking consistent with remaining runway distance.

MAIN GEAR TIRE FAILURE ON TAKE-OFF.

If main gear tire failure is suspected or confirmed, and speed is below decision speed, abort procedures should be followed, except that pilot discretion should determine amount of braking. The load on the remaining tires may be reduced by maintaining forward control column pressure and full lateral control sway from the failed tire to increase wing lift on the failed-tire side.

If take-off is continued, forward pressure on the control column and lateral control against the swerve direction will ease the tire loads of the remaining tires on that bogie.

MAIN GEAR TIRE FAILURE LANDING.

If a landing is to be made with a suspected or confirmed main gear tire failure, proceed as follows:

1. Landing weight - Reduce.
   Burn off excess fuel to reduce weight.
2. Normal approach procedures.
   Attempt to land on the side of the runway away from the failed tire.
3. Touchdown.
   After touchdown, lower nose wheels to runway and apply lateral control away from the failed tire.
4. Nose wheel steering switch - ENGAGE then FAIL SAFE.
5. Drag chute handle - DEPLOY.
6. Wheel brakes - Apply.

LANDING ON UNPREPARED SURFACES.

A landing should not be attempted on an unprepared surface.

LANDING WITH ANY GEAR UP OR UNLOCKED.

NOSE GEAR UP.

WARNING

If the nose gear cannot be lowered, eject rather than attempt an emergency landing.

BOTH MAIN GEARS UP OR UNLOCKED.

If the nose gear is down and locked but both main gears fail to extend and lock, a landing may be attempted at the pilot's discretion. Use a normal landing pattern with a minimum rate of descent just before touchdown.

If a landing is to be attempted, use the following procedure:

1. Reduce weight.
   Burn off all fuel above that required for at least one approach and go-around pattern.
2. Ground escape hatch jettison handle - Pull just before final approach.
3. Shoulder harness - LOCK.
4. Touchdown at 7-degree angle of attack.

NOTE

Nose wheel steering is inoperative and rudder travel may be restricted to ±3 degrees.

5. Drag chute handle - DEPLOY after nose wheels are on the runway.
6. Throttles - OFF.

T.O. 1B-70(X)A-1

MAIN GEAR DOWN AND LOCKED AND BOGIE UNSAFE.

If the nose gear and the main gears are down and locked, but a bogie is in any unsafe position as confirmed by chase plane or tower fly-by, a landing may be attempted at the pilot's discretion. Use a normal landing pattern with a minimum rate of descent just before touchdown, and touchdown at minimum speed. After nose wheels are on the runway, deploy drag chute and maintain heading with nose wheel steering.

BELLY LANDING.

If the landing gear cannot be lowered, a belly landing must not be made.

LANDING WITH CANARD FLAPS UP.

There is no alternate method of lowering the canard flaps. No special precautions during the landing pattern are required. Final approach and touchdown speeds should be increased by about 10 knots IAS.

EMERGENCY GROUND ESCAPE.

In case of an emergency requiring immediate evacuation from the airplane, such as a fire, shut down the engines and leave the airplane through the entrance door or the ground escape hatch. Unless rescue crews are at the site with ladders, use the descent device attached to the escape rope to reach the ground. (See figure 3-6 for emergency escape routes and exits.) Before abandoning the airplane, and depending upon the emergency, the following must be accomplished.

1. Flight status safety pin - Insert.
    Insert the flight status safety pin in the right console of each seat to safety the escape capsule ejection system.
2. Entrance door - Open.
3. Ground escape hatch - Jettison, if entrance door cannot be opened.
    Jettison the ground escape hatch by pulling either the hatch jettison handle on the pilot's console or the jettison handle on the left wall of the escape aisle. (See figure 1-34.)
4. Leave airplane by ladder or escape rope.
    Leave the airplane by a ladder put in place by the rescue crew, or if a ladder is not available, use the escape rope and descent device. Remove the escape ropes and descent devices from the stowage compartment forward of the entrance door. If the entrance door is used, insert and lock the pip pins on the escape ropes into the sockets above the door opening and throw the ropes out the door. If the entrance door cannot be used, leave the airplane through the ground escape hatch. When the escape hatch is used, throw the ropes out the hatch opening and over the leading edge of the canard. (The pip pins should not be used.)
5. Descent device - Grasp properly and slide to ground.
    After the escape ropes are extended, put one hand through the strap loop on the descent device (Sky Genie) and grasp the remainder of the strap with the other hand and slide to the ground.

    NOTE
    Do not grasp the end of the escape rope below the descent device, as this will stop the descent.

6. Get clear of the airplane.

T.O. 1B-70(X)A-1

EMERGENCY ENTRANCE.

The procedure to be used by rescue personnel when assisting the crew from the airplane following a crash landing is outlined in figure 3-6. If the airplane is still on the landing gear, the same procedure is used except it is necessary to use a safe and rapid means of reaching the entrance door, ground escape hatch jettison handle, or the ground escape hatch opening.

DITCHING.

> **WARNING**
> Under no circumstances should ditching be attempted.

THROTTLE SYSTEM MALFUNCTION.

SINGLE THROTTLE SYSTEM FAILURE.

Indication of a possible inoperative throttle servo system is by direct observation of the engine instruments when the throttles are moved. With any indication of a throttle servo system failure, proceed as follows:

1. Alternate throttle switch (affected engine) - Hold at INCR or DECR, as required.
   This changes the thrust setting of the corresponding engine, and turns off and isolates the normal throttle servo system.

   > **NOTE**
   > - Alternate throttle switch operation does not override the rpm lockup.
   > - Coordinated movement of the throttle and alternate throttle switch is not necessary.
   > - Do not move the throttle to OFF except for intentional engine shutdown, as this closes the fuel shutoff valve and shuts down the engine, even though the alternate throttle switch has been used.

COMPLETE THROTTLE SYSTEM FAILURE.

Simultaneous loss of all six throttle servo systems may be the result of a loss of essential ac bus power. If all throttles fail, proceed as follows:

1. All alternate throttle switches - Hold at INCR or DECR, as required. If the engines do not respond*:
   a. Engine shutdown and wheel brake arming switch - Check OFF.

   > **CAUTION**
   > To preclude inadvertent engine shutdown when using the alternate throttle switches, the engine shutdown and wheel brake arming switch must not be at its ARMED position in flight.

   b. Battery-inverter switch - ON. Break safety wire and move battery-inverter switch to ON so that emergency battery will power the alternate throttle switches.

   > **NOTE**
   > After being energized, the emergency battery requires 3 to 5 seconds before it will light the battery-inverter indicator light.

   c. All alternate throttles INCR or DECR as required.

---

*Airplane AF62-001

EMERGENCY GROUND ESCAPE
ESCAPE ROUTES AND EXITS

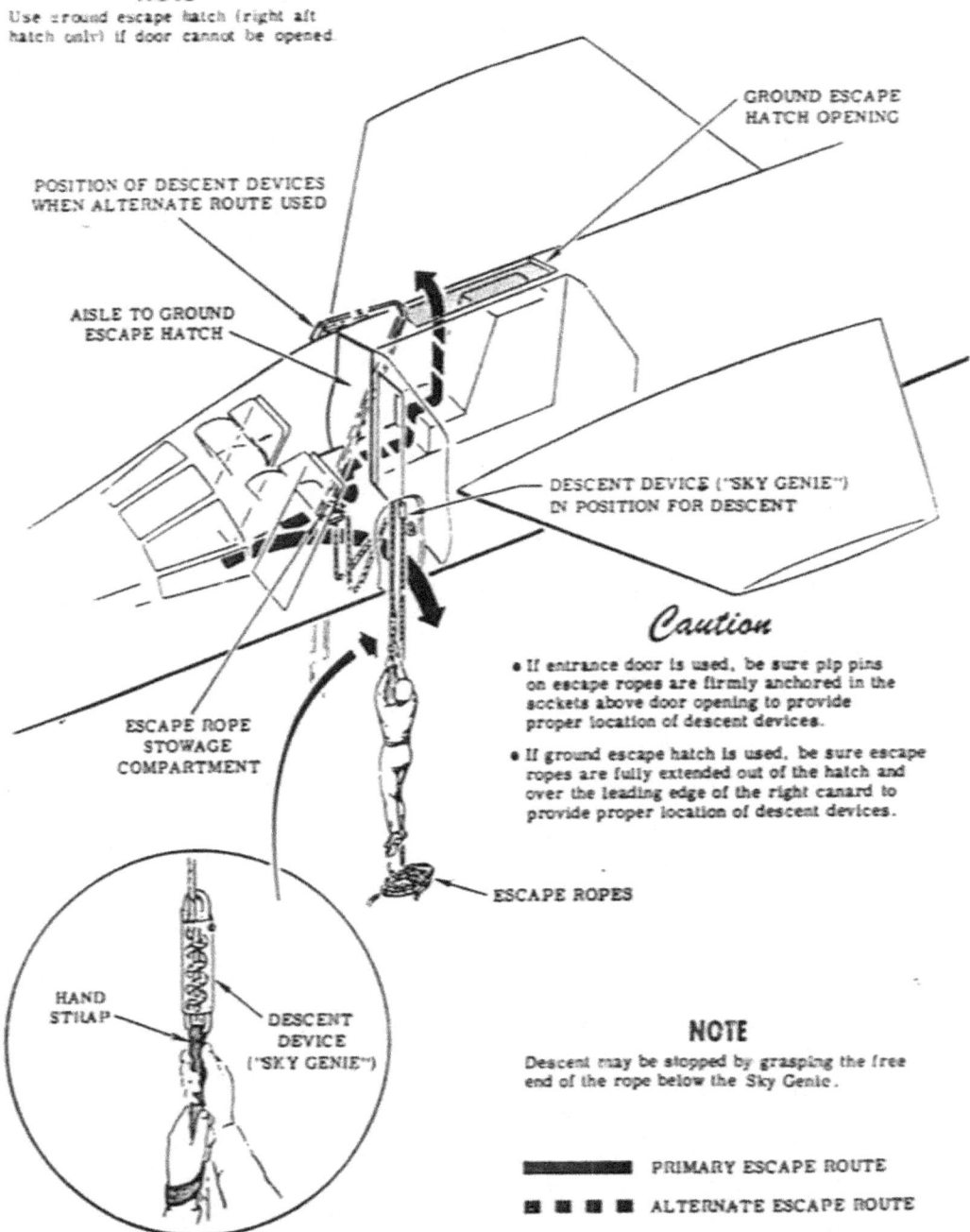

Figure 3-6 (Sheet 1 of 4)

T.O. 1B-70(X)A-1

EMERGENCY ENTRANCE - AIRPLANE

1 Gain access to crew compartment.

• Open entrance door, using door handle.

---OR---

• Unlatch access door on right side of airplane. Remove hatch jettison handle and fully extend cable to jettison hatch.

Warning

Keep all personnel clear of right aft escape hatch jettison path. Watch hatch path after jettisoning and remain clear.

---OR---

• Unscrew entrance door hinge access panels and remove hinge pins.

NOTE

If above methods of gaining entrance cannot be accomplished, remove the screw-attached emergency access panels (10 screws per panel) and disconnect and manually pull door pins.

---OR---

• Cut hole in skin within marked area. (Right side only.)

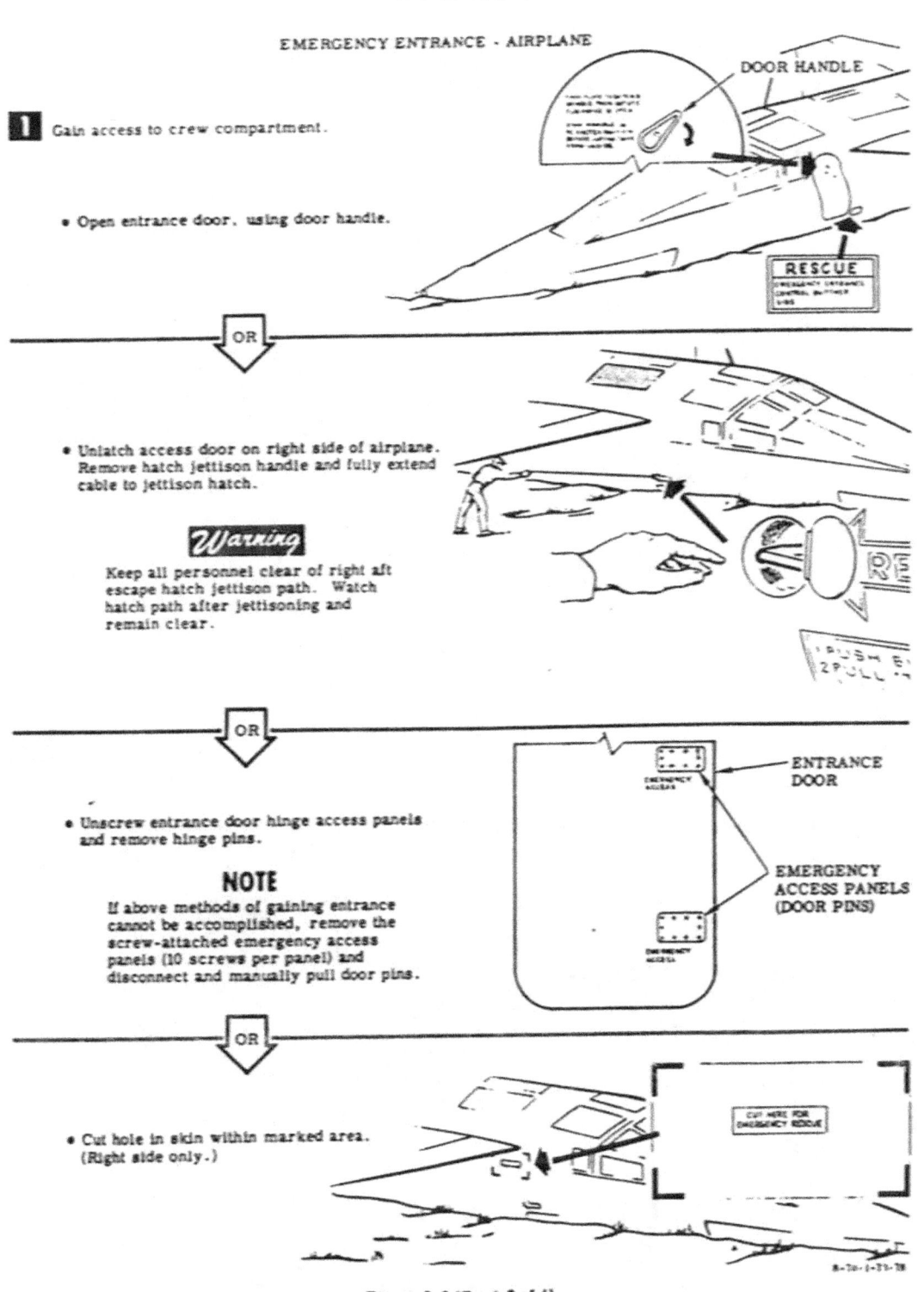

Figure 3-6 (Sheet 2 of 4)

T.O. 1B-70(X)A-1

SAFETYING CAPSULE
(Pilot's shown, copilot's similar)

2 Safetying capsule.

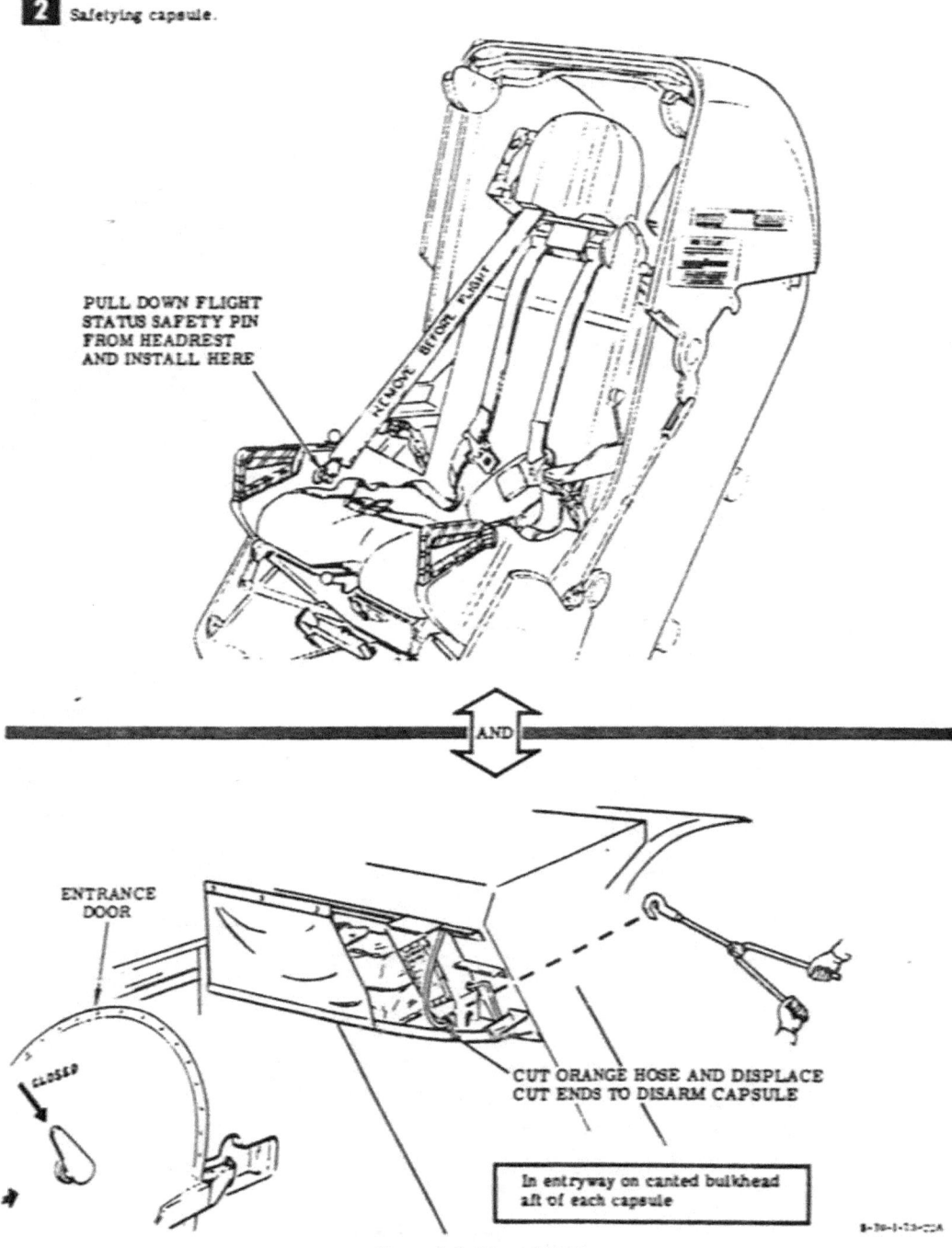

PULL DOWN FLIGHT
STATUS SAFETY PIN
FROM HEADREST
AND INSTALL HERE

AND

ENTRANCE DOOR

CUT ORANGE HOSE AND DISPLACE
CUT ENDS TO DISARM CAPSULE

In entryway on canted bulkhead
aft of each capsule

Figure 3-6 (Sheet 3 of 4)

This page intentionally left blank

T.O. 1B-70(X)A-1

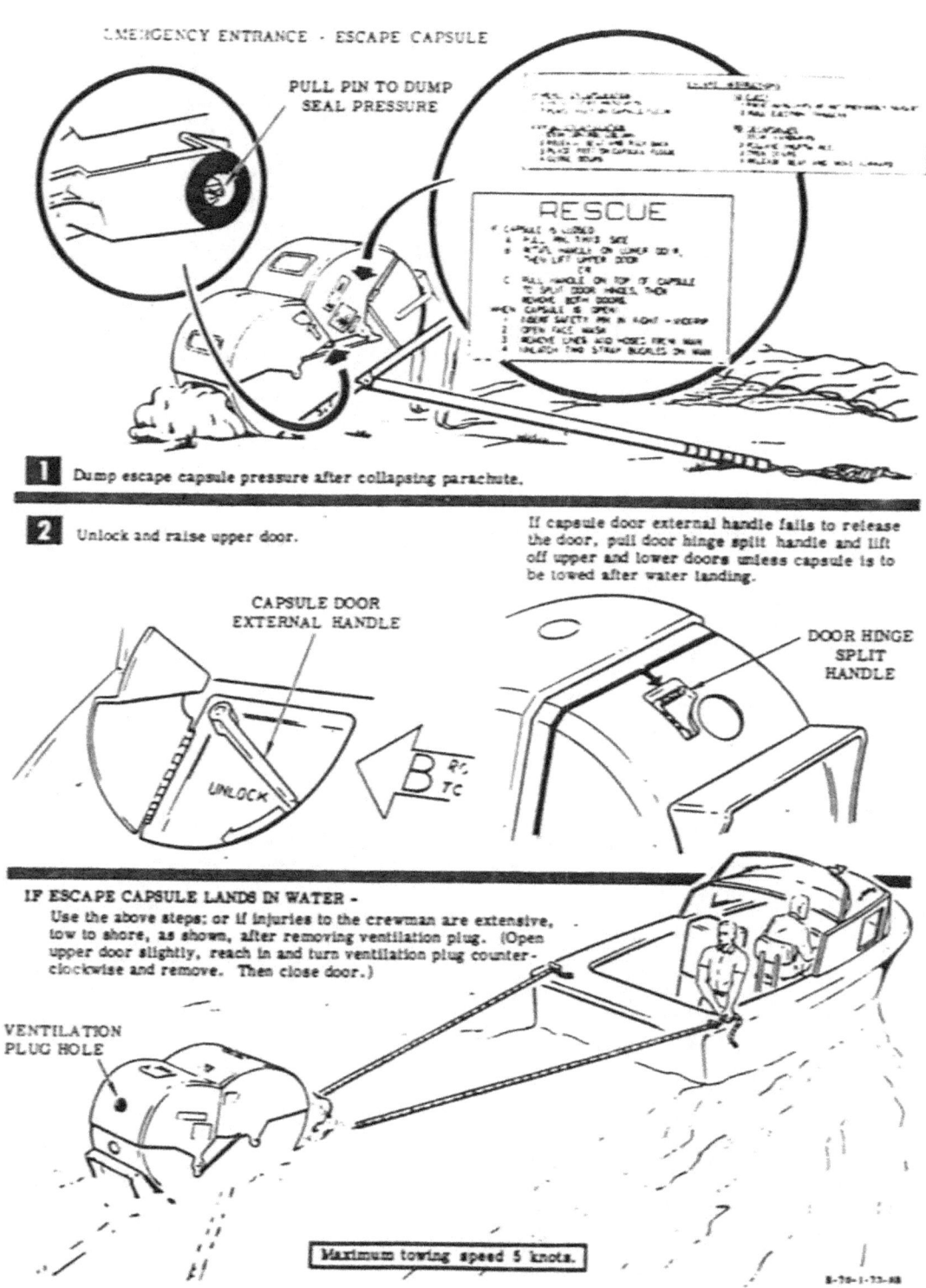

Figure 3-6 (Sheet 4 of 4)

T.O. 1B-70(X)A-1

2. When time and conditions permit, annunciator light test switch - Hold at BRIGHT or DIM momentarily to test for indications of essential ac bus power.
   a. If all annunciator lights remain out, proceed to step 3. Failure of lights to come on when test switch is used, indicates essential ac bus failure.
   b. If all annunciator lights come on when test switch is used, essential ac bus power is available. Therefore, proceed to step 4 in attempt to return to normal throttle control.
3. Throttle and fire detection bus selector switch - RH BUS.
   Break safety wire and move selector switch to RH BUS to transfer throttle servo system power from the essential ac bus to the right primary ac bus.

   CAUTION
   Do not select RH BUS position if essential ac bus power is available.

4. All throttles - Reposition to engine rpm.
5. Throttle reset button - Press.
   If the throttle servo systems are operating, the servo actuators will be adjusted to their respective throttle settings.
6. All throttles - As required.
   a. If engines do not respond, use alternate throttle switches to control thrust (emergency battery* on if required).
7. Battery-inverter switch* - ON, on final approach.
   Make sure emergency battery is energized on final to provide emergency power for alternate throttle use if necessary.

RETURNING TO NORMAL THROTTLE SYSTEM.

After an alternate throttle switch has been used, an attempt to return engine control to the normal throttle servo system can be made as follows:

1. Throttle (affected engine) - Reposition to engine rpm.

2. Throttle reset button - Press.
   If the normal throttle system is operating, the thrust control servo actuators will be adjusted to their respective throttle settings.

ENGINE SHUTDOWN WITH FAILED THROTTLE.

To shut down an engine with a failed throttle system, proceed as follows:

1. Alternate throttle switch (affected engine) - Hold at DECR until idle thrust is obtained.

   CAUTION
   During engine shutdown, when using an alternate throttle switch, do not move throttle to OFF until engine thrust is reduced to idle, or possible fuel system damage may occur.

2. Throttle (affected engine) - OFF.

ENGINE EXHAUST NOZZLE FAILURE.

PRIMARY EXHAUST NOZZLE FAILS OPEN.

Failure of a primary exhaust nozzle in the open direction is indicated by the corresponding primary nozzle position indicator and a lower-than-normal exhaust temperature. During afterburner operation, such a failure may cause afterburner flame-out.

*Airplane AF62-001

PRIMARY NOZZLE FAILS OPEN - ABOVE MACH 2.1, AUTO/MANUAL OR MANUAL AICS (AIRPLANE AF62-001).

1. Bypass wheels - Both aft as required to maintain shocks in crosshatch.
2. Engine rpm lockup switch - RELEASE.
3. Throttle (affected engine) - IDLE, and maintain shocks in crosshatch.
   a. If nozzle closes, throttle (affected engine) - 40 degrees, then proceed to step 5.
   b. If nozzle stays open, maintain 80% rpm on affected engine until engine is shut down after landing, or proceed to step 4.

   NOTE
   If unlocked idle rpm is above 80%, descend at unlocked idle until 80% rpm is obtained.

4. Throttle (affected engine) - OFF, maintain shocks in crosshatch, and abort flight.
5. Throat:
   If AUTO - Check schedule.
   If MANUAL - Both wheels aft to maintain throat at 0.2 Mach less than airplane Mach.
6. Engine rpm lockup switch - AUTO.
7. Throttle (affected engine) - 40 degrees.

   NOTE
   Advance throttle of affected engine to 40 degrees, to provide fuel flow for proper cooling of engine lube oil system. (See figure 5-2.)

PRIMARY NOZZLE FAILS OPEN - BELOW MACH 2.1, AUTO/MANUAL OR MANUAL AICS (AIRPLANE AF62-001).

1. Bypass area (affected inlet):
   If SUPERSONIC - Wheel aft to obtain 700, 1100, or 1800 square inches. For first throttle to be moved to IDLE, obtain 700 square inches; for second throttle, 1100 square inches; and for third throttle, 1800 square inches.
   If SUBSONIC - Check bypass area closed.

2. Engine rpm lockup switch - RELEASE.
3. Throttle (affected engine) - IDLE.
   a. If nozzle closes, throttle (affected engine) - 40 degrees, then proceed to step 5.
   b. If nozzle stays open, maintain 80% rpm on affected engine until engine is shut down after landing, or proceed to step 4.

   NOTE
   If unlocked idle rpm is above 80%, descend at unlocked idle until 80% rpm is obtained.

4. Throttle (affected engine) - OFF, and abort flight.
5. Throat - Check schedule.
6. Engine rpm lockup switch (above Mach 1.4) - AUTO.
7. Throttle (affected engine) - 40 degrees.

   NOTE
   Advance throttle of affected engine to 40 degrees, to provide fuel flow for proper cooling of engine lube oil system. (See figure 5-2.)

PRIMARY NOZZLE FAILS OPEN - ABOVE MACH 2.1, AUTOMATIC OR STANDBY AICS (AIRPLANE AF62-207).

1. Bypass area (affected inlet):
   If AUTO, duct performance switch - LOW.
   If STANDBY, bypass door standby switch - Down to maintain shock in crosshatch.
2. Engine rpm lockup switch - RELEASE.
3. Throttle (affected engine) - IDLE, and if affected inlet is in standby mode maintain shock in crosshatch.
4. Throat (affected inlet):
   If AUTO - Check schedule.
   If STANDBY, throat Mach schedule standby switch - Down to maintain throat at 0.2 Mach less than airplane Mach.
5. Throttle (affected engine):
   a. If nozzle closes, throttle (affected engine) - 40 degrees, then proceed to step 8.

T.O. 1B-70(X)A-1

   b. If nozzle remains open, maintain 80% rpm on affected engine until engine is shutdown after landing, or proceed to step 6.

> **NOTE**
> If unlocked idle rpm is above 80%, descend at unlocked idle until 80% rpm is obtained.

6. Throttle (affected engine) - OFF, and if affected inlet is in standby mode maintain shock in crosshatch.
7. Bypass door standby switch (if affected inlet is in automatic mode) - Hold down 1, 3, or 6 seconds.

   If the inlet for the engine being shut down is in automatic mode, hold the bypass door standby switch down for one second if only one engine is shut down; three seconds if two engines are shut down; and six seconds if three engines are shut down. This will bias the bypass door master cylinder from its normal rig position so that when the airplane is decelerating through approximately Mach 2.08 (AICS transfers from shock control to open loop control) the bypass doors will slowly open from their normal locked position of 500 square inches to approximately 700, 1100, or 1800 square inches (one, two, or three engines out).

8. Engine rpm lockup switch - AUTO.
9. Throttle (affected engine) - 40 degrees.

> **NOTE**
> Advance throttle of affected engine to 40 degrees, to provide fuel flow for proper cooling of engine lube oil system. (See figure 5-2.)

10. Duct performance switch (if affected inlet is in automatic mode) - NORM.

PRIMARY NOZZLE FAILS OPEN - BELOW MACH 2.1, AUTOMATIC OR STANDBY AICS (AIRPLANE AF62-207).

1. Bypass area (affected inlet):
   If SUPERSONIC, bypass door standby switch - Hold down 1, 3, or 6 seconds.

Hold the bypass door standby switch down for one second if only one throttle is to be moved to IDLE; three seconds for two throttles at IDLE; and six seconds for three throttles at IDLE. If the affected inlet is in automatic mode, this will bias the bypass door master cylinder from its normal rig position so that when the airplane is decelerating through approximately Mach 2.08 (AICS transfers from shock control to open loop control) the bypass doors will slowly open from their normal locked position of 500 square inches to approximately 700, 1100, or 1800 square inches (one, two, or three engines at IDLE or out). If the affected inlet is in standby mode, this will cause the bypass doors to open to approximately 700, 1100, or 1800 square inches, respectively.

   If SUBSONIC - Check both bypass areas closed.

2. Engine rpm lockup switch - RELEASE.
3. Throttle (affected engine) - IDLE.
4. Throats - If one inlet is in standby mode and the other in automatic mode, adjust standby throat to obtain same throat Mach schedule indicator reading as for the automatic throat. If both throats are automatic, check indicators stopped at approximately Mach 2.1.
5. Throttle (affected engine):
   a. If nozzle closes, throttle (affected engine) - 40 degrees, then proceed to step 8.
   b. If nozzle remains open, maintain 80% rpm on affected engine until engine is shut down after landing, or proceed to step 6.

> **NOTE**
> If unlocked idle rpm is above 80%, descend at unlocked idle until 80% rpm is obtained.

260

T.O. 1B-70(X)A-1

6. Throttle (affected engine) - OFF.
7. Bypass area (affected inlet):
   If SUPERSONIC, bypass door standby switch - As required to refine bypass to 700, 1100, or 1800 square inches.
   Move switch as required to obtain 700 square inches for one engine out; 1100 square inches for two engines out; and 1800 square inches for three engines out.
8. Engine rpm lockup switch (above Mach 1.4) - AUTO.
9. Throttle (affected engine) - 40 degrees.

   NOTE

   Advance throttle of affected engine to 40 degrees, to provide fuel flow for proper cooling of engine lube oil system. (See figure 5-2.)

PRIMARY EXHAUST NOZZLE FAILS CLOSED.

Failure of a primary exhaust nozzle in the closed direction is indicated by the corresponding primary nozzle position indicator. An overtemperature, compressor stall, and/or rpm drop also may occur. This type of failure may be caused by a failure in the primary nozzle section of the nozzle area control and also cuts off afterburner fuel flow.

PRIMARY NOZZLE FAILS CLOSED - ABOVE MACH 2.1, AUTO/MANUAL OR MANUAL AICS (AIRPLANE AF62-001).

1. Bypass wheels - Both aft to maintain shocks in crosshatch.
2. Engine rpm lockup switch - RELEASE.
3. Throttle (affected engine) - IDLE, and maintain shocks in crosshatch.
   a. If exhaust temperature remains within limits, throttle (affected engine) - 40 degrees.
   b. If exhaust temperature cannot be controlled, throttle (affected engine) - OFF.
4. Throat:
   If AUTO - Check schedule.
   If MANUAL - Both throat wheels aft to maintain throat at 0.2 Mach less than airplane Mach.
5. Engine rpm lockup switch - AUTO.
6. Throttle (affected engine) - 40 degrees.

   NOTE

   Advance throttle of affected engines to 40 degrees, to provide fuel flow for proper cooling of engine lube oil system. (See figure 5-2.)

PRIMARY NOZZLE FAILS CLOSED - BELOW MACH 2.1, AUTO/MANUAL OR MANUAL AICS (AIRPLANE AF62-001).

1. Bypass area (affected inlet):
   If SUPERSONIC - Wheel aft to obtain 700, 1100, or 1800 square inches. For first throttle to be moved to IDLE, obtain 700 square inches; for second throttle, 1100 square inches; and for third throttle, 1800 square inches.
   If SUBSONIC - Check bypass area closed.
2. Engine rpm lockup switch - RELEASE.
3. Throttle (affected engine) - IDLE.
   a. If exhaust temperature remains within limits, throttle (affected engine) - 40 degrees.
   b. If exhaust temperature cannot be controlled, throttle (affected engine) - OFF.
4. Throat - Check schedule.
5. Engine rpm lockup switch (above Mach 1.4) - AUTO.
6. Throttle (affected engine) - 40 degrees.

   NOTE

   Advance throttle of affected engine to 40 degrees, to provide fuel flow for proper cooling of engine lube oil system. (See figure 5-2.)

PRIMARY NOZZLE FAILS CLOSED - ABOVE MACH 2.1, AUTOMATIC OR STANDBY AICS (AIRPLANE AF62-207).

1. Bypass area (affected inlet):
   If AUTO, duct performance switch - LOW.
   If STANDBY, bypass door standby switch - Down to maintain shock in crosshatch.
2. Engine rpm lockup switch - RELEASE.
3. Throttle (affected engine) - IDLE, and if affected inlet is in standby mode maintain shock in crosshatch.

4. Throat (affected inlet):
   If AUTO - Check schedule.
   If STANDBY, throat Mach schedule standby switch - DOWN to maintain throat at 0.2 Mach less than airplane Mach.
5. Throttle (affected engine):
   a. If exhaust temperature remains within limits, throttle (affected engine) - 40 degrees. Proceed to step 8.
   b. If exhaust temperature cannot be controlled, proceed to step 6.
6. Throttle (affected engine) - OFF, and if affected inlet is in standby mode maintain shock in crosshatch.
7. Bypass door standby switch (if affected inlet is in automatic mode) - Hold down 1, 3, or 6 seconds.
   If the inlet for the engine being shut down is in automatic mode, hold the bypass door standby switch down for one second if only one engine is shut down; three seconds if two engines are shut down; and six seconds if three engines are shut down. This will bias the bypass door master cylinder from its normal rig position so that when the airplane is decelerating through approximately Mach 2.08 (AICS transfers from shock control to open loop control) the bypass doors will slowly open from their normal locked position of 500 square inches to approximately 700, 1100, or 1800 square inches (one, two, or three engines out).
8. Engine rpm lockup switch - AUTO.
9. Throttle (affected engine) - 40 degrees.

   NOTE

   Advance throttle of affected engine to 40 degrees, to provide fuel flow for proper cooling of engine lube oil system. (See figure 5-2.)

10. Duct performance switch (if affected inlet is in automatic mode - NORM.

NOZZLE FAILS CLOSED - BELOW MACH 2.1, AUTOMATIC OR STANDBY AICS (AIRPLANE AF62-207).

1. Bypass area (affected inlet):
   If SUPERSONIC, bypass door standby switch - Hold down 1, 3, or 6 seconds.
   Hold the bypass door standby switch down for one second if only one throttle is to be moved to IDLE; three seconds for two throttles at IDLE; and six seconds for three throttles at IDLE. If the affected inlet is in automatic mode, this will bias the bypass door master cylinder from its normal rig position so that when the airplane is decelerating through approximately Mach 2.08 (AICS transfers from shock control to open loop control) the bypass doors will slowly open from their normal locked position of 500 square inches to approximately 700, 1100, or 1800 square inches (one, two, or three engines at IDLE or out). If the affected inlet is in standby mode, this will cause the bypass doors to open to approximately 700, 1100, or 1800 square inches, respectively.
   If SUBSONIC - Check both bypass areas closed.
2. Engine rpm lockup switch - RELEASE.
3. Throttle (affected engine) - IDLE.
4. Throats - If one inlet is in standby mode and the other in automatic mode, adjust standby throat to obtain same throat Mach schedule indicator reading as for the automatic throat. If both throats are automatic, check indicators stopped at approximately Mach 2.1.
5. Throttle (affected engine):
   a. If exhaust temperature remains within limits, throttle (affected engine) - 40 degrees. Proceed to step 8.
   b. If exhaust temperature cannot be controlled, proceed to step 6.
6. Throttle (affected engine) - OFF.
7. Bypass area (affected inlet):
   If SUPERSONIC, bypass door standby switch - As required to refine bypass area to 700, 1100, or 1800 square inches.
   Move switch as required to obtain 700 square inches for one engine out; 1100 square inches for two engines out; and 1800 square inches for three engines out.

T.O. 1B-70(X)A-1

8. Engine rpm lockup switch (above Mach 1.4) - AUTO.
9. Throttle (affected engine) - 40 degrees.

> NOTE
> Advance throttle of affected engine to 40 degrees to provide fuel flow for proper cooling of engine lube oil system. (See figure 5-2.)

AFTERBURNER FAILURE.

During take-off, if an afterburner failure occurs before reaching decision speed, the take-off should be aborted because it must be assumed the cause of the failure is unknown and successive failure on the other engines also may occur. (Refer to "Engine Failure During Take-off, Abort" in this section.) If decision speed has been exceeded, continue the take-off. (Refer to "Engine Failure During Take-off, Take-off Continued" in this section.)

ENGINE OIL PRESSURE LOW.

The engine oil pressure caution light comes on when low oil pressure is sensed for any engine, and simultaneous illumination of an engine identification light shows which engine has the failure. The oil pressure caution light senses low pressure at the No. 2 bearing. If low engine oil pressure is indicated, the affected engine must be shut down immediately except during take-off. Refer to "Engine Failure" in this section for applicable engine shutdown procedures.

> NOTE
> - The oil pressure caution light goes out when the throttle is retarded to OFF, and the applicable engine identification light remains on.
>
> - The engine which is being shut down because of low oil pressure must be braked if engine rpm does not reduce to 22% within 5 minutes after the throttle is moved to OFF.

> CAUTION
> If more than one engine must be braked, airplane speed must be reduced to Mach 1.5 before the second engine can be braked.

ACCESSORY DRIVE SYSTEM FAILURE.

ACCESSORY DRIVE SYSTEM OIL PRESSURE FAILURE, OR GEARBOX OR TRANSMISSION SHAFT FAILURE.

The simultaneous illumination of the ADS caution light and an engine identification light indicates low oil pressure in an accessory drive system gearbox. If the failure is mechanical, (gearbox or transmission shaft) the hydraulic pump status indicator for the affected gearbox will show yellow, and if on engines 3 or 4, the respective generator out caution light will come on. If an accessory drive system oil system failure is indicated, the affected engine must be shut down immediately, except during take-off. Refer to "Engine Failure" in this section for applicable engine shutdown procedures.

> NOTE
> - The ADS oil pressure caution light goes out when the applicable throttle is retarded to OFF. The applicable engine identification light remains on.
>
> - The engine which is being shut down because of ADS oil pressure or gearbox or transmission shaft failure must be braked if engine rpm does not reduce to 22% within 5 minutes after the throttle is moved to OFF.

> CAUTION
> If more than one engine must be braked, airplane speed must be reduced to Mach 1.5 before the second engine can be braked.

Changed 25 June 1965

T.O. 1B-70(X)A-1

ACCESSORY DRIVE SYSTEM OIL PRESSURE FAILURE - TWO GEARBOXES SIMULTANEOUSLY.

The illumination of the ADS oil pressure caution light with simultaneous illumination of two specific engine identification lights (1 and 4, 2 and 5, or 3 and 6) is a possible indication of a failure in one of the gaseous nitrogen systems which pressurizes and inerts the lubricating system of the respective gearboxes.

> **NOTE**
> If the accessory drive oil pressure caution light and engine identification lights 2 and 5 come on, together with the tire and drag chute compartment overheat caution lights, loss of nitrogen system No. 2 is indicated.

Above 30,000 feet, loss of nitrogen pressure can cause cavitation of the lube pumps in the corresponding gearboxes. However, below 30,000 feet the gearbox lube pumps will not cavitate if nitrogen pressure is not available.

ADS OIL PRESSURE FAILURE - TWO GEARBOXES SIMULTANEOUSLY (ABOVE MACH 2.1), AUTO/MANUAL OR MANUAL AICS (AIRPLANE AF62-001).

If oil pressure failure in two gearboxes simultaneously is indicated during flight above Mach 2.1, proceed as follows:

> **NOTE**
> The ADS oil pressure caution light goes out when the applicable throttle is retarded to OFF. The applicable engine identification light remains on.

1. Bypass wheels - Both aft to maintain shocks in crosshatch.
2. Engine rpm lockup switch - RELEASE.
3. Throttles (affected engines) - IDLE, and maintain shocks in crosshatch.
4. Throat:
   If AUTO - Check both schedules.
   If MANUAL - Both throat wheels aft to maintain throat at 0.2 Mach less than airplane Mach.
5. Descend to below 30,000 feet, with throttles (good engines) - MIL.
   a. If the ADS oil pressure caution light and both engine identification lights go out when below 30,000 feet, a nitrogen system failure is indicated. Flight may be continued at any thrust setting below 30,000 feet. Accomplish step 6 only.
   b. If the ADS oil pressure caution light and the engine identification lights remain on, proceed to step 7.
6. Applicable primary generator switch - Cycle, if required.
   If engine 3 or 4 is affected, cycle corresponding primary generator switch to restore generator operation.
7. Throttles (affected engines) - OFF, and maintain shocks in crosshatch.
8. Engine emergency brake switches (affected engines) - ON, if required, and maintain shocks in crosshatch.

> **NOTE**
> The engines which are to be shut down must be braked if engine rpm does not reduce to 22% within 5 minutes after the throttles are moved to OFF.

> **CAUTION**
> Before the second engine can be braked, the airplane speed must be reduced to Mach 1.5 or below.

9. Engine emergency brake switches - OFF.
   Move switches to OFF after engine rpm has stabilized at 22% or below.
10. Engine rpm lockup switch - AUTO.
11. Throttles (affected engines) - 40 degrees, if brakes not used.

> **NOTE**
> If engine braking was not required, advance throttles of affected engines to 40 degrees, to provide fuel flow for proper cooling of engine lube oil system. (See figure 5-2.)

T.O. 1B-70(X)A-1

ADS OIL PRESSURE FAILURE - TWO GEARBOXES SIMULTANEOUSLY (BELOW MACH 2.1), AUTO/MANUAL OR MANUAL AICS (AIRPLANE AF62-001).

If oil pressure failure in two gearboxes simultaneously is indicated during flight below Mach 2.1, proceed as follows:

> **NOTE**
> The ADS oil pressure caution light goes out when the applicable throttle is retarded to OFF. The applicable engine identification light remains on.

1. Bypass area:
   If SUPERSONIC - Both wheels aft to obtain 700, 1100, or 1800 square inches.
   For first throttle to be moved to IDLE, obtain 700 square inches; for second throttle, 1100 square inches; and for third throttle, 1800 square inches.
   If SUBSONIC - Check both bypass areas closed.
2. Engine rpm lockup switch - RELEASE.
3. Throttles (affected engines) - IDLE.
4. Throat - Check both schedules.
5. Descend to below 30,000 feet, with throttles (good engines) - MIL.
   a. If the ADS oil pressure caution light and both engine identification lights go out when below 30,000 feet a nitrogen system failure is indicated. Flight may be continued at any thrust setting below 30,000 feet. Accomplish step 6 only.
   b. If the ADS oil pressure caution light and the engine identification lights remain on, proceed to step 7.
6. Applicable primary generator switch - Cycle, if required.
   If engine 3 or 4 is affected, cycle corresponding primary generator switch to restore generator operation.
7. Throttles (affected engines) - OFF.
8. Engine emergency brake switches (affected engines) - ON, if required.

> **NOTE**
> The engines which are to be shut down must be braked if engine rpm does not reduce to 22% within 5 minutes after the throttles are moved to OFF.

> **CAUTION**
> Before the second engine can be braked, the airplane speed must be reduced to Mach 1.5 or below.

9. Engine emergency brake switches - OFF.
   Move switches to OFF after engine rpm has stabilized at 22% or below.
10. Engine rpm lockup switch (above Mach 1.4) - AUTO.
11. Throttles (affected engines) - 40 degrees, if brakes not used.

> **NOTE**
> If engine braking was not required, advance throttles of affected engines to 40 degrees, to provide fuel flow for proper cooling of engine lube oil system. (See figure 5-2.)

ADS OIL PRESSURE FAILURE - TWO GEARBOXES SIMULTANEOUSLY (ABOVE MACH 2.1), AUTOMATIC OR STANDBY AICS (AIRPLANE AF62-207).

If oil pressure failure in two gearboxes simultaneously is indicated during flight above Mach 2.1, proceed as follows:

> **NOTE**
> The ADS oil pressure caution light goes out when the applicable throttle is retarded to OFF. The applicable engine identification light remains on.

1. Bypass area:
   If AUTO, duct performance switch - LOW.
   If STANDBY, bypass door standby switch - Down to maintain shock in crosshatch.
2. Engine rpm lockup switch - RELEASE.
3. Throttles (affected engines) - IDLE, and if either inlet is in standby mode maintain shock in crosshatch.

T.O. 1B-70(X)A-1

4. Throats:
   If AUTO - Check schedule.
   If STANDBY, throat Mach schedule standby switch - Down to maintain throat at 0.2 Mach less than airplane Mach.
5. Descend to below 30,000 feet, with throttles (good engines) - MIL.
   a. If the ADS oil pressure caution light and both engine identification lights go out when below 30,000 feet a nitrogen system failure is indicated. Flight may be continued at any thrust setting below 30,000 feet. Accomplish step 6 only.
   b. If the ADS oil pressure caution light and the engine identification lights remain on, proceed to step 7.
6. Applicable primary generator switch - Cycle, if required.
   If engine 3 or 4 is affected, cycle corresponding primary generator switch to restore generator operation.
7. Throttles (affected engines) - OFF.
8. Bypass door standby switch (if affected inlet is in automatic mode) - Hold down 1, 3, or 6 seconds.
   If an inlet is in automatic mode, hold the bypass door standby switch for that inlet down for one second if only one engine is shut down; three seconds if two engines are shut down; and six seconds if three engines are shut down. This will bias the bypass door master cylinder from its normal rig position so that when the airplane is decelerating through approximately Mach 2.08 (AICS transfers from shock control to open loop control) the bypass doors will slowly open from their normal locked position of 500 square inches to approximately 700, 1100, or 1800 square inches (one, two, or three engines out).
9. Engine emergency brake switches (affected engines) - ON, if required.

   NOTE
   The engines which are to be shut down must be braked if engine rpm does not reduce to 22% within 5 minutes after the throttles are moved to OFF.

   CAUTION
   Before the second engine can be braked, the airplane speed must be reduced to Mach 1.5 or below.

10. Engine emergency brake switch - OFF. Move switch to OFF after engine rpm has stabilized at 22% or below.
11. Engine rpm lockup switch - AUTO.
12. Throttles (affected engines) - 40 degrees, if brakes not used.

    NOTE
    If engine braking was not required, advance throttles of affected engines to 40 degrees, to provide fuel flow for proper cooling of engine lube oil system. (See figure 5-2.)

13. Duct performance switch (if either inlet is in automatic mode) - NORM.

ADS OIL PRESSURE FAILURE - TWO GEARBOXES SIMULTANEOUSLY (BELOW MACH 2.1), AUTOMATIC OR STANDBY AICS (AIRPLANE AF62-207).

If oil pressure failure in two gearboxes simultaneously is indicated during flight below Mach 2.1, proceed as follows:

    NOTE
    The ADS oil pressure caution light goes out when the applicable throttle is retarded to OFF. The applicable engine identification light remains on.

1. Bypass areas:
   If SUPERSONIC, bypass door standby switches - Hold both down 1, 3, or 6 seconds.
   Hold both bypass door standby switches down for one second if only one throttle per inlet is to be moved to IDLE; three seconds for two throttles per inlet at IDLE; and six seconds for three throttles per inlet at IDLE. If an affected inlet is in automatic mode, this will bias the bypass door master cylinder from its normal rig position so that when the air-

3-46

T.O. 1B-70(X)A-1

plane is decelerating through approximately Mach 2.08 (AICS transfers from shock control to open loop control) the bypass doors will slowly open from their normal locked position of 500 square inches to approximately 700, 1100, or 1800 square inches (one, two, or three engines at IDLE or out). If an affected inlet is in standby mode, this will cause the bypass doors to open to approximately 700, 1100, or 1800 square inches, respectively.

If SUBSONIC - Check both bypass areas closed.

2. Engine rpm lockup switch - RELEASE.
3. Throttles (affected engines) - IDLE.
4. Throats - If one inlet is in standby mode and the other in automatic, adjust standby throat to obtain same throat Mach schedule indicator reading as for the automatic throat. If both throats are automatic, check indicators stopped at approximately Mach 2.1.
5. Descend to below 30,000 feet, with throttles (good engines) - MIL.
    a. If the ADS oil pressure caution light and both engine identification lights go out when below 30,000 feet a nitrogen system failure is indicated. Flight may be continued at any thrust setting below 30,000 feet. Accomplish step 6 only.
    b. If the ADS oil pressure caution light and the engine identification lights remain on, proceed to step 7.
6. Applicable primary generator switch - Cycle, if required.
    If engine 3 or 4 is affected, cycle corresponding primary generator switch to restore generator operation.
7. Bypass areas:
    If SUPERSONIC, bypass door standby switches - Both as required to refine bypass areas to 700, 1100, or 1800 square inches.
    Move switches as required to obtain 700 square inches for one engine per inlet out; 1100 square inches for two engines per inlet out; and 1800 square inches for three engines per inlet out.

8. Throttles (affected engines) - OFF.
9. Engine emergency brake switches (affected engines) - ON, if required.

NOTE
The engines which are to be shut down must be braked if engine rpm does not reduce to 22% within 5 minutes after the throttles are moved to OFF.

CAUTION
Before the second engine can be braked, the airplane speed must be reduced to Mach 1.5 or below.

10. Engine emergency brake switches - OFF.
    Move switches to OFF after engine rpm has stabilized at 22% or below.
11. Engine rpm lockup switch (above Mach 1.4) - AUTO.
12. Throttles (affected engines) - 40 degrees, if brakes not used.

NOTE
If engine braking was not required, advance throttles of affected engines to 40 degrees, to provide fuel flow for proper cooling of engine lube oil system. (See figure 5-2.)

EXCESSIVE ENGINE OR ACCESSORY DRIVE SYSTEM GEARBOX VIBRATION.

If the vibration of any engine or accessory drive system gearbox is over 50 percent (5 mils peak-to-peak), the vibration caution light comes on and the affected engine or gearbox can be identified from the vibration indicator.

NOTE
The master caution light does not come on with the vibration caution light.

The steady-state vibration limit for the engine varies with engine speed; the gearbox vibration limit remains constant at 50 percent. (The 50 percent limit also applies to engine operation at 104% rpm.) Engine vibration limits are shown in figure 5-4.

During engine starts, high engine vibration can be disregarded until the engine has been accelerated and decelerated. Indications of high engine vibration also can be disregarded during throttle transients.

EXCESSIVE ENGINE OR ACCESSORY DRIVE SYSTEM GEARBOX VIBRATION - ABOVE MACH 2.1, AUTO/MANUAL OR MANUAL AICS (AIRPLANE AF62-001).

If excessive engine or ADS gearbox vibration occurs during flight above Mach 2.1, proceed as follows:

1. Bypass wheels - Both aft to maintain shocks in crosshatch.
2. Engine rpm lockup switch - RELEASE.
3. Throttle (affected engine) - IDLE, and maintain shocks in crosshatch.
4. Throat:
   If AUTO - Check schedule.
   If MANUAL - Both throat wheels aft to maintain throat at 0.2 Mach less than airplane Mach.
5. Start normal deceleration and descent as required, with throttles (good engines) - MIL.
   a. If vibration level remains excessive, proceed to step 6.
   b. If the vibration caution light goes out, leave throttle (affected engine) at IDLE.
6. Throttle (affected engine) - OFF, and maintain shocks in crosshatch.
7. Engine emergency brake switch (affected engine) - ON, if vibration is excessive, and maintain shocks in crosshatch.

CAUTION

Only one engine per inlet should be braked above Mach 1.5. This prevents the possibility of inducing continuous inlet buzz which could seriously affect airplane stability and control and could damage the engines and the inlet. Speed should be reduced to below Mach 1.5 before actuation of the brake for a second engine.

NOTE

The engine braking system is irreversible; therefore, the engine cannot be restarted after the emergency brake has been engaged.

8. Engine emergency brake switch - OFF. Move switch to OFF after engine rpm has stabilized at 22% or below.
9. Engine rpm lockup switch - AUTO.
10. Throttle (affected engine) - 40 degrees, if brake not used.

NOTE

If engine braking was not required, advance throttle of affected engine to 40 degrees, to provide fuel flow for proper cooling of engine lube oil system. (See figure 5-2.)

EXCESSIVE ENGINE OR ACCESSORY DRIVE SYSTEM GEARBOX VIBRATION - BELOW MACH 2.1, AUTO/MANUAL OR MANUAL AICS (AIRPLANE AF62-001).

If excessive engine or ADS gearbox vibration occurs during flight below Mach 2.1, proceed as follows:

1. Bypass area (affected inlet):
   If SUPERSONIC - Wheel aft to obtain 700, 1100, or 1800 square inches. For first throttle to be moved to IDLE, obtain 700 square inches; for second throttle, 1100 square inches; and for third throttle, 1800 square inches.
   If SUBSONIC - Check bypass area closed.
2. Engine rpm lockup switch - RELEASE.
3. Throttle (affected engine) - IDLE.
4. Throat - Check schedule.
5. Start normal deceleration and descent as required, with throttles (good engines) - MIL.
   a. If vibration level remains excessive, proceed to step 6.
   b. If the vibration caution light goes out, leave throttle (affected engine) at IDLE.
6. Throttle (affected engine) - OFF.
7. Engine emergency brake switch (affected engine) - ON, if vibration is excessive.

CAUTION

Only one engine per inlet should be braked above Mach 1.5. This prevents the possibility of inducing continuous inlet buzz which could seriously affect airplane stability and control and could damage the engines and the inlet. Speed should be reduced to below Mach 1.5 before actuation of the brake for a second engine.

NOTE
The engine braking system is irreversible; therefore, the engine cannot be restarted after the emergency brake has been engaged.

8. Engine emergency brake switch - OFF. Move switch to OFF after engine rpm has stabilized at 22% or below.
9. Engine rpm lockup switch (above Mach 1.4) - AUTO.
10. Throttle (affected engine) - 40 degrees, if brake not used.

NOTE
If engine braking was not required, advance throttle of affected engine to 40 degrees, to provide fuel flow for proper cooling of engine lube oil system. (See figure 5-2.)

EXCESSIVE ENGINE OR ACCESSORY DRIVE SYSTEM GEARBOX VIBRATION - ABOVE MACH 2.1, AUTOMATIC OR STANDBY AICS (AIRPLANE AF62-207).

If excessive engine or ADS gearbox vibration occurs during flight above Mach 2.1, proceed as follows:

1. Bypass area (affected inlet):
   If AUTO, duct performance switch - LOW.
   If STANDBY, bypass door standby switch - Down to maintain shock in crosshatch.
2. Engine rpm lockup switch - RELEASE.
3. Throttle (affected engine) - IDLE, and if affected inlet is in standby mode maintain shock in crosshatch.
4. Throat (affected inlet):
   If AUTO - Check schedule.
   If STANDBY, throat Mach schedule standby switch - Down to maintain throat at 0.2 Mach less than airplane Mach.
5. Start normal deceleration and descent as required, with throttles (good engines) - MIL.
   a. If vibration level remains excessive, proceed to step 6.
   b. If the vibration caution light goes out, leave throttle (affected engine) at IDLE.
6. Throttle (affected engine) - OFF, and if affected inlet is in standby mode maintain shock in crosshatch.
7. Bypass door standby switch (if affected inlet is in automatic mode) - Hold down 1, 3, or 6 seconds.
   If the inlet for the engine to be shut down is in automatic mode, hold the bypass door switch down for one second if only one engine is shut down; three seconds if two engines are shut down; and six seconds if three engines are shut down. This will bias the bypass door master cylinder from its normal rig position so that when the airplane is decelerating through approximately Mach 2.08 (AICS transfers from shock control to open loop control) the bypass doors will slowly open from the normal locked position of 500 square inches to approximately 700, 1100, or 1800 square inches (one, two, or three engines out).
8. Engine emergency brake switch (affected engine) - ON, if vibration is excessive, and maintain shock in crosshatch.

CAUTION
Only one engine per inlet should be braked above Mach 1.5. This prevents the possibility of inducing continuous inlet buzz which could seriously affect airplane stability and control and could damage the engines and the inlet. Speed should be reduced to below Mach 1.5 before actuation of the brake for a second engine.

NOTE
The engine braking system is irreversible; therefore, the engine cannot be restarted after the emergency brake has been engaged.

T.O. 1B-70(X)A-1

9. Engine emergency brake switch - OFF.
   Move switch to OFF after engine rpm has stabilized at 22% or below.
10. Engine rpm lockup switch - AUTO.
11. Throttle (affected engine) - 40 degrees, if brake not used.
12. Duct performance switch (if affected inlet is in automatic mode) - NORM.

EXCESSIVE ENGINE OR ACCESSORY DRIVE SYSTEM GEARBOX VIBRATION - BELOW MACH 2.1, AUTOMATIC OR STANDBY AICS (AIRPLANE AF62-207).

If excessive engine or ADS gearbox vibration occurs during flight below Mach 2.1, proceed as follows:

1. Bypass area (affected inlet):
   If SUPERSONIC, bypass door standby switch - Down 1, 3, or 6 seconds. Hold bypass door standby switch down for one second if only one throttle is to be moved to IDLE; three seconds for two throttles at IDLE; and six seconds for three throttles at IDLE. If the affected inlet is in the automatic mode, this will bias the bypass door master cylinder from its normal rig position so that when the airplane is decelerating through approximately Mach 2.08 (AICS transfers from shock control to open loop control) the bypass doors will slowly open from their normal locked position of 500 square inches to approximately 700, 1100, or 1800 or out). If the affected inlet is in standby mode, this will cause the bypass doors to open to approximately 700, 1100, or 1800 square inches (one, two, or three engines at IDLE or out). If the affected inlet is in standby mode, this will cause the bypass doors to open to approximately 700, 1100, or 1800 square inches, respectively.

   If SUBSONIC - Check both bypass areas closed.
2. Engine rpm lockup switch - RELEASE.
3. Throttle (affected engine) - IDLE.
4. Throats - If one inlet is in standby mode and the other in automatic, adjust standby throat to obtain same throat Mach schedule indicator reading as for the automatic throat. If both throats are automatic, check indicators stopped at approximately Mach 2.1.
5. Start normal deceleration and descent as required, with throttles (good engines) - MIL.
   a. If vibration level remains excessive, proceed to step 6.
   b. If the vibration caution light goes out, leave throttle (affected engine) at IDLE.
6. Bypass area (affected inlet):
   If SUPERSONIC, bypass door standby switch - As required to refine bypass area to 700, 1100, or 1800 square inches.
   Move switch as required to obtain 700 square inches for one engine out; 1100 square inches for two engines out; and 1800 square inches for three engines out.
7. Throttle (affected engine) - OFF.
8. Engine emergency brake switch (affected engine) - ON, if vibration is excessive.

   CAUTION
   Only one engine per inlet should be braked above Mach 1.5. This prevents the possibility of inducing continuous inlet buzz which could seriously affect airplane stability and control and could damage the engines and the inlet. Speed should be reduced to below Mach 1.5 before actuation of the brake for a second engine.

   NOTE
   The engine braking system is irreversible; therefore, the engine cannot be restarted after the emergency brake has been engaged.

9. Engine emergency brake switch - OFF.
   Move switch to OFF after engine rpm has stabilized at 22% or below.
10. Engine rpm lockup switch (above Mach 1.4) - AUTO.

T.O. 1B-70(X)A-1

11. Throttle (affected engine) - 40 degrees, if brake not used.

NOTE
If engine braking was not required, advance throttle of affected engine to 40 degrees, to provide fuel flow for proper cooling of engine lube oil system. (See figure 5-2.)

ENGINE OR ADS VIBRATION INDICATING SYSTEM FAILURE.

The vibration indicating system is relatively simple and the possibility of system failure is remote. In most cases, an indicating system failure will result in zero indicator readings. However, if a vibration pick-up or bracket is loose, or if there is a break in the shielding of the pick-up signal wire, an excessively high indicator reading results. If a pick-up is loose, the readings will respond to rpm changes; if the shielding is broken, rpm changes have no effect on the reading. If an in-flight failure of the vibration indicating system is suspected, the system test button can be used to check the operation. (This will not isolate a loose pick-up or broken shielding.) When the system is operating properly, pressing the test button causes the vibration caution light to come on, and makes both pointers on each indicator read somewhere between 75 percent and the sum of 75 percent plus the previous indicator reading (vibration pick-up).

AIR INDUCTION CONTROL SYSTEM EMERGENCY OPERATION.

FAILURE OF THROAT MACH SCHEDULE INDICATOR - ABOVE MACH 2.1 (AIRPLANE AF62-001).

If either throat Mach schedule indicator fails, or the respective throat indicator caution light comes on, use the following procedure:

1. Bypass wheels - Both aft to position and maintain shocks in crosshatch.
2. Maintain stabilized level flight.
3. Throat wheels - Both aft to maintain throats at 0.2 Mach less than airplane Mach.
4. Throat Mach schedule mode switches - Both MAN.
   a. If affected throat Mach schedule indicator resumes operation, stay in manual mode.
   b. If affected throat Mach schedule indicator does not resume operation, proceed to step 5.
5. Throat Mach schedule mode switches - Both OFF.
6. Throat Mach schedule standby switch (affected inlet) - Jog down to OPEN as necessary, maintaining shocks in crosshatch, until both bypass area indicator readings are the same.
7. Throttles - MIL.
8. Bypass wheels - Both aft toward OPEN to maintain shocks in crosshatch.
9. Throat Mach schedule standby switches - Both down to DECR to maintain throats at 0.2 Mach less than airplane Mach.

FAILURE OF THROAT MACH SCHEDULE INDICATOR - ABOVE MACH 2.1 (AIRPLANE AF62-207).

If either throat Mach schedule indicator fails (indicator fails to respond to changes in airplane Mach or moves erratically or to a hard-over position), proceed as follows:

1. AICS (affected inlet):
   If AUTO - No action necessary. If there is no accompanying indication of failure of the automatic mode, the affected inlet should be left in automatic mode. If STANDBY, bypass door standby switch - Move as necessary to set bypass area of affected inlet the same as for the other inlet, plus 100 square inches.
2. Throat Mach schedule standby switch (affected inlet) - Move as required to maintain the shock in the green arc.
3. Decelerate to Mach 1.0 or below.

Changed 25 June 1965

T.O. 1B-70(X)A-1

THROAT PANEL EXTENDED CAUTION LIGHT ON - BELOW MACH 1.5 (AIRPLANE AF62-001).

If either throat panel extended caution light comes on below Mach 1.5, indicating the inlet throat width is less than 39 inches, a large thrust loss will occur. If either light comes on during flight below Mach 1.5, proceed as follows:

WARNING
Do not take off if a throat panel extended caution light is on. An inlet throat size corresponding to a throat Mach schedule indicator reading 3.0 reduces available thrust to less than 25 percent of the normal thrust.

1. Throat mode switch (affected inlet) - Check OFF.
2. Throat Mach schedule standby switch (affected inlet) - Down until throat Mach schedule indicator for affected inlet reads 1.67 (throat full open).
3. Abort mission and land.

THROAT PANEL EXTENDED CAUTION LIGHT ON - BELOW MACH 1.4 (AIRPLANE AF62-207).

Illumination of a throat panel extended caution light during flight below Mach 1.4 indicates the affected throat is extended to less than 39 inches. Under such conditions, a large loss of thrust and engine compressor stall will occur unless corrective action is taken immediately. If either throat panel extended caution light comes on during flight below Mach 1.4, proceed as follows:

1. AICS mode switch (affected inlet) - STBY.
2. Throat Mach schedule standby switch (affected inlet) - Down until throat Mach schedule indicator for affected inlet reads 1.67 Mach (throat full open).

BYPASS DOOR OPEN CAUTION LIGHT ON - BELOW MACH 0.4 (AIRPLANE AF62-001).

If either bypass door open caution light comes on during flight below Mach 0.4, this indicates the bypass doors for the affected inlet are not fully closed. This could result in pressure conditions which would cause structural damage to the inlet in the area of the bypass plenum. If either light comes on during flight below Mach 0.4, proceed as follows:

1. Bypass door mode switch (affected inlet) - Check OFF.
2. Bypass standby system selector switch (affected inlet) - PRIMARY.
3. Bypass door standby switch (affected inlet) - Up to CLOSE.
   Hold switch up to CLOSE until bypass doors of affected inlet are fully closed and caution light goes out.
4. Bypass standby system selector switch (affected inlet) - ALTERNATE, if bypass doors did not close.
5. Bypass door standby switch (affected inlet) - Up to CLOSE.
   Hold switch up to CLOSE until bypass doors of affected inlet are fully closed and caution light goes out.

FAILURE OF SHOCK WAVE POSITION INDICATOR (AIRPLANE AF62-207).

If either shock wave position indicator fails (indicator needle is erratic or goes to a hard-over position and remains there) during flight with a started inlet, proceed as follows:

1. AICS (affected inlet):
   If AUTO - No action necessary.
      If there is no accompanying indication of failure of the automatic mode, the affected inlet should be left in automatic mode.
   If STANDBY, bypass door standby switch - Move as necessary to set bypass area of affected inlet the same as for the other inlet, plus 100 square inches.
2. Throat Mach schedule standby switch (affected inlet) - Move as required to obtain same throat Mach schedule indicator reading as for the other throat.
3. Decelerate to Mach 1.0 or below.

SHOCK AFT CAUTION LIGHT ON - BELOW MACH 0.7 (AIRPLANE AF62-207).

Illumination of a shock aft caution light during flight below Mach 0.7 indicates that the bypass doors are not fully closed. This could result in pressure conditions which would cause structural damage to the inlet in the area of the bypass plenum. If either light comes on below Mach 0.7, proceed as follows:

1. AICS mode switch (affected inlet) - STBY.
2. Bypass door standby switch (affected inlet) - Up until light goes out.

SHOCK AFT CAUTION LIGHT ON - STARTED INLET (AIRPLANE AF62-207).

Illumination of a shock aft caution light during flight with the inlets started indicates the shock position for the affected inlet is aft of a predetermined limit. This would result in loss of thrust and engine stall if allowed to continue. If either light comes on during started inlet flight, proceed as follows:

NOTE
If the inlets are in automatic mode, a light may go on momentarily due to a transient condition. If the light goes out, no corrective action is necessary.

1. Bypass area (affected inlet):
   If AUTO - Monitor. If not recovering, put inlet in standby mode.
   Check bypass area and shock wave position indicators of affected inlet. If bypass area is not decreasing, shock wave position indicator needle is not moving toward FDW and light remains on, put affected inlet in standby mode.
   If STANDBY, go to step 2.
2. Bypass door standby switch (affected inlet) - Up until shock aft caution light goes out.
3. Duct performance switch - NORM.

UNSTART AND/OR BUZZ.

NOTE
- If inlet unstart or buzz occurs, the engines may stall, flame out, or overtemp.
- The airplane will yaw away from and roll toward the unstarted or buzzing inlet.
- The duct unstart caution lights are inoperative when both throat Mach schedule indicators are at Mach 2.17 or less.

An unstarted inlet is indicated by the respective unstart caution light coming on. Buzz may or may not accompany an unstart.

BUZZ BELOW MACH 2.1 - MANUAL AICS (AIRPLANE AF62-001).

1. Bypass wheel (affected inlet) - Aft to position shock at top of green arc.
   If buzz caution light goes out, return to normal operation. If light remains on, proceed to step 2.

NOTE
Avoid opening bypass more than necessary, as engine stall could occur.

2. Engine rpm lockup switch - RELEASE.
3. Throttles (affected inlet) - As required.
   Retard throttles to IDLE or as necessary to maintain engines within operating limits.
4. Throat - Check schedule.
5. Engines (affected inlet) - If abnormal:
   a. Bypass wheel (affected inlet) - Aft.
   b. Throttles (affected engines) - OFF.

T.O. 1B-70(X)A-1

6. Throttles (affected engines) - 40 degrees.

   NOTE
   Advance throttles of affected engines to 40 degrees, to provide fuel flow for proper cooling of engine lube oil system. (See figure 5-2.)

7. Bypass wheel (affected inlet) - Forward to obtain 700, 1100, or 1800 square inches.
   For one engine shut down, obtain 700 square inches; for two engines, 1100 square inches; and for three engines, 1800 square inches.

8. Engine rpm lockup switch (above Mach 1.4) - AUTO.

BUZZ BELOW MACH 2.1 - AUTOMATIC OR STANDBY AICS (AIRPLANE AF62-207).

1. Bypass area (affected inlet):
   If AUTO - Monitor. If not increasing, go to standby mode.
      If bypass area is increasing, this indicates the automatic system is correcting the buzz condition. If the bypass area is not increasing or is decreasing, put affected inlet in standby mode.
   If STANDBY, bypass door standby switch - Move as necessary to position the shock wave of the affected inlet in the top of the green arc.

2. Engine rpm lockup switch - RELEASE.

3. Throttles (affected inlet) - As required.
   Move throttles to IDLE or as required to maintain engines within operating limits.

4. Throats - If one inlet is in standby mode and the other in automatic mode, adjust standby throat to obtain same throat Mach schedule indicator reading as for the automatic throat.

5. Engines (affected inlet) - If abnormal:
   a. Bypass door standby switch - Hold down 1, 3, or 6 seconds.
      Hold bypass door standby switch down for one second if only one engine is to be shut down; three seconds if two engines are to be shut down; and six seconds if three engines are to be shut down. This will bias the bypass door master cylinder from its normal rig position so that when the airplane is decelerating through approximately Mach 2.08 (AICS transfers from shock control to open loop control) the bypass doors will slowly open from their normal locked position of 500 square inches to approximately 700, 1100, or 1800 square inches (one, two, or three engines out).
   b. Throttles (affected engines) - OFF.

6. Throttles (affected engines) - 40 degrees.

   NOTE
   Advance throttles of affected engines to 40 degrees, to provide fuel flow for proper cooling of engine lube oil system. (See figure 5-2.)

7. Bypass door standby switch (affected inlet) - As required to refine bypass area to 700, 1100, or 1800 square inches.
   Move switch as required to obtain 700 square inches for one engine out; 1100 square inches for two engines out; and 1800 square inches for three engines out.

8. Engine rpm lockup switch (above Mach 1.4) - AUTO.

UNSTART WITH OR WITHOUT BUZZ - AUTO/MANUAL AICS (AIRPLANE AF62-001).

1. Bypass wheels - Both aft to position and maintain shocks in crosshatch.

   CAUTION
   Avoid opening bypass more than necessary, as engine stall could occur.

2. Engine rpm lockup switch - RELEASE.

3. Throttles (all engines) - As required, and maintain shocks in crosshatch.
   Retard throttles to IDLE or as necessary to maintain engines within operating limits.

4. Throat Mach schedule mode switch - Both MAN and adjust bypass wheels as necessary to maintain shocks in crosshatch.

3-46H

Changed 25 June 1965

T.O. 1B-70(X)A-1

5. Engines (affected inlet) - If abnormal, throttles of affected engines OFF and maintain shock in crosshatch.
6. Unstart and buzz caution lights - Check.
   a. If lights are out, proceed to step 7.
   b. If either caution light remains on, check both throat Mach at 0.4 Mach less than airplane Mach, and <u>slowly</u> roll both bypass wheels aft until light goes out or bottom of crosshatch is reached. (Do not bottom needles).

   NOTE
   If inlet cannot be restarted, switch to standby and reduce speed to below Mach 1.5.

7. Resume normal engine operation and maintain shocks in crosshatch.

   CAUTION
   If buzz accompanied the unstart condition and any engine had to be shut down, it must not be restarted. If buzz did not accompany the unstart condition, any engine which had been shut down may be restarted.

8. Engine rpm lockup switch - AUTO.
9. Throat wheels - Both forward to airplane Mach and adjust bypass wheels as necessary to maintain shocks in crosshatch.
10. Bypass wheels - Both forward as required to obtain desired shock position.

UNSTART WITH OR WITHOUT BUZZ - MANUAL AICS (AIRPLANE AF62-001).

1. Bypass wheels - Both aft to position and maintain shocks in crosshatch.

   CAUTION
   Avoid opening bypass more than necessary, as engine stall could occur.

2. Engine rpm lockup switch - RELEASE.
3. Throttles (all engines) - As required, and maintain shocks in crosshatch.
   Retard throttles to IDLE or as necessary to maintain engines within operating limits.

4. Throat wheels - Both aft to decrease throat Mach 0.3 to 0.4 Mach, and adjust bypass wheels as necessary to maintain shocks in crosshatch.
5. Engines (affected inlet) - If abnormal, throttles of affected engines OFF and maintain shocks in crosshatch.
6. Unstart and buzz caution lights - Check.
   a. If lights are out, proceed to step 7.
   b. If either caution light remains on, check both throat Mach at 0.4 Mach less than airplane Mach and <u>slowly</u> roll both bypass wheels aft until light goes out or bottom of crosshatch is reached. (Do not bottom needles.)

   NOTE
   If inlet cannot be restarted, switch to standby and reduce speed to below Mach 1.5.

7. Resume normal engine operation, and maintain shocks in crosshatch.

   CAUTION
   If buzz accompanied the unstart condition and any engine had to be shut down, it must not be restarted. If buzz did not accompany the unstart condition, any engine which had been shut down may be restarted.

8. Engine rpm lockup switch - AUTO.
9. Throat wheels - Both forward to airplane Mach and adjust bypass wheels as necessary to maintain shocks in crosshatch.
10. Bypass wheels - Both forward as required to obtain desired shock position.

UNSTART WITH OR WITHOUT BUZZ - AUTOMATIC OR STANDBY AICS (AIRPLANE AF62-207).

If Affected Inlet In Automatic Mode

1. Duct performance switch - NORM.
2. Bypass area and throat Mach schedule indicator - Monitor.

Changed 25 June 1965

T.O. 1B-70(X)A-1

a. If the inlet recovers, do only step 3.
   Inlet action toward recovery will be initially indicated by an increase in bypass area and a decrease in throat Mach schedule indicator reading. When recovery is complete, the unstart (and buzz) caution lights will go out.
b. If the inlet is not recovering, proceed to step 4.

3. AICS reset switch/light - Press momentarily. Check light out.
4. Duct performance switch and AICS mode switch (affected inlet) - LOW, then STBY.
   Rapidly and in sequence, move the duct performance switch to LOW, then the AICS mode switch for the affected inlet to STANDBY. If the mode switch is moved first or too long after the duct performance switch is moved to LOW, the bypass doors would tend to move at high rate toward the closed position, aggravating the unstart and buzz condition.

If Affected Inlet in Standby Mode

5. Bypass door standby switch (affected inlet) - Down to maintain shock in crosshatch.
6. Engine rpm lockup switch - RELEASE.
7. Throttles (all engines) - As required, and maintain shock for affected inlet in crosshatch.
8. Throat Mach schedule standby switch (affected inlet) - Down to maintain throat 0.3 to 0.4 Mach less than airplane Mach, and maintain shock for affected inlet in crosshatch.
9. Engines (affected inlet) - If abnormal, throttles of affected engines OFF, and maintain shock for affected inlet in crosshatch.
10. Unstart and buzz caution lights - Check.
    a. If lights are out, proceed to step 11.
    b. If either caution light remains on, check throat of affected inlet 0.3 to 0.4 Mach less than airplane Mach and slowly jog bypass door standby switch of affected inlet down until light goes out or bottom of crosshatch is reached. (Do not bottom needle.)

NOTE
If inlet cannot be restarted, reduce speed to below Mach 1.5.

11. Resume normal engine operation and maintain shock for affected inlet in crosshatch.

CAUTION
If buzz accompanied the unstart condition and any engine had to be shut down, it must not be restarted. If buzz did not accompany the unstart condition, any engine which had been shut down may be restarted.

12. Engine rpm lockup switch - AUTO.
13. Throat Mach schedule standby switch (affected inlet) - As required.
14. Bypass door standby switch (affected inlet) - Up, as required.
15. Duct performance switch - NORM.

CHANGE-OVER TO STANDBY AICS (AIRPLANE AF62-001).

If it becomes necessary to change the inlets from auto/manual or manual to standby mode of operation, proceed as follows:

1. All 4 mode switches - OFF.
   Check both bypass standby system selector switches at PRIMARY, or ALTERNATE if required.
2. Bypass door standby switches - Both down as required to position and maintain shocks in crosshatch.
3. Throat Mach schedule standby switches - Both down as required to decrease throat Mach 0.2 less than airplane Mach.
4. Throttles - MIL.
5. Bypass door standby switches - Both as required to maintain shocks in crosshatch or to obtain 700 square inches when speed is below Mach 2.1.
6. Throat Mach schedule standby switches - Both as required to maintain throat Mach 0.2 less than airplane Mach.

T.O. 1B-70(X)A-1

CHANGE-OVER TO STANDBY AICS (AIRPLANE AF62-207).

If it becomes necessary to change an inlet from automatic to standby mode of operation, proceed as follows:

1. Duct performance switch - LOW; then AICS mode switch (affected inlet) - STBY.
   Rapidly and in sequence, move the duct performance switch to LOW, then the AICS mode switch for the affected inlet to STBY. If the mode switch is moved first or too long after the duct performance switch is moved to LOW, the bypass doors would tend to move at high rate toward the closed position, inducing buzz or unstart.

   NOTE

   If it is necessary to move both inlets to standby mode, the change-over should be accomplished one inlet at a time. After the first inlet is put in standby mode (by accomplishing step 1, above), move the duct performance switch to NORM, then repeat step 1 for the second inlet.

2. Bypass area (affected inlet):
   IF ABOVE MACH 2.1, bypass door standby switch - Down to maintain shock in crosshatch.
   IF BELOW MACH 2.1, bypass door standby switch - Down 700, 1100, or 1800 square inches.
   Hold switch down to obtain 700 square inches for no engines or one engine out; 1100 square inches for two engines out; or 1800 square inches for three engines out.
3. Throat Mach schedule standby switch (affected inlet) - Down to maintain throat at 0.2 Mach less than airplane Mach.
4. Duct performance switch - NORM.
   If one inlet remains in automatic mode, move duct performance switch to NORM.
5. See "Emergency Deceleration - One or Both Inlets in Standby AICS (Airplane AF62-207)."

EMERGENCY DECELERATION - STANDBY AICS (AIRPLANE AF62-001).

SUPERSONIC ABOVE MACH 2.1.

Before Decelerating

Before beginning to decelerate from any airspeed above Mach 2.1, accomplish the following:

1. All four mode switches - OFF.
   Check both bypass standby system selector switches at PRIMARY, or ALTERNATE if required.
2. Bypass door standby switches - Both down to position and maintain shocks in crosshatch.
3. Throat Mach schedule standby switches - Both down to maintain throats at 0.2 Mach less than airplane Mach.
4. Throttles - MIL.
5. Bypass door standby switches - Both down to maintain shocks in crosshatch.

2.6 Mach

6. Bypass door standby switches - Both down as required.
7. Throat Mach schedule standby switches - Both down to maintain throats at 0.2 Mach less than airplane Mach.
8. Lateral bobweight switch - LOCK.

2.1 Mach

9. Throttles - 40 degrees or above.
10. Engine status - Check.
11. Bypass door standby switches - Both up to position shocks in green arc.
12. Throat Mach schedule standby switches - Both down to maintain throats at 0.2 Mach less than airplane Mach.
13. Fuel tank pump switches of empty tanks - Check OFF.

SUPERSONIC BELOW MACH 2.1.

Before decelerating from any supersonic airspeed below Mach 2.1, accomplish the following:

14. All four mode switches - OFF.

T.O. 1B-70(X)A-1

15. Bypass area - Check both 700, 1100, or 1800 square inches.
    For no engines or one engine out in an inlet, check bypass area 700 square inches; for two engines out, 1100 square inches; and for three engines out, 1800 square inches.
16. Throat Mach schedule standby switches - Both down to maintain throats at 0.2 Mach less than airplane Mach.
17. Throttles - MIL.

1.7 Mach

18. Throat Mach schedule standby switches - Both down until throats are full open (1.67).
19. Throat wheels - Both full aft.
20. Emergency heat exchanger water switch - OFF.
21. Pitot heater and windshield defogging switches - ON.

1.4 Mach

22. Wing tip position selector switch - ½.

NOTE

When the wing tips are raised, a slight nose-down trim change occurs.

23. Throttles - 40 degrees or above.
24. Engine rpm lockup switch - RELEASE.
25. Bypass door standby switches - Both up as required.
    For no engines out in one inlet, obtain 400 square inches; for one engine out, 700 square inches; for two engines out, 1100 square inches; and for three engines out, 1800 square inches.
26. Fuel tank pump switches of empty tanks - Check OFF.
27. Liquid nitrogen quantity - Check.
28. Secondary exhaust nozzle area standby pressure knob - Set to airplane altitude if engines are below 100% rpm.
29. Engine rpm - Maintain engines 3 and 4 at or above 87%.

1.0 Mach

30. Bypass door standby switches - Both up until bypass areas are full closed.

31. Bypass wheels - Both full forward.
32. Bypass standby system selector switches - Leave both at PRIMARY or ALTERNATE.

CAUTION

If the bypass standby system selector switches are moved to OFF, the actuators will center and the bypass doors will move to the position selected by the bypass wheels or to the position as determined by the bypass master cylinder.

33. Secondary exhaust nozzle area standby pressure knob - Set to field elevation.
34. Nose ramp switch - DOWN.
35. Anticollision light switch - ON.

0.95 Mach

36. Wing tip position selector switch - UP.

NOTE

When the wing tips are raised, a slight nose-down trim change occurs.

37. Ammonia, water, oxygen, and liquid nitrogen quantities - Check.
38. Electrical and hydraulics - Check. Check voltages, and hydraulic pressures, fluid levels, and pump indicators.
39. Fuel tank pump switches of empty tanks - Check OFF.
40. Engine rpm - Maintain engines 3 and 4 at or above 87%.

EMERGENCY DECELERATION - ONE OR BOTH INLETS IN STANDBY AICS (AIRPLANE AF62-207).

Before Decelerating

Before beginning to decelerate from any airspeed with one or both inlets in standby mode, accomplish the following:

1. Duct performance switch - Check NORM.
2. Bypass area:
   AUTO inlet - Check.
   STANDBY inlet, bypass door standby switch - Down to maintain shock in crosshatch.

3. Throat:
   AUTO inlet - Check schedule.
   STANDBY inlet, throat Mach schedule standby switch - Down to maintain throat at 0.2 Mach less than airplane Mach.
4. Throttles - MIL.

2.3 Mach

1. Throttles - 40 degrees or above.
2. Engine status - Check.
3. Bypass area:
   AUTO inlet - Check.
   STANDBY inlet, bypass door standby switch - Up to position shock in the green arc.
4. Throat:
   Auto inlet - Check.
   STANDBY inlet, bypass door standby switch - Down until throat Mach schedule indicator reads Mach 2.1.
5. Fuel tank pump switches of empty tanks - Check OFF.

2.0 Mach

1. Bypass area:
   AUTO inlet - Check closing to 500 square inches plus the bias if applied for engine-out condition.
   If all engines are operating, check bypass area closing to 500 square inches; with one engine out, closing to 700 square inches; with two engines out, closing to 1100 square inches; and with three engines out, closing to 1800 square inches.
   STANDBY inlet - Check 700, 1100, or 1800 square inches.
   For no engines out or one engine out, obtain 700 square inches; for two engines out, 1100 square inches; and for three engines out, 1800 square inches.
2. Throat trim power switch - OFF.

1.7 Mach

1. Emergency heat exchanger water switch - OFF.
2. Pitot heater and windshield defogging switches - ON.

1.4 Mach

1. Wing tip position selector switch - ½.

NOTE

When the wing tips are raised, a slight nose-down trim change occurs.

2. Throttles - 40 degrees or above.
3. Engine rpm lockup switch - RELEASE.
4. Fuel tank pump switches of empty tanks - Check OFF.
5. Liquid nitrogen quantity - Check.
6. Secondary exhaust nozzle area standby pressure knob - Set to airplane altitude if engines are below 100% rpm.
7. Engine rpm - Maintain engines 3 and 4 at or above 87%.
8. Bypass area:
   AUTO inlet - Check closing plus the bias if applied for engine-out condition.
   If all engines are operating, check bypass area closing to 0000; with one engine out, closing to 700 square inches; with two engines out, closing to 1100 square inches; and with three engines out, closing to 1800 square inches.

   STANDBY inlet - Check 400, 700, 1100, or 1800 square inches.
   For no engines out, obtain 400 square inches; one for engine out, 700 square inches; for two engines out, 1100 square inches; and for three engines out, 1800 square inches.

1.0 Mach

1. AICS mode switches - Both STBY.
2. Bypass door standby switches - Both down until bypass areas are fully closed.
3. Throat Mach schedule standby switches - Both down until throats are full open (throat Mach schedule indicators read 1.67).
4. Secondary exhaust nozzle area standby pressure knob - Set to field elevation.
5. Nose ramp switch - DOWN.
6. Anticollision light switch - ON.

T.O. 1B-70(X)A-1

.95 Mach

1. Wing tip position selector switch - UP.

   NOTE
   When the wing tips are raised, a slight nose-down trim change occurs.

2. Ammonia, water, oxygen, and liquid nitrogen quantities - Check.
3. Electrical and hydraulics - Check. Check voltages, and hydraulic pressures, fluid levels, and pump indicators.
4. Fuel tank pump switches of empty tanks - Check OFF.
5. Engine rpm - Maintain engines 3 and 4 at or above 87%.

AIR INDUCTION CONTROL SYSTEM COOLING SYSTEM FAILURE (AIRPLANE AF62-001).

The dual AICS cooling system automatically transfers from system No. 1 to system No. 2 in case of a malfunction. If the coolant caution light remains out after master caution light is pressed, the cooling system has transferred to system No. 2, and is functioning properly. If the coolant caution light remains on or comes back on, use the following procedure:

1. Bypass wheels - Both aft to position and maintain shocks in crosshatch.
2. Bypass door mode switches - Both OFF. Check both bypass standby system selector switches at PRIMARY, or ALTERNATE if required.
3. Throat Mach schedule mode switches - Both MAN.
4. Air induction control system package power switch - OFF.
5. Decelerate to Mach 1.5 or below, using standby bypass and manual throat control.
   a. Bypass door standby switches - Both down as required to maintain schedule below.
   b. Throat wheels - Both aft to maintain throat at 0.2 Mach less than airplane Mach.

AIRPLANE MACH NO.	BYPASS AREA NO. OF ENGINES OPERATING (REST WINDMILLING)			
	3	2	1	0
Above 2.8	400	500	600	700
at 2.8	500	650	800	900
2.6	600	800	1000	1200
Bobweight - LOCK				
2.4	700	950	1300	1800
2.1	700	700	1100	1800

1.7 Throat wheels - Both full aft.
Throat Mach schedule mode switches - Both OFF.
Emergency heat exchanger water switch - OFF.
Pitot heater and windshield defogging switches - ON.

1.4 Wing tip position selector switch - ½.

   NOTE
   When the wing tips are raised, a slight nose-down trim change occurs.

Engine rpm lockup switch - RELEASE.
Bypass door standby switches - Both up as required.

   For no engines out in one inlet, obtain 400 square inches; for one engine out, 700 square inches; for two engines out, 1100 square inches; and for three engines out, 1800 square inches.

Fuel tank pump switches of empty tanks - Check OFF.
Liquid nitrogen quantity - Check.
Secondary exhaust nozzle area standby pressure knob - Set to airplane altitude if engines are below 100% rpm.
Engine rpm - Maintain engines 3 and 4 at or above 87%.

1.0 Bypass door standby switches - Both up until bypass areas are full closed.
Bypass wheels - Both full forward.
Bypass standby system selector switches - Leave both at PRIMARY or ALTERNATE.

T.O. 1B-70(X)A-1

Secondary exhaust nozzle area standby pressure knob - Set to field elevation.
Nose ramp switch - DOWN.
Anticollision light switch - ON.
.95 Wing tip position selector switch - UP.

NOTE

When the wing tips are raised, a slight nose-down trim change occurs.

Ammonia, water, oxygen, and liquid nitrogen quantities - Check.
Electrical and hydraulics - Check.
  Check voltages, and hydraulic pressures, fluid levels and pump indicators.
Fuel tank pump switches of empty tanks - OFF.
Engine rpm - Maintain engines 3 and 4 at or above 87%.

AIR INDUCTION CONTROL SYSTEM COOLING SYSTEM FAILURE (AIRPLANE AF62-207).

The dual AICS cooling system automatically transfers from system No. 1 to system No. 2 in case of a malfunction. If the coolant caution light remains out after the master caution light is pressed, the cooling system has transferred to system No. 2 and is functioning properly. If the coolant light remains on or comes back on, use the following procedure:

1. Duct performance switch - LOW; then both AICS mode switches - STBY.
   Rapidly and in sequence move the duct performance switch to LOW, then both AICS mode switches simultaneously to STBY. If the mode switches are moved first or too long after the duct performance switch is moved to LOW, the bypass doors would tend to move at high rate toward the closed position, inducing buzz or unstart.

NOTE

If both mode switches cannot be moved simultaneously with ease and without any delay, the change-over to standby mode may be made one inlet at a time. After the first inlet is put in standby mode, move the duct performance switch back to NORM, then put the second inlet in standby mode.

2. Bypass door standby switches - Both down to maintain shocks in crosshatch.
3. AICS package power switch - OFF.

NOTE

This will disable the buzz and unstart warning systems.

4. Decelerate to Mach 1.5 or below.
   a. Bypass door standby switches - Both down as required to maintain schedule given below.
   b. Throat Mach schedule standby switches - Both down to maintain throats at 0.2 Mach less than airplane Mach.
   c. Throttles - MIL.

AIRPLANE MACH NO.	BYPASS AREA NO. OF ENGINES OPERATING (REST WINDMILLING)			
	3	2	1	0
Above 2.8	400	500	600	700
at 2.8	500	650	800	900
2.6	600	800	1000	1200
2.4	700	950	1300	1800
2.1	700	700	1100	1800

   1.7 Emergency heat exchanger water switch - OFF.
       Pitot heater and windshield defogging switches - ON.
   1.4 Wing tip position selector switch - ½.

NOTE

When the wing tips are raised, a slight nose-down trim change occurs.

Throttles - 40 degrees or above.
Engine rpm lockup switch - RELEASE.
Bypass door standby switches - Both up as required.
  For no engines out in one inlet, obtain 400 square inches; for one engine out, 700 square inches; for two engines out, 1100 square inches; and for three engines out, 1800 square inches.

T.O. 1B-70(X)A-1

Fuel tank pump switches of empty tanks - Check OFF.
Liquid nitrogen quantity - Check.
Secondary exhaust nozzle area standby pressure knob - Set to airplane altitude if engines are below 100% rpm.
Engine rpm - Maintain engines 3 and 4 at or above 87%.
1.0 Bypass door standby switches - Both down until doors are fully closed.
Throat Mach schedule standby switches - Both down until throats are full open (throat Mach schedule indicators read 1.67).
Secondary exhaust nozzle area standby pressure knob - Set to field elevation.
Nose ramp switch - DOWN.
Anticollision light switch - ON.
.95 Wing tip position selector switch - UP.

NOTE
When the wing tips are raised, a slight nose-down trim change occurs.

Ammonia, water, oxygen, and liquid nitrogen quantities - Check.
Electrical and hydraulics - Check.
  Check voltages, and hydraulic pressures, fluid levels, and pump indicators.
Fuel tank pump switches of empty tanks - Check OFF.
Engine rpm - Maintain engines 3 and 4 at or above 87%.

AIR INDUCTION CONTROL SYSTEM OPERATION WITH RIGHT PRIMARY AC BUS FAILED (AIRPLANE AF62-001).

Illumination of the No. 4 primary generator-out and the bus-tie open caution lights indicates loss of right primary ac bus power. If these lights come on, check for bus voltages with the ac voltmeter and voltmeter phase bus selector switches. If bus failure is definitely indicated, operate the air induction control system as follows:

NOTE
Failure of the right hand primary ac bus will result in loss of the following AICS functions:

- Automatic and manual modes.
- One buzz and one unstart warning system.
- Shock position indication.

1. Bypass door mode switches - Both OFF.
2. Throat Mach schedule mode switches - Both OFF.
3. Bypass standby system selector switches - Both PRIMARY, or ALTERNATE if required.
4. Decelerate to Mach 1.5 or below, using standby bypass and throat control.
   a. Bypass door standby switches - Both down as required to maintain schedule below.
   b. Throat Mach schedule standby switches - Both down to maintain throats at 0.2 Mach less than airplane Mach.
   c. Throttles - MIL.

AIRPLANE MACH NO.	BYPASS AREA			
	NO. OF ENGINES OPERATING (REST WINDMILLING)			
	3	2	1	0
Above 2.8	400	500	600	700
at 2.8	500	650	800	900
2.6	600	800	1000	1200
Bobweight - LOCK				
2.4	700	950	1300	1800
2.1	700	700	1100	1800

1.7 Throat Mach schedule standby switches - Both down until throat Mach schedule indicator is at 1.67.
Emergency heat exchanger water switch - OFF.
Pitot heater and windshield defogging switches - ON.
1.4 Wing tip position selector switch - ½.

NOTE
When the wing tips are raised, a slight nose-down trim change occurs.

Engine rpm lockup switch - RELEASE.
Bypass door standby switches - Both up as required.
   For no engines out in one inlet, obtain 400 square inches; for one engine out, 700 square inches; for two engines out, 1100 square inches; and for three engines out, 1800 square inches.
Fuel tank pump switches of empty tanks - Check OFF.
Liquid nitrogen quantity - Check.
Secondary exhaust nozzle area standby pressure knob - Set to airplane altitude if engines are below 100% rpm.
Engine rpm - Maintain engines 3 and 4 at or above 87%.

1.0 Bypass door standby switches - Both up until bypass areas are fully closed.
Secondary exhaust nozzle area standby pressure knob - Set to field elevation.
Nose ramp switch - DOWN.
Anticollision light switch - ON.

.95 Wing tip position selector switch - UP.

NOTE

When the wing tips are raised, a slight nose-down trim change occurs.

Ammonia, water, oxygen, and liquid nitrogen quantities - Check.
Electrical and hydraulics - Check.
   Check voltages, and hydraulic pressures, fluid levels, and pump indications.
Fuel tank pump switches of empty tanks - OFF.
Engine rpm - Maintain engines 3 and 4 at or above 87%.

This page intentionally left blank

T.O. 1B-70(X)A-1

FUEL SUPPLY SYSTEM FAILURE.

FUEL BOOST PUMP FAILURE.

Boost pump failures will not be known during flight. Failure of one boost pump does not affect fuel flow to the engines. With two boost pumps failed (one boost pump feeding the engines), normal engine operated can be maintained at all altitudes, however, power loss or engine instability may occur during afterburner take-off.

FUEL TRANSFER SYSTEM FAILURE.

Improper operation of the automatic fuel sequence system is indicated by:

- Fuel sequence strips fail to move down.
- Fuel sequence strips move down ahead of sequence.
- No. 3 tank (sump tank) strip falls below the green band.
- Sump tank low fuel level caution light on with fuel remaining in other tanks.

The fuel sequence is shown in figure 3-7. A faulty indicating system may be caused by a failed indicator, fuel probe or fuel control module. If it is determined that a fuel control module has failed, replacements may be made in flight. (See figure 3-8 for fuel control module replacement.) Spare fuel control modules are carried for tanks 1, 2, 3, 4, and 5. No replacement module is provided for left or right tanks 6, 7, or 8.

> NOTE
> Because either the left or right module of tanks 6, 7, or 8 controls the sequence of the left and right tanks, failure of either module will not prevent the remaining module from sequencing the next tank. The indication of the total fuel remaining may be incorrect.

If the fuel control module for tank No. 3 (sump tank) fails, it should be replaced to provide a continuous indication of the fuel remaining in this tank, and to permit operation of the sump tank low fuel level caution light.

FUEL INDICATING SYSTEM TEST.

The fuel quantity indicator test switch is used to diagnose improper operation of the fuel quantity indicating system.

> NOTE
> Holding the switch at either position should be limited to about 4 seconds to keep from cycling the fuel pumps and interrupting the normal fuel sequence.

If one indicator (sequence strip or selected quantity) does not respond when the test switch is used, but the others do, the indicator that did not respond has failed. If neither indicator responds, the probable cause is a failed fuel control module. If the indicators respond to the use of the test switch, but do not return to the original indication when the test switch is released,

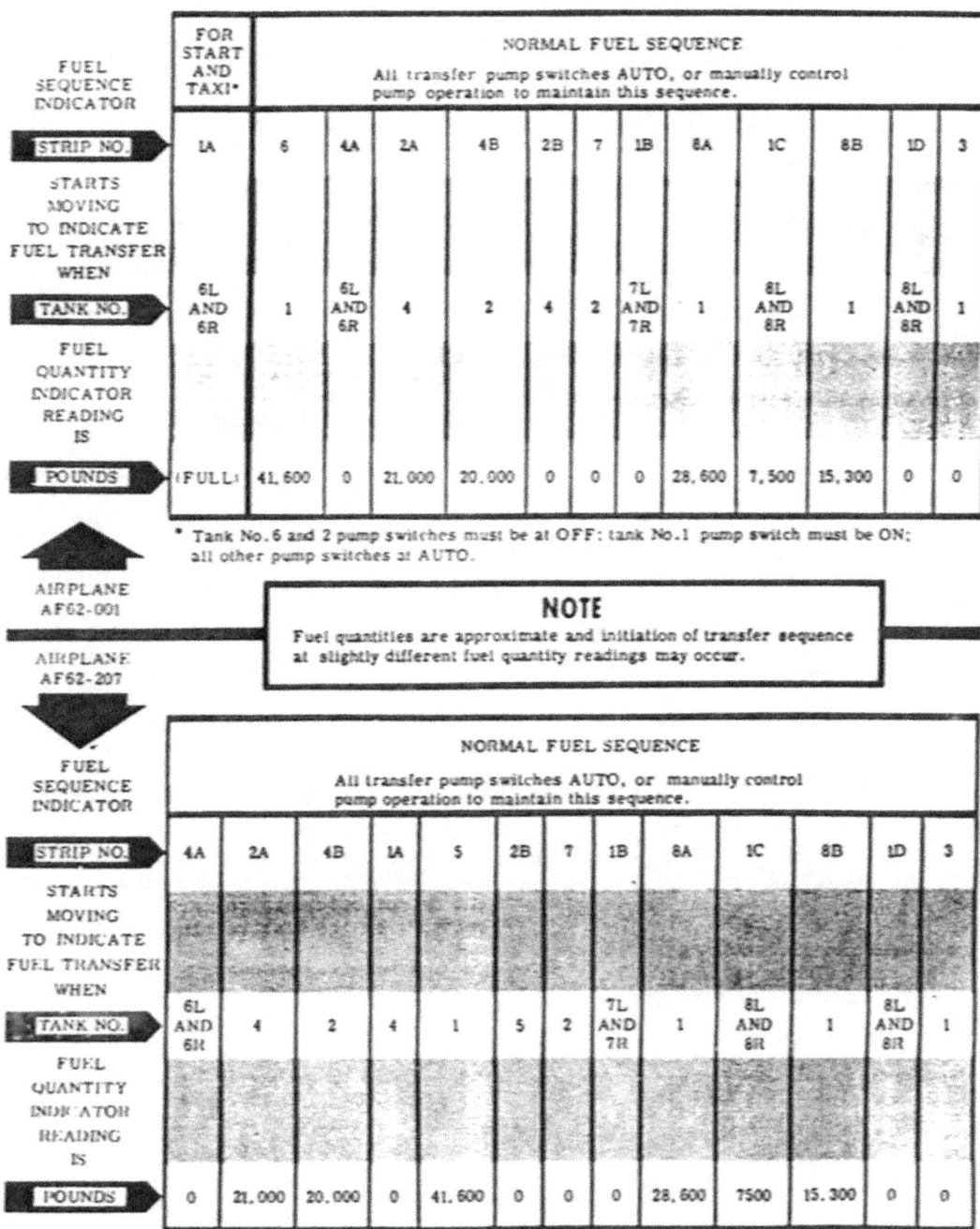

Figure 3-7

the probable cause is a tank unit circuit failure.

> **NOTE**
> When the yellow portion of any sequence strip appears, either at the top or bottom of the strip, a malfunction of that portion of the sequence indicator is indicated and using the test switch should have no effect on it. The other tank sequence strips should test normally.

SEQUENCE STRIP SHOWS FUEL NOT TRANSFERRING OR TRANSFERRING AHEAD OF SEQUENCE - OTHER THAN TANK 3.

1. If failure is indicated in tank 1 or 8, start return to base before trouble shooting.
2. Selected fuel tank quantity indicator knob - Rotate to applicable tank.
   - If indicator does not agree with sequence strip - Identify failed indicator with the test switch and proceed with normal fuel management.
   - If indicator agrees with sequence strip - Proceed to step 3.
3. Applicable fuel tank pump switch - OFF, if transferring ahead of schedule; ON, if not transferring.
   - If malfunction <u>is</u> corrected - Manually control fuel sequencing until back on sequence.
   - If malfunction <u>is not</u> corrected - Proceed to step 4.
4. Indicating system test switch - EMPTY, momentarily.

> **NOTE**
> Do not hold switch at EMPTY for more than 4 seconds.

- If the indicators do not test satisfactory, or drove rapidly to empty before the test switch was moved to EMPTY, the indicating system has malfunctioned. Proceed to step 5.
- If the indicators test satisfactory, proceed to step 6 if tank not transferring or to step 7 if transferring ahead of schedule.

5. If indicators have failed, use the following applicable procedure:
   - Sequence strips 1D, 2B, 4A, 4B, 5, 6, 7, 8A, or 8B - Manually control sequence and monitor tank 3 indication to detect when the affected tank is empty.

> **WARNING**
> If tank 3 indicates tank 8A or 8B is not transferring, land immediately.

   - Sequence strip 2A or 1C - Use all of the affected tank, and monitor tank 3 indication to detect when the tank is empty.

> **NOTE**
> If possible, select unused tank unit circuit on the applicable fuel control module or change the module. (See figure 3-8.)

   - Sequence strip 1A or 1B - Select unused tank unit circuit on the applicable fuel control module or change the module. (See figure 3-8.) If this is not done, or if the malfunction remains, abort the mission.

> **NOTE**
> Total fuel quantity may be erroneous.

6. If both indicators test satisfactory and transfer pumps have failed off:
   a. Turn on next forward tank segment in sequence.

T.O. 1B-70(X)A-1

FUEL CONTROL MODULE REPLACEMENT

NOTE
- Spare fuel control modules are provided for tanks 1, 2, 3, 4, and 5 only.
- When fuel control unit is pulled out, cockpit indications will be erroneous until control unit is back in place.

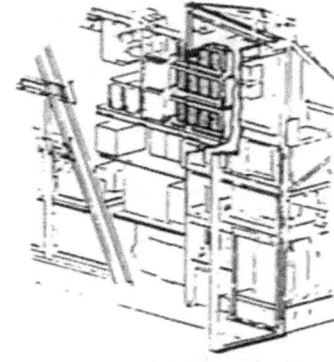

ELECTRONIC EQUIPMENT
COMPARTMENT (LEFT SIDE)

1 All fuel tank pump switches (except for tank transferring fuel) - OFF.

2 All associated fuel circuit breakers and circuit breaker switches - Check in and ON. (This may have been the cause of the malfunction.)

3 Release the four camlocks with screwdriver provided.

CAMLOCK SCREWDRIVER

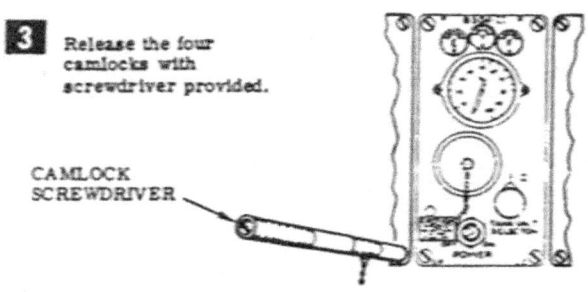

4 Turn wing camlock 1/4 turn to release latching handle. Pull latching handle out about 30 degrees.

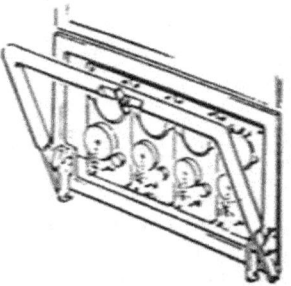

5 Pull fuel control unit out far enough to gain access to the spare module and electrical connections.

Caution
The fuel control unit will drop if pulled out too far.

6 Remove electrical connection and pull failed module from control unit. Install correct spare module for the position, hook up electrical connection, and stow failed module in spare position upside down. Slide control unit back into rack and secure.

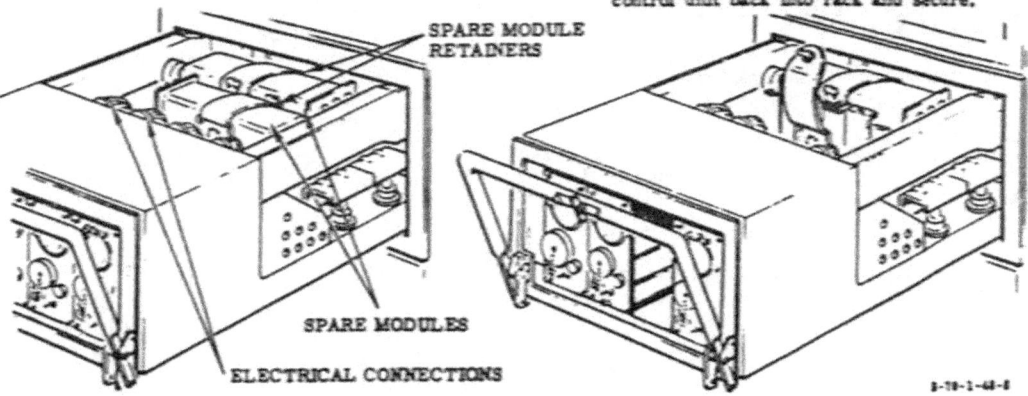

SPARE MODULE RETAINERS

SPARE MODULES

ELECTRICAL CONNECTIONS

Figure 3-8

T.O. 1B-70(X)A-1

   b. Manually control fuel sequence in normal alternating sequence, leaving an equal number of portions of upper and lower strips to balance fuel which will not transfer.
   c. Plan flight based on available fuel.

WARNING
Immediately abort mission if failure occurs at start of sequence of strips 1B, 1C, 1D, 8A, or 8B.

7. If both indicators test satisfactory and the transfer pumps have failed on, use the following applicable procedure:
   - If the failure is in tank 1 or 2 - Use the affected tank, manually alternating with an aft tank to maintain a balance of upper and lower strips.
   - If the failure is in tank 4 - Let the tank empty, then the sequence will continue automatically.
   - If the failure is in tank 5, 7, or 8:
     a. Refueling valve switch of applicable tank and of last aft tank that has emptied - OPEN.
     b. Use normal alternating sequence to maintain a balance of upper and lower strips.
     c. Affected tank refueling valve switch CLOSE and fuel tank pump switch ON when transfer of fuel from this tank is required.

SEQUENCE STRIP SHOWS TANK FILLING OTHER THAN TANK 3.

1. Selected fuel tank quantity indicator knob - Rotate to applicable tank.
   - If indicator does not agree with sequence strip - Identify failed indicator with the test switch and proceed with normal fuel management.
   - If indicator agrees with the sequence strip - Proceed to step 2.

2. Applicable refueling valve switch - CLOSE.
      a. If malfunction remains - Proceed to next step 3.
3. Indicating system test switch - FULL, momentarily.

NOTE
Do not hold switch at FULL for more than 4 seconds.

- If the indicators do not test satisfactory or drove rapidly to full before the test switch was moved to FULL, the indicating system has malfunctioned. Proceed to step 4.
- If the indicators test satisfactory, proceed to step 5.

4. If indicators have failed, use the following applicable procedure:
   - Sequence strips 1D, 2B, 4A, 4B, 6, 7, 8A, or 8B - Manually control sequence and monitor tank 3 indication to detect when the affected tank is empty.

WARNING
If tank 3 indicates tank 8A is not transferring, land immediately.

- Sequence strip 2A or 1C - Use all of the affected tank and monitor tank 3 indication to detect when the tank is empty.

NOTE
If possible, select unused tank unit circuit on the applicable fuel control module or change the module. (See figure 3-8.)

- Sequence strip 1A or 1B - Select unused tank unit circuit on the applicable fuel control module or change the module. (See figure 3-8.) If this is not done or the malfunction remains, abort the mission.

NOTE
Total fuel quantity may be erroneous.

5. If tank is filling, abort mission and:
   a. Applicable fuel tank pump switch – ON.
   b. All other fuel tank pump switches – OFF, except as necessary to maintain tank 3 below 30,000 pounds to control CG.

TANK 3 INDICATING ABNORMAL.

1. Start return to base before trouble shooting.
2. Selected fuel tank quantity indicator knob – Rotate to 3.
3. Indicating system test switch – Move to EMPTY momentarily.

NOTE
Do not hold switch at EMPTY for more than 4 seconds.

- If either the sequence strip or the selected fuel tank quantity indicator tests satisfactory – Proceed with normal fuel management.
- If both indicators do not test satisfactory, the indicating system has malfunctioned – Select unused tank unit circuit on tank 3 module and if the system is still unsatisfactory, change tank 3 module. (See figure 3-8.)
- If both indicators test satisfactory – Select unused tank unit circuit on tank 3 module. If malfunction is not corrected, abort mission and land immediately.

COOLING LOOP FUEL PUMP FAILURE.

Illumination of either cooling loop fuel pump caution light indicates failure of the corresponding cooling loop fuel pump, and the flight should be aborted.

CAUTION
The flight should be aborted when the cooling loop fuel pump caution light comes on, because failure of the remaining pump would stop the flow of cooling fuel through the cooling loop. As a result, subsequent failure of accessory drive systems and electrical generating system can occur, as well as overheating of the fluid systems that are cooled by the cooling loop.

EITHER COOLING LOOP FUEL PUMP CAUTION LIGHT ON.

1. Decelerate and descend.
2. Land at home base as soon as possible.

BOTH COOLING LOOP FUEL PUMP CAUTION LIGHTS ON.

1. Decelerate and descend using minimum rpm.
2. All non-essential electrical equipment – Off.
3. Reduce hydraulic requirements to the minimum.
4. Land as soon as possible.

T.O. 1B-70(X)A-1

TANK PRESSURIZATION AND FUEL INERTING SYSTEM FAILURE.

The fuel inerting caution light comes on when the liquid nitrogen quantity indicator shows less than 5 percent liquid nitrogen remaining and/or when pressure in the liquid nitrogen container is too low, or when fuel tank pressure is too low. Air venting of the fuel tanks can occur during descent below 40,000 feet if pressurization system fails. This condition is hazardous if fuel tank temperatures are above 400 degrees F at speeds above Mach 2.4.

FUEL INERTING CAUTION LIGHT ON (IF MACH 2.4 HAS BEEN EXCEEDED).

1. Fuel transfer pumps in empty tanks - Check OFF.
2. Altitude - If above 40,000 feet, descend to this altitude, if below 40,000 hold altitude constant to reduce temperature.
3. Airspeed - Reduce airspeed and fly at minimum safe speed consistent with the airplane weight for 15 minutes.
4. Abort mission and return to base.

NOTE
The fuel inerting caution light remains on until the caution light circuit is ground reset.

FUEL INERTING CAUTION LIGHT ON (IF MACH 2.4 HAS NOT BEEN EXCEEDED).

1. Abort mission and return to base.

ELECTRICAL POWER SYSTEM FAILURE.

PRIMARY GENERATOR FAILURE.

If either primary generator fails or has tripped, the respective generator-out caution light comes on. Abort mission and lower landing gear as follows:

1. Decelerate using normal procedures and return to base.
2. Engines 4, 5 and 6 - Maintain at 99% rpm until landing gear is down.
3. Landing gear handle - DOWN.
4. After touchdown - Monitor No. 2 utility system pumps; if one fails, advance other two engines with the operating No. 2 utility pumps to 80% rpm until airplane is stopped.

COMPLETE DC ELECTRICAL FAILURE (WHILE WEARING PRESSURE SUIT).

NOTE
Loss of complete dc power will cause rapid (within one minute) loss of pressurization because of dumping the door and hatch seal pressure.

In case of a complete loss of dc power above 40,000 feet, and ac power is still available, use the following procedure immediately:

> **CAUTION**
> Failure to use the following procedure when above 40,000 feet could cause overheat damage to the electronic equipment and full ram air temperature on the capsule. No cooling is provided for the ram air when the essential dc bus out and primary dc bus out caution lights are on.

1. Crew air shutoff handle - Unlock and pull up.
2. Cabin air switch - Hold at PEPPES-SUPE.
   Hold cabin air switch at PEPPES-SUPE to keep the emergency ram-air scoop closed.
3. Emergency descent - Initiate.
   a. Maintain inlets as required.
   b. Throttles - IDLE.
   c. Start maximum safe-G spiral descent.
   d. Cabin altitude - Monitor.
4. Cabin air switch - PURGE, when total temperature is below 160°F.
5. Use emergency cruise-back procedure. (Refer to "Return to Base Procedure After Environmental System Emergency - Ram-air Scoop Open" in this section.)

DC ELECTRICAL FAILURE BELOW 40,000 FEET.

In case of a complete loss of dc power below 40,000 feet, and ac power is still available, use the following procedure immediately:

> **CAUTION**
> No cooling is provided for the ram air when the essential dc bus out and primary dc bus out caution lights are on.

1. Cabin air switch - PURGE, when total temperature is below 160°F.
2. Abort mission and use emergency cruise-back procedure. (Refer to "Return to Base Procedure After Environmental System Emergency - Ram-air Scoop Open" in this section.)

EMERGENCY GENERATOR OPERATION (HYDRAULIC SYSTEM SATISFACTORY).

When the emergency generator switch is at AUTO, the emergency generator comes on automatically if both primary generators fail, or if the No. 3 generator fails and a bus-tie contactor is open. (The emergency generator-on caution light comes on when the emergency generator is engaged.)

If a failure causes the emergency generator to come on, abort mission and lower landing gear as follows:

1. Decelerate using normal procedures and return to base.
2. Engines 4, 5 and 6 - Maintain at 99% rpm until landing gear is down.
3. Landing gear handle - DOWN.
4. Manual emergency landing gear handle - UT SYS NO. 1 before touchdown.
5. If both primary generators are inoperative, accomplish the following*:
   a. Engine shutdown and wheel brake arming switch - Check OFF.

> **CAUTION**
> The engine shutdown and wheel brake arming switch must not be at ARMED in the air.

   b. Battery-inverter switch - ON. Break safety wire and move battery-inverter switch to ON.

> **NOTE**
> After being energized, the emergency battery will require 3 to 5

---

* Airplane AF62-001.

T.O. 1B-70(X)A-1

seconds before it will light the battery-inverter indicator light.

c. Battery-inverter switch - OFF after battery-inverter light comes on.

NOTE
- Moving the battery-inverter switch to OFF after emergency battery is energized stops battery until inverter is required.
- The battery-inverter light will go out, but the battery remains energized.

d. Battery-inverter switch - ON when required.

COMPLETE ELECTRICAL FAILURE (EMERGENCY BATTERY OPERATION).*

In case of a complete electrical failure, use the emergency battery-inverter system as follows:

1. Abort mission and set up return to home base.
2. Decelerate and raise wing tips as follows:
   a. Engine shutdown and wheel brake arming switch - Check OFF.

CAUTION
The engine shutdown and wheel brake arming switch must not be at ARMED in the air.

b. Battery-inverter switch - ON. Break safety wire and move battery-inverter switch to ON.

NOTE
After being energized, the emergency battery will require 3 to 5 seconds before it will light the battery-inverter indicator light.

c. Alternate throttle switches - Use no more than two at a time as required.
d. Wing tip emergency-up switch - Hold at WING TIP UP at least 5 seconds. The wing tip emergency-up switch must be held at either up position at least 5 seconds to ensure that wing tips are raised to full up.

CAUTION
Do not use wing tip and alternate throttle switches simultaneously because of the drain on the battery.

3. Nose ramp unlock handle - Pull, and maintain speed above 300 knots IAS until windshield is full down.
4. Lower landing gear as follows:
   a. Landing gear handle - DOWN.
   b. Manual emergency landing gear handle - UT SYS NO. 1 or UT SYS NO. 2.
5. Alternate throttle switches - DECR, then centered after touchdown. Move all alternate throttle switches to DECR after touchdown and hold to retard engines to idle, then release and check centered.
6. Check feet off brake pedals. Feet must be off brake pedals before step 7 to prevent inadvertent application of brakes.

---

* Airplane AF62-001

T.O. 1B-70(X)A-1

7. Engine shutdown and wheel brake arming switch - ARMED.

   CAUTION
   Do not touch alternate throttle switches when arming switch is at ARMED until engines are to be shut down. Inadvertent shutdown of the engines will cause the loss of all hydraulic power.

8. Apply brakes with extreme care as only manual braking is available.

   NOTE
   If the brakes fail, steer with alternate throttle switches after moving the engine shutdown and wheel brake arming switch to OFF to prevent accidently shutting off an engine.

   CAUTION
   Use brakes with extreme care as anti-skid is inoperative and only manual brakes are available.

9. Alternate throttle switches - Hold at DECR to shut down engines after airplane is stopped and chocked.

   NOTE
   The engine shutdown and wheel brake arming switch must be at ARMED before the alternate throttle switches can shut down the engines.

10. Accomplish normal after-shutdown procedures.

BUS-TIE CONTACTORS OPEN.

The bus-tie contactors are protective devices in the electrical system which open to isolate the right and left primary busses and the primary generators if certain faults occur in the system.

   NOTE
   When the bus-tie contactors are open, the attitude director and horizontal situation indicators will present erratic displays of heading and attitude. (Refer to "Erratic Operation of the Attitude Director and Horizontal Situation Indicators" in Section IV.)

If large unbalanced currents flow between the generators, the bus-tie contactors will open (indicated by only the bus-tie open caution light coming on), so that each primary generator will supply power to its respective bus. In addition, the contactors open to prevent a good generator from tripping off the line because of a fault on the other bus. If these electrical faults caused the contactors to open, the bus-tie contactor override switch should not be used in an attempt to close the contactors.

The contactors also open if both primary generators go off the line because engines 3 and 4 are shutdown or lost, or because of generator shutdown. Under these conditions, however, the override switch can be used to close the contactors if either primary generator subsequently has been brought back on the line. This permits the operating generator to power both primary busses.

   CAUTION
   If the contactors are open and one primary generator has been restored, use the override switch only if the contactors were opened by any of the following conditions:

   * Loss of both primary generators because of shutdown or loss of engines 3 and 4.

   * Shutdown of both primary generators.

   * Loss of one primary generator (which in itself did not cause contactors to open) and subsequent loss of

T.O. 1B-70(X)A-1

the other due to shutdown or loss of its engine.

If the contactors were opened by other conditions, do not use the override switch as possible loss of the remaining good generator can result.

If the bus-tie open caution light comes on as a result of known or suspected electrical faults, proceed as follows:

1. Descend to below 50,000 feet, using normal descent procedures.

If the bus-tie open caution light comes on as a result of known generator or engine (3 or 4) shutdown or loss, proceed as follows:

1. Descend to below 50,000 feet, using normal descent procedures.

2. Bus-tie contactor override switch - 3 GEN or 4 GEN.
   After one generator has been restored, the override switch should be held momentarily at its 3 GEN position if the No. 3 primary generator is operating, or at the 4 GEN position if the No. 4 generator is operating.

HYDRAULIC POWER SYSTEM FAILURE.

Symptoms of a hydraulic power system failure are the same for both primary and utility hydraulic systems. Impending failure of a hydraulic system may be indicated by low pressure readings or pressure fluctuations. The individual hydraulic pump status indicators change from green to yellow to indicate which hydraulic pump has failed. A failed system is indicated by the appropriate pressure gage reading.

PRIMARY HYDRAULIC SYSTEM FAILURE.

The primary hydraulic systems power the following:

NO. 1 PRIMARY	NO. 2 PRIMARY
1/2 Elevon dual supply	1/2 Elevon dual supply
1/2 Rudder dual supply	1/2 Rudder dual supply
1/2 Canard flap dual supply	1/2 Canard flap dual supply
1/2 Wing fold dual supply	1/2 Wing fold dual supply
Pitch augmentation	Roll augmentation (primary roll trim)
Yaw 1 augmentation	Yaw 2 augmentation
One fuel boost pump	One fuel boost pump
No. 1 Cooling loop fuel pump	No. 2 Cooling loop fuel pump
Two tank 7 transfer pumps	Two tank 7 transfer pumps
Two tank 8 transfer pumps	Two tank 8 transfer pumps
One tank 5 transfer pump*	One tank 5 transfer pump*

*Airplane AF62-207

This page intentionally left blank

T.O. 1B-70(X)A-1

PARTIAL FAILURE OF PRIMARY HYDRAULIC SYSTEM.

In case of a partial failure of both primary hydraulic systems, such as failure of one hydraulic pump in each of the primary hydraulic systems, the flight controls will respond slower than normal because of the reduced hydraulic flow. Failure of two hydraulic pumps in each of the primary hydraulic systems reduces control rate to 1/2 at 100 percent rpm and to 1/3 at IDLE. For partial failure of the primary hydraulic systems, accomplish the following:

1. Abort mission and land.
2. Keep rpm on engines with good pumps as high as conditions permit.
3. Use minimum control movements.
4. Reduce non-essential demands on the primary hydraulic systems.

COMPLETE FAILURE OF EITHER PRIMARY HYDRAULIC SYSTEM.

Failure of one primary hydraulic system does not affect the rate capability of the flight control system, flaps, and wing fold. However, system power or hinge moments are reduced by one-half except for canard flaps and wing fold which are operationally unaffected. Partial flight control augmentation is lost depending on which system has failed. Two fuel transfer pumps, one boost pump and one cooling loop fuel pump will be inoperative with one primary hydraulic system failed. However, the fuel and cooling systems are not operationally affected. If either primary hydraulic system fails, proceed as follows:

1. Abort mission, decelerate and land.
2. Monitor good primary hydraulic system.
3. Turn off all non-essential equipment.
4. Refrain from making abrupt control movements.

UTILITY HYDRAULIC SYSTEM FAILURE.

The utility hydraulic systems power the following:

NO. 1 UTILITY	NO. 2 UTILITY
Standby AICS	Standby AICS
Automatic and manual AICS* Automatic AICS†	Nose ramp
Brakes	Brakes
Drag chute	Drag chute
Ram air scoop	Ram air scoop
Landing gear (includes bogie fold if sys No. 2 not available)	Bogie fold
Landing gear (emergency manual (No. 1)	Landing gear (emergency manual No. 2)
Nose wheel steering	Landing gear (emergency lowering switch at DOWN)
Nose wheel steering (emergency manual No. 1)	Nose wheel steering (emergency lowering switch at DOWN)
1/2 of fuel transfer pumps in tanks 1, 2, 4, 6L, 6R	Nose wheel steering (emergency manual No. 2)
	1/2 of fuel transfer pumps in tanks 1, 2, 4, 6L, 6R.

---

*Airplane AF62-001
†Airplane AF62-207

T.O. 1B-70(X)A-1

NO. 1 UTILITY	NO. 2 UTILITY
One fuel boost pump	
Yaw gearing changer	Emergency generator
	Yaw gearing changer (Emergency manual No. 2 or emergency lowering switch at DOWN)

For various combinations of No. 1 and No. 2 utility hydraulic system pump failures, see figure 3-9.

NITROGEN SYSTEM FAILURE.

LIQUID NITROGEN SYSTEM FAILURE.

Refer to "Tank Pressurization and Fuel Inerting System Failure" in this section.

GASEOUS NITROGEN SYSTEM FAILURE.

There is no direct indication in the crew compartment of a failure in the three independent gaseous nitrogen systems which pressurize and inert the lubricating system of each accessory drive gearbox, the engine hydraulic systems, and the liquid coolant tank for the landing gear and drag chute compartment cooling systems. Satisfactory performance of these systems, as well as that of the related electrical and hydraulic power supply systems, indicates proper operation of the gaseous nitrogen systems. (Refer to "Accessory Drive System Oil Pressure Failure - Two Gearboxes Simultaneously", "Tire and/or Drag Chute Compartment Overheat Caution Light On", and "Engine Exhaust Nozzle Failure" in this section.) However, a possible indication of a failed nitrogen system is when the accessory drive system oil pressure caution light comes on with engine identification lights 1 and 4, 2 and 5, or 3 and 6.

NOTE

If the accessory drive oil pressure caution light and engine identification lights 2 and 5 come one, together with the tire and drag chute compartment overheat caution lights, loss of nitrogen system No. 2 is indicated.

If a nitrogen system failure is suspected as a result of malfunctions occuring in the systems it pressurizes, and if time and conditions permit, check the quantity in each of the three nitrogen bottles by means of the gaseous nitrogen quantity indicator and system selector on the ground test panel in the electronic equipment compartment. If a related system fails as the result of a suspected nitrogen system failure, retard the throttles of the engines of the affected accessory drive gearboxes to IDLE. Reduce altitude to below 30,000 feet. If the accessory drive system oil pressure caution light and the engine identification lights go out after altitude is reduced, the nitrogen system has failed. With the nitrogen system failed, the airplane may be flown at a reduced altitude and at any thrust setting to the destination. However if the lights remain on below 30,000 feet, shut down the affected engine and refer to the applicable system emergency procedure in this section.

3-58 Changed 25 June 1965

T.O. 1B-70(X)A-1

UTILITY HYDRAULIC SYSTEM FAILURES

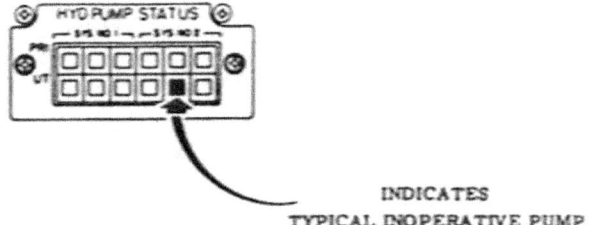

INDICATES
TYPICAL INOPERATIVE PUMP

NO. 1 UTILITY HYDRAULIC SYSTEM FAILURE.

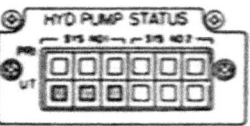

Caution

Standby system must be used to control the inlets when No. 1 utility system fails, as the automatic and manual systems are inoperative.

1. Change inlet control to standby system - Refer to AICS emergency operation in this section.
2. Tank No. 1 - Transfer fuel from tank to reduce fuel level to 12,000 pounds.
3. Engines 4, 5, and 6 - Maintain at 99½ rpm until landing gear is down.
4. Landing gear:
    a. Landing gear handle - DOWN. (If gear lowers, proceed to step 5.)
    b. Manual emergency landing gear handle - UT SYS NO 2. *
       Landing gear emergency lowering switch - DOWN.†
5. After touchdown, if one primary generator inoperative or emergency generator on.
    a. Monitor No. 2 utility hydraulic system pumps.
    b. If one pump fails, advance throttles of engines with good No 2 utility hydraulic system pumps to 80% rpm until airplane is stopped and chocked.

* Airplane AF62-001
† Airplane AF62-207

Figure 3-9 (Sheet 1 of 7)

T.O. 1B-70(X)A-1

NO. 2 UTILITY HYDRAULIC SYSTEM FAILURE.

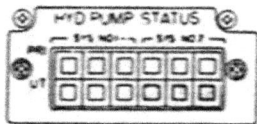

Caution
Emergency generator will be inoperative with No. 2 utility hydraulic system failure.

1. Nose ramp unlock handle - Pull and maintain airspeed above 300 knots IAS until windshield is full down.
2. Tank No. 1 - Transfer fuel from tank to reduce fuel level to 12,000 pounds.
3. Landing gear -
   a. Landing gear handle - DOWN.
   b. Manual emergency landing gear handle - UT SYS NO 1.
4. If one primary generator is inoperative, accomplish the following:*
   a. Engine shutdown and wheel brake arming switch - Check OFF.

Caution
The engine shutdown and wheel brake arming switch must not be at ARMED in the air.

   b. Battery-inverter switch - ON, on final approach.

NOTE
Emergency battery requires 3 to 5 seconds to become fully energized.

   c. Battery-inverter switch - OFF after battery-inverter light comes on. The battery-inverter light will go out, but the battery remains energized.
   d. Battery-inverter switch - ON when required.

* Airplane AF62-001

Figure 3-9 (Sheet 2 of 7)

T.O. 1B-70(X)A-1

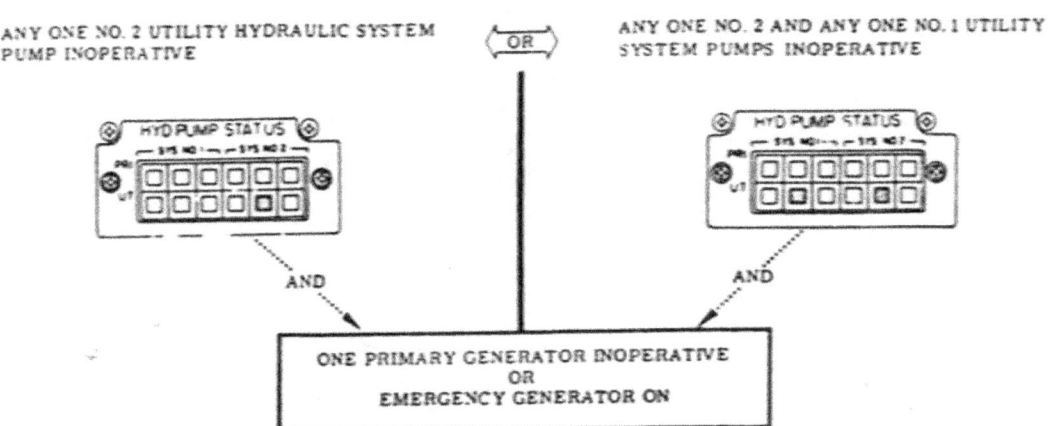

1. Decelerate using normal procedures and set up return to base.

2. Engines with good No. 2 utility system pumps - Maintain above 80% rpm until airplane has landed and is stopped and chocked.

3. Manual emergency landing gear handle - UT SYS NO 1.

4. Landing gear handle - DOWN.

Figure 3-9 (Sheet 3 of 7)

T.O. 1B-70(X)A-1

BOTH UTILITY HYDRAULIC SYSTEMS FAILED (LANDING GEAR DOWN)

THE FOLLOWING ARE INOPERATIVE:
- NOSE WHEEL STEERING
- WHEEL BRAKES
- DRAG CHUTE
- FUEL TRANSFER PUMPS IN TANKS 1, 2, 4, AND 6
- UPPER BOOST PUMP

NOTE
- Emergency generator will not operate.
- Rudder travel is limited to ± 3 degrees.

1. Throttles - Below Mach 0.5, leave engines 3 and 4 at IDLE; engines 1 and 6 at or near maximum thrust; use engines 2 and 5 for thrust control.
2. Engine shutdown and wheel brake arming switch - Check OFF, before touchdown.*

Caution

The engine shutdown and wheel brake arming switch must not be at ARMED in the air.

3. Battery-inverter switch - ON, before touchdown.*

NOTE
Emergency battery requires 3 to 5 seconds to become fully energized.

4. Battery-inverter switch - OFF after battery-inverter light comes on.*
   The battery-inverter light will go out, but the battery remains energized.
5. Battery-inverter switch - ON when required.*
6. Fly a 270 knot IAS final approach and plan so as not to go around.

Warning

If either throat panel extended caution light is on, a large thrust loss will occur.

7. Use minimum rate of descent just before touchdown, and touchdown at minimum speed because the bogies are in an intermediate folded position.
8. After touchdown, shutdown engines 2, 4 and 5.
9. Use flight controls and outboard engines for steering during landing roll.
10. Shutdown remaining engines as required.

*Airplane AF62-001

Figure 3-9 (Sheet 4 of 7)

T.O. 1B-70(X)A-1

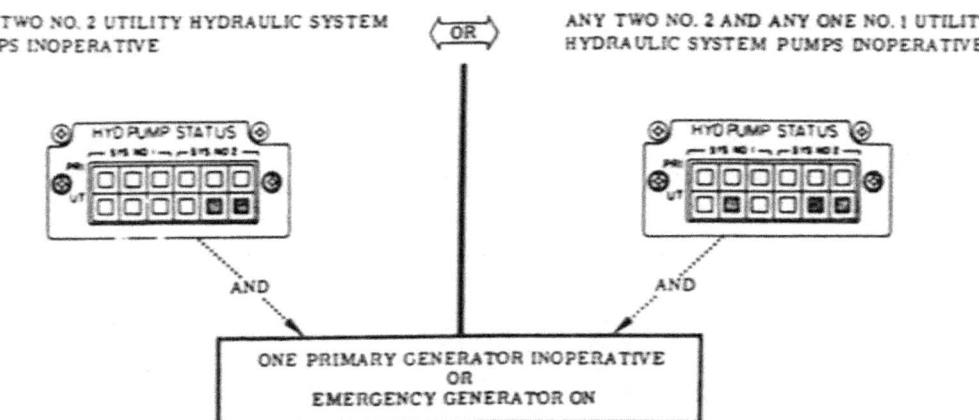

1. Change inlet control to standby system - Refer to AICS emergency operation in this section.

   NOTE
   Use of standby system is a precautionary measure.

2. Decelerate using normal procedures and set up return to base.

3. Engine with good No. 2 utility system pump - Maintain at 100% rpm until inlets are secured.

4. Engine with good No. 2 utility system pump - Maintain at or above 90% rpm until airplane has landed and is stopped and chocked.

5. Manual emergency landing gear handle - UT SYS NO 1.

6. Landing gear handle - DOWN.

Figure 3-9 (Sheet 5 of 7)

T.O. 1B-70(X)A-1

ANY ONE NO. 2 AND ANY TWO NO. 1 UTILITY HYDRAULIC SYSTEM PUMPS INOPERATIVE.

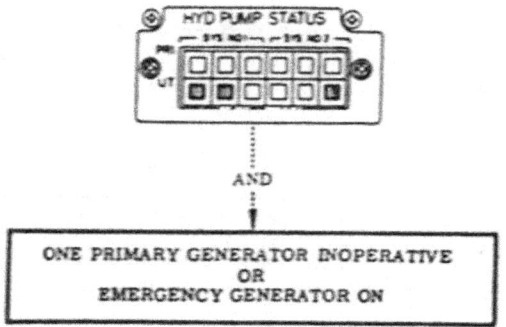

1. Change inlet control to standby system - Refer to AICS emergency operation in this section.

2. Decelerate using normal procedures and set up return to base.

3. Engines with good No. 2 utility system pumps - Maintain above 80% rpm until airplane has landed and is stopped and chocked.

4. Manual emergency landing gear handle - UT SYS NO 1

5. Landing gear handle - DOWN.

Figure 3-9 (Sheet 6 of 7)

T.O. 1B-70(X)A-1

ANY ONE NO. 2 PUMP AND NO. 1 UTILITY HYDRAULIC SYSTEM INOPERATIVE.

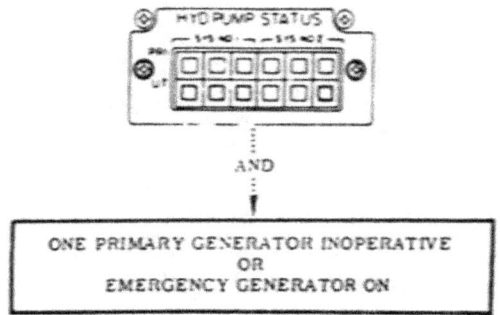

Caution

Standby system must be used to control the inlets when No. 1 utility system fails, as the automatic and manual systems are inoperative.

1. Change inlet control to standby system - Refer to AICS emergency operation in this section.
2. Tank No. 1 - Transfer fuel from tank to reduce fuel level to 12,000 pounds.
3. Engines with good No. 2 utility system pumps - Maintain at 100% rpm until inlets are secured.
4. Emergency generator switch - OFF, just prior to gear extension.
5. Landing gear:
   a. Landing gear handle - DOWN. If gear lowers, proceed to step 6.
   b. Manual emergency landing gear handle - UT SYS NO 2. *
      Landing gear emergency lowering switch - DOWN. †
6. Emergency generator switch - AUTO, after gear is down.
7. Engines with good No. 2 utility system pumps - Maintain at 80% rpm until airplane has landed and is stopped and chocked.

* Airplane AF62-001
† Airplane AF62-207

Figure 3-9 (Sheet 7 of 7)

This page intentionally left blank

T.O. 1B-70(X)A-1

FLIGHT CONTROL SYSTEM FAILURE.

PRIMARY HYDRAULIC SYSTEM FAILURE.

Refer to "Hydraulic Power System Failure" in this section.

> **WARNING**
> If complete hydraulic failure occurs, control of the airplane is impossible and the crew must eject. An attempt should be made, however, to reach a lower altitude and a suitable ejection area before ejection.

NO. 1 OR NO. 2 PRIMARY HYDRAULIC SYSTEM FAILURE.

> **NOTE**
> - If No. 1 primary hydraulic system fails, pitch augmentation, and No. 1 yaw augmentation are inoperative.
> - If No. 2 primary hydraulic system fails, roll augmentation, primary roll trim, and No. 2 yaw augmentation are inoperative.

1. Abort mission and land.
2. Monitor the good primary hydraulic system.
3. Use minimum control movements.
4. Decelerate to subsonic speed.

ONE OR MORE PUMPS FAILED IN EACH PRIMARY HYDRAULIC SYSTEM.

> **NOTE**
> Failure of two hydraulic pumps in each of the primary hydraulic systems reduces control rate to 1/2 at 100 percent rpm and to 1/3 at IDLE.

For partial failure in each primary hydraulic systems, accomplish the following:

1. Abort mission and land.
2. Keep rpm on engines with good pumps as high as conditions permit.
3. Use minimum control movements.
4. Reduce non-essential demands on the primary hydraulic systems.

FLIGHT CONTROL ARTIFICIAL-FEEL SYSTEM FAILURE.

Artificial-feel failure is indicated by an increase or decrease of control forces which causes overcontrolling, and poor control centering. If an artificial-feel failure occurs:

1. Manually control fuel sequence to obtain most forward CG.
2. Airspeed - As required.
   Adjust airspeed as required to relieve possible oscillations of the airplane.
3. If control cannot be maintained - Ejection is recommended.

FLIGHT AUGMENTATION CONTROL SYSTEM FAILURE.

All augmentation is lost if the right primary ac bus fails. The pitch and roll channels of the flight augmentation control system (FACS) have an automatic disengage feature. The yaw channels, however, can only be manually disengaged.

> **CAUTION**
> If oscillation of the airplane occurs, manually disengage the FACS.

Augmentation system disengagement or failure is indicated by illumination of

T.O. 1B-70(X)A-1

the applicable augmentation system caution light and by reduced damping of the airplane.

> NOTE
> Failure of the No. 1 primary hydraulic system centers the pitch augmentation system and locks the No. 1 yaw augmentation system. Roll augmentation is centered and the No. 2 yaw augmentation system is locked if the No. 2 primary hydraulic system fails.

When an augmentation system caution light comes on:

1. Applicable augmentation power switch - Recycle ON.
2. Augmentation engage button - After 3 minutes, push during trimmed 1-G flight.

> NOTE
> Waiting three minutes before attempting re-engagement of the augmentation system permits the augmentation system differential servos to return to a neutral position. This will prevent any violent maneuvers when the augmentation system is re-engaged.

3. Augmentation caution lights - Check.
   a. If light remains out, augmentation has re-engaged.
   b. If light remains on, or comes back on (no electrical or hydraulic failure) the particular augmentation system has failed.

TRIM FAILURE.

> NOTE
> - Primary roll trim is inoperative whenever roll augmentation is lost or turned off.
> - Primary pitch trim is inoperative whenever pitch augmentation power is lost.

RUNAWAY PITCH TRIM.

In case of runaway pitch trim, the following procedures should be used:

1. Apply force necessary to hold control column.
2. Standby trim pitch switch (center console) - As required.

> NOTE
> Use of the standby trim pitch switch automatically disengages the primary pitch trim system.

> CAUTION
> Do not attempt to use the primary pitch trim if a malfunction exists in the primary pitch trim system.

3. Standby pitch trim arming switch (left console) - OFF.

> NOTE
> When the standby pitch trim arming switch is moved to OFF, the primary trim pitch switch circuit is re-engaged and the standby pitch trim system is inoperative.

   a. If runaway pitch trim stops, use primary trim pitch switch as required.

3-64

4. Standby pitch trim arming switch (left console) - ALT ARMED.

   NOTE

   With the standby pitch trim arming switch at ALT ARMED or OFF, pitch trim control is not available from the trim button on the capsule emergency descent control grip, and the mission should be aborted.

5. Standby trim pitch switch (center console) - Use to retrim until trim is stabilized.
   a. If runaway pitch trim reoccurs, move standby pitch trim arming switch to OFF and continue flight as required.

A flaps-up landing should be planned if the runaway trim has required the use of push force on the control wheel, because the trim change caused by lowering the flaps is nose-up and will increase the push force required. If pull force results from runaway trim, flaps should be used. (Refer to "Takeoff and Landing Emergencies" in this section for flaps-up landing procedure.)

LATERAL BOBWEIGHT FAILURE.*

If the lateral bobweight fails to unlock, as indicated by excessive negative dihedral effect or by the lateral bobweight indicator, do not exceed Mach 2.6. If the lateral bobweight fails to lock, as indicated by the indicator or by marginal directional damping, descend at minimum practical speed. Do not exceed Mach 0.7 below 20,000 feet.

CANARD FLAP PRESSURE CAUTION LIGHT ON.

If the canard flap pressure caution light comes on:

1. Flap handle - Check UP.
2. Airspeed - Reduce to below 270 knots IAS.

3. Abort mission and land flaps up with approach speed increased 10 knots IAS.

CANARD FLAP SYSTEM EMERGENCY OPERATION.

There is no emergency system for operation of the canard flaps. If flaps cannot be lowered, increase approach speed by 10 knots IAS.

WING TIP FOLD SYSTEM EMERGENCY OPERATION.

   NOTE
   - If asymmetric wing tip operation is suspected when lowering the wing tips (excessive roll), immediately move wing tip position selector switch to UP in an attempt to return wing tips to full-up position.
   - If an asymmetric wing tip position occurs and both tips cannot be raised by emergency procedures, the raised wing tip should be lowered to the position that provides a symmetrical configuration. A landing can be attempted with both wing tips half down. (Refer to "Emergency Procedures With Wing Tips Half Down" in this section.)

   WARNING
   Do not attempt a landing with asymmetric wing tips,

---

* Airplane AF62-001

T.O. 1B-70(X)A-1

as unsafe flight characteristics will be encountered at low speeds.

EMERGENCY RAISING OF WING TIPS.

If the wing tips are folded and cannot be raised to the full-up position when using the normal mode of operation:

NOTE

The wing tip emergency-up system controls are on the ground test panel in the electronic equipment compartment.

1. Wing tip position selector switch - Check UP.
2. Wing tip fold mode switch - ALTR.
   a. If wing tips raise, do only steps 3 and 4.
   b. If wing tips do not raise, proceed to step 3.
3. Wing tip emergency-up system reset switch - Check OFF.
4. <u>Simultaneously</u> hold wing tip emergency-up power selector switch and wing tip emergency-up switch at each of the following positions for about 5 seconds.
   a. Wing tip emergency-up power selector switch - ESSENTIAL BUS or PRIMARY BUS.
   b. Wing tip emergency-up switch - Either WING TIP UP position.
   c. If wing tips do not raise, try all combinations, holding each for about 5 seconds.

NOTE

Once the tips have been raised using the emergency-up system, additional wing tip positioning cannot be obtained until the system has been reset.

   d. If wing tips still fail to raise, proceed to step 5.*
5. Engine shutdown and wheel brake arming switch* - Check OFF.

CAUTION

The engine shutdown and wheel brake arming switch must not be at ARMED in the air.

6. Battery-inverter switch* - ON.

NOTE

Allow 3 to 5 seconds for emergency battery to become fully activated.

7. Wing tip emergency-up switch - Hold at either WING TIP UP position for about 5 seconds.
8. After wing tips are full up, battery-inverter switch* - OFF, until further use is required.

WING TIP POSITION INDICATOR SHOWS BARBER POLE (TIPS NOT IN TRANSIT).

If wing tips are not in transit and the wing tip position indicator shows barber pole and the essential ac bus is normal, the wing tips may be hunting (moving up and down slightly) near the selected position. Wing tip hunting occurs in small enough increments so the airplane does not respond to these fluctuations. If a barber pole condition occurs:

1. Wing tip fold mode switch - ALTR. Wing tip position indicator should now show selected position.
2. Raise wing tips using normal procedures.
3. Wing tip emergency-up system reset switch - Check OFF.

---

* Airplane AF62-001

T.O. 1B-70(X)A-1

4. After wing tips are in the full up position and before landing, <u>simultaneously</u> hold the following switches at the positions indicated for about 5 seconds.
   a. Wing tip emergency-up power selector switch - Hold at either ESSENTIAL BUS or PRIMARY BUS position.
   b. Wing tip emergency-up switch - Hold at either WING TIP UP position.
   c. If tip emergency system not-reset caution light remains out, try all combinations of preceeding steps a and b for about 5 seconds each.

<u>EMERGENCY PROCEDURES WITH WING TIPS HALF DOWN</u>.

If the wing tips are lowered to the one-half position and cannot be repositioned to full up, a landing is possible. Stabilized subsonic flight can be maintained at any speed with the tips at the one-half position. With the wing tips in one-half position, the landing should be planned using a flat fast approach. (A high touchdown speed is required even at the lightest gross weights to keep the tips from contacting the ground.) Only two-thirds normal elevon control is available since the outer two elevon segments are "locked out" when the tips are not fully up. The high pattern speeds required will tend to counteract the reduced elevon control. If a landing is required with the wing tips half down, use the following procedure:

1. Reduce weight.
   Burn off all fuel above that required for at least one approach and go-around pattern.
2. Set up a heavy-weight flaps-down landing pattern with touchdown spesd at maximum tire limit speed.

   WARNING
   Keep bank angle less than 4 degrees to prevent wing tips contacting the runway.

3. Lower nose gear as quickly as possible after main gear touchdown to increase wing tip clearance.

4. Follow normal stopping procedure.

<u>EMERGENCY PROCEDURES WITH WING TIPS FULL DOWN</u>.

WARNING
If the wing tips are fully down and cannot be raised, a landing must not be attempted.

If the wing tips cannot be raised from full down, and fuel and time permit, the following procedure is recommended:

1. Manually control fuel sequence to obtain most forward CG.
2. Loiter at about 35,000 feet and 450 knots IAS until ready to eject.
3. Airspeed - Reduce as low as possible.
4. Eject.

<u>LANDING GEAR EMERGENCY OPERATION</u>.

<u>LANDING GEAR WARNING LIGHT ON ABOVE GEAR-DOWN LIMIT AIRSPEED</u>.

If the landing gear warning light (in the landing gear handle knot) comes on during flight, proceed as follows:

1. Airspeed - Reduce.
   Slow airplane to below gear-down limit airspeed.
2. Landing gear handle - Check UP.
3. Landing gear and landing gear door position - Check.
   Have gear and gear door position check by the tower on a fly-by, or by chase plane.
4. Landing gear handle - DOWN.

3-6

T.O. 1B-70(X)A-1

LANDING GEAR EMERGENCY LOWERING.

> NOTE
> There is no mechanical means of lowering the landing gear.

In case of a malfunction of the normal landing gear system, and the gear fails to extend and lock down after the landing gear handle is moved to DOWN, use the following procedure:

1. Have chase plane check gear configuration. Leave handle at DOWN.
2. Utility hydraulic system pressure gages - Check.
    a. If failure exists, refer to "Hydraulic Power System Failure" in this section.
    b. If No. 2 utility system is pressurized, proceed to step 3.
3. Landing gear emergency lowering switch - DOWN.
4. Manual emergency landing gear handle - UT SYS NO. 1.
5. Manual emergency landing gear handle - UT SYS NO. 2.

AUTOMATIC BRAKING SYSTEM FAILURE.

If the brake control caution light comes on, leave the wheel brake control switch at AUTOMATIC and use rapid on and off technique for braking. If deceleration is not felt, release the pedals and move the wheel brake control switch to MANUAL and use same on-and-off technique for braking. Be careful not to skid the tires, as skid protection is not available when at MANUAL and may not be available when at AUTOMATIC.

> CAUTION
> Apply manual braking with extreme care to prevent destruction of the tires.

NOSE WHEEL STEERING SYSTEM FAILURE.

If the nose wheels fail to follow the rudder pedals, proceed as follows:

> CAUTION
> If nose wheel steering fails (disengages) at ground speeds above 30 knots, do not attempt to re-engage until at a safe taxi speed as the disengagement may have been caused by a hard-over signal.

1. Nose wheel steering engage switch - ENGAGE then FAIL SAFE.
    Momentarily move the nose wheel steering engage switch to ENGAGE then FAIL SAFE to engage nose wheel steering if it has disengaged.
2. Landing gear emergency lowering switch - DOWN, if No. 1 utility system failed.
    Move landing gear emergency lowering switch to DOWN to provide No. 2 utility hydraulic system pressure for nose wheel steering.
3. If hard-over signal occurs when ENGAGE selected, nose wheel steering selector switch - OFF.

TIRE AND/OR DRAG CHUTE COMPARTMENT OVERHEAT CAUTION LIGHT ON.

Tire or drag chute overheating could be caused by a fire in either compartment or a failure of the following systems:
* Cooling fuel loop system.
* Landing gear and drag chute compartment cooling system.
* #2 gaseous nitrogen system.

If either caution light comes on, use the following procedure:

> NOTE
> The tire overheat caution light heat sensor contacts the tire only when the gear is retracted.

1. (Deleted)

T.O. 1B-70(X)A-1

2. Airspeed - Reduce until light goes out, or to below gear-down limit airspeed.
   a. If caution lights go out, continue flight below Mach 1.5.

   > **CAUTION**
   > When the drag chute compartment overheat caution light comes on, assume that the drag chutes are damaged.

   b. If tire overheat caution light stays on, proceed to step 3.
3. Landing gear handle - DOWN.
   Move landing gear handle DOWN and leave gear extended ten minutes to cool the tires. If possible, have chase plane check wheel wells for indications of fire. If fire is confirmed, leave gear extended and return to base.

WINDSHIELD NOSE RAMP EMERGENCY OPERATION

If the windshield nose ramp cannot be raised, the range is reduced but it is still possible to fly at supersonic speeds; and the mission requirements other than range are not affected.

> **CAUTION**
> Sustained operation above Mach 2.5 with the windshield down causes deterioration of the inner windshield glass edge attachment bonds and inner layer.

WINDSHIELD NOSE RAMP EMERGENCY LOWERING.

If the nose ramp fails to lower when the windshield nose ramp switch is moved to DOWN, proceed as follows:

> **NOTE**
> - Loss of hydraulic pressure does not affect the emergency lowering of the nose ramp.

- The windshield nose ramp cannot be raised after the emergency release handle has been pulled.

1. Nose ramp switch - Recycle.
2. Nose ramp unlock handle - Pull above 300 knots IAS.
   To ensure full engagement of windshield downlock, the handle must be pulled at speeds above 300 knots IAS.

CENTRAL AIR DATA SYSTEM FAILURE.

A central air data system failure is indicated by the air data and set nozzle altitude caution lights coming on, and/or different readings between the standby and vertical scale indicators.

Illumination of the air data caution light indicates only electrical failure or failure of the altitude monitor circuit, and does not necessarily indicate a failure in the IAS, Mach, or altitude rate portions of the central air data system. The following airplane and engine systems are affected, but not necessarily lost:
- Anticollision lights
- Engine rpm lock-up
- Engine secondary nozzle controls
- Altitude/vertical velocity indicators
- Airspeed-Mach number indicators
- Flight augmentation control system
- Flight director computer

3-69

T.O. 1B-70(X)A-1

- Auxiliary gyro platform system
- Landing gear warning system
- Air induction control system*

CAUTION

The central air data system ground test panel should not be used in flight. If used, false conditions will be introduced to the central air data system which will affect other airplane systems.

NOTE

The air induction control system for Airplane AF62-207 has its own local Mach sensing system; therefore, central air data system failure will not affect throat Mach schedule indicator presentations on this airplane.

If air data and set nozzle altitude caution lights come on:

NOTE

- When the central air data system (CADS) fails, the CADS monitor puts the flight augmentation control system on fixed gains.
- The bypass door open -caution lights will be inoperative.

1. Change inlet control to manual if at automatic.*
   a. Bypass wheels - Both aft toward OPEN as required to position and maintain shocks in crosshatch.
   b. Throat wheels - Both aft toward DECR to maintain throat at Mach 0.2 less than airplane Mach.
   c. Both throat Mach schedule mode switches - MAN.
2. Secondary exhaust nozzle standby pressure knob - To airplane altitude.

CAUTION

Incorrect operation of the knob could lead to the simultaneous failure of the secondary exhaust nozzles of the six engines.

3. Standby altimeters and airspeed indicators - Cross check with vertical scale indicators.
4. Decelerate and manually compute Mach.

NOTE

For Airplane AF62-207, if the air induction control system is being operated in the automatic mode, the throat Mach schedule indicator readings can be used to determine airplane Mach.

5. If all vertical scale indicators (except angle of attack and G) are inoperative:
   a. Speed stability switch - Check OFF.
   b. Engine rpm lockup switch - RELEASE below Mach 1.4.
   c. Landing gear warning unreliable.

ENVIRONMENTAL SYSTEMS EMERGENCY OPERATION.

LOSS OF CABIN PRESSURE.

Cabin pressurization loss is indicated by the cabin pressure altimeter, cabin over 10,000 feet caution light coming on, cabin flood flow caution light coming on, or possibility of the cabin over 42,000 feet warning light coming on. If the cabin over 42,000 feet warning light comes on, the crew must encapsulate immediately (unless wearing pressure suit) and decelerate and descend as required. Use the following procedures.

CABIN OVER 10,000 FEET CAUTION LIGHT ON.

1. Oxygen masks on or face piece closed.

2. Cabin air switch - Hold at REPRESSURE.
   Hold switch until cabin altitude is below 26,500 feet and release to OFF. If cabin altitude does not decrease, proceed to step 3.

---

*Airplane AF62-001.

T.O. 1B-70(X)A-1

3. Bleed air leak override switch - OPEN, if engines 2, 3, 4, and 5 are below 87% rpm. Proceed to step 4.

CAUTION

The OPEN position of the bleed air switch overrides the bleed air leak detection system in the environmental control equipment compartment and opens a valve to supply compressor bleed air (from engines 2, 3, 4, and 5) to the environmental system. As a result, operation of these engines above 87% rpm at this time may cause excessive bleed air temperatures in the compartment if a failure of the duct system had occurred. Therefore, if bleed air switch is at OPEN and rpm of engines 2, 3, 4, and 5 must be increased above 87%, return switch to AUTO or CLOSE before advancing throttles. This will prevent potential damage to units in the environmental control equipment compartment.

4. Cabin air switch - Hold at REPRESSURE.
   Hold switch until cabin altitude is below 26,500 feet and release to OFF. If cabin altitude does not decrease, proceed to step 5.
5. Crew air shutoff handle - Pull up.
6. If electronic equipment compartment overheat caution light comes on, cabin air switch - PURGE.
7. Decelerate and descend at 400 knots IAS minimum to an altitude not requiring pressurization.
8. Return to base with ram air scoop open.

ELECTRONIC EQUIPMENT AIR OVERHEAT CAUTION LIGHT ON AND/OR ELECTRONIC EQUIPMENT AIR TEMPERATURE ABOVE 70°F (CABIN ALTITUDE BELOW 10,000 FEET WITH CABIN AIRFLOW).

In case of an electronic equipment overheat condition (as indicated by the electronic equipment air overheat caution light coming on, or excessive temperature rise indication on the electronic equipment air temperature gage) with cabin pressure normal and airflow from the cabin air outlets, use the following steps, in order, until the situation is corrected:

1. Emergency heat exchanger water switch - ON.
2. Auxiliary cooling switch - ON.
   a. If caution light stays on, or temperature does not decrease in 30 seconds, proceed to step 4.
3. Crew air shutoff handle - Pull up if crew air temperature is excessive.
4. If below 40,000 feet, Freon temperature controller reset button - Press if compressor lockout light is on.

NOTE

The compressor reset button and lockout light are on the Freon temperature controller in the electronic equipment compartment.

5. Emergency deceleration and descent.
6. When subsonic:
   a. Cabin air switch - PURGE.
   b. Refrigeration switch - OFF.
7. Crew air shutoff handle - Push down.

EXCESSIVE CABIN TEMPERATURE.

In case of excessive cabin temperature with the electronic equipment air overheat caution light off and the electronic equipment air temperature gage below 70°F, use the following steps, in order, until the situation is corrected:

1. Cabin temperature knob - COLD.
2. Cabin temperature selector switch - MANUAL.
3. Cabin temperature selector switch - OFF.
4. Crew air shutoff handle - Pull or adjust.
5. Decelerate and descend, if required.

Changed 25 June 1965

T.O. 1B-70(X)A-1

LOSS OF CABIN AIRFLOW.

If stoppage of the recirculation air occurs, as indicated by lack of airflow from the crew air outlets and electronic equipment overheat light coming on, use the following steps in order, until the situation is corrected.

1. Air recirculating fan thermal protection override switch - OVERRIDE. If no air, proceed to step 2.
2. Cabin air switch - PURGE.
3. Make emergency descent and return to base at subsonic speed.

WINDSHIELD ICING AND FOGGING.

In case of windshield icing or fogging, use the following steps in order until the situation is corrected:

1. Engines 2, 3, 4, and 5 - Above 90% rpm, and climb to 35,000 feet.
2. Windshield anti-ice and rain removal switches - ON.
3. Cabin temperature knob - Towards HOT.
4. Crew air shutoff handle - Push in.
5. Cabin temperature selector switch - MANUAL.
6. Pitot heater switch - Check ON.
7. Make slow descent, keeping engines 2, 3, 4, and 5 at 90% rpm.

RETURN TO BASE PROCEDURE AFTER ENVIRONMENTAL SYSTEM EMERGENCY - РАМ-AIR SCOOP OPEN.

If return to base is required because of an environmental system emergency, accomplish the following:

1. Airspeed and altitude - Maintain 0.9 to 0.95 Mach between 25,000 and 35,000 feet.

   NOTE
   • If these speeds and altitudes are impractical, cruise within the following alternates: sea level to 35,000 feet and 310 to 410 knots IAS.

   • With auxiliary cooling switch at AMMONIA EMER OFF or both dc bus out caution lights on, maintain total temperature less than 30°F. This may require a lower Mach number.

2. Cabin temperature knob - Adjust. If no change in temperature occurs when adjusting the cabin temperature knot, there will be no windshield anti-ice and rain removal air available during landing.
3. Electronic equipment air temperature gage - Check below 60°F. If marginal, cruise-back should be at about 35,000 feet.

   NOTE
   Electronic equipment air overheat caution light is inoperative if PURGE position of cabin air switch is selected (ram-air scoop open).

4. Ammonia quantity gage - Check. If ammonia is low, favor high side of altitude band.

   The minimum amount of ammonia required for final descent and landing, when over the field, is 150 pounds. Advise base there will be no cooling to electronic equipment, and ground cooling units must be available at end of landing roll.

5. Water quantity gage - Check.
   a. If water is low, favor high side of altitude band.
      The minimum amount of water required for final descent and landing, when over the field, is 600 pounds.
   b. Refrigeration switch - OFF.

3-72

Changed 25 June 1965

T.O. 1B-70(X)A-1

6. Final descent - Start before the following:
   a. Ammonia quantity reaches 150 pounds.
   b. Water quantity reaches 600 pounds.

APPROACH AND LANDING - RAM-AIR SCOOP OPEN.

If an in-flight emergency has made it necessary to use emergency ram-air, accomplish the following, and land with the scoop open.

1. Crew air shutoff handle - Pull up.
2. Airspeed - Maintain 240 knots IAS minimum until final approach.

DURING LANDING ROLL - RAM-AIR SCOOP OPEN.

If an in-flight emergency has made it necessary to use emergency ram-air, accomplish the following during the landing roll:

1. Auxiliary cooling switch - Check ON. (If ammonia odor is excessive, move switch to AMMONIA EMER OFF.)
2. Refrigeration switch - OFF.
3. Air recirculating fan switch - Check ON. (OFF if ammonia supply depleted or both dc bus out caution lights on.)
4. Air recirculating fan thermal protection override switch - OVERRIDE.
5. Cabin air switch - Momentarily at REPRESSURE.
6. With airflow and ammonia cooling, continue to taxi. With no airflow and/or if electronic equipment compartment temperature is above 80 F, shut down.

OXYGEN SYSTEM EMERGENCY OPERATION.

If there are symptoms of hypoxia or other signs of insufficient oxygen, one or more of the following procedures should be used until satisfactory conditions are obtained:

1. Check all hose connections.
2. Check fit of oxygen mask or face piece.
3. Emergency oxygen actuator knob ("green apple") - Pull.
4. Manually encapsulate and remove mask or open face piece.
   Refer to "Crew Encapsulation" in this section.
5. Descend to altitude not requiring pressurization as soon as possible.

LOSS OF HATCH DURING FLIGHT.

If an escape hatch is lost:

1. Cabin air switch - PURGE.
2. Encapsulate, if necessary.
   Refer to "Crew Encapsulation" in this section.

CAUTION AND WARNING LIGHTS.

A list of the placard-type caution and warning lights with corresponding conditions and actions is shown in figure 3-10.

ABBREVIATED CHECKLIST.

The abbreviated checklist is in T.O. 1B-70(X)A-1CL-1.

Changed 25 June 1965

T. O. 1B-70(X)A-1

CAUTION AND WARNING LIGHTS

LIGHT	CONDITION	ACTION
BAILOUT	Pilot pushed bailout button.	• Handgrips - Raise. • Triggers - Squeeze.
ENCAPSULATE	Pilot actuated encapsulate caution light switch or encapsulated.	• Control column - Manually stow. • Handgrips - Raise. • Heel pedals - Press back.
CREW ENCAPSULATED	Copilot encapsulated.	------
CABIN OVER 42 000	Cabin altitude exceeds 42,000 feet.	• Cabin air switch - PURGE. • Start descent (400 KIAS minimum). • Without pressure suit, encapsulate.
FIRE	Fire and/or overheat in accessory drive system or engine compartment.	• Adjust inlets as required. • Refer to applicable procedure on page 3-16A.
NOSE STEER ON	Nose wheel steering is engaged and hydraulic pressure is available.	------
CAB OVER 10,000	Cabin altitude exceeds 10,000 feet.	• Refer to applicable precedure on page 3-70.
#3 or #4 ENG GEN OUT	Corresponding primary generator inoperative.	• Decelerate using normal procedures and return to base. • Refer to applicable procedure on page 3-53 for landing.
ESSENTIAL DC BUS OUT	Essential dc bus inoperative.	• Descend below 50,000 feet and return to base.
EMER GEN ON	Emergency generator powering essential busses.	• Decelerate using normal procedures and return to base. • Refer to applicable procedure on page 3-54 for landing.
CABIN FLOOD FLOW	Ram-air scoop is open and air recirculating fans are inoperative.	• Decelerate and descend (400 KIAS minimum). • Refer to applicable procedure on page 3-70.
PRIMARY DC BUS OUT (AIR DATA and SET NOZ ALT lights also come on)	Cabin goes to 40,000 feet. Ram-air scoop opens. Refrigeration system and vertical scale indicators (except angle-of-attack and G) inoperative. Auto AICS*, primary pitch trim, TACAN, ILS, and CADS inoperative. Flight augmentation control system on fixed gain. Engine rpm locked up.	• AICS* - Go to MAN. • Secondary exhaust nozzle standby pressure knob - Airplane altitude. • Standby airspeed and altitude - Crosscheck. • Decelerate (400 KIAS minimum), and manually compute Mach.* • Cabin air switch - Leave at OFF or PURGE. • Crew air shutoff handle - Pull.
BUS TIE OPEN	Right and left primary busses and generators are separated.	• Refer to applicable procedure on page 3-56.

*Airplane AF62-001

Figure 3-10 (Sheet 1 of 4)

Changed 25 June 1965

T.O. 1B-70(X)A-1

LIGHT	CONDITION	ACTION
EE OVERHEAT	High inlet air temperature or low air flow to electronic equipment compartment.	• Emergency heat exchanger water switch - ON. • Auxiliary cooling switch - ON if light not off in 30 seconds. • Refer to applicable procedure on page 3-71.
CHUTE OVERHEAT	Drag chute compartment overheated.	• Decelerate to Mach 1.5 or less. • Refer to applicable procedure on page 3-68.
#1 or #2 COOLING FUEL PUMP	Inoperative pump.	• Decelerate and descend. • Land at home base as soon as possible.
ROLL AUG	Roll and primary roll trim inoperative.	• Recycle augmentation power switch to ON. • Wait 3 minutes. • In level trimmed flight, push engage button.
YAW AUG 1 or YAW AUG 2	Yaw augmentation is reduced to 1/2 authority.	• Recycle respective yaw augmentation power switch. • Press engage button.
WATER AMMONIA	Water below 2500 pounds or ammonia below 250 pounds. If quantities are all right, water tank air pressure is low.	• Decelerate to subsonic speed. • Make final descent before water reaches 600 pounds and ammonia reaches 150 pounds.
TIRE OVERHEAT	Tires overheated (when gear up).	• Decelerate to Mach 1.5 or less. • Refer to applicable procedure on page 3-68.
PITCH AUG	Pitch augmentation inoperative.	• Recycle augmentation power switch to ON. • Wait 3 minutes. • In level trimmed flight, push engage button.
OVSP ARMED	Engine overspeed available.	• Disarm after take-off.
ENGINE OIL PRESS	Engine oil pressure low.	• Adjust inlets as required. • Refer to applicable procedure on page 3-43.
AGPS ALIGNING	On the ground, auxiliary gyro platform is aligning.	• Auxiliary gyro platform alignment switch - Check at OPERATE.
BRAKE CONTROL	Manual braking selected or malfunction of automatic braking. If manual braking not selected, skid protection may be lost.	• Brake within extreme caution. • Switch to MANUAL if brakes are inoperative.

Figure 3-10 (Sheet 2 of 4)

T. O. 1B-70(X)A-1

LIGHT	CONDITION	ACTION
LH or RH BYPASS DOOR OPEN *	Bypass doors not closed below Mach 0.4 and 8,000 feet.	• Standby system selector switch - PRIMARY. • Bypass standby switches - CLOSE. • Refer to applicable procedure on page 3-46F.
LH or RH BUZZ	Low frequency pressure fluctuations. Inlet is unstarted above Mach 2.0.	• Refer to applicable procedure on page 3-46G.
LH or RH UNSTART	Normal shock wave expelled from inlet.	• Refer to applicable procedure on page 3-46G.
AIR START ON	Air start ignition is on.	• Air start switch - OFF if not in use.
ADS	Low accessory drive system oil pressure for engine indicated.	• Adjust inlet as required. • Refer to applicable procedure on page 3-43.
SUMP FUEL LOW	Sump tank fuel level below 21,000 pounds.	• Manually transfer fuel or land.
FUEL INERTING	Nitrogen quantity or pressure low.	• Empty tank pumps - OFF. • Descend to 40,000 feet. • Refer to applicable procedure on page 3-53.
LH or RH THROAT PNL EXT	Throat panel less than full open below Mach 1.5* (1.4†).	• Throat Mach schedule standby switch* - DECR. • AICS mode switch - STBY. • Throat Mach schedule switch† - DCR. • Abort mission and land at home base.
AICS COOL	No. 1 AICS cooling system has malfunctioned.	• Master caution light - Push. • If AICS COOL light stays on, refer to applicable procedure on page 3-46Q.
RH or LH THROAT INDICATOR *	Throat Mach schedule indicator unreliable.	• Maintain stabilized level flight. • Refer to applicable procedure on page 3-46E.
LH or RH SHOCK AFT †	With started inlet, shock wave aft of predetermined limit.	• Refer to applicable procedure on page 3-46G.
	Bypass doors not fully closed below Mach 0.7.	• AICS mode - STBY • Bypass-Up until light goes out
LDG LT EXTENDED	(Landing light system temporarily inoperative).	- - - - - -
FLAP PRESS	Canard flaps not powered up by both hydraulic systems.	• Reduce airspeed to below 270 KIAS • Make flaps-up landing.
BLEED AIR LEAK	Pressure in environmental control equipment compartment exceeds 3 psi (± 0.25).	• Bleed air leak override switch - CLOSE.

*Airplane AF62-001
†Airplane AF62-207

Figure 3-10 (Sheet 3 of 4)

T.O. 1B-70(X)A-1

LIGHT	CONDITION	ACTION
AIR DATA (SET NOZ ALT light also comes on)	Automatic AICS unreliable.* Nozzle area pressure signal failed, area on standby. Flight augmentation control system on fixed gain.	• AICS* - Go to MAN. • Secondary exhaust nozzle standby pressure knob - Set to airplane altitude. • Standby airspeed and altimeter - Crosscheck. • Decelerate and manually compute Mach. • Refer to applicable procedure on page 3-69.
SET NOZ ALT	Nozzle area pressure signal failed, area on standby.	• Secondary exhaust nozzle standby pressure knob - Set to airplane altitude.
VIBRATION HIGH * VIB HI LIGHTS †	Engine and/or accessory drive system vibration over 50 percent.	• Adjust inlet - As required. • Refer to applicable procedure on page 3-46A.
COOL MALF	Instrumentation cooling malfunctioning.	• If COOL MALF light does not go out in 30 seconds, select system not on. • If both systems out after 2 minutes, master switch-OFF; decelerate to Mach 1.8 or less.
INSTRM OFF	Instrumentation master switch OFF, or loss of power.	• Master switch - ON. • Push restart button for 120 seconds of emergency data if required. • If both systems out after 2 minutes, master switch-OFF; decelerate to Mach 1.8 or less.
LN$_2$ LOW	Light inoperative	- - - - - -

* Airplane AF62-001
† Airplane AF62-207

Figure 3-10 (Sheet 4 of 4)

T.O. 1B-70(X)A-1

LOSS OF CABIN AIRFLOW.

If stoppage of the recirculation air occurs, as indicated by lack of airflow from the crew air outlets and electronic equipment overheat light coming on, use the following steps in order, until the situation is corrected.

1. Air recirculating fan thermal protection override switch - OVERRIDE. If no air, proceed to step 2.
2. Cabin air switch - PURGE.
3. Make emergency descent and return to base at subsonic speed.

WINDSHIELD ICING AND FOGGING.

In case of windshield icing or fogging, use the following steps in order until the situation is corrected:

1. Engines 2, 3, 4, and 5 - Above 90% rpm, and climb to 35,000 feet.
2. Windshield anti-ice and rain removal switches - ON.
3. Cabin temperature knob - Towards HOT.
4. Crew air shutoff handle - Push in.
5. Cabin temperature selector switch - MANUAL.
6. Pitot heater switch - Check ON.
7. Make slow descent, keeping engines 2, 3, 4, and 5 at 90% rpm.

RETURN TO BASE PROCEDURE AFTER ENVIRONMENTAL SYSTEM EMERGENCY - RAM-AIR SCOOP OPEN.

If return to base is required because of an environmental system emergency, accomplish the following:

1. Airspeed and altitude - Maintain 0.9 to 0.95 Mach between 25,000 and 35,000 feet.

   NOTE
   - If these speeds and altitudes are impractical, cruise within the following alternates: sea level to 35,000 feet and 310 to 410 knots IAS.
   - With auxiliary cooling switch at AMMONIA EMER OFF or both dc bus out caution lights on, maintain total temperature less than 30°F. This may require a lower Mach number.

2. Cabin temperature knob - Adjust. If no change in temperature occurs when adjusting the cabin temperature knob, there will be no windshield anti-ice and rain removal air available during landing.
3. Electronic equipment air temperature gage - Check below 60°F. If marginal, cruise-back should be at about 35,000 feet.

   NOTE
   Electronic equipment air overheat caution light is inoperative if PURGE position of cabin air switch is selected (ram-air scoop open).

4. Ammonia quantity gage - Check. If ammonia is low, favor high side of altitude band.
   The minimum amount of ammonia required for final descent and landing, when over the field, is 150 pounds. Advise base there will be no cooling to electronic equipment, and ground cooling units must be available at end of landing roll.
5. Water quantity gage - Check.
   a. If water is low, favor high side of altitude band.
      The minimum amount of water required for final descent and landing, when over the field, is 600 pounds.
   b. Refrigeration switch - OFF.

T.O. 1B-70(X)A-1

SECTION IV

AUXILIARY EQUIPMENT

TABLE OF CONTENTS	PAGE		PAGE
Environmental Systems	4-1	Oxygen Systems	4-28
Electronic Equipment Cooling System	4-13	Navigation Equipment	4-31
Drag Chute and Landing Gear Compartments Cooling System	4-14	Single-point Pressure Refueling System	4-47
Communication and Associated Electronic Equipment	4-16	Flight Test Instrumentation	4-49
		Miscellaneous Equipment	4-54
Lighting Equipment	4-25		

ENVIRONMENTAL SYSTEMS.

AIR CONDITIONING AND PRESSURIZATION SYSTEM.

Hot engine compressor air (1170°F maximum), extracted from the final stage of engines No. 2, 3, 4, and 5, is used for pressurization, ventilation, heating, rain removal, anti-icing, driving the Freon compressor of the refrigeration system, powering pneumatic components, and cooling environmental control components. (See figure 4-1.) An auxiliary cooling and pressurization system augments the Freon refrigeration system, and has a retractable ram-air scoop atop the forward fuselage that operates manually or automatically to supply ram air for emergency cooling and pressurization. The various systems are controlled or armed by switches in the crew compartment.

The engine compressor bleed air is collected in a single duct which passes forward through the fuselage fuel tanks to the environmental control equipment compartment. In the compartment the duct divides into three branches. These three branches provide high temperature air (about 1000°F), moderate temperature air (750°F to 850°F), and low temperature air (250°F maximum at sea level).

The high-temperature air branch goes to a crew compartment air-to-air heater and to windshield anti-icing system nozzles through a pressure and temperature limiting valve and shutoff valve. (The air for either right or left windshield can be shut off as desired.)

The air for the low temperature branch passes through a bleed air heat exchanger (water boiler) that reduces the temperature of the hot engine bleed air by using its heat to boil water. The steam formed is vented overboard. The low-temperature air is used to cool environmental control system components, pressurize the water tanks, pressurize the secondary pressurization system (entrance door and escape hatch seals), and provide pressurization and ventilation for the crew compartment and electronic equipment compartment. The pressurization system maintains an 8000-foot altitude cabin when above this altitude. (See figure 4-2.) Air from the low-temperature branch is mixed with engine bleed air that bypasses the bleed air heat exchanger to provide moderate temperature air for the moderate temperature branch.

Changed 25 June 1965

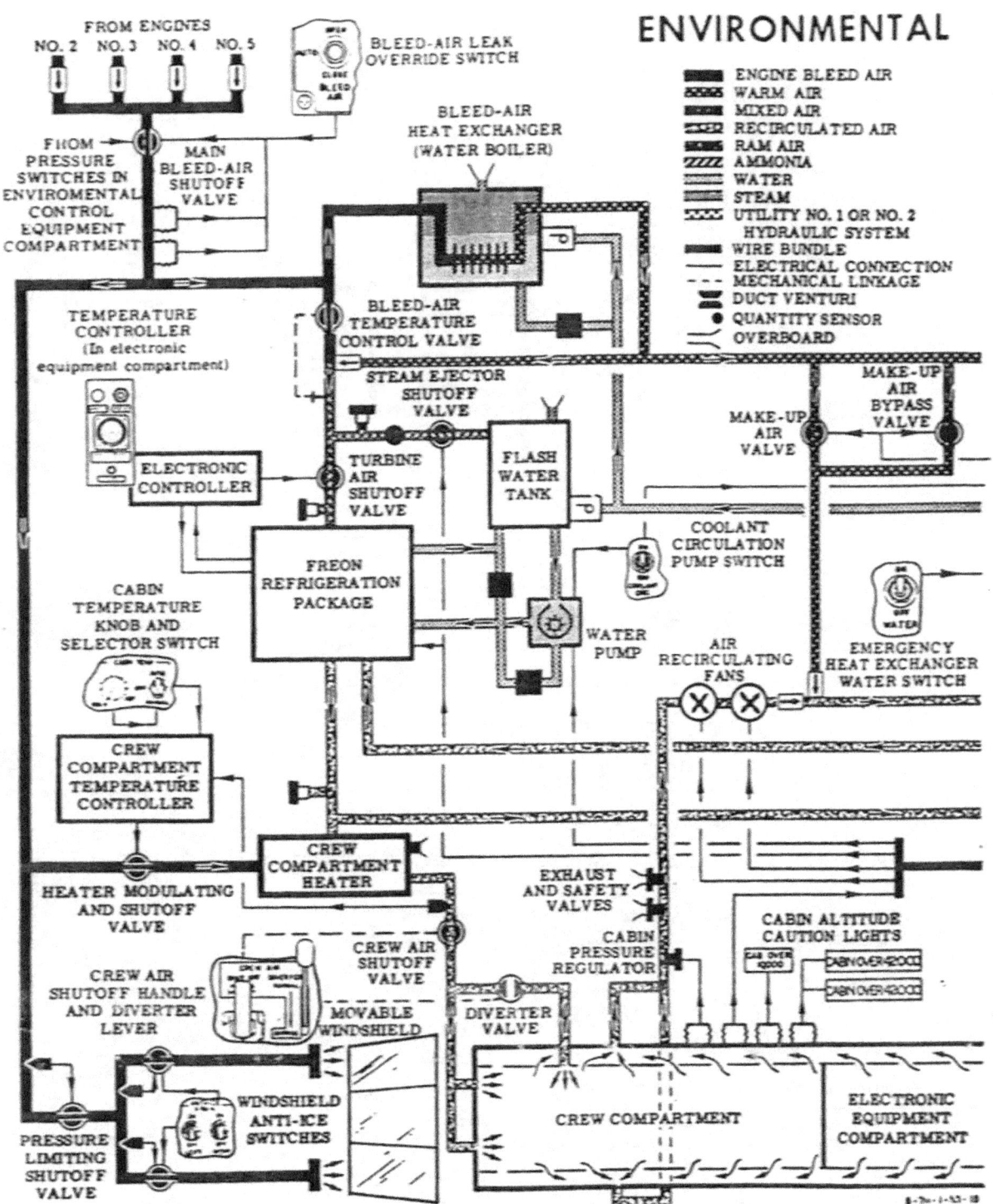

Figure 4-1 (Sheet 1 of 2)

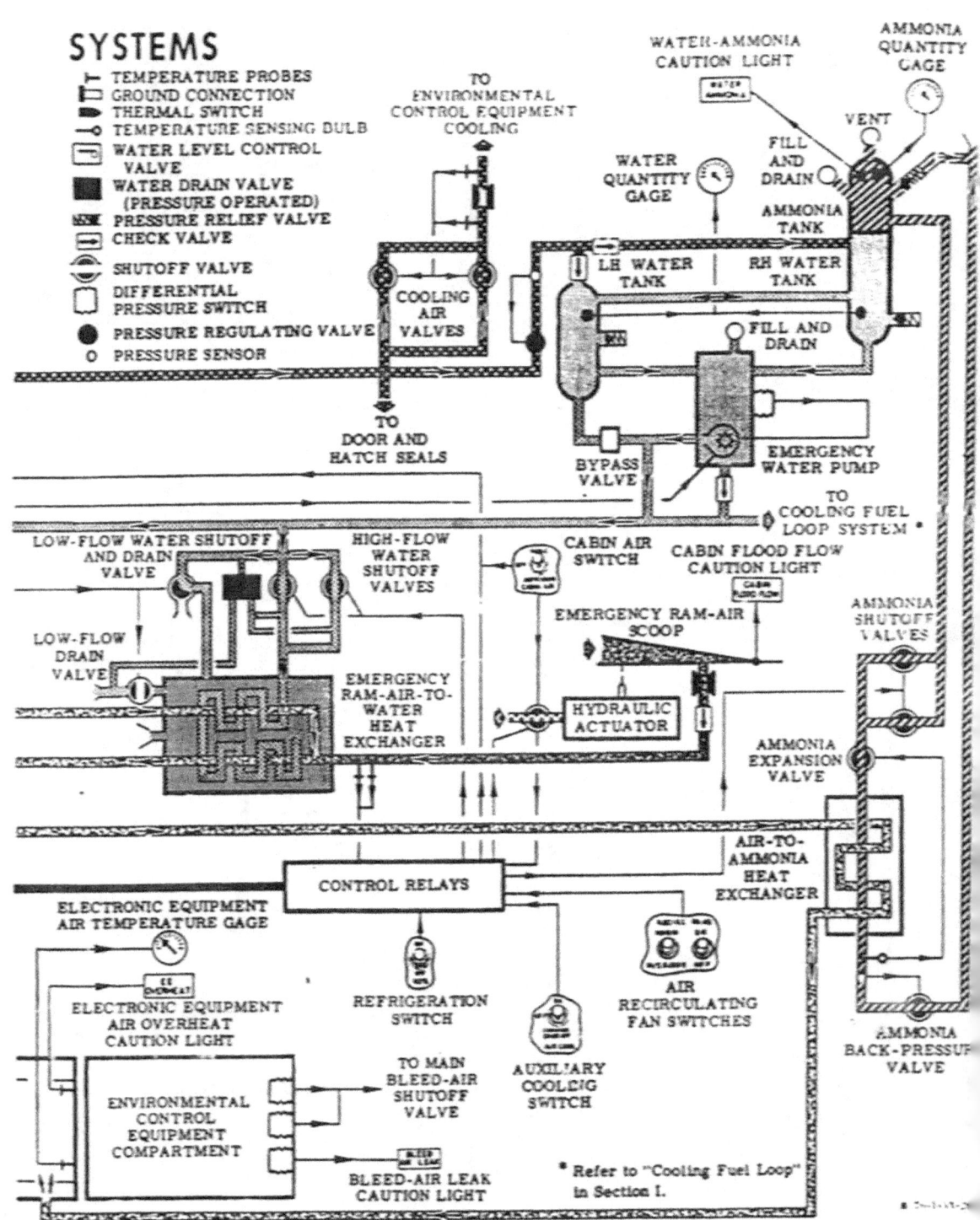

Figure 4-1 (Sheet 2 of 2)

CABIN PRESSURE SCHEDULE

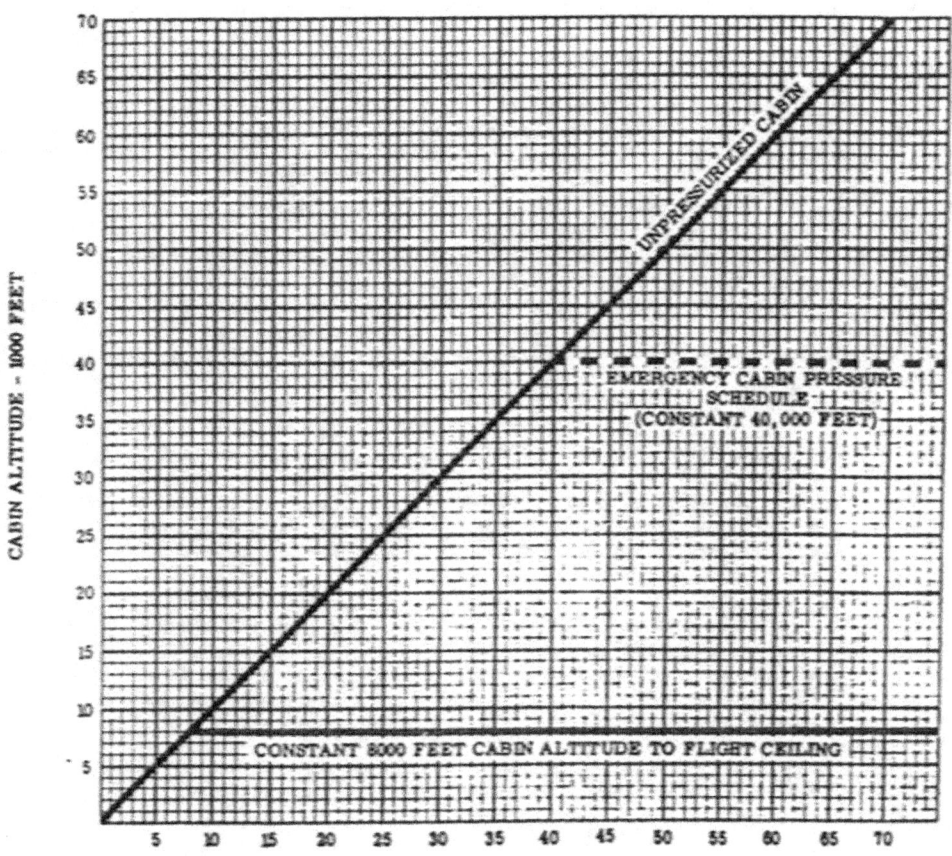

Figure 4-2

T.O. 1B-70(X)A-1

The moderate temperature air branch provides airflow for the steam ejector of a flash water tank and drives a Freon compressor turbine in the refrigeration package.

Recirculation air is exhausted from the crew compartment and electronic compartment through a thin perforated metal transpiration wall into the return portion of the air recirculation system. The air recirculation system is powered by two fans in series. For normal flight operations, the recirculation air for the crew and electronic equipment compartments is cooled by the refrigeration system. The airflow supplied to the crew compartment is heated by an air-to-air type heater using the engine compressor bleed air. The electronic equipment compartment and the instruments on the instrument panel are also cooled by the recirculated air passing through the air-to-ammonia heat exchanger. A fabric dust cover, installed when the crew entrance door is latched open, keeps dust and debris out of the airplane, and prevents the loss of cooling air out the open door. With the cover in place, the cooling air is forced to flow around the electrical equipment in the pilot's and copilot's consoles and any other equipment not receiving direct cooling, and out through the transpiration wall to return to the system.

For ground operation, and also in case of an emergency, additional cooling for the electronic equipment compartment is available through an auxiliary ammonia cooling system. A ram-air-to-water heat exchanger provides supplementary cooling of the recirculating air during normal operation at conditions of high speed flight. The ram-air-to-water heat exchanger provides primary cooling under conditions requiring emergency ram air. Cabin pressure regulator and safety valves are in the recirculation air system. The main bleed air shutoff valve is automatically closed in case of leakage of engine bleed air and pressure build-up in the fuel tank conduit, environmental control equipment compartment, or in the duct in the flight control area. The main bleed air shutoff valve can be reopened manually if the condition causing the valve to close automatically is not indicated to be a bleed air leak. All water lines which could be subjected to freezing have electric heaters. The environmental system is controlled by switches in the crew compartment. Indicators and caution lights permit monitoring of the system. Both cooled and heated air for the crew compartment and the electronic equipment compartment can be supplied during static ground operations, through the ground air conditioning inlet in the fuselage just forward of the left inlet duct.

ENGINE BLEED AIR LEAK DETECTION SYSTEM.

This system is designed to detect any leakage of bleed air from the main engine bleed air duct into the fuel tank area, environment control equipment compartment, and the flight control area. Basically, the detection system includes a main shutoff valve, a bleed air leak override switch, a bleed air leak caution light, and five pressure-sensing detection switches. Leakage of bleed air into a conduit surrounding that portion of the duct in the fuel tank area, and into a shroud surrounding the portion of the duct in the flight control area, is detected by two of these switches on the duct. Leakage into the environmental control equipment compartment from the duct is detected by two switches in the compartment. All four switches are set to sense a maximum pressure of 1 ± 0.2 psi above ambient, and to send a signal to close the main bleed-air shutoff valve if this pressure is exceeded. The fifth switch, also in the environment control equipment compartment, is set at 3 ± 0.25 psi above ambient to illuminate the caution light in the crew compartment, to indicate an overpressure condition (which may be presumed to be a bleed air leak) in this compartment. The bleed air leak override switch is used to reopen the main bleed air shutoff valve if the overpressure condition in the environmental control equipment compartment appears to be due to something other than a bleed air leak. For example, a transient pressure rise sufficient to actuate the pressure switches, can occur in the environmental control equipment compartment when the emergency ram air scoop is extended and retracted during high Mach flights. This condition comes about because the positive pressure build-up in front of the scoop during extension and retraction momentarily flows into

Changed 25 June 1965

the environmental control equipment compartment through the opening left by the closeout door that is momentarily open during the 3-second transition period. If the more serious condition of overpressure occurs due to a bleed air duct leak in the fuel tank or flight control areas, there is no light indication, and the shutoff valve cannot be reopened in flight.

REFRIGERATION SYSTEMS.

During normal operation, cooling of the recirculation air is accomplished primarily by the Freon system in the refrigeration package, and is supplemented by the emergency ram-air-to-water heat exchanger and the ammonia refrigerated auxiliary cooling system. During conditions requiring emergency ram air operation, cooling of the ram air is accomplished primarily by the emergency ram-air-to-water heat exchanger, and is supplemented by the auxiliary cooling system, and the Freon system if it is still operating. The auxiliary cooling system cools the air supplied to the electronic equipment only.

The Freon system includes an evaporator heat exchanger, condenser heat exchanger using water for cooling from a flash water tank, subcooler heat exchanger, dryer and strainer, turbine-driven-compressor, and various control valves and temperature sensors.

Temperature of recirculating supply air to the crew compartment and electronic equipment compartment can be regulated by manual or automatic control of the Freon system. However, the system is presently set for manual (full cold) operation, so that only cool recirculating air leaves the Freon system in the refrigeration package. The automatic control has been bypassed electrically. Recirculated air passes through the evaporator heat exchanger in the Freon system where it is cooled, and returns to the crew compartment and the electronic equipment compartment. Water from the flash water tank is pumped through the Freon condenser heat exchanger where the heat of the compressor and evaporator is transferred to the water. The water is returned to the flash water tank where it is flashed into steam and vented overboard. The water level in the flash water tank is maintained by water from the water storage tanks through a float type water level control valve. Engine bleed air from the moderate temperature air branch drives the Freon compressor turbine and the steam ejector that reduces the boiling point of water in the flash tank, before being exhausted overboard.

The auxiliary cooling system uses ammonia to cool recirculating air for the electronic equipment compartment during taxiing, take-off and landing operations, during in-flight equipment overheat conditions, and to cool ram air during emergency ram air operations. The system includes a pressurized supply tank and quantity indicator, an air-to-ammonia heat exchanger, and valves and sensors. The air supplied to the electronic equipment compartment passes through the ammonia heat exchanger and through and around the electronic equipment. Auxiliary cooling is manually controlled during ground operations when low engine rpm would not supply sufficient bleed air to drive the Freon compressor turbine for adequate cooling of the electronic equipment.

CAUTION

Use of the normal refrigeration (Freon) system during taxiing could damage the Freon compressor because of inadequate bearing cooling.

Adequate crew compartment cooling is provided during taxiing and take-off operation through the air recirculation system by the recirculating fans that help to draw cooling air from the electronic equipment compartment, forward to the crew members. In flight, during normal operation, the auxiliary cooling system is used to augment the Freon refrigeration system whenever the recirculated air temperature entering the electronic equipment compartment is high or the air weight flow is inadequate. These conditions are indicated by an electronic equipment air temperature gage, and by illumination of a caution light in the crew compartment that alerts the crew to turn on the system. Refer to "Auxiliary Cooling Switch", "Electronic Equipment Air Temperature Gage", and "Electronic Equipment Air

Overheat Caution Light" in this section. The auxiliary cooling system is activated automatically during all emergency ram air operations to further cool the ram air before it enters the electronic equipment compartment.

EMERGENCY RAM AIR OPERATION.

The emergency ram air scoop may be opened and closed manually or is opened automatically to provide emergency cooling, emergency pressurization, or to purge the crew compartment of smoke or other contaminates. Emergency ram air operation is capable of maintaining a 40,000 foot altitude pressure schedule in the crew compartment and electronic equipment compartment. The ram air scoop can be actuated by a switch in the crew compartment (refer to "Cabin Air Switch" in this section), or will open automatically upon signal from pressure switches in the crew compartment if crew compartment or electronic equipment compartment pressure decreases to below 35,000 feet pressure altitude. During emergency ram air operation, ram air flows through the emergency ram-air-to-water heat exchanger and Freon evaporator of the refrigeration package, and travels through the re-circulating-air ducting into the crew and electronic equipment compartments in the same manner as in normal circulation, except that all of the air is vented overboard through the safety valves after passing through the electronic equipment and crew compartments. The auxiliary cooling system is automatically activated during emergency ram air operations. The series of events that occur following automatic operation of the ram air scoop are the same as those that occur during the PURGE function of the cabin air switch. Emergency ram air operation is terminated by positioning the cabin air switch to REPRESSURE.

DEFOGGING SYSTEMS.

FIXED WINDSHIELD DEFOGGING.

The front and side panels of the fixed windshield are protected from fogging by a transparent electrical heating film deposited on the glass between the glass laminations. The heating action of this film maintains the glass surface temperature above the cabin dew point to prevent condensation. The front and side panels of the pilot's fixed windshield and the front and side panels of the co-pilot's fixed windshield are powered by different electrical busses. A thermal switch, attached to the inner surface of each glass (two for the fixed windshield front panel) controls the temperature of the glass when the defogging system is on to protect the glass from overheating.

MOVABLE WINDSHIELD DEFOGGING.

The windshield air gap filtering and drying system removes moisture, dust, and other contaminants from the air gap between the fixed and the movable windshield to prevent fogging and maintain visibility. The system consists of two subsystems: an automatic air breathing subsystem working on differential pressure, and a back-up blower-powered air circulation subsystem. Air moving through either subsystem passes through filters and dehumidifiers.

The automatic air breathing subsystem draws in or expells outside air from the forward equipment compartment. During descent, or as the windshield is raised, air from the forward compartment is drawn in through a filter and dehumidifier into the windshield air gap. A check valve allows additional filtered air to enter directly into the windshield air gap when required. During climb, or as the windshield is lowered, air is forced out through the dehumidifier and filter into the forward compartment. A check valve allows additional air to be expelled from the windshield air gap when required.

The blower-powered air circulation subsystem is turned on by the windshield defogging switch in the crew compartment. The blower draws air in from the windshield air gap through a filter and dehumidifier and returns clean, dry air to the air gap through a check valve. The blower also provides air circulation to the air space in the aft side windows.

ANTI-ICING AND RAIN REMOVAL SYSTEM.

Engine compressor bleed air from the high-temperature branch provides anti-icing and rain removal for the outer surface of the movable windshield. The high-temperature air is ejected through

T.O. 1B-70(X)A-1

two nozzles at the forward edge of the moveable windshield; one for the pilot's side and one for the copilot's side. Separate switches in the crew compartment permit individual or simultaneous nozzle airflow. Increased airflow from either nozzle can be obtained by closing the other. Over-heating of the glass is prevented by a thermal switch for each nozzle which closes the nozzle valve if the air temperature exceeds 600°F. Additional protection is provided by a supply duct thermal switch which shuts off the air to the nozzles if the air temperature exceeds 700°F at that location.

ENVIRONMENTAL SYSTEMS CONTROLS AND INDICATORS.

CREW COMPARTMENT AIR OUTLETS.

Pressurization, ventilation, cooling, and heating air enters the crew compartment through various air outlets. (See figure 1-2.) The pilot and copilot each have a manually adjustable "eyeball-type" air outlet on the outboard side of the instrument panel shroud, a manually adjustable air outlet on the control column, a manually adjustable air outlet above the side console at the forward end, and a nonadjustable foot air outlet beside each rudder pedal. This single diverter air outlet is behind the pilot's capsule.

COOLANT CIRCULATION PUMP SWITCH.

The coolant circulation pump switch (3, figure 1-9) on the co-pilot's console, receives power from the right primary ac bus* (essential ac bus†). Moving the switch from OFF to ON turns on the coolant circulation (water) pump for the flash water tank for the refrigeration package condenser. The ON position also places the emergency water pump in a standby condition by arming the water tank pressure switch so the pump will automatically operate if water tank pressure decreases to below 15 psi.

PITOT HEATER SWITCH.

The two-position pitot heater switch (29 figure 1-9), on the copilot's console, receives power from the essential ac bus.

---
*Airplane AF62-001
†Airplane AF62-207

Moving the switch from OFF to ON supplies power to the electrical heater in the pitot head in the pitot boom.

NOTE

Above Mach 1.4, aerodynamic heating will provide pitot heating and the switch should be moved to OFF.

WINDSHIELD ANTI-ICE AND RAIN REMOVAL SWITCHES.

Two windshield anti-ice and rain removal switches (4, figure 1-9), one for the left (pilot's) windshield and one for the right (copilot's) windshield, are side-by-side on the copilot's console. The copilot's switch receives power from the right primary dc bus and the pilot's switch receives power from the essential dc bus. Moving the selected switch from OFF to ON opens a temperature-controlled valve to permit hot engine bleed air to flow over the outer surface of the corresponding area of the movable windshield. However, if the air temperature in the line exceeds 600°F, the valve closes automatically to prevent overheating the windshield. A pressure-limiting and temperature-controlled shutoff valve in the windshield anti-ice and rain removal line closes if the supply air exceeds 700°F or when both windshield anti-ice and rain removal switches are at OFF. The switches can be operated simultaneously or individually, depending upon conditions. Increased airflow through the nozzles can be obtained by operating the switches individually.

WINDSHIELD DEFOGGING SWITCH.

The two-position windshield defogging switch (5, figure 1-9) is on the copilot's console. Moving the switch from OFF to ON supplies electrical power to the fan in the movable windshield defogging system and to a transparent, electrically conductive coating in the front and side panels of the pilot's and copilot's fixed windshield. The heaters in the pilot's front and side panels and the fan are powered by the essential ac bus. The heaters in the copilot's front and side panels of the windshield are powered by the right primary ac bus. The glass areas are protected from an over-

Changed 25 June 1965

heat condition when the defogging switch is ON by thermal switches attached to the inner surface of the glass. These thermal switches permit heating if the glass temperature is below 92°F. and shut off the heaters if the glass temperature exceeds 112°F.

CABIN TEMPERATURE KNOB.

The cabin temperature knob (26, figure 1-9), on the copilot's console, controls crew compartment supply air temperature. The knob can be adjusted to any position between the two extreme COLD and HOT positions. (The range of supply air temperature is from 42°F to 105°F.) Rotating the knob clockwise increases the temperature of crew compartment supply air. Counterclockwise rotation of the knob decreases the temperature of the crew compartment supply air. The knob receives power from the right primary ac bus and works in conjunction with the cabin temperature selector switch. When the selector switch is at AUTO, the crew compartment supply air temperature will be maintained automatically at the temperature level selected by the position of the knob. When the selector switch is at MANUAL, the knob is turned to manually control the crew compartment supply air temperature.

CABIN TEMPERATURE SELECTOR SWITCH.

The three-position cabin temperature selector switch (6, figure 1-9), on the copilot's console, selects the mode of cabin supply air temperature control. The switch receives power from the right primary ac bus. With the switch at AUTO, the temperature selected by the cabin temperature knob is maintained automatically. Moving the switch to MANUAL provides manual control of the crew compartment supply air temperature through the cabin temperature knob in case of a malfunction of the automatic control. Moving the switch to OFF shuts off the crew compartment supply air heating system by closing the heater modulating and shutoff valve.

REFRIGERATION SWITCH.

The two-position refrigeration switch (7, figure 1-9), on the copilot's console, receives power from the right primary dc and ac busses. Moving the switch to ON turns on the refrigeration package through control relays, and controls and puts the flash water tank steam ejector valve (which is controlled by a pressure switch) on standby. The refrigeration switch is mechanically latched at ON and must be pulled out before it can be moved to OFF. Moving the switch to OFF turns off engine bleed air in the refrigeration package, and the flash water tank steam ejector shutoff valve. This routes additional engine bleed air to the windshield anti-ice and rain removal system if required.

AIR RECIRCULATING FAN SWITCH.

The two-position air recirculating fan switch (22, figure 1-3), on the pilot's instrument panel, controls both fans in the cabin air recirculation system. Moving the switch to ON turns on both air recirculation fans in the air recirculation dict. One fan is powered by the right primary ac bus and the other fan is powered by the left primary ac bus. The fans are shut off automatically if emergency ram air is automatically initiated, if the cabin air switch is at PURGE, or if there is an overheat condition in the fans.

AIR RECIRCULATING FAN THERMAL PROTECTION OVERRIDE SWITCH.

The two-position thermal protection override switch (23, figure 1-3), is on the pilot's instrument panel. With the switch at NORMAL, thermal protection is provided for the two air recirculating fans in case of a fan overheat condition. However, in case of an emergency and the fans are required after fan shutdown by the thermal protection device, moving the switch OVERRIDE bypasses the thermal protector and permits operation of the fans.

The thermal protection override switch is mechanically latched at NORMAL and must be pulled out before it can be moved to the OVERRIDE position.

CAUTION

Use of the thermal protection override switch should be limited to landing and taxiing to prevent destruction of the fan.

T.O. 1B-70(X)A-1

NOTE

For all normal operation, the switch should be at NORMAL.

BLEED AIR LEAK OVERRIDE SWITCH.

The bleed air leak override switch (25, figure 1-3) on the pilot's instrument panel, is used for overriding the two pressure switches in the environmental control equipment compartment, and for reopening the main bleed air shutoff valve if it had closed automatically due to an overpressure condition in this compartment. If the overpressure is due to a duct leak in the fuel tank or flight control area, the switch will not open the shutoff valve. The switch is labeled OPEN, AUTO, and CLOSE. The OPEN position performs the override function of reopening the valve. With the switch at AUTO, the bleed air leak detection system functions in the normal manner. The CLOSE position is used to manually close the main bleed air shutoff valve. The bleed air leak override switch receives power from the right primary ac and essential ac busses.

NOTE

If the bleed air leak caution light comes on and stays on, the switch should be immediately moved to CLOSE.

CABIN AIR SWITCH.

The three-position cabin air switch (24, figure 1-3), on the pilot's instrument panel receives power from the right primary ac and essential ac busses. Moving the switch to PURGE opens the emergency ram-air scoop (hydraulically operated), turns off the air recirculation fans if on, initiates full cold operation of the emergency ram-air to water heat exchanger by opening the normally closed high-flow stage water shutoff valves to admit water (if ram air is above 170°F), turns on ammonia for emergency refrigeration (air-to-ammonia) heat exchanger, shuts off engine bleed air to the air recirculation system, resets cabin pressure safety valves to 40,000-foot altitude pressure schedule, and opens an exhaust valve if the airplane is below about 40,000 feet. (The cabin flood flow caution light comes on whenever the emergency ram-air scoop is opened.) Moving the switch to OFF cancels all of the purge functions if cabin altitude is below 26,500 feet.

NOTE

Duration of steady-state emergency ram-air operation is limited by the water and ammonia consumption. At high altitude and high speeds, it is limited to about 2 minutes. After the 2-minute limit, decelerate and descend as required. The water and ammonia quantity gages must be monitored.

Holding the switch at REPRESSURE terminates the 40,000-foot cabin schedule by closing the safety valves, and closes the emergency ram-air scoop, and opens the make-up air valve and the make-up air bypass valve to provide rapid repressurization of the cabin. The switch should be held at REPRESSURE until the cabin altitude is below 26,500 feet, then released. In addition to canceling all of the purge functions, the REPRESSURE position of the switch also is used momentarily if a gradual loss of pressurization is discovered and then should be used each time the cabin over 10,000 feet caution light comes on. The cabin air switch is spring-loaded from REPRESSURE to OFF. It is mechanically latched at OFF and must be pulled out before it can be moved to PURGE. Refer to "Emergency Ram Air Operation" in this section.

NOTE

If the crew compartment and electronic equipment compartment do not repressurize, the engine bleed air leak detection system may have closed the main shutoff valve. In this event, if the bleed air leak caution light is out, the bleed air leak override switch should be moved to OPEN. The four inboard engines should be throttled back, and airspeed reduced. This will help to lower bleed air temperature if the duct had failed in the environmental control equipment compartment.

Changed 25 June 1965

T.O. 1B-70(X)A-1

EMERGENCY HEAT EXCHANGER WATER SWITCH.

The emergency heat exchanger water switch (2, figure 1-9) on the co-pilot's console, controls operation of the low flow stage water shutoff and drain valve and low flow stage drain valve of the emergency ram-air-to-water heat exchanger. Moving the switch to ON opens the low flow stage water shutoff and drain valve to supply water to the ram-air-to-water heat exchanger, and closes the low flow stage drain valve. Moving the switch to OFF closes the low flow stage water shutoff and drain valve to stop the flow of water and allow excess water to drain overboard from the heat exchanger through the valve. At the same time, the low flow stage drain valve opens to permit additional drainage at the heat exchanger. The switch receives power from the essential dc bus.

NOTE

The emergency heat exchanger water switch should be moved to ON only at speeds above Mach 1.7. At lower speeds, the water is not required, and the water would drain overboard and possibly freeze and break off of the airplane.

CREW AIR DIVERTER LEVER.

The crew air diverter lever (15, figure 1-9), on the copilot's console, mechanically controls a valve in the crew compartment supply air duct. Moving the lever forward to NORMAL supplies full air to the various crew outlets. Moving the lever aft to BYPASS diverts 30 percent of the air into the aisle behind the pilot's capsule.

NOTE

Leave air diverter lever at NORMAL at all times and control airflow with the crew air shutoff handle.

CREW AIR SHUTOFF HANDLE.

The crew air shutoff "T" handle (19, figure 1-9), on the copilot's console, has a ratchet type lock and mechanically controls an air shutoff valve in the crew compartment supply air branch to vary airflow to the crew compartment. The handle is pulled up to close the valve which diverts all of the cabin airflow to the electronic equipment compartment when engines No. 2, 3, 4, and 5 are below 81% rpm. The handle is rotated and pushed down to open the valve if engines No. 2, 3, 4, and 5 are operating above 81% rpm or if engines No. 3 and 4 are operating above 87% rpm.

NOTE

The handle should be pulled up whenever the refrigeration system is not operating, ground air conditioning is not available, and the air recirculation fans are on to route all airflow to the electronic equipment compartment.

QUANTITY GAGES TEST BUTTON.

The ammonia, water, and oxygen quantity gages are tested simultaneously by a button (20A, figure 1-3). The button is on the pilot's instrument panel and receives power from the essential ac bus. Pressing and holding the button in causes the pointers of the ammonia, water, and oxygen quantity gages to move towards "0". When the button is released, all pointers should return to the previous indication.

FREON COMPRESSOR LOCKOUT INDICATOR LIGHT AND RESET BUTTON.

The compressor lockout indicator light and the compressor reset button are side-by-side on the Freon temperature controller, forward of the circuit breaker panels on a rack in the electronic equipment compartment. The light comes on if the refrigeration package Freon compressor is shut down automatically as the result of Freon overtemperature or overpressure, or because of overspeed of the compressor turbine. If the lockout light is on, the reset button may be used in an attempt to restore compressor operation. The reset button is effective only if the Freon pressure or temperature has decreased to acceptable limits. If a turbine overspeed condition caused the compressor lockout, the reset button will not re-engage the compressor, and the malfunction must be corrected before the compressor is operable. The

T.O. 1B-70(X)A-1

refrigeration package compressor lockout and reset circuits are powered by the right primary dc bus.

ELECTRONIC EQUIPMENT AIR TEMPERATURE GAGE.

Refer to "Electronic Equipment Cooling System Controls and Indicators" in this section.

CABIN PRESSURE ALTIMETER.

The cabin pressure altimeter (26, figure 1-3), on the pilot's instrument panel, has a range of 0 to 80,000 feet. The cabin altimeter indicates cabin altitude and operates by cabin pressure.

AMMONIA QUANTITY GAGE.

Refer to "Electronic Equipment Cooling System Controls and Indicators" in this section.

WATER QUANTITY GAGE.

The water quantity gage (20, figure 1-3), on the pilot's instrument panel, has a range of 0 to 5000 pounds in 100-pound increments. The gage is powered by the essential ac bus and indicates the total quantity of water available in both storage tanks for the air conditioning and pressurization system. A yellow band on the gage shows the range of limited water supply. The upper end of the band is the minimum quantity necessary for an emergency descent and return to the base. (The water-ammonia caution light also comes on when the gage pointer is below this point.) The lower end of the band is the minimum quantity of water necessary for final descent and landing. The gage can be tested by the quantity gages test button.

WATER-AMMONIA CAUTION LIGHT.

The placard-type water ammonia caution light (1, figure 1-7) on the center console, is powered by the essential ac bus. The light comes on to show "WATER-AMMONIA" when water quantity decreases below 2500 pounds, or ammonia quantity decreases below 250 pounds, or when the emergency water pump is operating (due to pressure in the water tanks decreasing below 15 psi).

NOTE

The light will not come on to indicate pump operation, as a result of low pressure in the water tanks, when the coolant circulation pump switch is at OFF. The light will come on to indicate low quantity water or ammonia regardless of the position of the coolant circulation pump switch.

If the coolant circulation pump switch is ON during engine start, the light will be on. The light should go out within 10 minutes after any one of the four inboard engines is above 71% rpm (indicating enough bleed air is available to pressurize the water tanks above 15 psi).

CABIN OVER 10,000 FEET CAUTION LIGHT.

The placard-type cabin over 10,000 feet caution light (1, figure 1-7), on the center console is powered by the essential ac bus. The light comes on to show "CAB OVER 10,000" whenever the cabin pressure altitude is above 10,000 feet.

ELECTRONIC EQUIPMENT AIR OVERHEAT CAUTION LIGHT.

Refer to "Electronic Equipment Cooling System Controls and Indicators" in this section.

BLEED AIR LEAK CAUTION LIGHT.

This placard-type light (5, figure 1-7) on the center console, comes on to read BLEED AIR LEAK when there is a leakage of engine bleed air in the environmental control equipment compartment sufficient to cause a pressure buildup that exceeds 3±0.25 psi over ambient. The light is powered by the right primary ac and essential ac busses.

CABIN FLOOD FLOW CAUTION LIGHT.

The placard-type cabin flood flow caution light (1, figure 1-7), on the center console, is powered by the essential ac bus. The light comes on to show "CABIN FLOOD FLOW" whenever the emergency ram-air scoop is open.

DRAG CHUTE COMPARTMENT OVERHEAT CAUTION LIGHT.

Refer to "Drag Chute and Landing Gear Compartments Cooling System" in this section.

CABIN OVER 42,000 FEET WARNING LIGHTS.

Two placard-type cabin over 42,000 feet warning lights (3, figure 1-3 and 12, figure 1-4), one on the pilot's and one on the copilot's instrument panel, are powered by the essential ac bus. The lights come on to show "CABIN OVER 42000" if the cabin altitude exceeds 42,000 feet.

WARNING
Crew must encapsulate immediately if the cabin over 42,000 feet warning lights come on and initiate an emergency descent to an altitude not requiring pressurization.

NORMAL OPERATION OF ENVIRONMENTAL SYSTEMS.

These procedures are included in normal operation in Section II because a certain relationship must be maintained between normal procedures and operation of the environmental systems.

EMERGENCY OPERATION OF ENVIRONMENTAL SYSTEMS.

Refer to "Environmental Systems Emergency Operation" in Section III.

ESCAPE CAPSULE PRESSURIZATION SYSTEM.

Each capsule is automatically sealed and pressurized, if required by the altitude, whenever the capsule doors are closed. However, if pressurization is not required, only the seals are pressurized. Each capsule pressurization system is independent of the airplane-system and consists of four 1800 psi pressurization cylinders, two on the back of each capsule and two under the seat of each capsule. These cylinders contain a breathable mixture of 60 percent oxygen and 40 percent nitrogen. The mixture, after passing through a pressure controller, is used to inflate the capsule shell and door seals and for pressurizing the capsule interior. The exact endurance time for the capsule pressurization system cannot be given because of the many variables possible at each situation.

Typically, however, it is possible to encapsulate at the maximum flight altitude, trapping ambient pressure, then accomplish an emergency descent to 40,000 feet, followed by decapsulation. At this point, it is possible to re-encapsulate for an immediate ejection while again trapping ambient pressure. A pressure relief valve prevents over-pressurization. A system pressure gage and filler valve is located in the capsule. The capsule pressurization system is shown in figure 4-3.

CAPSULE SEAL DEFLATE BUTTON.

A yellow and black striped capsule seal deflate button (figure 1-36), is flush with the inside left wall of each capsule. A decal below the button is

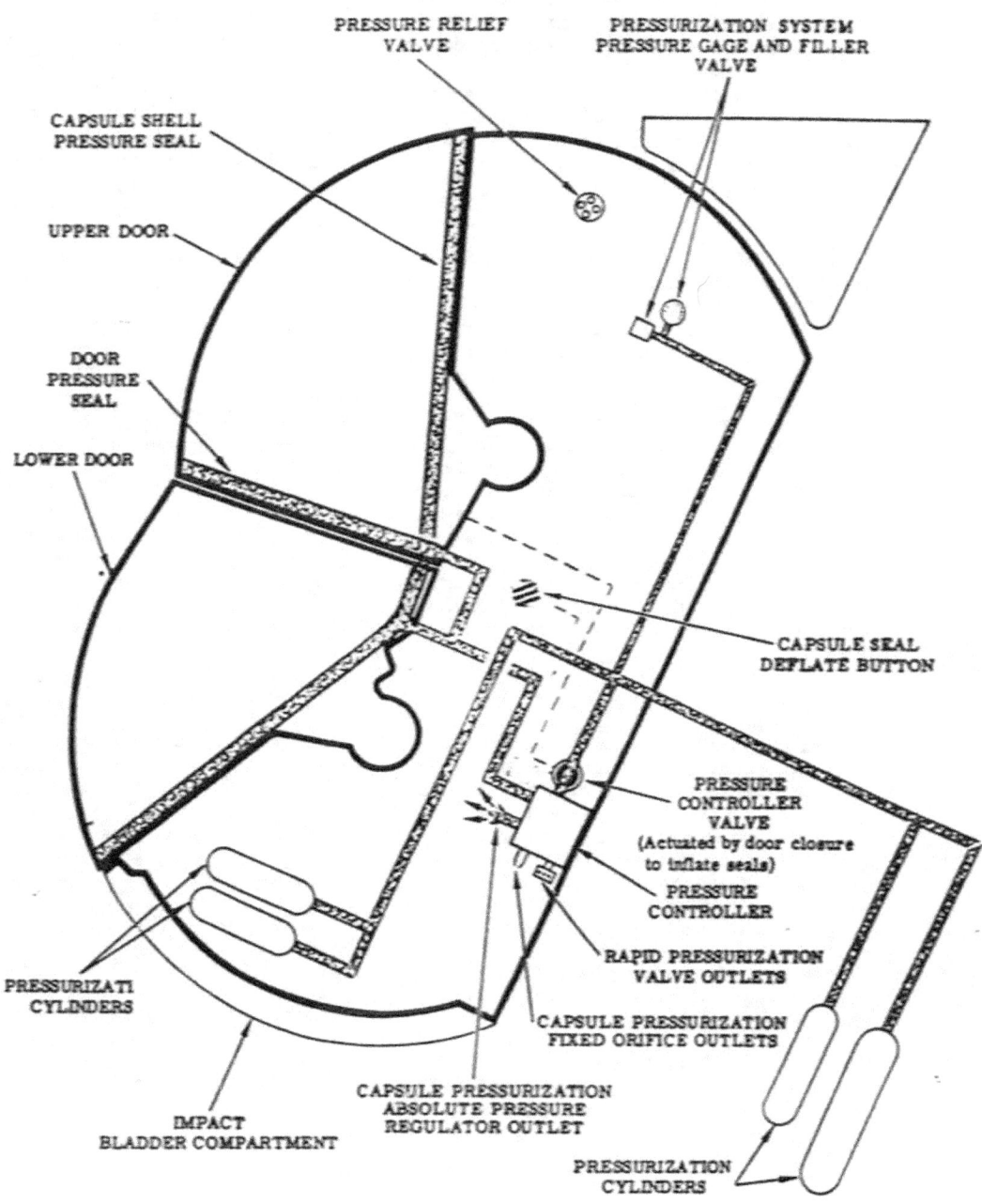

Figure 4-3

T.O. 1B-70(X)A-1

marked "SEAL DEFLATE." Pressing the button to a latched position shuts off the pressure controller and dumps the seal pressure so that the capsule doors may be opened. The button and the pressure controller are automatically recocked when the capsule doors are opened. A pin protrudes through the capsule wall from the back of the button for external use.

CAPSULE PRESSURIZATION CYLINDER PRESSURE GAGE AND FILLER VALVE.

The capsule pressurization cylinder pressure gage and the filler valve (figure 1-36) are mounted as a unit in the upper right rear corner of each capsule. The mounting area of the gage is painted grey and the filler valve is painted maroon and is marked "PRESS." The gage indicates the pressure in the cylinders. During servicing, the required pressure on the gage for the prevailing cabin temperature is determined by using a temperature-pressure chart to ensure a full system.

CAPSULE PRESSURE RELIEF VALVE.

A capsule pressure relief valve (figure 1-36), on the upper inside left corner of each capsule, opens when the capsule internal pressure exceeds 9.4(±.2) psi or when the external pressure exceeds the internal pressure by 0.5(±.2) psi. Pushing in and rotating the end of the valve aligns ON or OFF with an index mark. Rotating the end counterclockwise to ON provides the relief valve function. The valve should be normally left at ON. The OFF position should not be used.

CAUTION

Manual use of the pressure relief valve is for maintenance testing only and must be on as indicated by alignment of ON with the index mark.

ELECTRONIC EQUIPMENT COOLING SYSTEM.

Air for cooling the electronic equipment is provided by a branch of the cabin air recirculation system. The air passes through an air-to-ammonia heat exchanger. After passing through the heat exchanger, the air passes into the electronic equipment compartment and over a temperature sensor and a cooling effect detector. Air is exhausted from the compartment through the transpiration wall to the recirculation air return duct. The air-to-ammonia heat exchanger is put into operation by a switch in the crew compartment. An electronic equipment over-temperature condition is sensed by a temperature sensor and cooling effect detector located in the compartment and is indicated by a temperature gage and caution light in the crew compartment.

ELECTRONIC EQUIPMENT COOLING SYSTEM CONTROLS AND INDICATORS.

AUXILIARY COOLING SWITCH.

The three-position auxiliary cooling switch (30, figure 1-9), on the copilot's console, receives power from the primary and essential dc busses. The switch is mechanically latched at OFF and must be pulled out before it can be moved to the ON or AMMONIA EMER OFF positions. If an electronic equipment compartment overheat condition is indicated by the electronic equipment air temperature gage or caution light, the switch should be moved to ON. Moving the switch to ON starts the ammonia auxiliary cooling system. The ammonia quantity gage must be monitored when the switch is at ON. Moving the switch to AMMONIA EMER OFF shuts off the ammonia flow. The AMMONIA EMER OFF position should be used only in case there is excessive ammonia odor in the crew compartment and emergency ram-air is required. Moving the switch to OFF shuts off the ammonia auxiliary cooling system.

Changed 25 June 1965

T.O. 1B-70(X)A-1

CABIN AIR SWITCH.

Refer to "Environmental Systems Controls and Indicators" in this section.

QUANTITY GAGES TEST BUTTON.

Refer to "Environmental Systems Controls and Indicators" in this section.

ELECTRONIC EQUIPMENT AIR TEMPERATURE GAGE.

The electronic equipment air temperature gage (19, figure 1-3), on the pilot's instrument panel, is powered by the essential ac bus. The gage is marked "EE TEMP" and is calibrated in 10° increments from 0 to 100°F. The gage indicates the temperature of the supply air to the electronic equipment.

AMMONIA QUANTITY GAGE.

The ammonia quantity gage (21, figure 1-3), on the pilot's instrument panel, has a range of 0 to 700 pounds in 10-pound increments. The gage is powered by the essential ac bus and indicates the quantity of ammonia available for auxiliary cooling. A yellow band on the gage shows the range of limited ammonia supply. The upper end of the band is the minimum quantity necessary for an emergency descent and return to the base. (The water-ammonia caution light also comes on when the gage pointer is below this point.) The lower end of the band is the minimum quantity of ammonia necessary for final descent and landing. The gage can be tested by the quantity gages test button.

WATER QUANTITY GAGE.

Refer to "Environmental Systems Controls and Indicators" in this section.

ELECTRONIC EQUIPMENT AIR OVERHEAT CAUTION LIGHT.

The placard-type electronic equipment air overheat caution light (1, figure 1-7), on the center console, is powered by the essential ac bus. The light comes on to show "EE OVERHEAT" if the temperature or weight flow of air over the electronic equipment is inadequate. This light is inoperative during ram air operation.

CABIN FLOOD FLOW CAUTION LIGHT.

Refer to "Environmental Systems Controls and Indicators" in this section.

WATER-AMMONIA CAUTION LIGHT.

Refer to "Environmental Systems Controls and Indicators" in this section.

NORMAL OPERATION OF ELECTRONIC EQUIPMENT COOLING SYSTEM.

These procedures are included in normal operation in Section II because a certain relationship must be maintained between normal procedures and operation of the electronic equipment cooling system.

EMERGENCY OPERATION OF ELECTRONIC EQUIPMENT COOLING SYSTEM.

Refer to "Environmental Systems Emergency Operation" in Section III.

DRAG CHUTE AND LANDING GEAR COMPARTMENTS COOLING SYSTEM.

A separate cooling system for the drag chute and gear compartments provides cooling for the drag chutes and the

Changed 25 June 1965

DRAG CHUTE AND LANDING GEAR COMPARTMENTS COOLING SYSTEM

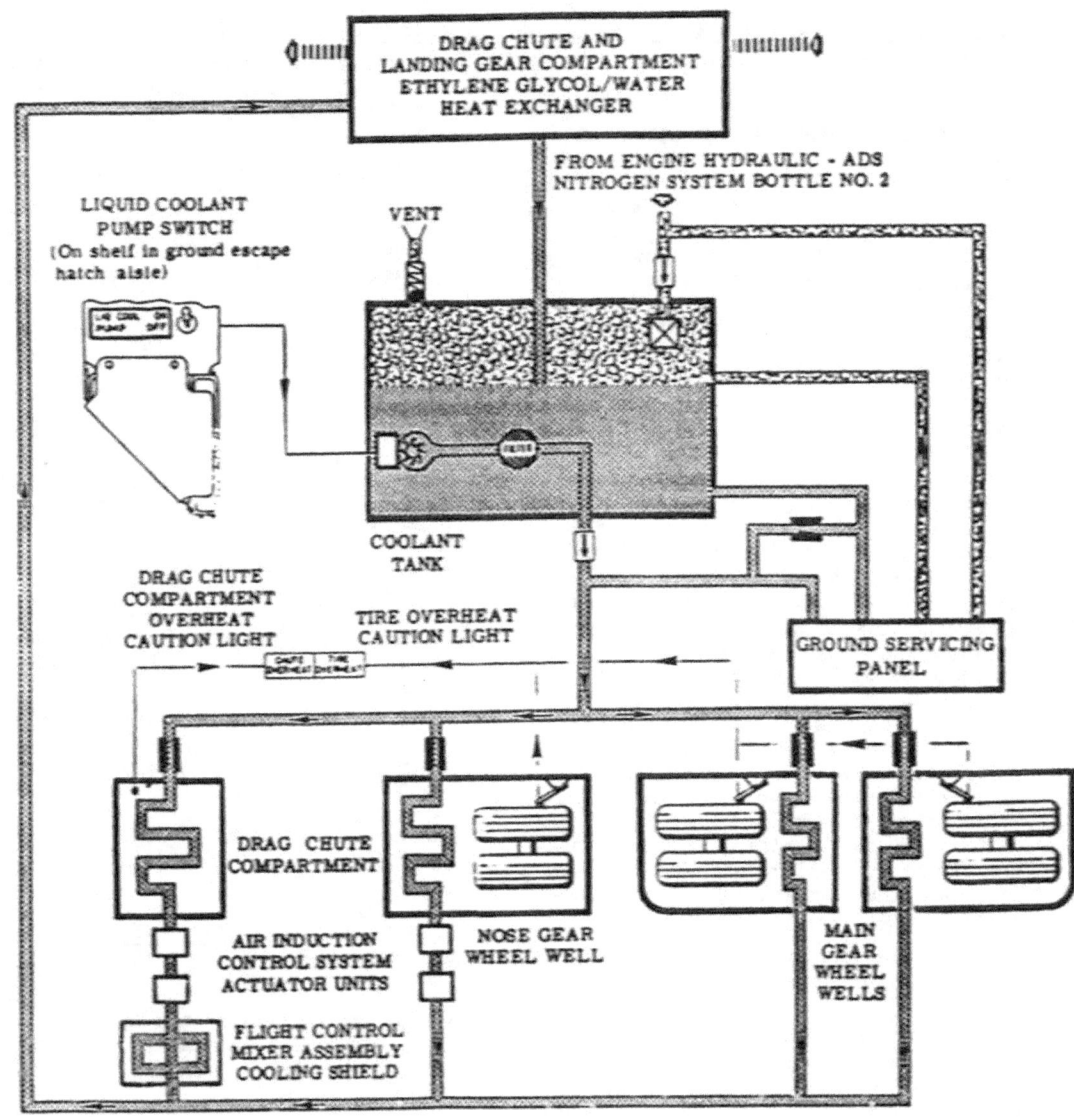

Figure 4-4

T.O. 1B-70(X)A-1

nose and main gear tires. (See figure 4-4.) This cooling system, using ethylene glycol and water flowing through the walls of the compartments, includes a coolant tank pressurized by nitrogen from the No. 2 engine-accessory drive system nitrogen supply bottle (refer to "Nitrogen Systems" in Section I), a pump, a coolant-to-fuel heat exchanger, and associated valves and temperature sensors. The coolant picks up the compartment heat, passes through and is cooled by the heat exchanger (which uses cooling loop fuel), and returns to the tank to repeat its cycle. (Refer to "Fuel Supply System" in Section I.) A drag chute compartment overheat condition is indicated by a caution light in the crew compartment. The nose and main gear tire overheat caution light comes on if the tires are overheated.

LIQUID COOLANT PUMP SWITCH.

This switch controls operation of the coolant pump for drag chute and landing gear compartments, and the air induction control system actuator cooling systems. (See figure 4-4.) Moving the switch from OFF to ON turns on the coolant pump. The switch is mechanically latched at both positions and must be pulled out to move the switch in either direction. The liquid coolant pump switch receives power from the right primary ac bus, and is on a shelf on the inboard side of the ground escape hatch aisle.

DRAG CHUTE COMPARTMENT OVERHEAT CAUTION LIGHT.

The placard-type drag chute compartment overheat caution light (1, figure 1-7), on the center console, is powered by the essential ac bus. The light comes on to show "CHUTE OVERHEAT" when the temperature of the drag chute compartment walls is above about 250°F. When the overheat light comes on, landing procedures should be planned on the assumption the drag chutes are damaged.

TIRE OVERHEAT CAUTION LIGHT.

The placard-type tire overheat caution light (1, figure 1-7), on the center console, is powered by the essential ac bus. The light comes on to show "TIRE OVERHEAT" when any of the temperature sensors against the nose and main gear tires record a temperature over about 275°F. (This temperature is below the blowoff temperature of the wheel thermal plug.) As a result of the sensor mounting, the sensor does not contact the tire when the gear is not up and locked. The sensor for the nose wheel tires does not contact the tires until 10 minutes after the nose gear has retracted.

NORMAL OPERATION OF DRAG CHUTE AND LANDING GEAR COMPARTMENTS COOLING SYSTEM.

The drag chute and gear compartment cooling system is put into operation when the coolant circulation pump is turned ON. Refer to "Normal Operation of Environmental Systems" in this section.

COMMUNICATION AND ASSOCIATED ELECTRONIC EQUIPMENT.

TABLE OF COMMUNICATIONS AND ASSOCIATED ELECTRONIC EQUIPMENT.

See figure 4-5. See figure 1-1 for antenna locations.

UHF COMMAND RADIO - AN/ARC-50.

Two independent UHF command radio systems provide air-to-air and air-to-ground communications between the frequencies of 225 to 399.95 megacycles. Two identical transmitters and receivers are used, controlled by two separate control panels: one on the center console and one on the pilot's console. The transmitter audio signal is directed through the AN/AIC-18 communications amplifier. Two separate receivers (a

4-16   Changed 25 June 1965

T. O. 1B-70(X)A-1

COMMUNICATION AND ASSOCIATED ELECTRONIC EQUIPMENT

TYPE	DESIGNATION (AN)	FUNCTION	RANGE	CONTROL LOCATION
UHF RADIO (COMMAND)	ARC-50	TWO-WAY VOICE COMMUNICATION	LINE OF SIGHT	LEFT CONSOLE AND CENTER CONSOLE
INTERCOM SYSTEM	AIC-18	CONTROLS AND SELECTS ALL AUDIO SIGNALS	NOT APPLICABLE	CENTER CONSOLE
TACAN	ARN-65	AZIMUTH BEARING AND DISTANCE	APPROXIMATELY 200 MILES	CENTER CONSOLE
ILS	ARN-58	LOCALIZER, GLIDESLOPE DEVIATIONS, AND MARKER BEACON	APPROXIMATELY 200 MILES	CENTER CONSOLE
IFF (SIF)	APX-46	AUTOMATIC IDENTIFICATION	APPROXIMATELY 200 MILES	RIGHT CONSOLE

Figure 4-3

main and a guard receiver) are used with each radio system. The main receivers normally carry out all reception functions. Guard receivers are ground-tuned to a particular guard frequency and cannot be changed without removing the control panel. The main receivers are tuneable through the same frequency range as the transmitters, while the guard receiver frequency range is from 238.0 to 248.0 megacycles (normally set to 243.0 megacycles). Any one of twenty preset frequencies can be instantly selected. These frequencies are recorded on two frequency cards, one in a holder on each side of the center console. In addition, operating frequencies can be selected manually without disturbing the preset frequencies. Whenever a new frequency is selected, the transmitter and receiver are tuned automatically to the new frequency. This tuning cycle requires about 4 seconds, and completion of the tuning cycle is signaled by an audio tone heard in the headset. Two UHF antennas are used. A switch permits manual selection of either antenna. Automatic antenna selection is initiated by the antenna receiving the first usable signal. The command radios are powered by the essential ac bus or the right primary ac bus.

NOTE
A 60-second waiting period is required before the UHF radio will return to normal operation after an electrical power interruption, even though the interruption is only momentary.

UHF COMMAND RADIO CONTROLS.

NOTE
Identical controls are provided for each command radio. Because a selector switch determines which set is operating, only the controls of the selected set affect UHF operation.

Manual-Preset-Guard Sliding Selector and Frequency Selector Knobs.

The sliding selector (25, figure 1-7 and 9, figure 1-8) on each UHF radio control panel controls the method of command radio frequency selection. It is operated by sliding the control through a limited arc across the face of the panel. This control has three positions: MANUAL, PRESET, and GUARD, and is arranged so that when it is in any one position, the other two positions are masked by a semitransparent green glass. When the sliding selector is placed in the MANUAL position, a mask is removed from in front of each of the five windows across the top of the panel, revealing numerals that make up the operating frequency.

Beneath each of the five windows is a small knob which, when rotated, changes the number and the frequency. (See 22, figure 1-7 and 8, figure 1-8.) This makes it possible to manually select 3500 frequencies within the range of 225.0 to 399.95 megacycles.

While the sliding selector is in the MANUAL position, preset channel selection is deactivated and the main receiver and transmitter may be tuned manually by the five frequency knobs. Sliding the selector to PRESET masks the five small windows, deactivates the manually selected frequency, and activates one of the 20 preset channels controlled by the channel selector switch. Regardless of the position used, anytime a frequency is changed, about 4 seconds is required for the tuning mechanism to complete the tuning cycle. Both reception and transmission are inoperative during the tuning cycle, which is indicated by a tone signal heard in the headset. When the tuning cycle is completed, the tone signal ceases. Placing the sliding selector in the GUARD position automatically tunes the main transmitter and main receiver to the guard frequency set up before the installation of the equipment.

T.O. 1B-70(X)A-1

UHF Channel Selector Knob.

A rotary-type selector knob (29, figure 1-7; 23, figure 1-8), on each UHF radio control panel is used to select any one of 20 preset frequencies by channel number. When the knob is rotated, channel numbers from 1 through 20 appear in the channel indicator window, directly above the knob. This window is masked when the selector knob is in any position other than PRESET.

UHF Function Switch.

A four-position rotary-type function switch, (28, figure 1-7; 11, figure 1-8) is on each UHF radio control panel. The set is inoperative with the switch in the OFF position. When the switch is moved to MAIN, the transmitter and main receiver are activated. (A warm-up period of approximately 3 minutes is required before the radio set can be operated.) The guard receiver is in stand-by condition, and the guard frequency will only be received if it is one of the preset frequencies or if it is manually set up. In the BOTH position, the set transmitter and both the main and guard receivers are energized and both the main and guard receivers are energized and heard simultaneously. The ADF position is currently inoperative and is covered.

Intercom Function Selector Switch.

Refer to "Intercom System - AN/AIC-18" in this section.

Intercom-Microphone Switches.

Refer to "Intercom System - AN/AIC-18" in this section.

UHF Mixer Switch.

Refer to "Intercom System - AN/AIC-18" in this section.

UHF Modulation Selector Switch.

The two-position modulation selector switch (50, figure 1-7; 26, figure 1-8) on each UHF radio control panel is inoperative.

UHF Transmitter Power Output Knob.

A ten-position rotary knob (49, figure 1-7, 25, figure 1-8), on each UHF panel controls the transmitter power in steps of 8.9 decibels, permitting power output reductions up to 80 decibels as required by the tactical situation. The knob positions are marked in the window directly above the knob. Positions A and 10 are maximum power output positions with power decreasing as the numbers in the window decrease. The number 1 position is minimum power output. Normal operation is obtained with the knob in the number 10 or A position (maximum power output). The knob should be left in one of these two positions.

Volume Control Knob.

The volume knob (46, figure 1-7, 24, figure 1-8), on each UHF radio control panel, is inoperative. UHF volume is controlled by the UHF mixer switch, volume control and the master volume control knobs on the intercom control panels. (Refer to "Intercom System - AN/AIC-18" in this section.)

UHF Antenna Selector Switch.

The three-position antenna selector switch (36, figure 1-7) is on the center console. When the switch is at UPPER or LOWER, UHF transmission and reception is through the antenna on top or on the bottom of the fuselage, respectively. When the switch is at AUTO, operation is through the antenna first receiving a sufficiently strong signal. This antenna circuit will remain activated and is used for the next UHF transmission from the airplane. However, because the next transmission may be made at a later time, on a different frequency, or to a different ground station, the retained antenna circuit may not be the antenna to use. Therefore, manual selection of the other antenna may be necessary. The antenna selector switch receives power from the essential dc bus.

Changed 25 June 1965

T.O. 1B-70(X)A-1

Escape Capsule Microphone Switch.

Refer to "Escape Capsule Communications" in this section.

NORMAL OPERATION OF UHF COMMAND RADIO.

1. Frequencies - Check.
   Before take-off, check frequency to be used against those listed on the frequency cards.
2. Manual-preset-guard sliding selector - Check.
   Check operation of transmitter and main receiver with sliding selector in each position.

   NOTE
   No transmission will be made on emergency (distress) frequency channels except for emergency purposes in order to prevent transmission of messages that could be construed as actual emergency messages.

3. UHF function switch - BOTH.
   Check operation of the guard receiver, using the BOTH position of the function switch.
4. Initial channel selection - Complete.
   For initial channel selection, select a channel other than the one to be used until the warm-up power is completed, or after warm-up, switch to another channel and then back to the channel desired. Reduced performance can result because of mistuning if the desired channel is selected before the warm-up period is completed.
5. Antenna selector switch - AUTO.
6. Volume control knobs - Set.
   Adjust volume controls on the intercom control panels.
7. Manual-preset-guard sliding selector - Set as desired.
   For manual selection of a frequency that is not in the preset channels, move sliding selector to MANUAL. The five windows across the top of the panel will open and, by using the five knobs directly beneath each window, establish desired frequency. (The function switch must be at MAIN or BOTH for this operation.) To obtain transmission and reception of guard frequency only, move sliding selector to GUARD.

   NOTE
   * This procedure places the equipment in condition to receive. Transmissions on the same frequency are obtained by pressing the intercom-microphone switch to the MIC position; however, if it is desired to change the transmitter frequency, the intercom-microphone switch should be released before the frequency is changed. About 4 seconds should elapse before transmission begins on a new frequency.
   * Do not select a frequency less than 225.0 mc. The transmitter will attempt to tune this frequency; and after 90 seconds, the transmitter will shut down. To restore transmission, turn the function switch to OFF, wait 30 seconds, then select a higher frequency.

   CAUTION
   Do not move antenna selector switch while the intercom-microphone switch is pressed as damage to the antenna selector circuit will occur.

8. Transmitter power output knob - As desired.
   Select proper power output according to tactical requirements (normally position A or 10).
9. UHF mixer switch - Pull.
10. Intercom function selector switch - UHF.
11. Intercom-microphone switch - Press to MIC and talk, release to listen.

    NOTE
    The intercom-microphone switch must be released when transmission is complete to receive reply, except when intercom "HOT MIC" mixer

4-20

T.O. 1B-70(X)A-1

switch is used. This switch overrides the intercom-microphone switch.

To turn the UHF command radio off, move the function switch to OFF.

EMERGENCY OPERATION OF UHF COMMAND RADIO.

Sudden Loss of Transmission and/or Reception.

If UHF communication is lost while on one of the two sets, switch to the other UHF set. The second UHF set is always ready to operate and will be available for use without delay providing the proper frequency has been selected. The normal (4 seconds) tuning delay exists if the frequency has to be set up. If neither command radio will transmit or receive satisfactorily within the range of the equipment, the automatic antenna switching unit may not have selected the proper antenna. In this event, move the antenna selector switch to the LOWER or UPPER position to re-establish communication. If communication cannot be established, move the switch to AUTO and follow instructions given under "Radio Not Operating" in this section.

Radio Not Operating.

In the case of apparent command radio failure, attempt operation using an alternate position of the sliding selector and/or function switch. Turn equipment off for several minutes; then turn function switch to type of operation desired. This will restore operation of the protective relay if the tuning mechanism was responsible for the failure. Check the circuit breaker panel for a tripped condition of any of seven AN/ARC-50 circuit breakers. Any one tripped AN/ARC-50 circuit breaker will cause operational failure of the UHF set.

INTERCOM SYSTEM -AN/AIC-18.

This transistorized intercom set completes the airplane communication system when integrated with the TACAN and ILS navigation equipment and the UHF command radio equipment. The TACAN, ILS, IFF, and UHF transmitters and receivers, along with the intercom amplifier, provide air-to-air and air-to-ground communications, as well as intercom operation between crew positions, and the monitoring of any combination of radio and navigation signals. Two modes of transmission are available through a switch on each control wheel. Three internal and four external positions are provided for intercom operation. Two of the internal positions are in the crew compartment and the third is in the electronic equipment compartment. An external intercom plug-in receptacle is in each wheel well and one is on the bottom of the fuselage at the external electrical power receptacle. A switch in the crew compartment interconnects the flight stations to the external receptacles for communications with ground personnel. The landing gear audio warning signal is directed through the intercom system to the headset. This high volume signal cannot be adjusted and will override all other signals. It can be turned off by a separate switch in the landing gear system. (Refer to "Landing Gear System" in Section I.) Mixing switches permit individual or simultaneous monitoring of all communication signals. When the associated mixer switch is pulled out, the individual receiver is monitored; and the corresponding transmitter will be keyed when the microphone switch on the control wheels is pressed. A single mixer switch provides for hand-free (hot mike), intercom. Also hot mike operation is automatically provided when any one of the following occurs: bail-out warning light button is pressed, encapsulate caution light switch is placed at ON, or when the doors of one or both escape capsules are closed. The intercom system is powered by the ground tow dc bus or the right primary dc bus.

Changed 25 June 1965

INTERCOM GROUND CREW OUTLETS.

Two-way communication is provided between ground crew and flight crew through one internal and four external plug-in receptacles. One intercom receptacle is in each wheel well, one at the external electrical power receptacle, and one on the radio equipment rack in the electronic equipment compartment. Portable intercom equipment must be used in conjunction with each intercom outlet. Fully transistorized amplifier units provide microphone and headset amplification for each outlet. (The receptacle on the radio equipment rack differs from the other intercom receptacles in that it uses the nose wheel well receptacle unit for amplifying the signals to that station.) A spring-loaded switch on the radio rack must be held at its INT position for microphone operation from the radio equipment rack position. Automatic gain control circuitry lessens distortion during operation.

INTERCOM FUNCTION SELECTOR SWITCH.

A switch (14, figure 1-7) on each intercom control panel selects the operating function of the communication systems. The switch has six positions but only the three labeled "UHF 1," "UHF 2," and "INT" are used. Either UHF position provides for both radio transmission and intercom operation. (The UHF 1 position selects the command radio controlled by the UHF panel on the center console; the UHF 2 position selects the command radio controlled by the UHF panel on the pilot's console.) The switch on each control wheel controls the type of communication selected. Therefore, the function selector switch may remain in a UHF position at all times. Rotation of this knob to the INT position shuts off all other circuits except the intercom circuit and the landing gear audio warning signal.

MIXER SWITCHES.

Each intercom control panel has eight switches (9, 10, 12, 13, 15, 16, 18, and 19, figure 1-7), six of which are used for controlling the mixed-signal listen facility and two for hot microphone operation of the intercom set. These push-pull type switches provide signal monitoring and hot microphone operation. They can be rotated to provide individual volume control for adjusting specific output. The switches are identified as "MXR BCN," "ILS," "UHF 1," "UHF 2," "TACAN," "INT," "HOT MIC ON-OFF," and "HOT MIC VOL."

NOTE
- The "HOT MIC ON-OFF" switch does not incorporate volume control circuitry. However, the "HOT MIC VOL" switch controls the volume of the hot microphone and it is necessary that both switches be pulled out for proper operation.
- Any one or combination of signals may be received simultaneously by pulling out the appropriate mixer switch, regardless of the position of the function selector switch. The selected volume control can be used to adjust the individual audio level. Audio level adjustment can also be controlled by the intercom master volume control. Pushing the individual mixer switch shuts off the corresponding signal. However, the "INT" mixer switch is inoperative when the function selector switch is at INT or the "HOT MIC" mixer switch is pulled up.

VOLUME CONTROL KNOBS.

Volume control knobs adjust the audio levels of incoming communication signals. Each mixer switch, when pulled out, becomes a volume control for its individual unit, except the "HOT MIC" switch. A separate switch (9, figure 1-7) is provided for control of the "HOT MIC" volume. In addition, a master volume control knob (17, figure 1-7) permits simultaneous audio level control of all communication signals.

T.O. 1B-70(X)A-1

CALL BUTTON.

The call button (11, figure 1-7), on each intercom control panel, is a momentary push-button switch that permits the calling station to interrupt all intercom functions at a high audio level; and the other crew station can be contacted without pressing the intercom-microphone switch. It is used primarily in an emergency.

INTERCOM-MICROPHONE SWITCHES.

A two-position, trigger-type switch (1, figure 1-11) is on the outboard grip of each control wheel. Pressing the switch to the microphone (MIC) position, with the associated intercom mixer button and intercom function selector switch at the UHF position, initiates radio transmission. Pressing the switch to the intercom (INTER) position initiates normal intercom operation only. With the intercom function selector switch at INT, pressing the trigger switch to either MIC or INTER will initiate intercom operation while prohibiting UHF radio transmission.

GROUND INTERCOM SWITCH.

A two-position switch (12, figure 1-9) on the copilot's console controls intercom between the ground crew intercom outlets and the crew compartment. Moving the switch to the ON position permits conversation with ground crew personnel whenever the applicable microphone switches are pressed.

NORMAL OPERATION OF INTERCOM SYSTEM.

For intercom operation only, proceed as follows:

1. Intercom function selector switch - UHF or INT.

   NOTE
   The function selector may remain at the UHF position at all times because radio transmissions and interphone operations are controlled by the interphone-microphone switch on each control wheel.

2. "INT" mixer switch - Pull out.
3. Other mixer switches - Push in.

   NOTE
   Mixer switches are pulled out for on, pushed in for off.

4. Intercom-microphone switch - INTER.

   NOTE
   Individual volume control is connected to the mixer switches.

For intercom call operation, proceed as follows:

1. Call button - Hold and talk.

   NOTE
   - All other stations receive the message regardless of the position of the mixer switches or function selector switch.
   - When the call button is used, it overrides the intercom-microphone switch and prevents transmission of intercom conversation over the command radio.
   - No signal mixing is possible during call operation.
   - Call button must be released to hear replies.

For monitoring all communication signals, proceed as follows:

1. Intercom function selector switch - INT or UHF.
2. Desired mixer switches - Pull out.

   NOTE
   Several signals can be monitored simultaneously by pulling out the corresponding mixer switch.

3. Volume control knobs - As desired.

IDENTIFICATION RADAR (IFF) - AN/APX-46.

The AN/APX-46 identification radar set provides selective identification of the airplane in response to IFF interrogations. The set includes an RT 556/APX-46 receiver-transmitter, a C-1158/APX

T.O. 1B-70(X)A-1

control panel, a C-1128/APX-25 SIF coder-group control panel, an antenna switching unit, and two antennas. The constant rate automatic antenna switching unit provides optimum reception and transmission of IFF signals. The IFF set receives power from the essential ac and dc busses.

NOTE
A 60-second waiting period is required before the IFF will return to normal operation after an electrical power interruption, even though the interruption is only momentary.

Operation of the IFF in either LOW or NORM positions provides automatic switching to the emergency mode when the encapsulate switch is ON, when the bailout button is pressed, or when the capsule doors are closed. The IFF will continue to transmit until the encapsulate switch is moved to RESET, then OFF (except when the bailout button has been used).

IDENTIFICATION RADAR CONTROLS.

The AN/APX-46 identification radar controls are on the two panels (labeled IFF and SIF) located on the copilot's console. The IFF control panel has a master switch, mode 2 and mode 3 switches, and an identification of position(I/P) reply switch. The master switch (24, figure 1-9) has five positions: OFF, STDBY, LOW, NORM, and EMERGENCY. Selection of the STDBY position will warm up the set.

NOTE
Transmission of reply is disabled in the STDBY position.

The set operates throughout its maximum range when NORM is selected, and range is reduced when the LOW position is selected. With the switch in either the NORM or LOW position, the set responds only to challenges correctly coded for the mode or modes selected. With the master switch at EMERGENCY, a coded reply will be automatically transmitted in response to any challenge.

NOTE
To move the master switch to EMERGENCY, the emergency interlock button (23, figure 1-9), below the switch, must be pressed and held while the switch is being moved.

The mode 2 switch (10, figure 1-9) has MODE 2 and OUT positions. The mode 3 switch (10, figure 1-9) has MODE 3 and OUT positions. The position of mode 2 and mode 3 switches determines the IFF reply-to-ground or air-borne equipment interrogations. Mode 1 always is operating, regardless of the positions of the mode switches and coder knobs. The three-position identification of position (I/P) reply switch (11, figure 1-9) controls the distinct type of position transmission. With the I/P switch at OUT, no position reply will be sent. When the I/P switch is at MIC, a position reply will be sent if the mode switches are on when the intercom-microphone switch on the control wheel is pressed to MIC and for 30 seconds after. Holding the switch at I/P automatically transmits a position reply. The SIF (selective identification feature) control panel contains two concentric rotary coder knobs (9, figure 1-9), mode 1 knobs and mode 3 knobs. The mode 1 inner knob has positions 0 through 7. The mode 3 inner and outer knobs have positions 0 through 7. The positions selected on each set of knobs determine the specific selected identification reply to be sent.

OPERATION OF IDENTIFICATION RADAR.

NOTE
Check that the IFF frequency counters have been set to the proper identification frequency channels before take-off.

1. IFF master switch - STDBY.
   The switch should be at STDBY for a 3-minute warm-up period.

2. IFF I/P reply switch - OUT.

NOTE

Use I/P or MIC positions only when directed by the traffic controller.

3. IFF mode switches - As required.
4. SIF coder knobs - As required.

NOTE

The mode and code to be used for IFF operation at a specified time and place will usually be directed by an authorized agency before take-off, on departure, or in flight. However, in the absence of specific instructions, the following is recommended:

   a. Mode 1 - All switches OUT, set SIF mode 1 coder knobs to 00.
   b. Mode 2 - Set IFF mode 2 switch to OUT.
   c. Mode 3 - Set IFF mode switch to MODE 3 and set SIF mode 3 outer coder knob at 0 and inner coder knob at 5.

5. IFF master switch - NORMAL.

NOTE

The low position (low sensitivity) should be used only when directed by the traffic controller.

6. IFF identification of position switch - I/P or MIC, as directed. Move the position reply switch to the I/P or MIC position when directed by the traffic controller.
7. IFF master switch - OFF. To turn the IFF set off, rotate the IFF master switch counterclockwise to OFF.

To use the IFF in case of an emergency, proceed as follows:

NOTE

With the IFF at either NORMAL or LOW, the emergency mode of operation of the IFF is automatically actuated when either capsule is closed or when the encapsulate caution light switch is at ON, or when the bail-out warning light button is pressed.

1. SIF mode 1 coder knobs - 00.
2. IFF mode 3 switch - MODE 3.
3. SIF mode 3 coder knobs - 77.
4. IFF master switch - EMERGENCY.

NOTE

The IFF emergency interlock button must be pressed before rotating the IFF master switch to EMERGENCY. A reply will then be made automatically in response to a mode 1 or mode 2 challenge.

ESCAPE CAPSULE COMMUNICATIONS.

Air-to-air and air-to-ground communications as well as intercom is available following encapsulation, providing the UHF communication and the intercom systems are operating. Hand-free (hot mike) operation of the microphone is provided as soon as either escape capsule is closed, and establishes intercom between pilot and copilot only. Each escape capsule has a push-button microphone switch (figure 1-36) mounted on the left wall of the capsule. When this switch is pressed, radio communications can be maintained on the frequency or frequencies set up on the UHF control panel before encapsulation. The microphone switch must be released to hear any UHF replies. Volume control remains as adjusted before encapsulation. The emergency mode of IFF operation is also actuated automatically when either capsule is closed providing IFF master switch is at either NORMAL or LOW.

LIGHTING EQUIPMENT.

EXTERIOR LIGHTING.

The navigation lights, in each wing tip, consist of forward and side-mounted colored lights and an aft-facing white light. Three red anticollision lights,

T.O. 1B-70(X)A-1

one on the top of the fuselage and two below the intake ducts, retract flush with the skin of the airplane when not in use. The dual landing lights and the auxiliary landing and taxi light, under the crew compartment, retract flush for streamlining and protection. Cutout circuits, controlled by signals from the air data computer, automatically prevent extending the landing lights, the auxiliary landing and taxi light, or the anticollision lights above certain speeds and/or altitudes. A caution light in the crew compartment shows when the landing lights are extended above the altitude and airspeed limits. The exterior lights are shown in figure 1-1.

LANDING LIGHT SWITCH.

The two-position landing light switch (27, figure 1-7), on the center console, receives power from the right primary ac bus. The ON position of the switch is powered only if the airplane is below 8000 feet or the airspeed is less than 250 knots IAS. Moving the switch to ON opens the landing light doors and extends and turns on both landing lights. Moving the switch to OFF turns off and retracts the landing lights and closes the landing light doors.

CAUTION

The landing lights must be retracted above 250 knots IAS and 8000 feet altitude to prevent damage to the lights.

AUXILIARY LANDING AND TAXI LIGHT SWITCH.

The two-position auxiliary light switch (1, figure 1-6), on the overhead panel, receives power from the right primary ac bus. The ON position of the switch is powered only if the airplane is below 8000 feet and the airspeed is less than 250 knots IAS. Moving the switch to ON in flight extends the light to about 72 degrees and turns on the light. The light also is angled about 20 degrees to the left. When the main gear touches down, or if the switch is moved to ON on the ground, the light extends an additional 10 degrees to direct the light beam further ahead and to one side of the airplane. Moving the switch to OFF turns off and retracts the auxiliary landing and taxi light.

CAUTION

The auxiliary landing and taxi light must be retracted above 250 knots IAS and 8000 feet to prevent damage to the light.

ANTICOLLISION LIGHT SWITCH.

The two-position anticollision light switch (12, figure 1-6), on the overhead panel, receives power from the right primary ac bus if the airspeed is below approximately Mach 1.1. Moving the switch to ON extends and turns on the three anticollision lights and starts them rotating. Moving the switch to OFF turns off the lights and retracts them. If the lights are extended and the airspeed is increased above the limit airspeed, the lights retract automatically. The anticollision light switch is mechanically latched in the OFF position and must be pulled out before it can be moved to ON.

NOTE

The anti-collision light should be turned OFF during flight through conditions of reduced visibility where the pilot could experience vertigo as a result of the rotating reflections of the light against the clouds. In addition, the light would be ineffective as an anticollision light during these conditions since it could not be observed by pilots of other airplanes.

NAVIGATION LIGHT SWITCH.

The two-position navigation light switch (2, figure 1-6), on the overhead panel, receives power from the ground tow ac

T.O. 1B-70(X)A-1

bus. Moving the switch to ON turns on the wing tip navigation lights. Moving the switch to OFF turns the lights off. The navigation light switch is mechanically latched in the OFF position and must be pulled out before it can be moved to ON.

LANDING LIGHT EXTENDED CAUTION LIGHT.

The placard-type landing light extended caution light (5, figure 1-7), on the center console, is powered by the essential ac bus. The light comes on to show "LDG LT EXTENDED" if the auxiliary landing and taxi light and/or the landing lights are not fully retracted when the airplane is above 8000 feet or 250 knots IAS.

INTERIOR LIGHTING.

The control panels and edge-lighted instruments have white nonglare indirect lighting from bulbs imbedded in the plastic panels. Individual rheostats in the crew compartment permit separate indirect lighting control of the pilot's instrument panel; copilot's instrument panel; center instrument panel; and the side consoles, center console, and overhead panel. Floodlights are provided for the instrument panel, the side consoles, the center aisle console, and the overhead panel. The instrument panel floodlights and console floodlights are separately controlled. Utility lights, with self-contained switches, fit into a socket on both the pilot's and copilot's consoles for general crew compartment lighting. The utility lights can be removed from their sockets to light areas not normally lighted by other interior lights. Four nondimmable floodlights are in the electronic equipment compartment ceiling. Spare bulbs are stored in a compartment in the pilot's console. (See 18, figure 1-8.)

PILOT'S FLIGHT INSTRUMENT INDIRECT LIGHT SWITCH AND RHEOSTAT.

The pilot's flight instrument indirect light switch and rheostat (10, figure 1-6), on the overhead panel, controls the indirect lighting of the pilot's instrument panel. It is marked "FLIGHT INST" and receives power from the essential ac bus. The combination switch and rheostat knob is turned clockwise from OFF to turn the lights on and increase the brightness. Turning the knob counterclockwise dims the lights, and full counterclockwise rotation to OFF turns the lights off.

COPILOT'S FLIGHT INSTRUMENT INDIRECT LIGHT SWITCH AND RHEOSTAT.

The copilot's flight instrument indirect light switch and rheostat (6, figure 1-6), on the overhead panel, controls the indirect lighting of the copilot's instrument panel. It is marked "FLIGHT INST" and receives power from the essential ac bus. The combination switch and rheostat knob is turned clockwise from OFF to turn the lights on to increase the brightness. Turning the knob counterclockwise dims the lights, and full counterclockwise rotation to OFF turns the lights off.

ENGINE INSTRUMENT INDIRECT LIGHT SWITCH AND RHEOSTAT.

The engine instrument indirect light switch and rheostat (5, figure 1-6), on the overhead panel, controls the indirect lighting of the center instrument panel. It is marked "ENGINE INST" and receives power from the essential ac bus. The combination switch and rheostat knob is turned clockwise from OFF to turn the lights on and increase the brightness. Turning the knob counterclockwise dims the lights, and full counterclockwise rotation to OFF turns the lights off.

Changed 30 November 1964

T.O. 1B-70(X)A-1

OVERHEAD, PEDESTAL, AND CONSOLE
INDIRECT LIGHT SWITCH AND RHEOSTAT.

The overhead, pedestal, and console indirect light switch and rheostat (3, figure 1-6), on the overhead panel, controls the indirect lighting of the overhead panel, center console (pedestal), and pilot's and copilot's consoles. The switch receives power from the essential ac bus. The combination switch and rheostat knob is turned clockwise from OFF to turn the lights on and increase the brightness. Turning the knob counterclockwise dims the lights, and full counterclockwise rotation to OFF turns the lights off.

INSTRUMENT PANEL FLOODLIGHT SWITCH AND RHEOSTAT.

The instrument panel floodlight switch and rheostat (11, figure 1-6), on the overhead panel, is marked "INST FLOOD" and receives power from the ground tow ac bus. The combination switch and rheostat knob is turned clockwise from OFF to turn on the six floodlights under the instrument panel shroud and increase the brightness. Turning the knob counterclockwise dims the lights, and full counterclockwise rotation to OFF turns the lights off.

CONSOLE FLOODLIGHT SWITCH AND RHEOSTAT.

The console floodlight switch and rheostat (4, figure 1-6), on the overhead panel, is marked "CONSOLE FLOOD" and receives power from ground tow ac bus. The combination switch and rheostat knob is turned clockwise from OFF to turn on and increase the brightness of the four floodlights over both the pilot's and copilot's consoles and the four overhead floodlights which light the center console and the overhead panel. Turning the knob counterclockwise dims the lights, and full counterclockwise rotation to OFF turns the lights off.

CONSOLE UTILITY LIGHTS.

The portable utility lights (17, figure 1-8 and 17, figure 1-9), one on both the pilot's and copilot's console, are powered by the essential dc bus. The end cap of each utility light is also a switch and rheostat with BRIGHT, DIM, and OFF positions. Turning the end clockwise from OFF turns on the light and increases the brightness. Turning the end counterclockwise dims the light, and full counterclockwise rotation to OFF turns the light off.

ELECTRONIC EQUIPMENT COMPARTMENT
UTILITY FLOODLIGHT AND SWITCH.

The utility floodlights in the electronic equipment compartment are powered by the essential ac bus. The lights are controlled by a two-position switch on the right side, on the corner of the escape aisle leading to the ground escape hatch. The switch is marked "UTILITY LIGHT" and is mounted in a recess. Moving the switch to ON turns on the floodlights in the electronic equipment compartment. Moving the switch to OFF turns off the lights.

OXYGEN SYSTEM.

Each crew member has his own complete liquid oxygen system. Each system has a converter-storage container and an air heat exchanger to convert the liquid to a gas which is warmed to make it suitable for breathing. Either converter can supply gaseous oxygen to the other crew member through interconnecting lines and check valves. The changeover is automatic and occurs if there is a 12 psi differential between systems. Each individual system is controlled by a toggle valve in the crew compartment. The liquid oxygen is stored in two 10-liter vacuum-insulated Thermos bottle type converter containers in the crew compartment. (See 6, figure 1-1.) For servicing, the converter containers are removed. A

4-28

Changed 30 November 1964

quantity gage in the crew compartment shows the total quantity of liquid oxygen in both containers. Container pressure, necessary to force out the liquid when demanded by the system, is provided by converting some of the liquid to gas and using this gas pressure in the container. Gaseous oxygen, at a pressure of about 70 psi, is delivered from the converters to the escape capsules. The 70 psi oxygen is then routed to an automatic oxygen regulator under each seat. The oxygen regulator supplies 100 percent oxygen at a pressure of 2.0 to 60 inches of water, depending on altitude, to the personal-lead disconnect. The oxygen personal leads, connected to the personal-lead disconnect, also has a 2.1 pressure reducer installed to reduce the pressure to between zero and 30 inches of water depending on altitude. The liquid oxygen system supplies breathable oxygen at a rate that depends on cabin altitude and crew demand. An oxygen mask test button is provided in each capsule. Liquid oxygen duration is shown in figure 4-6. An emergency oxygen system in each capsule provides additional gaseous oxygen in case of an emergency. See figure 1-37 for liquid oxygen specifications.

OXYGEN SYSTEM CONTROLS AND INDICATOR.

OXYGEN TOGGLE VALVES.

Two oxygen toggle valves (6, figure 1-8; 8, figure 1-9), one on each console, control their respective oxygen system shutoff valve. Moving the toggle to ON mechanically opens the valve to supply oxygen to the respective oxygen mask hose whether the mask is being worn or not. The OFF position of the toggle shuts off the respective system.

OXYGEN MASK TEST BUTTONS.

The push-to-test buttons, one on the front of each seat, permit checking the fit of the oxygen mask. Pushing the button applies an oxygen pressure of 11 to 16 inches of water to the respective oxygen mask to check for leaks.

QUANTITY GAGES TEST BUTTON.

Refer to "Environmental Systems Controls and Indicators" in this section.

LIQUID OXYGEN QUANTITY GAGE.

The liquid oxygen quantity gage (18, figure 1-3), on the pilot's instrument panel, has a range of 0 to 20 liters, in one-liter increments. The gage is powered by the essential ac bus and indicates the amount of liquid oxygen in both storage containers. An operational check of the gage can be made by means of the quantity gages test button.

ESCAPE CAPSULE OXYGEN SYSTEM (EMERGENCY OXYGEN SYSTEM).

A gaseous emergency oxygen system is incorporated within each escape capsule. The dual purpose system is used as an emergency breathing system when it is manually actuated by pulling the emergency knob ("green apple") or as an ejection-escape breathing system when actuated automatically upon ejection. Each system consists of a 14.1 cubic foot supply of gaseous oxygen in a cylinder below the seat, (at a pressure of 1800 psi) and a filler and pressure gage assembly. The gaseous oxygen is ported into an oxygen pressure reducer in the capsule. The 1800 psi is reduced to 70 psi before leaving the pressure reducer. When the emergency oxygen system is activated, pressure from this system presses against a check valve which shuts off the normal liquid oxygen supply system. Once the emergency oxygen system is activated, it is not possible to change back to the liquid oxygen system until the emergency system pressure is reduced to less than that of the liquid oxygen system which permits the check valve to open. The emergency oxygen system is sufficient

T.O. 1B-70(X)A-1

OXYGEN DURATION-HOURS

Crew: 2
100 percent oxygen to mask - Constant 70 psi flow to regulator

CABIN ALTITUDE - 1000 FEET	20	18	16	14	12	10	8	6	4	2	BELOW 2
35 AND ABOVE	56.4	50.8	45.2	39.5	33.8	28.2	22.6	16.9	11.3	5.6	
30	40.8	37.6	33.4	29.3	25.1	20.8	16.7	12.5	8.4	4.2	
25	31.3	28.2	25.0	21.9	18.8	15.7	12.5	9.4	6.3	3.1	
20	24.5	22.0	19.6	17.2	14.7	12.3	9.8	7.4	4.9	2.5	DESCEND TO ALTITUDE NOT REQUIRING OXYGEN
15	19.8	17.8	15.9	13.9	11.9	9.9	7.9	5.9	4.0	2.0	
10	15.9	14.3	12.7	11.1	9.5	7.9	6.4	4.8	3.2	1.6	
8	14.5	13.0	11.6	10.1	8.7	7.2	5.8	4.3	2.9	1.5	
6	12.8	11.5	10.3	9.0	7.7	6.4	5.1	3.8	2.6	1.3	
4	12.3	11.1	9.8	8.6	7.4	6.1	4.9	3.7	2.5	1.2	
2	11.1	10.0	8.9	7.8	6.7	5.5	4.4	3.3	2.2	1.1	
SEA LEVEL	10.2	9.2	8.2	7.1	6.1	5.1	4.1	3.1	2.0	1.0	

LITERS

Crew: 2
In pressure suits (Airplane AF62-001)

CABIN ALTITUDE - 1000 FEET	20	18	16	14	12	10	8	6	4	2	BELOW 2
55 AND ABOVE	14.0	13.0	11.0	10.0	9.0	7.0	6.0	4.0	3.0	1.0	
50	15.0	13.0	12.0	10.0	9.0	7.0	6.0	4.0	3.0	1.0	
45	21.0	19.0	17.0	15.0	13.0	10.0	8.0	6.0	4.0	2.0	
40	32.0	29.0	26.0	23.0	19.0	16.0	13.0	10.0	6.5	3.0	
35	30.0	27.0	24.0	21.0	18.0	15.0	12.0	9.0	6.0	3.0	DESCEND TO ALTITUDE NOT REQUIRING OXYGEN
30	24.0	21.0	19.0	16.0	14.0	12.0	9.0	7.0	5.0	2.0	
25	18.0	16.0	15.0	13.0	11.0	9.0	7.0	5.0	4.0	2.0	
20	14.0	13.0	11.0	10.0	8.0	7.0	6.0	4.0	3.0	1.0	
15	11.0	10.0	9.0	8.0	7.0	6.0	4.0	3.0	2.0	1.0	
10	9.0	8.0	7.0	6.0	5.0	4.0	3.5	3.0	2.0	1.0	
8	8.0	7.0	6.0	6.0	5.0	4.0	3.0	2.0	2.0	.8	
5	7.0	6.0	6.0	5.0	4.0	3.5	3.0	2.0	1.0	1.0	
SEA LEVEL	6.0	5.0	5.0	4.0	3.5	3.0	2.0	2.0	1.0	.5	

LITERS

Liquid Oxygen Converter-Container - Two Type GCU - 18/A (10 liters each)

Figure 4-6

for about 20 minutes. See figure 1-37 for gaseous oxygen specifications.

CAPSULE EMERGENCY OXYGEN ACTUATOR KNOB ("GREEN APPLE").

A round green emergency oxygen actuator knob, (figure 1-37), called a "green apple" is on the forward edge of each seat at the centerline. Pulling the knob up opens a valve in the oxygen pressure reducer to activate the emergency oxygen system. The knob cannot shut off the emergency oxygen system.

CAPSULE EMERGENCY OXYGEN PRESSURE GAGE AND FILLER VALVE.

An emergency oxygen pressure gage and a filler valve (figure 1-37) are mounted as a unit in the upper right rear corner of each capsule. The gage has a range from REFILL to 2500 psi. The range from REFILL to 1800 (full) is a red band, and from 1800 (full) to 2500 is a green band. The mounting area of the gage and filler valve is painted green and marked "OXY." The filler valve is just below the gage.

OXYGEN SYSTEM PREFLIGHT CHECK.

Before take-off, the oxygen system should be checked as follows:

NOTE
Any reference to oxygen controls and indicators applies to both pilot and copilot.

1. Liquid oxygen quantity gage - Check.
   Check liquid oxygen quantity gage for adequate oxygen for the mission. (Full condition is 20 liters.)
2. Emergency oxygen cylinder pressure gage - Check.
   Check emergency oxygen cylinder pressure gage for a minimum reading of 1800 psi at 70 degrees F.
3. Oxygen toggle valve - Check OFF.
4. Oxygen flow - Check.
   Uncap outlet port of the pressure reducer valve and move oxygen toggle valve to ON. Oxygen should flow freely out the uncapped port. Move oxygen toggle valve to OFF after checking.

CAUTION
Do not allow oxygen to flow freely out of port for more than 10 seconds, otherwise the oxygen regulator may be damaged.

5. Oxygen mask and hoses - Put on and connect as shown in figure 4-7.
6. Oxygen toggle valve - ON.
7. Oxygen mask test button - Press momentarily.
   Momentarily press the test button to check the mask fit.

NORMAL OPERATION OF OXYGEN SYSTEM.

Operation of the respective oxygen system is automatic after the pilot's or copilot's oxygen toggle valves are moved to ON.

OXYGEN SYSTEM EMERGENCY OPERATION.

Refer to "Oxygen System Emergency Operation" in Section III.

NAVIGATION EQUIPMENT.

TACAN - AN/ARN-65.

The TACAN set is an air navigational system which provides cockpit displays of distance and bearing to a selected VORTAC or TACAN surface beacon. This range and bearing information is reliable up to a line-of-sight distance of approximately 200 nautical miles.

NOTE
Improperly adjusted or malfunctioning ground or airborne TACAN equipment may "lock-on" to a false bearing. Therefore, during flight, verify TACAN bearing information when possible by cross-checking with ground radar, airborne radar or VOR.

T.O. 1B-70(X)A-1

OXYGEN HOSE HOOK-UP

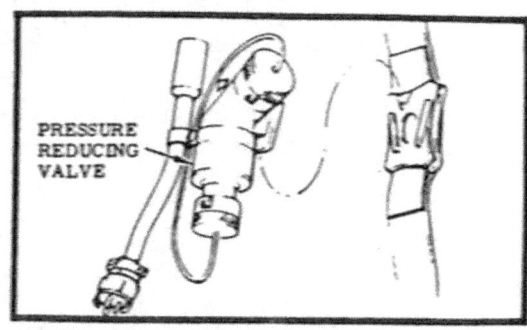

1 Insert connector into mounting plate attached to the restraint harness. Check that connector is properly inserted and that lock pin is engaged.

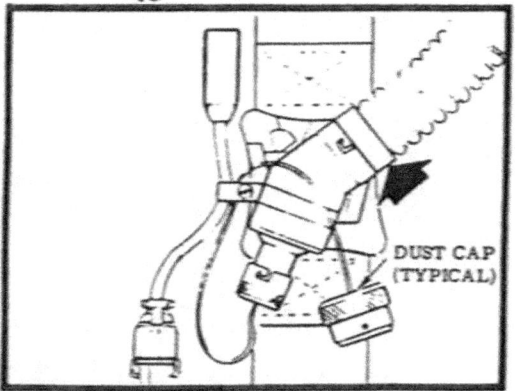

2 Remove dust cap and insert male bayonet connection, on the oxygen mask hose, into connector. Turn bayonet to lock prongs.

3 Remove dust cap and connect female bayonet connection, on seat oxygen hose, onto bottom of connector. Turn bayonet to lock prongs. Attach dust caps together.

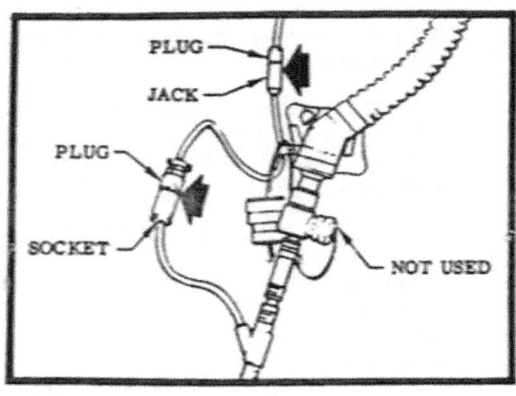

4 Connect plug from oxygen mask to jack on the connector, and connect plug on connector to socket from seat.

5 After connecting plug and socket, lock together by rotating shell on plug to engage socket.

Figure 4-7

T.O. 1B-70(X)A-1

The major components of the TACAN set are a transceiver, an indicator coupler (flight director computer), a control panel, and two antennas. The antennas are selected automatically through the antenna selector unit. The unit will automatically select the antenna which first receives a satisfactory signal. The TACAN transceiver automatically transmits an interrogation signal, which is received by the selected surface beacon and returned to the airplane. Distance, bearing, and course signals are then sent to the indicator coupler (flight director computer), which processes the signals and couples them to the indicators in the cockpit. The TACAN surface beacon identification signals are transmitted every 38 seconds and can be heard in the headsets. The TACAN set is powered by the right primary ac and dc busses.

NOTE
A 60-second waiting period is required before the TACAN will return to normal operation after an electrical power interruption, even though the power interruption is only momentary.

TACAN CHANNEL SELECTOR SWITCH.

The channel selector switch (31, figure 1-7), on the center console, permits selection of any one of 126 channels. These channels cover the transmitting frequency range of 1025 to 1150 megacycles and the receiving frequency range of 962 to 1024 and 1151 to 1213 megacycles with a one megacycle separation. The receiver frequency is automatically set at the same time a transmitting frequency is selected. The switch consists of a large circular serrated knob and small handle. The circular knob selects the first two digits and the handle selects the third digit of a desired channel. A window above the handle displays the selected channel.

TACAN VOLUME CONTROL KNOB.

This knob (32, figure 1-7), on the center console, is inoperative; TACAN volume is regulated through the TACAN mixer switches on the intercom control panels. (Refer to "Intercom System - AN/AIC-18" in this section.)

TACAN FUNCTION SWITCH.

A three-position rotary switch (30, figure 1-7), on the center console, controls power to the set and the mode of operation. With the switch at the REC (receive) position, the system presents bearing and audio identification information. With the switch at T/R (transmit/receive), the system presents bearing, distance, and audio identification information as well as all transmitting operations. When the switch is OFF, the system is off. The switch receives power from the right primary dc bus.

COMMAND CONTROL SWITCH.

Refer to "Flight Director System" in this section.

FLIGHT DIRECTOR MODE SELECTOR SWITCH.

Refer to "Flight Director System" in this section.

INTERCOM TACAN MIXER SWITCH.

Refer to "Intercom System - AN/AIC-18" in this section.

ATTITUDE DIRECTOR INDICATOR SELECTOR SWITCH.

Refer to "Flight Director System" in this section.

HORIZONTAL SITUATION INDICATORS (HSI).

Refer to "Flight Director System" in this section.

ATTITUDE DIRECTOR INDICATORS (ADI).

Refer to "Flight Director System" in this section.

OPERATION OF TACAN.

NOTE
The following procedures put only the TACAN set into operation.

T.O. 1B-70(X)A-1

Refer to "Flight Director System" in this section for procedures on use of TACAN in the various flight director modes.

1. TACAN function switch - REC or T/R, as desired.
    After moving function switch from OFF, allow a 3-minute warm-up.
2. TACAN channel selector switch - Set.
3. Intercom TACAN mixer switch - Pull out.
    Rotate mixer switch, as desired, for volume control.
4. TACAN function switch - OFF.
    To shut off TACAN, move function switch to OFF.

INSTRUMENT LANDING SYSTEM (ILS).

The three instrument landing functions are provided by the AN/ARN-58 radio receiving set. This receiving set includes an R-843/ARN-58 localizer receiver with necessary instruments, an R-844/ARN-58 glide slope and marker beacon receiver and a control panel. These receivers, together with antennas, indicators (attitude director and horizontal situation indicators), and display coupler (part of the flight director computer) comprise a complete instrument landing system. Guidance signals are received from ground transmitters and displayed on the attitude director, horizontal situation, and the marker beacon indicators. The displays shown are localizer deviations, localizer command steering, glide slope deviation, glide slope command steering and marker beacon interception. Visual and aural indications are provided when the airplane passes over a 75-megacycle transmitter providing airway and/or airfield identification (airway marker or runway approach marker). All components of the instrument landing system receive power from the right primary dc bus.

ILS FREQUENCY SELECTOR KNOB.

The ILS frequency selector knob (35, figure 1-7), on the center console, is used to select the desired localizer frequency. The knob permits selection of localizer frequencies through the range of 108.1 to 111.9 megacycles in 200-kilocycle steps. The localizer frequency selected is displayed through a window to the left of the knob. Glide slope frequencies are automatically tuned with the selection of a localizer frequency and range from 329.3 to 335.0 megacycles in 300-kilocycle steps. (Glide slope frequencies are not displayed.)

ILS POWER SWITCH.

The two-position ILS power switch (33, figure 1-7) is on the center console. When the switch is moved to POWER, the ILS system receives power from the right primary dc bus.

ILS VOLUME KNOB.

This knob (34, figure 1-7) on the center console is inoperative, and ILS volume is controlled by rotating the ILS mixer switches on the intercom control panels. (Refer to "Intercom System - AN/AIC-18" in this section.)

COMMAND CONTROL SWITCH.

Refer to "Flight Director System" in this section.

FLIGHT DIRECTOR MODE SELECTOR SWITCH.

Refer to "Flight Director System" in this section.

INTERCOM ILS MIXER SWITCH.

Refer to "Intercom System - AN/AIC-18" in this system.

ATTITUDE DIRECTOR INDICATOR SELECTOR SWITCH.

Refer to "Flight Director System" in this section.

HORIZONTAL SITUATION INDICATORS (HSI).

Refer to "Flight Director System" in this section.

ATTITUDE DIRECTOR INDICATORS (ADI).

Refer to "Flight Director System" in this section.

ALTITUDE HOLD SWITCH.

Refer to "Flight Director System" in this section.

MARKER BEACON INDICATOR LIGHTS.

Two placard-type indicator lights (33, figure 1-3 and 24, figure 1-4) are illuminated by the marker beacon receiver when the airplane passes over a 75-megacycle marker beacon transmitter. One marker beacon indicator light is on the pilot's instrument panel; the other is on the copilot's instrument panel. In addition to these lights, a tone in the headsets indicates when the airplane is passing over a marker beacon, if the intercom marker beacon mixer switch has been pulled up. (Refer to "Intercom System - AN/AIC-18" in this section.) The marker beacon indicator lights are powered by the essential ac bus.

OPERATION OF INSTRUMENT LANDING SYSTEM.

NOTE
The following procedures place only the ILS set into operation. Refer to "Flight Director System" in this section for procedures covering approaches.

1. ILS power switch - POWER.
2. ILS frequency selector knob - Set desired frequency.
3. Intercom ILS mixer switch - Pull out and rotate for desired volume.
4. Altitude hold switch - As required.

NOTE
If the ILS approach mode comes through the air data computer beam sensor circuit while the flight director mode selector switch is at ILS, the altitude hold circuit automatically disengages.

5. Marker beacon mixer switch - Pull out.
6. ILS power switch - OFF.
   To shut off ILS, move power switch to OFF.

AUXILIARY GYRO PLATFORM SYSTEM (AGPS).

The auxiliary gyro platform system provides pitch, roll, and heading reference information to the attitude director indicators and the flight director computer. It also supplies heading reference information to the horizontal situation indicators and to the TACAN system. The gyro system compensates for gyro drift as well as maneuvering and acceleration changes of the airplane to furnish a constant vertical and horizontal reference to the flight instruments. During take-off, when acceleration changes are the greatest, the vertical reference is maintained independent of forward acceleration. In flight, airspeed information from the central air data system is used by the auxiliary gyro platform system to maintain the vertical and horizontal references. The auxiliary gyro platform system is backed up by the standby attitude system which supplies an attitude reference to the pilot's standby attitude indicator at all times. Manually selecting the standby attitude system supplies attitude reference information to the flight director computer and to the copilot's attitude director indicator, as well as the pilot's standby attitude indicator.

Heading information is manually selected. Magnetic variation is manually inserted and is mixed with magnetic heading information to provide true north heading indications. Magnetic variation can be inserted at any time and is displayed through a digital indicator on the auxiliary gyro platform system control panel. Local latitude can be set manually any time. A digital latitude indicator on the auxiliary gyro platform control panel displays latitude.

NOTE

Magnetic variation and latitude must be changed periodically during flight as dictated by speed and heading.

A meter-type indicator displays the deviation between the magnetic heading output shaft and the magnetic heading sensed by the remote magnetic heading indicator. On initial erection of the auxiliary gyro platform system, the great circle heading computer is aligned automatically to the sensed magnetic heading of the airplane when essential ac bus power is initially applied to the auxiliary gyro platform system. Erroneous magnetic interference, however, can cause incorrect alignment of the great circle heading computer. Realignment of the great circle heading computer can be accomplished at anytime before take-off.

AUXILIARY GYRO PLATFORM MODE SWITCH.

The four-position mode switch (15, figure 1-8), on the pilot's console, is used to select the desired heading modes which are displayed on the horizontal situation and attitude director indicators. When the switch is in the GREAT CIRCLE position, heading with respect to an arbitrarily selected earth's great circle is displayed. The great circle heading is corrected automatically for earth's rate with latitude information manually inserted into the auxiliary gyro platform system. Great circle heading is automatically aligned with the magnetic heading of the airplane, unless magnetic variation has been inserted by the pilot, in which case the great circle heading is aligned with the true north heading. When the switch is at TRUE, heading, with respect to magnetic headings plus or minus manually inserted magnetic variation, is displayed. When the switch is moved to MAG, a heading with respect to the earth's magnetic north, sensed by the remote magnetic heading detector and stabilized by a gyro is displayed. With the switch in the DERATED MAG position, the heading is the same as in the MAG position except that it is fast responding and is not gyro stabilized. Loss of gyro stabilization cause inaccuracies in the derated magnetic position; however, it is still usable in an emergency. Derated magnetic heading is derived directly from the remote magnetic heading detector. The mode switch must be placed in DERATED MAG for heading information when the auxiliary gyro platform fails. The switch is powered by the essential ac bus.

AUXILIARY GYRO PLATFORM ALIGNMENT SWITCH.

Normal operation of the auxiliary gyro platform system is controlled by a two-position switch (20, figure 1-8) on the pilot's console. With the switch in the OPERATE position, essential ac bus power is applied to the gyro platform and initial erection and alignment of the gyro platform takes place. At the same time, the auxiliary gyro platform system aligning light comes on and remains on until the system has been brought up to normal operating condition. When the auxiliary gyro platform has reached the normal operating condition (after about three minutes), the aligning light goes out. (Heading should be within ±2 degrees of a known airplane position.) If the heading is not within limits, realignment of the great circle heading can be accomplished by moving the alignment switch to the REALIGN GREAT CIRCLE position for about 30 seconds. The aligning light comes on and remains on until the switch is repositioned to the OPERATE position. Realignment of the great circle heading computer may be accomplished at any time before take-off. The auxiliary gyro platform alignment switch must be returned to OPERATE to resume normal operation of the gyro platform.

NOTE
- No alignment will occur in flight if the auxiliary gyro platform alignment switch is set at the REALIGN GREAT CIRCLE position. However, the auxiliary gyro platform system aligning light will come on.
- Erroneous initial alignment of the auxiliary gyro platform may be caused by interference from magnetic material, such as steel hangars, etc, or from magnetic fields generated from power lines, transformers, etc. Realignment should be attempted after the airplane has been moved from these influencing factors.

AUXILIARY GYRO PLATFORM LATITUDE SETTING KNOB AND INDICATOR.

Changes in latitude must be inserted into the gyro platform system by the latitude setting knob (13, figure 1-8) and the latitude is read from a digital indicator (12, figure 1-8) on the pilot's console. The indicator displays latitude in degrees and tenths of degrees. With an increase in north latitude or a decrease in south latitude, the knob should be rotated clockwise towards N INCR. The knob is rotated counterclockwise towards S INCR for an increase in south latitude or a decrease in north latitude. As the knob is rotated, it mechanically changes the appropriate (north or south) degrees of latitude that appear in the latitude indicator. The position of knob, in turn applies electronic signals, which correspond to its existing latitude reading, to the gyro platform system.

AUXILIARY GYRO PLATFORM MAGNETIC VARIATION SETTING KNOB AND INDICATOR.

Changes in magnetic variation must be inserted into the auxiliary gyro platform system by the magnetic variation setting knob (21, figure 1-8) and the variation is read from a digital indicator (22, figure 1-8) on the pilot's console. The indicator displays magnetic variation in degrees and tenths of degrees. The knob is rotated clockwise toward EAST for a decrease in variation and counterclockwise toward WEST for an increase in variation. When the knob is rotated, it mechanically changes the degrees of variation that appear in the magnetic variation indicator. Position of the magnetic variation setting knob provides a correction to magnetic heading to produce true north heading outputs to the attitude director and horizontal situation indicators when TRUE (true north) heading is selected on the auxiliary gyro platform system mode switch.

AUXILIARY GYRO PLATFORM HEADING SLEW KNOB.

A pull-out knob (19, figure 1-8), on the pilot's console, is used to manually slew great circle heading outputs rapidly to any desired heading. The knob is coupled directly to the heading slew pot and is spring-loaded to OFF. Pulling the knob out cuts off the earth's rate correction information and then rotating the knob towards INCR or DCR applies positive or negative slewing respectively of the great circle heading. Slewing speed is dependent upon how far the knob is turned.

NOTE
Slewing is available only when the mode switch is at GREAT CIRCLE.

T.O. 1B-70(X)A-1

HORIZONTAL SITUATION INDICATORS (HSI).

Refer to "Flight Director System" in this section.

ATTITUDE DIRECTOR INDICATORS (ADI).

Refer to "Flight Director System" in this section.

AUXILIARY GYRO PLATFORM MAGNETIC HEADING SYNCHRONIZATION INDICATOR.

The magnetic heading synchronization indicator (14, figure 1-8), on the pilot's console, continually displays the deviation between the magnetic heading output shaft of the auxiliary gyro platform system and the heading as sensed by the remote magnetic heading detector. The indicator receives power from the essential ac bus.

AUXILIARY GYRO PLATFORM SYSTEM ALIGNING LIGHT.

The auxiliary gyro platform system aligning light (1, figure 1-7), on the center console, receives power from the primary dc bus. The light (labeled "AGPS ALIGNING") comes on when power is applied to the auxiliary gyro platform system and remains on during the initial aligning cycle (about three minutes). The light goes out when the gyro platform is aligned and in normal operating condition. Whenever the alignment setting switch is placed in its REALIGN GREAT CIRCLE position, the aligning light comes on and remains on until the alignment switch is moved to the OPERATE position.

AUXILIARY GYRO PLATFORM SYSTEM OPERATION.

NOTE
The auxiliary gyro platform system is automatically erected within three minutes after the essential ac bus is powered. (Auxiliary gyro platform alignment switch must be at OPERATE.)

To operate system, proceed as follows:

1. Auxiliary gyro platform mode switch - GREAT CIRCLE.
   The mode switch should be at GREAT CIRCLE for initial alignment.
   The auxiliary gyro platform system is automatically aligned during the initial erection cycle to the magnetic heading (or to the true north heading if magnetic variation is inserted manually).
2. Auxiliary gyro platform alignment switch - OPERATE.
   Note that the aligning light is on. Light will go out when the initial erection and alignment cycle is completed.
3. Magnetic variation setting knob - Set local magnetic variation.
4. Latitude setting knob - Set local latitude.
5. Magnetic heading synchronization indicator - Check centered.
6. Heading slew knob - Check off.

To realign the great circle heading, proceed as follows:

NOTE
Realignment can be accomplished only on the ground.

1. Mode switch - GREAT CIRCLE.
2. Magnetic variation setting knob - Set to local magnetic variation.
3. Latitude setting knob - Set to local latitude.
4. Alignment switch - REALIGN GREAT CIRCLE.
   The alignment switch should remain in this position for at least 30 seconds. The auxiliary gyro platform system aligning light should be on.
5. Alignment switch - OPERATE.
   Move alignment switch to OPERATE and note that the aligning light is out.

T.O. 1B-70(X)A-1

6. Heading slew knob - Select great circle heading.
   Slewing of the great circle heading can be accomplished on the ground or during flight.
7. Heading slew knob - Check OFF.

FLIGHT DIRECTOR SYSTEM.

The flight director system, using a CPU-27/A flight director computer, provides a selection of navigation signals to the attitude director and horizontal situation indicators. The system is powered by the right primary ac and dc busses and the essential ac bus.

FLIGHT DIRECTOR COMPUTER - CPU-27/A.

The electronic CPU-27/A flight director computer combines the altitude, heading, attitude, and radio navigation information and presents it on the attitude director. The computer combines heading, roll, course, and localizer signals for roll indications and altitude, pitch, and glideslope signals for pitch indications. The computer is controlled by a switching arrangement, which puts the computer into any one of five modes (four major modes and one submode). The combination of input signals used is determined by the mode selected which changes the input signals for the proper programming of flight paths to fit the particular flight profile. Depending on the mode of operation selected, the computer supplies either command heading steering, localizer steering or TACAN signals to the attitude director indicator bank steering bar. The computer also supplies glide slope deviation signals to the glide slope indicator or glide slope steering signals to the pitch steering bar. Balancing of various input signals will center the bank and pitch steering bars of the attitude director indicator. With no steering or deviation signals selected (the computer on stand-by), bias signals drive the steering bars out of view. (The bank steering bar is used to show sideslip when on standby, and PILOT is selected.) The computer also serves as a coupler for signals going to the integrated flight displays and must be on though not functioning. There is also one submode, altitude hold,
which may be used with any of the major modes except ILS APP. (Refer to "Altitude Hold Switch" in this section.) The flight director computer is powered by the right primary ac bus.

FLIGHT DIRECTOR MODE SELECTOR SWITCH.

The five-position rotary switch (29, figure 1-3), on the pilot's instrument panel, selects the mode of operation of the flight director computer. When the switch is at STBY, the pointers and warning flags on the attitude director indicators are driven out of view by a signal from the flight director computer. (Refer to "Flight Test Instrumentation" in this section.) With the switch at ILS, localizer deviation from the ILS localizer receiver is sent to the flight director computer and combined with roll information to produce an ILS heading error which is displayed by the attitude director indicator bank steering bar. This mode is normally selected after letdown but before reaching the glide slope beam. When the bank steering bar is centered, the airplane is "on course." When "on course" for an instrument landing, the flight director mode switch can be moved to the ILS APP. By watching the downward movement of the pitch steering bar, the glide slope interception can be anticipated and the descent prepared. In the event of a go-around with the switch at ILS or ILS APP, the back course of the ILS can be flown or the switch can be moved to MAN HDG and a predetermined heading flown. The same information is used in the TACAN mode as in the ILS or ILS APP modes except that distance information is added. Distance from TACAN station to the airplane is displayed in the range window of the horizontal situation indicator in nautical miles. The ILS, ILS APP, and MAN HDG modes are read primarily from the attitude director indicators, while the TACAN mode is read from the horizontal situation indicator. The mode selector switch receives power from the right primary dc bus.

Changed 30 November 1964

4-39

ATTITUDE DIRECTOR INDICATOR SELECTOR SWITCH.

The attitude director indicator selector switch (28, figure 1-3), on the pilot's instrument panel, is used to select the pitch and roll signal sources for the attitude director indicators and the flight director computer. The switch is mechanically latched in the NORMAL position and must be pulled out before it can be moved to STBY. When the switch is at NORMAL, essential ac bus power is supplied to the pilot's attitude director indicator and right primary ac bus power is supplied to the copilot's attitude director indicator. At the same time, attitude signals are supplied by the auxiliary gyro platform system indicating heading, pitch, and roll information on both attitude director indicators. The flight director system supplies navigation information to both attitude director indicators also. When the switch is moved to the STBY position, the stand-by gyro provides attitude information to the pilot's stand-by attitude indicator, the copilot's attitude director indicator and the flight director computer. The attitude director indicator selector switch receives power from the right primary dc bus.

COMMAND CONTROL SWITCH.

This two-position command control switch (30, figure 1-3), on the pilot's instrument panel, is used to determine whether the pilot or copilot has control of heading and course settings on the horizontal situation indicator, and control of command airspeed, Mach, or altitude settings. When the switch is at PILOT or COPILOT, the horizontal situation indicator, the altitude-vertical velocity indicator, and the airspeed-Mach number indicator on the respective panel (pilot's or copilot's) become "master" indicators. (Refer to "Flight Test Instrumentation" in this section.) The corresponding indicators on the other instrument panel then become "slave" indicators. As a result, when a setting is changed on a master indicator, an equal change is produced automatically on the corresponding slave indicator. (Setting changes cannot be made using the slave indicator.)

The command control switch receives power from the right primary dc bus.

ALTITUDE HOLD SWITCH.

The two-position altitude hold switch (31, figure 1-3), is on the pilot's instrument panel. The switch, magnetically held in the ON position, engages the altitude hold mode in the flight director computer. The air data computer sends altitude information to the flight director computer. Altitude changes from the air data computer are combined with pitch information from the auxiliary gyro platform system or from the pitch and roll gyros to provide a steering signal for steering to the engaged altitude. This steering signal is displayed by the pitch steering bar on the attitude director indicator. By flying the pitch steering bar, the desired altitude can be maintained up to a deviation of ±500 feet. If the altitude deviation exceeds 500 feet, the altitude hold circuit is changed automatically by an amount equal to the deviation beyond 500 feet, as indicated on the altitude - vertical velocity indicator. Holding the pitch steering bar in line with the miniature airplane on the attitude director indicator maintains the airplane at the engaged altitude. Altitude hold can be selected during any of the flight director modes except the ILS APP mode. The altitude hold switch is automatically moved to OFF, and the hold circuit disengaged, when the ILS APP mode is selected, or when a strong approach signal is received by the glide slope receiver when the mode selector switch is at ILS. Electrical power for the altitude hold switch is received from the right primary dc bus.

ATTITUDE DIRECTOR INDICATORS (ADI).

There are two attitude director indicators (2, figure 1-3; 10, figure 1-4; and figure 4-8): one on the pilot's instrument panel and one on the co-pilot's instrument panel. Each presents roll and pitch attitude, heading, turn and slip information, computed steering information in relation to a command heading or course, glide slope displacement for instrument landings, and computed steering information to intercept localizer courses, ILS glide slopes, and TACAN. An added scale on the cover glass provides sideslip information in degrees. This pictorial-type instrument combines displays of pitch, roll, and heading on a universally mounted sphere which serves as a reference for a miniature airplane. The miniature airplane symbol (9, figure 4-8), fastened to the instrument frame, is always in proper physical relation to the simulated earth, horizon, and sky areas of the sphere. The sphere, receiving information from the auxiliary gyro platform system, is free to rotate 360 degrees about all axes. (Refer to "Auxiliary Gyro Platform System (AGPS)" in this section.) The horizon is represented as a solid line and is graduated in 5-degree increments which represents airplane heading. A pitch trim knob (10, figure 4-8) rotates the sphere vertically to position the desired horizon line reference with respect to the miniature airplane. A fade feature gradually cancels the amount of horizon line displacement when the airplane approaches 90 degrees of climb or dive. The bank pointers (5, figure 4-8), extending from the top to the bottom of the sphere face, measure bank angle on a semicircular bank scale below the sphere, graduated in 10-degree increments.

Movement of two long steering bars, perpendicular to each other, displays flight director computer command information and/or movement around the pitch and roll axes or sideslip information. The pitch steering bar (horizontal bar) (8, figure 4-8) is an indication of steering error and provides a guide for steering to the glide slope or a selected altitude. The bank steering bar (vertical bar) (7, figure 4-8) provides a guide for steering to a selected course, selected heading, ILS localizer beam, TACAN or number of degrees sideslip. When centered, the bars indicate "on course" or "correct turn to course." The attitude director indicator bank steering bar moves in the direction of heading correction necessary to maintain a desired track. To center the bank steering bar, the airplane must be turned in the direction of bank steering bar. When proper angle of interception has been reached, the bank steering bar automatically centers. As the airplane approaches the desired heading selected on the horizontal situation indicator, the bank steering bar will deviate in the opposite direction and the airplane must again be turned toward the vertical bar to center the bar. A warning flag appears in conjunction with the bank steering bar if the deviation signal is unreliable when the flight director mode selector switch is at TACAN, ILS or ILS APP. A separate turn rate gyro supplies turn information to a conventional turn needle (11, figure 4-8) at the bottom of the attitude director indicator. The turn needle is calibrated so that one standard needle-width turn will accomplish a 360-degree turn in four minutes (1-1/2 degree per second rate-of-turn). Slip information is presented by a conventional ball slip indicator (12, figure 4-8) directly above the turn needle.

The glide slope indicator (3, figure 4-8) on the left side of the instrument operates only when the flight director mode selector switch is at ILS or ILS APP and measures the magnitude of deviation from the center of the glide slope beam. The glide slope deviation scale (4, figure 4-8) indicates amount of deviation from the glide slope, and the dots are spaced one-half beam-width apart. When the glide slope indicator is aligned with the center index, the airplane is on the glide slope.

If power fails in the stand-by vertical gyro on the attitude director indicator, a power-off flag (1, figure 4-8) appears in the face of the indicator. (The word "OFF" is printed on the flag.)

The sphere in the copilot's attitude indicator will tumble or oscillate if the bus-tie contactors open.

T.O. 1B-70(X)A-1

FLIGHT DIRECTOR MODES

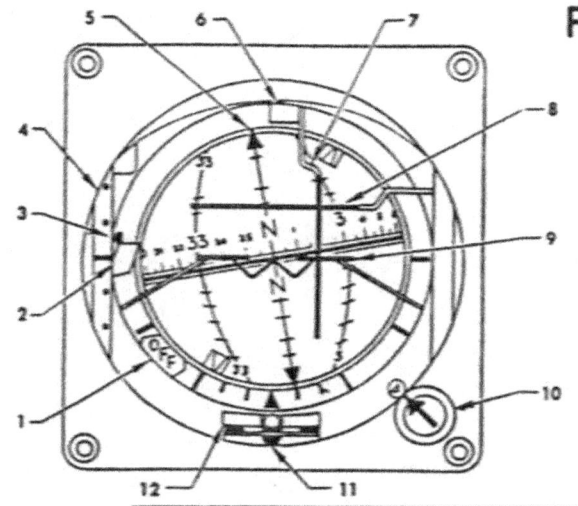

Warning

In the absence of a usable signal (indicated by the appearance of applicable warning flag), related presentations on both indicators are unreliable.

1. ATTITUDE WARNING FLAG
2. GLIDE SLOPE WARNING FLAG
3. GLIDE SLOPE INDICATOR
4. GLIDE SLOPE DEVIATION SCALE
5. BANK POINTERS
6. COURSE WARNING FLAG
7. BANK STEERING BAR
8. PITCH STEERING BAR
9. MINIATURE AIRPLANE
10. PITCH TRIM KNOB
11. TURN INDICATOR
12. SLIP INDICATOR

MAJOR MODE	ATTITUDE DIRECTOR INDICATOR				
	GLIDE SLOPE INDICATOR	BANK STEERING BAR	PITCH STEERING BAR	COURSE WARNING	GLIDE SLOPE WARNING
* MAN HDG	OUT OF VIEW	COMMAND HEADING STEERING	OUT OF VIEW	OUT OF VIEW WITH USABLE STEERING SIGNAL	OUT OF VIEW
* TACAN	OUT OF VIEW	COURSE SET STEERING	OUT OF VIEW	OUT OF VIEW WITH USABLE TACAN SIGNAL	OUT OF VIEW
* ILS	OUT OF VIEW	LOCALIZER STEERING	OUT OF VIEW	OUT OF VIEW WITH USABLE LOCALIZER SIGNAL	OUT OF VIEW
ILS APPROACH	GLIDE SLOPE DEVIATION	LOCALIZER STEERING	GLIDE SLOPE STEERING	OUT OF VIEW WITH USABLE LOCALIZER SIGNAL	OUT OF VIEW WITH USABLE GLIDE SLOPE SIGNAL
STBY	OUT OF VIEW	OUT OF VIEW	OUT OF VIEW	OUT OF VIEW	OUT OF VIEW

NOTE

* Altitude hold switch can be used in any mode except the ILS approach

Figure 4-8 (Sheet 1 of 2)

T. O. 1B-70(X)A-1

....and Pilot Indicator Presentations

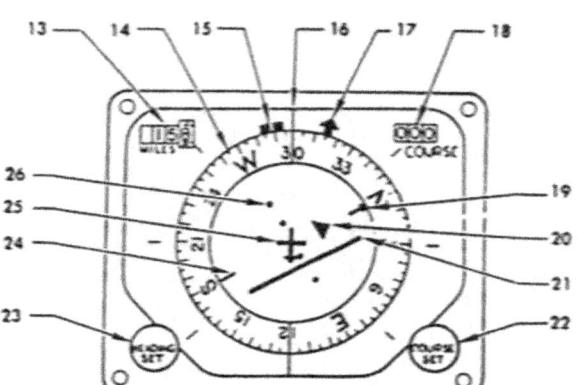

13. RANGE INDICATOR
14. COMPASS CARD
15. HEADING MARKER
16. LUBBER LINE
17. BEARING POINTER
18. COURSE SELECTOR WINDOW
19. COURSE ARROW (HEAD)
20. TO-FROM INDICATOR
21. COURSE DEVIATION INDICATOR
22. COURSE SET KNOB
23. HEADING SET KNOB
24. COURSE ARROW (TAIL)
25. MINIATURE AIRPLANE
26. COURSE DEVIATION SCALE

HORIZONTAL SITUATION INDICATOR					
HEADING MARKER	COURSE ARROW	COURSE DEVIATION INDICATOR	TO-FROM INDICATOR	BEARING POINTER	RANGE INDICATOR
SET BY PILOT	SET TO TACAN BEARING	TACAN DEVIATION	FUNCTION OF TACAN SIGNAL	TACAN BEARING	TACAN DISTANCE
NO FUNCTION	SET TO TACAN BEARING	TACAN DEVIATION	FUNCTION OF TACAN SIGNAL	TACAN BEARING	TACAN DISTANCE
NO FUNCTION	SET TO LOCALIZER COURSE	LOCALIZER DEVIATION	FUNCTION OF TACAN SIGNAL	TACAN BEARING	TACAN DISTANCE
NO FUNCTION	SET TO LOCALIZER COURSE	LOCALIZER DEVIATION	FUNCTION OF TACAN SIGNAL	TACAN BEARING	TACAN DISTANCE
NO FUNCTION	SET TO TACAN BEARING	TACAN DEVIATION	FUNCTION OF TACAN SIGNAL	TACAN BEARING	TACAN DISTANCE

Figure 4-8 (Sheet 2 of 2)

T.O. 1B-70(X)A-1

Whenever electrical signals from the navigational receiver are weak or unreliable for operation of the bank steering bar, the course warning flag (6, figure 4-8) appears on the face of the indicator. If signals from the glide slope receiver are weak or unreliable for operation of the glide slope indicator, the glide slope warning flag (2, figure 4-8) appears on the face of the indicator. (This flag is electrically driven from view during the TACAN and MAN HDG mode of operation.) The pilot's attitude director indicator receives power from the essential ac bus and the copilot's attitude director indicator receives power from the right primary ac bus.

HORIZONTAL SITUATION INDICATORS (HSI).

The horizontal situation indicator (34, figure 1-3; 25, figure 1-4; and figure 4-8), on the pilot's and copilot's instrument panels, is a multipurpose indicator that displays heading, course, course deviation, TACAN bearing and range, command heading and course, and instrument landing indications in various flight director system modes. Airplane heading is displayed on a rotating compass card (14, figure 4-8) marked in 5-degree increments through 360 degrees. The compass card is driven by signals from the auxiliary gyro platform system, which are read against a fixed reference marker called a lubber line (16, figure 4-8) at the top of the dial. Reciprocal heading is read under the lubber line at the bottom of the dial. Command heading and course can be inserted manually by rotating the corresponding knobs on the lower portion of the instrument. A double-bar rectangular index (heading marker) (15, figure 4-8) can be rotated around the outer edge of the compass card by the heading set knob (23, figure 4-8) and indicates the selected command heading. Clockwise rotation of the heading set knob moves the command heading index clockwise, and counterclockwise rotation moves the index counterclockwise. In the MAN HDG or TACAN modes of operation of the flight director computer, the command heading index can be set by the heading set knob on the horizontal situation indicator. Once the index is set, it will synchronize and rotate with the compass card. In the ILS or ILS APP modes, the command heading index is automatically aligned with the airplane heading, and turning the heading set knob will have no effect on the command heading index position. A course arrow (19 and 24, figure 4-8) that rotates inside the compass card displays desired course or track and can be set by turning the course set knob (22, figure 4-8). Since the TACAN is related to magnetic north, the auxiliary gyro platform system heading selector switch should be on MAG when using the course displays. Clockwise rotation of the course set knob moves the course arrow clockwise. The course selected also is displayed on a three-digit counter in the course selector window (18, figure 4-8). Once the course arrow is set, it rotates with the compass card. The center section of the course arrow, called a course deviation indicator (21, figure 4-8) is movable in a lateral motion and remains parallel to the course arrow, indicating the position of the airplane in relation to the selected course. The course deviation indicator also rotates in conjunction with the course arrow.

NOTE

The heading signals displayed on the pilot's horizontal situation indicator and the copilot's attitude director indicator are connected in parallel and the copilot's horizontal situation indicator and the pilot's attitude director indicator are connected in parallel. When the command control switch is set at either PILOT or COPILOT, the corresponding horizontal situation indicator becomes the "master" and the other the "slave" unit. Rotating the heading set or course set knob on the "master" indicator selects heading or course on both indicators. The set knobs on the "slave" indicator are inoperative.

An indication to determine whether a selected course is to or from a radio station is displayed by the location of a triangular to-from indicator (20, figure 4-8) above or below the miniature airplane symbol (25, figure 4-8). With the triangular to-from indicator on the same side as the course arrow, the course set is toward the radio station; and if on the opposite side of the course arrow, the course set is away from the station. The bearing pointer (17, figure 4-8), rotating about the compass card, indicates the direction of the selected ground station relative to the airplane. The angle between the fixed lubber line and the bearing arrow is the relative bearing to the station. The bearing arrow is remotely operated by electrical signals from TACAN. A four-digit (three of which are used) range indicator (13, figure 4-8) displays the slant range, in nautical miles, from the radio station. In any flight director mode other than TACAN, the window is masked; also, if distance is greater than 200 miles, the window will be masked in the TACAN mode also. Range signals are received directly from the TACAN equipment to the horizontal situation indicators. The pilot's horizontal situation indicator is powered by the essential ac bus and the copilot's horizontal situation indicator is powered by the right primary ac bus. Both horizontal situation indicators also receive power from the instrument ac bus.

ERRATIC OPERATION OF THE ATTITUDE DIRECTOR AND HORIZONTAL SITUATION INDICATORS.

Loss of the auxiliary gyro platform system gyro, instrument ac bus, or opening of the bus-tie contactors will affect the operation of the attitude director and horizontal situation indicators.

Loss of the auxiliary gyro platform system gyro will cause incorrect heading and attitude information to be sent to the attitude director and horizontal situation indicators. Attitude information for the pilot's stand-by attitude indicator and the copilot's attitude director indicator is available from the stand-by gyro, and derated magnetic heading information is available to the attitude director and horizontal situation indicators. If the instrument ac bus is lost, no distance information will be displayed on the horizontal situation indicators and the command function will be by the master horizontal situation indicator only. Also, the loss of the instrument ac bus will cause the loss of altitude hold capability (in the altitude hold mode only) of the attitude director and horizontal situation indicators. (Refer to "Altitude Hold Switch" in this section.) Heading and attitude information continues to be displayed on the attitude director and horizontal situation indicators.

Should the bus-tie contactors open (as indicated by the bus-tie open caution light coming on), errors will creep into the attitude director and horizontal situation indicators, due to out-of-phase electrical power supply. Attitude information is available from the stand-by circuit to the pilot's stand-by attitude indicator and the copilot's attitude director indicator. The compass card on the pilot's horizontal situation indicator will tend to oscillate, however, the heading information can be used for rough course computations. Heading information displayed on the copilot's attitude director and horizontal situation indicators cannot be used. Usable rate-of-turn information will be displayed on the attitude director indicators.

NOTE

With the bus-tie contactors open, the sphere in the attitude director indicators and the heading card in the horizontal situation indicators will oscillate or spin.

OPERATION OF FLIGHT DIRECTOR SYSTEM.

Dead Reckoning Navigation.

To select and fly a particular magnetic heading, use the following procedure:

1. Flight director mode selector switch - MAN HDG.
2. Command control switch - As desired.
3. Horizontal situation indicator heading set knob - Set.
    Align command heading marker with the desired magnetic heading on the horizontal situation indicator compass card.
4. Turn to the desired heading.

Maintain heading by keeping the horizontal situation indicator command heading index under the lubber line and the attitude director indicator bank steering bar centered.

TACAN Navigation.

To fly toward or away from a TACAN station but not on a preselected radial, use the following procedure:

NOTE

During flight, verify TACAN bearing information when possible by cross-checking with ground radar, airborne radar, or VOR.

1. TACAN function switch - T/R.
2. TACAN channel selector switch - Select desired station channel.
3. Flight director mode selector switch - TACAN.
4. Command control switch - As desired.
5. Horizontal situation indicator course set knob - Set.
    Set desired course in the course window. Course arrow will align to the selected course on the compass card at the same time. Course deviation indicator will indicate the position of the airplane in relation to the selected course. Steer airplane by centering the bank steering bar on the attitude director indicator.
6. Auxiliary gyro platform mode switch - Set as desired.
7. Wind drift correction - Check.
    Steer airplane to keep the horizontal situation indicator course deviation indicator centered to the course arrow. (Course arrow may be offset from the lubber line to show wind drift correction.) Monitor that the bank steering bar on the attitude director indicator is centered.
8. Distance from radio station - Monitor.
    Check the range indicator on the horizontal situation indicator as necessary. (The TACAN function switch must be at the T/R position to obtain range indications.)

To fly a selected TACAN radial to or from a station, use the following procedure:

NOTE

During flight, verify TACAN bearing information when possible by cross-checking with ground radar, airborne radar, or VOR.

1. Repeat steps 1 through 4.
2. Horizontal situation indicator course set knob - Set.
    Rotate horizontal situation indicator course set knob until the course arrow is aligned with the desired radial heading on the compass card. Course window should indicate the same course reading and the course deviation indicator will indicate airplane position from the selected radial. Attitude director indicator bank steering bar will show angle of course interception.
3. Attitude director indicator bank steering bar - Center.
    Turn airplane to center the attitude director indicator bank steering bar. Reduce bank angle, as necessary, to keep the bank steering bar centered. The bank steering bar should remain centered when on course.

T.O. 1B-70(X)A-1

4. Wind drift correction - Check. Steer airplane to keep the horizontal situation indicator deviation indicator centered, and rotate the heading set knob as required to align the command heading index with the lubber line. Maintain drift-corrected heading by keeping the attitude director indicator bank steering bar centered.

5. Distance from TACAN station - Check. Check the range indicator on the horizontal situation indicator as necessary. (The TACAN function switch must be in the T/R position to obtain slant range information.)

SINGLE-POINT PRESSURE REFUELING SYSTEM.

The fuel tanks are serviced on the ground through the single-point refueling system from a receptacle on the right side of the fuselage, forward of the main gear well. (There is no alternate means of refueling.) Refueling system controls permit selective automatic refueling of the tanks. The airplane normally is refueled at a flow rate of 600 gallons per minute. To ensure that the fuel tanks remain inert, during refueling the incoming fuel passes through a deaeration unit before entering the airplane. Gaseous nitrogen is injected into the fuel as it flows into the deaeration unit to remove oxygen dissolved in the fuel.

Fuel enters the tanks through tank-mounted refueling level control shutoff valves. As each tank becomes full, the valves automatically close to shutoff the refueling flow to the tank. Each shutoff valve has a remote, tank-mounted level control pilot valve which responds to the fuel level in the tank to control operation of the shutoff valve. Because the level control shutoff and pilot valves have dual floats, solenoids, and diaphragms, a single failure will not prevent the valve from shutting off the fuel flow. Except for tank No. 3, which has normally open level control valves, all tanks have normally closed level control shutoff valves. Refueling pressure opens the normally open valves and, when electrical power is applied, also opens the normally closed valves. Electrical circuits to the refueling valves are controlled by switches on the instrument panel and are completed when the lever over the refueling receptacle cap is lifted in order to remove the cap. A level control valve test system is used at the start of refueling to determine if the valves are operating properly. The single-point refueling system is shown schematically in figure 4-9. See figure 1-11 for fuel tank capacities, and figure 1-32 for fuel specifications.

NOTE
The refueling system also is used to defuel the airplane.

REFUELING VALVE SWITCHES.

The seven refueling valve switches (21, figure 1-3), on the copilot's instrument panel, provide selective control of the refueling system. Each switch controls operation of the refueling level control valves in its corresponding tank. The valves in left and right tanks of the same number are controlled by a single switch. Because tank No. 3 (sump tank) always is refilled, no refueling valve switch is provided for this tank.

NOTE
Tank No. 5 is not used on Airplane AF62-001, therefore the No. 5 refueling level control valve circuit is inoperative on this airplane.

For complete automatic refueling of all fuel tanks, each refueling valve switch should be at AUTO. This permits the normally closed level control valves to open when refueling pressure is applied.

NOTE
All refueling control valve switches must be set at AUTO after any refueling operation to ensure proper operation of the fuel system.

SINGLE-POINT REFUELING SYSTEM

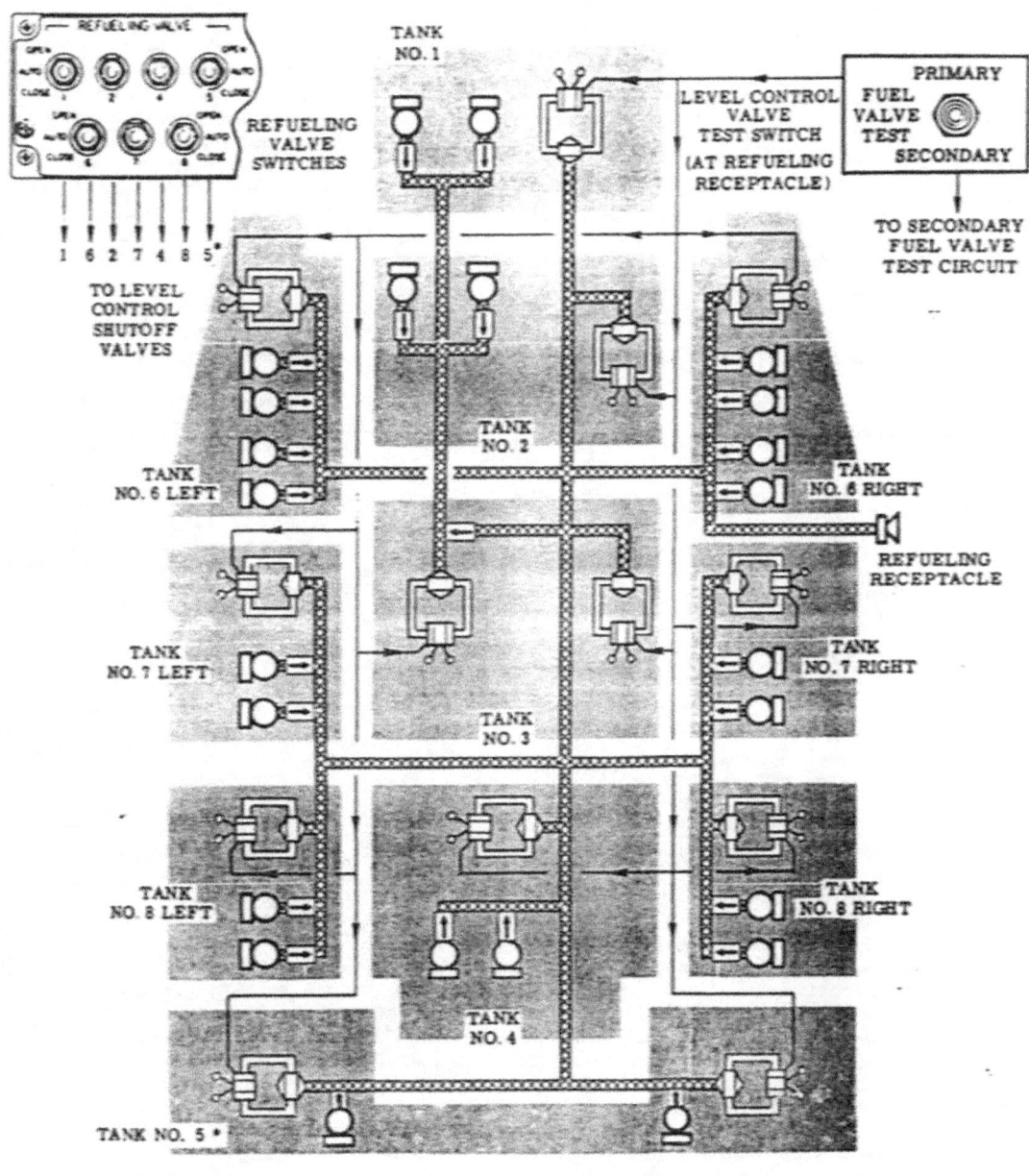

Figure 4-9

T.O. 1B-70(X)A-1

For partial refueling of the airplane, the refueling valve switches of tanks not to be filled are placed at CLOSE to keep the level control valves in the corresponding tanks closed during refueling. The OPEN position of the refueling valve switches allows the valves in the corresponding tanks to open when the tanks are not full.

NOTE

The OPEN position is for maintenance purposes and special inflight operations only. This position should be used in flight only on specific instructions because fuel sequencing will be affected.

The refueling valve switches receive power from the primary fuel and defuel ac bus.

REFUELING LEVEL CONTROL VALVE TEST SWITCH.

The three-position refueling level control valve test switch in the refueling receptacle compartment is used by ground personnel at the start of refueling to test level control valve shutoff operation. (The valves are tested when refueling pressure is applied and fuel is flowing.) When the test switch is held at PRIMARY, the primary portions of the dual level control valves should close; holding the test switch at SECONDARY closes the secondary portions of the valves. Refueling flow will stop as each position is selected, if the corresponding portions of the level control valves are operating properly. The test switch receives power from the primary fuel and defuel ac bus. It is spring-loaded to its center off position and is effective only when the refueling level control valve switches on the copilot's instrument panel are at AUTO.

FLIGHT TEST INSTRUMENTATION.

The flight test instrumentation is recorded by two digital and one analog tape recorders installed in a controlled environment instrumentation package in the weapons bay. Selection and operation of the flight test instrumentation equipment are controlled by switches in the crew compartment. Each digital recorder provides 32 minutes of recording time (giving a total of 64 minutes of recording time), and the analog recorder provides 64 minutes of recording time. A cabin tape recorder operates when the instrumentation system is recording, and is used for recording panel response data and preselected parameters during flight. It is located aft of the crew compartment. A voice track* is available on this recorder to record either intercom or radio communications when the recorder is on. This permits identification of test conditions or general comments to be made part of the data taken. The cabin recorder provides either 12 1/2 or 25 minutes* (16 minutes†) of recording time, depending on the tape speed selected before flight. Airspeed, vertical "G", and altitude are recorded on a VGH recorder. The VGH recorder is a 3-channel oscillograph type continuous trace strip recorder. This recorder provides about 1 1/2 hours of recording time. Four landing cameras*, used to photograph landing data, are located as follows: one on each main gear strut door focused on the bogie of the opposite gear, and two in the forward fuselage, one focused on the nose gear and one pointing down to photograph airplane drift in relation to the runway. Each of the three cameras focused on the gear has 40-seconds of film, and the camera used to photograph drift has one minute of film. Data is recorded from various pickups throughout the airplane and certain data is telemetered to ground stations during flight. A portable battery-powered tape recorder records intercom and all voice communications to and from the airplane, and also has a mike to permit additional pilot comments prior to or after each flight. (The portable tape recorder, on a shelf behind the copilot's capsule, provides about 4 1/4 hours of recording time with a rechargeable battery that provides 5 to 10 hours of running time. The recorder should be started prior to the flight and turned off after the flight by switches on the recorder.) A 16-mm movie camera on the ceiling of the pilot's compartment photographs the center and pilot's instrument panels when the camera is on and data is being recorded. (A total of 33 minutes of movie film is carried in the camera.) A switch on the pilot's capsule auto-

---
*Airplane AF62-001
†Airplane AF62-207

T.O. 1B-70(X)A-1

matically provides continuous data recording and movies when the pilot encapsulates.

The instrumentation systems are powered by the flight test instrumentation bus which receives power from the right primary ac bus except the movie camera which receives power directly from the right primary ac bus.

The cabin recorder and landing camera* systems however, are powered by the right primary dc bus. For these systems, the instrumentation master switch does not have to be on to permit operation.

INSTRUMENTATION CONTROLS.

INSTRUMENTATION MASTER SWITCH.

The two-position master switch (42, figure 1-3) on the pilot's instrument panel receives power from the instrumentation bus. Moving the switch to ON turns on the instrumentation package cooling system and applies power to the analog, digital and telemetering systems. The switch is mechanically latched at ON and must be pulled out before it can be moved to OFF.

TELEMETERING SWITCH.

The two-position telemetering switch (43, figure 1-3) on the pilot's instrument panel receives power from the instrumentation bus. Moving the switch to XMT transmits data to ground stations. Moving the switch to STBY keeps the transmitter warmed up ready to transmit when required.

NOTE
Do not move the telemetering switch to XMT until just prior to start to take-off run.

CAMERA SWITCH.

The two-position camera switch (41, figure 1-3) on the pilot's instrument panel receives power from both the right primary ac bus and the instrumentation bus. With the switch at READY, the movie camera will operate whenever a recorder is operating, or when the pilot's capsule is closed. Moving the switch to OFF turns off the movie camera and disconnects the camera from the record switches.

DIGITAL RECORDER SELECTOR SWITCH.

The three-position digital recorder selector switch (44, figure 1-3) on the pilot's instrument panel receives power from the instrumentation bus. When the switch is at AUTO, and either record switch is used, data is recorded first on recorder "A"; then, when this recorder runs out of tape (about 50 percent of the remaining tape on the digital tape remaining indicator), recorder "B" is started automatically. Moving the selector switch to either REC A or REC B permits manual selection of either digital tape recorder. The switch is mechanically latched at all three positions and must be pulled out before it can be moved to a new position.

INSTRUMENTATION PACKAGE COOLING SYSTEM SELECTOR SWITCH.

The three-position cooling system selector switch (38, figure 1-3) on the pilot's instrument panel receives power from the instrumentation bus. When the switch is at AUTO, the environment of the instrumentation package is normally controlled by the number one instrumentation cooling system. However, if this system fails to maintain the proper pressure or temperature in the package, the number two cooling system automatically takes over and the number one system is shut off. Moving the selector switch to either No. 1 or No. 2 overrides the automatic selection and permits manual selection of either cooling system. The switch is mechanically latched at all three positions and must be pulled out before it can be moved to a new position.

*Airplane AF62-001

T.O. 1B-70(X)A-1

MAIN GEAR DOWN AND LOCKED AND BOGIE UNSAFE.

If the nose gear and the main gears are down and locked, but a bogie is in any unsafe position as confirmed by chase plane or tower fly-by, a landing may be attempted at the pilot's discretion. Use a normal landing pattern with a minimum rate of descent just before touchdown, and touchdown at minimum speed. After nose wheels are on the runway, deploy drag chute and maintain heading with nose wheel steering.

BELLY LANDING.

If the landing gear cannot be lowered, a belly landing must not be made.

LANDING WITH CANARD FLAPS UP.

There is no alternate method of lowering the canard flaps. No special precautions during the landing pattern are required. Final approach and touchdown speeds should be increased by about 10 knots IAS.

EMERGENCY GROUND ESCAPE.

In case of an emergency requiring immediate evacuation from the airplane, such as a fire, shut down the engines and leave the airplane through the entrance door or the ground escape hatch. Unless rescue crews are at the site with ladders, use the descent device attached to the escape rope to reach the ground. (See figure 3-6 for emergency escape routes and exits.) Before abandoning the airplane, and depending upon the emergency, the following must be accomplished.

1. Flight status safety pin - Insert.
   Insert the flight status safety pin in the right console of each seat to safety the escape capsule ejection system.
2. Entrance door - Open.
3. Ground escape hatch - Jettison, if entrance door cannot be opened. Jettison the ground escape hatch by pulling either the hatch jettison handle on the pilot's console or the jettison handle on the left wall of the escape aisle. (See figure 1-34.)
4. Leave airplane by ladder or escape rope.
   Leave the airplane by a ladder put in place by the rescue crew, or if a ladder is not available, use the escape rope and descent device. Remove the escape ropes and descent devices from the stowage compartment forward of the entrance door. If the entrance door is used, insert and lock the pip pins on the escape ropes into the sockets above the door opening and throw the ropes out the door. If the entrance door cannot be used, leave the airplane through the ground escape hatch. When the escape hatch is used, throw the ropes out the hatch opening and over the leading edge of the canard. (The pip pins should not be used.)
5. Descent device - Grasp properly and slide to ground.
   After the escape ropes are extended, put one hand through the strap loop on the descent device (Sky Genie) and grasp the remainder of the strap with the other hand and slide to the ground.

   NOTE
   Do not grasp the end of the escape rope below the descent device, as this will stop the descent.

6. Get clear of the airplane.

T.O. 1B-70(X)A-1

EMERGENCY ENTRANCE.

The procedure to be used by rescue personnel when assisting the crew from the airplane following a crash landing is outlined in figure 3-6. If the airplane is still on the landing gear, the same procedure is used except it is necessary to use a safe and rapid means of reaching the entrance door, ground escape hatch jettison handle, or the ground escape hatch opening.

DITCHING.

WARNING
Under no circumstances should ditching be attempted.

THROTTLE SYSTEM MALFUNCTION.

SINGLE THROTTLE SYSTEM FAILURE.

Indication of a possible inoperative throttle servo system is by direct observation of the engine instruments when the throttles are moved. With any indication of a throttle servo system failure, proceed as follows:

1. Alternate throttle switch (affected engine) - Hold at INCR or DECR, as required.
   This changes the thrust setting of the corresponding engine, and turns off and isolates the normal throttle servo system.

   NOTE
   - Alternate throttle switch operation does not override the rpm lockup.
   - Coordinated movement of the throttle and alternate throttle switch is not necessary.
   - Do not move the throttle to OFF except for intentional engine shutdown, as this closes the fuel shutoff valve and shuts down the engine, even though the alternate throttle switch has been used.

COMPLETE THROTTLE SYSTEM FAILURE.

Simultaneous loss of all six throttle servo systems may be the result of a loss of essential ac bus power. If all throttles fail, proceed as follows:

1. All alternate throttle switches - Hold at INCR or DECR, as required. If the engines do not respond*:
   a. Engine shutdown and wheel brake arming switch - Check OFF.

   CAUTION
   To preclude inadvertent engine shutdown when using the alternate throttle switches, the engine shutdown and wheel brake arming switch must not be at its ARMED position in flight.

   b. Battery-inverter switch - ON. Break safety wire and move battery-inverter switch to ON so that emergency battery will power the alternate throttle switches.

   NOTE
   After being energized, the emergency battery requires 3 to 5 seconds before it will light the battery-inverter indicator light.

   c. All alternate throttles INCR or DECR as required.

---

*Airplane AF62-001

3-34   Changed 25 June 1965

T.O. 1B-70(X)A-1

EMERGENCY GROUND ESCAPE
ESCAPE ROUTES AND EXITS

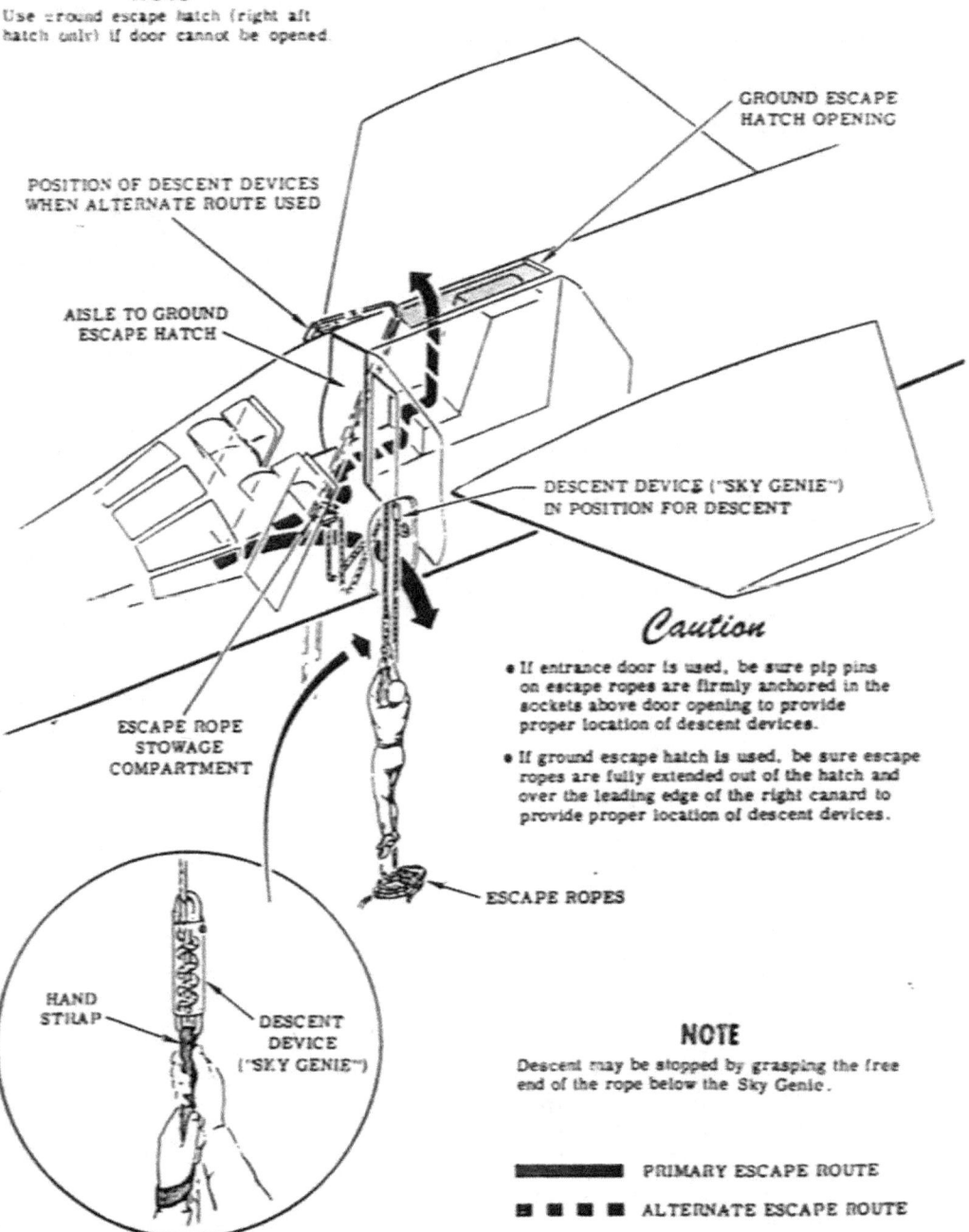

Figure 3-6 (Sheet 1 of 4)

T.O. 1B-70(X)A-1

EMERGENCY ENTRANCE - AIRPLANE

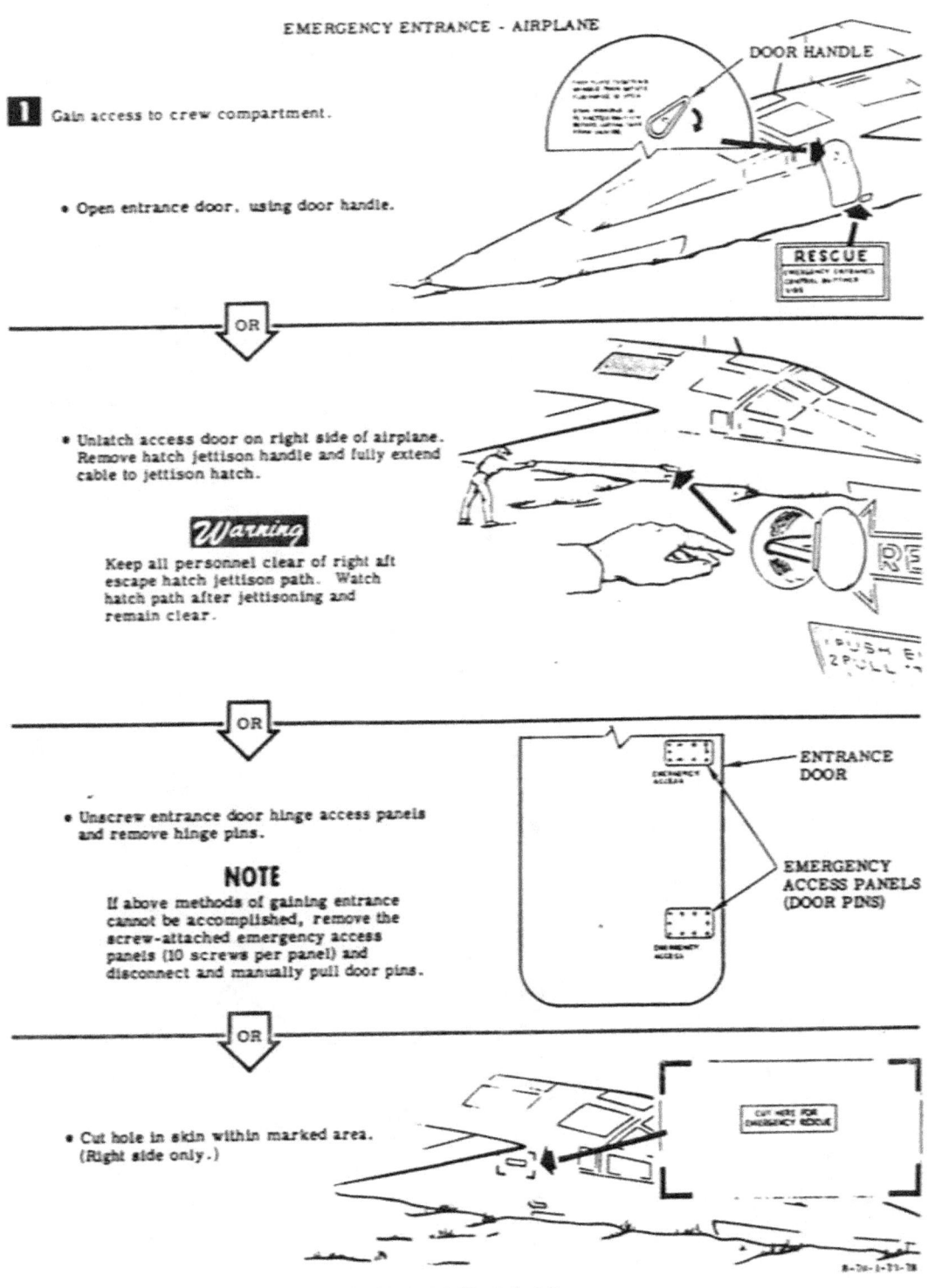

1 Gain access to crew compartment.

- Open entrance door, using door handle.

―OR―

- Unlatch access door on right side of airplane. Remove hatch jettison handle and fully extend cable to jettison hatch.

Warning

Keep all personnel clear of right aft escape hatch jettison path. Watch hatch path after jettisoning and remain clear.

―OR―

- Unscrew entrance door hinge access panels and remove hinge pins.

NOTE

If above methods of gaining entrance cannot be accomplished, remove the screw-attached emergency access panels (10 screws per panel) and disconnect and manually pull door pins.

―OR―

- Cut hole in skin within marked area. (Right side only.)

Figure 3-6 (Sheet 2 of 4)

Changed 30 November 1964

T.O. 1B-70(X)A-1

SAFETYING CAPSULE
(Pilot's shown, copilot's similar)

2 Safetying capsule.

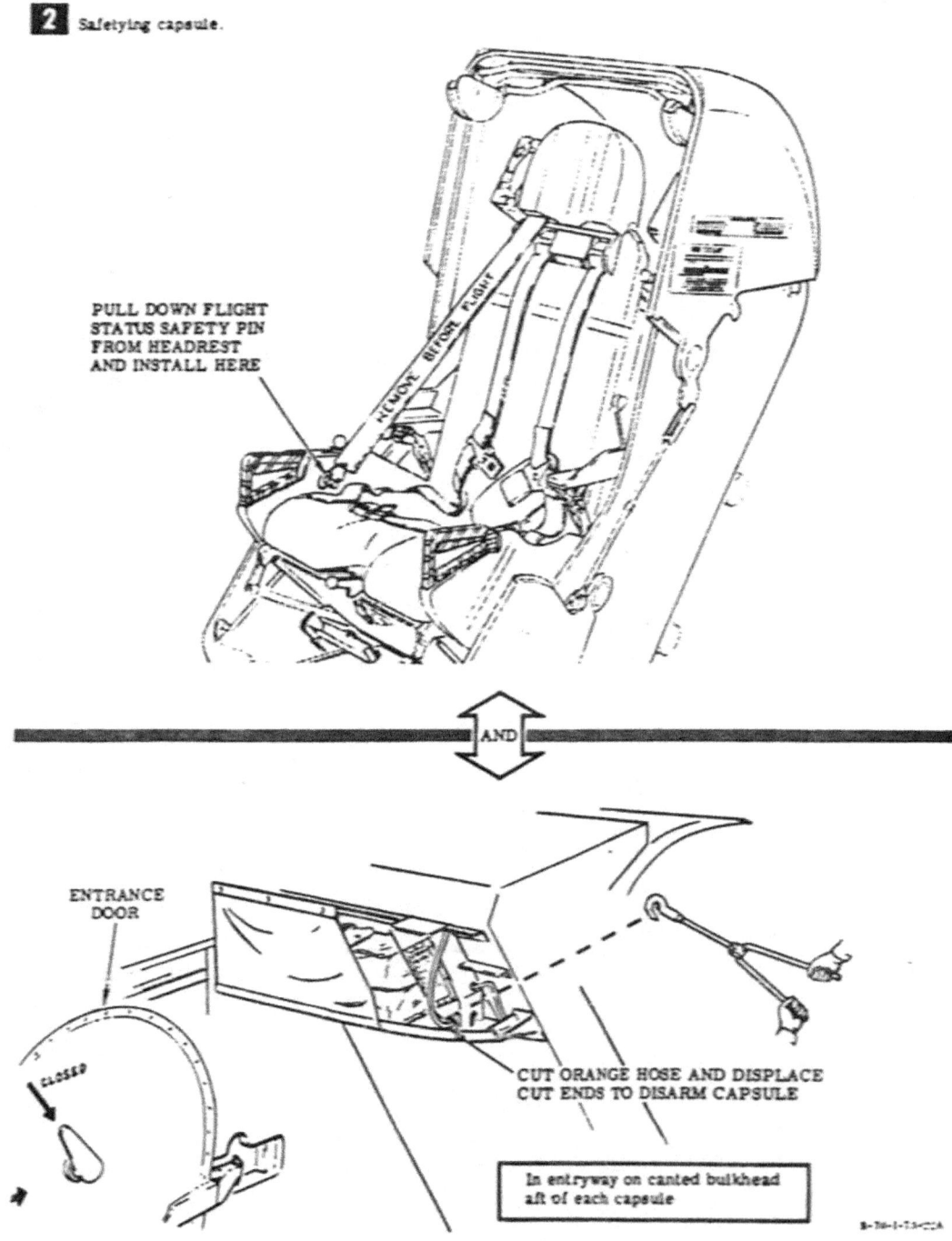

Figure 3-6 (Sheet 3 of 4)

T.O. 1B-70(X)A-1

EMERGENCY ENTRANCE - ESCAPE CAPSULE

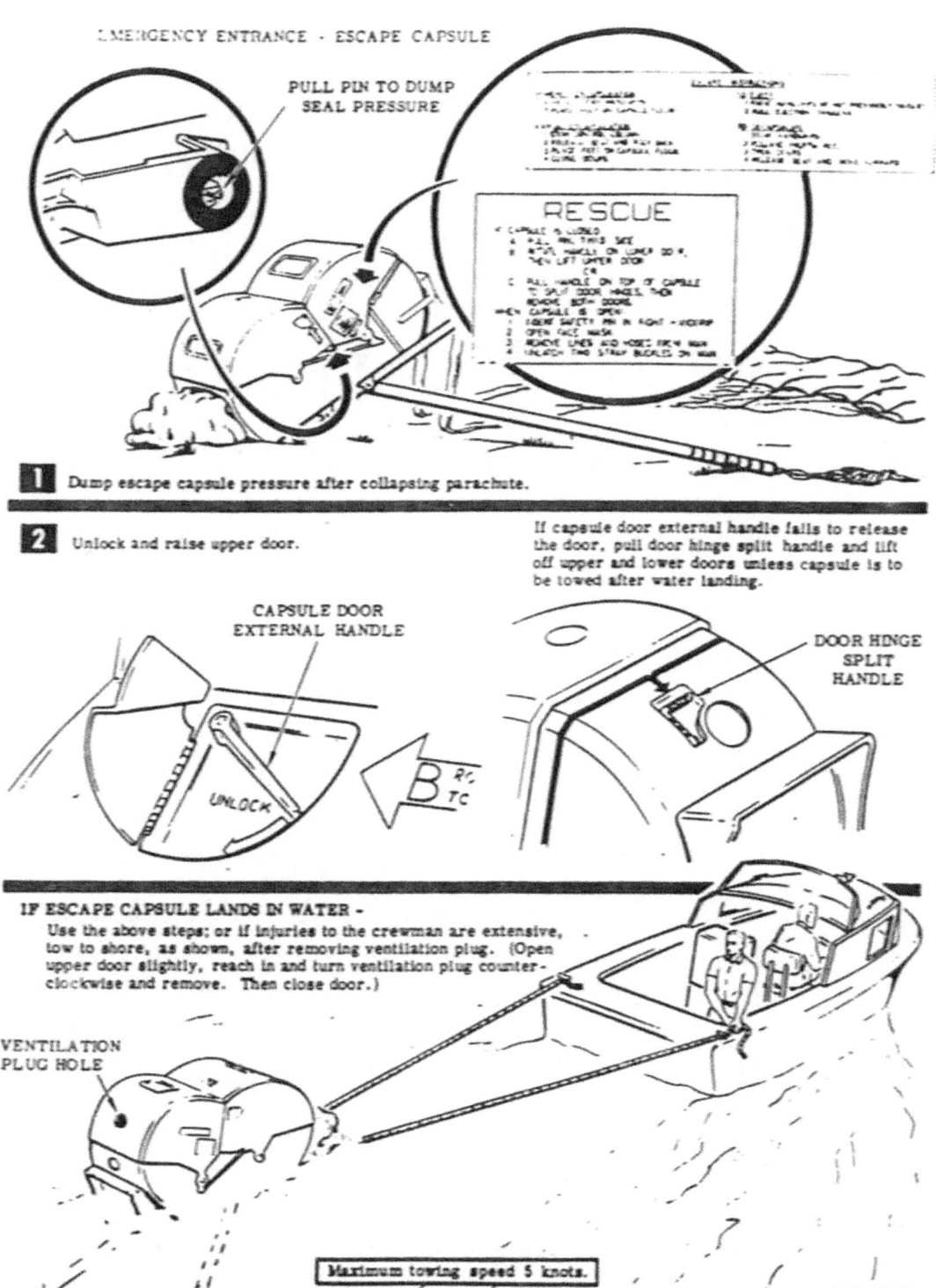

1. Dump escape capsule pressure after collapsing parachute.

2. Unlock and raise upper door.

If capsule door external handle fails to release the door, pull door hinge split handle and lift off upper and lower doors unless capsule is to be towed after water landing.

IF ESCAPE CAPSULE LANDS IN WATER -
Use the above steps; or if injuries to the crewman are extensive, tow to shore, as shown, after removing ventilation plug. (Open upper door slightly, reach in and turn ventilation plug counterclockwise and remove. Then close door.)

Maximum towing speed 5 knots.

Figure 3-6 (Sheet 4 of 4)

Changed 30 November 1964

T.O. 1B-70(X)A-1

2. When time and conditions permit, annunciator light test switch - Hold at BRIGHT or DIM momentarily to test for indications of essential ac bus power.
   a. If all annunciator lights remain out, proceed to step 3. Failure of lights to come on when test switch is used, indicates essential ac bus failure.
   b. If all annunciator lights come on when test switch is used, essential ac bus power is available. Therefore, proceed to step 4 in attempt to return to normal throttle control.
3. Throttle and fire detection bus selector switch - RH BUS.
   Break safety wire and move selector switch to RH BUS to transfer throttle servo system power from the essential ac bus to the right primary ac bus.

   CAUTION
   Do not select RH BUS position if essential ac bus power is available.

4. All throttles - Reposition to engine rpm.
5. Throttle reset button - Press.
   If the throttle servo systems are operating, the servo actuators will be adjusted to their respective throttle settings.
6. All throttles - As required.
   a. If engines do not respond, use alternate throttle switches to control thrust (emergency battery* on if required).
7. Battery-inverter switch* - ON, on final approach.
   Make sure emergency battery is energized on final to provide emergency power for alternate throttle use if necessary.

RETURNING TO NORMAL THROTTLE SYSTEM.

After an alternate throttle switch has been used, an attempt to return engine control to the normal throttle servo system can be made as follows:

1. Throttle (affected engine) - Reposition to engine rpm.

*Airplane AF62-001

2. Throttle reset button - Press.
   If the normal throttle system is operating, the thrust control servo actuators will be adjusted to their respective throttle settings.

ENGINE SHUTDOWN WITH FAILED THROTTLE.

To shut down an engine with a failed throttle system, proceed as follows:

1. Alternate throttle switch (affected engine) - Hold at DECR until idle thrust is obtained.

   CAUTION
   During engine shutdown, when using an alternate throttle switch, do not move throttle to OFF until engine thrust is reduced to idle, or possible fuel system damage may occur.

2. Throttle (affected engine) - OFF.

ENGINE EXHAUST NOZZLE FAILURE.

PRIMARY EXHAUST NOZZLE FAILS OPEN.

Failure of a primary exhaust nozzle in the open direction is indicated by the corresponding primary nozzle position indicator and a lower-than-normal exhaust temperature. During afterburner operation, such a failure may cause afterburner flame-out.

T.O. 1B-70(X)A-1

PRIMARY NOZZLE FAILS OPEN - ABOVE MACH 2.1, AUTO/MANUAL OR MANUAL AICS (AIRPLANE AF62-001).

1. Bypass wheels - Both aft as required to maintain shocks in crosshatch.
2. Engine rpm lockup switch - RELEASE.
3. Throttle (affected engine) - IDLE, and maintain shocks in crosshatch.
   a. If nozzle closes, throttle (affected engine) - 40 degrees, then proceed to step 5.
   b. If nozzle stays open, maintain 80% rpm on affected engine until engine is shut down after landing, or proceed to step 4.

   NOTE
   If unlocked idle rpm is above 80%, descend at unlocked idle until 80% rpm is obtained.

4. Throttle (affected engine) - OFF, maintain shocks in crosshatch, and abort flight.
5. Throat:
   If AUTO - Check schedule.
   If MANUAL - Both wheels aft to maintain throat at 0.2 Mach less than airplane Mach.
6. Engine rpm lockup switch - AUTO.
7. Throttle (affected engine) - 40 degrees.

   NOTE
   Advance throttle of affected engine to 40 degrees, to provide fuel flow for proper cooling of engine lube oil system. (See figure 5-2.)

PRIMARY NOZZLE FAILS OPEN - BELOW MACH 2.1, AUTO/MANUAL OR MANUAL AICS (AIRPLANE AF62-001).

1. Bypass area (affected inlet):
   If SUPERSONIC - Wheel aft to obtain 700, 1100, or 1800 square inches. For first throttle to be moved to IDLE, obtain 700 square inches; for second throttle, 1100 square inches; and for third throttle, 1800 square inches.
   If SUBSONIC - Check bypass area closed.

2. Engine rpm lockup switch - RELEASE.
3. Throttle (affected engine) - IDLE.
   a. If nozzle closes, throttle (affected engine) - 40 degrees, then proceed to step 5.
   b. If nozzle stays open, maintain 80% rpm on affected engine until engine is shut down after landing, or proceed to step 4.

   NOTE
   If unlocked idle rpm is above 80%, descend at unlocked idle until 80% rpm is obtained.

4. Throttle (affected engine) - OFF, and abort flight.
5. Throat - Check schedule.
6. Engine rpm lockup switch (above Mach 1.4) - AUTO.
7. Throttle (affected engine) - 40 degrees.

   NOTE
   Advance throttle of affected engine to 40 degrees, to provide fuel flow for proper cooling of engine lube oil system. (See figure 5-2.)

PRIMARY NOZZLE FAILS OPEN - ABOVE MACH 2.1, AUTOMATIC OR STANDBY AICS (AIRPLANE AF62-207).

1. Bypass area (affected inlet):
   If AUTO, duct performance switch - LOW.
   If STANDBY, bypass door standby switch - Down to maintain shock in crosshatch.
2. Engine rpm lockup switch - RELEASE.
3. Throttle (affected engine) - IDLE, and if affected inlet is in standby mode maintain shock in crosshatch.
4. Throat (affected inlet):
   If AUTO - Check schedule.
   If STANDBY, throat Mach schedule standby switch - Down to maintain throat at 0.2 Mach less than airplane Mach.
5. Throttle (affected engine):
   a. If nozzle closes, throttle (affected engine) - 40 degrees, then proceed to step 8.

T.O. 1B-70(X)A-1

b. If nozzle remains open, maintain 80% rpm on affected engine until engine is shutdown after landing, or proceed to step 6.

NOTE

If unlocked idle rpm is above 80%, descend at unlocked idle until 80% rpm is obtained.

6. Throttle (affected engine) - OFF, and if affected inlet is in standby mode maintain shock in crosshatch.
7. Bypass door standby switch (if affected inlet is in automatic mode) - Hold down 1, 3, or 6 seconds.

If the inlet for the engine being shut down is in automatic mode, hold the bypass door standby switch down for one second if only one engine is shut down; three seconds if two engines are shut down; and six seconds if three engines are shut down. This will bias the bypass door master cylinder from its normal rig position so that when the airplane is decelerating through approximately Mach 2.08 (AICS transfers from shock control to open loop control) the bypass doors will slowly open from their normal locked position of 500 square inches to approximately 700, 1100, or 1800 square inches (one, two, or three engines out).

8. Engine rpm lockup switch - AUTO.
9. Throttle (affected engine) - 40 degrees.

NOTE

Advance throttle of affected engine to 40 degrees, to provide fuel flow for proper cooling of engine lube oil system. (See figure 5-2.)

10. Duct performance switch (if affected inlet is in automatic mode) - NORM.

PRIMARY NOZZLE FAILS OPEN - BELOW MACH 2.1, AUTOMATIC OR STANDBY AICS (AIRPLANE AF62-207).

1. Bypass area (affected inlet):
   If SUPERSONIC, bypass door standby switch - Hold down 1, 3, or 6 seconds.

Hold the bypass door standby switch down for one second if only one throttle is to be moved to IDLE; three seconds for two throttles at IDLE; and six seconds for three throttles at IDLE. If the affected inlet is in automatic mode, this will bias the bypass door master cylinder from its normal rig position so that when the airplane is decelerating through approximately Mach 2.08 (AICS transfers from shock control to open loop control) the bypass doors will slowly open from their normal locked position of 500 square inches to approximately 700, 1100, or 1800 square inches (one, two, or three engines at IDLE or out). If the affected inlet is in standby mode, this will cause the bypass doors to open to approximately 700, 1100, or 1800 square inches, respectively.

If SUBSONIC - Check both bypass areas closed.

2. Engine rpm lockup switch - RELEASE.
3. Throttle (affected engine) - IDLE.
4. Throats - If one inlet is in standby mode and the other in automatic mode, adjust standby throat to obtain same throat Mach schedule indicator reading as for the automatic throat. If both throats are automatic, check indicators stopped at approximately Mach 2.1.
5. Throttle (affected engine):
   a. If nozzle closes, throttle (affected engine) - 40 degrees, then proceed to step 8.
   b. If nozzle remains open, maintain 80% rpm on affected engine until engine is shut down after landing, or proceed to step 6.

NOTE

If unlocked idle rpm is above 80%, descend at unlocked idle until 80% rpm is obtained.

T.O. 1B-70(X)A-1

6. Throttle (affected engine) - OFF.
7. Bypass area (affected inlet):
   If SUPERSONIC, bypass door standby switch - As required to refine bypass to 700, 1100, or 1800 square inches.
   Move switch as required to obtain 700 square inches for one engine out; 1100 square inches for two engines out; and 1800 square inches for three engines out.
8. Engine rpm lockup switch (above Mach 1.4) - AUTO.
9. Throttle (affected engine) - 40 degrees.

NOTE

Advance throttle of affected engine to 40 degrees, to provide fuel flow for proper cooling of engine lube oil system. (See figure 5-2.)

PRIMARY EXHAUST NOZZLE FAILS CLOSED.

Failure of a primary exhaust nozzle in the closed direction is indicated by the corresponding primary nozzle position indicator. An overtemperature, compressor stall, and/or rpm drop also may occur. This type of failure may be caused by a failure in the primary nozzle section of the nozzle area control and also cuts off afterburner fuel flow.

PRIMARY NOZZLE FAILS CLOSED - ABOVE MACH 2.1, AUTO/MANUAL OR MANUAL AICS (AIRPLANE AF62-001).

1. Bypass wheels - Both aft to maintain shocks in crosshatch.
2. Engine rpm lockup switch - RELEASE.
3. Throttle (affected engine) - IDLE, and maintain shocks in crosshatch.
   a. If exhaust temperature remains within limits, throttle (affected engine) - 40 degrees.
   b. If exhaust temperature cannot be controlled, throttle (affected engine) - OFF.
4. Throat:
   If AUTO - Check schedule.
   If MANUAL - Both throat wheels aft to maintain throat at 0.2 Mach less than airplane Mach.
5. Engine rpm lockup switch - AUTO.

6. Throttle (affected engine) - 40 degrees.

NOTE

Advance throttle of affected engines to 40 degrees, to provide fuel flow for proper cooling of engine lube oil system. (See figure 5-2.)

PRIMARY NOZZLE FAILS CLOSED - BELOW MACH 2.1, AUTO/MANUAL OR MANUAL AICS (AIRPLANE AF62-001).

1. Bypass area (affected inlet):
   If SUPERSONIC - Wheel aft to obtain 700, 1100, or 1800 square inches. For first throttle to be moved to IDLE, obtain 700 square inches; for second throttle, 1100 square inches; and for third throttle, 1800 square inches.
   If SUBSONIC - Check bypass area closed.
2. Engine rpm lockup switch - RELEASE.
3. Throttle (affected engine) - IDLE.
   a. If exhaust temperature remains within limits, throttle (affected engine) - 40 degrees.
   b. If exhaust temperature cannot be controlled, throttle (affected engine) - OFF.
4. Throat - Check schedule.
5. Engine rpm lockup switch (above Mach 1.4) - AUTO.
6. Throttle (affected engine) - 40 degrees.

NOTE

Advance throttle of affected engine to 40 degrees, to provide fuel flow for proper cooling of engine lube oil system. (See figure 5-2.)

PRIMARY NOZZLE FAILS CLOSED - ABOVE MACH 2.1, AUTOMATIC OR STANDBY AICS (AIRPLANE AF62-207).

1. Bypass area (affected inlet):
   If AUTO, duct performance switch - LOW.
   If STANDBY, bypass door standby switch - Down to maintain shock in crosshatch.
2. Engine rpm lockup switch - RELEASE.
3. Throttle (affected engine) - IDLE, and if affected inlet is in standby mode maintain shock in crosshatch.

4. Throat (affected inlet):
   If AUTO - Check schedule.
   If STANDBY, throat Mach schedule standby switch - DOWN to maintain throat at 0.2 Mach less than airplane Mach.
5. Throttle (affected engine):
   a. If exhaust temperature remains within limits, throttle (affected engine) - 40 degrees. Proceed to step 8.
   b. If exhaust temperature cannot be controlled, proceed to step 6.
6. Throttle (affected engine) - OFF, and if affected inlet is in standby mode maintain shock in crosshatch.
7. Bypass door standby switch (if affected inlet is in automatic mode) - Hold down 1, 3, or 6 seconds.
   If the inlet for the engine being shut down is in automatic mode, hold the bypass door standby switch down for one second if only one engine is shut down; three seconds if two engines are shut down; and six seconds if three engines are shut down. This will bias the bypass door master cylinder from its normal rig position so that when the airplane is decelerating through approximately Mach 2.08 (AICS transfers from shock control to open loop control) the bypass doors will slowly open from their normal locked position of 500 square inches to approximately 700, 1100, or 1800 square inches (one, two, or three engines out).
8. Engine rpm lockup switch - AUTO.
9. Throttle (affected engine) - 40 degrees.

   NOTE
   Advance throttle of affected engine to 40 degrees, to provide fuel flow for proper cooling of engine lube oil system. (See figure 5-2.)

10. Duct performance switch (if affected inlet is in automatic mode - NORM.

NOZZLE FAILS CLOSED - BELOW MACH 2.1, AUTOMATIC OR STANDBY AICS (AIRPLANE AF62-207).

1. Bypass area (affected inlet):
   If SUPERSONIC, bypass door standby switch - Hold down 1, 3, or 6 seconds.
   Hold the bypass door standby switch down for one second if only one throttle is to be moved to IDLE; three seconds for two throttles at IDLE; and six seconds for three throttles at IDLE. If the affected inlet is in automatic mode, this will bias the bypass door master cylinder from its normal rig position so that when the airplane is decelerating through approximately Mach 2.08 (AICS transfers from shock control to open loop control) the bypass doors will slowly open from their normal locked position of 500 square inches to approximately 700, 1100, or 1800 square inches (one, two, or three engines at IDLE or out). If the affected inlet is in standby mode, this will cause the bypass doors to open to approximately 700, 1100, or 1800 square inches, respectively.
   If SUBSONIC - Check both bypass areas closed.
2. Engine rpm lockup switch - RELEASE.
3. Throttle (affected engine) - IDLE.
4. Throats - If one inlet is in standby mode and the other in automatic mode, adjust standby throat to obtain same throat Mach schedule indicator reading as for the automatic throat. If both throats are automatic, check indicators stopped at approximately Mach 2.1.
5. Throttle (affected engine):
   a. If exhaust temperature remains within limits, throttle (affected engine) - 40 degrees. Proceed to step 8.
   b. If exhaust temperature cannot be controlled, proceed to step 6.
6. Throttle (affected engine) - OFF.
7. Bypass area (affected inlet):
   If SUPERSONIC, bypass door standby switch - As required to refine bypass area to 700, 1100, or 1800 square inches.
   Move switch as required to obtain 700 square inches for one engine out; 1100 square inches for two engines out; and 1800 square inches for three engines out.

T.O. 1B-70(X)A-1

8. Engine rpm lockup switch (above Mach 1.4) - AUTO.
9. Throttle (affected engine) - 40 degrees.

    NOTE

    Advance throttle of affected engine to 40 degrees to provide fuel flow for proper cooling of engine lube oil system. (See figure 5-2.)

AFTERBURNER FAILURE.

During take-off, if an afterburner failure occurs before reaching decision speed, the take-off should be aborted because it must be assumed the cause of the failure is unknown and successive failure on the other engines also may occur. (Refer to "Engine Failure During Take-off, Abort" in this section.) If decision speed has been exceeded, continue the take-off. (Refer to "Engine Failure During Take-off, Take-off Continued" in this section.)

ENGINE OIL PRESSURE LOW.

The engine oil pressure caution light comes on when low oil pressure is sensed for any engine, and simultaneous illumination of an engine identification light shows which engine has the failure. The oil pressure caution light senses low pressure at the No. 2 bearing. If low engine oil pressure is indicated, the affected engine must be shut down immediately except during take-off. Refer to "Engine Failure" in this section for applicable engine shutdown procedures.

    NOTE

    - The oil pressure caution light goes out when the throttle is retarded to OFF, and the applicable engine identification light remains on.

    - The engine which is being shut down because of low oil pressure must be braked if engine rpm does not reduce to 22% within 5 minutes after the throttle is moved to OFF.

    CAUTION

    If more than one engine must be braked, airplane speed must be reduced to Mach 1.5 before the second engine can be braked.

ACCESSORY DRIVE SYSTEM FAILURE.

ACCESSORY DRIVE SYSTEM OIL PRESSURE FAILURE, OR GEARBOX OR TRANSMISSION SHAFT FAILURE.

The simultaneous illumination of the ADS caution light and an engine identification light indicates low oil pressure in an accessory drive system gearbox. If the failure is mechanical, (gearbox or transmission shaft) the hydraulic pump status indicator for the affected gearbox will show yellow, and if on engines 3 or 4, the respective generator out caution light will come on. If an accessory drive system oil system failure is indicated, the affected engine must be shut down immediately, except during take-off. Refer to "Engine Failure" in this section for applicable engine shutdown procedures.

    NOTE

    - The ADS oil pressure caution light goes out when the applicable throttle is retarded to OFF. The applicable engine identification light remains on.

    - The engine which is being shut down because of ADS oil pressure or gearbox or transmission shaft failure must be braked if engine rpm does not reduce to 22% within 5 minutes after the throttle is moved to OFF.

    CAUTION

    If more than one engine must be braked, airplane speed must be reduced to Mach 1.5 before the second engine can be braked.

Changed 25 June 1965

3-43

T.O. 1B-70(X)A-1

ACCESSORY DRIVE SYSTEM OIL PRESSURE FAILURE - TWO GEARBOXES SIMULTANEOUSLY.

The illumination of the ADS oil pressure caution light with simultaneous illumination of two specific engine identification lights (1 and 4, 2 and 5, or 3 and 6) is a possible indication of a failure in one of the gaseous nitrogen systems which pressurizes and inerts the lubricating system of the respective gearboxes.

NOTE
If the accessory drive oil pressure caution light and engine identification lights 2 and 5 come on, together with the tire and drag chute compartment overheat caution lights, loss of nitrogen system No. 2 is indicated.

Above 30,000 feet, loss of nitrogen pressure can cause cavitation of the lube pumps in the corresponding gearboxes. However, below 30,000 feet the gearbox lube pumps will not cavitate if nitrogen pressure is not available.

ADS OIL PRESSURE FAILURE - TWO GEARBOXES SIMULTANEOUSLY (ABOVE MACH 2.1), AUTO/MANUAL OR MANUAL AICS (AIRPLANE AF62-001).

If oil pressure failure in two gearboxes simultaneously is indicated during flight above Mach 2.1, proceed as follows:

NOTE
The ADS oil pressure caution light goes out when the applicable throttle is retarded to OFF. The applicable engine identification light remains on.

1. Bypass wheels - Both aft to maintain shocks in crosshatch.
2. Engine rpm lockup switch - RELEASE.
3. Throttles (affected engines) - IDLE, and maintain shocks in crosshatch.
4. Throat:
   If AUTO - Check both schedules.
   If MANUAL - Both throat wheels aft to maintain throat at 0.2 Mach less than airplane Mach.
5. Descend to below 30,000 feet, with throttles (good engines) - MIL.
   a. If the ADS oil pressure caution light and both engine identification lights go out when below 30,000 feet, a nitrogen system failure is indicated. Flight may be continued at any thrust setting below 30,000 feet. Accomplish step 6 only.
   b. If the ADS oil pressure caution light and the engine identification lights remain on, proceed to step 7.
6. Applicable primary generator switch - Cycle, if required.
   If engine 3 or 4 is affected, cycle corresponding primary generator switch to restore generator operation.
7. Throttles (affected engines) - OFF, and maintain shocks in crosshatch.
8. Engine emergency brake switches (affected engines) - ON, if required, and maintain shocks in crosshatch.

NOTE
The engines which are to be shut down must be braked if engine rpm does not reduce to 22% within 5 minutes after the throttles are moved to OFF.

CAUTION
Before the second engine can be braked, the airplane speed must be reduced to Mach 1.5 or below.

9. Engine emergency brake switches - OFF.
   Move switches to OFF after engine rpm has stabilized at 22% or below.
10. Engine rpm lockup switch - AUTO.
11. Throttles (affected engines) - 40 degrees, if brakes not used.

NOTE
If engine braking was not required, advance throttles of affected engines to 40 degrees, to provide fuel flow for proper cooling of engine lube oil system. (See figure 5-2.)

T.O. 1B-70(X)A-1

ADS OIL PRESSURE FAILURE - TWO GEARBOXES SIMULTANEOUSLY (BELOW MACH 2.1), AUTO/MANUAL OR MANUAL AICS (AIRPLANE AF62-001).

If oil pressure failure in two gearboxes simultaneously is indicated during flight below Mach 2.1, proceed as follows:

> **NOTE**
> The ADS oil pressure caution light goes out when the applicable throttle is retarded to OFF. The applicable engine identification light remains on.

1. Bypass area:
    If SUPERSONIC - Both wheels aft to obtain 700, 1100, or 1800 square inches.
    For first throttle to be moved to IDLE, obtain 700 square inches; for second throttle, 1100 square inches; and for third throttle, 1800 square inches.
    If SUBSONIC - Check both bypass areas closed.
2. Engine rpm lockup switch - RELEASE.
3. Throttles (affected engines) - IDLE.
4. Throat - Check both schedules.
5. Descend to below 30,000 feet, with throttles (good engines) - MIL.
    a. If the ADS oil pressure caution light and both engine identification lights go out when below 30,000 feet a nitrogen system failure is indicated. Flight may be continued at any thrust setting below 30,000 feet. Accomplish step 6 only.
    b. If the ADS oil pressure caution light and the engine identification lights remain on, proceed to step 7.
6. Applicable primary generator switch - Cycle, if required.
    If engine 3 or 4 is affected, cycle corresponding primary generator switch to restore generator operation.
7. Throttles (affected engines) - OFF.
8. Engine emergency brake switches (affected engines) - ON, if required.

> **NOTE**
> The engines which are to be shut down must be braked if engine rpm does not reduce to 22% within 5 minutes after the throttles are moved to OFF.

> **CAUTION**
> Before the second engine can be braked, the airplane speed must be reduced to Mach 1.5 or below.

9. Engine emergency brake switches - OFF.
    Move switches to OFF after engine rpm has stabilized at 22% or below.
10. Engine rpm lockup switch (above Mach 1.4) - AUTO.
11. Throttles (affected engines) - 40 degrees, if brakes not used.

> **NOTE**
> If engine braking was not required, advance throttles of affected engines to 40 degrees, to provide fuel flow for proper cooling of engine lube oil system. (See figure 5-2.)

ADS OIL PRESSURE FAILURE - TWO GEARBOXES SIMULTANEOUSLY (ABOVE MACH 2.1), AUTOMATIC OR STANDBY AICS (AIRPLANE AF62-207).

If oil pressure failure in two gearboxes simultaneously is indicated during flight above Mach 2.1, proceed as follows:

> **NOTE**
> The ADS oil pressure caution light goes out when the applicable throttle is retarded to OFF. The applicable engine identification light remains on.

1. Bypass area:
    If AUTO, duct performance switch - LOW.
    If STANDBY, bypass door standby switch - Down to maintain shock in crosshatch.
2. Engine rpm lockup switch - RELEASE.
3. Throttles (affected engines) - IDLE, and if either inlet is in standby mode maintain shock in crosshatch.

Changed 25 June 1965

T.O. 1B-70(X)A-1

4. Throats:
   If AUTO - Check schedule.
   If STANDBY, throat Mach schedule standby switch - Down to maintain throat at 0.2 Mach less than airplane Mach.
5. Descend to below 30,000 feet, with throttles (good engines) - MIL.
   a. If the ADS oil pressure caution light and both engine identification lights go out when below 30,000 feet a nitrogen system failure is indicated. Flight may be continued at any thrust setting below 30,000 feet. Accomplish step 6 only.
   b. If the ADS oil pressure caution light and the engine identification lights remain on, proceed to step 7.
6. Applicable primary generator switch - Cycle, if required.
   If engine 3 or 4 is affected, cycle corresponding primary generator switch to restore generator operation.
7. Throttles (affected engines) - OFF.
8. Bypass door standby switch (if affected inlet is in automatic mode) - Hold down 1, 3, or 6 seconds.
   If an inlet is in automatic mode, hold the bypass door standby switch for that inlet down for one second if only one engine is shut down; three seconds if two engines are shut down; and six seconds if three engines are shut down. This will bias the bypass door master cylinder from its normal rig position so that when the airplane is decelerating through approximately Mach 2.08 (AICS transfers from shock control to open loop control) the bypass doors will slowly open from their normal locked position of 500 square inches to approximately 700, 1100, or 1800 square inches (one, two, or three engines out).
9. Engine emergency brake switches (affected engines) - ON, if required.

   NOTE
   The engines which are to be shut down must be braked if engine rpm does not reduce to 22% within 5 minutes after the throttles are moved to OFF.

   CAUTION
   Before the second engine can be braked, the airplane speed must be reduced to Mach 1.5 or below.

10. Engine emergency brake switch - OFF.
    Move switch to OFF after engine rpm has stabilized at 22% or below.
11. Engine rpm lockup switch - AUTO.
12. Throttles (affected engines) - 40 degrees, if brakes not used.

    NOTE
    If engine braking was not required, advance throttles of affected engines to 40 degrees, to provide fuel flow for proper cooling of engine lube oil system. (See figure 5-2.)

13. Duct performance switch (if either inlet is in automatic mode) - NORM.

ADS OIL PRESSURE FAILURE - TWO GEARBOXES SIMULTANEOUSLY (BELOW MACH 2.1), AUTOMATIC OR STANDBY AICS (AIRPLANE AF62-207).

If oil pressure failure in two gearboxes simultaneously is indicated during flight below Mach 2.1, proceed as follows:

NOTE
The ADS oil pressure caution light goes out when the applicable throttle is retarded to OFF. The applicable engine identification light remains on.

1. Bypass areas:
   If SUPERSONIC, bypass door standby switches - Hold both down 1, 3, or 6 seconds.
   Hold both bypass door standby switches down for one second if only one throttle per inlet is to be moved to IDLE; three seconds for two throttles per inlet at IDLE; and six seconds for three throttles per inlet at IDLE. If an affected inlet is in automatic mode, this will bias the bypass door master cylinder from its normal rig position so that when the air-

3-46

T.O. 1B-70(X)A-1

plane is decelerating through approximately Mach 2.08 (AICS transfers from shock control to open loop control) the bypass doors will slowly open from their normal locked position of 500 square inches to approximately 700, 1100, or 1800 square inches (one, two, or three engines at IDLE or out). If an affected inlet is in standby mode, this will cause the bypass doors to open to approximately 700, 1100, or 1800 square inches, respectively.
   If SUBSONIC - Check both bypass areas closed.
2. Engine rpm lockup switch - RELEASE.
3. Throttles (affected engines) - IDLE.
4. Throats - If one inlet is in standby mode and the other in automatic, adjust standby throat to obtain same throat Mach schedule indicator reading as for the automatic throat. If both throats are automatic, check indicators stopped at approximately Mach 2.1.
5. Descend to below 30,000 feet, with throttles (good engines) - MIL.
   a. If the ADS oil pressure caution light and both engine identification lights go out when below 30,000 feet a nitrogen system failure is indicated. Flight may be continued at any thrust setting below 30,000 feet. Accomplish step 6 only.
   b. If the ADS oil pressure caution light and the engine identification lights remain on, proceed to step 7.
6. Applicable primary generator switch - Cycle, if required.
   If engine 3 or 4 is affected, cycle corresponding primary generator switch to restore generator operation.
7. Bypass areas:
   If SUPERSONIC, bypass door standby switches - Both as required to refine bypass areas to 700, 1100, or 1800 square inches.
   Move switches as required to obtain 700 square inches for one engine per inlet out; 1100 square inches for two engines per inlet out; and 1800 square inches for three engines per inlet out.

8. Throttles (affected engines) - OFF.
9. Engine emergency brake switches (affected engines) - ON, if required.

NOTE
The engines which are to be shut down must be braked if engine rpm does not reduce to 22% within 5 minutes after the throttles are moved to OFF.

CAUTION
Before the second engine can be braked, the airplane speed must be reduced to Mach 1.5 or below.

10. Engine emergency brake switches - OFF.
    Move switches to OFF after engine rpm has stabilized at 22% or below.
11. Engine rpm lockup switch (above Mach 1.4) - AUTO.
12. Throttles (affected engines) - 40 degrees, if brakes not used.

NOTE
If engine braking was not required, advance throttles of affected engines to 40 degrees, to provide fuel flow for proper cooling of engine lube oil system. (See figure 5-2.)

EXCESSIVE ENGINE OR ACCESSORY DRIVE SYSTEM GEARBOX VIBRATION.

If the vibration of any engine or accessory drive system gearbox is over 50 percent (5 mils peak-to-peak), the vibration caution light comes on and the affected engine or gearbox can be identified from the vibration indicator.

NOTE
The master caution light does not come on with the vibration caution light.

The steady-state vibration limit for the engine varies with engine speed; the gearbox vibration limit remains constant at 50 percent. (The 50 percent limit also applies to engine operation at 104% rpm.) Engine vibration limits are shown in figure 5-4.

T.O. 1B-70(X)A-1

During engine starts, high engine vibration can be disregarded until the engine has been accelerated and decelerated. Indications of high engine vibration also can be disregarded during throttle transients.

EXCESSIVE ENGINE OR ACCESSORY DRIVE SYSTEM GEARBOX VIBRATION - ABOVE MACH 2.1, AUTO/MANUAL OR MANUAL AICS (AIRPLANE AF62-001).

If excessive engine or ADS gearbox vibration occurs during flight above Mach 2.1, proceed as follows:

1. Bypass wheels - Both aft to maintain shocks in crosshatch.
2. Engine rpm lockup switch - RELEASE.
3. Throttle (affected engine) - IDLE, and maintain shocks in crosshatch.
4. Throat:
   If AUTO - Check schedule.
   If MANUAL - Both throat wheels aft to maintain throat at 0.2 Mach less than airplane Mach.
5. Start normal deceleration and descent as required, with throttles (good engines) - MIL.
   a. If vibration level remains excessive, proceed to step 6.
   b. If the vibration caution light goes out, leave throttle (affected engine) at IDLE.
6. Throttle (affected engine) - OFF, and maintain shocks in crosshatch.
7. Engine emergency brake switch (affected engine) - ON, if vibration is excessive, and maintain shocks in crosshatch.

CAUTION
Only one engine per inlet should be braked above Mach 1.5. This prevents the possibility of inducing continuous inlet buzz which could seriously affect airplane stability and control and could damage the engines and the inlet. Speed should be reduced to below Mach 1.5 before actuation of the brake for a second engine.

NOTE
The engine braking system is irreversible; therefore, the engine cannot be restarted after the emergency brake has been engaged.

8. Engine emergency brake switch - OFF. Move switch to OFF after engine rpm has stabilized at 22% or below.
9. Engine rpm lockup switch - AUTO.
10. Throttle (affected engine) - 40 degrees, if brake not used.

NOTE
If engine braking was not required, advance throttle of affected engine to 40 degrees, to provide fuel flow for proper cooling of engine lube oil system. (See figure 5-2.)

EXCESSIVE ENGINE OR ACCESSORY DRIVE SYSTEM GEARBOX VIBRATION - BELOW MACH 2.1, AUTO/MANUAL OR MANUAL AICS (AIRPLANE AF62-001).

If excessive engine or ADS gearbox vibration occurs during flight below Mach 2.1, proceed as follows:

1. Bypass area (affected inlet):
   If SUPERSONIC - Wheel aft to obtain 700, 1100, or 1800 square inches. For first throttle to be moved to IDLE, obtain 700 square inches; for second throttle, 1100 square inches; and for third throttle, 1800 square inches.
   If SUBSONIC - Check bypass area closed.
2. Engine rpm lockup switch - RELEASE.
3. Throttle (affected engine) - IDLE.
4. Throat - Check schedule.
5. Start normal deceleration and descent as required, with throttles (good engines) - MIL.
   a. If vibration level remains excessive, proceed to step 6.
   b. If the vibration caution light goes out, leave throttle (affected engine) at IDLE.
6. Throttle (affected engine) - OFF.
7. Engine emergency brake switch (affected engine) - ON, if vibration is excessive.

CAUTION
Only one engine per inlet should be braked above Mach 1.5. This prevents the

possibility of inducing continuous inlet buzz which could seriously affect airplane stability and control and could damage the engines and the inlet. Speed should be reduced to below Mach 1.5 before actuation of the brake for a second engine.

NOTE

The engine braking system is irreversible; therefore, the engine cannot be restarted after the emergency brake has been engaged.

8. Engine emergency brake switch - OFF. Move switch to OFF after engine rpm has stabilized at 22% or below.
9. Engine rpm lockup switch (above Mach 1.4) - AUTO.
10. Throttle (affected engine) - 40 degrees, if brake not used.

NOTE

If engine braking was not required, advance throttle of affected engine to 40 degrees, to provide fuel flow for proper cooling of engine lube oil system. (See figure 5-2.)

EXCESSIVE ENGINE OR ACCESSORY DRIVE SYSTEM GEARBOX VIBRATION - ABOVE MACH 2.1, AUTOMATIC OR STANDBY AICS (AIRPLANE AF62-207).

If excessive engine or ADS gearbox vibration occurs during flight above Mach 2.1, proceed as follows:

1. Bypass area (affected inlet):
   If AUTO, duct performance switch - LOW.
   If STANDBY, bypass door standby switch - Down to maintain shock in crosshatch.
2. Engine rpm lockup switch - RELEASE.
3. Throttle (affected engine) - IDLE, and if affected inlet is in standby mode maintain shock in crosshatch.
4. Throat (affected inlet):
   If AUTO - Check schedule.
   If STANDBY, throat Mach schedule standby switch - Down to maintain throat at 0.2 Mach less than airplane Mach.

5. Start normal deceleration and descent as required, with throttles (good engines) - MIL.
   a. If vibration level remains excessive, proceed to step 6.
   b. If the vibration caution light goes out, leave throttle (affected engine) at IDLE.
6. Throttle (affected engine) - OFF, and if affected inlet is in standby mode maintain shock in crosshatch.
7. Bypass door standby switch (if affected inlet is in automatic mode) - Hold down 1, 3, or 6 seconds. If the inlet for the engine to be shut down is in automatic mode, hold the bypass door switch down for one second if only one engine is shut down; three seconds if two engines are shut down; and six seconds if three engines are shut down. This will bias the bypass door master cylinder from its normal rig position so that when the airplane is decelerating through approximately Mach 2.08 (AICS transfers from shock control to open loop control) the bypass doors will slowly open from the normal locked position of 500 square inches to approximately 700, 1100, or 1800 square inches (one, two, or three engines out).
8. Engine emergency brake switch (affected engine) - ON, if vibration is excessive, and maintain shock in crosshatch.

CAUTION

Only one engine per inlet should be braked above Mach 1.5. This prevents the possibility of inducing continuous inlet buzz which could seriously affect airplane stability and control and could damage the engines and the inlet. Speed should be reduced to below Mach 1.5 before actuation of the brake for a second engine.

NOTE

The engine braking system is irreversible; therefore, the engine cannot be restarted after the emergency brake has been engaged.

T.O. 1B-70(X)A-1

9. Engine emergency brake switch - OFF.
   Move switch to OFF after engine
   rpm has stabilized at 22% or below.
10. Engine rpm lockup switch - AUTO.
11. Throttle (affected engine) - 40
    degrees, if brake not used.
12. Duct performance switch (if affected
    inlet is in automatic mode) - NORM.

EXCESSIVE ENGINE OR ACCESSORY DRIVE SYSTEM GEARBOX VIBRATION - BELOW MACH 2.1, AUTOMATIC OR STANDBY AICS (AIRPLANE AF62-207).

If excessive engine or ADS gearbox vibration occurs during flight below Mach 2.1, proceed as follows:

1. Bypass area (affected inlet):
   If SUPERSONIC, bypass door standby switch - Down 1, 3, or 6 seconds.
   Hold bypass door standby switch down for one second if only one throttle is to be moved to IDLE;
   three seconds for two throttles at IDLE; and six seconds for three throttles at IDLE. If the affected inlet is in the automatic mode, this will bias the bypass door master cylinder from its normal rig position so that when the airplane is decelerating through approximately Mach 2.08 (AICS transfers from shock control to open loop control) the bypass doors will slowly open from their normal locked position of 500 square inches to approximately 700, 1100, or 1800 or out). If the affected inlet is in standby mode, this will cause the bypass doors to open to approximately 700, 1100, or 1800 square inches (one, two, or three engines at IDLE or out). If the affected inlet is in standby mode, this will cause the bypass doors to open to approximately 700, 1100, or 1800 square inches, respectively.

   If SUBSONIC - Check both bypass areas closed.
2. Engine rpm lockup switch - RELEASE.
3. Throttle (affected engine) - IDLE.

4. Throats - If one inlet is in standby mode and the other in automatic, adjust standby throat to obtain same throat Mach schedule indicator reading as for the automatic throat. If both throats are automatic, check indicators stopped at approximately Mach 2.1.
5. Start normal deceleration and descent as required, with throttles (good engines) - MIL.
   a. If vibration level remains excessive, proceed to step 6.
   b. If the vibration caution light goes out, leave throttle (affected engine) at IDLE.
6. Bypass area (affected inlet):
   If SUPERSONIC, bypass door standby switch - As required to refine bypass area to 700, 1100, or 1800 square inches.
   Move switch as required to obtain 700 square inches for one engine out; 1100 square inches for two engines out; and 1800 square inches for three engines out.
7. Throttle (affected engine) - OFF.
8. Engine emergency brake switch (affected engine) - ON, if vibration is excessive.

   CAUTION
   Only one engine per inlet should be braked above Mach 1.5. This prevents the possibility of inducing continuous inlet buzz which could seriously affect airplane stability and control and could damage the engines and the inlet. Speed should be reduced to below Mach 1.5 before actuation of the brake for a second engine.

   NOTE
   The engine braking system is irreversible; therefore, the engine cannot be restarted after the emergency brake has been engaged.

9. Engine emergency brake switch - OFF.
   Move switch to OFF after engine rpm has stabilized at 22% or below.
10. Engine rpm lockup switch (above Mach 1.4) - AUTO.

11. Throttle (affected engine) - 40 degrees, if brake not used.

    NOTE
    If engine braking was not required, advance throttle of affected engine to 40 degrees, to provide fuel flow for proper cooling of engine lube oil system. (See figure 5-2.)

ENGINE OR ADS VIBRATION INDICATING SYSTEM FAILURE.

The vibration indicating system is relatively simple and the possibility of system failure is remote. In most cases, an indicating system failure will result in zero indicator readings. However, if a vibration pick-up or bracket is loose, or if there is a break in the shielding of the pick-up signal wire, an excessively high indicator reading results. If a pick-up is loose, the readings will respond to rpm changes; if the shielding is broken, rpm changes have no effect on the reading. If an in-flight failure of the vibration indicating system is suspected, the system test button can be used to check the operation. (This will not isolate a loose pick-up or broken shielding.) When the system is operating properly, pressing the test button causes the vibration caution light to come on, and makes both pointers on each indicator read somewhere between 75 percent and the sum of 75 percent plus the previous indicator reading (vibration pick-up).

AIR INDUCTION CONTROL SYSTEM EMERGENCY OPERATION.

FAILURE OF THROAT MACH SCHEDULE INDICATOR - ABOVE MACH 2.1 (AIRPLANE AF62-001).

If either throat Mach schedule indicator fails, or the respective throat indicator caution light comes on, use the following procedure:

1. Bypass wheels - Both aft to position and maintain shocks in crosshatch.
2. Maintain stabilized level flight.
3. Throat wheels - Both aft to maintain throats at 0.2 Mach less than airplane Mach.
4. Throat Mach schedule mode switches - Both MAN.
   a. If affected throat Mach schedule indicator resumes operation, stay in manual mode.
   b. If affected throat Mach schedule indicator does not resume operation, proceed to step 5.
5. Throat Mach schedule mode switches - Both OFF.
6. Throat Mach schedule standby switch (affected inlet) - Jog down to OPEN as necessary, maintaining shocks in crosshatch, until both bypass area indicator readings are the same.
7. Throttles - MIL.
8. Bypass wheels - Both aft toward OPEN to maintain shocks in crosshatch.
9. Throat Mach schedule standby switches - Both down to DECR to maintain throats at 0.2 Mach less than airplane Mach.

FAILURE OF THROAT MACH SCHEDULE INDICATOR - ABOVE MACH 2.1 (AIRPLANE AF62-207).

If either throat Mach schedule indicator fails (indicator fails to respond to changes in airplane Mach or moves erratically or to a hard-over position), proceed as follows:

1. AICS (affected inlet):
   If AUTO - No action necessary. If there is no accompanying indication of failure of the automatic mode, the affected inlet should be left in automatic mode. If STANDBY, bypass door standby switch - Move as necessary to set bypass area of affected inlet the same as for the other inlet, plus 100 square inches.
2. Throat Mach schedule standby switch (affected inlet) - Move as required to maintain the shock in the green arc.
3. Decelerate to Mach 1.0 or below.

T.O. 1B-70(X)A-1

THROAT PANEL EXTENDED CAUTION LIGHT ON - BELOW MACH 1.5 (AIRPLANE AF62-001).

If either throat panel extended caution light comes on below Mach 1.5, indicating the inlet throat width is less than 39 inches, a large thrust loss will occur. If either light comes on during flight below Mach 1.5, proceed as follows:

WARNING
Do not take off if a throat panel extended caution light is on. An inlet throat size corresponding to a throat Mach schedule indicator reading 3.0 reduces available thrust to less than 25 percent of the normal thrust.

1. Throat mode switch (affected inlet) - Check OFF.
2. Throat Mach schedule standby switch (affected inlet) - Down until throat Mach schedule indicator for affected inlet reads 1.67 (throat full open).
3. Abort mission and land.

THROAT PANEL EXTENDED CAUTION LIGHT ON - BELOW MACH 1.4 (AIRPLANE AF62-207).

Illumination of a throat panel extended caution light during flight below Mach 1.4 indicates the affected throat is extended to less than 39 inches. Under such conditions, a large loss of thrust and engine compressor stall will occur unless corrective action is taken immediately. If either throat panel extended caution light comes on during flight below Mach 1.4, proceed as follows:

1. AICS mode switch (affected inlet) - STBY.
2. Throat Mach schedule standby switch (affected inlet) - Down until throat Mach schedule indicator for affected inlet reads 1.67 Mach (throat full open).

BYPASS DOOR OPEN CAUTION LIGHT ON - BELOW MACH 0.4 (AIRPLANE AF62-001).

If either bypass door open caution light comes on during flight below Mach 0.4, this indicates the bypass doors for the affected inlet are not fully closed.

This could result in pressure conditions which would cause structural damage to the inlet in the area of the bypass plenum. If either light comes on during flight below Mach 0.4, proceed as follows:

1. Bypass door mode switch (affected inlet) - Check OFF.
2. Bypass standby system selector switch (affected inlet) - PRIMARY.
3. Bypass door standby switch (affected inlet) - Up to CLOSE.
   Hold switch up to CLOSE until bypass doors of affected inlet are fully closed and caution light goes out.
4. Bypass standby system selector switch (affected inlet) - ALTERNATE, if bypass doors did not close.
5. Bypass door standby switch (affected inlet) - Up to CLOSE.
   Hold switch up to CLOSE until bypass doors of affected inlet are fully closed and caution light goes out.

FAILURE OF SHOCK WAVE POSITION INDICATOR (AIRPLANE AF62-207).

If either shock wave position indicator fails (indicator needle is erratic or goes to a hard-over position and remains there) during flight with a started inlet, proceed as follows:

1. AICS (affected inlet):
   If AUTO - No action necessary.
      If there is no accompanying indication of failure of the automatic mode, the affected inlet should be left in automatic mode.
   If STANDBY, bypass door standby switch - Move as necessary to set bypass area of affected inlet the same as for the other inlet, plus 100 square inches.
2. Throat Mach schedule standby switch (affected inlet) - Move as required to obtain same throat Mach schedule indicator reading as for the other throat.
3. Decelerate to Mach 1.0 or below.

T.O. 1B-70(X)A-1

SHOCK AFT CAUTION LIGHT ON - BELOW MACH 0.7 (AIRPLANE AF62-207).

Illumination of a shock aft caution light during flight below Mach 0.7 indicates that the bypass doors are not fully closed. This could result in pressure conditions which would cause structural damage to the inlet in the area of the bypass plenum. If either light comes on below Mach 0.7, proceed as follows:

1. AICS mode switch (affected inlet) - STBY.
2. Bypass door standby switch (affected inlet) - Up until light goes out.

SHOCK AFT CAUTION LIGHT ON - STARTED INLET (AIRPLANE AF62-207).

Illumination of a shock aft caution light during flight with the inlets started indicates the shock position for the affected inlet is aft of a predetermined limit. This would result in loss of thrust and engine stall if allowed to continue. If either light comes on during started inlet flight, proceed as follows:

NOTE

If the inlets are in automatic mode, a light may go on momentarily due to a transient condition. If the light goes out, no corrective action is necessary.

1. Bypass area (affected inlet):
    If AUTO - Monitor. If not recovering, put inlet in standby mode.
    Check bypass area and shock wave position indicators of affected inlet. If bypass area is not decreasing, shock wave position indicator needle is not moving toward FDW and light remains on, put affected inlet in standby mode.
    If STANDBY, go to step 2.
2. Bypass door standby switch (affected inlet) - Up until shock aft caution light goes out.
3. Duct performance switch - NORM.

UNSTART AND/OR BUZZ.

NOTE
- If inlet unstart or buzz occurs, the engines may stall, flame out, or overtemp.
- The airplane will yaw away from and roll toward the unstarted or buzzing inlet.
- The duct unstart caution lights are inoperative when both throat Mach schedule indicators are at Mach 2.17 or less.

An unstarted inlet is indicated by the respective unstart caution light coming on. Buzz may or may not accompany an unstart.

BUZZ BELOW MACH 2.1 - MANUAL AICS (AIRPLANE AF62-001).

1. Bypass wheel (affected inlet) - Aft to position shock at top of green arc.
    If buzz caution light goes out, return to normal operation. If light remains on, proceed to step 2.

NOTE
Avoid opening bypass more than necessary, as engine stall could occur.

2. Engine rpm lockup switch - RELEASE.
3. Throttles (affected inlet) - As required.
    Retard throttles to IDLE or as necessary to maintain engines within operating limits.
4. Throat - Check schedule.
5. Engines (affected inlet) - If abnormal:
    a. Bypass wheel (affected inlet) - Aft.
    b. Throttles (affected engines) - OFF.

Changed 25 June 1965

3-460

T.O. 1B-70(X)A-1

6. Throttles (affected engines) - 40 degrees.

   NOTE
   Advance throttles of affected engines to 40 degrees, to provide fuel flow for proper cooling of engine lube oil system. (See figure 5-2.)

7. Bypass wheel (affected inlet) - Forward to obtain 700, 1100, or 1800 square inches.
   For one engine shut down, obtain 700 square inches; for two engines, 1100 square inches; and for three engines, 1800 square inches.

8. Engine rpm lockup switch (above Mach 1.4) - AUTO.

BUZZ BELOW MACH 2.1 - AUTOMATIC OR STANDBY AICS (AIRPLANE AF62-207).

1. Bypass area (affected inlet):
   If AUTO - Monitor. If not increasing, go to standby mode.
   If bypass area is increasing, this indicates the automatic system is correcting the buzz condition. If the bypass area is not increasing or is decreasing, put affected inlet in standby mode.
   If STANDBY, bypass door standby switch - Move as necessary to position the shock wave of the affected inlet in the top of the green arc.

2. Engine rpm lockup switch - RELEASE.

3. Throttles (affected inlet) - As required.
   Move throttles to IDLE or as required to maintain engines within operating limits.

4. Throats - If one inlet is in standby mode and the other in automatic mode, adjust standby throat to obtain same throat Mach schedule indicator reading as for the automatic throat.

5. Engines (affected inlet) - If abnormal:
   a. Bypass door standby switch - Hold down 1, 3, or 6 seconds.
      Hold bypass door standby switch down for one second if only one engine is to be shut down; three seconds if two engines are to be shut down; and six seconds if three engines are to be shut down. This will bias the bypass door master cylinder from its normal rig position so that when the airplane is decelerating through approximately Mach 2.08 (AICS transfers from shock control to open loop control) the bypass doors will slowly open from their normal locked position of 500 square inches to approximately 700, 1100, or 1800 square inches (one, two, or three engines out).
   b. Throttles (affected engines) - OFF.

6. Throttles (affected engines) - 40 degrees.

   NOTE
   Advance throttles of affected engines to 40 degrees, to provide fuel flow for proper cooling of engine lube oil system. (See figure 5-2.)

7. Bypass door standby switch (affected inlet) - As required to refine bypass area to 700, 1100, or 1800 square inches.
   Move switch as required to obtain 700 square inches for one engine out; 1100 square inches for two engines out; and 1800 square inches for three engines out.

8. Engine rpm lockup switch (above Mach 1.4) - AUTO.

UNSTART WITH OR WITHOUT BUZZ - AUTO/MANUAL AICS (AIRPLANE AF62-001).

1. Bypass wheels - Both aft to position and maintain shocks in crosshatch.

   CAUTION
   Avoid opening bypass more than necessary, as engine stall could occur.

2. Engine rpm lockup switch - RELEASE.

3. Throttles (all engines) - As required, and maintain shocks in crosshatch.
   Retard throttles to IDLE or as necessary to maintain engines within operating limits.

4. Throat Mach schedule mode switch - Both MAN and adjust bypass wheels as necessary to maintain shocks in crosshatch.

T.O. 1B-70(X)A-1

5. Engines (affected inlet) - If abnormal, throttles of affected engines OFF and maintain shock in crosshatch.
6. Unstart and buzz caution lights - Check.
   a. If lights are out, proceed to step 7.
   b. If either caution light remains on, check both throat Mach at 0.4 Mach less than airplane Mach, and slowly roll both bypass wheels aft until light goes out or bottom of crosshatch is reached. (Do not bottom needles).

   NOTE

   If inlet cannot be restarted, switch to standby and reduce speed to below Mach 1.5.

7. Resume normal engine operation and maintain shocks in crosshatch.

   CAUTION

   If buzz accompanied the unstart condition and any engine had to be shut down, it must not be restarted. If buzz did not accompany the unstart condition, any engine which had been shut down may be restarted.

8. Engine rpm lockup switch - AUTO.
9. Throat wheels - Both forward to airplane Mach and adjust bypass wheels as necessary to maintain shocks in crosshatch.
10. Bypass wheels - Both forward as required to obtain desired shock position.

UNSTART WITH OR WITHOUT BUZZ - MANUAL AICS (AIRPLANE AF62-001).

1. Bypass wheels - Both aft to position and maintain shocks in crosshatch.

   CAUTION

   Avoid opening bypass more than necessary, as engine stall could occur.

2. Engine rpm lockup switch - RELEASE.
3. Throttles (all engines) - As required, and maintain shocks in crosshatch.
   Retard throttles to IDLE or as necessary to maintain engines within operating limits.

4. Throat wheels - Both aft to decrease throat Mach 0.3 to 0.4 Mach, and adjust bypass wheels as necessary to maintain shocks in crosshatch.
5. Engines (affected inlet) - If abnormal, throttles of affected engines OFF and maintain shocks in crosshatch.
6. Unstart and buzz caution lights - Check.
   a. If lights are out, proceed to step 7.
   b. If either caution light remains on, check both throat Mach at 0.4 Mach less than airplane Mach and slowly roll both bypass wheels aft until light goes out or bottom of crosshatch is reached. (Do not bottom needles.)

   NOTE

   If inlet cannot be restarted, switch to standby and reduce speed to below Mach 1.5.

7. Resume normal engine operation, and maintain shocks in crosshatch.

   CAUTION

   If buzz accompanied the unstart condition and any engine had to be shut down, it must not be restarted. If buzz did not accompany the unstart condition, any engine which had been shut down may be restarted.

8. Engine rpm lockup switch - AUTO.
9. Throat wheels - Both forward to airplane Mach and adjust bypass wheels as necessary to maintain shocks in crosshatch.
10. Bypass wheels - Both forward as required to obtain desired shock position.

UNSTART WITH OR WITHOUT BUZZ - AUTOMATIC OR STANDBY AICS (AIRPLANE AF62-207).

If Affected Inlet In Automatic Mode

1. Duct performance switch - NORM.
2. Bypass area and throat Mach schedule indicator - Monitor.

a. If the inlet recovers, do only step 3. Inlet action toward recovery will be initially indicated by an increase in bypass area and a decrease in throat Mach schedule indicator reading. When recovery is complete, the unstart (and buzz) caution lights will go out.
b. If the inlet is not recovering, proceed to step 4.
3. AICS reset switch/light - Press momentarily. Check light out.
4. Duct performance switch and AICS mode switch (affected inlet) - LOW, then STBY.
Rapidly and in sequence, move the duct performance switch to LOW, then the AICS mode switch for the affected inlet to STANDBY. If the mode switch is moved first or too long after the duct performance switch is moved to LOW, the bypass doors would tend to move at high rate toward the closed position, aggravating the unstart and buzz condition.

If Affected Inlet in Standby Mode

5. Bypass door standby switch (affected inlet) - Down to maintain shock in crosshatch.
6. Engine rpm lockup switch - RELEASE.
7. Throttles (all engines) - As required, and maintain shock for affected inlet in crosshatch.
8. Throat Mach schedule standby switch (affected inlet) - Down to maintain throat 0.3 to 0.4 Mach less than airplane Mach, and maintain shock for affected inlet in crosshatch.
9. Engines (affected inlet) - If abnormal, throttles of affected engines OFF, and maintain shock for affected inlet in crosshatch.
10. Unstart and buzz caution lights - Check.
a. If lights are out, proceed to step 11.
b. If either caution light remains on, check throat of affected inlet 0.3 to 0.4 Mach less than airplane Mach and slowly jog bypass door standby switch of affected inlet down until light goes out or bottom of crosshatch is reached. (Do not bottom needle.)

NOTE
If inlet cannot be restarted, reduce speed to below Mach 1.5.

11. Resume normal engine operation and maintain shock for affected inlet in crosshatch.

CAUTION
If buzz accompanied the unstart condition and any engine had to be shut down, it must not be restarted. If buzz did not accompany the unstart condition, any engine which had been shut down may be restarted.

12. Engine rpm lockup switch - AUTO.
13. Throat Mach schedule standby switch (affected inlet) - As required.
14. Bypass door standby switch (affected inlet) - Up, as required.
15. Duct performance switch - NORM.

CHANGE-OVER TO STANDBY AICS (AIRPLANE AF62-001).

If it becomes necessary to change the inlets from auto/manual or manual to standby mode of operation, proceed as follows:

1. All 4 mode switches - OFF.
Check both bypass standby system selector switches at PRIMARY, or ALTERNATE if required.
2. Bypass door standby switches - Both down as required to position and maintain shocks in crosshatch.
3. Throat Mach schedule standby switches - Both down as required to decrease throat Mach 0.2 less than airplane Mach.
4. Throttles - MIL.
5. Bypass door standby switches - Both as required to maintain shocks in crosshatch or to obtain 700 square inches when speed is below Mach 2.1.
6. Throat Mach schedule standby switches - Both as required to maintain throat Mach 0.2 less than airplane Mach.

T.O. 1B-70(X)A-1

CHANGE-OVER TO STANDBY AICS (AIRPLANE AF62-207).

If it becomes necessary to change an inlet from automatic to standby mode of operation, proceed as follows:

1. Duct performance switch - LOW; then AICS mode switch (affected inlet) - STBY.

   Rapidly and in sequence, move the duct performance switch to LOW, then the AICS mode switch for the affected inlet to STBY. If the mode switch is moved first or too long after the duct performance switch is moved to LOW, the bypass doors would tend to move at high rate toward the closed position, inducing buzz or unstart.

   NOTE

   If it is necessary to move both inlets to standby mode, the change-over should be accomplished one inlet at a time. After the first inlet is put in standby mode (by accomplishing step 1, above), move the duct performance switch to NORM, then repeat step 1 for the second inlet.

2. Bypass area (affected inlet):
   IF ABOVE MACH 2.1, bypass door standby switch - Down to maintain shock in crosshatch.
   IF BELOW MACH 2.1, bypass door standby switch - Down 700, 1100, or 1800 square inches.

   Hold switch down to obtain 700 square inches for no engines or one engine out; 1100 square inches for two engines out; or 1800 square inches for three engines out.

3. Throat Mach schedule standby switch (affected inlet) - Down to maintain throat at 0.2 Mach less than airplane Mach.
4. Duct performance switch - NORM.
   If one inlet remains in automatic mode, move duct performance switch to NORM.
5. See "Emergency Deceleration - One or Both Inlets in Standby AICS (Airplane AF62-207)."

EMERGENCY DECELERATION - STANDBY AICS (AIRPLANE AF62-001).

SUPERSONIC ABOVE MACH 2.1.

Before Decelerating

Before beginning to decelerate from any airspeed above Mach 2.1, accomplish the following:

1. All four mode switches - OFF.
   Check both bypass standby system selector switches at PRIMARY, or ALTERNATE if required.
2. Bypass door standby switches - Both down to position and maintain shocks in crosshatch.
3. Throat Mach schedule standby switches - Both down to maintain throats at 0.2 Mach less than airplane Mach.
4. Throttles - MIL.
5. Bypass door standby switches - Both down to maintain shocks in crosshatch.

2.6 Mach

6. Bypass door standby switches - Both down as required.
7. Throat Mach schedule standby switches - Both down to maintain throats at 0.2 Mach less than airplane Mach.
8. Lateral bobweight switch - LOCK.

2.1 Mach

9. Throttles - 40 degrees or above.
10. Engine status - Check.
11. Bypass door standby switches - Both up to position shocks in green arc.
12. Throat Mach schedule standby switches - Both down to maintain throats at 0.2 Mach less than airplane Mach.
13. Fuel tank pump switches of empty tanks - Check OFF.

SUPERSONIC BELOW MACH 2.1.

Before decelerating from any supersonic airspeed below Mach 2.1, accomplish the following:

14. All four mode switches - OFF.

Changed 25 June 1965

T.O. 1B-70(X)A-1

15. Bypass area - Check both 700, 1100, or 1800 square inches.
    For no engines or one engine out in an inlet, check bypass area 700 square inches; for two engines out, 1100 square inches; and for three engines out, 1800 square inches.
16. Throat Mach schedule standby switches - Both down to maintain throats at 0.2 Mach less than airplane Mach.
17. Throttles - MIL.

1.7 Mach

18. Throat Mach schedule standby switches - Both down until throats are full open (1.67).
19. Throat wheels - Both full aft.
20. Emergency heat exchanger water switch - OFF.
21. Pitot heater and windshield defogging switches - ON.

1.4 Mach

22. Wing tip position selector switch - ½.

NOTE

When the wing tips are raised, a slight nose-down trim change occurs.

23. Throttles - 40 degrees or above.
24. Engine rpm lockup switch - RELEASE.
25. Bypass door standby switches - Both up as required.
    For no engines out in one inlet, obtain 400 square inches; for one engine out, 700 square inches; for two engines out, 1100 square inches; and for three engines out, 1800 square inches.
26. Fuel tank pump switches of empty tanks - Check OFF.
27. Liquid nitrogen quantity - Check.
28. Secondary exhaust nozzle area standby pressure knob - Set to airplane altitude if engines are below 100% rpm.
29. Engine rpm - Maintain engines 3 and 4 at or above 87%.

1.0 Mach

30. Bypass door standby switches - Both up until bypass areas are full closed.

31. Bypass wheels - Both full forward.
32. Bypass standby system selector switches - Leave both at PRIMARY or ALTERNATE.

CAUTION

If the bypass standby system selector switches are moved to OFF, the actuators will center and the bypass doors will move to the position selected by the bypass wheels or to the position as determined by the bypass master cylinder.

33. Secondary exhaust nozzle area standby pressure knob - Set to field elevation.
34. Nose ramp switch - DOWN.
35. Anticollision light switch - ON.

0.95 Mach

36. Wing tip position selector switch - UP.

NOTE

When the wing tips are raised, a slight nose-down trim change occurs.

37. Ammonia, water, oxygen, and liquid nitrogen quantities - Check.
38. Electrical and hydraulics - Check. Check voltages, and hydraulic pressures, fluid levels, and pump indicators.
39. Fuel tank pump switches of empty tanks - Check OFF.
40. Engine rpm - Maintain engines 3 and 4 at or above 87%.

EMERGENCY DECELERATION - ONE OR BOTH INLETS IN STANDBY AICS (AIRPLANE AF62-207).

Before Decelerating

Before beginning to decelerate from any airspeed with one or both inlets in standby mode, accomplish the following:

1. Duct performance switch - Check NORM.
2. Bypass area:
   AUTO inlet - Check.
   STANDBY inlet, bypass door standby switch - Down to maintain shock in crosshatch.

T.O. 1B-70(X)A-1

3. Throat:
   AUTO inlet - Check schedule.
   STANDBY inlet, throat Mach schedule standby switch - Down to maintain throat at 0.2 Mach less than airplane Mach.
4. Throttles - MIL.

2.3 Mach

1. Throttles - 40 degrees or above.
2. Engine status - Check.
3. Bypass area:
   AUTO inlet - Check.
   STANDBY inlet, bypass door standby switch - Up to position shock in the green arc.
4. Throat:
   Auto inlet - Check.
   STANDBY inlet, bypass door standby switch - Down until throat Mach schedule indicator reads Mach 2.1.
5. Fuel tank pump switches of empty tanks - Check OFF.

2.0 Mach

1. Bypass area:
   AUTO inlet - Check closing to 500 square inches plus the bias if applied for engine-out condition.
      If all engines are operating, check bypass area closing to 500 square inches; with one engine out, closing to 700 square inches; with two engines out, closing to 1100 square inches; and with three engines out, closing to 1800 square inches.
   STANDBY inlet - Check 700, 1100, or 1800 square inches.
      For no engines out or one engine out, obtain 700 square inches; for two engines out, 1100 square inches; and for three engines out, 1800 square inches.
2. Throat trim power switch - OFF.

1.7 Mach

1. Emergency heat exchanger water switch - OFF.
2. Pitot heater and windshield defogging switches - ON.

1.4 Mach

1. Wing tip position selector switch - ½.

NOTE
When the wing tips are raised, a slight nose-down trim change occurs.

2. Throttles - 40 degrees or above.
3. Engine rpm lockup switch - RELEASE.
4. Fuel tank pump switches of empty tanks - Check OFF.
5. Liquid nitrogen quantity - Check.
6. Secondary exhaust nozzle area standby pressure knob - Set to airplane altitude if engines are below 100% rpm.
7. Engine rpm - Maintain engines 3 and 4 at or above 87%.
8. Bypass area:
   AUTO inlet - Check closing plus the bias if applied for engine-out condition.
      If all engines are operating, check bypass area closing to 0000; with one engine out, closing to 700 square inches; with two engines out, closing to 1100 square inches; and with three engines out, closing to 1800 square inches.

   STANDBY inlet - Check 400, 700, 1100, or 1800 square inches.
      For no engines out, obtain 400 square inches; one for engine out, 700 square inches; for two engines out, 1100 square inches; and for three engines out, 1800 square inches.

1.0 Mach

1. AICS mode switches - Both STBY.
2. Bypass door standby switches - Both down until bypass areas are fully closed.
3. Throat Mach schedule standby switches - Both down until throats are full open (throat Mach schedule indicators read 1.67).
4. Secondary exhaust nozzle area standby pressure knob - Set to field elevation.
5. Nose ramp switch - DOWN.
6. Anticollision light switch - ON.

T.O. 1B-70(X)A-1

.95 Mach

1. Wing tip position selector switch - UP.

   NOTE
   When the wing tips are raised, a slight nose-down trim change occurs.

2. Ammonia, water, oxygen, and liquid nitrogen quantities - Check.
3. Electrical and hydraulics - Check. Check voltages, and hydraulic pressures, fluid levels, and pump indicators.
4. Fuel tank pump switches of empty tanks - Check OFF.
5. Engine rpm - Maintain engines 3 and 4 at or above 87%.

AIR INDUCTION CONTROL SYSTEM COOLING SYSTEM FAILURE (AIRPLANE AF62-001).

The dual AICS cooling system automatically transfers from system No. 1 to system No. 2 in case of a malfunction. If the coolant caution light remains out after master caution light is pressed, the cooling system has transferred to system No. 2, and is functioning properly. If the coolant caution light remains on or comes back on, use the following procedure:

1. Bypass wheels - Both aft to position and maintain shocks in crosshatch.
2. Bypass door mode switches - Both OFF. Check both bypass standby system selector switches at PRIMARY, or ALTERNATE if required.
3. Throat Mach schedule mode switches - Both MAN.
4. Air induction control system package power switch - OFF.
5. Decelerate to Mach 1.5 or below, using standby bypass and manual throat control.
   a. Bypass door standby switches - Both down as required to maintain schedule below.
   b. Throat wheels - Both aft to maintain throat at 0.2 Mach less than airplane Mach.

AIRPLANE MACH NO.	BYPASS AREA NO. OF ENGINES OPERATING (REST WINDMILLING)			
	3	2	1	0
Above 2.8	400	500	600	700
at 2.8	500	650	800	900
2.6	600	800	1000	1200

Bobweight - LOCK

2.4	700	950	1300	1800
2.1	700	700	1100	1800

1.7 Throat wheels - Both full aft.
Throat Mach schedule mode switches - Both OFF.
Emergency heat exchanger water switch - OFF.
Pitot heater and windshield defogging switches - ON.

1.4 Wing tip position selector switch - ½.

   NOTE
   When the wing tips are raised, a slight nose-down trim change occurs.

Engine rpm lockup switch - RELEASE.
Bypass door standby switches - Both up as required.

For no engines out in one inlet, obtain 400 square inches; for one engine out, 700 square inches; for two engines out, 1100 square inches; and for three engines out, 1800 square inches.

Fuel tank pump switches of empty tanks - Check OFF.
Liquid nitrogen quantity - Check.
Secondary exhaust nozzle area standby pressure knob - Set to airplane altitude if engines are below 100% rpm.
Engine rpm - Maintain engines 3 and 4 at or above 87%.

1.0 Bypass door standby switches - Both up until bypass areas are full closed.
Bypass wheels - Both full forward.
Bypass standby system selector switches - Leave both at PRIMARY or ALTERNATE.

T.O. 1B-70(X)A-1

Secondary exhaust nozzle area standby pressure knob - Set to field elevation.
Nose ramp switch - DOWN.
Anticollision light switch - ON.
.95 Wing tip position selector switch - UP.

NOTE

When the wing tips are raised, a slight nose-down trim change occurs.

Ammonia, water, oxygen, and liquid nitrogen quantities - Check.
Electrical and hydraulics - Check.
Check voltages, and hydraulic pressures, fluid levels and pump indicators.
Fuel tank pump switches of empty tanks - OFF.
Engine rpm - Maintain engines 3 and 4 at or above 87%.

AIR INDUCTION CONTROL SYSTEM COOLING SYSTEM FAILURE (AIRPLANE AF62-207).

The dual AICS cooling system automatically transfers from system No. 1 to system No. 2 in case of a malfunction. If the coolant caution light remains out after the master caution light is pressed, the cooling system has transferred to system No. 2 and is functioning properly. If the coolant light remains on or comes back on, use the following procedure:

1. Duct performance switch - LOW; then both AICS mode switches - STBY.
   Rapidly and in sequence move the duct performance switch to LOW, then both AICS mode switches simultaneously to STBY. If the mode switches are moved first or too long after the duct performance switch is moved to LOW, the bypass doors would tend to move at high rate toward the closed position, inducing buzz or unstart.

NOTE

If both mode switches cannot be moved simultaneously with ease and without any delay, the change-over to standby mode may be made one inlet at a time. After the first inlet is put in standby mode, move the duct performance switch back to NORM, then put the second inlet in standby mode.

2. Bypass door standby switches - Both down to maintain shocks in crosshatch.
3. AICS package power switch - OFF.

NOTE

This will disable the buzz and unstart warning systems.

4. Decelerate to Mach 1.5 or below.
   a. Bypass door standby switches - Both down as required to maintain schedule given below.
   b. Throat Mach schedule standby switches - Both down to maintain throats at 0.2 Mach less than airplane Mach.
   c. Throttles - MIL.

AIRPLANE MACH NO.	BYPASS AREA NO. OF ENGINES OPERATING (REST WINDMILLING)			
	3	2	1	0
Above 2.8	400	500	600	700
at 2.8	500	650	800	900
2.6	600	800	1000	1200
2.4	700	950	1300	1800
2.1	700	700	1100	1800

1.7 Emergency heat exchanger water switch - OFF.
Pitot heater and windshield defogging switches - ON.
1.4 Wing tip position selector switch - ½.

NOTE

When the wing tips are raised, a slight nose-down trim change occurs.

Throttles - 40 degrees or above.
Engine rpm lockup switch - RELEASE.
Bypass door standby switches - Both up as required.
For no engines out in one inlet, obtain 400 square inches; for one engine out, 700 square inches; for two engines out, 1100 square inches; and for three engines out, 1800 square inches.

407

T.O. 1B-70(X)A-1

Fuel tank pump switches of empty tanks - Check OFF.
Liquid nitrogen quantity - Check.
Secondary exhaust nozzle area standby pressure knob - Set to airplane altitude if engines are below 100% rpm.
Engine rpm - Maintain engines 3 and 4 at or above 87%.
1.0 Bypass door standby switches - Both down until doors are fully closed.
Throat Mach schedule standby switches - Both down until throats are full open (throat Mach schedule indicators read 1.67).
Secondary exhaust nozzle area standby pressure knob - Set to field elevation.
Nose ramp switch - DOWN.
Anticollision light switch - ON.
.95 Wing tip position selector switch - UP.

NOTE
When the wing tips are raised, a slight nose-down trim change occurs.

Ammonia, water, oxygen, and liquid nitrogen quantities - Check.
Electrical and hydraulics - Check.
  Check voltages, and hydraulic pressures, fluid levels, and pump indicators.
Fuel tank pump switches of empty tanks - Check OFF.
Engine rpm - Maintain engines 3 and 4 at or above 87%.

AIR INDUCTION CONTROL SYSTEM OPERATION WITH RIGHT PRIMARY AC BUS FAILED (AIRPLANE AF62-001).

Illumination of the No. 4 primary generator-out and the bus-tie open caution lights indicates loss of right primary ac bus power. If these lights come on, check for bus voltages with the ac voltmeter and voltmeter phase bus selector switches. If bus failure is definitely indicated, operate the air induction control system as follows:

NOTE
Failure of the right hand primary ac bus will result in loss of the following AICS functions:

● Automatic and manual modes.

● One buzz and one unstart warning system.

● Shock position indication.

1. Bypass door mode switches - Both OFF.
2. Throat Mach schedule mode switches - Both OFF.
3. Bypass standby system selector switches - Both PRIMARY, or ALTERNATE if required.
4. Decelerate to Mach 1.5 or below, using standby bypass and throat control.
   a. Bypass door standby switches - Both down as required to maintain schedule below.
   b. Throat Mach schedule standby switches - Both down to maintain throats at 0.2 Mach less than airplane Mach.
   c. Throttles - MIL.

AIRPLANE MACH NO.	BYPASS AREA NO. OF ENGINES OPERATING (REST WINDMILLING)			
	3	2	1	0
Above 2.8	400	500	600	700
at 2.8	500	650	800	900
2.6	600	800	1000	1200
Bobweight - LOCK				
2.4	700	950	1300	1800
2.1	700	700	1100	1800

1.7 Throat Mach schedule standby switches - Both down until throat Mach schedule indicator is at 1.67.
Emergency heat exchanger water switch - OFF.
Pitot heater and windshield defogging switches - ON.
1.4 Wing tip position selector switch - ½.

NOTE
When the wing tips are raised, a slight nose-down trim change occurs.

Changed 25 June 1965

T.O. 1B-70(X)A-1

Engine rpm lockup switch - RELEASE.
Bypass door standby switches - Both up as required.
   For no engines out in one inlet, obtain 400 square inches; for one engine out, 700 square inches; for two engines out, 1100 square inches; and for three engines out, 1800 square inches.
Fuel tank pump switches of empty tanks - Check OFF.
Liquid nitrogen quantity - Check.
Secondary exhaust nozzle area standby pressure knob - Set to airplane altitude if engines are below 100% rpm.
Engine rpm - Maintain engines 3 and 4 at or above 87%.

1.0 Bypass door standby switches - Both up until bypass areas are fully closed.

Secondary exhaust nozzle area standby pressure knob - Set to field elevation.
Nose ramp switch - DOWN.
Anticollision light switch - ON.

.95 Wing tip position selector switch - UP.

NOTE

When the wing tips are raised, a slight nose-down trim change occurs.

Ammonia, water, oxygen, and liquid nitrogen quantities - Check.
Electrical and hydraulics - Check.
   Check voltages, and hydraulic pressures, fluid levels, and pump indications.
Fuel tank pump switches of empty tanks - OFF.
Engine rpm - Maintain engines 3 and 4 at or above 87%.

This page intentionally left blank

T.O. 1B-70(X)A-1

FUEL SUPPLY SYSTEM FAILURE.

FUEL BOOST PUMP FAILURE.

Boost pump failures will not be known during flight. Failure of one boost pump does not affect fuel flow to the engines. With two boost pumps failed (one boost pump feeding the engines), normal engine operated can be maintained at all altitudes, however, power loss or engine instability may occur during afterburner take-off.

FUEL TRANSFER SYSTEM FAILURE.

Improper operation of the automatic fuel sequence system is indicated by:

- Fuel sequence strips fail to move down.
- Fuel sequence strips move down ahead of sequence.
- No. 3 tank (sump tank) strip falls below the green band.
- Sump tank low fuel level caution light on with fuel remaining in other tanks.

The fuel sequence is shown in figure 3-7. A faulty indicating system may be caused by a failed indicator, fuel probe or fuel control module. If it is determined that a fuel control module has failed, replacements may be made in flight. (See figure 3-8 for fuel control module replacement.) Spare fuel control modules are carried for tanks 1, 2, 3, 4, and 5. No replacement module is provided for left or right tanks 6, 7, or 8.

NOTE
Because either the left or right module of tanks 6, 7, or 8 controls the sequence of the left and right tanks, failure of either module will not prevent the remaining module from sequencing the next tank. The indication of the total fuel remaining may be incorrect.

If the fuel control module for tank No. 3 (sump tank) fails, it should be replaced to provide a continuous indication of the fuel remaining in this tank, and to permit operation of the sump tank low fuel level caution light.

FUEL INDICATING SYSTEM TEST.

The fuel quantity indicator test switch is used to diagnose improper operation of the fuel quantity indicating system.

NOTE
Holding the switch at either position should be limited to about 4 seconds to keep from cycling the fuel pumps and interrupting the normal fuel sequence.

If one indicator (sequence strip or selected quantity) does not respond when the test switch is used, but the others do, the indicator that did not respond has failed. If neither indicator responds, the probable cause is a failed fuel control module. If the indicators respond to the use of the test switch, but do not return to the original indication when the test switch is released,

T.C. 1F-70(X)A-1

FUEL SEQUENCE CHART
(FUEL SYSTEM FULLY SERVICED)

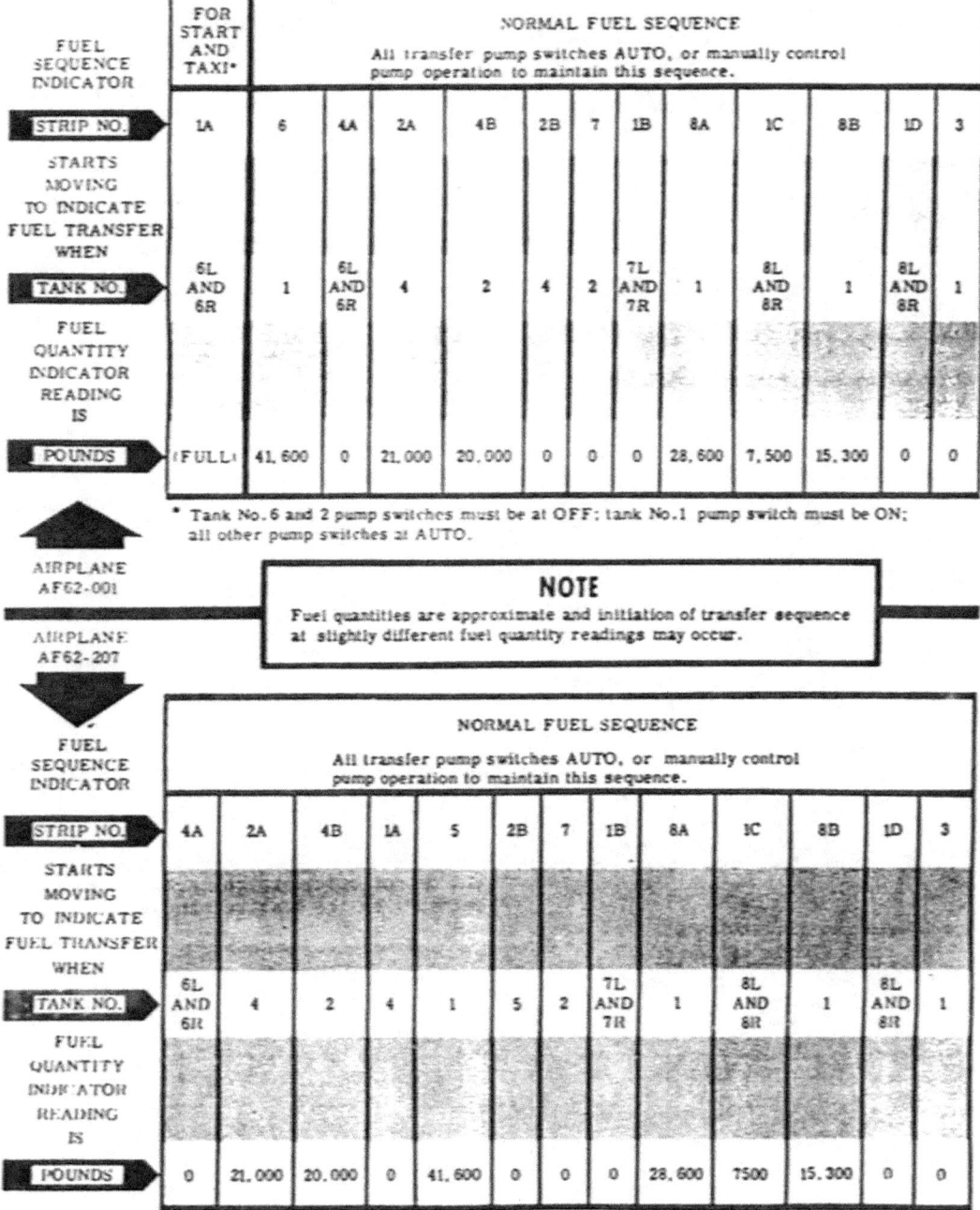

Figure 3-7

T.O. 1B-70(X)A-1

the probable cause is a tank unit circuit failure.

> **NOTE**
> When the yellow portion of any sequence strip appears, either at the top or bottom of the strip, a malfunction of that portion of the sequence indicator is indicated and using the test switch should have no effect on it. The other tank sequence strips should test normally.

SEQUENCE STRIP SHOWS FUEL NOT TRANSFERRING OR TRANSFERRING AHEAD OF SEQUENCE - OTHER THAN TANK 3.

1. If failure is indicated in tank 1 or 8, start return to base before trouble shooting.
2. Selected fuel tank quantity indicator knob - Rotate to applicable tank.
   - If indicator does not agree with sequence strip - Identify failed indicator with the test switch and proceed with normal fuel management.
   - If indicator agrees with sequence strip - Proceed to step 3.
3. Applicable fuel tank pump switch - OFF, if transferring ahead of schedule; ON, if not transferring.
   - If malfunction <u>is</u> corrected - Manually control fuel sequencing until back on sequence.
   - If malfunction <u>is not</u> corrected - Proceed to step 4.
4. Indicating system test switch - EMPTY, momentarily.

> **NOTE**
> Do not hold switch at EMPTY for more than 4 seconds.

   - If the indicators do not test satisfactory, or drove rapidly to empty before the test switch was moved to EMPTY, the indicating system has malfunctioned. Proceed to step 5.
   - If the indicators test satisfactory, proceed to step 6 if tank not transferring or to step 7 if transferring ahead of schedule.
5. If indicators have failed, use the following applicable procedure:
   - Sequence strips 1D, 2B, 4A, 4B, 5, 6, 7, 8A, or 8B - Manually control sequence and monitor tank 3 indication to detect when the affected tank is empty.

> **WARNING**
> If tank 3 indicates tank 8A or 8B is not transferring, land immediately.

   - Sequence strip 2A or 1C - Use all of the affected tank, and monitor tank 3 indication to detect when the tank is empty.

> **NOTE**
> If possible, select unused tank unit circuit on the applicable fuel control module or change the module. (See figure 3-8.)

   - Sequence strip 1A or 1B - Select unused tank unit circuit on the applicable fuel control module or change the module. (See figure 3-8.) If this is not done, or if the malfunction remains, abort the mission.

> **NOTE**
> Total fuel quantity may be erroneous.

6. If both indicators test satisfactory and transfer pumps have failed off:
   a. Turn on next forward tank segment in sequence.

3-49

T.O. 1B-70(X)A-1

FUEL CONTROL MODULE REPLACEMENT

NOTE
- Spare fuel control modules are provided for tanks 1, 2, 3, 4, and 5 only.
- When fuel control unit is pulled out, cockpit indications will be erroneous until control unit is back in place.

1 All fuel tank pump switches (except for tank transferring fuel) - OFF.

2 All associated fuel circuit breakers and circuit breaker switches - Check in and ON. (This may have been the cause of the malfunction.)

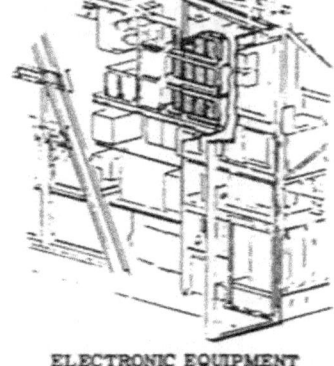

ELECTRONIC EQUIPMENT COMPARTMENT (LEFT SIDE)

3 Release the four camlocks with screwdriver provided.

CAMLOCK SCREWDRIVER

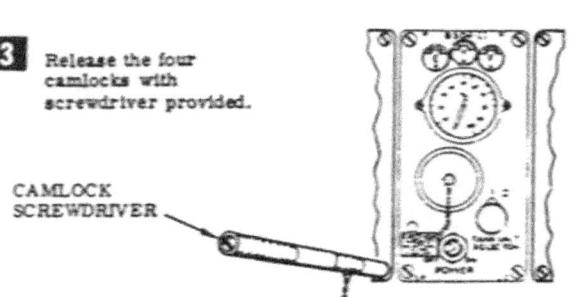

4 Turn wing camlock 1/4 turn to release latching handle. Pull latching handle out about 30 degrees.

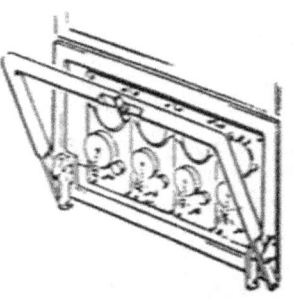

5 Pull fuel control unit out far enough to gain access to the spare module and electrical connections.

Caution
The fuel control unit will drop if pulled out too far.

6 Remove electrical connection and pull failed module from control unit. Install correct spare module for the position, hook up electrical connection, and stow failed module in spare position upside down. Slide control unit back into rack and secure.

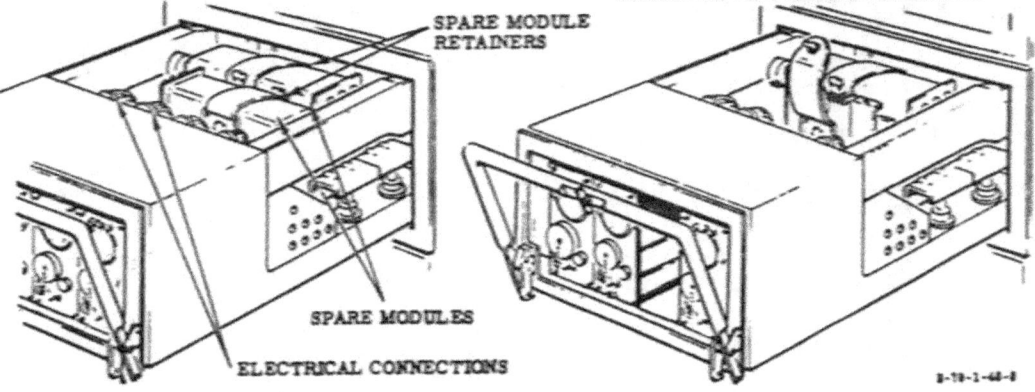

SPARE MODULE RETAINERS

SPARE MODULES

ELECTRICAL CONNECTIONS

Figure 3-8

T.O. 1B-70(X)A-1

b. Manually control fuel sequence in normal alternating sequence, leaving an equal number of portions of upper and lower strips to balance fuel which will not transfer.
c. Plan flight based on available fuel.

WARNING
Immediately abort mission if failure occurs at start of sequence of strips 1B, 1C, 1D, 8A, or 8B.

7. If both indicators test satisfactory and the transfer pumps have failed on, use the following applicable procedure:
   - If the failure is in tank 1 or 2 - Use the affected tank, manually alternating with an aft tank to maintain a balance of upper and lower strips.
   - If the failure is in tank 4 - Let the tank empty, then the sequence will continue automatically.
   - If the failure is in tank 5, 7, or 8:
      a. Refueling valve switch of applicable tank and of last aft tank that has emptied - OPEN.
      b. Use normal alternating sequence to maintain a balance of upper and lower strips.
      c. Affected tank refueling valve switch CLOSE and fuel tank pump switch ON when transfer of fuel from this tank is required.

SEQUENCE STRIP SHOWS TANK FILLING OTHER THAN TANK 3.

1. Selected fuel tank quantity indicator knob - Rotate to applicable tank.
   - If indicator does not agree with sequence strip - Identify failed indicator with the test switch and proceed with normal fuel management.
   - If indicator agrees with the sequence strip - Proceed to step 2.

2. Applicable refueling valve switch - CLOSE.
   a. If malfunction remains - Proceed to next step 3.
3. Indicating system test switch - FULL, momentarily.

NOTE
Do not hold switch at FULL for more than 4 seconds.

- If the indicators do not test satisfactory or drove rapidly to full before the test switch was moved to FULL, the indicating system has malfunctioned. Proceed to step 4.
- If the indicators test satisfactory, proceed to step 5.

4. If indicators have failed, use the following applicable procedure:
   - Sequence strips 1D, 2B, 4A, 4B, 6, 7, 8A, or 8B - Manually control sequence and monitor tank 3 indication to detect when the affected tank is empty.

WARNING
If tank 3 indicates tank 8A is not transferring, land immediately.

- Sequence strip 2A or 1C - Use all of the affected tank and monitor tank 3 indication to detect when the tank is empty.

NOTE
If possible, select unused tank unit circuit on the applicable fuel control module or change the module. (See figure 3-8.)

- Sequence strip 1A or 1B - Select unused tank unit circuit on the

T.O. 1B-70(X)A-1

applicable fuel control module or change the module. (See figure 3-8.) If this is not done or the malfunction remains, abort the mission.

> **NOTE**
> Total fuel quantity may be erroneous.

5. If tank is filling, abort mission and:
   a. Applicable fuel tank pump switch - ON.
   b. All other fuel tank pump switches - OFF, except as necessary to maintain tank 3 below 30,000 pounds to control CG.

TANK 3 INDICATING ABNORMAL.

1. Start return to base before trouble shooting.
2. Selected fuel tank quantity indicator knob - Rotate to 3.
3. Indicating system test switch - Move to EMPTY momentarily.

> **NOTE**
> Do not hold switch at EMPTY for more than 4 seconds.

- If either the sequence strip or the selected fuel tank quantity indicator tests satisfactory - Proceed with normal fuel management.
- If both indicators do not test satisfactory, the indicating system has malfunctioned - Select unused tank unit circuit on tank 3 module and if the system is still unsatisfactory, change tank 3 module. (See figure 3-8.)
- If both indicators test satisfactory - Select unused tank unit circuit on tank 3 module. If malfunction is not corrected, abort mission and land immediately.

COOLING LOOP FUEL PUMP FAILURE.

Illumination of either cooling loop fuel pump caution light indicates failure of the corresponding cooling loop fuel pump, and the flight should be aborted.

> **CAUTION**
> The flight should be aborted when the cooling loop fuel pump caution light comes on, because failure of the remaining pump would stop the flow of cooling fuel through the cooling loop. As a result, subsequent failure of accessory drive systems and electrical generating system can occur, as well as overheating of the fluid systems that are cooled by the cooling loop.

EITHER COOLING LOOP FUEL PUMP CAUTION LIGHT ON.

1. Decelerate and descend.
2. Land at home base as soon as possible.

BOTH COOLING LOOP FUEL PUMP CAUTION LIGHTS ON.

1. Decelerate and descend using minimum rpm.
2. All non-essential electrical equipment - Off.
3. Reduce hydraulic requirements to the minimum.
4. Land as soon as possible.

T.O. 1B-70(X)A-1

TANK PRESSURIZATION AND FUEL INERTING SYSTEM FAILURE.

The fuel inerting caution light comes on when the liquid nitrogen quantity indicator shows less than 5 percent liquid nitrogen remaining and/or when pressure in the liquid nitrogen container is too low, or when fuel tank pressure is too low. Air venting of the fuel tanks can occur during descent below 40,000 feet if pressurization system fails. This condition is hazardous if fuel tank temperatures are above 400 degrees F at speeds above Mach 2.4.

FUEL INERTING CAUTION LIGHT ON (IF MACH 2.4 HAS BEEN EXCEEDED).

1. Fuel transfer pumps in empty tanks - Check OFF.
2. Altitude - If above 40,000 feet, descend to this altitude, if below 40,000 hold altitude constant to reduce temperature.
3. Airspeed - Reduce airspeed and fly at minimum safe speed consistent with the airplane weight for 15 minutes.
4. Abort mission and return to base.

> NOTE
> The fuel inerting caution light remains on until the caution light circuit is ground reset.

FUEL INERTING CAUTION LIGHT ON (IF MACH 2.4 HAS NOT BEEN EXCEEDED).

1. Abort mission and return to base.

ELECTRICAL POWER SYSTEM FAILURE.

PRIMARY GENERATOR FAILURE.

If either primary generator fails or has tripped, the respective generator-out caution light comes on. Abort mission and lower landing gear as follows:

1. Decelerate using normal procedures and return to base.
2. Engines 4, 5 and 6 - Maintain at 99% rpm until landing gear is down.
3. Landing gear handle - DOWN.
4. After touchdown - Monitor No. 2 utility system pumps; if one fails, advance other two engines with the operating No. 2 utility pumps to 80% rpm until airplane is stopped.

COMPLETE DC ELECTRICAL FAILURE (WHILE WEARING PRESSURE SUIT).

> NOTE
> Loss of complete dc power will cause rapid (within one minute) loss of pressurization because of dumping the door and hatch seal pressure.

In case of a complete loss of dc power above 40,000 feet, and ac power is still available, use the following procedure immediately:

> **CAUTION**
> Failure to use the following procedure when above 40,000 feet could cause overheat damage to the electronic equipment and full ram air temperature on the capsule. No cooling is provided for the ram air when the essential dc bus out and primary dc bus out caution lights are on.

1. Crew air shutoff handle - Unlock and pull up.
2. Cabin air switch - Hold at PEPPES-SUPE.
   Hold cabin air switch at PEPPES-SUPE to keep the emergency ram-air scoop closed.
3. Emergency descent - Initiate.
   a. Maintain inlets as required.
   b. Throttles - IDLE.
   c. Start maximum safe-G spiral descent.
   d. Cabin altitude - Monitor.
4. Cabin air switch - PURGE, when total temperature is below 160°F.
5. Use emergency cruise-back procedure. (Refer to "Return to Base Procedure After Environmental System Emergency - Ram-air Scoop Open" in this section.)

DC ELECTRICAL FAILURE BELOW 40,000 FEET.

In case of a complete loss of dc power below 40,000 feet, and ac power is still available, use the following procedure immediately:

> **CAUTION**
> No cooling is provided for the ram air when the essential dc bus out and primary dc bus out caution lights are on.

1. Cabin air switch - PURGE, when total temperature is below 160°F.
2. Abort mission and use emergency cruise-back procedure. (Refer to "Return to Base Procedure After Environmental System Emergency - Ram-air Scoop Open" in this section.)

EMERGENCY GENERATOR OPERATION (HYDRAULIC SYSTEM SATISFACTORY).

When the emergency generator switch is at AUTO, the emergency generator comes on automatically if both primary generators fail, or if the No. 3 generator fails and a bus-tie contactor is open. (The emergency generator-on caution light comes on when the emergency generator is engaged.)

If a failure causes the emergency generator to come on, abort mission and lower landing gear as follows:

1. Decelerate using normal procedures and return to base.
2. Engines 4, 5 and 6 - Maintain at 99% rpm until landing gear is down.
3. Landing gear handle - DOWN.
4. Manual emergency landing gear handle - UT SYS NO. 1 before touchdown.
5. If both primary generators are inoperative, accomplish the following*:
   a. Engine shutdown and wheel brake arming switch - Check OFF.

> **CAUTION**
> The engine shutdown and wheel brake arming switch must not be at ARMED in the air.

   b. Battery-inverter switch - ON.
      Break safety wire and move battery-inverter switch to ON.

> **NOTE**
> After being energized, the emergency battery will require 3 to 5

---

* Airplane AF62-001.

T.O. 1B-70(X)A-1

seconds before it will light the battery-inverter indicator light.

c. Battery-inverter switch - OFF after battery-inverter light comes on.

NOTE
- Moving the battery-inverter switch to OFF after emergency battery is energized stops battery until inverter is required.
- The battery-inverter light will go out, but the battery remains energized.

d. Battery-inverter switch - ON when required.

COMPLETE ELECTRICAL FAILURE (EMERGENCY BATTERY OPERATION).*

In case of a complete electrical failure, use the emergency battery-inverter system as follows:

1. Abort mission and set up return to home base.
2. Decelerate and raise wing tips as follows:
   a. Engine shutdown and wheel brake arming switch - Check OFF.

CAUTION
The engine shutdown and wheel brake arming switch must not be at ARMED in the air.

b. Battery-inverter switch - ON. Break safety wire and move battery-inverter switch to ON.

NOTE
After being energized, the emergency battery will require 3 to 5 seconds before it will light the battery-inverter indicator light.

c. Alternate throttle switches - Use no more than two at a time as required.
d. Wing tip emergency-up switch - Hold at WING TIP UP at least 5 seconds. The wing tip emergency-up switch must be held at either up position at least 5 seconds to ensure that wing tips are raised to full up.

CAUTION
Do not use wing tip and alternate throttle switches simultaneously because of the drain on the battery.

3. Nose ramp unlock handle - Pull, and maintain speed above 300 knots IAS until windshield is full down.
4. Lower landing gear as follows:
   a. Landing gear handle - DOWN.
   b. Manual emergency landing gear handle - UT SYS NO. 1 or UT SYS NO. 2.
5. Alternate throttle switches - DECR, then centered after touchdown. Move all alternate throttle switches to DECR after touchdown and hold to retard engines to idle, then release and check centered.
6. Check feet off brake pedals. Feet must be off brake pedals before step 7 to prevent inadvertent application of brakes.

---

* Airplane AF62-001

T.O. 1B-70(X)A-1

7. Engine shutdown and wheel brake arming switch - ARMED.

   CAUTION
   Do not touch alternate throttle switches when arming switch is at ARMED until engines are to be shut down. Inadvertent shutdown of the engines will cause the loss of all hydraulic power.

8. Apply brakes with extreme care as only manual braking is available.

   NOTE
   If the brakes fail, steer with alternate throttle switches after moving the engine shutdown and wheel brake arming switch to OFF to prevent accidently shutting off an engine.

   CAUTION
   Use brakes with extreme care as anti-skid is inoperative and only manual brakes are available.

9. Alternate throttle switches - Hold at DECR to shut down engines after airplane is stopped and chocked.

   NOTE
   The engine shutdown and wheel brake arming switch must be at ARMED before the alternate throttle switches can shut down the engines.

10. Accomplish normal after-shutdown procedures.

BUS-TIE CONTACTORS OPEN.

The bus-tie contactors are protective devices in the electrical system which open to isolate the right and left primary busses and the primary generators if certain faults occur in the system.

NOTE
When the bus-tie contactors are open, the attitude director and horizontal situation indicators will present erratic displays of heading and attitude. (Refer to "Erratic Operation of the Attitude Director and Horizontal Situation Indicators" in Section IV.)

If large unbalanced currents flow between the generators, the bus-tie contactors will open (indicated by only the bus-tie open caution light coming on), so that each primary generator will supply power to its respective bus. In addition, the contactors open to prevent a good generator from tripping off the line because of a fault on the other bus. If these electrical faults caused the contactors to open, the bus-tie contactor override switch should not be used in an attempt to close the contactors.

The contactors also open if both primary generators go off the line because engines 3 and 4 are shutdown or lost, or because of generator shutdown. Under these conditions, however, the override switch can be used to close the contactors if either primary generator subsequently has been brought back on the line. This permits the operating generator to power both primary busses.

CAUTION
If the contactors are open and one primary generator has been restored, use the override switch only if the contactors were opened by any of the following conditions:

- Loss of both primary generators because of shutdown or loss of engines 3 and 4.

- Shutdown of both primary generators.

- Loss of one primary generator (which in itself did not cause contactors to open) and subsequent loss of

T.O. 1B-70(X)A-1

the other due to shutdown or loss of its engine.

If the contactors were opened by other conditions, do not use the override switch as possible loss of the remaining good generator can result.

If the bus-tie open caution light comes on as a result of known or suspected electrical faults, proceed as follows:

1. Descend to below 50,000 feet, using normal descent procedures.

If the bus-tie open caution light comes on as a result of known generator or engine (3 or 4) shutdown or loss, proceed as follows:

1. Descend to below 50,000 feet, using normal descent procedures.

2. Bus-tie contactor override switch - 3 GEN or 4 GEN.
   After one generator has been restored, the override switch should be held momentarily at its 3 GEN position if the No. 3 primary generator is operating, or at the 4 GEN position if the No. 4 generator is operating.

HYDRAULIC POWER SYSTEM FAILURE.

Symptoms of a hydraulic power system failure are the same for both primary and utility hydraulic systems. Impending failure of a hydraulic system may be indicated by low pressure readings or pressure fluctuations. The individual hydraulic pump status indicators change from green to yellow to indicate which hydraulic pump has failed. A failed system is indicated by the appropriate pressure gage reading.

PRIMARY HYDRAULIC SYSTEM FAILURE.

The primary hydraulic systems power the following:

NO. 1 PRIMARY	NO. 2 PRIMARY
1/2 Elevon dual supply	1/2 Elevon dual supply
1/2 Rudder dual supply	1/2 Rudder dual supply
1/2 Canard flap dual supply	1/2 Canard flap dual supply
1/2 Wing fold dual supply	1/2 Wing fold dual supply
Pitch augmentation	Roll augmentation (primary roll trim)
Yaw 1 augmentation	Yaw 2 augmentation
One fuel boost pump	One fuel boost pump
No. 1 Cooling loop fuel pump	No. 2 Cooling loop fuel pump
Two tank 7 transfer pumps	Two tank 7 transfer pumps
Two tank 8 transfer pumps	Two tank 8 transfer pumps
One tank 5 transfer pump*	One tank 5 transfer pump*

*Airplane AF62-207

This page intentionally left blank

T.O. 1B-70(X)A-1

PARTIAL FAILURE OF PRIMARY HYDRAULIC SYSTEM.

In case of a partial failure of both primary hydraulic systems, such as failure of one hydraulic pump in each of the primary hydraulic systems, the flight controls will respond slower than normal because of the reduced hydraulic flow. Failure of two hydraulic pumps in each of the primary hydraulic systems reduces control rate to 1/2 at 100 percent rpm and to 1/3 at IDLE. For partial failure of the primary hydraulic systems, accomplish the following:

1. Abort mission and land.
2. Keep rpm on engines with good pumps as high as conditions permit.
3. Use minimum control movements.
4. Reduce non-essential demands on the primary hydraulic systems.

COMPLETE FAILURE OF EITHER PRIMARY HYDRAULIC SYSTEM.

Failure of one primary hydraulic system does not affect the rate capability of the flight control system, flaps, and wing fold. However, system power or hinge moments are reduced by one-half except for canard flaps and wing fold which are operationally unaffected. Partial flight control augmentation is lost depending on which system has failed. Two fuel transfer pumps, one boost pump and one cooling loop fuel pump will be inoperative with one primary hydraulic system failed. However, the fuel and cooling systems are not operationally affected. If either primary hydraulic system fails, proceed as follows:

1. Abort mission, decelerate and land.
2. Monitor good primary hydraulic system.
3. Turn off all non-essential equipment.
4. Refrain from making abrupt control movements.

UTILITY HYDRAULIC SYSTEM FAILURE.

The utility hydraulic systems power the following:

NO. 1 UTILITY	NO. 2 UTILITY
Standby AICS	Standby AICS
Automatic and manual AICS* Automatic AICS†	Nose ramp
Brakes	Brakes
Drag chute	Drag chute
Ram air scoop	Ram air scoop
Landing gear (includes bogie fold if sys No. 2 not available)	Bogie fold
Landing gear (emergency manual (No. 1)	Landing gear (emergency manual No. 2)
Nose wheel steering	Landing gear (emergency lowering switch at DOWN)
Nose wheel steering (emergency manual No. 1)	Nose wheel steering (emergency lowering switch at DOWN)
1/2 of fuel transfer pumps in tanks 1, 2, 4, 6L, 6R	Nose wheel steering (emergency manual No. 2)
	1/2 of fuel transfer pumps in tanks 1, 2, 4, 6L, 6R.

---

*Airplane AF62-001
†Airplane AF62-207

T.O. 1B-70(X)A-1

NO. 1 UTILITY	NO. 2 UTILITY
One fuel boost pump	
Yaw gearing changer	Emergency generator
	Yaw gearing changer (Emergency manual No. 2 or emergency lowering switch at DOWN)

For various combinations of No. 1 and No. 2 utility hydraulic system pump failures, see figure 3-9.

NITROGEN SYSTEM FAILURE.

LIQUID NITROGEN SYSTEM FAILURE.

Refer to "Tank Pressurization and Fuel Inerting System Failure" in this section.

GASEOUS NITROGEN SYSTEM FAILURE.

There is no direct indication in the crew compartment of a failure in the three independent gaseous nitrogen systems which pressurize and inert the lubricating system of each accessory drive gearbox, the engine hydraulic systems, and the liquid coolant tank for the landing gear and drag chute compartment cooling systems. Satisfactory performance of these systems, as well as that of the related electrical and hydraulic power supply systems, indicates proper operation of the gaseous nitrogen systems. (Refer to "Accessory Drive System Oil Pressure Failure - Two Gearboxes Simultaneously", "Tire and/or Drag Chute Compartment Overheat Caution Light On", and "Engine Exhaust Nozzle Failure" in this section.) However, a possible indication of a failed nitrogen system is when the accessory drive system oil pressure caution light comes on with engine identification lights 1 and 4, 2 and 5, or 3 and 6.

NOTE
If the accessory drive oil pressure caution light and engine identification lights 2 and 5 come one, together with the tire and drag chute compartment overheat caution lights, loss of nitrogen system No. 2 is indicated.

If a nitrogen system failure is suspected as a result of malfunctions occuring in the systems it pressurizes, and if time and conditions permit, check the quantity in each of the three nitrogen bottles by means of the gaseous nitrogen quantity indicator and system selector on the ground test panel in the electronic equipment compartment. If a related system fails as the result of a suspected nitrogen system failure, retard the throttles of the engines of the affected accessory drive gearboxes to IDLE. Reduce altitude to below 30,000 feet. If the accessory drive system oil pressure caution light and the engine identification lights go out after altitude is reduced, the nitrogen system has failed. With the nitrogen system failed, the airplane may be flown at a reduced altitude and at any thrust setting to the destination. However if the lights remain on below 30,000 feet, shut down the affected engine and refer to the applicable system emergency procedure in this section.

T.O. 1B-70(X)A-1

UTILITY HYDRAULIC SYSTEM FAILURES

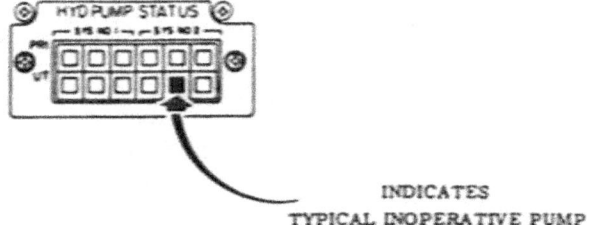

INDICATES TYPICAL INOPERATIVE PUMP

NO. 1 UTILITY HYDRAULIC SYSTEM FAILURE.

Caution

Standby system must be used to control the inlets when No. 1 utility system fails, as the automatic and manual systems are inoperative.

1. Change inlet control to standby system - Refer to AICS emergency operation in this section.
2. Tank No. 1 - Transfer fuel from tank to reduce fuel level to 12,000 pounds.
3. Engines 4, 5, and 6 - Maintain at 99½ rpm until landing gear is down.
4. Landing gear:
   a. Landing gear handle - DOWN. (If gear lowers, proceed to step 5.)
   b. Manual emergency landing gear handle - UT SYS NO 2. *
   Landing gear emergency lowering switch - DOWN.†
5. After touchdown, if one primary generator inoperative or emergency generator on.
   a. Monitor No. 2 utility hydraulic system pumps.
   b. If one pump fails, advance throttles of engines with good No 2 utility hydraulic system pumps to 80% rpm until airplane is stopped and chocked.

* Airplane AF62-001
† Airplane AF62-207

Figure 3-9 (Sheet 1 of 7)

Changed 25 June 1965

T.O. 1B-70(X)A-1

NO. 2 UTILITY HYDRAULIC SYSTEM FAILURE.

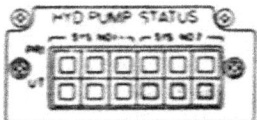

Caution

Emergency generator will be inoperative with No. 2 utility hydraulic system failure.

1. Nose ramp unlock handle - Pull and maintain airspeed above 300 knots IAS until windshield is full down.
2. Tank No. 1 - Transfer fuel from tank to reduce fuel level to 12,000 pounds.
3. Landing gear -
    a. Landing gear handle - DOWN.
    b. Manual emergency landing gear handle - UT SYS NO 1.
4. If one primary generator is inoperative, accomplish the following:*
    a. Engine shutdown and wheel brake arming switch - Check OFF.

Caution

The engine shutdown and wheel brake arming switch must not be at ARMED in the air.

   b. Battery-inverter switch - ON, on final approach.

NOTE

Emergency battery requires 3 to 5 seconds to become fully energized.

   c. Battery-inverter switch - OFF after battery-inverter light comes on. The battery-inverter light will go out, but the battery remains energized.
   d. Battery-inverter switch - ON when required.

* Airplane AF62-001

Figure 3-9 (Sheet 2 of 7)

T.O. 1B-70(X)A-1

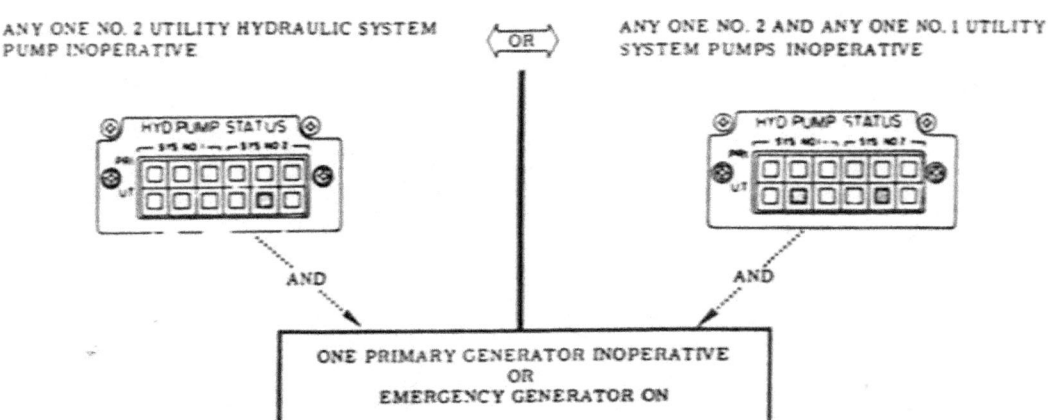

1. Decelerate using normal procedures and set up return to base.
2. Engines with good No. 2 utility system pumps - Maintain above 80% rpm until airplane has landed and is stopped and chocked.
3. Manual emergency landing gear handle - UT SYS NO 1.
4. Landing gear handle - DOWN.

Figure 3-9 (Sheet 3 of 7)

T.O. 1B-70(X)A-1

BOTH UTILITY HYDRAULIC SYSTEMS FAILED (LANDING GEAR DOWN)

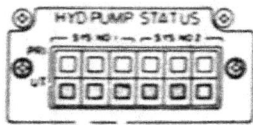

THE FOLLOWING ARE INOPERATIVE:
- NOSE WHEEL STEERING
- WHEEL BRAKES
- DRAG CHUTE
- FUEL TRANSFER PUMPS IN TANKS 1, 2, 4, AND 6
- UPPER BOOST PUMP

NOTE
- Emergency generator will not operate.
- Rudder travel is limited to ± 3 degrees.

1. Throttles - Below Mach 0.5, leave engines 3 and 4 at IDLE; engines 1 and 6 at or near maximum thrust; use engines 2 and 5 for thrust control.
2. Engine shutdown and wheel brake arming switch - Check OFF, before touchdown.*

Caution

The engine shutdown and wheel brake arming switch must not be at ARMED in the air.

3. Battery-inverter switch - ON, before touchdown.*

NOTE
Emergency battery requires 3 to 5 seconds to become fully energized.

4. Battery-inverter switch - OFF after battery-inverter light comes on. *
   The battery-inverter light will go out, but the battery remains energized.
5. Battery-inverter switch - ON when required. *
6. Fly a 270 knot IAS final approach and plan so as not to go around.

Warning

If either throat panel extended caution light is on, a large thrust loss will occur.

7. Use minimum rate of descent just before touchdown, and touchdown at minimum speed because the bogies are in an intermediate folded position.
8. After touchdown, shutdown engines 2, 4 and 5.
9. Use flight controls and outboard engines for steering during landing roll.
10. Shutdown remaining engines as required.

* Airplane AF62-001

Figure 3-9 (Sheet 4 of 7)

3-62   Changed 25 June 1965

T.O. 1B-70(X)A-1

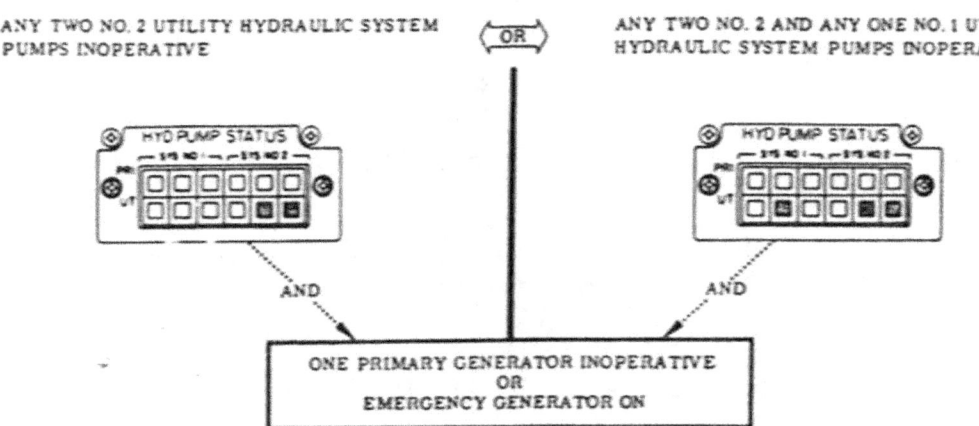

1. Change inlet control to standby system - Refer to AICS emergency operation in this section.

NOTE

Use of standby system is a precautionary measure.

2. Decelerate using normal procedures and set up return to base.

3. Engine with good No. 2 utility system pump - Maintain at 100% rpm until inlets are secured.

4. Engine with good No. 2 utility system pump - Maintain at or above 90% rpm until airplane has landed and is stopped and chocked.

5. Manual emergency landing gear handle - UT SYS NO 1.

6. Landing gear handle - DOWN.

Figure 3-9 (Sheet 5 of 7)

T.O. 1B-70(X)A-1

ANY ONE NO. 2 AND ANY TWO NO. 1 UTILITY HYDRAULIC SYSTEM PUMPS INOPERATIVE.

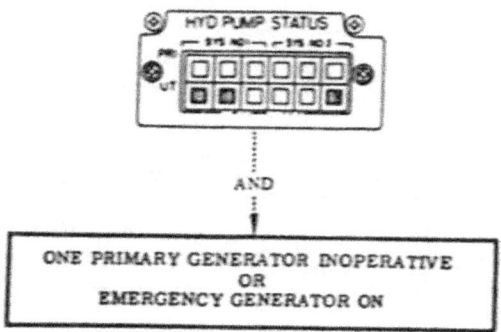

AND

ONE PRIMARY GENERATOR INOPERATIVE
OR
EMERGENCY GENERATOR ON

1. Change inlet control to standby system - Refer to AICS emergency operation in this section.

2. Decelerate using normal procedures and set up return to base.

3. Engines with good No. 2 utility system pumps - Maintain above 80% rpm until airplane has landed and is stopped and chocked.

4. Manual emergency landing gear handle - UT SYS NO 1.

5. Landing gear handle - DOWN.

Figure 3-9 (Sheet 6 of 7)

T.O. 1B-70(X)A-1

ANY ONE NO. 2 PUMP AND NO. 1 UTILITY HYDRAULIC SYSTEM INOPERATIVE.

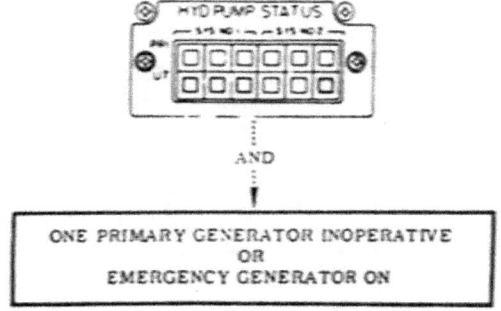

AND

ONE PRIMARY GENERATOR INOPERATIVE
OR
EMERGENCY GENERATOR ON

Caution

Standby system must be used to control the inlets when No. 1 utility system fails, as the automatic and manual systems are inoperative.

1. Change inlet control to standby system - Refer to AICS emergency operation in this section.
2. Tank No. 1 - Transfer fuel from tank to reduce fuel level to 12,000 pounds.
3. Engines with good No. 2 utility system pumps - Maintain at 100% rpm until inlets are secured.
4. Emergency generator switch - OFF, just prior to gear extension.
5. Landing gear:
    a. Landing gear handle - DOWN. If gear lowers, proceed to step 6.
    b. Manual emergency landing gear handle - UT SYS NO 2. *
       Landing gear emergency lowering switch - DOWN. †
6. Emergency generator switch - AUTO, after gear is down.
7. Engines with good No. 2 utility system pumps - Maintain at 80% rpm until airplane has landed and is stopped and chocked.

* Airplane AF62-001
† Airplane AF62-207

Figure 3-9 (Sheet 7 of 7)

This page intentionally left blank

T.O. 1B-70(X)A-1

FLIGHT CONTROL SYSTEM FAILURE.

PRIMARY HYDRAULIC SYSTEM FAILURE.

Refer to "Hydraulic Power System Failure" in this section.

> **WARNING**
> If complete hydraulic failure occurs, control of the airplane is impossible and the crew must eject. An attempt should be made, however, to reach a lower altitude and a suitable ejection area before ejection.

NO. 1 OR NO. 2 PRIMARY HYDRAULIC SYSTEM FAILURE.

> **NOTE**
> - If No. 1 primary hydraulic system fails, pitch augmentation, and No. 1 yaw augmentation are inoperative.
> - If No. 2 primary hydraulic system fails, roll augmentation, primary roll trim, and No. 2 yaw augmentation are inoperative.

1. Abort mission and land.
2. Monitor the good primary hydraulic system.
3. Use minimum control movements.
4. Decelerate to subsonic speed.

ONE OR MORE PUMPS FAILED IN EACH PRIMARY HYDRAULIC SYSTEM.

> **NOTE**
> Failure of two hydraulic pumps in each of the primary hydraulic systems reduces control rate to 1/2 at 100 percent rpm and to 1/3 at IDLE.

For partial failure in each primary hydraulic systems, accomplish the following:

1. Abort mission and land.
2. Keep rpm on engines with good pumps as high as conditions permit.
3. Use minimum control movements.
4. Reduce non-essential demands on the primary hydraulic systems.

FLIGHT CONTROL ARTIFICIAL-FEEL SYSTEM FAILURE.

Artificial-feel failure is indicated by an increase or decrease of control forces which causes overcontrolling, and poor control centering. If an artificial-feel failure occurs:

1. Manually control fuel sequence to obtain most forward CG.
2. Airspeed - As required.
   Adjust airspeed as required to relieve possible oscillations of the airplane.
3. If control cannot be maintained - Ejection is recommended.

FLIGHT AUGMENTATION CONTROL SYSTEM FAILURE.

All augmentation is lost if the right primary ac bus fails. The pitch and roll channels of the flight augmentation control system (FACS) have an automatic disengage feature. The yaw channels, however, can only be manually disengaged.

> **CAUTION**
> If oscillation of the airplane occurs, manually disengage the FACS.

Augmentation system disengagement or failure is indicated by illumination of

T.O. 1B-70(X)A-1

the applicable augmentation system caution light and by reduced damping of the airplane.

> **NOTE**
> Failure of the No. 1 primary hydraulic system centers the pitch augmentation system and locks the No. 1 yaw augmentation system. Roll augmentation is centered and the No. 2 yaw augmentation system is locked if the No. 2 primary hydraulic system fails.

When an augmentation system caution light comes on:

1. Applicable augmentation power switch - Recycle ON.
2. Augmentation engage button - After 3 minutes, push during trimmed 1-G flight.

> **NOTE**
> Waiting three minutes before attempting re-engagement of the augmentation system permits the augmentation system differential servos to return to a neutral position. This will prevent any violent maneuvers when the augmentation system is re-engaged.

3. Augmentation caution lights - Check.
   a. If light remains out, augmentation has re-engaged.
   b. If light remains on, or comes back on (no electrical or hydraulic failure) the particular augmentation system has failed.

TRIM FAILURE.

> **NOTE**
> - Primary roll trim is inoperative whenever roll augmentation is lost or turned off.
> - Primary pitch trim is inoperative whenever pitch augmentation power is lost.

RUNAWAY PITCH TRIM.

In case of runaway pitch trim, the following procedures should be used:

1. Apply force necessary to hold control column.
2. Standby trim pitch switch (center console) - As required.

> **NOTE**
> Use of the standby trim pitch switch automatically disengages the primary pitch trim system.

> **CAUTION**
> Do not attempt to use the primary pitch trim if a malfunction exists in the primary pitch trim system.

3. Standby pitch trim arming switch (left console) - OFF.

> **NOTE**
> When the standby pitch trim arming switch is moved to OFF, the primary trim pitch switch circuit is re-engaged and the standby pitch trim system is inoperative.

   a. If runaway pitch trim stops, use primary trim pitch switch as required.

3-64

4. Standby pitch trim arming switch (left console) - ALT ARMED.

   NOTE
   With the standby pitch trim arming switch at ALT ARMED or OFF, pitch trim control is not available from the trim button on the capsule emergency descent control grip, and the mission should be aborted.

5. Standby trim pitch switch (center console) - Use to retrim until trim is stabilized.
   a. If runaway pitch trim reoccurs, move standby pitch trim arming switch to OFF and continue flight as required.

A flaps-up landing should be planned if the runaway trim has required the use of push force on the control wheel, because the trim change caused by lowering the flaps is nose-up and will increase the push force required. If pull force results from runaway trim, flaps should be used. (Refer to "Take-off and Landing Emergencies" in this section for flaps-up landing procedure.)

LATERAL BOBWEIGHT FAILURE.*

If the lateral bobweight fails to unlock, as indicated by excessive negative dihedral effect or by the lateral bobweight indicator, do not exceed Mach 2.6. If the lateral bobweight fails to lock, as indicated by the indicator or by marginal directional damping, descend at minimum practical speed. Do not exceed Mach 0.7 below 20,000 feet.

CANARD FLAP PRESSURE CAUTION LIGHT ON.

If the canard flap pressure caution light comes on:

1. Flap handle - Check UP.
2. Airspeed - Reduce to below 270 knots IAS.

3. Abort mission and land flaps up with approach speed increased 10 knots IAS.

CANARD FLAP SYSTEM EMERGENCY OPERATION.

There is no emergency system for operation of the canard flaps. If flaps cannot be lowered, increase approach speed by 10 knots IAS.

WING TIP FOLD SYSTEM EMERGENCY OPERATION.

NOTE
- If asymmetric wing tip operation is suspected when lowering the wing tips (excessive roll), immediately move wing tip position selector switch to UP in an attempt to return wing tips to full-up position.
- If an asymmetric wing tip position occurs and both tips cannot be raised by emergency procedures, the raised wing tip should be lowered to the position that provides a symmetrical configuration. A landing can be attempted with both wing tips half down. (Refer to "Emergency Procedures With Wing Tips Half Down" in this section.)

WARNING
Do not attempt a landing with asymmetric wing tips,

---

* Airplane AF62-001

T.O. 1B-70(X)A-1

as unsafe flight characteristics will be encountered at low speeds.

EMERGENCY RAISING OF WING TIPS.

If the wing tips are folded and cannot be raised to the full-up position when using the normal mode of operation:

NOTE
The wing tip emergency-up system controls are on the ground test panel in the electronic equipment compartment.

1. Wing tip position selector switch - Check UP.
2. Wing tip fold mode switch - ALTR.
   a. If wing tips raise, do only steps 3 and 4.
   b. If wing tips do not raise, proceed to step 3.
3. Wing tip emergency-up system reset switch - Check OFF.
4. <u>Simultaneously</u> hold wing tip emergency-up power selector switch and wing tip emergency-up switch at each of the following positions for about 5 seconds.
   a. Wing tip emergency-up power selector switch - ESSENTIAL BUS or PRIMARY BUS.
   b. Wing tip emergency-up switch - Either WING TIP UP position.
   c. If wing tips do not raise, try all combinations, holding each for about 5 seconds.

NOTE
Once the tips have been raised using the emergency-up system, additional wing tip positioning cannot be obtained until the system has been reset.

   d. If wing tips still fail to raise, proceed to step 5.*
5. Engine shutdown and wheel brake arming switch* - Check OFF.

CAUTION
The engine shutdown and wheel brake arming switch must not be at ARMED in the air.

6. Battery-inverter switch* - ON.

NOTE
Allow 3 to 5 seconds for emergency battery to become fully activated.

7. Wing tip emergency-up switch - Hold at either WING TIP UP position for about 5 seconds.
8. After wing tips are full up, battery-inverter switch* - OFF, until further use is required.

WING TIP POSITION INDICATOR SHOWS BARBER POLE (TIPS NOT IN TRANSIT).

If wing tips are not in transit and the wing tip position indicator shows barber pole and the essential ac bus is normal, the wing tips may be hunting (moving up and down slightly) near the selected position. Wing tip hunting occurs in small enough increments so the airplane does not respond to these fluctuations. If a barber pole condition occurs:

1. Wing tip fold mode switch - ALTR. Wing tip position indicator should now show selected position.
2. Raise wing tips using normal procedures.
3. Wing tip emergency-up system reset switch - Check OFF.

---

* Airplane AF62-001

T.O. 1B-70(X)A-1

4. After wing tips are in the full up position and before landing, simultaneously hold the following switches at the positions indicated for about 5 seconds.
   a. Wing tip emergency-up power selector switch - Hold at either ESSENTIAL BUS or PRIMARY BUS position.
   b. Wing tip emergency-up switch - Hold at either WING TIP UP position.
   c. If tip emergency system not-reset caution light remains out, try all combinations of pre-ceeding steps a and b for about 5 seconds each.

EMERGENCY PROCEDURES WITH WING TIPS HALF DOWN.

If the wing tips are lowered to the one-half position and cannot be re-positioned to full up, a landing is possible. Stabilized subsonic flight can be maintained at any speed with the tips at the one-half position. With the wing tips in one-half position, the landing should be planned using a flat fast approach. (A high touchdown speed is required even at the lightest gross weights to keep the tips from contact-ing the ground.) Only two-thirds normal elevon control is available since the outer two elevon segments are "locked out" when the tips are not fully up. The high pattern speeds required will tend to counteract the reduced elevon control. If a landing is required with the wing tips half down, use the follow-ing procedure:

1. Reduce weight.
   Burn off all fuel above that re-quired for at least one approach and go-around pattern.
2. Set up a heavy-weight flaps-down landing pattern with touchdown speed at maximum tire limit speed.

   WARNING
   Keep bank angle less than 4 degrees to prevent wing tips contacting the runway.

3. Lower nose gear as quickly as pos-sible after main gear touchdown to increase wing tip clearance.

4. Follow normal stopping procedure.

EMERGENCY PROCEDURES WITH WING TIPS FULL DOWN.

   WARNING
   If the wing tips are fully down and cannot be raised, a landing must not be at-tempted.

If the wing tips cannot be raised from full down, and fuel and time permit, the following procedure is recommended:

1. Manually control fuel sequence to obtain most forward CG.
2. Loiter at about 35,000 feet and 450 knots IAS until ready to eject.
3. Airspeed - Reduce as low as possible.
4. Eject.

LANDING GEAR EMERGENCY OPERATION.

LANDING GEAR WARNING LIGHT ON ABOVE GEAR-DOWN LIMIT AIRSPEED.

If the landing gear warning light (in the landing gear handle knot) comes on during flight, proceed as follows:

1. Airspeed - Reduce.
   Slow airplane to below gear-down limit airspeed.
2. Landing gear handle - Check UP.
3. Landing gear and landing gear door position - Check.
   Have gear and gear door position check by the tower on a fly-by, or by chase plane.
4. Landing gear handle - DOWN.

T.O. 1B-70(X)A-1

LANDING GEAR EMERGENCY LOWERING.

> NOTE
> There is no mechanical means of lowering the landing gear.

In case of a malfunction of the normal landing gear system, and the gear fails to extend and lock down after the landing gear handle is moved to DOWN, use the following procedure:

1. Have chase plane check gear configuration. Leave handle at DOWN.
2. Utility hydraulic system pressure gages - Check.
   a. If failure exists, refer to "Hydraulic Power System Failure" in this section.
   b. If No. 2 utility system is pressurized, proceed to step 3.
3. Landing gear emergency lowering switch - DOWN.
4. Manual emergency landing gear handle - UT SYS NO. 1.
5. Manual emergency landing gear handle - UT SYS NO. 2.

AUTOMATIC BRAKING SYSTEM FAILURE.

If the brake control caution light comes on, leave the wheel brake control switch at AUTOMATIC and use rapid on and off technique for braking. If deceleration is not felt, release the pedals and move the wheel brake control switch to MANUAL and use same on-and-off technique for braking. Be careful not to skid the tires, as skid protection is not available when at MANUAL and may not be available when at AUTOMATIC.

> CAUTION
> Apply manual braking with extreme care to prevent destruction of the tires.

NOSE WHEEL STEERING SYSTEM FAILURE.

If the nose wheels fail to follow the rudder pedals, proceed as follows:

> CAUTION
> If nose wheel steering fails (disengages) at ground speeds above 30 knots, do not attempt to re-engage until at a safe taxi speed as the disengagement may have been caused by a hard-over signal.

1. Nose wheel steering engage switch - ENGAGE then FAIL SAFE.
   Momentarily move the nose wheel steering engage switch to ENGAGE then FAIL SAFE to engage nose wheel steering if it has disengaged.
2. Landing gear emergency lowering switch - DOWN, if No. 1 utility system failed.
   Move landing gear emergency lowering switch to DOWN to provide No. 2 utility hydraulic system pressure for nose wheel steering.
3. If hard-over signal occurs when ENGAGE selected, nose wheel steering selector switch - OFF.

TIRE AND/OR DRAG CHUTE COMPARTMENT OVERHEAT CAUTION LIGHT ON.

Tire or drag chute overheating could be caused by a fire in either compartment or a failure of the following systems:
- Cooling fuel loop system.
- Landing gear and drag chute compartment cooling system.
- #2 gaseous nitrogen system.

If either caution light comes on, use the following procedure:

> NOTE
> The tire overheat caution light heat sensor contacts the tire only when the gear is retracted.

1. (Deleted)

T.O. 1B-70(X)A-1

2. Airspeed - Reduce until light goes out, or to below gear-down limit airspeed.
   a. If caution lights go out, continue flight below Mach 1.5.

   CAUTION
   When the drag chute compartment overheat caution light comes on, assume that the drag chutes are damaged.

   b. If tire overheat caution light stays on, proceed to step 3.
3. Landing gear handle - DOWN.
   Move landing gear handle DOWN and leave gear extended ten minutes to cool the tires. If possible, have chase plane check wheel wells for indications of fire. If fire is confirmed, leave gear extended and return to base.

WINDSHIELD NOSE RAMP EMERGENCY OPERATION

If the windshield nose ramp cannot be raised, the range is reduced but it is still possible to fly at supersonic speeds; and the mission requirements other than range are not affected.

   CAUTION
   Sustained operation above Mach 2.5 with the windshield down causes deterioration of the inner windshield glass edge attachment bonds and inner layer.

WINDSHIELD NOSE RAMP EMERGENCY LOWERING.

If the nose ramp fails to lower when the windshield nose ramp switch is moved to DOWN, proceed as follows:

   NOTE
   • Loss of hydraulic pressure does not affect the emergency lowering of the nose ramp.

   • The windshield nose ramp cannot be raised after the emergency release handle has been pulled.

1. Nose ramp switch - Recycle.
2. Nose ramp unlock handle - Pull above 300 knots IAS.
   To ensure full engagement of windshield downlock, the handle must be pulled at speeds above 300 knots IAS.

CENTRAL AIR DATA SYSTEM FAILURE.

A central air data system failure is indicated by the air data and set nozzle altitude caution lights coming on, and/or different readings between the standby and vertical scale indicators.

Illumination of the air data caution light indicates only electrical failure or failure of the altitude monitor circuit, and does not necessarily indicate a failure in the IAS, Mach, or altitude rate portions of the central air data system. The following airplane and engine systems are affected, but not necessarily lost:
• Anticollision lights
• Engine rpm lock-up
• Engine secondary nozzle controls
• Altitude/vertical velocity indicators
• Airspeed-Mach number indicators
• Flight augmentation control system
• Flight director computer

3-69

T.O. 1B-70(X)A-1

- Auxiliary gyro platform system
- Landing gear warning system
- Air induction control system*

CAUTION

The central air data system ground test panel should not be used in flight. If used, false conditions will be introduced to the central air data system which will affect other airplane systems.

NOTE

The air induction control system for Airplane AF62-207 has its own local Mach sensing system; therefore, central air data system failure will not affect throat Mach schedule indicator presentations on this airplane.

If air data and set nozzle altitude caution lights come on:

NOTE

- When the central air data system (CADS) fails, the CADS monitor puts the flight augmentation control system on fixed gains.
- The bypass door open caution lights will be inoperative.

1. Change inlet control to manual if at automatic.*
   a. Bypass wheels - Both aft toward OPEN as required to position and maintain shocks in crosshatch.
   b. Throat wheels - Both aft toward DECR to maintain throat at Mach 0.2 less than airplane Mach.
   c. Both throat Mach schedule mode switches - MAN.
2. Secondary exhaust nozzle standby pressure knob - To airplane altitude.

CAUTION

Incorrect operation of the knob could lead to the simultaneous failure of the secondary exhaust nozzles of the six engines.

3. Standby altimeters and airspeed indicators - Cross check with vertical scale indicators.
4. Decelerate and manually compute Mach.

NOTE

For Airplane AF62-207, if the air induction control system is being operated in the automatic mode, the throat Mach schedule indicator readings can be used to determine airplane Mach.

5. If all vertical scale indicators (except angle of attack and G) are inoperative:
   a. Speed stability switch - Check OFF.
   b. Engine rpm lockup switch - RELEASE below Mach 1.4.
   c. Landing gear warning unreliable.

ENVIRONMENTAL SYSTEMS EMERGENCY OPERATION.

LOSS OF CABIN PRESSURE.

Cabin pressurization loss is indicated by the cabin pressure altimeter, cabin over 10,000 feet caution light coming on, cabin flood flow caution light coming on, or possibility of the cabin over 42,000 feet warning light coming on. If the cabin over 42,000 feet warning light comes on, the crew must encapsulate immediately (unless wearing pressure suit) and decelerate and descend as required. Use the following procedures.

CABIN OVER 10,000 FEET CAUTION LIGHT ON.

1. Oxygen masks on or face piece closed.
2. Cabin air switch - Hold at REPRESSURE.

   Hold switch until cabin altitude is below 26,500 feet and release to OFF. If cabin altitude does not decrease, proceed to step 3.

---

*Airplane AF62-001.

3-70

Changed 25 June 1965

T.O. 1B-70(X)A-1

3. Bleed air leak override switch - OPEN, if engines 2, 3, 4, and 5 are below 87% rpm. Proceed to step 4.

CAUTION
The OPEN position of the bleed air switch overrides the bleed air leak detection system in the environmental control equipment compartment and opens a valve to supply compressor bleed air (from engines 2, 3, 4, and 5) to the environmental system. As a result, operation of these engines above 87% rpm at this time may cause excessive bleed air temperatures in the compartment if a failure of the duct system had occurred. Therefore, if bleed air switch is at OPEN and rpm of engines 2, 3, 4, and 5 must be increased above 87%, return switch to AUTO or CLOSE before advancing throttles. This will prevent potential damage to units in the environmental control equipment compartment.

4. Cabin air switch - Hold at REPRESSURE.
   Hold switch until cabin altitude is below 26,500 feet and release to OFF. If cabin altitude does not decrease, proceed to step 5.
5. Crew air shutoff handle - Pull up.
6. If electronic equipment compartment overheat caution light comes on, cabin air switch - PURGE.
7. Decelerate and descend at 400 knots IAS minimum to an altitude not requiring pressurization.
8. Return to base with ram air scoop open.

ELECTRONIC EQUIPMENT AIR OVERHEAT CAUTION LIGHT ON AND/OR ELECTRONIC EQUIPMENT AIR TEMPERATURE ABOVE 70°F (CABIN ALTITUDE BELOW 10,000 FEET WITH CABIN AIRFLOW).

In case of an electronic equipment overheat condition (as indicated by the electronic equipment air overheat caution light coming on, or excessive temperature rise indication on the electronic equipment air temperature gage) with cabin pressure normal and airflow from the cabin air outlets, use the following steps, in order, until the situation is corrected:

1. Emergency heat exchanger water switch - ON.
2. Auxiliary cooling switch - ON.
   a. If caution light stays on, or temperature does not decrease in 30 seconds, proceed to step 4.
3. Crew air shutoff handle - Pull up if crew air temperature is excessive.
4. If below 40,000 feet, Freon temperature controller reset button - Press if compressor lockout light is on.

NOTE
The compressor reset button and lockout light are on the Freon temperature controller in the electronic equipment compartment.

5. Emergency deceleration and descent.
6. When subsonic:
   a. Cabin air switch - PURGE.
   b. Refrigeration switch - OFF.
7. Crew air shutoff handle - Push down.

EXCESSIVE CABIN TEMPERATURE.

In case of excessive cabin temperature with the electronic equipment air overheat caution light off and the electronic equipment air temperature gage below 70°F, use the following steps, in order, until the situation is corrected:

1. Cabin temperature knob - COLD.
2. Cabin temperature selector switch - MANUAL.
3. Cabin temperature selector switch - OFF.
4. Crew air shutoff handle - Pull or adjust.
5. Decelerate and descend, if required.

Changed 25 June 1965

T.O. 1B-70(X)A-1

LOSS OF CABIN AIRFLOW.

If stoppage of the recirculation air occurs, as indicated by lack of airflow from the crew air outlets and electronic equipment overheat light coming on, use the following steps in order, until the situation is corrected.

1. Air recirculating fan thermal protection override switch - OVERRIDE. If no air, proceed to step 2.
2. Cabin air switch - PURGE.
3. Make emergency descent and return to base at subsonic speed.

WINDSHIELD ICING AND FOGGING.

In case of windshield icing or fogging, use the following steps in order until the situation is corrected:

1. Engines 2, 3, 4, and 5 - Above 90% rpm, and climb to 35,000 feet.
2. Windshield anti-ice and rain removal switches - ON.
3. Cabin temperature knob - Towards HOT.
4. Crew air shutoff handle - Push in.
5. Cabin temperature selector switch - MANUAL.
6. Pitot heater switch - Check ON.
7. Make slow descent, keeping engines 2, 3, 4, and 5 at 90% rpm.

RETURN TO BASE PROCEDURE AFTER ENVIRONMENTAL SYSTEM EMERGENCY - RAM-AIR SCOOP OPEN.

If return to base is required because of an environmental system emergency, accomplish the following:

1. Airspeed and altitude - Maintain 0.9 to 0.95 Mach between 25,000 and 35,000 feet.

   NOTE
   - If these speeds and altitudes are impractical, cruise within the following alternates: sea level to 35,000 feet and 310 to 410 knots IAS.
   - With auxiliary cooling switch at AMMONIA EMER OFF or both dc bus out caution lights on, maintain total temperature less than 30°F. This may require a lower Mach number.

2. Cabin temperature knob - Adjust. If no change in temperature occurs when adjusting the cabin temperature knob, there will be no windshield anti-ice and rain removal air available during landing.
3. Electronic equipment air temperature gage - Check below 60°F. If marginal, cruise-back should be at about 35,000 feet.

   NOTE
   Electronic equipment air overheat caution light is inoperative if PURGE position of cabin air switch is selected (ram-air scoop open).

4. Ammonia quantity gage - Check. If ammonia is low, favor high side of altitude band.
   The minimum amount of ammonia required for final descent and landing, when over the field, is 150 pounds. Advise base there will be no cooling to electronic equipment, and ground cooling units must be available at end of landing roll.
5. Water quantity gage - Check.
   a. If water is low, favor high side of altitude band.
      The minimum amount of water required for final descent and landing, when over the field, is 600 pounds.
   b. Refrigeration switch - OFF.

3-72

Changed 25 June 1965

6. Final descent - Start before the following:
   a. Ammonia quantity reaches 150 pounds.
   b. Water quantity reaches 600 pounds.

APPROACH AND LANDING - RAM-AIR SCOOP OPEN.

If an in-flight emergency has made it necessary to use emergency ram-air, accomplish the following, and land with the scoop open.

1. Crew air shutoff handle - Pull up.
2. Airspeed - Maintain 240 knots IAS minimum until final approach.

DURING LANDING ROLL - RAM-AIR SCOOP OPEN.

If an in-flight emergency has made it necessary to use emergency ram-air, accomplish the following during the landing roll:

1. Auxiliary cooling switch - Check ON. (If ammonia odor is excessive, move switch to AMMONIA EMER OFF.)
2. Refrigeration switch - OFF.
3. Air recirculating fan switch - Check ON. (OFF if ammonia supply depleted or both dc bus out caution lights on.)
4. Air recirculating fan thermal protection override switch - OVERRIDE.
5. Cabin air switch - Momentarily at REPRESSURE.
6. With airflow and ammonia cooling, continue to taxi. With no airflow and/or if electronic equipment compartment temperature is above 80 F, shut down.

OXYGEN SYSTEM EMERGENCY OPERATION.

If there are symptoms of hypoxia or other signs of insufficient oxygen, one or more of the following procedures should be used until satisfactory conditions are obtained:

1. Check all hose connections.
2. Check fit of oxygen mask or face piece.
3. Emergency oxygen actuator knob ("green apple") - Pull.
4. Manually encapsulate and remove mask or open face piece.
   Refer to "Crew Encapsulation" in this section.
5. Descend to altitude not requiring pressurization as soon as possible.

LOSS OF HATCH DURING FLIGHT.

If an escape hatch is lost:

1. Cabin air switch - PURGE.
2. Encapsulate, if necessary.
   Refer to "Crew Encapsulation" in this section.

CAUTION AND WARNING LIGHTS.

A list of the placard-type caution and warning lights with corresponding conditions and actions is shown in figure 3-10.

ABBREVIATED CHECKLIST.

The abbreviated checklist is in T.O. 1B-70(X)A-1CL-1.

T.O. 1B-70(X)A-1

CAUTION AND WARNING LIGHTS

LIGHT	CONDITION	ACTION
BAILOUT	Pilot pushed bailout button.	• Handgrips - Raise. • Triggers - Squeeze.
ENCAPSULATE	Pilot actuated encapsulate caution light switch or encapsulated.	• Control column - Manually stow. • Handgrips - Raise. • Heel pedals - Press back.
CREW ENCAPSULATED	Copilot encapsulated.	-------
CABIN OVER 42 000	Cabin altitude exceeds 42,000 feet.	• Cabin air switch - PURGE. • Start descent (400 KIAS minimum). • Without pressure suit, encapsulate.
FIRE	Fire and/or overheat in accessory drive system or engine compartment.	• Adjust inlets as required. • Refer to applicable procedure on page 3-16A.
NOSE STEER ON	Nose wheel steering is engaged and hydraulic pressure is available.	-------
CAB OVER 10,000	Cabin altitude exceeds 10,000 feet.	• Refer to applicable precedure on page 3-70.
#3 or #4 ENG GEN OUT	Corresponding primary generator inoperative.	• Decelerate using normal procedures and return to base. • Refer to applicable procedure on page 3-53 for landing.
ESSENTIAL DC BUS OUT	Essential dc bus inoperative.	• Descend below 50,000 feet and return to base.
EMER GEN ON	Emergency generator powering essential busses.	• Decelerate using normal procedures and return to base. • Refer to applicable procedure on page 3-54 for landing.
CABIN FLOOD FLOW	Ram-air scoop is open and air recirculating fans are inoperative.	• Decelerate and descend (400 KIAS minimum). • Refer to applicable procedure on page 3-70.
PRIMARY DC BUS OUT (AIR DATA and SET NOZ ALT lights also come on)	Cabin goes to 40,000 feet. Ram-air scoop opens. Refrigeration system and vertical scale indicators (except angle-of-attack and G) inoperative. Auto AICS*, primary pitch trim, TACAN, ILS, and CADS inoperative. Flight augmentation control system on fixed gain. Engine rpm locked up.	• AICS* - Go to MAN. • Secondary exhaust nozzle standby pressure knob - Airplane altitude. • Standby airspeed and altitude - Crosscheck. • Decelerate (400 KIAS minimum), and manually compute Mach.* • Cabin air switch - Leave at OFF or PURGE. • Crew air shutoff handle - Pull.
BUS TIE OPEN	Right and left primary busses and generators are separated.	• Refer to applicable procedure on page 3-56.

*Airplane AF62-001

Figure 3-10 (Sheet 1 of 4)

T. O. 1B-70(X)A-1

LIGHT	CONDITION	ACTION
EE OVERHEAT	High inlet air temperature or low air flow to electronic equipment compartment.	• Emergency heat exchanger water switch - ON. • Auxiliary cooling switch - ON if light not off in 30 seconds. • Refer to applicable procedure on page 3-71.
CHUTE OVERHEAT	Drag chute compartment overheated.	• Decelerate to Mach 1.5 or less. • Refer to applicable procedure on page 3-68.
#1 or #2 COOLING FUEL PUMP	Inoperative pump.	• Decelerate and descend. • Land at home base as soon as possible.
ROLL AUG	Roll and primary roll trim inoperative.	• Recycle augmentation power switch to ON. • Wait 3 minutes. • In level trimmed flight, push engage button.
YAW AUG 1 or YAW AUG 2	Yaw augmentation is reduced to 1/2 authority.	• Recycle respective yaw augmentation power switch. • Press engage button.
WATER AMMONIA	Water below 2500 pounds or ammonia below 250 pounds. If quantities are all right, water tank air pressure is low.	• Decelerate to subsonic speed. • Make final descent before water reaches 600 pounds and ammonia reaches 150 pounds.
TIRE OVERHEAT	Tires overheated (when gear up).	• Decelerate to Mach 1.5 or less. • Refer to applicable procedure on page 3-68.
PITCH AUG	Pitch augmentation inoperative.	• Recycle augmentation power switch to ON. • Wait 3 minutes. • In level trimmed flight, push engage button.
OVSP ARMED	Engine overspeed available.	• Disarm after take-off.
ENGINE OIL PRESS	Engine oil pressure low.	• Adjust inlets as required. • Refer to applicable procedure on page 3-43.
AGPS ALIGNING	On the ground, auxiliary gyro platform is aligning.	• Auxiliary gyro platform alignment switch - Check at OPERATE.
BRAKE CONTROL	Manual braking selected or malfunction of automatic braking. If manual braking not selected, skid protection may be lost.	• Brake within extreme caution. • Switch to MANUAL if brakes are inoperative.

Figure 3-10 (Sheet 2 of 4)

T. O. 1B-70(X)A-1

LIGHT	CONDITION	ACTION
LH or RH BYPASS DOOR OPEN •	Bypass doors not closed below Mach 0.4 and 8,000 feet.	• Standby system selector switch - PRIMARY. • Bypass standby switches - CLOSE. • Refer to applicable procedure on page 3-46F.
LH or RH BUZZ	Low frequency pressure fluctuations. Inlet is unstarted above Mach 2.0.	• Refer to applicable procedure on page 3-46G.
LH or RH UNSTART	Normal shock wave expelled from inlet.	• Refer to applicable procedure on page 3-46G.
AIR START ON	Air start ignition is on.	• Air start switch - OFF if not in use.
ADS	Low accessory drive system oil pressure for engine indicated.	• Adjust inlet as required. • Refer to applicable procedure on page 3-43.
SUMP FUEL LOW	Sump tank fuel level below 21,000 pounds.	• Manually transfer fuel or land.
FUEL INERTING	Nitrogen quantity or pressure low.	• Empty tank pumps - OFF. • Descend to 40,000 feet. • Refer to applicable procedure on page 3-53.
LH or RH THROAT PNL EXT	Throat panel less than full open below Mach 1.5* (1.4†).	• Throat Mach schedule standby switch* - DECR. • AICS mode switch - STBY. • Throat Mach schedule switch† - DCR. • Abort mission and land at home base.
AICS COOL	No. 1 AICS cooling system has malfunctioned.	• Master caution light - Push. • If AICS COOL light stays on, refer to applicable procedure on page 3-46Q.
RH or LH THROAT INDICATOR •	Throat Mach schedule indicator unreliable.	• Maintain stabilized level flight. • Refer to applicable procedure on page 3-46E.
LH or RH SHOCK AFT †	With started inlet, shock wave aft of predetermined limit.	• Refer to applicable procedure on page 3-46G.
	Bypass doors not fully closed below Mach 0.7.	• AICS mode - STBY • Bypass - Up until light goes out
LDG LT EXTENDED	(Landing light system temporarily inoperative).	- - - - -
FLAP PRESS	Canard flaps not powered up by both hydraulic systems.	• Reduce airspeed to below 270 KIAS • Make flaps-up landing.
BLEED AIR LEAK	Pressure in environmental control equipment compartment exceeds 3 psi (± 0.25).	• Bleed air leak override switch - CLOSE.

*Airplane AF62-001
†Airplane AF62-207

Figure 3-10 (Sheet 3 of 4)

T.O. 1B-70(X)A-1

LIGHT	CONDITION	ACTION
AIR DATA (SET NOZ ALT light also comes on)	Automatic AICS unreliable.* Nozzle area pressure signal failed, area on standby. Flight augmentation control system on fixed gain.	• AICS* - Go to MAN. • Secondary exhaust nozzle standby pressure knob - Set to airplane altitude. • Standby airspeed and altimeter - Crosscheck. • Decelerate and manually compute Mach.* • Refer to applicable procedure on page 3-69.
SET NOZ ALT	Nozzle area pressure signal failed, area on standby.	• Secondary exhaust nozzle standby pressure knob - Set to airplane altitude.
VIBRATION HIGH * VIB HI LIGHTS †	Engine and/or accessory drive system vibration over 50 percent.	• Adjust inlet - As required. • Refer to applicable procedure on page 3-46A.
COOL MALF	Instrumentation cooling malfunctioning.	• If COOL MALF light does not go out in 30 seconds, select system not on. • If both systems out after 2 minutes, master switch-OFF; decelerate to Mach 1.8 or less.
INSTRM OFF	Instrumentation master switch OFF, or loss of power.	• Master switch - ON. • Push restart button for 120 seconds of emergency data if required. • If both systems out after 2 minutes, master switch-OFF; decelerate to Mach 1.8 or less.
LN₂ LOW	Light inoperative	--------

* Airplane AF62-001
† Airplane AF62-207

Figure 3-10 (Sheet 4 of 4)

T.O. 1B-70(X)A-1

LOSS OF CABIN AIRFLOW.

If stoppage of the recirculation air occurs, as indicated by lack of airflow from the crew air outlets and electronic equipment overheat light coming on, use the following steps in order, until the situation is corrected.

1. Air recirculating fan thermal protection override switch - OVERRIDE. If no air, proceed to step 2.
2. Cabin air switch - PURGE.
3. Make emergency descent and return to base at subsonic speed.

WINDSHIELD ICING AND FOGGING.

In case of windshield icing or fogging, use the following steps in order until the situation is corrected:

1. Engines 2, 3, 4, and 5 - Above 90% rpm, and climb to 35,000 feet.
2. Windshield anti-ice and rain removal switches - ON.
3. Cabin temperature knob - Towards HOT.
4. Crew air shutoff handle - Push in.
5. Cabin temperature selector switch - MANUAL.
6. Pitot heater switch - Check ON.
7. Make slow descent, keeping engines 2, 3, 4, and 5 at 90% rpm.

RETURN TO BASE PROCEDURE AFTER ENVIRONMENTAL SYSTEM EMERGENCY - RAM-AIR SCOOP OPEN.

If return to base is required because of an environmental system emergency, accomplish the following:

1. Airspeed and altitude - Maintain 0.9 to 0.95 Mach between 25,000 and 35,000 feet.

NOTE
- If these speeds and altitudes are impractical, cruise within the following alternates: sea level to 35,000 feet and 310 to 410 knots IAS.
- With auxiliary cooling switch at AMMONIA EMER OFF or both dc bus out caution lights on, maintain total temperature less than 30°F. This may require a lower Mach number.

2. Cabin temperature knob - Adjust. If no change in temperature occurs when adjusting the cabin temperature knob, there will be no windshield anti-ice and rain removal air available during landing.
3. Electronic equipment air temperature gage - Check below 60°F. If marginal, cruise-back should be at about 35,000 feet.

NOTE
Electronic equipment air overheat caution light is inoperative if PURGE position of cabin air switch is selected (ram-air scoop open).

4. Ammonia quantity gage - Check. If ammonia is low, favor high side of altitude band.
   The minimum amount of ammonia required for final descent and landing, when over the field, is 150 pounds. Advise base there will be no cooling to electronic equipment, and ground cooling units must be available at end of landing roll.
5. Water quantity gage - Check.
   a. If water is low, favor high side of altitude band.
      The minimum amount of water required for final descent and landing, when over the field, is 600 pounds.
   b. Refrigeration switch - OFF.

T.O. 1B-70(X)A-1

SECTION IV

AUXILIARY EQUIPMENT

TABLE OF CONTENTS	PAGE		PAGE
Environmental Systems	4-1	Oxygen Systems	4-28
Electronic Equipment Cooling System	4-13	Navigation Equipment	4-31
Drag Chute and Landing Gear Compartments Cooling System	4-14	Single-point Pressure Refueling System	4-47
Communication and Associated Electronic Equipment	4-16	Flight Test Instrumentation	4-49
Lighting Equipment	4-25	Miscellaneous Equipment	4-54

ENVIRONMENTAL SYSTEMS.

AIR CONDITIONING AND PRESSURIZATION SYSTEM.

Hot engine compressor air (1170°F maximum), extracted from the final stage of engines No. 2, 3, 4, and 5, is used for pressurization, ventilation, heating, rain removal, anti-icing, driving the Freon compressor of the refrigeration system, powering pneumatic components, and cooling environmental control components. (See figure 4-1.) An auxiliary cooling and pressurization system augments the Freon refrigeration system, and has a retractable ram-air scoop atop the forward fuselage that operates manually or automatically to supply ram air for emergency cooling and pressurization. The various systems are controlled or armed by switches in the crew compartment.

The engine compressor bleed air is collected in a single duct which passes forward through the fuselage fuel tanks to the environmental control equipment compartment. In the compartment the duct divides into three branches. These three branches provide high temperature air (about 1000°F), moderate temperature air (750°F to 850°F), and low temperature air (250°F maximum at sea level)

The high-temperature air branch goes to a crew compartment air-to-air heater and to windshield anti-icing system nozzles through a pressure and temperature limiting valve and shutoff valve. (The air for either right or left windshield can be shut off as desired.)

The air for the low temperature branch passes through a bleed air heat exchanger (water boiler) that reduces the temperature of the hot engine bleed air by using its heat to boil water. The steam formed is vented overboard. The low-temperature air is used to cool environmental control system components, pressurize the water tanks, pressurize the secondary pressurization system (entrance door and escape hatch seals), and provide pressurization and ventilation for the crew compartment and electronic equipment compartment. The pressurization system maintains an 8000-foot altitude cabin when above this altitude. (See figure 4-2.) Air from the low-temperature branch is mixed with engine bleed air that bypasses the bleed air heat exchanger to provide moderate temperature air for the moderate temperature branch.

Changed 25 June 1965

T.O. 1B-70(X)A-1

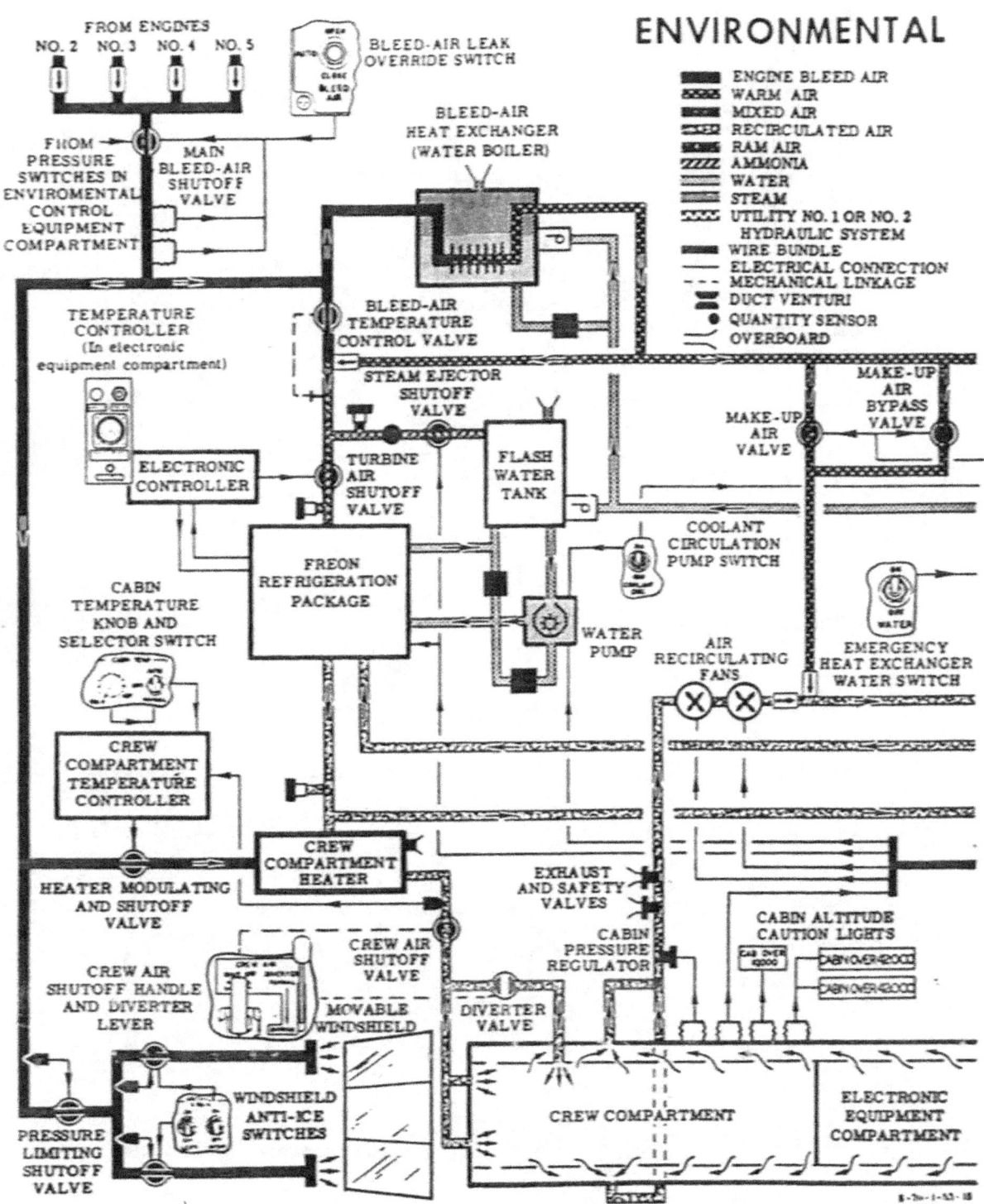

Figure 4-1 (Sheet 1 of 2)

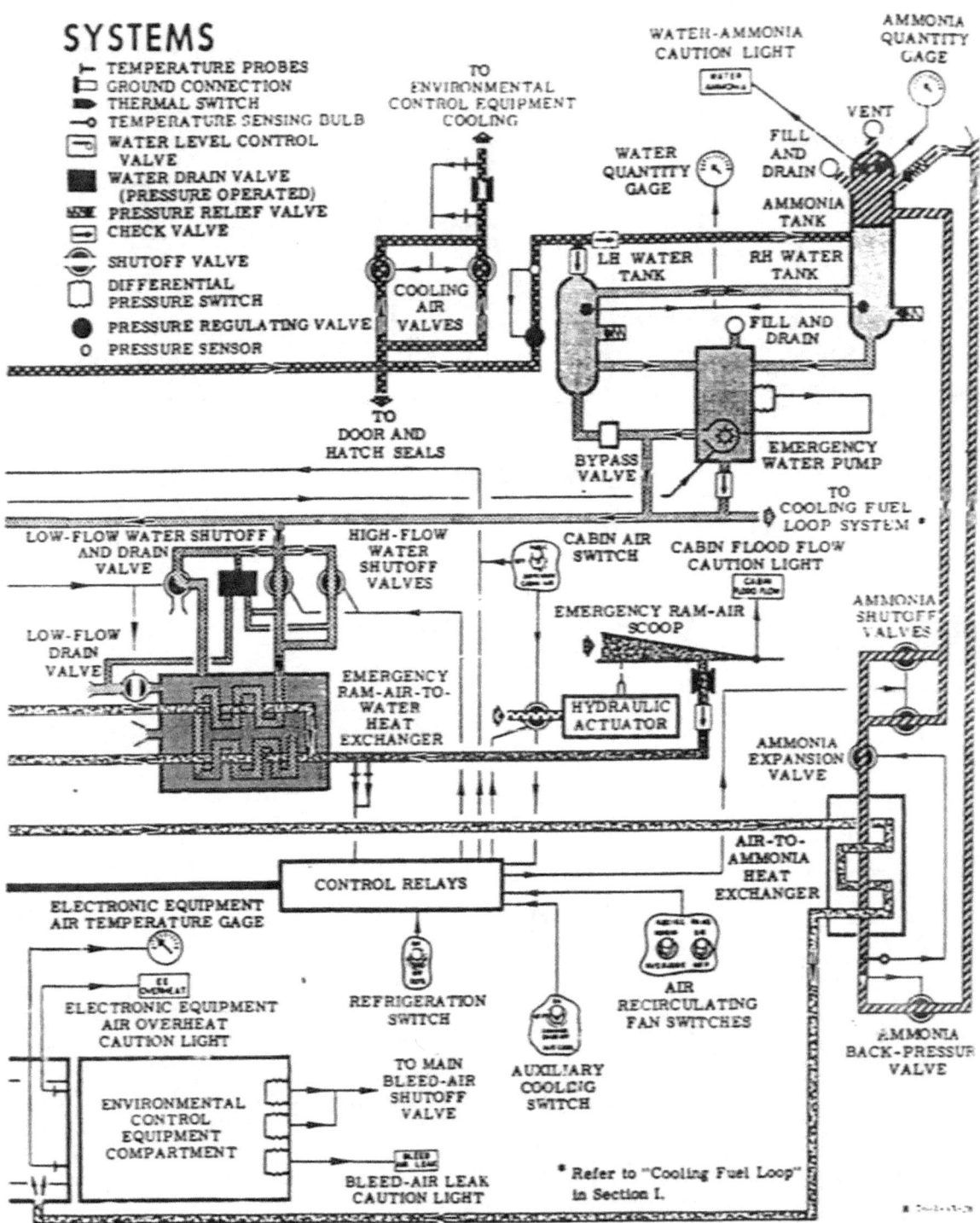

Figure 4-1 (Sheet 2 of 2)

CABIN PRESSURE SCHEDULE

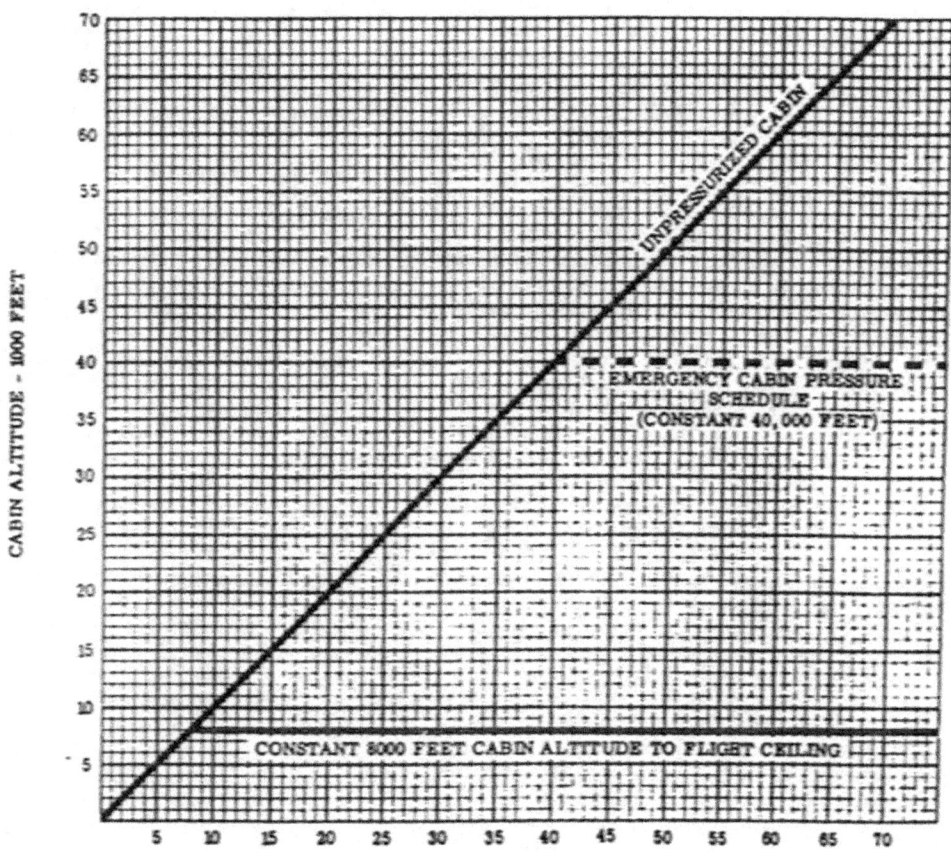

Figure 4-2

The moderate temperature air branch provides airflow for the steam ejector of a flash water tank and drives a Freon compressor turbine in the refrigeration package.

Recirculation air is exhausted from the crew compartment and electronic compartment through a thin perforated metal transpiration wall into the return portion of the air recirculation system. The air recirculation system is powered by two fans in series. For normal flight operations, the recirculation air for the crew and electronic equipment compartments is cooled by the refrigeration system. The airflow supplied to the crew compartment is heated by an air-to-air type heater using the engine compressor bleed air. The electronic equipment compartment and the instruments on the instrument panel are also cooled by the recirculated air passing through the air-to-ammonia heat exchanger. A fabric dust cover, installed when the crew entrance door is latched open, keeps dust and debris out of the airplane, and prevents the loss of cooling air out the open door. With the cover in place, the cooling air is forced to flow around the electrical equipment in the pilot's and copilot's consoles and any other equipment not receiving direct cooling, and out through the transpiration wall to return to the system.

For ground operation, and also in case of an emergency, additional cooling for the electronic equipment compartment is available through an auxiliary ammonia cooling system. A ram-air-to-water heat exchanger provides supplementary cooling of the recirculating air during normal operation at conditions of high speed flight. The ram-air-to-water heat exchanger provides primary cooling under conditions requiring emergency ram air. Cabin pressure regulator and safety valves are in the recirculation air system. The main bleed air shutoff valve is automatically closed in case of leakage of engine bleed air and pressure build-up in the fuel tank conduit, environmental control equipment compartment, or in the duct in the flight control area. The main bleed air shutoff valve can be reopened manually if the condition causing the valve to close automatically is not indicated to be a bleed air leak. All water lines which could be subjected to freezing have electric heaters. The environmental system is controlled by switches in the crew compartment. Indicators and caution lights permit monitoring of the system. Both cooled and heated air for the crew compartment and the electronic equipment compartment can be supplied during static ground operations, through the ground air conditioning inlet in the fuselage just forward of the left inlet duct.

ENGINE BLEED AIR LEAK DETECTION SYSTEM.

This system is designed to detect any leakage of bleed air from the main engine bleed air duct into the fuel tank area, environment control equipment compartment, and the flight control area. Basically, the detection system includes a main shutoff valve, a bleed air leak override switch, a bleed air leak caution light, and five pressure-sensing detection switches. Leakage of bleed air into a conduit surrounding that portion of the duct in the fuel tank area, and into a shroud surrounding the portion of the duct in the flight control area, is detected by two of these switches on the duct. Leakage into the environmental control equipment compartment from the duct is detected by two switches in the compartment. All four switches are set to sense a maximum pressure of 1 ± 0.2 psi above ambient, and to send a signal to close the main bleed-air shutoff valve if this pressure is exceeded. The fifth switch, also in the environment control equipment compartment, is set at 3 ± 0.25 psi above ambient to illuminate the caution light in the crew compartment, to indicate an overpressure condition (which may be presumed to be a bleed air leak) in this compartment. The bleed air leak override switch is used to reopen the main bleed air shutoff valve if the overpressure condition in the environmental control equipment compartment appears to be due to something other than a bleed air leak. For example, a transient pressure rise sufficient to actuate the pressure switches, can occur in the environmental control equipment compartment when the emergency ram air scoop is extended and retracted during high Mach flights. This condition comes about because the positive pressure build-up in front of the scoop during extension and retraction momentarily flows into

T.O. 1B-70(X)A-1

the environmental control equipment compartment through the opening left by the closeout door that is momentarily open during the 3-second transition period. If the more serious condition of overpressure occurs due to a bleed air duct leak in the fuel tank or flight control areas, there is no light indication, and the shutoff valve cannot be reopened in flight.

REFRIGERATION SYSTEMS.

During normal operation, cooling of the recirculation air is accomplished primarily by the Freon system in the refrigeration package, and is supplemented by the emergency ram-air-to-water heat exchanger and the ammonia refrigerated auxiliary cooling system. During conditions requiring emergency ram air operation, cooling of the ram air is accomplished primarily by the emergency ram-air-to-water heat exchanger, and is supplemented by the auxiliary cooling system, and the Freon system if it is still operating. The auxiliary cooling system cools the air supplied to the electronic equipment only.

The Freon system includes an evaporator heat exchanger, condenser heat exchanger using water for cooling from a flash water tank, subcooler heat exchanger, dryer and strainer, turbine-driven-compressor, and various control valves and temperature sensors.

Temperature of recirculating supply air to the crew compartment and electronic equipment compartment can be regulated by manual or automatic control of the Freon system. However, the system is presently set for manual (full cold) operation, so that only cool recirculating air leaves the Freon system in the refrigeration package. The automatic control has been bypassed electrically. Recirculated air passes through the evaporator heat exchanger in the Freon system where it is cooled, and returns to the crew compartment and the electronic equipment compartment. Water from the flash water tank is pumped through the Freon condenser heat exchanger where the heat of the compressor and evaporator is transferred to the water. The water is returned to the flash water tank where it is flashed into steam and vented overboard. The water level in the flash water tank is maintained by water from the water storage tanks through a float type water level control valve. Engine bleed air from the moderate temperature air branch drives the Freon compressor turbine and the steam ejector that reduces the boiling point of water in the flash tank, before being exhausted overboard.

The auxiliary cooling system uses ammonia to cool recirculating air for the electronic equipment compartment during taxiing, take-off and landing operations, during in-flight equipment overheat conditions, and to cool ram air during emergency ram air operations. The system includes a pressurized supply tank and quantity indicator, an air-to-ammonia heat exchanger, and valves and sensors. The air supplied to the electronic equipment compartment passes through the ammonia heat exchanger and through and around the electronic equipment. Auxiliary cooling is manually controlled during ground operations when low engine rpm would not supply sufficient bleed air to drive the Freon compressor turbine for adequate cooling of the electronic equipment.

CAUTION

Use of the normal refrigeration (Freon) system during taxiing could damage the Freon compressor because of inadequate bearing cooling.

Adequate crew compartment cooling is provided during taxiing and take-off operation through the air recirculation system by the recirculating fans that help to draw cooling air from the electronic equipment compartment, forward to the crew members. In flight, during normal operation, the auxiliary cooling system is used to augment the Freon refrigeration system whenever the recirculated air temperature entering the electronic equipment compartment is high or the air weight flow is inadequate. These conditions are indicated by an electronic equipment air temperature gage, and by illumination of a caution light in the crew compartment that alerts the crew to turn on the system. Refer to "Auxiliary Cooling Switch", "Electronic Equipment Air Temperature Gage", and "Electronic Equipment Air

T.O. 1B-70(X)A-1

Overheat Caution Light" in this section. The auxiliary cooling system is activated automatically during all emergency ram air operations to further cool the ram air before it enters the electronic equipment compartment.

EMERGENCY RAM AIR OPERATION.

The emergency ram air scoop may be opened and closed manually or is opened automatically to provide emergency cooling, emergency pressurization, or to purge the crew compartment of smoke or other contaminates. Emergency ram air operation is capable of maintaining a 40,000 foot altitude pressure schedule in the crew compartment and electronic equipment compartment. The ram air scoop can be actuated by a switch in the crew compartment (refer to "Cabin Air Switch" in this section), or will open automatically upon signal from pressure switches in the crew compartment if crew compartment or electronic equipment compartment pressure decreases to below 35,000 feet pressure altitude. During emergency ram air operation, ram air flows through the emergency ram-air-to-water heat exchanger and Freon evaporator of the refrigeration package, and travels through the recirculating-air ducting into the crew and electronic equipment compartments in the same manner as in normal circulation, except that all of the air is vented overboard through the safety valves after passing through the electronic equipment and crew compartments. The auxiliary cooling system is automatically activated during emergency ram air operations. The series of events that occur following automatic operation of the ram air scoop are the same as those that occur during the PURGE function of the cabin air switch. Emergency ram air operation is terminated by positioning the cabin air switch to REPRESSURE.

DEFOGGING SYSTEMS.

FIXED WINDSHIELD DEFOGGING.

The front and side panels of the fixed windshield are protected from fogging by a transparent electrical heating film deposited on the glass between the glass laminations. The heating action of this film maintains the glass surface temperature above the cabin dew point to prevent condensation. The front and side panels of the pilot's fixed windshield and the front and side panels of the co-pilot's fixed windshield are powered by different electrical busses. A thermal switch, attached to the inner surface of each glass (two for the fixed windshield front panel) controls the temperature of the glass when the defogging system is on to protect the glass from overheating.

MOVABLE WINDSHIELD DEFOGGING.

The windshield air gap filtering and drying system removes moisture, dust, and other contaminants from the air gap between the fixed and the movable windshield to prevent fogging and maintain visibility. The system consists of two subsystems: an automatic air breathing subsystem working on differential pressure, and a back-up blower-powered air circulation subsystem. Air moving through either subsystem passes through filters and dehumidifiers.

The automatic air breathing subsystem draws in or expells outside air from the forward equipment compartment. During descent, or as the windshield is raised, air from the forward compartment is drawn in through a filter and dehumidifier into the windshield air gap. A check valve allows additional filtered air to enter directly into the windshield air gap when required. During climb, or as the windshield is lowered, air is forced out through the dehumidifier and filter into the forward compartment. A check valve allows additional air to be expelled from the windshield air gap when required.

The blower-powered air circulation subsystem is turned on by the windshield defogging switch in the crew compartment. The blower draws air in from the windshield air gap through a filter and dehumidifier and returns clean, dry air to the air gap through a check valve. The blower also provides air circulation to the air space in the aft side windows.

ANTI-ICING AND RAIN REMOVAL SYSTEM.

Engine compressor bleed air from the high-temperature branch provides anti-icing and rain removal for the outer surface of the movable windshield. The high-temperature air is ejected through

Changed 25 June 1965

T.O. 1B-70(X)A-1

two nozzles at the forward edge of the moveable windshield; one for the pilot's side and one for the copilot's side. Separate switches in the crew compartment permit individual or simultaneous nozzle airflow. Increased airflow from either nozzle can be obtained by closing the other. Over-heating of the glass is prevented by a thermal switch for each nozzle which closes the nozzle valve if the air temperature exceeds 600°F. Additional protection is provided by a supply duct thermal switch which shuts off the air to the nozzles if the air temperature exceeds 700°F at that location.

ENVIRONMENTAL SYSTEMS CONTROLS AND INDICATORS.

CREW COMPARTMENT AIR OUTLETS.

Pressurization, ventilation, cooling, and heating air enters the crew compartment through various air outlets. (See figure 1-2.) The pilot and copilot each have a manually adjustable "eyeball-type" air outlet on the outboard side of the instrument panel shroud, a manually adjustable air outlet on the control column, a manually adjustable air outlet above the side console at the forward end, and a nonadjustable foot air outlet beside each rudder pedal. This single diverter air outlet is behind the pilot's capsule.

COOLANT CIRCULATION PUMP SWITCH.

The coolant circulation pump switch (3, figure 1-9) on the co-pilot's console, receives power from the right primary ac bus* (essential ac bus†). Moving the switch from OFF to ON turns on the coolant circulation (water) pump for the flash water tank for the refrigeration package condenser. The ON position also places the emergency water pump in a standby condition by arming the water tank pressure switch so the pump will automatically operate if water tank pressure decreases to below 15 psi.

PITOT HEATER SWITCH.

The two-position pitot heater switch (29 figure 1-9), on the copilot's console, receives power from the essential ac bus.

*Airplane AF62-001
†Airplane AF62-207

Moving the switch from OFF to ON supplies power to the electrical heater in the pitot head in the pitot boom.

NOTE

Above Mach 1.4, aerodynamic heating will provide pitot heating and the switch should be moved to OFF.

WINDSHIELD ANTI-ICE AND RAIN REMOVAL SWITCHES.

Two windshield anti-ice and rain removal switches (4, figure 1-9), one for the left (pilot's) windshield and one for the right (copilot's) windshield, are side-by-side on the copilot's console. The copilot's switch receives power from the right primary dc bus and the pilot's switch receives power from the essential dc bus. Moving the selected switch from OFF to ON opens a temperature-controlled valve to permit hot engine bleed air to flow over the outer surface of the corresponding area of the movable windshield. However, if the air temperature in the line exceeds 600°F, the valve closes automatically to prevent overheating the windshield. A pressure-limiting and temperature-controlled shutoff valve in the windshield anti-ice and rain removal line closes if the supply air exceeds 700°F or when both windshield anti-ice and rain removal switches are at OFF. The switches can be operated simultaneously or individually, depending upon conditions. Increased airflow through the nozzles can be obtained by operating the switches individually.

WINDSHIELD DEFOGGING SWITCH.

The two-position windshield defogging switch (5, figure 1-9) is on the co-pilot's console. Moving the switch from OFF to ON supplies electrical power to the fan in the movable windshield defogging system and to a transparent, electrically conductive coating in the front and side panels of the pilot's and copilot's fixed windshield. The heaters in the pilot's front and side panels and the fan are powered by the essential ac bus. The heaters in the copilot's front and side panels of the windshield are powered by the right primary ac bus. The glass areas are protected from an over-

Changed 25 June 1965

heat condition when the defogging switch is ON by thermal switches attached to the inner surface of the glass. These thermal switches permit heating if the glass temperature is below 92°F. and shut off the heaters if the glass temperature exceeds 112°F.

CABIN TEMPERATURE KNOB.

The cabin temperature knob (28, figure 1-9), on the copilot's console, controls crew compartment supply air temperature. The knob can be adjusted to any position between the two extreme COLD and HOT positions. (The range of supply air temperature is from 42°F to 105°F.) Rotating the knob clockwise increases the temperature of crew compartment supply air. Counterclockwise rotation of the knob decreases the temperature of the crew compartment supply air. The knob receives power from the right primary ac bus and works in conjunction with the cabin temperature selector switch. When the selector switch is at AUTO, the crew compartment supply air temperature will be maintained automatically at the temperature level selected by the position of the knob. When the selector switch is at MANUAL, the knob is turned to manually control the crew compartment supply air temperature.

CABIN TEMPERATURE SELECTOR SWITCH.

The three-position cabin temperature selector switch (6, figure 1-9), on the copilot's console, selects the mode of cabin supply air temperature control. The switch receives power from the right primary ac bus. With the switch at AUTO, the temperature selected by the cabin temperature knob is maintained automatically. Moving the switch to MANUAL provides manual control of the crew compartment supply air temperature through the cabin temperature knob in case of a malfunction of the automatic control. Moving the switch to OFF shuts off the crew compartment supply air heating system by closing the heater modulating and shutoff valve.

REFRIGERATION SWITCH.

The two-position refrigeration switch (7, figure 1-9), on the copilot's console, receives power from the right primary dc and ac busses. Moving the switch to ON turns on the refrigeration package through control relays, and controls and puts the flash water tank steam ejector valve (which is controlled by a pressure switch) on standby. The refrigeration switch is mechanically latched at ON and must be pulled out before it can be moved to OFF. Moving the switch to OFF turns off engine bleed air in the refrigeration package, and the flash water tank steam ejector shutoff valve. This routes additional engine bleed air to the windshield anti-ice and rain removal system if required.

AIR RECIRCULATING FAN SWITCH.

The two-position air recirculating fan switch (22, figure 1-3), on the pilot's instrument panel, controls both fans in the cabin air recirculation system. Moving the switch to ON turns on both air recirculation fans in the air recirculation dict. One fan is powered by the right primary ac bus and the other fan is powered by the left primary ac bus. The fans are shut off automatically if emergency ram air is automatically initiated, if the cabin air switch is at PURGE, or if there is an overheat condition in the fans.

AIR RECIRCULATING FAN THERMAL PROTECTION OVERRIDE SWITCH.

The two-position thermal protection override switch (23, figure 1-3), is on the pilot's instrument panel. With the switch at NORMAL, thermal protection is provided for the two air recirculating fans in case of a fan overheat condition. However, in case of an emergency and the fans are required after fan shutdown by the thermal protection device, moving the switch OVERRIDE bypasses the thermal protector and permits operation of the fans.

The thermal protection override switch is mechanically latched at NORMAL and must be pulled out before it can be moved to the OVERRIDE position.

CAUTION

Use of the thermal protection override switch should be limited to landing and taxiing to prevent destruction of the fan.

NOTE

For all normal operation, the switch should be at NORMAL.

BLEED AIR LEAK OVERRIDE SWITCH.

The bleed air leak override switch (25, figure 1-3) on the pilot's instrument panel, is used for overriding the two pressure switches in the environmental control equipment compartment, and for reopening the main bleed air shutoff valve if it had closed automatically due to an overpressure condition in this compartment. If the overpressure is due to a duct leak in the fuel tank or flight control area, the switch will not open the shutoff valve. The switch is labeled OPEN, AUTO, and CLOSE. The OPEN position performs the override function of reopening the valve. With the switch at AUTO, the bleed air leak detection system functions in the normal manner. The CLOSE position is used to manually close the main bleed air shutoff valve. The bleed air leak override switch receives power from the right primary ac and essential ac busses.

NOTE

If the bleed air leak caution light comes on and stays on, the switch should be immediately moved to CLOSE.

CABIN AIR SWITCH.

The three-position cabin air switch (24, figure 1-3), on the pilot's instrument panel receives power from the right primary ac and essential ac busses. Moving the switch to PURGE opens the emergency ram-air scoop (hydraulically operated), turns off the air recirculation fans if on, initiates full cold operation of the emergency ram-air to water heat exchanger by opening the normally closed high-flow stage water shutoff valves to admit water (if ram air is above 170°F), turns on ammonia for emergency refrigeration (air-to-ammonia) heat exchanger, shuts off engine bleed air to the air recirculation system, resets cabin pressure safety valves to 40,000-foot altitude pressure schedule, and opens an exhaust valve if the airplane is below about 40,000 feet. (The cabin flood flow caution light comes on whenever the emergency ram-air scoop is opened.) Moving the switch to OFF cancels all of the purge functions if cabin altitude is below 26,500 feet.

NOTE

Duration of steady-state emergency ram-air operation is limited by the water and ammonia consumption. At high altitude and high speeds, it is limited to about 2 minutes. After the 2-minute limit, decelerate and descend as required. The water and ammonia quantity gages must be monitored.

Holding the switch at REPRESSURE terminates the 40,000-foot cabin schedule by closing the safety valves, and closes the emergency ram-air scoop, and opens the make-up air valve and the make-up air bypass valve to provide rapid repressurization of the cabin. The switch should be held at REPRESSURE until the cabin altitude is below 26,500 feet, then released. In addition to canceling all of the purge functions, the REPRESSURE position of the switch also is used momentarily if a gradual loss of pressurization is discovered and then should be used each time the cabin over 10,000 feet caution light comes on. The cabin air switch is spring-loaded from REPRESSURE to OFF. It is mechanically latched at OFF and must be pulled out before it can be moved to PURGE. Refer to "Emergency Ram Air Operation" in this section.

NOTE

If the crew compartment and electronic equipment compartment do not repressurize, the engine bleed air leak detection system may have closed the main shutoff valve. In this event, if the bleed air leak caution light is out, the bleed air leak override switch should be moved to OPEN. The four inboard engines should be throttled back, and airspeed reduced. This will help to lower bleed air temperature if the duct had failed in the environmental control equipment compartment.

T.O. 1B-70(X)A-1

EMERGENCY HEAT EXCHANGER WATER SWITCH.

The emergency heat exchanger water switch (2, figure 1-9) on the co-pilot's console, controls operation of the low flow stage water shutoff and drain valve and low flow stage drain valve of the emergency ram-air-to-water heat exchanger. Moving the switch to ON opens the low flow stage water shutoff and drain valve to supply water to the ram-air-to-water heat exchanger, and closes the low flow stage drain valve. Moving the switch to OFF closes the low flow stage water shutoff and drain valve to stop the flow of water and allow excess water to drain overboard from the heat exchanger through the valve. At the same time, the low flow stage drain valve opens to permit additional drainage at the heat exchanger. The switch receives power from the essential dc bus.

NOTE

The emergency heat exchanger water switch should be moved to ON only at speeds above Mach 1.7. At lower speeds, the water is not required, and the water would drain overboard and possibly freeze and break off of the airplane.

CREW AIR DIVERTER LEVER.

The crew air diverter lever (15, figure 1-9), on the copilot's console, mechanically controls a valve in the crew compartment supply air duct. Moving the lever forward to NORMAL supplies full air to the various crew outlets. Moving the lever aft to BYPASS diverts 30 percent of the air into the aisle behind the pilot's capsule.

NOTE

Leave air diverter lever at NORMAL at all times and control airflow with the crew air shutoff handle.

CREW AIR SHUTOFF HANDLE.

The crew air shutoff "T" handle (19, figure 1-9), on the copilot's console, has a ratchet type lock and mechanically controls an air shutoff valve in the crew compartment supply air branch to vary airflow to the crew compartment. The handle is pulled up to close the valve which diverts all of the cabin airflow to the electronic equipment compartment when engines No. 2, 3, 4, and 5 are below 81% rpm. The handle is rotated and pushed down to open the valve if engines No. 2, 3, 4, and 5 are operating above 81% rpm or if engines No. 3 and 4 are operating above 87% rpm.

NOTE

The handle should be pulled up whenever the refrigeration system is not operating, ground air conditioning is not available, and the air recirculation fans are on to route all airflow to the electronic equipment compartment.

QUANTITY GAGES TEST BUTTON.

The ammonia, water, and oxygen quantity gages are tested simultaneously by a button (20A, figure 1-3). The button is on the pilot's instrument panel and receives power from the essential ac bus. Pressing and holding the button in causes the pointers of the ammonia, water, and oxygen quantity gages to move towards "0". When the button is released, all pointers should return to the previous indication.

FREON COMPRESSOR LOCKOUT INDICATOR LIGHT AND RESET BUTTON.

The compressor lockout indicator light and the compressor reset button are side-by-side on the Freon temperature controller, forward of the circuit breaker panels on a rack in the electronic equipment compartment. The light comes on if the refrigeration package Freon compressor is shut down automatically as the result of Freon overtemperature or overpressure, or because of overspeed of the compressor turbine. If the lockout light is on, the reset button may be used in an attempt to restore compressor operation. The reset button is effective only if the Freon pressure or temperature has decreased to acceptable limits. If a turbine overspeed condition caused the compressor lockout, the reset button will not re-engage the compressor, and the malfunction must be corrected before the compressor is operable. The

Changed 25 June 1965

T.O. 1B-70(X)A-1

refrigeration package compressor lockout and reset circuits are powered by the right primary dc bus.

ELECTRONIC EQUIPMENT AIR TEMPERATURE GAGE.

Refer to "Electronic Equipment Cooling System Controls and Indicators" in this section.

CABIN PRESSURE ALTIMETER.

The cabin pressure altimeter (26, figure 1-3), on the pilot's instrument panel, has a range of 0 to 80,000 feet. The cabin altimeter indicates cabin altitude and operates by cabin pressure.

AMMONIA QUANTITY GAGE.

Refer to "Electronic Equipment Cooling System Controls and Indicators" in this section.

WATER QUANTITY GAGE.

The water quantity gage (20, figure 1-3), on the pilot's instrument panel, has a range of 0 to 5000 pounds in 100-pound increments. The gage is powered by the essential ac bus and indicates the total quantity of water available in both storage tanks for the air conditioning and pressurization system. A yellow band on the gage shows the range of limited water supply. The upper end of the band is the minimum quantity necessary for an emergency descent and return to the base. (The water-ammonia caution light also comes on when the gage pointer is below this point.) The lower end of the band is the minimum quantity of water necessary for final descent and landing. The gage can be tested by the quantity gages test button.

WATER-AMMONIA CAUTION LIGHT.

The placard-type water ammonia caution light (1, figure 1-7) on the center console, is powered by the essential ac bus. The light comes on to show "WATER-AMMONIA" when water quantity decreases below 2500 pounds, or ammonia quantity decreases below 250 pounds, or when the emergency water pump is operating (due to pressure in the water tanks decreasing below 15 psi).

NOTE

The light will not come on to indicate pump operation, as a result of low pressure in the water tanks, when the coolant circulation pump switch is at OFF. The light will come on to indicate low quantity water or ammonia regardless of the position of the coolant circulation pump switch.

If the coolant circulation pump switch is ON during engine start, the light will be on. The light should go out within 10 minutes after any one of the four inboard engines is above 71% rpm (indicating enough bleed air is available to pressurize the water tanks above 15 psi).

CABIN OVER 10,000 FEET CAUTION LIGHT.

The placard-type cabin over 10,000 feet caution light (1, figure 1-7), on the center console is powered by the essential ac bus. The light comes on to show "CAB OVER 10,000" whenever the cabin pressure altitude is above 10,000 feet.

ELECTRONIC EQUIPMENT AIR OVERHEAT CAUTION LIGHT.

Refer to "Electronic Equipment Cooling System Controls and Indicators" in this section.

BLEED AIR LEAK CAUTION LIGHT.

This placard-type light (5, figure 1-7) on the center console, comes on to read BLEED AIR LEAK when there is a leakage of engine bleed air in the environmental control equipment compartment sufficient to cause a pressure buildup that exceeds 3±0.25 psi over ambient. The light is powered by the right primary ac and essential ac busses.

T.O. 1B-70(X)A-1

CABIN FLOOD FLOW CAUTION LIGHT.

The placard-type cabin flood flow caution light (1, figure 1-7), on the center console, is powered by the essential ac bus. The light comes on to show "CABIN FLOOD FLOW" whenever the emergency ram-air scoop is open.

DRAG CHUTE COMPARTMENT OVERHEAT CAUTION LIGHT.

Refer to "Drag Chute and Landing Gear Compartments Cooling System" in this section.

CABIN OVER 42,000 FEET WARNING LIGHTS.

Two placard-type cabin over 42,000 feet warning lights (3, figure 1-3 and 12, figure 1-4), one on the pilot's and one on the copilot's instrument panel, are powered by the essential ac bus. The lights come on to show "CABIN OVER 42000" if the cabin altitude exceeds 42,000 feet.

WARNING
Crew must encapsulate immediately if the cabin over 42,000 feet warning lights come on and initiate an emergency descent to an altitude not requiring pressurization.

NORMAL OPERATION OF ENVIRONMENTAL SYSTEMS.

These procedures are included in normal operation in Section II because a certain relationship must be maintained between normal procedures and operation of the environmental systems.

EMERGENCY OPERATION OF ENVIRONMENTAL SYSTEMS.

Refer to "Environmental Systems Emergency Operation" in Section III.

ESCAPE CAPSULE PRESSURIZATION SYSTEM.

Each capsule is automatically sealed and pressurized, if required by the altitude, whenever the capsule doors are closed. However, if pressurization is not required, only the seals are pressurized. Each capsule pressurization system is independent of the airplane-system and consists of four 1800 psi pressurization cylinders, two on the back of each capsule and two under the seat of each capsule. These cylinders contain a breathable mixture of 60 percent oxygen and 40 percent nitrogen. The mixture, after passing through a pressure controller, is used to inflate the capsule shell and door seals and for pressurizing the capsule interior. The exact endurance time for the capsule pressurization system cannot be given because of the many variables possible at each situation.

Typically, however, it is possible to encapsulate at the maximum flight altitude, trapping ambient pressure, then accomplish an emergency descent to 40,000 feet, followed by decapsulation. At this point, it is possible to re-encapsulate for an immediate ejection while again trapping ambient pressure. A pressure relief valve prevents over-pressurization. A system pressure gage and filler valve is located in the capsule. The capsule pressurization system is shown in figure 4-3.

CAPSULE SEAL DEFLATE BUTTON.

A yellow and black striped capsule seal deflate button (figure 1-36), is flush with the inside left wall of each capsule. A decal below the button is

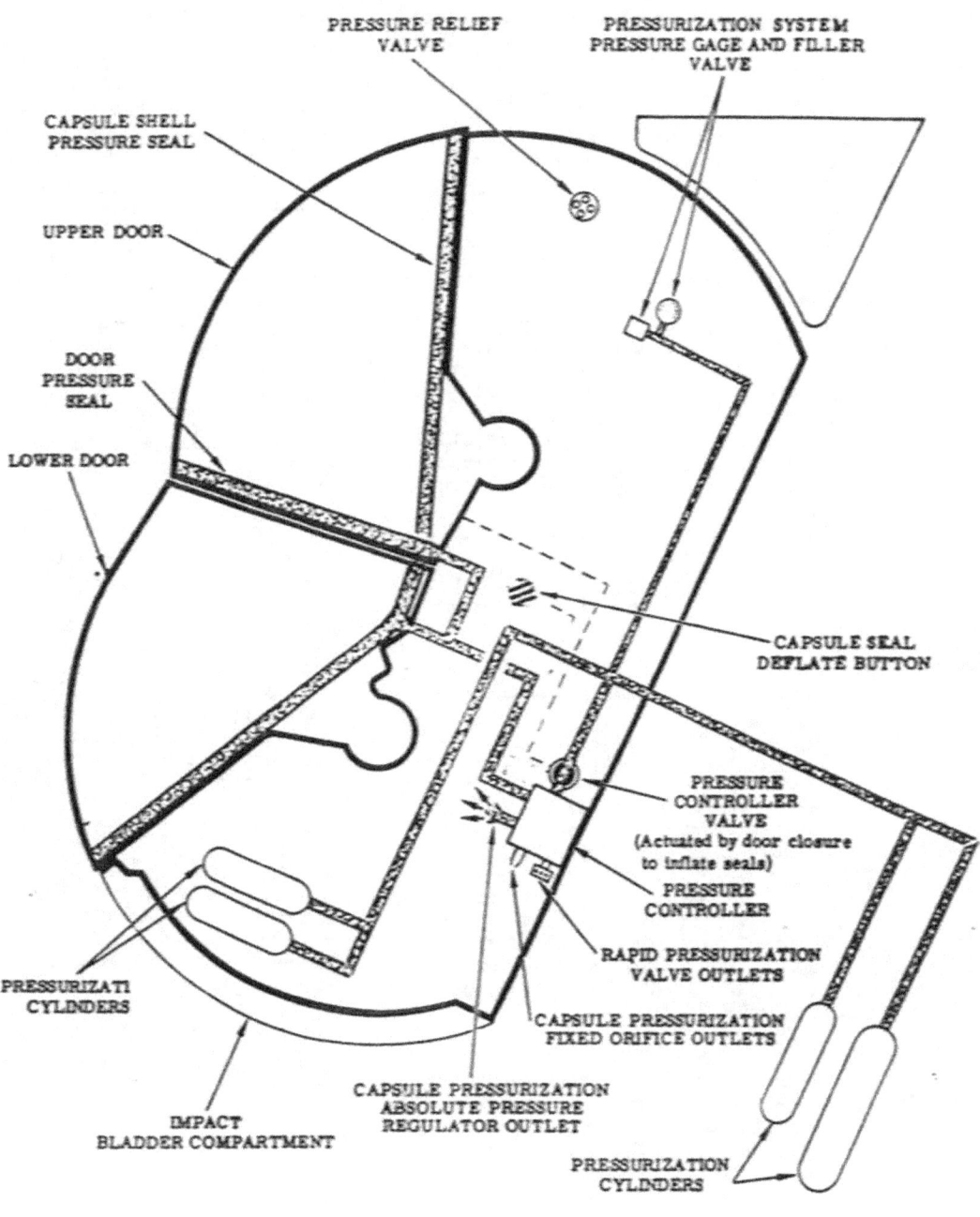

Figure 4-3

marked "SEAL DEFLATE." Pressing the button to a latched position shuts off the pressure controller and dumps the seal pressure so that the capsule doors may be opened. The button and the pressure controller are automatically recocked when the capsule doors are opened. A pin protrudes through the capsule wall from the back of the button for external use.

CAPSULE PRESSURIZATION CYLINDER PRESSURE GAGE AND FILLER VALVE.

The capsule pressurization cylinder pressure gage and the filler valve (figure 1-36) are mounted as a unit in the upper right rear corner of each capsule. The mounting area of the gage is painted grey and the filler valve is painted maroon and is marked "PRESS." The gage indicates the pressure in the cylinders. During servicing, the required pressure on the gage for the prevailing cabin temperature is determined by using a temperature-pressure chart to ensure a full system.

CAPSULE PRESSURE RELIEF VALVE.

A capsule pressure relief valve (figure 1-36), on the upper inside left corner of each capsule, opens when the capsule internal pressure exceeds 9.4($\pm$.2) psi or when the external pressure exceeds the internal pressure by 0.5($\pm$.2) psi. Pushing in and rotating the end of the valve aligns ON or OFF with an index mark. Rotating the end counterclockwise to ON provides the relief valve function. The valve should be normally left at ON. The OFF position should not be used.

CAUTION
Manual use of the pressure relief valve is for maintenance testing only and must be on as indicated by alignment of ON with the index mark.

ELECTRONIC EQUIPMENT COOLING SYSTEM.

Air for cooling the electronic equipment is provided by a branch of the cabin air recirculation system. The air passes through an air-to-ammonia heat exchanger. After passing through the heat exchanger, the air passes into the electronic equipment compartment and over a temperature sensor and a cooling effect detector. Air is exhausted from the compartment through the transpiration wall to the recirculation air return duct. The air-to-ammonia heat exchanger is put into operation by a switch in the crew compartment. An electronic equipment over-temperature condition is sensed by a temperature sensor and cooling effect detector located in the compartment and is indicated by a temperature gage and caution light in the crew compartment.

ELECTRONIC EQUIPMENT COOLING SYSTEM CONTROLS AND INDICATORS.

AUXILIARY COOLING SWITCH.

The three-position auxiliary cooling switch (30, figure 1-9), on the copilot's console, receives power from the primary and essential dc busses. The switch is mechanically latched at OFF and must be pulled out before it can be moved to the ON or AMMONIA EMER OFF positions. If an electronic equipment compartment overheat condition is indicated by the electronic equipment air temperature gage or caution light, the switch should be moved to ON. Moving the switch to ON starts the ammonia auxiliary cooling system. The ammonia quantity gage must be monitored when the switch is at ON. Moving the switch to AMMONIA EMER OFF shuts off the ammonia flow. The AMMONIA EMER OFF position should be used only in case there is excessive ammonia odor in the crew compartment and emergency ram-air is required. Moving the switch to OFF shuts off the ammonia auxiliary cooling system.

T.O. 1B-70(X)A-1

CABIN AIR SWITCH.

Refer to "Environmental Systems Controls and Indicators" in this section.

QUANTITY GAGES TEST BUTTON.

Refer to "Environmental Systems Controls and Indicators" in this section.

ELECTRONIC EQUIPMENT AIR TEMPERATURE GAGE.

The electronic equipment air temperature gage (19, figure 1-3), on the pilot's instrument panel, is powered by the essential ac bus. The gage is marked "EE TEMP" and is calibrated in 10° increments from 0 to 100°F. The gage indicates the temperature of the supply air to the electronic equipment.

AMMONIA QUANTITY GAGE.

The ammonia quantity gage (21, figure 1-3), on the pilot's instrument panel, has a range of 0 to 700 pounds in 10-pound increments. The gage is powered by the essential ac bus and indicates the quantity of ammonia available for auxiliary cooling. A yellow band on the gage shows the range of limited ammonia supply. The upper end of the band is the minimum quantity necessary for an emergency descent and return to the base. (The water-ammonia caution light also comes on when the gage pointer is below this point.) The lower end of the band is the minimum quantity of ammonia necessary for final descent and landing. The gage can be tested by the quantity gages test button.

WATER QUANTITY GAGE.

Refer to "Environmental Systems Controls and Indicators" in this section.

ELECTRONIC EQUIPMENT AIR OVERHEAT CAUTION LIGHT.

The placard-type electronic equipment air overheat caution light (1, figure 1-7), on the center console, is powered by the essential ac bus. The light comes on to show "EE OVERHEAT" if the temperature or weight flow of air over the electronic equipment is inadequate. This light is inoperative during ram air operation.

CABIN FLOOD FLOW CAUTION LIGHT.

Refer to "Environmental Systems Controls and Indicators" in this section.

WATER-AMMONIA CAUTION LIGHT.

Refer to "Environmental Systems Controls and Indicators" in this section.

NORMAL OPERATION OF ELECTRONIC EQUIPMENT COOLING SYSTEM.

These procedures are included in normal operation in Section II because a certain relationship must be maintained between normal procedures and operation of the electronic equipment cooling system.

EMERGENCY OPERATION OF ELECTRONIC EQUIPMENT COOLING SYSTEM.

Refer to "Environmental Systems Emergency Operation" in Section III.

DRAG CHUTE AND LANDING GEAR COMPARTMENTS COOLING SYSTEM.

A separate cooling system for the drag chute and gear compartments provides cooling for the drag chutes and the

Changed 25 June 1965

DRAG CHUTE AND LANDING GEAR COMPARTMENTS COOLING SYSTEM

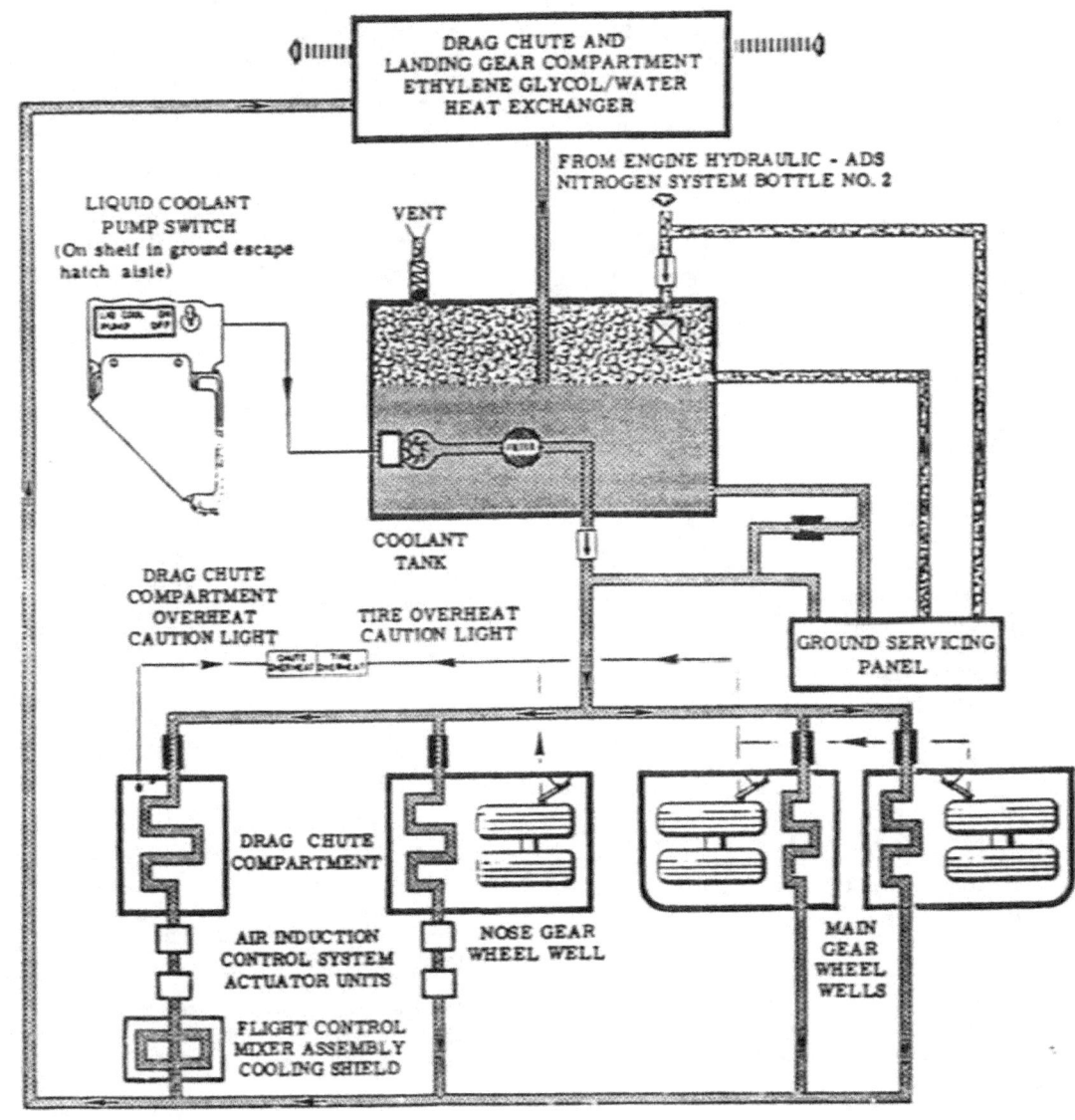

Figure 4-4

nose and main gear tires. (See figure 4-4.) This cooling system, using ethylene glycol and water flowing through the walls of the compartments, includes a coolant tank pressurized by nitrogen from the No. 2 engine-accessory drive system nitrogen supply bottle (refer to "Nitrogen Systems" in Section I), a pump, a coolant-to-fuel heat exchanger, and associated valves and temperature sensors. The coolant picks up the compartment heat, passes through and is cooled by the heat exchanger (which uses cooling loop fuel), and returns to the tank to repeat its cycle. (Refer to "Fuel Supply System" in Section I.) A drag chute compartment overheat condition is indicated by a caution light in the crew compartment. The nose and main gear tire overheat caution light comes on if the tires are overheated.

LIQUID COOLANT PUMP SWITCH.

This switch controls operation of the coolant pump for drag chute and landing gear compartments, and the air induction control system actuator cooling systems. (See figure 4-4.) Moving the switch from OFF to ON turns on the coolant pump. The switch is mechanically latched at both positions and must be pulled out to move the switch in either direction. The liquid coolant pump switch receives power from the right primary ac bus, and is on a shelf on the inboard side of the ground escape hatch aisle.

DRAG CHUTE COMPARTMENT OVERHEAT CAUTION LIGHT.

The placard-type drag chute compartment overheat caution light (1, figure 1-7), on the center console, is powered by the essential ac bus. The light comes on to show "CHUTE OVERHEAT" when the temperature of the drag chute compartment walls is above about 250°F. When the overheat light comes on, landing procedures should be planned on the assumption the drag chutes are damaged.

TIRE OVERHEAT CAUTION LIGHT.

The placard-type tire overheat caution light (1, figure 1-7), on the center console, is powered by the essential ac bus. The light comes on to show "TIRE OVERHEAT" when any of the temperature sensors against the nose and main gear tires record a temperature over about 275°F. (This temperature is below the blowoff temperature of the wheel thermal plug.) As a result of the sensor mounting, the sensor does not contact the tire when the gear is not up and locked. The sensor for the nose wheel tires does not contact the tires until 10 minutes after the nose gear has retracted.

NORMAL OPERATION OF DRAG CHUTE AND LANDING GEAR COMPARTMENTS COOLING SYSTEM.

The drag chute and gear compartment cooling system is put into operation when the coolant circulation pump is turned ON. Refer to "Normal Operation of Environmental Systems" in this section.

COMMUNICATION AND ASSOCIATED ELECTRONIC EQUIPMENT.

TABLE OF COMMUNICATIONS AND ASSOCIATED ELECTRONIC EQUIPMENT.

See figure 4-5. See figure 1-1 for antenna locations.

UHF COMMAND RADIO - AN/ARC-50.

Two independent UHF command radio systems provide air-to-air and air-to-ground communications between the frequencies of 225 to 399.95 megacycles. Two identical transmitters and receivers are used, controlled by two separate control panels: one on the center console and one on the pilot's console. The transmitter audio signal is directed through the AN/AIC-18 communications amplifier. Two separate receivers (a

COMMUNICATION AND ASSOCIATED ELECTRONIC EQUIPMENT

TYPE	DESIGNATION (AN)	FUNCTION	RANGE	CONTROL LOCATION
UHF RADIO (COMMAND)	ARC-50	TWO-WAY VOICE COMMUNICATION	LINE OF SIGHT	LEFT CONSOLE AND CENTER CONSOLE
INTERCOM SYSTEM	AIC-18	CONTROLS AND SELECTS ALL AUDIO SIGNALS	NOT APPLICABLE	CENTER CONSOLE
TACAN	ARN-65	AZIMUTH BEARING AND DISTANCE	APPROXIMATELY 200 MILES	CENTER CONSOLE
ILS	ARN-58	LOCALIZER, GLIDESLOPE DEVIATIONS, AND MARKER BEACON	APPROXIMATELY 200 MILES	CENTER CONSOLE
IFF (SIF)	APX-46	AUTOMATIC IDENTIFICATION	APPROXIMATELY 200 MILES	RIGHT CONSOLE

T.O. 1B-70(X)A-1

main and a guard receiver) are used with each radio system. The main receivers normally carry out all reception functions. Guard receivers are ground-tuned to a particular guard frequency and cannot be changed without removing the control panel. The main receivers are tuneable through the same frequency range as the transmitters, while the guard receiver frequency range is from 238.0 to 248.0 megacycles (normally set to 243.0 megacycles). Any one of twenty preset frequencies can be instantly selected. These frequencies are recorded on two frequency cards, one in a holder on each side of the center console. In addition, operating frequencies can be selected manually without disturbing the preset frequencies. Whenever a new frequency is selected, the transmitter and receiver are tuned automatically to the new frequency. This tuning cycle requires about 4 seconds, and completion of the tuning cycle is signaled by an audio tone heard in the headset. Two UHF antennas are used. A switch permits manual selection of either antenna. Automatic antenna selection is initiated by the antenna receiving the first usable signal. The command radios are powered by the essential ac bus or the right primary ac bus.

NOTE

A 60-second waiting period is required before the UHF radio will return to normal operation after an electrical power interruption, even though the interruption is only momentary.

UHF COMMAND RADIO CONTROLS.

NOTE

Identical controls are provided for each command radio. Because a selector switch determines which set is operating, only the controls of the selected set affect UHF operation.

Manual-Preset-Guard Sliding Selector and Frequency Selector Knobs.

The sliding selector (25, figure 1-7 and 9, figure 1-8) on each UHF radio control panel controls the method of command radio frequency selection. It is operated by sliding the control through a limited arc across the face of the panel. This control has three positions: MANUAL, PRESET, and GUARD, and is arranged so that when it is in any one position, the other two positions are masked by a semitransparent green glass. When the sliding selector is placed in the MANUAL position, a mask is removed from in front of each of the five windows across the top of the panel, revealing numerals that make up the operating frequency.

Beneath each of the five windows is a small knob which, when rotated, changes the number and the frequency. (See 22, figure 1-7 and 8, figure 1-8.) This makes it possible to manually select 3500 frequencies within the range of 225.0 to 399.95 megacycles.

While the sliding selector is in the MANUAL position, preset channel selection is deactivated and the main receiver and transmitter may be tuned manually by the five frequency knobs. Sliding the selector to PRESET masks the five small windows, deactivates the manually selected frequency, and activates one of the 20 preset channels controlled by the channel selector switch. Regardless of the position used, anytime a frequency is changed, about 4 seconds is required for the tuning mechanism to complete the tuning cycle. Both reception and transmission are inoperative during the tuning cycle, which is indicated by a tone signal heard in the headset. When the tuning cycle is completed, the tone signal ceases. Placing the sliding selector in the GUARD position automatically tunes the main transmitter and main receiver to the guard frequency set up before the installation of the equipment.

T.O. 1B-70(X)A-1

UHF Channel Selector Knob.

A rotary-type selector knob (29, figure 1-7; 23, figure 1-8), on each UHF radio control panel is used to select any one of 20 preset frequencies by channel number. When the knob is rotated, channel numbers from 1 through 20 appear in the channel indicator window, directly above the knob. This window is masked when the selector knob is in any position other than PRESET.

UHF Function Switch.

A four-position rotary-type function switch, (28, figure 1-7; 11, figure 1-8) is on each UHF radio control panel. The set is inoperative with the switch in the OFF position. When the switch is moved to MAIN, the transmitter and main receiver are activated. (A warm-up period of approximately 3 minutes is required before the radio set can be operated.) The guard receiver is in stand-by condition, and the guard frequency will only be received if it is one of the preset frequencies or if it is manually set up. In the BOTH position, the set transmitter and both the main and guard receivers are energized and both the main and guard receivers are energized and heard simultaneously. The ADF position is currently inoperative and is covered.

Intercom Function Selector Switch.

Refer to "Intercom System - AN/AIC-18" in this section.

Intercom-Microphone Switches.

Refer to "Intercom System - AN/AIC-18" in this section.

UHF Mixer Switch.

Refer to "Intercom System - AN/AIC-18" in this section.

UHF Modulation Selector Switch.

The two-position modulation selector switch (50, figure 1-7, 26, figure 1-8) on each UHF radio control panel is inoperative.

UHF Transmitter Power Output Knob.

A ten-position rotary knob (49, figure 1-7, 25, figure 1-8), on each UHF panel controls the transmitter power in steps of 8.9 decibels, permitting power output reductions up to 80 decibels as required by the tactical situation. The knob positions are marked in the window directly above the knob. Positions A and 10 are maximum power output positions with power decreasing as the numbers in the window decrease. The number 1 position is minimum power output. Normal operation is obtained with the knob in the number 10 or A position (maximum power output). The knob should be left in one of these two positions.

Volume Control Knob.

The volume knob (46, figure 1-7, 24, figure 1-8), on each UHF radio control panel, is inoperative. UHF volume is controlled by the UHF mixer switch, volume control and the master volume control knobs on the intercom control panels. (Refer to "Intercom System - AN/AIC-18" in this section.)

UHF Antenna Selector Switch.

The three-position antenna selector switch (36, figure 1-7) is on the center console. When the switch is at UPPER or LOWER, UHF transmission and reception is through the antenna on top or on the bottom of the fuselage, respectively. When the switch is at AUTO, operation is through the antenna first receiving a sufficiently strong signal. This antenna circuit will remain activated and is used for the next UHF transmission from the airplane. However, because the next transmission may be made at a later time, on a different frequency, or to a different ground station, the retained antenna circuit may not be the antenna to use. Therefore, manual selection of the other antenna may be necessary. The antenna selector switch receives power from the essential dc bus.

Changed 25 June 1965

T.O. 1B-70(X)A-1

Escape Capsule Microphone Switch.

Refer to "Escape Capsule Communications" in this section.

NORMAL OPERATION OF UHF COMMAND RADIO.

1. Frequencies - Check.
   Before take-off, check frequency to be used against those listed on the frequency cards.
2. Manual-preset-guard sliding selector - Check.
   Check operation of transmitter and main receiver with sliding selector in each position.

   NOTE
   No transmission will be made on emergency (distress) frequency channels except for emergency purposes in order to prevent transmission of messages that could be construed as actual emergency messages.

3. UHF function switch - BOTH.
   Check operation of the guard receiver, using the BOTH position of the function switch.
4. Initial channel selection - Complete.
   For initial channel selection, select a channel other than the one to be used until the warm-up power is completed, or after warm-up, switch to another channel and then back to the channel desired. Reduced performance can result because of mistuning if the desired channel is selected before the warm-up period is completed.
5. Antenna selector switch - AUTO.
6. Volume control knobs - Set.
   Adjust volume controls on the intercom control panels.
7. Manual-preset-guard sliding selector - Set as desired.
   For manual selection of a frequency that is not in the preset channels, move sliding selector to MANUAL. The five windows across the top of the panel will open and, by using the five knobs directly beneath each window, establish desired frequency. (The function switch must be at MAIN or BOTH for this operation.) To obtain transmission and reception of guard frequency only, move sliding selector to GUARD.

   NOTE
   - This procedure places the equipment in condition to receive. Transmissions on the same frequency are obtained by pressing the intercom-microphone switch to the MIC position; however, if it is desired to change the transmitter frequency, the intercom-microphone switch should be released before the frequency is changed. About 4 seconds should elapse before transmission begins on a new frequency.
   - Do not select a frequency less than 225.0 mc. The transmitter will attempt to tune this frequency; and after 90 seconds, the transmitter will shut down. To restore transmission, turn the function switch to OFF, wait 30 seconds, then select a higher frequency.

   CAUTION
   Do not move antenna selector switch while the intercom-microphone switch is pressed as damage to the antenna selector circuit will occur.

8. Transmitter power output knob - As desired.
   Select proper power output according to tactical requirements (normally position A or 10).
9. UHF mixer switch - Pull.
10. Intercom function selector switch - UHF.
11. Intercom-microphone switch - Press to MIC and talk, release to listen.

    NOTE
    The intercom-microphone switch must be released when transmission is complete to receive reply, except when intercom "HOT MIC" mixer

L-20

switch is used. This switch overrides the intercom-microphone switch.

To turn the UHF command radio off, move the function switch to OFF.

EMERGENCY OPERATION OF UHF COMMAND RADIO.

Sudden Loss of Transmission and/or Reception.

If UHF communication is lost while on one of the two sets, switch to the other UHF set. The second UHF set is always ready to operate and will be available for use without delay providing the proper frequency has been selected. The normal (4 seconds) tuning delay exists if the frequency has to be set up. If neither command radio will transmit or receive satisfactorily within the range of the equipment, the automatic antenna switching unit may not have selected the proper antenna. In this event, move the antenna selector switch to the LOWER or UPPER position to re-establish communication. If communication cannot be established, move the switch to AUTO and follow instructions given under "Radio Not Operating" in this section.

Radio Not Operating.

In the case of apparent command radio failure, attempt operation using an alternate position of the sliding selector and/or function switch. Turn equipment off for several minutes; then turn function switch to type of operation desired. This will restore operation of the protective relay if the tuning mechanism was responsible for the failure. Check the circuit breaker panel for a tripped condition of any of seven AN/ARC-50 circuit breakers. Any one tripped AN/ARC-50 circuit breaker will cause operational failure of the UHF set.

INTERCOM SYSTEM -AN/AIC-18.

This transistorized intercom set completes the airplane communication system when integrated with the TACAN and ILS navigation equipment and the UHF command radio equipment. The TACAN, ILS, IFF, and UHF transmitters and receivers, along with the intercom amplifier, provide air-to-air and air-to-ground communications, as well as intercom operation between crew positions, and the monitoring of any combination of radio and navigation signals. Two modes of transmission are available through a switch on each control wheel. Three internal and four external positions are provided for intercom operation. Two of the internal positions are in the crew compartment and the third is in the electronic equipment compartment. An external intercom plug-in receptacle is in each wheel well and one is on the bottom of the fuselage at the external electrical power receptacle. A switch in the crew compartment interconnects the flight stations to the external receptacles for communications with ground personnel. The landing gear audio warning signal is directed through the intercom system to the headset. This high volume signal cannot be adjusted and will override all other signals. It can be turned off by a separate switch in the landing gear system. (Refer to "Landing Gear System" in Section I.) Mixing switches permit individual or simultaneous monitoring of all communication signals. When the associated mixer switch is pulled out, the individual receiver is monitored; and the corresponding transmitter will be keyed when the microphone switch on the control wheels is pressed. A single mixer switch provides for hand-free (hot mike), intercom. Also hot mike operation is automatically provided when any one of the following occurs: bail-out warning light button is pressed, encapsulate caution light switch is placed at ON, or when the doors of one or both escape capsules are closed. The intercom system is powered by the ground tow dc bus or the right primary dc bus.

T.O. 1B-70(X)A-1

INTERCOM GROUND CREW OUTLETS.

Two-way communication is provided between ground crew and flight crew through one internal and four external plug-in receptacles. One intercom receptacle is in each wheel well, one at the external electrical power receptacle, and one on the radio equipment rack in the electronic equipment compartment. Portable intercom equipment must be used in conjunction with each intercom outlet. Fully transistorized amplifier units provide microphone and headset amplification for each outlet. (The receptacle on the radio equipment rack differs from the other intercom receptacles in that it uses the nose wheel well receptacle unit for amplifying the signals to that station.) A spring-loaded switch on the radio rack must be held at its INT position for microphone operation from the radio equipment rack position. Automatic gain control circuitry lessens distortion during operation.

INTERCOM FUNCTION SELECTOR SWITCH.

A switch (14, figure 1-7) on each intercom control panel selects the operating function of the communication systems. The switch has six positions but only the three labeled "UHF 1," "UHF 2," and "INT" are used. Either UHF position provides for both radio transmission and intercom operation. (The UHF 1 position selects the command radio controlled by the UHF panel on the center console; the UHF 2 position selects the command radio controlled by the UHF panel on the pilot's console.) The switch on each control wheel controls the type of communication selected. Therefore, the function selector switch may remain in a UHF position at all times. Rotation of this knob to the INT position shuts off all other circuits except the intercom circuit and the landing gear audio warning signal.

MIXER SWITCHES.

Each intercom control panel has eight switches (9, 10, 12, 13, 15, 16, 18, and 19, figure 1-7), six of which are used for controlling the mixed-signal listen facility and two for hot microphone operation of the intercom set. These push-pull type switches provide signal monitoring and hot microphone operation. They can be rotated to provide individual volume control for adjusting specific output. The switches are identified as "MXR BCN," "ILS," "UHF 1," "UHF 2," "TACAN," "INT," "HOT MIC ON-OFF," and "HOT MIC VOL."

NOTE
- The "HOT MIC ON-OFF" switch does not incorporate volume control circuitry. However, the "HOT MIC VOL" switch controls the volume of the hot microphone and it is necessary that both switches be pulled out for proper operation.
- Any one or combination of signals may be received simultaneously by pulling out the appropriate mixer switch, regardless of the position of the function selector switch. The selected volume control can be used to adjust the individual audio level. Audio level adjustment can also be controlled by the intercom master volume control. Pushing the individual mixer switch shuts off the corresponding signal. However, the "INT" mixer switch is inoperative when the function selector switch is at INT or the "HOT MIC" mixer switch is pulled up.

VOLUME CONTROL KNOBS.

Volume control knobs adjust the audio levels of incoming communication signals. Each mixer switch, when pulled out, becomes a volume control for its individual unit, except the "HOT MIC" switch. A separate switch (9, figure 1-7) is provided for control of the "HOT MIC" volume. In addition, a master volume control knob (17, figure 1-7) permits simultaneous audio level control of all communication signals.

1-22

T.O. 1B-70(X)A-1

CALL BUTTON.

The call button (11, figure 1-7), on each intercom control panel, is a momentary push-button switch that permits the calling station to interrupt all intercom functions at a high audio level; and the other crew station can be contacted without pressing the intercom-microphone switch. It is used primarily in an emergency.

INTERCOM-MICROPHONE SWITCHES.

A two-position, trigger-type switch (1, figure 1-11) is on the outboard grip of each control wheel. Pressing the switch to the microphone (MIC) position, with the associated intercom mixer button and intercom function selector switch at the UHF position, initiates radio transmission. Pressing the switch to the intercom (INTER) position initiates normal intercom operation only. With the intercom function selector switch at INT, pressing the trigger switch to either MIC or INTER will initiate intercom operation while prohibiting UHF radio transmission.

GROUND INTERCOM SWITCH.

A two-position switch (12, figure 1-9) on the copilot's console controls intercom between the ground crew intercom outlets and the crew compartment. Moving the switch to the ON position permits conversation with ground crew personnel whenever the applicable microphone switches are pressed.

NORMAL OPERATION OF INTERCOM SYSTEM.

For intercom operation only, proceed as follows:

1. Intercom function selector switch - UHF or INT.

    NOTE
    The function selector may remain at the UHF position at all times because radio transmissions and interphone operations are controlled by the interphone-microphone switch on each control wheel.

2. "INT" mixer switch - Pull out.
3. Other mixer switches - Push in.

    NOTE
    Mixer switches are pulled out for on, pushed in for off.

4. Intercom-microphone switch - INTER.

    NOTE
    Individual volume control is connected to the mixer switches.

For intercom call operation, proceed as follows:

1. Call button - Hold and talk.

    NOTE
    - All other stations receive the message regardless of the position of the mixer switches or function selector switch.
    - When the call button is used, it overrides the intercom-microphone switch and prevents transmission of intercom conversation over the command radio.
    - No signal mixing is possible during call operation.
    - Call button must be released to hear replies.

For monitoring all communication signals, proceed as follows:

1. Intercom function selector switch - INT or UHF.
2. Desired mixer switches - Pull out.

    NOTE
    Several signals can be monitored simultaneously by pulling out the corresponding mixer switch.

3. Volume control knobs - As desired.

IDENTIFICATION RADAR (IFF) - AN/APX-46.

The AN/APX-46 identification radar set provides selective identification of the airplane in response to IFF interrogations. The set includes an RT 556/APX-46 receiver-transmitter, a C-1158/APX control panel, a C-1128/APX-25 SIF coder-group control panel, an antenna switching unit, and two antennas. The constant rate automatic antenna switching unit provides optimum reception and transmission of IFF signals. The IFF set receives power from the essential ac and dc busses.

NOTE
A 60-second waiting period is required before the IFF will return to normal operation after an electrical power interruption, even though the interruption is only momentary.

Operation of the IFF in either LOW or NORM positions provides automatic switching to the emergency mode when the encapsulate switch is ON, when the bailout button is pressed, or when the capsule doors are closed. The IFF will continue to transmit until the encapsulate switch is moved to RESET, then OFF (except when the bailout button has been used).

IDENTIFICATION RADAR CONTROLS.

The AN/APX-46 identification radar controls are on the two panels (labeled IFF and SIF) located on the copilot's console. The IFF control panel has a master switch, mode 2 and mode 3 switches, and an identification of position(I/P) reply switch. The master switch (24, figure 1-9) has five positions: OFF, STDBY, LOW, NORM, and EMERGENCY. Selection of the STDBY position will warm up the set.

NOTE
Transmission of reply is disabled in the STDBY position.

The set operates throughout its maximum range when NORM is selected, and range is reduced when the LOW position is selected. With the switch in either the NORM or LOW position, the set responds only to challenges correctly coded for the mode or modes selected. With the master switch at EMERGENCY, a coded reply will be automatically transmitted in response to any challenge.

NOTE
To move the master switch to EMERGENCY, the emergency interlock button (23, figure 1-9), below the switch, must be pressed and held while the switch is being moved.

The mode 2 switch (10, figure 1-9) has MODE 2 and OUT positions. The mode 3 switch (10, figure 1-9) has MODE 3 and OUT positions. The position of mode 2 and mode 3 switches determines the IFF reply-to-ground or air-borne equipment interrogations. Mode 1 always is operating, regardless of the positions of the mode switches and coder knobs. The three-position identification of position (I/P) reply switch (11, figure 1-9) controls the distinct type of position transmission. With the I/P switch at OUT, no position reply will be sent. When the I/P switch is at MIC, a position reply will be sent if the mode switches are on when the intercom-microphone switch on the control wheel is pressed to MIC and for 30 seconds after. Holding the switch at I/P automatically transmits a position reply. The SIF (selective identification feature) control panel contains two concentric rotary coder knobs (9, figure 1-9), mode 1 knobs and mode 3 knobs. The mode 1 inner knob has positions 0 through 7. The mode 3 inner and outer knobs have positions 0 through 7. The positions selected on each set of knobs determine the specific selected identification reply to be sent.

OPERATION OF IDENTIFICATION RADAR.

NOTE
Check that the IFF frequency counters have been set to the proper identification frequency channels before take-off.

1. IFF master switch - STDBY.
   The switch should be at STDBY for a 3-minute warm-up period.

2. IFF I/P reply switch - OUT.

NOTE

Use I/P or MIC positions only when directed by the traffic controller.

3. IFF mode switches - As required.
4. SIF coder knobs - As required.

NOTE

The mode and code to be used for IFF operation at a specified time and place will usually be directed by an authorized agency before take-off, on departure, or in flight. However, in the absence of specific instructions, the following is recommended:

   a. Mode 1 - All switches OUT, set SIF mode 1 coder knobs to 00.
   b. Mode 2 - Set IFF mode 2 switch to OUT.
   c. Mode 3 - Set IFF mode switch to MODE 3 and set SIF mode 3 outer coder knob at 0 and inner coder knob at 5.

5. IFF master switch - NORMAL.

NOTE

The low position (low sensitivity) should be used only when directed by the traffic controller.

6. IFF identification of position switch - I/P or MIC, as directed. Move the position reply switch to the I/P or MIC position when directed by the traffic controller.
7. IFF master switch - OFF. To turn the IFF set off, rotate the IFF master switch counterclockwise to OFF.

To use the IFF in case of an emergency, proceed as follows:

NOTE

With the IFF at either NORMAL or LOW, the emergency mode of operation of the IFF is automatically actuated when either capsule is closed or when the encapsulate caution light switch is at ON, or when the bail-out warning light button is pressed.

1. SIF mode 1 coder knobs - 00.
2. IFF mode 3 switch - MODE 3.
3. SIF mode 3 coder knobs - 77.
4. IFF master switch - EMERGENCY.

NOTE

The IFF emergency interlock button must be pressed before rotating the IFF master switch to EMERGENCY. A reply will then be made automatically in response to a mode 1 or mode 2 challenge.

ESCAPE CAPSULE COMMUNICATIONS.

Air-to-air and air-to-ground communications as well as intercom is available following encapsulation, providing the UHF communication and the intercom systems are operating. Hand-free (hot mike) operation of the microphone is provided as soon as either escape capsule is closed, and establishes intercom between pilot and copilot only. Each escape capsule has a push-button microphone switch (figure 1-36) mounted on the left wall of the capsule. When this switch is pressed, radio communications can be maintained on the frequency or frequencies set up on the UHF control panel before encapsulation. The microphone switch must be released to hear any UHF replies. Volume control remains as adjusted before encapsulation. The emergency mode of IFF operation is also actuated automatically when either capsule is closed providing IFF master switch is at either NORMAL or LOW.

LIGHTING EQUIPMENT.

EXTERIOR LIGHTING.

The navigation lights, in each wing tip, consist of forward and side-mounted colored lights and an aft-facing white light. Three red anticollision lights,

T.O. 1B-70(X)A-1

one on the top of the fuselage and two below the intake ducts, retract flush with the skin of the airplane when not in use. The dual landing lights and the auxiliary landing and taxi light, under the crew compartment, retract flush for streamlining and protection. Cutout circuits, controlled by signals from the air data computer, automatically prevent extending the landing lights, the auxiliary landing and taxi light, or the anticollision lights above certain speeds and/or altitudes. A caution light in the crew compartment shows when the landing lights are extended above the altitude and airspeed limits. The exterior lights are shown in figure 1-1.

LANDING LIGHT SWITCH.

The two-position landing light switch (27, figure 1-7), on the center console, receives power from the right primary ac bus. The ON position of the switch is powered only if the airplane is below 8000 feet or the airspeed is less than 250 knots IAS. Moving the switch to ON opens the landing light doors and extends and turns on both landing lights. Moving the switch to OFF turns off and retracts the landing lights and closes the landing light doors.

CAUTION

The landing lights must be retracted above 250 knots IAS and 8000 feet altitude to prevent damage to the lights.

AUXILIARY LANDING AND TAXI LIGHT SWITCH.

The two-position auxiliary light switch (1, figure 1-6), on the overhead panel, receives power from the right primary ac bus. The ON position of the switch is powered only if the airplane is below 8000 feet and the airspeed is less than 250 knots IAS. Moving the switch to ON in flight extends the light to about 72 degrees and turns on the light. The light also is angled about 20 degrees to the left. When the main gear touches down, or if the switch is moved to ON on the ground, the light extends an additional 10 degrees to direct the light beam further ahead and to one side of the airplane. Moving the switch to OFF turns off and retracts the auxiliary landing and taxi light.

CAUTION

The auxiliary landing and taxi light must be retracted above 250 knots IAS and 8000 feet to prevent damage to the light.

ANTICOLLISION LIGHT SWITCH.

The two-position anticollision light switch (12, figure 1-6), on the overhead panel, receives power from the right primary ac bus if the airspeed is below approximately Mach 1.1. Moving the switch to ON extends and turns on the three anticollision lights and starts them rotating. Moving the switch to OFF turns off the lights and retracts them. If the lights are extended and the airspeed is increased above the limit airspeed, the lights retract automatically. The anticollision light switch is mechanically latched in the OFF position and must be pulled out before it can be moved to ON.

NOTE

The anti-collision light should be turned OFF during flight through conditions of reduced visibility where the pilot could experience vertigo as a result of the rotating reflections of the light against the clouds. In addition, the light would be ineffective as an anticollision light during these conditions since it could not be observed by pilots of other airplanes.

NAVIGATION LIGHT SWITCH.

The two-position navigation light switch (2, figure 1-6), on the overhead panel, receives power from the ground tow ac

4-26

T.O. 1B-70(X)A-1

bus. Moving the switch to ON turns on the wing tip navigation lights. Moving the switch to OFF turns the lights off. The navigation light switch is mechanically latched in the OFF position and must be pulled out before it can be moved to ON.

LANDING LIGHT EXTENDED CAUTION LIGHT.

The placard-type landing light extended caution light (5, figure 1-7), on the center console, is powered by the essential ac bus. The light comes on to show "LDG LT EXTENDED" if the auxiliary landing and taxi light and/or the landing lights are not fully retracted when the airplane is above 8000 feet or 250 knots IAS.

INTERIOR LIGHTING.

The control panels and edge-lighted instruments have white nonglare indirect lighting from bulbs imbedded in the plastic panels. Individual rheostats in the crew compartment permit separate indirect lighting control of the pilot's instrument panel; copilot's instrument panel; center instrument panel; and the side consoles, center console, and overhead panel. Floodlights are provided for the instrument panel, the side consoles, the center aisle console, and the overhead panel. The instrument panel floodlights and console floodlights are separately controlled. Utility lights, with self-contained switches, fit into a socket on both the pilot's and copilot's consoles for general crew compartment lighting. The utility lights can be removed from their sockets to light areas not normally lighted by other interior lights. Four nondimmable floodlights are in the electronic equipment compartment ceiling. Spare bulbs are stored in a compartment in the pilot's console. (See 18, figure 1-8.)

PILOT'S FLIGHT INSTRUMENT INDIRECT LIGHT SWITCH AND RHEOSTAT.

The pilot's flight instrument indirect light switch and rheostat (10, figure 1-6), on the overhead panel, controls the indirect lighting of the pilot's instrument panel. It is marked "FLIGHT INST" and receives power from the essential ac bus. The combination switch and rheostat knob is turned clockwise from OFF to turn the lights on and increase the brightness. Turning the knob counterclockwise dims the lights, and full counterclockwise rotation to OFF turns the lights off.

COPILOT'S FLIGHT INSTRUMENT INDIRECT LIGHT SWITCH AND RHEOSTAT.

The copilot's flight instrument indirect light switch and rheostat (6, figure 1-6), on the overhead panel, controls the indirect lighting of the copilot's instrument panel. It is marked "FLIGHT INST" and receives power from the essential ac bus. The combination switch and rheostat knob is turned clockwise from OFF to turn the lights on to increase the brightness. Turning the knob counterclockwise dims the lights, and full counterclockwise rotation to OFF turns the lights off.

ENGINE INSTRUMENT INDIRECT LIGHT SWITCH AND RHEOSTAT.

The engine instrument indirect light switch and rheostat (5, figure 1-6), on the overhead panel, controls the indirect lighting of the center instrument panel. It is marked "ENGINE INST" and receives power from the essential ac bus. The combination switch and rheostat knob is turned clockwise from OFF to turn the lights on and increase the brightness. Turning the knob counterclockwise dims the lights, and full counterclockwise rotation to OFF turns the lights off.

T.O. 1B-70(X)A-1

OVERHEAD, PEDESTAL, AND CONSOLE
INDIRECT LIGHT SWITCH AND RHEOSTAT.

The overhead, pedestal, and console indirect light switch and rheostat (3, figure 1-6), on the overhead panel, controls the indirect lighting of the overhead panel, center console (pedestal), and pilot's and copilot's consoles. The switch receives power from the essential ac bus. The combination switch and rheostat knob is turned clockwise from OFF to turn the lights on and increase the brightness. Turning the knob counterclockwise dims the lights, and full counterclockwise rotation to OFF turns the lights off.

INSTRUMENT PANEL FLOODLIGHT SWITCH AND RHEOSTAT.

The instrument panel floodlight switch and rheostat (11, figure 1-6), on the overhead panel, is marked "INST FLOOD" and receives power from the ground tow ac bus. The combination switch and rheostat knob is turned clockwise from OFF to turn on the six floodlights under the instrument panel shroud and increase the brightness. Turning the knob counterclockwise dims the lights, and full counterclockwise rotation to OFF turns the lights off.

CONSOLE FLOODLIGHT SWITCH AND RHEOSTAT.

The console floodlight switch and rheostat (4, figure 1-6), on the overhead panel, is marked "CONSOLE FLOOD" and receives power from ground tow ac bus. The combination switch and rheostat knob is turned clockwise from OFF to turn on and increase the brightness of the four floodlights over both the pilot's and copilot's consoles and the four overhead floodlights which light the center console and the overhead panel. Turning the knob counterclockwise dims the lights, and full counterclockwise rotation to OFF turns the lights off.

CONSOLE UTILITY LIGHTS.

The portable utility lights (17, figure 1-8 and 17, figure 1-9), one on both the pilot's and copilot's console, are powered by the essential dc bus. The end cap of each utility light is also a switch and rheostat with BRIGHT, DIM, and OFF positions. Turning the end clockwise from OFF turns on the light and increases the brightness. Turning the end counterclockwise dims the light, and full counterclockwise rotation to OFF turns the light off.

ELECTRONIC EQUIPMENT COMPARTMENT
UTILITY FLOODLIGHT AND SWITCH.

The utility floodlights in the electronic equipment compartment are powered by the essential ac bus. The lights are controlled by a two-position switch on the right side, on the corner of the escape aisle leading to the ground escape hatch. The switch is marked "UTILITY LIGHT" and is mounted in a recess. Moving the switch to ON turns on the floodlights in the electronic equipment compartment. Moving the switch to OFF turns off the lights.

OXYGEN SYSTEM.

Each crew member has his own complete liquid oxygen system. Each system has a converter-storage container and an air heat exchanger to convert the liquid to a gas which is warmed to make it suitable for breathing. Either converter can supply gaseous oxygen to the other crew member through interconnecting lines and check valves. The changeover is automatic and occurs if there is a 12 psi differential between systems. Each individual system is controlled by a toggle valve in the crew compartment. The liquid oxygen is stored in two 10-liter vacuum-insulated Thermos bottle type converter containers in the crew compartment. (See 6, figure 1-1.) For servicing, the converter containers are removed. A quantity gage in the crew compartment shows the total quantity of liquid oxygen in both containers. Container pressure, necessary to force out the liquid when demanded by the system, is provided by converting some of the liquid to gas and using this gas pressure in the container. Gaseous oxygen, at a pressure of about 70 psi, is delivered from the converters to the escape capsules. The 70 psi oxygen is then routed to an automatic oxygen regulator under each seat. The oxygen regulator supplies 100 percent oxygen at a pressure of 2.0 to 60 inches of water, depending on altitude, to the personal-lead disconnect. The oxygen personal leads, connected to the personal-lead disconnect, also has a 2.1 pressure reducer installed to reduce the pressure to between zero and 30 inches of water depending on altitude. The liquid oxygen system supplies breathable oxygen at a rate that depends on cabin altitude and crew demand. An oxygen mask test button is provided in each capsule. Liquid oxygen duration is shown in figure 4-6. An emergency oxygen system in each capsule provides additional gaseous oxygen in case of an emergency. See figure 1-37 for liquid oxygen specifications.

OXYGEN SYSTEM CONTROLS AND INDICATOR.

OXYGEN TOGGLE VALVES.

Two oxygen toggle valves (6, figure 1-8; 8, figure 1-9), one on each console, control their respective oxygen system shutoff valve. Moving the toggle to ON mechanically opens the valve to supply oxygen to the respective oxygen mask hose whether the mask is being worn or not. The OFF position of the toggle shuts off the respective system.

OXYGEN MASK TEST BUTTONS.

The push-to-test buttons, one on the front of each seat, permit checking the fit of the oxygen mask. Pushing the button applies an oxygen pressure of 11 to 16 inches of water to the respective oxygen mask to check for leaks.

QUANTITY GAGES TEST BUTTON.

Refer to "Environmental Systems Controls and Indicators" in this section.

LIQUID OXYGEN QUANTITY GAGE.

The liquid oxygen quantity gage (18, figure 1-3), on the pilot's instrument panel, has a range of 0 to 20 liters, in one-liter increments. The gage is powered by the essential ac bus and indicates the amount of liquid oxygen in both storage containers. An operational check of the gage can be made by means of the quantity gages test button.

ESCAPE CAPSULE OXYGEN SYSTEM (EMERGENCY OXYGEN SYSTEM).

A gaseous emergency oxygen system is incorporated within each escape capsule. The dual purpose system is used as an emergency breathing system when it is manually actuated by pulling the emergency knob ("green apple") or as an ejection-escape breathing system when actuated automatically upon ejection. Each system consists of a 14.1 cubic foot supply of gaseous oxygen in a cylinder below the seat, (at a pressure of 1800 psi) and a filler and pressure gage assembly. The gaseous oxygen is ported into an oxygen pressure reducer in the capsule. The 1800 psi is reduced to 70 psi before leaving the pressure reducer. When the emergency oxygen system is activated, pressure from this system presses against a check valve which shuts off the normal liquid oxygen supply system. Once the emergency oxygen system is activated, it is not possible to change back to the liquid oxygen system until the emergency system pressure is reduced to less than that of the liquid oxygen system which permits the check valve to open. The emergency oxygen system is sufficient

T.O. 1B-70(X)A-1

OXYGEN DURATION-HOURS

Crew: 2
100 percent oxygen to mask - Constant 70 psi flow to regulator

CABIN ALTITUDE - 1000 FEET

	20	18	16	14	12	10	8	6	4	2	BELOW 2
35 AND ABOVE	56.4	50.8	45.2	39.5	33.8	28.2	22.6	16.9	11.3	5.6	DESCEND TO ALTITUDE NOT REQUIRING OXYGEN
30	40.8	37.6	33.4	29.3	25.1	20.8	16.7	12.5	8.4	4.2	
25	31.3	28.2	25.0	21.9	18.8	15.7	12.5	9.4	6.3	3.1	
20	24.5	22.0	19.6	17.2	14.7	12.3	9.8	7.4	4.9	2.5	
15	19.8	17.8	15.9	13.9	11.9	9.9	7.9	5.9	4.0	2.0	
10	15.9	14.3	12.7	11.1	9.5	7.9	6.4	4.8	3.2	1.6	
8	14.5	13.0	11.6	10.1	8.7	7.2	5.8	4.3	2.9	1.5	
6	12.8	11.5	10.3	9.0	7.7	6.4	5.1	3.8	2.6	1.3	
4	12.3	11.1	9.8	8.6	7.4	6.1	4.9	3.7	2.5	1.2	
2	11.1	10.0	8.9	7.8	6.7	5.5	4.4	3.3	2.2	1.1	
SEA LEVEL	10.2	9.2	8.2	7.1	6.1	5.1	4.1	3.1	2.0	1.0	

LITERS

Crew: 2
In pressure suits (Airplane AF62-001)

CABIN ALTITUDE - 1000 FEET

	20	18	16	14	12	10	8	6	4	2	BELOW 2
55 AND ABOVE	14.0	13.0	11.0	10.0	9.0	7.0	6.0	4.0	3.0	1.0	DESCEND TO ALTITUDE NOT REQUIRING OXYGEN
50	15.0	13.0	12.0	10.0	9.0	7.0	6.0	4.0	3.0	1.0	
45	21.0	19.0	17.0	15.0	13.0	10.0	8.0	6.0	4.0	2.0	
40	32.0	29.0	26.0	23.0	19.0	16.0	13.0	10.0	6.5	3.0	
35	30.0	27.0	24.0	21.0	18.0	15.0	12.0	9.0	6.0	3.0	
30	24.0	21.0	19.0	16.0	14.0	12.0	9.0	7.0	5.0	2.0	
25	18.0	16.0	15.0	13.0	11.0	9.0	7.0	5.0	4.0	2.0	
20	14.0	13.0	11.0	10.0	8.0	7.0	6.0	4.0	3.0	1.0	
15	11.0	10.0	9.0	8.0	7.0	6.0	4.0	3.0	2.0	1.0	
10	9.0	8.0	7.0	6.0	5.0	4.0	3.5	3.0	2.0	1.0	
8	8.0	7.0	6.0	6.0	5.0	4.0	3.0	2.0	2.0	.8	
5	7.0	6.0	6.0	5.0	4.0	3.5	3.0	2.0	1.0	1.0	
SEA LEVEL	6.0	5.0	5.0	4.0	3.5	3.0	2.0	2.0	1.0	.5	

LITERS

Liquid Oxygen Converter-Container - Two Type GCU - 18/A (10 liters each)

Figure 4-6

for about 20 minutes. See figure 1-37 for gaseous oxygen specifications.

CAPSULE EMERGENCY OXYGEN ACTUATOR KNOB ("GREEN APPLE").

A round green emergency oxygen actuator knob, (figure 1-37), called a "green apple" is on the forward edge of each seat at the centerline. Pulling the knob up opens a valve in the oxygen pressure reducer to activate the emergency oxygen system. The knob cannot shut off the emergency oxygen system.

CAPSULE EMERGENCY OXYGEN PRESSURE GAGE AND FILLER VALVE.

An emergency oxygen pressure gage and a filler valve (figure 1-37) are mounted as a unit in the upper right rear corner of each capsule. The gage has a range from REFILL to 2500 psi. The range from REFILL to 1800 (full) is a red band, and from 1800 (full) to 2500 is a green band. The mounting area of the gage and filler valve is painted green and marked "OXY." The filler valve is just below the gage.

OXYGEN SYSTEM PREFLIGHT CHECK.

Before take-off, the oxygen system should be checked as follows:

NOTE
Any reference to oxygen controls and indicators applies to both pilot and copilot.

1. Liquid oxygen quantity gage - Check.
   Check liquid oxygen quantity gage for adequate oxygen for the mission. (Full condition is 20 liters.)
2. Emergency oxygen cylinder pressure gage - Check.
   Check emergency oxygen cylinder pressure gage for a minimum reading of 1800 psi at 70 degrees F.
3. Oxygen toggle valve - Check OFF.
4. Oxygen flow - Check.
   Uncap outlet port of the pressure reducer valve and move oxygen toggle valve to ON. Oxygen should flow freely out the uncapped port. Move oxygen toggle valve to OFF after checking.

CAUTION
Do not allow oxygen to flow freely out of port for more than 10 seconds, otherwise the oxygen regulator may be damaged.

5. Oxygen mask and hoses - Put on and connect as shown in figure 4-7.
6. Oxygen toggle valve - ON.
7. Oxygen mask test button - Press momentarily.
   Momentarily press the test button to check the mask fit.

NORMAL OPERATION OF OXYGEN SYSTEM.

Operation of the respective oxygen system is automatic after the pilot's or copilot's oxygen toggle valves are moved to ON.

OXYGEN SYSTEM EMERGENCY OPERATION.

Refer to "Oxygen System Emergency Operation" in Section III.

NAVIGATION EQUIPMENT.

TACAN - AN/ARN-65.

The TACAN set is an air navigational system which provides cockpit displays of distance and bearing to a selected VORTAC or TACAN surface beacon. This range and bearing information is reliable up to a line-of-sight distance of approximately 200 nautical miles.

NOTE
Improperly adjusted or malfunctioning ground or airborne TACAN equipment may "lock-on" to a false bearing. Therefore, during flight, verify TACAN bearing information when possible by cross-checking with ground radar, airborne radar or VOR.

T. O. 1B-70(X)A-1

OXYGEN HOSE HOOK-UP

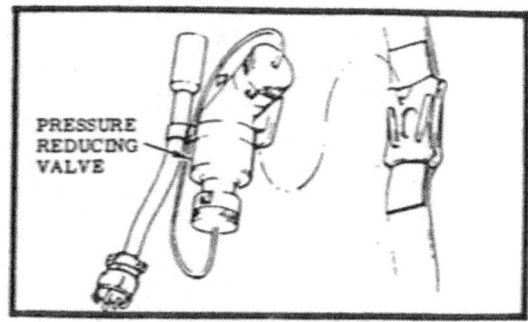

1 Insert connector into mounting plate attached to the restraint harness. Check that connector is properly inserted and that lock pin is engaged.

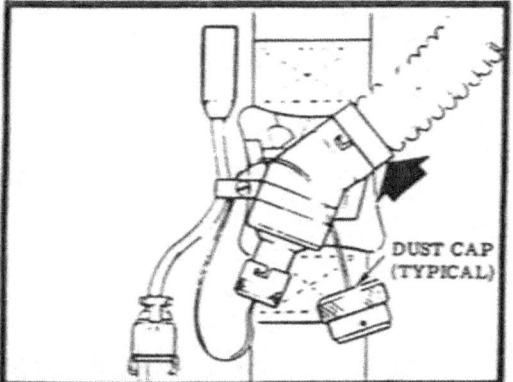

2 Remove dust cap and insert male bayonet connection, on the oxygen mask hose, into connector. Turn bayonet to lock prongs.

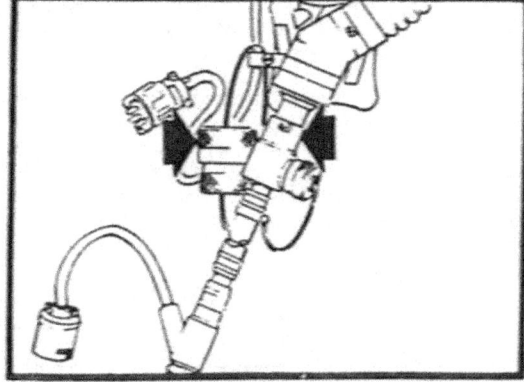

3 Remove dust cap and connect female bayonet connection, on seat oxygen hose, onto bottom of connector. Turn bayonet to lock prongs. Attach dust caps together.

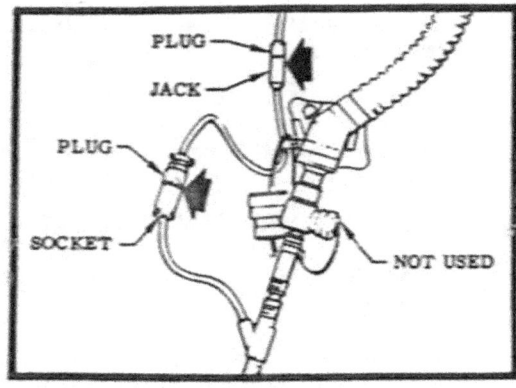

4 Connect plug from oxygen mask to jack on the connector, and connect plug on connector to socket from seat.

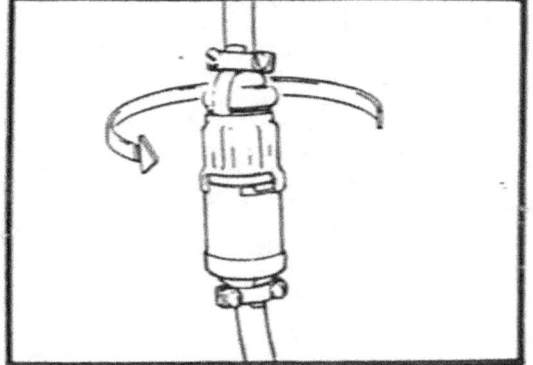

5 After connecting plug and socket, lock together by rotating shell on plug to engage socket.

Figure 4-7

The major components of the TACAN set are a transceiver, an indicator coupler (flight director computer), a control panel, and two antennas. The antennas are selected automatically through the antenna selector unit. The unit will automatically select the antenna which first receives a satisfactory signal. The TACAN transceiver automatically transmits an interrogation signal, which is received by the selected surface beacon and returned to the airplane. Distance, bearing, and course signals are then sent to the indicator coupler (flight director computer), which processes the signals and couples them to the indicators in the cockpit. The TACAN surface beacon identification signals are transmitted every 38 seconds and can be heard in the headsets. The TACAN set is powered by the right primary ac and dc busses.

NOTE
A 60-second waiting period is required before the TACAN will return to normal operation after an electrical power interruption, even though the power interruption is only momentary.

TACAN CHANNEL SELECTOR SWITCH.

The channel selector switch (31, figure 1-7), on the center console, permits selection of any one of 126 channels. These channels cover the transmitting frequency range of 1025 to 1150 megacycles and the receiving frequency range of 962 to 1024 and 1151 to 1213 megacycles with a one megacycle separation. The receiver frequency is automatically set at the same time a transmitting frequency is selected. The switch consists of a large circular serrated knob and small handle. The circular knob selects the first two digits and the handle selects the third digit of a desired channel. A window above the handle displays the selected channel.

TACAN VOLUME CONTROL KNOB.

This knob (32, figure 1-7), on the center console, is inoperative; TACAN volume is regulated through the TACAN mixer switches on the intercom control panels. (Refer to "Intercom System - AN/AIC-18" in this section.)

TACAN FUNCTION SWITCH.

A three-position rotary switch (30, figure 1-7), on the center console, controls power to the set and the mode of operation. With the switch at the REC (receive) position, the system presents bearing and audio identification information. With the switch at T/R (transmit/receive), the system presents bearing, distance, and audio identification information as well as all transmitting operations. When the switch is OFF, the system is off. The switch receives power from the right primary dc bus.

COMMAND CONTROL SWITCH.

Refer to "Flight Director System" in this section.

FLIGHT DIRECTOR MODE SELECTOR SWITCH.

Refer to "Flight Director System" in this section.

INTERCOM TACAN MIXER SWITCH.

Refer to "Intercom System - AN/AIC-18" in this section.

ATTITUDE DIRECTOR INDICATOR SELECTOR SWITCH.

Refer to "Flight Director System" in this section.

HORIZONTAL SITUATION INDICATORS (HSI).

Refer to "Flight Director System" in this section.

ATTITUDE DIRECTOR INDICATORS (ADI).

Refer to "Flight Director System" in this section.

OPERATION OF TACAN.

NOTE
The following procedures put only the TACAN set into operation.

Refer to "Flight Director System" in this section for procedures on use of TACAN in the various flight director modes.

1. TACAN function switch - REC or T/R, as desired.
    After moving function switch from OFF, allow a 3-minute warm-up.
2. TACAN channel selector switch - Set.
3. Intercom TACAN mixer switch - Pull out.
    Rotate mixer switch, as desired, for volume control.
4. TACAN function switch - OFF.
    To shut off TACAN, move function switch to OFF.

INSTRUMENT LANDING SYSTEM (ILS).

The three instrument landing functions are provided by the AN/ARN-58 radio receiving set. This receiving set includes an R-843/ARN-58 localizer receiver with necessary instruments, an R-844/ARN-58 glide slope and marker beacon receiver and a control panel. These receivers, together with antennas, indicators (attitude director and horizontal situation indicators), and display coupler (part of the flight director computer) comprise a complete instrument landing system. Guidance signals are received from ground transmitters and displayed on the attitude director, horizontal situation, and the marker beacon indicators. The displays shown are localizer deviations, localizer command steering, glide slope deviation, glide slope command steering and marker beacon interception. Visual and aural indications are provided when the airplane passes over a 75-megacycle transmitter providing airway and/or airfield identification (airway marker or runway approach marker). All components of the instrument landing system receive power from the right primary dc bus.

ILS FREQUENCY SELECTOR KNOB.

The ILS frequency selector knob (35, figure 1-7), on the center console, is used to select the desired localizer frequency. The knob permits selection of localizer frequencies through the range of 108.1 to 111.9 megacycles in 200-kilocycle steps. The localizer frequency selected is displayed through a window to the left of the knob. Glide slope frequencies are automatically tuned with the selection of a localizer frequency and range from 329.3 to 335.0 megacycles in 300-kilocycle steps. (Glide slope frequencies are not displayed.)

ILS POWER SWITCH.

The two-position ILS power switch (33, figure 1-7) is on the center console. When the switch is moved to POWER, the ILS system receives power from the right primary dc bus.

ILS VOLUME KNOB.

This knob (34, figure 1-7) on the center console is inoperative, and ILS volume is controlled by rotating the ILS mixer switches on the intercom control panels. (Refer to "Intercom System - AN/AIC-18" in this section.)

COMMAND CONTROL SWITCH.

Refer to "Flight Director System" in this section.

FLIGHT DIRECTOR MODE SELECTOR SWITCH.

Refer to "Flight Director System" in this section.

INTERCOM ILS MIXER SWITCH.

Refer to "Intercom System - AN/AIC-18" in this system.

T.O. 1B-70(X)A-1

ATTITUDE DIRECTOR INDICATOR SELECTOR SWITCH.

Refer to "Flight Director System" in this section.

HORIZONTAL SITUATION INDICATORS (HSI).

Refer to "Flight Director System" in this section.

ATTITUDE DIRECTOR INDICATORS (ADI).

Refer to "Flight Director System" in this section.

ALTITUDE HOLD SWITCH.

Refer to "Flight Director System" in this section.

MARKER BEACON INDICATOR LIGHTS.

Two placard-type indicator lights (33, figure 1-3 and 24, figure 1-4) are illuminated by the marker beacon receiver when the airplane passes over a 75-megacycle marker beacon transmitter. One marker beacon indicator light is on the pilot's instrument panel; the other is on the copilot's instrument panel. In addition to these lights, a tone in the headsets indicates when the airplane is passing over a marker beacon, if the intercom marker beacon mixer switch has been pulled up. (Refer to "Intercom System - AN/AIC-18" in this section.) The marker beacon indicator lights are powered by the essential ac bus.

OPERATION OF INSTRUMENT LANDING SYSTEM.

NOTE
The following procedures place only the ILS set into operation. Refer to "Flight Director System" in this section for procedures covering approaches.

1. ILS power switch - POWER.
2. ILS frequency selector knob - Set desired frequency.
3. Intercom ILS mixer switch - Pull out and rotate for desired volume.
4. Altitude hold switch - As required.

NOTE
If the ILS approach mode comes through the air data computer beam sensor circuit while the flight director mode selector switch is at ILS, the altitude hold circuit automatically disengages.

5. Marker beacon mixer switch - Pull out.
6. ILS power switch - OFF.
To shut off ILS, move power switch to OFF.

AUXILIARY GYRO PLATFORM SYSTEM (AGPS).

The auxiliary gyro platform system provides pitch, roll, and heading reference information to the attitude director indicators and the flight director computer. It also supplies heading reference information to the horizontal situation indicators and to the TACAN system. The gyro system compensates for gyro drift as well as maneuvering and acceleration changes of the airplane to furnish a constant vertical and horizontal reference to the flight instruments. During take-off, when acceleration changes are the greatest, the vertical reference is maintained independent of forward acceleration. In flight, airspeed information from the central air data system is used by the auxiliary gyro platform system to maintain the vertical and horizontal references. The auxiliary gyro platform system is backed up by the standby attitude system which supplies an attitude reference to the pilot's standby attitude indicator at all times. Manually selecting the standby attitude system supplies attitude reference information to the flight director computer and to the copilot's attitude director indicator, as well as the pilot's standby attitude indicator.

Heading information is manually selected. Magnetic variation is manually inserted and is mixed with magnetic heading information to provide true north heading indications. Magnetic variation can be inserted at any time and is displayed through a digital indicator on the auxiliary gyro platform system control panel. Local latitude can be set manually any time. A digital latitude indicator on the auxiliary gyro platform control panel displays latitude.

NOTE
Magnetic variation and latitude must be changed periodically during flight as dictated by speed and heading.

A meter-type indicator displays the deviation between the magnetic heading output shaft and the magnetic heading sensed by the remote magnetic heading indicator. On initial erection of the auxiliary gyro platform system, the great circle heading computer is aligned automatically to the sensed magnetic heading of the airplane when essential ac bus power is initially applied to the auxiliary gyro platform system. Erroneous magnetic interference, however, can cause incorrect alignment of the great circle heading computer. Realignment of the great circle heading computer can be accomplished at anytime before take-off.

AUXILIARY GYRO PLATFORM MODE SWITCH.

The four-position mode switch (15, figure 1-8), on the pilot's console, is used to select the desired heading modes which are displayed on the horizontal situation and attitude director indicators. When the switch is in the GREAT CIRCLE position, heading with respect to an arbitrarily selected earth's great circle is displayed. The great circle heading is corrected automatically for earth's rate with latitude information manually inserted into the auxiliary gyro platform system. Great circle heading is automatically aligned with the magnetic heading of the airplane, unless magnetic variation has been inserted by the pilot, in which case the great circle heading is aligned with the true north heading. When the switch is at TRUE, heading, with respect to magnetic headings plus or minus manually inserted magnetic variation, is displayed. When the switch is moved to MAG, a heading with respect to the earth's magnetic north, sensed by the remote magnetic heading detector and stabilized by a gyro is displayed. With the switch in the DERATED MAG position, the heading is the same as in the MAG position except that it is fast responding and is not gyro stabilized. Loss of gyro stabilization cause inaccuracies in the derated magnetic position; however, it is still usable in an emergency. Derated magnetic heading is derived directly from the remote magnetic heading detector. The mode switch must be placed in DERATED MAG for heading information when the auxiliary gyro platform fails. The switch is powered by the essential ac bus.

AUXILIARY GYRO PLATFORM ALIGNMENT SWITCH.

Normal operation of the auxiliary gyro platform system is controlled by a two-position switch (20, figure 1-8) on the pilot's console. With the switch in the OFFRATE position, essential ac bus power is applied to the gyro platform and initial erection and alignment of the gyro platform takes place. At the same time, the auxiliary gyro platform system aligning light comes on and remains on until the system has been brought up to normal operating condition. When the auxiliary gyro platform has reached the normal operating condition (after about three minutes), the aligning light goes out. (Heading should be within ±2 degrees of a known airplane position.) If the heading is not within limits, realignment of the great circle heading can be accomplished by moving the alignment switch to the REALIGN GREAT CIRCLE position for about 30 seconds. The aligning light comes on

T.O. 1B-70(X)A-1

and remains on until the switch is repositioned to the OPERATE position. Realignment of the great circle heading computer may be accomplished at any time before take-off. The auxiliary gyro platform alignment switch must be returned to OPERATE to resume normal operation of the gyro platform.

NOTE
- No alignment will occur in flight if the auxiliary gyro platform alignment switch is set at the REALIGN GREAT CIRCLE position. However, the auxiliary gyro platform system aligning light will come on.
- Erroneous initial alignment of the auxiliary gyro platform may be caused by interference from magnetic material, such as steel hangars, etc, or from magnetic fields generated from power lines, transformers, etc. Realignment should be attempted after the airplane has been moved from these influencing factors.

AUXILIARY GYRO PLATFORM LATITUDE SETTING KNOB AND INDICATOR.

Changes in latitude must be inserted into the gyro platform system by the latitude setting knob (13, figure 1-8) and the latitude is read from a digital indicator (12, figure 1-8) on the pilot's console. The indicator displays latitude in degrees and tenths of degrees. With an increase in north latitude or a decrease in south latitude, the knob should be rotated clockwise towards N INCR. The knob is rotated counterclockwise towards S INCR for an increase in south latitude or a decrease in north latitude. As the knob is rotated, it mechanically changes the appropriate (north or south) degrees of latitude that appear in the latitude indicator. The position of knob, in turn applies electronic signals, which correspond to its existing latitude reading, to the gyro platform system.

AUXILIARY GYRO PLATFORM MAGNETIC VARIATION SETTING KNOB AND INDICATOR.

Changes in magnetic variation must be inserted into the auxiliary gyro platform system by the magnetic variation setting knob (21, figure 1-8) and the variation is read from a digital indicator (22, figure 1-8) on the pilot's console. The indicator displays magnetic variation in degrees and tenths of degrees. The knob is rotated clockwise toward EAST for a decrease in variation and counterclockwise toward WEST for an increase in variation. When the knob is rotated, it mechanically changes the degrees of variation that appear in the magnetic variation indicator. Position of the magnetic variation setting knob provides a correction to magnetic heading to produce true north heading outputs to the attitude director and horizontal situation indicators when TRUE (true north) heading is selected on the auxiliary gyro platform system mode switch.

AUXILIARY GYRO PLATFORM HEADING SLEW KNOB.

A pull-out knob (19, figure 1-8), on the pilot's console, is used to manually slew great circle heading outputs rapidly to any desired heading. The knob is coupled directly to the heading slew pot and is spring-loaded to OFF. Pulling the knob out cuts off the earth's rate correction information and then rotating the knob towards INCR or DCR applies positive or negative slewing respectively of the great circle heading. Slewing speed is dependent upon how far the knob is turned.

NOTE
Slewing is available only when the mode switch is at GREAT CIRCLE.

T.O. 1B-70(X)A-1

HORIZONTAL SITUATION INDICATORS (HSI).

Refer to "Flight Director System" in this section.

ATTITUDE DIRECTOR INDICATORS (ADI).

Refer to "Flight Director System" in this section.

AUXILIARY GYRO PLATFORM MAGNETIC HEADING SYNCHRONIZATION INDICATOR.

The magnetic heading synchronization indicator (14, figure 1-8), on the pilot's console, continually displays the deviation between the magnetic heading output shaft of the auxiliary gyro platform system and the heading as sensed by the remote magnetic heading detector. The indicator receives power from the essential ac bus.

AUXILIARY GYRO PLATFORM SYSTEM ALIGNING LIGHT.

The auxiliary gyro platform system aligning light (1, figure 1-7), on the center console, receives power from the primary dc bus. The light (labeled "AGPS ALIGNING") comes on when power is applied to the auxiliary gyro platform system and remains on during the initial aligning cycle (about three minutes). The light goes out when the gyro platform is aligned and in normal operating condition. Whenever the alignment setting switch is placed in its REALIGN GREAT CIRCLE position, the aligning light comes on and remains on until the alignment switch is moved to the OPERATE position.

AUXILIARY GYRO PLATFORM SYSTEM OPERATION.

NOTE
The auxiliary gyro platform system is automatically erected within three minutes after the essential ac bus is powered. (Auxiliary gyro platform alignment switch must be at OPERATE.)

To operate system, proceed as follows:

1. Auxiliary gyro platform mode switch - GREAT CIRCLE.
   The mode switch should be at GREAT CIRCLE for initial alignment.
   The auxiliary gyro platform system is automatically aligned during the initial erection cycle to the magnetic heading (or to the true north heading if magnetic variation is inserted manually).
2. Auxiliary gyro platform alignment switch - OPERATE.
   Note that the aligning light is on. Light will go out when the initial erection and alignment cycle is completed.
3. Magnetic variation setting knob - Set local magnetic variation.
4. Latitude setting knob - Set local latitude.
5. Magnetic heading synchronization indicator - Check centered.
6. Heading slew knob - Check off.

To realign the great circle heading, proceed as follows:

NOTE
Realignment can be accomplished only on the ground.

1. Mode switch - GREAT CIRCLE.
2. Magnetic variation setting knob - Set to local magnetic variation.
3. Latitude setting knob - Set to local latitude.
4. Alignment switch - REALIGN GREAT CIRCLE.
   The alignment switch should remain in this position for at least 30 seconds. The auxiliary gyro platform system aligning light should be on.
5. Alignment switch - OPERATE.
   Move alignment switch to OPERATE and note that the aligning light is out.

T.O. 1B-70(X)A-1

6. Heading slew knob - Select great circle heading.
   Slewing of the great circle heading can be accomplished on the ground or during flight.
7. Heading slew knob - Check OFF.

FLIGHT DIRECTOR SYSTEM.

The flight director system, using a CPU-27/A flight director computer, provides a selection of navigation signals to the attitude director and horizontal situation indicators. The system is powered by the right primary ac and dc busses and the essential ac bus.

FLIGHT DIRECTOR COMPUTER - CPU-27/A.

The electronic CPU-27/A flight director computer combines the altitude, heading, attitude, and radio navigation information and presents it on the attitude director. The computer combines heading, roll, course, and localizer signals for roll indications and altitude, pitch, and glideslope signals for pitch indications. The computer is controlled by a switching arrangement, which puts the computer into any one of five modes (four major modes and one submode). The combination of input signals used is determined by the mode selected which changes the input signals for the proper programming of flight paths to fit the particular flight profile. Depending on the mode of operation selected, the computer supplies either command heading steering, localizer steering or TACAN signals to the attitude director indicator bank steering bar. The computer also supplies glide slope deviation signals to the glide slope indicator or glide slope steering signals to the pitch steering bar. Balancing of various input signals will center the bank and pitch steering bars of the attitude director indicator. With no steering or deviation signals selected (the computer on stand-by), bias signals drive the steering bars out of view. (The bank steering bar is used to show sideslip when on standby, and PILOT is selected.) The computer also serves as a coupler for signals going to the integrated flight displays and must be on though not functioning. There is also one submode, altitude hold, which may be used with any of the major modes except ILS APP. (Refer to "Altitude Hold Switch" in this section.) The flight director computer is powered by the right primary ac bus.

FLIGHT DIRECTOR MODE SELECTOR SWITCH.

The five-position rotary switch (29, figure 1-3), on the pilot's instrument panel, selects the mode of operation of the flight director computer. When the switch is at STBY, the pointers and warning flags on the attitude director indicators are driven out of view by a signal from the flight director computer. (Refer to "Flight Test Instrumentation" in this section.) With the switch at ILS, localizer deviation from the ILS localizer receiver is sent to the flight director computer and combined with roll information to produce an ILS heading error which is displayed by the attitude director indicator bank steering bar. This mode is normally selected after letdown but before reaching the glide slope beam. When the bank steering bar is centered, the airplane is "on course." When "on course" for an instrument landing, the flight director mode switch can be moved to the ILS APP. By watching the downward movement of the pitch steering bar, the glide slope interception can be anticipated and the descent prepared. In the event of a go-around with the switch at ILS or ILS APP, the back course of the ILS can be flown or the switch can be moved to MAN HDG and a predetermined heading flown. The same information is used in the TACAN mode as in the ILS or ILS APP modes except that distance information is added. Distance from TACAN station to the airplane is displayed in the range window of the horizontal situation indicator in nautical miles. The ILS, ILS APP, and MAN HDG modes are read primarily from the attitude director indicators, while the TACAN mode is read from the horizontal situation indicator. The mode selector switch receives power from the right primary dc bus.

Changed 30 November 1964

T.O. 1B-70(X)A-1

ATTITUDE DIRECTOR INDICATOR SELECTOR SWITCH.

The attitude director indicator selector switch (28, figure 1-3), on the pilot's instrument panel, is used to select the pitch and roll signal sources for the attitude director indicators and the flight director computer. The switch is mechanically latched in the NORMAL position and must be pulled out before it can be moved to STBY. When the switch is at NORMAL, essential ac bus power is supplied to the pilot's attitude director indicator and right primary ac bus power is supplied to the copilot's attitude director indicator. At the same time, attitude signals are supplied by the auxiliary gyro platform system indicating heading, pitch, and roll information on both attitude director indicators. The flight director system supplies navigation information to both attitude director indicators also. When the switch is moved to the STBY position, the standby gyro provides attitude information to the pilot's stand-by attitude indicator, the copilot's attitude director indicator and the flight director computer. The attitude director indicator selector switch receives power from the right primary dc bus.

COMMAND CONTROL SWITCH.

This two-position command control switch (30, figure 1-3), on the pilot's instrument panel, is used to determine whether the pilot or copilot has control of heading and course settings on the horizontal situation indicator, and control of command airspeed, Mach, or altitude settings. When the switch is at PILOT or COPILOT, the horizontal situation indicator, the altitude-vertical velocity indicator, and the airspeed-Mach number indicator on the respective panel (pilot's or copilot's) become "master" indicators. (Refer to "Flight Test Instrumentation" in this section.) The corresponding indicators on the other instrument panel then become "slave" indicators. As a result, when a setting is changed on a master indicator, an equal change is produced automatically on the corresponding slave indicator. (Setting changes cannot be made using the slave indicator.)

The command control switch receives power from the right primary dc bus.

ALTITUDE HOLD SWITCH.

The two-position altitude hold switch (31, figure 1-3), is on the pilot's instrument panel. The switch, magnetically held in the ON position, engages the altitude hold mode in the flight director computer. The air data computer sends altitude information to the flight director computer. Altitude changes from the air data computer are combined with pitch information from the auxiliary gyro platform system or from the pitch and roll gyros to provide a steering signal for steering to the engaged altitude. This steering signal is displayed by the pitch steering bar on the attitude director indicator. By flying the pitch steering bar, the desired altitude can be maintained up to a deviation of ±500 feet. If the altitude deviation exceeds 500 feet, the altitude hold circuit is changed automatically by an amount equal to the deviation beyond 500 feet, as indicated on the altitude - vertical velocity indicator. Holding the pitch steering bar in line with the miniature airplane on the attitude director indicator maintains the airplane at the engaged altitude. Altitude hold can be selected during any of the flight director modes except the ILS APP mode. The altitude hold switch is automatically moved to OFF, and the hold circuit disengaged, when the ILS APP mode is selected, or when a strong approach signal is received by the glide slope receiver when the mode selector switch is at ILS. Electrical power for the altitude hold switch is received from the right primary dc bus.

ATTITUDE DIRECTOR INDICATORS (ADI).

There are two attitude director indicators (2, figure 1-3; 10, figure 1-4; and figure 4-8): one on the pilot's

4-40   Changed 30 November 1964 instrument panel and one on the copilot's instrument panel. Each presents roll and pitch attitude, heading, turn and slip information, computed steering information in relation to a command heading or course, glide slope displacement for instrument landings, and computed steering information to intercept localizer courses, ILS glide slopes, and TACAN. An added scale on the cover glass provides sideslip information in degrees. This pictorial-type instrument combines displays of pitch, roll, and heading on a universally mounted sphere which serves as a reference for a miniature airplane. The miniature airplane symbol (9, figure 4-8), fastened to the instrument frame, is always in proper physical relation to the simulated earth, horizon, and sky areas of the sphere. The sphere, receiving information from the auxiliary gyro platform system, is free to rotate 360 degrees about all axes. (Refer to "Auxiliary Gyro Platform System (AGPS)" in this section.) The horizon is represented as a solid line and is graduated in 5-degree increments which represents airplane heading. A pitch trim knob (10, figure 4-8) rotates the sphere vertically to position the desired horizon line reference with respect to the miniature airplane. A fade feature gradually cancels the amount of horizon line displacement when the airplane approaches 90 degrees of climb or dive. The bank pointers (5, figure 4-8), extending from the top to the bottom of the sphere face, measure bank angle on a semicircular bank scale below the sphere, graduated in 10-degree increments.

Movement of two long steering bars, perpendicular to each other, displays flight director computer command information and/or movement around the pitch and roll axes or sideslip information. The pitch steering bar (horizontal bar) (8, figure 4-8) is an indication of steering error and provides a guide for steering to the glide slope or a selected altitude. The bank steering bar (vertical bar) (7, figure 4-8) provides a guide for steering to a selected course, selected heading, ILS localizer beam, TACAN or number of degrees sideslip. When centered, the bars indicate "on course" or "correct turn to course." The attitude director indicator bank steering bar moves in the direction of heading correction necessary to maintain a desired track. To center the bank steering bar, the airplane must be turned in the direction of bank steering bar. When proper angle of interception has been reached, the bank steering bar automatically centers. As the airplane approaches the desired heading selected on the horizontal situation indicator, the bank steering bar will deviate in the opposite direction and the airplane must again be turned toward the vertical bar to center the bar. A warning flag appears in conjunction with the bank steering bar if the deviation signal is unreliable when the flight director mode selector switch is at TACAN, ILS or ILS APP. A separate turn rate gyro supplies turn information to a conventional turn needle (11, figure 4-8) at the bottom of the attitude director indicator. The turn needle is calibrated so that one standard needle-width turn will accomplish a 360-degree turn in four minutes (1-1/2 degree per second rate-of-turn). Slip information is presented by a conventional ball slip indicator (12, figure 4-8) directly above the turn needle.

The glide slope indicator (3, figure 4-8) on the left side of the instrument operates only when the flight director mode selector switch is at ILS or ILS APP and measures the magnitude of deviation from the center of the glide slope beam. The glide slope deviation scale (4, figure 4-8) indicates amount of deviation from the glide slope, and the dots are spaced one-half beam-width apart. When the glide slope indicator is aligned with the center index, the airplane is on the glide slope.

If power fails in the stand-by vertical gyro on the attitude director indicator, a power-off flag (1, figure 4-8) appears in the face of the indicator. (The word "OFF" is printed on the flag.)

The sphere in the copilot's attitude indicator will tumble or oscillate if the bus-tie contactors open.

FLIGHT DIRECTOR MODES

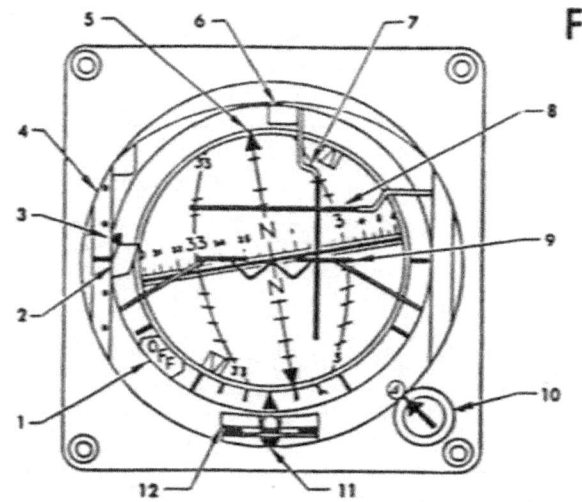

Warning

In the absence of a usable signal (indicated by the appearance of applicable warning flag), related presentations on both indicators are unreliable.

1. ATTITUDE WARNING FLAG
2. GLIDE SLOPE WARNING FLAG
3. GLIDE SLOPE INDICATOR
4. GLIDE SLOPE DEVIATION SCALE
5. BANK POINTERS
6. COURSE WARNING FLAG
7. BANK STEERING BAR
8. PITCH STEERING BAR
9. MINIATURE AIRPLANE
10. PITCH TRIM KNOB
11. TURN INDICATOR
12. SLIP INDICATOR

MAJOR MODE	ATTITUDE DIRECTOR INDICATOR				
	GLIDE SLOPE INDICATOR	BANK STEERING BAR	PITCH STEERING BAR	COURSE WARNING	GLIDE SLOPE WARNING
*MAN HDG	OUT OF VIEW	COMMAND HEADING STEERING	OUT OF VIEW	OUT OF VIEW WITH USABLE STEERING SIGNAL	OUT OF VIEW
*TACAN	OUT OF VIEW	COURSE SET STEERING	OUT OF VIEW	OUT OF VIEW WITH USABLE TACAN SIGNAL	OUT OF VIEW
*ILS	OUT OF VIEW	LOCALIZER STEERING	OUT OF VIEW	OUT OF VIEW WITH USABLE LOCALIZER SIGNAL	OUT OF VIEW
ILS APPROACH	GLIDE SLOPE DEVIATION	LOCALIZER STEERING	GLIDE SLOPE STEERING	OUT OF VIEW WITH USABLE LOCALIZER SIGNAL	OUT OF VIEW WITH USABLE GLIDE SLOPE SIGNAL
STBY	OUT OF VIEW	OUT OF VIEW	OUT OF VIEW	OUT OF VIEW	OUT OF VIEW

NOTE

*Altitude hold switch can be used in any mode except the ILS approach

Figure 4-8 (Sheet 1 of 2)

T.O. 1B-70(X)A-1

....and Pilot Indicator Presentations

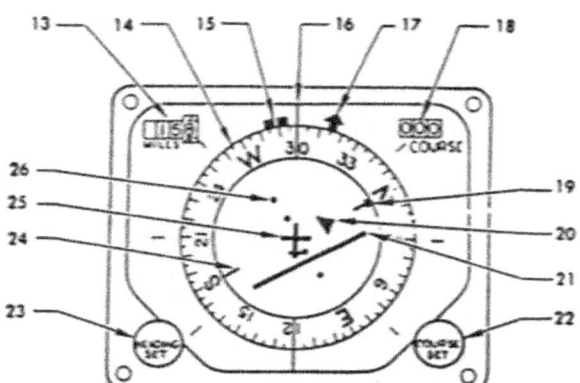

13. RANGE INDICATOR
14. COMPASS CARD
15. HEADING MARKER
16. LUBBER LINE
17. BEARING POINTER
18. COURSE SELECTOR WINDOW
19. COURSE ARROW (HEAD)
20. TO-FROM INDICATOR
21. COURSE DEVIATION INDICATOR
22. COURSE SET KNOB
23. HEADING SET KNOB
24. COURSE ARROW (TAIL)
25. MINIATURE AIRPLANE
26. COURSE DEVIATION SCALE

HORIZONTAL SITUATION INDICATOR					
HEADING MARKER	COURSE ARROW	COURSE DEVIATION INDICATOR	TO-FROM INDICATOR	BEARING POINTER	RANGE INDICATOR
SET BY PILOT	SET TO TACAN BEARING	TACAN DEVIATION	FUNCTION OF TACAN SIGNAL	TACAN BEARING	TACAN DISTANCE
NO FUNCTION	SET TO TACAN BEARING	TACAN DEVIATION	FUNCTION OF TACAN SIGNAL	TACAN BEARING	TACAN DISTANCE
NO FUNCTION	SET TO LOCALIZER COURSE	LOCALIZER DEVIATION	FUNCTION OF TACAN SIGNAL	TACAN BEARING	TACAN DISTANCE
NO FUNCTION	SET TO LOCALIZER COURSE	LOCALIZER DEVIATION	FUNCTION OF TACAN SIGNAL	TACAN BEARING	TACAN DISTANCE
NO FUNCTION	SET TO TACAN BEARING	TACAN DEVIATION	FUNCTION OF TACAN SIGNAL	TACAN BEARING	TACAN DISTANCE

Figure 4-6 (Sheet 2 of 2)

T.O. 1B-70(X)A-1

Whenever electrical signals from the navigational receiver are weak or unreliable for operation of the bank steering bar, the course warning flag (6, figure 4-8) appears on the face of the indicator. If signals from the glide slope receiver are weak or unreliable for operation of the glide slope indicator, the glide slope warning flag (2, figure 4-8) appears on the face of the indicator. (This flag is electrically driven from view during the TACAN and MAN HDG mode of operation.) The pilot's attitude director indicator receives power from the essential ac bus and the copilot's attitude director indicator receives power from the right primary ac bus.

HORIZONTAL SITUATION INDICATORS (HSI).

The horizontal situation indicator (34, figure 1-3; 25, figure 1-4; and figure 4-8), on the pilot's and copilot's instrument panels, is a multipurpose indicator that displays heading, course, course deviation, TACAN bearing and range, command heading and course, and instrument landing indications in various flight director system modes. Airplane heading is displayed on a rotating compass card (14, figure 4-8) marked in 5-degree increments through 360 degrees. The compass card is driven by signals from the auxiliary gyro platform system, which are read against a fixed reference marker called a lubber line (16, figure 4-8) at the top of the dial. Reciprocal heading is read under the lubber line at the bottom of the dial. Command heading and course can be inserted manually by rotating the corresponding knobs on the lower portion of the instrument. A double-bar rectangular index (heading marker) (15, figure 4-8) can be rotated around the outer edge of the compass card by the heading set knob (23, figure 4-8) and indicates the selected command heading. Clockwise rotation of the heading set knob moves the command heading index clockwise, and counterclockwise rotation moves the index counterclockwise. In the MAN HDG or TACAN modes of operation of the flight director computer, the command heading index can be set by the heading set knob on the horizontal situation indicator. Once the index is set, it will synchronize

and rotate with the compass card. In the ILS or ILS APP modes, the command heading index is automatically aligned with the airplane heading, and turning the heading set knob will have no effect on the command heading index position. A course arrow (19 and 24, figure 4-8) that rotates inside the compass card displays desired course or track and can be set by turning the course set knob (22, figure 4-8). Since the TACAN is related to magnetic north, the auxiliary gyro platform system heading selector switch should be on MAG when using the course displays. Clockwise rotation of the course set knob moves the course arrow clockwise. The course selected also is displayed on a three-digit counter in the course selector window (18, figure 4-8). Once the course arrow is set, it rotates with the compass card. The center section of the course arrow, called a course deviation indicator (21, figure 4-8) is movable in a lateral motion and remains parallel to the course arrow, indicating the position of the airplane in relation to the selected course. The course deviation indicator also rotates in conjunction with the course arrow.

NOTE

The heading signals displayed on the pilot's horizontal situation indicator and the copilot's attitude director indicator are connected in parallel and the copilot's horizontal situation indicator and the pilot's attitude director indicator are connected in parallel. When the command control switch is set at either PILOT or COPILOT, the corresponding horizontal situation indicator becomes the "master" and the other the "slave" unit. Rotating the heading set or course set knob

T.O. 1B-70(X)A-1

on the "master" indicator selects heading or course on both indicators. The set knobs on the "slave" indicator are inoperative.

An indication to determine whether a selected course is to or from a radio station is displayed by the location of a triangular to-from indicator (20, figure 4-8) above or below the miniature airplane symbol (25, figure 4-8). With the triangular to-from indicator on the same side as the course arrow, the course set is toward the radio station; and if on the opposite side of the course arrow, the course set is away from the station. The bearing pointer (17, figure 4-8), rotating about the compass card, indicates the direction of the selected ground station relative to the airplane. The angle between the fixed lubber line and the bearing arrow is the relative bearing to the station. The bearing arrow is remotely operated by electrical signals from TACAN. A four-digit (three of which are used) range indicator (13, figure 4-8) displays the slant range, in nautical miles, from the radio station. In any flight director mode other than TACAN, the window is masked; also, if distance is greater than 200 miles, the window will be masked in the TACAN mode also. Range signals are received directly from the TACAN equipment to the horizontal situation indicators. The pilot's horizontal situation indicator is powered by the essential ac bus and the copilot's horizontal situation indicator is powered by the right primary ac bus. Both horizontal situation indicators also receive power from the instrument ac bus.

ERRATIC OPERATION OF THE ATTITUDE DIRECTOR AND HORIZONTAL SITUATION INDICATORS.

Loss of the auxiliary gyro platform system gyro, instrument ac bus, or opening of the bus-tie contactors will affect the operation of the attitude director and horizontal situation indicators.

Loss of the auxiliary gyro platform system gyro will cause incorrect heading and attitude information to be sent to the attitude director and horizontal situation indicators. Attitude information for the pilot's stand-by attitude indicator and the copilot's attitude director indicator is available from the stand-by gyro, and derated magnetic heading information is available to the attitude director and horizontal situation indicators. If the instrument ac bus is lost, no distance information will be displayed on the horizontal situation indicators and the command function will be by the master horizontal situation indicator only. Also, the loss of the instrument ac bus will cause the loss of altitude hold capability (in the altitude hold mode only) of the attitude director and horizontal situation indicators. (Refer to "Altitude Hold Switch" in this section.) Heading and attitude information continues to be displayed on the attitude director and horizontal situation indicators.

Should the bus-tie contactors open (as indicated by the bus-tie open caution light coming on), errors will creep into the attitude director and horizontal situation indicators, due to out-of-phase electrical power supply. Attitude information is available from the stand-by circuit to the pilot's stand-by attitude indicator and the copilot's attitude director indicator. The compass card on the pilot's horizontal situation indicator will tend to oscillate, however, the heading information can be used for rough course computations. Heading information displayed on the copilot's attitude director and horizontal situation indicators cannot be used. Usable rate-of-turn information will be displayed on the attitude director indicators.

NOTE

With the bus-tie contactors open, the sphere in the attitude director indicators and the heading card in the horizontal situation indicators will oscillate or spin.

This page intentionally left blank

T.O. 1B-70(X)A-1

OPERATION OF FLIGHT DIRECTOR SYSTEM.

Dead Reckoning Navigation.

To select and fly a particular magnetic heading, use the following procedure:

1. Flight director mode selector switch - MAN HDG.
2. Command control switch - As desired.
3. Horizontal situation indicator heading set knob - Set.
    Align command heading marker with the desired magnetic heading on the horizontal situation indicator compass card.
4. Turn to the desired heading.

Maintain heading by keeping the horizontal situation indicator command heading index under the lubber line and the attitude director indicator bank steering bar centered.

TACAN Navigation.

To fly toward or away from a TACAN station but not on a preselected radial, use the following procedure:

NOTE

During flight, verify TACAN bearing information when possible by cross-checking with ground radar, airborne radar, or VOR.

1. TACAN function switch - T/R.
2. TACAN channel selector switch - Select desired station channel.
3. Flight director mode selector switch - TACAN.
4. Command control switch - As desired.
5. Horizontal situation indicator course set knob - Set.
    Set desired course in the course window. Course arrow will align to the selected course on the compass card at the same time. Course deviation indicator will indicate the position of the airplane in relation to the selected course. Steer airplane by centering the bank steering bar on the attitude director indicator.
6. Auxiliary gyro platform mode switch - Set as desired.
7. Wind drift correction - Check.
    Steer airplane to keep the horizontal situation indicator course deviation indicator centered to the course arrow. (Course arrow may be offset from the lubber line to show wind drift correction.) Monitor that the bank steering bar on the attitude director indicator is centered.
8. Distance from radio station - Monitor.
    Check the range indicator on the horizontal situation indicator as necessary. (The TACAN function switch must be at the T/R position to obtain range indications.)

To fly a selected TACAN radial to or from a station, use the following procedure:

NOTE

During flight, verify TACAN bearing information when possible by cross-checking with ground radar, airborne radar, or VOR.

1. Repeat steps 1 through 4.
2. Horizontal situation indicator course set knob - Set.
    Rotate horizontal situation indicator course set knob until the course arrow is aligned with the desired radial heading on the compass card. Course window should indicate the same course reading and the course deviation indicator will indicate airplane position from the selected radial. Attitude director indicator bank steering bar will show angle of course interception.
3. Attitude director indicator bank steering bar - Center.
    Turn airplane to center the attitude director indicator bank steering bar. Reduce bank angle, as necessary, to keep the bank steering bar centered. The bank steering bar should remain centered when on course.

This page intentionally left blank

T.O. 1B-70(X)A-1

4. Wind drift correction - Check. Steer airplane to keep the horizontal situation indicator deviation indicator centered, and rotate the heading set knob as required to align the command heading index with the lubber line. Maintain drift-corrected heading by keeping the attitude director indicator bank steering bar centered.

5. Distance from TACAN station - Check. Check the range indicator on the horizontal situation indicator as necessary. (The TACAN function switch must be in the T/R position to obtain slant range information.)

SINGLE-POINT PRESSURE REFUELING SYSTEM.

The fuel tanks are serviced on the ground through the single-point refueling system from a receptacle on the right side of the fuselage, forward of the main gear well. (There is no alternate means of refueling.) Refueling system controls permit selective automatic refueling of the tanks. The airplane normally is refueled at a flow rate of 600 gallons per minute. To ensure that the fuel tanks remain inert, during refueling the incoming fuel passes through a deaeration unit before entering the airplane. Gaseous nitrogen is injected into the fuel as it flows into the deaeration unit to remove oxygen dissolved in the fuel.

Fuel enters the tanks through tank-mounted refueling level control shutoff valves. As each tank becomes full, the valves automatically close to shutoff the refueling flow to the tank. Each shutoff valve has a remote, tank-mounted level control pilot valve which responds to the fuel level in the tank to control operation of the shutoff valve. Because the level control shutoff and pilot valves have dual floats, solenoids, and diaphragms, a single failure will not prevent the valve from shutting off the fuel flow. Except for tank No. 3, which has normally open level control valves, all tanks have normally closed level control shutoff valves. Refueling pressure opens the normally open valves and, when electrical power is applied, also opens the normally closed valves. Electrical circuits to the refueling valves are controlled by switches on the instrument panel and are completed when the lever over the refueling receptacle cap is lifted in order to remove the cap. A level control valve test system is used at the start of refueling to determine if the valves are operating properly. The single-point refueling system is shown schematically in figure 4-9. See figure 1-11 for fuel tank capacities, and figure 1-32 for fuel specifications.

NOTE
The refueling system also is used to defuel the airplane.

REFUELING VALVE SWITCHES.

The seven refueling valve switches (21, figure 1-3), on the copilot's instrument panel, provide selective control of the refueling system. Each switch controls operation of the refueling level control valves in its corresponding tank. The valves in left and right tanks of the same number are controlled by a single switch. Because tank No. 3 (sump tank) always is refilled, no refueling valve switch is provided for this tank.

NOTE
Tank No. 5 is not used on Airplane AF62-001, therefore the No. 5 refueling level control valve circuit is inoperative on this airplane.

For complete automatic refueling of all fuel tanks, each refueling valve switch should be at AUTO. This permits the normally closed level control valves to open when refueling pressure is applied.

NOTE
All refueling control valve switches must be set at AUTO after any refueling operation to ensure proper operation of the fuel system.

T.O. 1B-70(X)A-1

SINGLE-POINT REFUELING SYSTEM

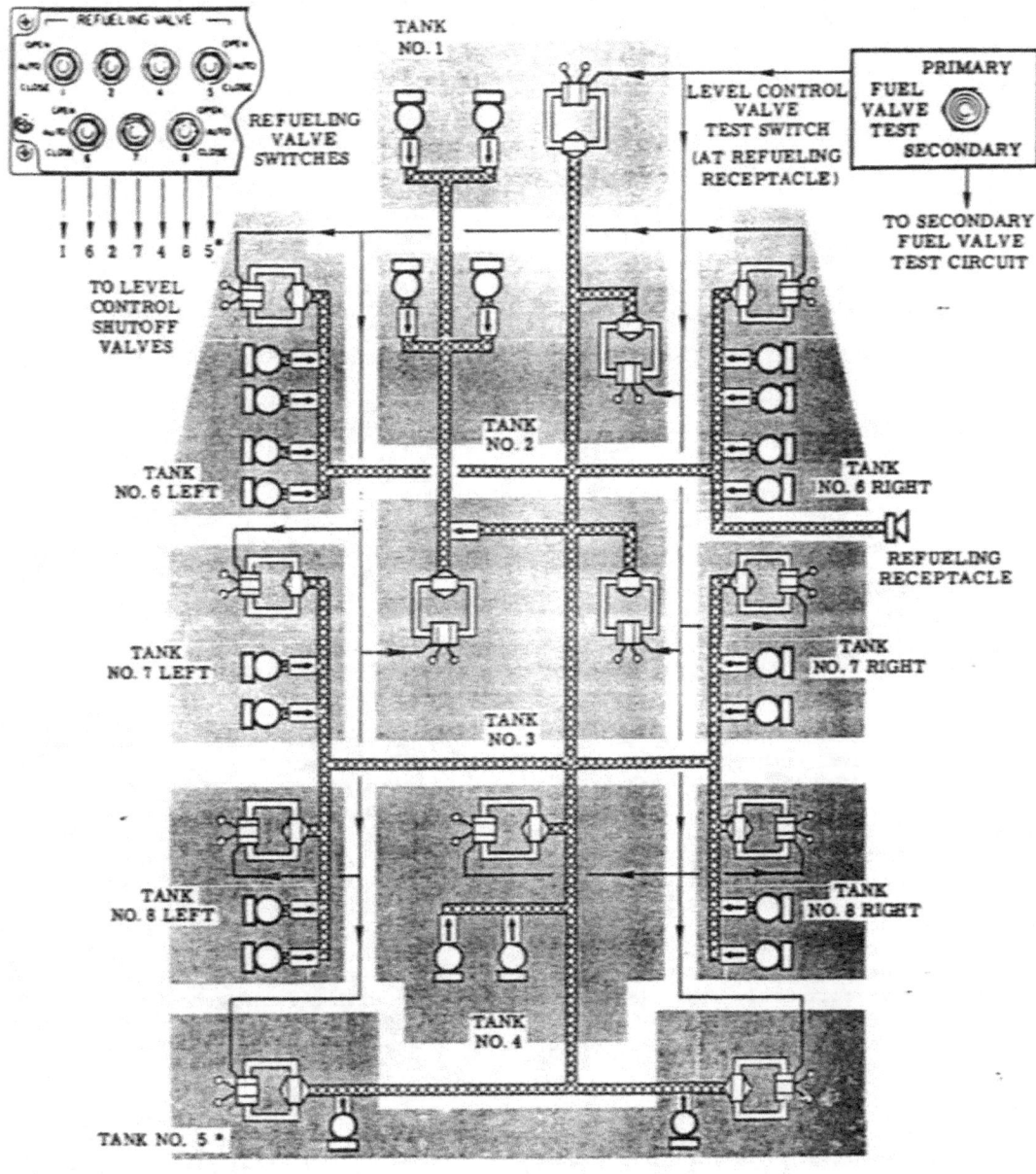

Figure 4-9

T.O. 1B-70(X)A-1

For partial refueling of the airplane, the refueling valve switches of tanks not to be filled are placed at CLOSE to keep the level control valves in the corresponding tanks closed during refueling. The OPEN position of the refueling valve switches allows the valves in the corresponding tanks to open when the tanks are not full.

NOTE

The OPEN position is for maintenance purposes and special in-flight operations only. This position should be used in flight only on specific instructions because fuel sequencing will be affected.

The refueling valve switches receive power from the primary fuel and defuel ac bus.

REFUELING LEVEL CONTROL VALVE TEST SWITCH.

The three-position refueling level control valve test switch in the refueling receptacle compartment is used by ground personnel at the start of refueling to test level control valve shutoff operation. (The valves are tested when refueling pressure is applied and fuel is flowing.) When the test switch is held at PRIMARY, the primary portions of the dual level control valves should close; holding the test switch at SECONDARY closes the secondary portions of the valves. Refueling flow will stop as each position is selected, if the corresponding portions of the level control valves are operating properly. The test switch receives power from the primary fuel and defuel ac bus. It is spring-loaded to its center off position and is effective only when the refueling level control valve switches on the copilot's instrument panel are at AUTO.

FLIGHT TEST INSTRUMENTATION.

The flight test instrumentation is recorded by two digital and one analog tape recorders installed in a controlled environment instrumentation package in the weapons bay. Selection and operation of the flight test instrumentation equipment are controlled by switches in the crew compartment. Each digital recorder provides 32 minutes of recording time (giving a total of 64 minutes of recording time), and the analog recorder provides 64 minutes of recording time. A cabin tape recorder operates when the instrumentation system is recording, and is used for recording panel response data and preselected parameters during flight. It is located aft of the crew compartment. A voice track* is available on this recorder to record either intercom or radio communications when the recorder is on. This permits identification of test conditions or general comments to be made part of the data taken. The cabin recorder provides either 12 1/2 or 25 minutes* (16 minutes†) of recording time, depending on the tape speed selected before flight. Airspeed, vertical "G", and altitude are recorded on a VGH recorder. The VGH recorder is a 3-channel oscillograph type continuous trace strip recorder. This recorder provides about 1 1/2 hours of recording time. Four landing cameras*, used to photograph landing data, are located as follows: one on each main gear strut door focused on the bogie of the opposite gear, and two in the forward fuselage, one focused on the nose gear and one pointing down to photograph airplane drift in relation to the runway. Each of the three cameras focused on the gear has 40-seconds of film, and the camera used to photograph drift has one minute of film. Data is recorded from various pickups throughout the airplane and certain data is telemetered to ground stations during flight. A portable battery-powered tape recorder records intercom and all voice communications to and from the airplane, and also has a mike to permit additional pilot comments prior to or after each flight. (The portable tape recorder, on a shelf behind the copilot's capsule, provides about 4 1/4 hours of recording time with a rechargeable battery that provides 5 to 10 hours of running time. The recorder should be started prior to the flight and turned off after the flight by switches on the recorder.) A 16-mm movie camera on the ceiling of the pilot's compartment photographs the center and pilot's instrument panels when the camera is on and data is being recorded. (A total of 33 minutes of movie film is carried in the camera.) A switch on the pilot's capsule auto-

---
*Airplane AF62-001
†Airplane AF62-207

Changed 25 June 1965

matically provides continuous data recording and movies when the pilot encapsulates.

The instrumentation systems are powered by the flight test instrumentation bus which receives power from the right primary ac bus except the movie camera which receives power directly from the right primary ac bus.

The cabin recorder and landing camera* systems however, are powered by the right primary dc bus. For these systems, the instrumentation master switch does not have to be on to permit operation.

INSTRUMENTATION CONTROLS.

INSTRUMENTATION MASTER SWITCH.

The two-position master switch (42, figure 1-3) on the pilot's instrument panel receives power from the instrumentation bus. Moving the switch to ON turns on the instrumentation package cooling system and applies power to the analog, digital and telemetering systems. The switch is mechanically latched at ON and must be pulled out before it can be moved to OFF.

TELEMETERING SWITCH.

The two-position telemetering switch (43, figure 1-3) on the pilot's instrument panel receives power from the instrumentation bus. Moving the switch to XMT transmits data to ground stations. Moving the switch to STBY keeps the transmitter warmed up ready to transmit when required.

> NOTE
> Do not move the telemetering switch to XMT until just prior to start to take-off run.

CAMERA SWITCH.

The two-position camera switch (41, figure 1-3) on the pilot's instrument panel receives power from both the right primary ac bus and the instrumentation bus. With the switch at READY, the movie camera will operate whenever a recorder is operating, or when the pilot's capsule is closed. Moving the switch to OFF turns off the movie camera and disconnects the camera from the record switches.

DIGITAL RECORDER SELECTOR SWITCH.

The three-position digital recorder selector switch (44, figure 1-3) on the pilot's instrument panel receives power from the instrumentation bus. When the switch is at AUTO, and either record switch is used, data is recorded first on recorder "A"; then, when this recorder runs out of tape (about 50 percent of the remaining tape on the digital tape remaining indicator), recorder "B" is started automatically. Moving the selector switch to either REC A or REC B permits manual selection of either digital tape recorder. The switch is mechanically latched at all three positions and must be pulled out before it can be moved to a new position.

INSTRUMENTATION PACKAGE COOLING SYSTEM SELECTOR SWITCH.

The three-position cooling system selector switch (38, figure 1-3) on the pilot's instrument panel receives power from the instrumentation bus. When the switch is at AUTO, the environment of the instrumentation package is normally controlled by the number one instrumentation cooling system. However, if this system fails to maintain the proper pressure or temperature in the package, the number two cooling system automatically takes over and the number one system is shut off. Moving the selector switch to either No. 1 or No. 2 overrides the automatic selection and permits manual selection of either cooling system. The switch is mechanically latched at all three positions and must be pulled out before it can be moved to a new position.

---

*Airplane AF62-001

INTERVAL RECORD SWITCH.

The three-position interval record switch (50, figure 1-3) on the pilot's instrument panel receives power from the instrumentation bus. When the switch is at SHORT, 5 seconds of data is recorded every 15 or 30 seconds, depending on a time selection made in the instrumentation package. When the switch is at LONG, 5 seconds of data is recorded every 2 or 4 minutes, depending on a preselected time made in the instrumentation package. The data is recorded by the digital and/or analog tape recorders as selected. If the camera switch is at READY, the movie camera also will start when data is being recorded. The switch is mechanically latched at OFF and must be pulled out before it can be moved to either of the other positions. When the switch is at OFF, data is only recorded when either record switch is used or when the pilot's capsule doors are closed. Using either record switch or closing the doors on the pilot's capsule bypasses the interval setting of the interval switch and provides continuous data recording.

RECORDING SYSTEM SELECTOR SWITCH.

The rotary, three-position recording system selector switch (46, figure 1-3) on the pilot's instrument panel receives power from the instrumentation bus. Turning the switch to DIGITAL, BOTH, or ANALOG selects the respective tape recording system required or simultaneous use of both. When the selector is at any of the three positions, either or both indicator lights show which recorder is operating.

RECORDING RESTART BUTTON.

The restart button (47, figure 1-3) on the pilot's instrument panel receives power from the instrumentation bus. In case of an automatic shutdown of the instrumentation package because of an environmental system failure, momentarily pushing the button will provide 2 minutes of instrumentation recording time. Recording should be delayed for about 30 seconds after pushing the button, to let the equipment warm up. However, if recording is critical, it can be started immediately after pushing the button, and all digital data should be satisfactory. If time still remains in the 2 minute time limit, the instrumentation master switch must be moved to OFF to reduce the heat in the package. The master switch must be moved to ON prior to pressing the restart button for the next recording.

CAUTION

Damage to the instrumentation equipment in the package could occur if this type of operation is continued beyond the first 2 minutes.

PILOT'S RECORD BUTTON.

The pilot's record button (5, figure 1-11) on the pilot's control wheel receives power from the instrumentation bus. Pressing the button, after the switches on the instrumentation panel are set, records data as long as the button is held down. If the button is pressed momentarily, 5 seconds of data will be recorded. The pilot's record button overrides the setting of the interval record switch.

PILOT'S EVENT MARKER BUTTON.

The pilot's event marker button (4, figure 1-11) on the pilot's control wheel receives power from the instrumentation bus. Pressing the button causes a unique word to be recorded. The button must be held down for at least 1/4 second to ensure the word is recorded.

COPILOT'S RECORD SWITCH.

The three-position copilot's record switch (14, figure 1-4) on the copilot's instrument panel receives power from the instrumentation bus, and is spring-loaded from MOM to OFF. Moving the switch to ON permits continuous recording of data by the copilot on the recorder selected by the pilot's control. Holding the switch at MOM records data as long as the switch is held. If the switch is moved to MOM momentarily, 5 seconds of data will be recorded. The record switch overrides the setting of the interval record switch on the pilot's instrumentation control panel. The copilot's record switch should be checked at OFF before

Changed 25 June 1965

T.O. 1B-70(X)A-1

the master switch is moved to ON to prevent inadvertent use of tape prior to flight. Indicator lights next to the switch show which recorder is being used.

ENGINE-ADS VIBRATION RECORD SELECTOR SWITCH.

The 7-position engine-ADS vibration record selector switch (15, figure 1-3) on the pilot's instrument panel receives power from the instrumentation bus when the instrumentation master switch is at ON. Moving the selector switch to AUTO and using either record switch records data from all engines and ADS in sequence on two tracks of the analog recorder. One track records engine vibration, which is telemetered to the ground, and the other track records ADS vibration which is not telemetered. To ensure that data from all engines and ADS has been recorded when the selector switch is at AUTO, either record switch must be on for at least 32 seconds. Moving the switch to 1 through 6, and holding a record switch on, records data only from the selected engine-ADS and requires about 4 seconds to obtain that data. Data as selected by the selector switch is continuously telemetered to the ground if the instrumentation master switch is on and the telemeter switch is at XMT. If the interval record switch is at either of the interval positions, vibration data will be recorded, but it will be incomplete if the selector switch is at AUTO because of the time required. (5 seconds of data recorded every 15 or 60 seconds will be insufficient.) The vibration indicators operate continuously whenever the engines are running and are not dependent on instrumentation power or switch positions.

LANDING CAMERA SWITCH.*

A two-position landing camera switch (12A, figure 1-4) receives power from the right primary dc bus. Moving the switch to ON turns on the four landing cameras to record landing data. Moving the switch to OFF turns the cameras off. The instrumentation master switch does not have to be on.

---
* Airplane AF62-001

VGH RECORDER SWITCH.

The two-position VGH recorder switch (13A, figure 1-9) on the copilot's console receives power from the right primary dc bus. Moving the switch to ON turns on the VGH recorder which records airspeed, vertical "G", and altitude. Moving the switch to OFF turns off the recorder. The instrumentation master switch does not have to be on.

CABIN RECORDER SWITCH.

The cabin recorder switch (22C, figure 1-5) on the center instrument panel receives power from the right primary dc bus. Moving the switch to READY arms the cabin tape recorder to record data when the pilot's record button is pushed. Moving the switch to OFF prevents operation of the cabin recorder when the pilot's record button is pushed.

FLIGHT DIRECTOR MODE SELECTOR SWITCH.

The five-position rotary switch (29, figure 1-3), on the pilot's instrument panel, selects the mode of operation of the flight director computer. When the switch is at STBY and the command control switch is at PILOT, the bank steering bar on the attitude director indicator can be used to indicate up to 3 degrees right or left sideslip on both the pilot's and copilot's attitude director indicators. The mode selector switch receives power from the right primary dc bus. For other functions of the flight director mode selector switch, refer to "Flight Director System" in this section.

COMMAND CONTROL SWITCH.

The two-position command control switch (30, figure 1-3), on the pilot's instrument panel, is used in conjunction with the flight director mode switch. When the switch is at PILOT and the flight director mode selector switch is at STBY, the bank steering bar on the attitude director indicator can be used to

4-52

Changed 25 June 1965

T.O. 1B-70(X)A-1

indicate up to 3 degrees right or left sideslip on both the pilot's and copilot's attitude director indicators. The command control switch receives power from the right primary dc bus. For other functions of the command control switch, refer to "Flight Director System" in this section.

INSTRUMENTATION INDICATORS.

DIGITAL TAPE REMAINING INDICATOR.

The digital tape remaining dial indicator (45, figure 1-3) on the pilot's instrument panel shows the total percentage of tape remaining on both digital recorders. The indicator is powered by the instrumentation bus. The indicator is marked from 0 to 100 percent, in 25-percent increments. (Each digital recorder has 50 percent of the tape supply.)

ANALOG TAPE REMAINING INDICATOR.

The analog tape remaining dial indicator (36, figure 1-3) on the pilot's instrument panel shows the percentage of tape remaining on the analog recorder. The indicator is powered by the instrumentation bus. The indicator is marked from 0 to 100 percent, in 25-percent increments.

TIME RESET BUTTON.

The time reset button (2, figure 1-5) is mounted below the instrument panel shroud. This push-button receives power from the instrumentation bus. Pushing the button returns the time code generator to a count of zero. The counter should also be turned to zero at this time so both will be in "sync."

DIGITAL RECORD INDICATOR LIGHTS.

The three digital record indicator lights (48, figure 1-3, 16, figure 1-4, and 24, figure 1-5) one on the pilot's instrument panel, one next to the correlation counter and one on the copilot's instrument panel are powered by

the instrumentation bus. The lights come on (green) steady or flashing when either digital recorder is operating. If the lights do not come on when the record button or switch is used, the digital recorder is not operating. This could be caused by the tape being exhausted.

ANALOG RECORD INDICATOR LIGHTS.

The three analog record indicator lights (49, figure 1-3, 15, figure 1-4, and 3, figure 1-5) one on the pilot's instrumentation control panel, one next to the correlation counter and one on the copilot's instrumentation control panel are powered by the instrumentation bus. The lights come on (green) steady or flashing when the analog recorder is operating. If the lights do not come on, the analog recorder is not operating.

CABIN RECORDER INDICATOR LIGHT.

The cabin recorder indicator light (22A, figure 1-5) on the center instrument panel is powered by the right primary dc bus. The light is green and comes on whenever the cabin recorder is recording.

INSTRUMENTATION OFF CAUTION LIGHT.

The instrumentation off caution light (51, figure 1-3), on the pilot's instrument panel, is powered by the instrumentation bus. The placard-type light comes on to show "INSTRM OFF" when power is available but the master switch is OFF. The light also comes on if a malfunction in the instrumentation package causes an automatic power shutoff.

INSTRUMENTATION PACKAGE COOLING MALFUNCTION CAUTION LIGHT.

The cooling malfunction caution light (51, figure 1-3), on the pilot's instrument panel, is powered by the

Changed 25 June 1965

instrumentation bus. The placard-type light comes on to show "COOL MALF" if the environment (pressurization or cooling) in the instrumentation package is out of limits for any continuous interval of 20 seconds. Also, control will switch over automatically to cooling system No. 2. If the cooling malfunction light stays on, instrumentation package power will be turned off automatically after about 100 seconds. (This will be indicated by the instrumentation off master light coming on.)

INSTRUMENTATION PACKAGE COOLING SYSTEM INDICATOR LIGHTS.

The two cooling system indicator lights (51, figure 1-3) on the pilot's instrument panel are powered by the instrumentation bus. One placard-type light comes on to show "COOL 1 ON" when the instrumentation package cooling system No. 1 is being used; the other light comes on to show "COOL 2 ON" when cooling system No. 1 has failed and the automatic changeover to cooling system No. 2 has been accomplished. Only one light will be on at a time.

INSTRUMENTATION PACKAGE LIQUID NITROGEN LOW CAUTION LIGHT.

The liquid nitrogen low caution light (51, figure 1-3) on the pilot's instrument panel is inoperative.

CORRELATION COUNTER.

The six digit correlation counter (1, figure 1-5) below the instrument panel shroud is powered by the instrumentation bus. The counter displays total elapsed time in seconds for correlation of recorded data. The counter, connected directly to the time code generator of the digital system, counts continuously and records on the tape after the instrumentation master switch is at ON. Setting up the counter requires holding down the correlation time and counter reset button (2, figure 1-5) until all zeros are displayed on the counter, then releasing the reset button. This starts the counter and the time code generator simultaneously so both will record the same time values. Any interruption of of instrumentation power will destroy this "sync" and the counter must be reset to the time code generator.

MISCELLANEOUS EQUIPMENT.

MAP CASE.

The map case, beneath the center console, is for stowage of flight manuals, enroute charts, letdown charts, and the letdown chart holder.

LETDOWN CHART HOLDER.

The transparent letdown chart holder holds one letdown chart and can be plugged into the pilot's instrument panel to present a selected letdown chart for ready reference. (See 7, figure 1-3.) When not in use, it is stored in the map case.

RELIEF CONTAINER.

The one-pint capacity relief container is stowed beneath the center console.

MOORING.

A mooring adapter is installed on the drag brace pin on the nose gear to attach the mooring cables. Four cables are used to moor the airplane. Fittings on each end of the cable attach to the mooring adapter and to mooring anchors in the ramp.

Changed 25 June 1965

T.O. 1B-70(X)A-1

PROTECTIVE SOLAR SHIELD.

The protective solar shield is used by ground personnel to reduce the temperature in the crew compartment while the airplane is parked. The solar shield, which is a thin, white, vinyl-coated, nylon fabric, snaps to the interior frame of the windshield.

PROTECTIVE COVERS.

Removable covers include engine air inlet covers, tail pipe covers, a pitot boom cover, engine inlet boundary layer airflow outlet covers, a wing walkway protective cover, mats for use in the air inlets, and miscellaneous plugs for external openings.

CREW ENTRANCE DUST COVER.

A fabric dust cover hooks into the crew entrance door opening after the door is opened and latched. This cover has a zippered opening that permits entering and leaving the airplane without removal of the cover. In addition to keeping blowing dust and debris out of the airplane, the cover forces the cooling air around electrical equipment not having direct cooling. If the cover is not installed, the cooling air goes out the door and not through the transpiration wall past the electrical equipment in the pilot's and copilot's consoles.

This page intentionally left blank

T.O. 1B-70(X)A-1

SECTION V

OPERATING LIMITATIONS

TABLE OF CONTENTS	PAGE		PAGE
Minimum Crew Requirements	5-1	Ground Speed Limitations	5-14
Instrument Markings	5-1	Prohibited Maneuvers	5-14
Engine Limitations	5-1	Acceleration Limitations	5-14
Airspeed Limitations	5-6	Center-of-Gravity Limitations	5-14
Inlet Limitations	5-11	Weight Limitations	5-14

MINIMUM CREW REQUIREMENTS.

The minimum crew required is a pilot and a copilot.

INSTRUMENT MARKINGS.

Careful attention must be given to the instrument markings (figure 5-1), because these limitations are not necessarily repeated in this or any other section.

ENGINE LIMITATIONS.

The engine limitations shown in figure 5-1 are based on use of JP-6 fuel.

THRUST DEFINITIONS.

MAXIMUM THRUST.

Maximum Thrust is defined as the thrust obtained at 100% rpm with the throttle at MAX A/B (maximum afterburner) and is not time-limited.

> NOTE
> During selected overspeed (104% rpm) operation, which can be used for take-off when ambient temperature is above 50°F, Maximum Thrust also is attained. (Refer to "Selected Overspeed Limits" in this section.)

MILITARY THRUST.

Military Thrust is defined as the thrust obtained at 100% rpm with the throttle at MIL (full throttle without afterburner) and is not time-limited.

NORMAL THRUST.

Normal Thrust is defined as the minimum thrust obtained at 100% rpm with the throttle at the 40-degree mark on the quadrant (sea-level static conditions). The same throttle setting produces Normal Thrust at altitude. This thrust rating is not time-limited.

SELECTED OVERSPEED LIMITS.

Selected overspeed (104% rpm) operation, with the throttle at OVSP, can be used for take-off only if ambient temperature is above 50°F. Selected overspeed is limited to 5 minutes per take-off and must be disengaged before attaining Mach 0.6 (one hour cumulative). Maximum allowable continuous engine speed during selected overspeed operation is 105% rpm. The transient overspeed limits permitted during selected overspeed are 105% rpm to 106% rpm for 2 minutes cumulative. Any operation above 106% rpm is prohibited. If the overspeed limits are exceeded on the ground, the engine must be shut down. If these limits are exceeded in flight, retard the throttle out of OVSP in an attempt

T. O. 1B-70(X)A-1

INSTRUMENT MARKINGS

NOTE
ENGINE LIMITATIONS ARE BASED ON JP-6 FUEL

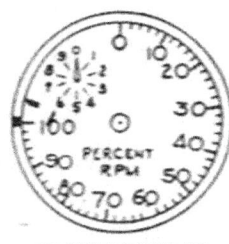

TACHOMETER (6)

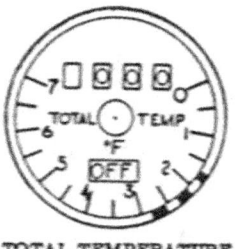

TOTAL TEMPERATURE
GAGE

▬ 99% TO 101%   NORMAL 100% RPM OPERATION
   103% TO 105%   NORMAL SELECTED OVERSPEED
▬ 106%   REJECT OVERSPEED

▋▋ 157° F TO 313° F   TOTAL TEMPERATURE-
   EXHAUST TEMPERATURE
   RELATIONSHIP*

NOTE
Normal operating range is 60% to 101% rpm.

* FOR TIME LIMITS REFER TO EXHAUST
  TEMPERATURE LIMITS.

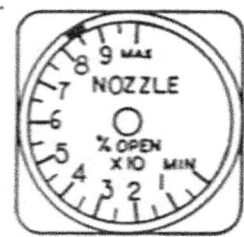

PRIMARY EXHAUST NOZZLE
POSITION INDICATOR (6)

▬ 81-1/2 PERCENT TO   NORMAL OPERATING
   86-1/2 PERCENT   RANGE FOR TAKE-OFF

   87 PERCENT TO   OVERSPEED RANGE FOR
   91 PERCENT   TAKE-OFF

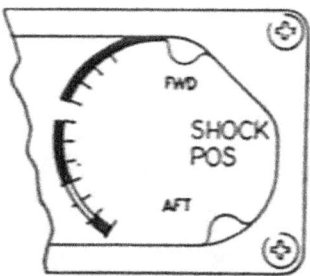

SHOCK WAVE POSITION
INDICATOR (2)

▬ DANGER (INLET UNSTARTED)
   CAUTION
▬ NORMAL
☐ POSITION OF SHOCK DOWNSTREAM
  OF NORMAL (AFT)
▬ RESTART

Figure 5-1 (Sheet 1 of 2)

T.O. 1B-70(X)A-1

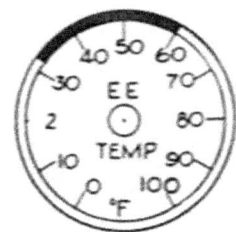

ELECTRONIC EQUIPMENT
AIR TEMPERATURE GAGE

■ 32°F TO 60°F   NORMAL
▨ 60°F TO 100°F   CAUTION

AMMONIA QUANTITY
GAGE

150 LB TO 250 LB   CAUTION

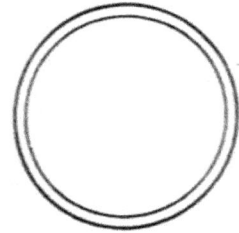

EXHAUST TEMPERATURE GAGE

REFER TO CONFIDENTIAL SUPPLEMENT,
T.O. 1B-70(X)A-1A

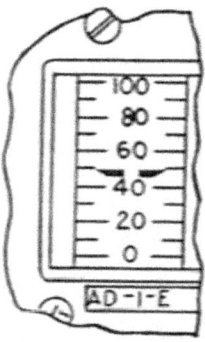

ENGINE—ADS VIBRATION INDICATOR (6)

▬   50 PERCENT   MAXIMUM
    (ENGINE AT 104 % RPM)

▬   50 PERCENT (ADS)   MAXIMUM

WATER QUANTITY GAGE

▮ 600 LB TO 2500 LB   MINIMUM

HYDRAULIC PRESSURE GAGE (4)

■ 3800 PSI TO 4200 PSI   NORMAL
▨ 4200 PSI TO 4250 PSI   MAXIMUM

Figure 5-1 (Sheet 2 of 2)

to reduce the rpm below 105%. If necessary, continue to retard the throttle to keep the rpm within limits. If retarding the throttle to IDLE fails to lower the rpm, the engine must be shut down.

CAUTION
Improper or excessive use of selected overspeed can result in reduced turbine life and premature turbine replacement.

NOTE
The duration of selected overspeed operation must be entered in the Form 781 (or equivalent).

ENGINE OVERSPEED LIMITATIONS.

For all steady-state engine operations other than selected overspeed, the maximum allowable continuous engine speed is 101% rpm. Transient overspeed limits are 102% to 105% rpm for 5 minutes; 105% to 106% rpm for 2 minutes cumulative. Any operation above 106% rpm is prohibited. If the overspeed limits are exceeded on the ground, the engine must be shut down. If these limits are exceeded in flight, retard the throttle in an attempt to reduce the rpm below 101%. If retarding the throttle to IDLE fails to lower the rpm, the engine must be shut down. (Refer to "Engine Windmilling RPM Limit" in this section.) The engine must be inspected for damage if the overspeed limits are exceeded. If 106% rpm is exceeded, a complete inspection of the compressor and turbine sections, and bench testing of the main fuel control are necessary.

NOTE
The amount and duration of engine overspeed and all time above 101% rpm must be entered in the Form 781 (or equivalent), so that prescribed engine inspections can be made.

ENGINE WINDMILLING LIMITS.

ENGINE WINDMILLING RPM LIMIT.

If an engine is shut down because of engine oil pressure failure or excessive uncontrollable vibration, the engine must not windmill above 22% rpm. (Engage engine brake and/or reduce airspeed to keep rpm of windmilling engine below 22%.)

ENGINE WINDMILLING TIME LIMITS.

See figure 5-2 for windmilling time limits.

AFTERBURNER LIGHT-OFF TIME AND RPM DROP LIMITS.

Afterburner light-off should occur within 4 seconds after the throttle is moved from MIL to MIN A/B. (Afterburner light-off normally will require only about 3 seconds.) An rpm drop up to 4.5% rpm is permissible during afterburner light-off.

ENGINE ACCELERATION LIMITS.

At sea-level, the engine should accelerate from Idle to Military Thrust within 9 seconds, and from Military Thrust to Maximum Thrust within 7 seconds. At low altitude, if the throttle is advanced directly from IDLE to MAX A/B when speed is below 150 knots IAS, Maximum Thrust should be attained within 13 seconds. Deviation in excess of the given times should be recorded in Form 781 (or equivalent).

ENGINE EMERGENCY WINDMILL BRAKE LIMITS.

Above Mach 1.5, only one engine per inlet should be braked. This prevents a possible continuous inlet buzz which can seriously affect airplane stability and control, and can damage the engines and inlet. If a second engine in the same inlet must be shut down and braked, speed must be reduced to below Mach 1.5 before the emergency brake on second engine is engaged. Refer to "Use of Engine Windmill Braking" in Section III.

T.O. 1B-70(X)A-1

ENGINE WINDMILLING TIME LIMITS

AIRPLANE MACH NO.	THROTTLE CONDITION				
	THROTTLE OFF		THROTTLE IDLE - RPM UNLOCKED		THROTTLE - IDLE THRU MIL, RPM LOCKED-UP OR THROTTLE - 40 DEG THRU MIL, RPM UNLOCKED
	WINDMILLING TIME LIMITS	MINIMUM COOLING TIME *	WINDMILLING TIME LIMITS	MINIMUM COOLING TIME *	
2.0 AND ABOVE	1/2 MINUTE	1 MINUTE	1 MINUTE	2 MINUTES	WINDMILLING TIME UNLIMITED
1.0 TO 2.0	1 MINUTE	2 MINUTES	3 MINUTES	6 MINUTES	
0.75 TO 1.0	2 MINUTES	2 MINUTES	WINDMILLING TIME UNLIMITED		
0.5 TO 0.75	5 MINUTES	5 MINUTES			
LESS THAN 0.5	UNLIMITED IF RPM ABOVE 8% 5 MINUTES IF RPM BELOW 8% †		MOVE THROTTLE TO OFF BELOW MACH 0.5. OPEN THROTTLE JUST LONG ENOUGH FOR AIR START ATTEMPTS.		

NOTE

Windmilling limits based on engine being free to rotate, with proper operation of engine lube oil system, and adequate fuel flow when throttle is not OFF.

* Maintain minimum cooling time with throttle at 45 degrees to repeat windmilling time at given throttle condition. (Additional fuel flow for engine lube oil cooling is provided by 45-degree throttle setting.)

† Requires post-flight inspection of engine lube oil filters and filters and No. 2 climb and dive scavange screens.

Figure 5-2

T.O. 1B-70(X)A-1

EXHAUST TEMPERATURE LIMITS.

Refer to the Confidential Supplement, T.O. 1B-70(X)A-1A, for exhaust temperature limits.

SECONDARY EXHAUST NOZZLE SHROUD LIMITS.

Refer to the Confidential Supplement, T.O. 1B-70(X)A-1A, for secondary exhaust nozzle shroud limits.

ENGINE AND ACCESSORY DRIVE SYSTEM VIBRATION LIMITS.

The steady-state vibration limits for the engine and accessory drive system are shown in figure 5-4. The engine vibration limit varies with engine rpm; the ADS limit remains constant.

CAUTION
Refer to "Excessive Engine or Accessory Drive System Gearbox Vibration" in Section III for procedure to be followed if the engine or ADS vibration limits are exceeded.

Because each engine and each ADS gearbox has its own normal operation steady-state vibration level, a change from this level, even though it is below the vibration limit, may indicate trouble. As a result, if a gradual increase in vibration level is noted, a ground check of the effected engine or gearbox is warranted. (Refer to "Engine-Accessory Drive System Vibration" in Section VII.)

ENGINE IGNITION SYSTEM LIMITS.

To prolong ignition unit service life, the ignition circuit is limited to 90 seconds of continuous operation. A minimum cooling period of 2 minutes is necessary before the ignition can be used again. The total operating time limit for the ignition system during any 30-minute period is 10 minutes below Mach 2.0, and 4 minutes above Mach 2.0.

AIRSPEED LIMITATIONS.

It should be noted that the limit airspeeds are attainable in level flight, and under most conditions, at less than maximum engine thrust. Therefore, approach to these limits should be made with caution. During operation at or near these limits, avoid maneuvers that tend to rapidly increase speed, such as accelerations, dives, abrupt thrust increases, etc.

MAXIMUM ALLOWABLE AIRSPEED.

Refer to the Confidential Supplement, T.O. 1B-70(X)A-1A, for maximum allowable airspeeds.

LANDING GEAR LOWERING SPEED.

The maximum allowable landing gear lowering speed is shown in figure 5-5.

CAUTION
Flight with the landing gear extended above gear-down limit speed will cause structural and component operating mechanism damage.

Avoid retracting or lowering the landing gear at load factors greater or less than 1.0G. Undue loads on the gear during cycling tend to decrease the service life unnecessarily.

CAUTION
Do not sideslip the airplane during gear extension or retraction as structural damage to the gear doors and operating mechanism can result.

T.O. 1B-70(X)A-1

SECONDARY EXHAUST NOZZLE SHROUD LIMITS

REFER TO CONFIDENTIAL SUPPLEMENT, T.O. 1B-70(X)A-1A

Figure 5-3

T. O. 1B-70(X)A-1

ENGINE AND ACCESSORY DRIVE SYSTEM VIBRATION LIMITS

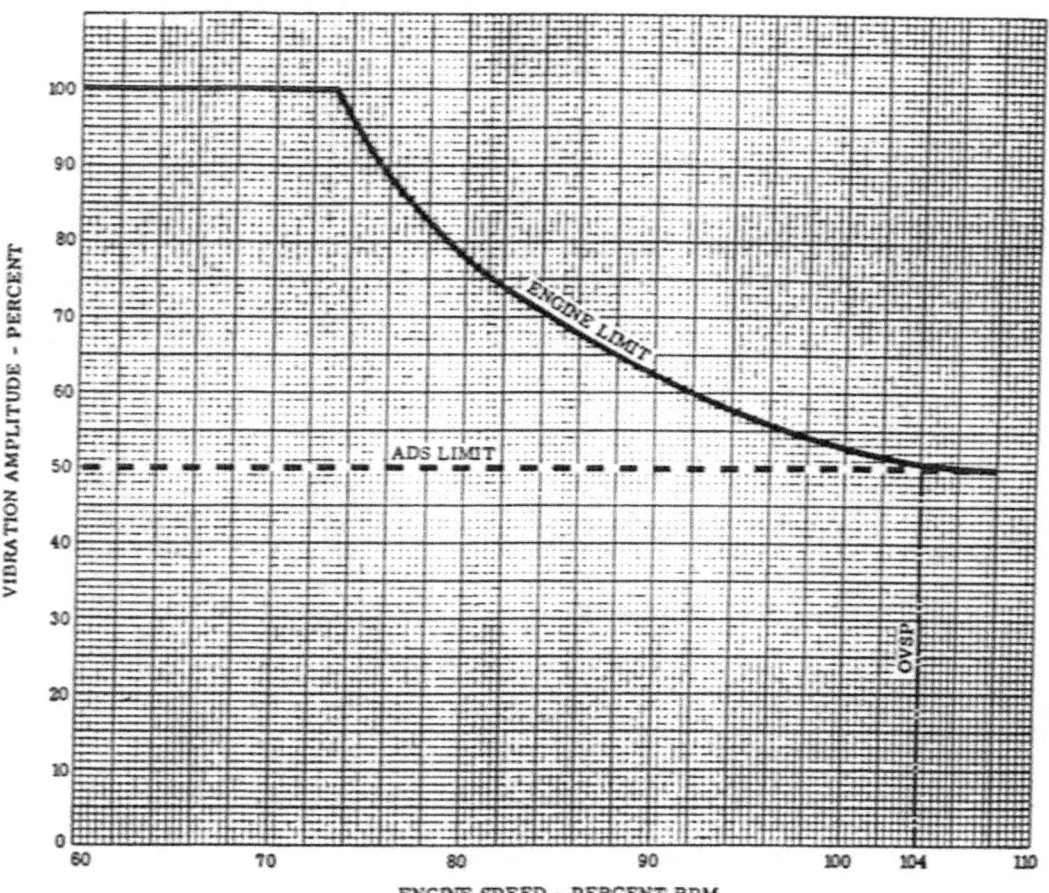

NOTE

Engine - ADS vibration indicators show vibration amplitude in percent, with the scale maximum of 100 percent corresponding to a peak-to-peak vibration displacement of 10 mils.

Figure 5-4

T.O. 1B-70(X)A-1

LANDING GEAR LOWERING LIMITS

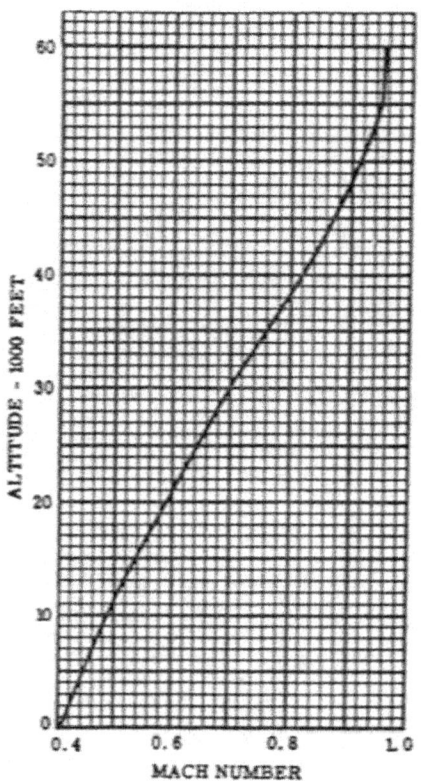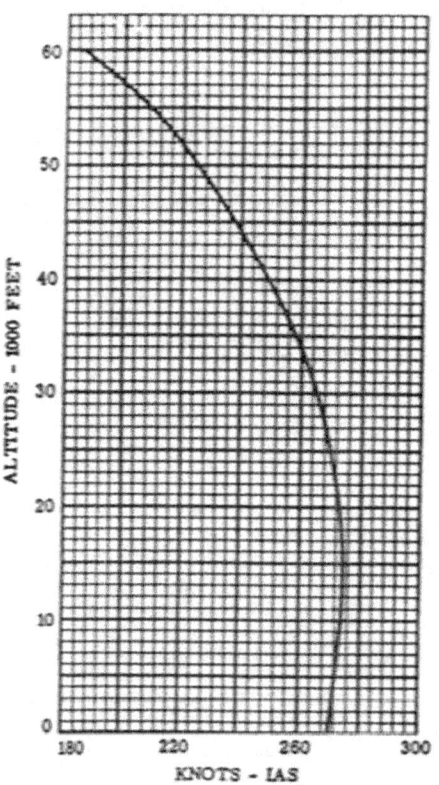

Figure 5-5

T.O. 1B-70(X)A-1

FLAP LOWERING SPEED.

The maximum allowable flap lowering speed is 270 knots IAS or Mach 0.6, whichever is lower.

> **CAUTION**
> Flight above 270 knots IAS or Mach 0.6 with the flaps extended, will cause structural and component operating mechanism damage.

LANDING LIGHT AND AUXILIARY LANDING AND TAXI LIGHT EXTENSION SPEED.

Extension of the landing light or the auxiliary landing and taxi light above the limit airspeed or altitude is prevented by the central air data system. However, if this automatic circuitry fails, the maximum allowable airspeed and altitude for lowering the lights is 250 knots IAS below 8,000 feet altitude. Damage to the lights is likely to occur if these limits are exceeded.

ANTICOLLISION LIGHT EXTENSION SPEED.

Extension of the anticollision lights above the limit airspeed is prevented by the central air data system. However, if this automatic circuitry fails, the maximum allowable airspeed for extending the anticollision lights is 325 knots IAS or Mach 1.15, whichever is lower. Damage to the lights will occur from heat effects if the lights are extended above this speed.

WING TIP FOLD OPERATING SPEEDS.

The wing tips must be at the $\frac{1}{2}$ position at airspeeds between Mach 0.95 (or 400 knots IAS, whichever is lower) and Mach 1.4. Above Mach 1.4, the wing tips must be full down. A tolerance of ±.05 Mach number is allowed for operating procedure and technique.

> **CAUTION**
> Avoid operating the wing tips during maneuvering flight, in rough or turbulent air, or during changes in G to prevent damage to the wing tip folding mechanism and/or airplane structure.

DRAG CHUTE OPERATING SPEEDS.

The drag chutes should be deployed after nose gear touchdown and at speeds below 220 knots IAS. If the drag chutes are deployed above 220 knots IAS, structural damage to airplane and/or chutes will occur.

> **CAUTION**
> To prevent slowing the airplane to below landing speed, the drag chutes must not be deployed until after touchdown. If inadvertent deployment does occur, the chutes must be jettisoned.

Minimum drag chute deployment speed is 100 knots IAS. Actuation of the drag chute handle below this speed results in incomplete deployment and loss of effectiveness. Minimum jettison speed for the drag chutes is 60 knots IAS.

> **CAUTION**
> To avoid possible structural damage to the upper wing surface, do not jettison the drag chutes at speeds below 60 knots. Failure to jettison the chutes results in engine exhaust damage to the drag chute risers, which requires inspection and/or replacement before subsequent flights.

T.O. 1B-70(X)A-1

WINDSHIELD NOSE RAMP POSITIONING SPEED.

The two-position nose ramp may be raised at any flight speed. It is desirable to avoid high-speed flight with the nose ramp in the down position because of the resulting high windshield temperatures and increase in airplane drag.

>NOTE
>
>Performance data in Appendix I reflects supersonic operation with the nose ramp in the up position only.

INLET LIMITATIONS.

Information on airplane attitude limitations for maintaining a started inlet will be supplied when available.

Changed 25 June 1965

T.O. 1B-70(X)A-1

MAXIMUM ALLOWABLE AIRSPEED

REFER TO CONFIDENTIAL SUPPLEMENT, T.O. 1B-70(X)A-1A

Figure 5-6

(Figure 5-7 deleted)

T.O. 1B-70(X)A-1

(All data deleted from page 5-13)

T.O. 1B-70(X)A-1

GROUND SPEED LIMITATIONS.

TAKE-OFF, LANDING, AND TAXI SPEEDS.

To prevent tire damage, the maximum allowable ground speed recommended during take-off or landing is 240 knots. Before take-off, following a period of excessive taxiing, have the tire temperatures checked to ensure that they are cool enough (below 200°F) for safe operation.

MAXIMUM TURNING SPEEDS DURING TAXIING.

To prevent structural damage, the following recommended maximum turning speeds should be observed during taxiing:

NOSE WHEEL STEERING SELECTOR SWITCH AT TAXI

RUDDER PEDAL TRAVEL	NOSE WHEEL ANGLE (DEGREES)	MAXIMUM TURNING SPEED
Full	58	9 mph
7/8	43	12 mph
3/4	34	15 mph
1/2	18	20 mph

NOSE WHEEL STEERING SELECTOR SWITCH AT TAKE-OFF LDG

RUDDER PEDAL TRAVEL	NOSE WHEEL ANGLE (DEGREES)	MAXIMUM TURNING SPEED
Full	35	14 mph
3/4	18	20 mph
1/2	8	31 mph

PROHIBITED MANEUVERS.

Aerobatic maneuvers of any kind are strictly prohibited. This includes intentional spins, snap rolls, vertical stalls, and steep dives, as well as any maneuver resulting in excessive accelerations. Violent or abrupt control movements should be avoided.

ACCELERATION LIMITATIONS.

Refer to the Confidential Supplement, T.O. 1B-70(X)A-1A, for acceleration limitations.

CAUTION
Do not exceed 1.15 G during or after an engine or accessory drive system compartment fire.

CENTER-OF-GRAVITY LIMITATIONS.

Refer to the Confidential Supplement, T.O. 1B-70(X)A-1A, for center-of-gravity limitations.

WEIGHT LIMITATIONS.

Refer to the Confidential Supplement, T.O. 1B-70(X)A-1A, for weight limitations.

NOTE
Refer to the Confidential Supplement, T.O. 1B-70(X)A-1A, for Section VI, Flight Characteristics.

T.O. 1B-70(X)A-1

SECTION VII

SYSTEMS OPERATION

TABLE OF CONTENTS	PAGE		PAGE
Wing Tip Operation	7-1	Minimum Afterburner Instability . . .	.7-3
Inlet Reaction Upon Decapsulation	7-3	Engine-Accessory Drive System Vibration	.7-3

WING TIP OPERATION.

At airspeeds between 400 knots IAS or Mach 0.95 (whichever is lower) and Mach 1.4, the wing tips must be one-half down. Above Mach 1.4, the wing tips must be full down. (See figure 2-7.)

NOTE
- On Airplane AF62-001, wing tip down positions are: ½, 25 degrees; DOWN, 65 degrees.
- On Airplane AF62-207, wing tip down positions are: ½, 30 degrees; DOWN, 70 degrees.

During acceleration, before Mach 0.95 or 400 knots IAS is exceeded, lower the wing tips to the one-half position. As the wing tips are lowered, a slight roll may be felt if one tip lowers slower than the other. If excessive roll occurs, immediately raise the wing tips. After the wing tips are in position, as shown by the indicators, continue acceleration. Above Mach 1.4, the wing tips should be full down.

NOTE
When the wing tips are lowered to each folded position, a slight nose up trim change occurs.

After the wing tips are full down on Airplane AF62-001, continue acceleration to Mach 2.6 and unlock the lateral bobweight by holding the lateral bobweight switch at FREE for about 3 seconds and checking that the lateral bobweight indicator shows FREE.

WARNING
Do not attempt flight at Mach 2.6 or above with the wing tips full down and the lateral bobweight locked, as undesirable maneuvering characteristics will result.

NOTE
Before moving the lateral bobweight switch to FREE, check that the bobweight indicator shows LOCKED. This verifies that the bobweight switch has not been moved accidentally.

If the indicator shows FREE before the bobweight switch is moved to FREE, hold the switch at LOCK until the indicator shows LOCKED, then hold the switch at FREE for 3 seconds. Check that the bobweight indicator now shows FREE. During the deceleration, when Mach 2.6 is reached, move the lateral bobweight switch to LOCK and check that the lateral bobweight indicator shows LOCKED.

NOTE
If indicator shows FREE, pulse lateral bobweight switch towards FREE until bobweight indicator shows LOCKED.

At Mach 1.4 raise wing tips to 1/2, then full up below Mach 0.95 or 400 knots IAS. After the wing tips are up, continue deceleration and descent as required.

NOTE
Raising the wing tips causes a slight nose down trim change.

T.O. 1B-70(X)A-1

(Figure 7-1 deleted)

INLET REACTION UPON DECAPSULATION.

Encapsulation, followed by the initial use of the throttle retard button on the emergency descent control grip by either occupant, causes the throats and bypass doors to go to the emergency position to help maintain stable airflow to the engines. The inlet emergency condition will remain locked in electrically as long as an occupant who used his throttle retard button remains encapsulated. In addition, the action which causes the inlets to be driven to the emergency position in effect biases the throats and bypass doors off their normal trim positions. Then, after decapsulation, full normal throat and bypass door travel could not be obtained except by use of the throat and bypass door standby switches. In view of the preceding, the following actions are required in conjunction with encapsulation and decapsulation:

a. If both occupants encapsulate and one presses his throttle retard button, the other occupant also should press his throttle retard button at least once. This will ensure that the inlets remain in the emergency position until both occupants have decapsulated.

b. If either occupant encapsulated and pressed his throttle retard button, the AICS must be operated only in the standby mode after decapsulation (throat and bypass door mode switches at OFF*; AICS mode switches at STBY†).

MINIMUM AFTERBURNER INSTABILITY.

During operation in the minimum afterburner range (throttle between the 61- and 70-degree settings on the quadrant), unstable combustion may occur. This instability can be recognized by low-frequency oscillations (1/2 to 1 cps) on the primary exhaust nozzle position indicator, exhaust temperature gage, and tachometer of the affected engine. (Representative peak-to-peak ranges of these indicator oscillations are: nozzle position, 10 percent; exhaust temperature, 110° C; and rpm 3%.) Instability should not be detrimental to the engine, however, if an instability condition is allowed to persist,

*Airplane AF62-001
†Airplane AF62-207

compressor stalls and/or engine flameout can result. Therefore, to prevent possible instability, operation in the minimum afterburner range should be avoided, unless required for specific tests. If it is necessary to use minimum afterburner thrust settings and instability is encountered, advance the throttle beyond the 70-degree setting or shut down the afterburner.

ENGINE-ACCESSORY DRIVE SYSTEM VIBRATION.

The vibration indicating system permits engine and/or accessory drive system gearbox vibrations to be monitored by the flight crew to determine existing operating conditions or to indicate impending trouble. Each engine and gearbox has a vibration level that is normal for steady-state operation. If this normal level gradually increases over a number of flights, some form of mechanical deterioration has occurred. As a result, a ground check of the affected unit is required, even through the vibration indicator reading has remained within the acceptable limits. If the vibration limits are exceeded (except for transient conditions), serious mechanical unbalance is indicated, and immediate thrust reduction and possible shutdown is necessary. (See figure 5-4 for the engine and ADS steady-state vibration limits, and refer to "Excessive Engine or Accessory Drive System Gearbox Vibration" in Section III for applicable emergency procedures.)

Normal engines, at steady-state conditions, should have vibration displacements (peak-to-peak) of 1 to 3 mils at 100% rpm, and 4 to 7 mils between 70% and 80% rpm. (These correspond to engine vibration indicator readings of 10 to 30 percent, and 40 to 70 percent, respectively.) During transient rpm changes, indicator readings of 50 to 90 percent can be expected. Transient readings above 50 percent also may be expected during engine start, during throttle changes, and may appear above Mach 2 as the result of changes to the inlet shock position. These transient indications can be disregarded if they return to normal when steady-state operation is resumed. When starting an engine which has not been cooled adequately (such cooling may take more than an hour), a vibration reading of 100 percent may be encountered. This high vibration may last 5 minutes or more unless the engine is accelerated to 80%-90% rpm and then returned to idle. Some YJ-93 engines develop a 520 cps vibration mode during rapid throttle bursts. Therefore, to prevent this particular vibration, the following throttle technique is recommended for making throttle bursts from IDLE to MIL (or greater): Accelerate to 80% to 90% rpm, and hold this speed long enough to observe stable rpm. If vibration is within limits, accelerate engine to throttle position as required. (During all flight conditions where flight idle is greater than 80% rpm, throttle movements are unrestricted.)

Accessory drive system gearbox vibration indicator readings for steady-state conditions are about 10 or 20 percent. These readings will exceed 50 percent during engine speed changes, but should return to normal with steady-state operation.

The vibration level of each engine and ADS gearbox should be noted at steady-state 100% rpm operation. Any marked increase in these levels should be reported to ensure the required ground check.

NOTE
Refer to the Confidential Supplement, T.O. 1B-70(X)A-1A, for Appendix I, Performance Data.

Warships DVD Series

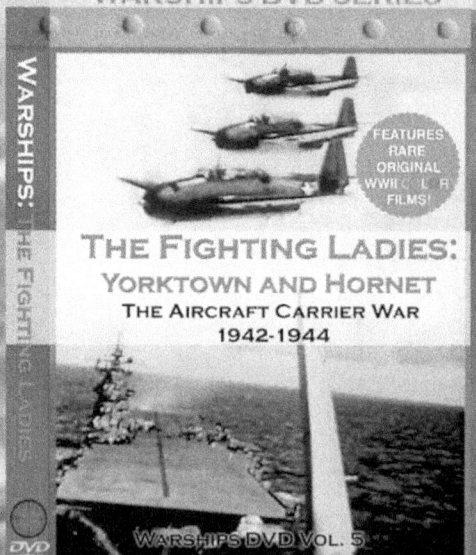

Now Available!

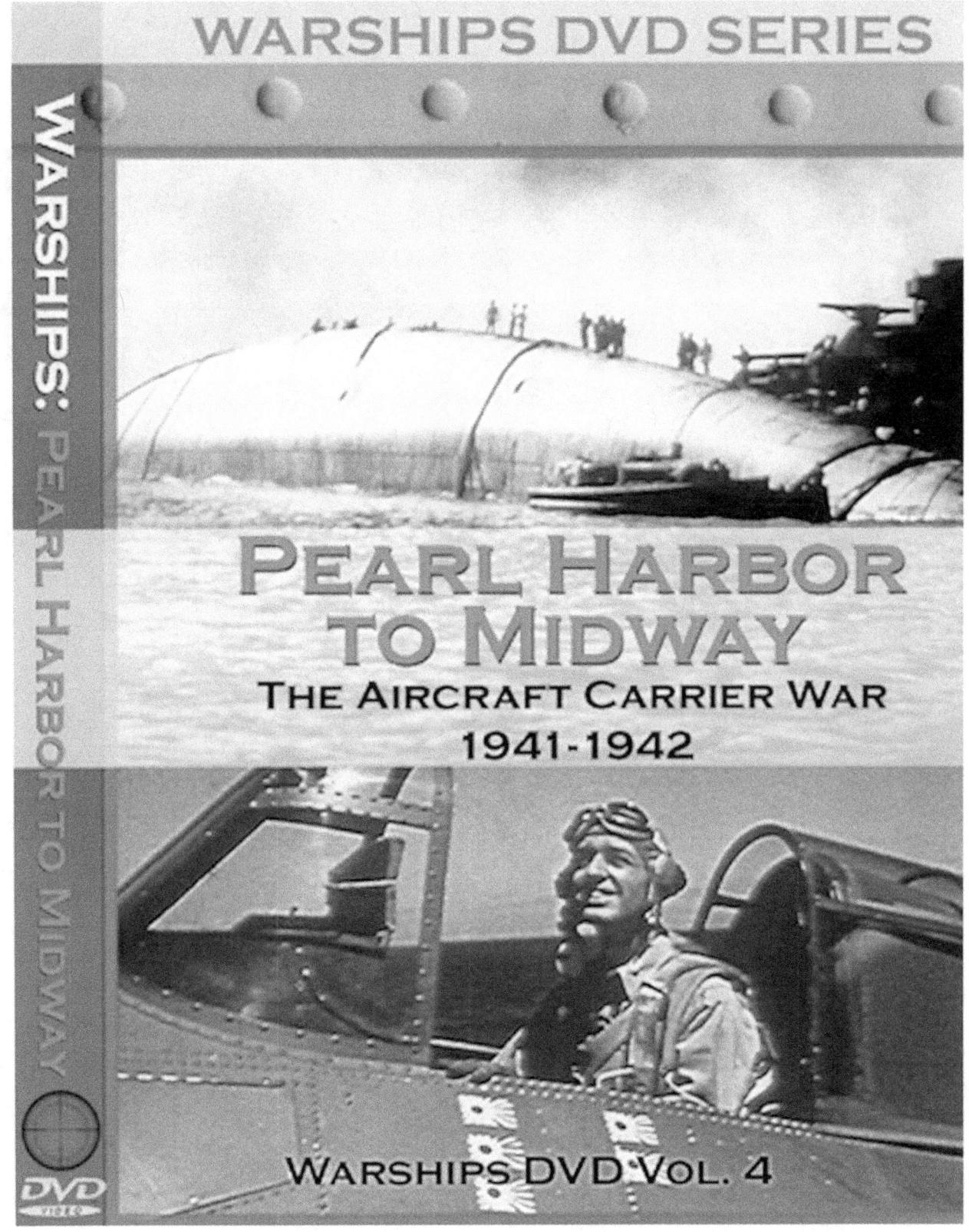

HISTORIC U.S. NAVY FILMS ON DVD!

WARSHIPS DVD SERIES

AIRCRAFT CARRIER MISHAPS
SAFETY AND TRAINING FILMS

—PERISCOPEFILM.COM—

NOW AVAILABLE ON DVD!

Aircraft At War DVD Series

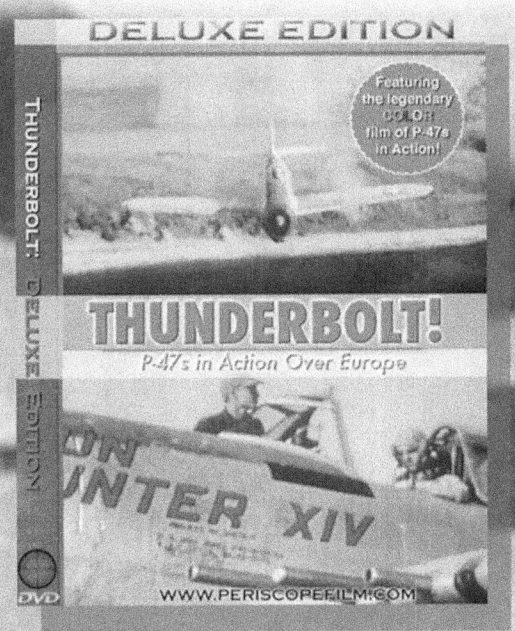
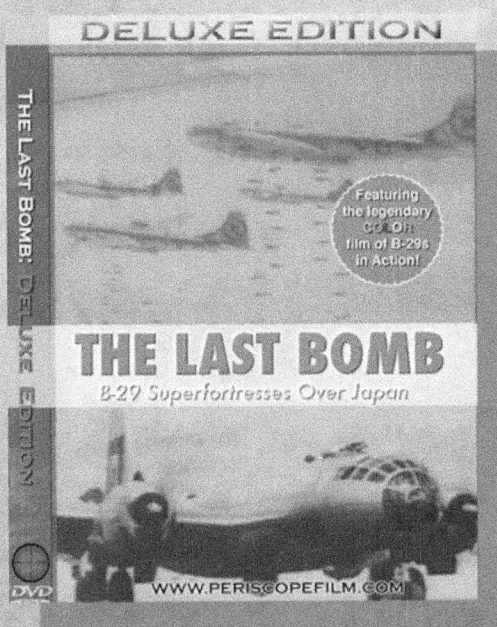
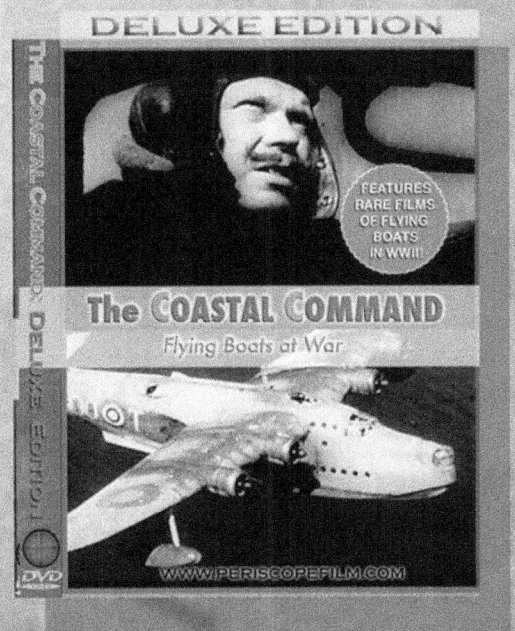

Now Available!

Epic Battles of WWII

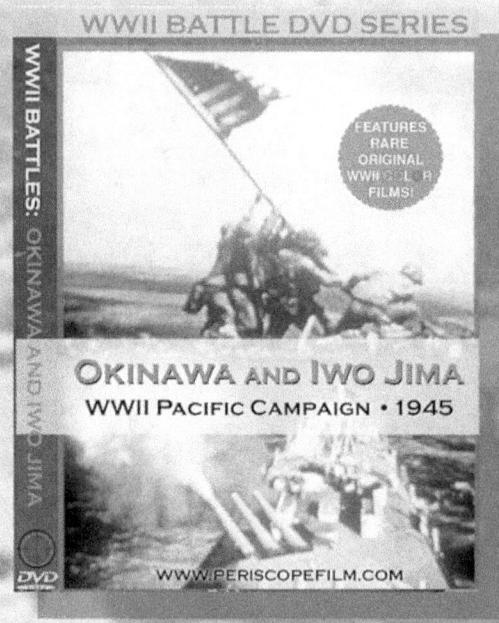

Now Available on DVD!

RESTRICTED
FILE B

TECHNICAL ORDER No. HAC 01-197-SP

HUGHES XF-11
PILOT'S FLIGHT OPERATING INSTRUCTIONS

Originally Published by the U.S. Army Air Force
Reprinted by Periscope Film LLC

NOW AVAILABLE!

SPRUCE GOOSE

HUGHES FLYING BOAT MANUAL

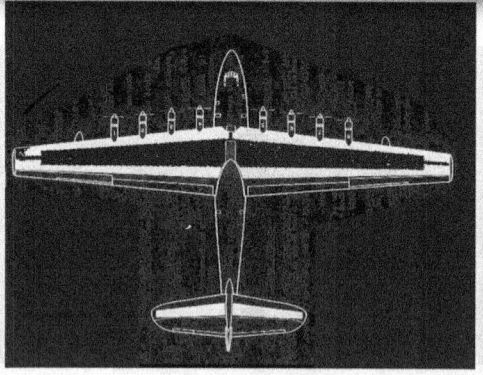

~~RESTRICTED~~

Originally Published by the War Department
Reprinted by Periscope Film LLC

NOW AVAILABLE!